THE AMERICAN
CIVIL RIGHTS
MOVEMENT

READINGS & INTERPRETATIONS

RAYMOND D'ANGELO
ST. JOSEPH'S COLLEGE

McGraw-Hill/Dushkin

A Division of The McGraw-Hill Companies

Book Team

Vice President and Publisher *Jeffrey L. Hahn*
List Manager *Theodore Knight*
Developmental Editor *Ava Suntoke*
Production Manager *Brenda S. Filley*
Director of Technology *Jonathan Stowe*
Designers *Charles Vitelli, Eldis N. Lima*
Typesetting Supervisor *Juliana Arbo*
Permissions Editor *Rose Gleich*
Proofreading Editor *Robin N. Charney*
Copier Coordinator *Larry Killian*

McGraw-Hill/Dushkin

A Division of The McGraw-Hill Companies

Cover Marchers along Route 80 in the Selma-to-Montgomery march for voters' rights, Alabama, 1965. © 1999 Vernon Merritt/Black Star

Cover Design *Lara M. Johnson, Michael Campbell*

The acknowledgment section for this book begins on page 590 and is considered an extension of the copyright page.

Library of Congress Control Number 00-134371

ISBN 0-07-239987-2

Printed in the United States of America

12345678FGRFGR54321

http://www.mhhe.com

To Herbert Douglas, master teacher and friend

About the Author

Raymond D'Angelo received his B.A. in history from Duquesne University, an M.A. from the New School for Social Research, and a Ph.D. in sociology from Bryn Mawr College. He teaches sociology at St. Joseph's College, New York, where he is chair of the Department of Social Sciences. A recent recipient of a National Endowment for the Humanities award, he has also received two fellowships from the National Science Foundation and a research award from the National Institute for Justice. He has contributed entries for the *Arena Review: Journal for the Study of Sport and Sociology* and for *Civil Rights in the United States*. He lives with his wife and two children in Connecticut, where he is active in historic preservation.

Contents in Brief

Contents

Chapter 2 From Resistance to a Social Movement   *113*

PART II The Modern Civil Rights Movement

Chapter 3 **Brown** *and Beyond: Rising Expectations, 1953–1959*   **222**

Introduction   222

Chapter 4 Student Activism and the Emergence of a Mass Movement   279

Chapter 5 The Militant Years, 1966–1968   *360*

PART III Civil Rights Issues after "The Movement"

Chapter 6 Integration or Segregation?   *462*

Preface

❧❧

At the dawn of the twentieth century, sociologist W. E. B. Du Bois wrote, "the problem of the twentieth century is the problem of the color-line." The American civil rights movement dramatized the spirit of these words in a massive struggle that changed—and continues to change—many parts of American society.

In part, the idea of a civil rights movement reader grew out of my own teaching experience. For many years I have assigned some of these readings to students in race and ethnic relations classes at a liberal arts college in New York. Initially, trying to engage students in a meaningful dialogue about race relations led me to assign more readings on the civil rights movement. Students responded positively to learning about segregation and its challenges.

The goal of *The American Civil Rights Movement: Readings and Interpretations* is to offer students a collection of readings that establishes a chronological and thematic framework to conceptualize and understand the movement. The reader is organized in a way that students will find understandable as well as intellectually challenging. This book contains 51 readings and six essays that craft a historical interpretation of the civil rights movement. Each reading has been selected because it contributes in a unique way to the picture of the whole movement. The distinction of this reader is that it is comprehensive and it has depth.

The book is organized in three parts containing six chapters. An author's essay introduces the student to each chapter and provides a perspective that unifies the readings in that chapter. Each section contains primary source readings from significant movement participants along with scholarly analyses from historians and sociologists.

The popular paradigm for the civil rights movement—the *Brown* decision in 1954 to King's assassination in 1968—misses the longer, more complete view of the civil rights struggle. This perspective of civil rights history offers a look at the social origins of the tradition of protest in the black community. In the reader, social and historical origins are linked to the modern movement of the 1950s and 1960s to show continuity as well as structural analysis. This straddling of the past and present allows students to think about the privileges of everyday life with an appreciation of the struggle that became a social movement. One cannot comprehend race relations today without this knowledge. When understood in its context, the past in turn helps us understand the present, which prepares us for the future.

From a sociohistorical perspective, three themes emerge in the reader. The first is the sociological imagination. According to C. Wright Mills, history involves the major structures and activities that unfold over time and space. The sociological imagination is that intersection of personal lives and the broader forces of history. History affects biography—the lives of people. Thus biography occurs in the context of history. Mills's sociological imagination is a unifying theme guiding one to understand and appreciate the significance of the civil rights movement. The movement offers us a case study of the problem of injustice, which was not simply an individual trap but the result of the destructive historical condition of segregation reaching beyond ordinary citizens. Personal problems of victimization by racism and discrimination became a "public issue" with the widespread recognition that the aggregate number of individual problems threatened American society as a whole. The collective response grew into an organized movement, a public issue. To understand the civil rights movement, this reader urges students to look beyond individual cases of prejudice and inequality, analyzing social conditions to understand why the movement became a public issue. The sociological imagination is evident in each of the sections.

The second theme is the protest of ordinary people against racism and injustice. This suggests that the civil rights movement was driven by the courage and conviction of ordinary citizens who listened to leaders, and at times pushed them in the right direction. Different forms of protest are described throughout the book. In some places the ideological debate of protest strategy is discussed, while other readings document and describe the protest. Some of the selections critique strategy and movement action, while others praise the form of protest.

A third theme is the dynamic tension between local and national forces. Local black communities organizing for protest invigorated themselves with support and sometimes leadership from national organizations. For the most part, this contributed to movement success, although at times there was conflict between local and national organizations. The National Association for the Advancement of Colored People (NAACP) played a significant role. Decades before the mass civil rights movement began with the Montgomery bus boycott in 1955, the NAACP dominated national civil rights efforts with its plan to attack segregation through the courts. From the early part of the twentieth century, through the 1950s and 1960s and into contemporary America, the NAACP has provided financial resources, a legal platform, and other types of assistance to the civil rights struggle. The dynamic tension stemming from local communities of African Americans working together with national organizations like the NAACP provided the energy and framework of the movement.

These themes are presented in six chapters, each of which develops around its own topical theme reflected in the introductory essay. In the first part, "Visions of Freedom and Civil Rights: Beginnings," the long-term sociohistorical perspective is examined. Chapter 1, "The Architecture of Segregation," emphasizes that segregation was a social and economic system designed to exploit blacks. This chapter considers the historical context in which early forms of African American resistance to segregation developed. The architecture of segregation was ensured by the constant threat of lynching, but, amazingly, from the era of segregation emerged the early forms of resistance that were the origins of the civil rights struggle.

"From Resistance to a Social Movement," chapter 2, tells the story of a developing formal social movement in the context of the conditions and structural factors of race relations preceding the landmark *Brown* decision. Indeed, factors including the role of the black press, nascent rising expectations for many blacks, national politics, America's war experiences, and segregation itself all contributed significantly to the civil rights movement. Although not well understood, these factors formed both a psychological and organizational framework out of which the civil rights movement as it is broadly recognized today developed into the twentieth century's most defining area of social change.

The readings in this chapter illustrate how historical conditions linked the ordinary people of the South to emerging national leaders like the charismatic Martin Luther King and little-known Ella Baker. Local African American resistance to segregation was supported greatly by the NAACP. Out of the architecture of segregation emerged architects of desegregation and integration.

Part II, "The Modern Civil Rights Movement," is presented in three chapters, organized chronologically and thematically. The readings in "*Brown* and Beyond: Rising Expectations, 1953–1959," chapter 3, characterize the nonviolent resistance that was fueled by a groundswell of support from ordinary people who had never before been politically active. The chapter covers three major civil rights events: the *Brown* decision, the Montgomery bus boycott, and integrating Central High School in Little Rock, Arkansas. The theme of the dynamics of local and national forces working to change the culture of segregation is explored in the Montgomery and Little Rock case studies.

Chapter 4, "Student Activism and the Emergence of a Mass Movement: 1960–1965," documents the role that young college students played in the movement. Starting with the North Carolina sit-ins and moving to the freedom riders and formation of the Student Nonviolent Coordinating Society (SNCC), the early 1960s civil rights struggle became a mass movement. National and local tensions again came to a head in conflicts in Albany, Georgia, and Birmingham, Alabama. The 1963 March on Washington and eventual passage of civil rights acts highlight the movement during this time.

"The Militant Years, 1966–1968," chapter 5 contains readings that document the conflicts and changes, including the role of Malcolm X and Black Power. In these years, the earlier civil rights coalition was challenged by the idea of militancy. After the assassination of King no other African American leader could galvanize the struggle and continue the modern civil rights movement.

The final part, "Civil Rights Issues after 'the Movement,'" examines the paradox that although many blacks benefited from the movement, many others were left behind; it seemed that poor blacks living in segregated areas of cities were not much better off than they had been before the movement. The paradox also extends to middle-class blacks for whom success was accompanied by modern, covert forms of racism. White backlash to the consequences of the movement became apparent in national politics, as national leaders began to reverse some of the civil rights gains of the 1960s. Nowhere was this more apparent than in the controversy over affirmative action.

Chapter 6, "Integration or Segregation?" is intended to stimulate students to reflect upon the movement and its consequences. Although the struggle for civil rights as a social movement dissolved in 1968, the issues have become part of another historical period with new conditions and new problems.

I hope students enjoy the combination of idealism and realism along with the sense of perpetual vitality that comes from the study of the civil rights movement. No matter what our superficial distinctions, we in America, students and nonstudents, stand to benefit from learning about the civil rights struggle. I would like to see Ella Baker, Charles Houston Hamilton, and E. D. Nixon become household names. They represent the depth and dignity of the civil rights movement, for they never confused the headlines with the real meaning of civil rights work. I hope that the study of the American civil rights movement will enhance students' understanding of American culture especially the values of freedom and equality—civil rights. It is central to understand the meaning of American democracy.

Additional resources, including well-researched Web sites, are provided at the end of each chapter. Finally, an instructor's manual is available for this reader. It contains summaries of the readings along with suggested discussion topics and possible examination questions.

I welcome any comments, criticisms, and suggestions to improve this reader. Please contact me at rdangelo@sjcny.edu.

Acknowledgments

This reader would not have been possible without many stimulating discussions about race and the civil rights movement with the following people; they provided ideas, support, and criticisms that brought the project to life: Julie Armstrong, Valdosta State University; the late Alan Babich, St. Joseph's College; Jack Bloom, Indiana University/Northwest; Herbert Douglas, Rowan State University; Ellen Casper Flood, Marymount College; Lee W. Formwalt, Organization of American Historians; Gregory Freeland, California Lutheran University; Charles Gallagher, Georgia State University; Graham Hodges, Colgate University; Charles Holmes, Tougaloo College; and Chris Waldrep, Eastern Illinois University.

Special thanks go to Ted Knight, list manager of the Taking Sides series at McGraw-Hill/Dushkin, who understood the vision of the book from the start and offered me the opportunity to see it realized, and also to Ava Suntoke, my patient and tireless editor. A lot more goes into the book production process than meets the eye. Thanks for a job well done to all those at McGraw-Hill/Dushkin's production department: Charlie Vitelli and others involved with cover and interior design; Juliana Arbo and the typesetters; and Robin Charney, the proofreader. Additional thanks to my friend Ken Jacoby for his interest in the civil rights movement and the reader.

In particular I am indebted to Patricia Sullivan (W. E. B. Du Bois Institute at Harvard University) and Waldo Martin (University of California, Berkeley) for their influence and leadership at a recent summer NEH Institute seminar, "Teaching the History of the Civil Rights Movement."

Parents play an important role in the lives of their children, indeed, my work and life are possible because of the environment of unqualified love and support my parents provided. This project, of course, would not have been possible without the love and inspiration of my wife, Susan, and children, Adam and Olivia.

The administration of St. Joseph's College provided me the adjusted schedule and support to put this project together. A special thanks to the college library staff, who was especially accommodating and helpful. Additional thanks to the many students over the years who have shown an interest in the civil rights movement.

Finally, and most importantly, I would like to pay tribute to all those who risked their lives and livelihoods in the struggle for freedom and justice, thereby making the civil rights movement a reality. You have made America a better place for all. Your full story needs to be told.

Raymond D'Angelo

Chapter 1

The Architecture of Segregation

The drive for civil rights and human dignity for African Americans began before the Supreme Court outlawed school segregation in *Brown v. Board of Education* and before Rosa Parks refused to give up her seat on a public bus in Montgomery. It began within the structure of Southern segregation. After the Civil War, which brought emancipation and Reconstruction, white power was restored in the South. Segregation, buttressed by racist intimidation and violence, became the social system designed by white Southerners to separate the races in every sphere of life and to achieve total dominance over blacks. Often referred to as the "Jim Crow" system, segregation began in 1877 following the end of the Reconstruction period of American history. The term Jim Crow came from an 1830s minstrel show character who danced without crossing his feet. The tradition began in 1843 when white minstrels applied black cork to their faces and performed a song-and-dance act across American cities. One of the performers, Thomas Dartmouth "Daddy" Rice, imitated a black man from Kentucky singing and dancing to a song that ended in the chorus,

> Weel about and turn about and do jis so,
> Eb'ry time I weel about I jump Jim Crow.

Negative stereotypes of blacks laughing, dancing, and serving whites became standard cultural images.

Jim Crow laws were passed by Southern state legislatures and created a racial caste system in the American South. They embodied subservience and second-class status. Civil rights historian Waldo Martin in *Brown v. Board of Education: A Brief History with Documents* (1998:3, Reading 3.1) notes that fighting Jim Crow was, like abolitionism, a war waged by a dissenting black minority and its stalwart white supporters, a multifaceted and far-reaching struggle. Like the nineteenth-century war against slavery, the struggle against Jim Crow embodied moral as well as political and economic issues.

The first half of the twentieth century saw the foundations of a movement to change the structure of American society, especially in the South. The vehicles of change include the black press, outside influences (new black experiences in both major wars), urbanization, organized labor, and increasing federal presence during those decades. These structural factors would determine the direction and scope of the modern civil rights movement. Rising expectations of African Americans were reflected in church organizations, membership in the growing NAACP (National Association for the Advancement of Colored People), labor unions, and organizations like the Southern Negro Youth Congress (SNYC).

Organizationally, the drive for civil rights grew out of existing groups in the black community. Those clubs, church groups, and other African American organizations, in turn, developed to become means of resistance and accommodation to segregation. Improving one's life entailed a conscious, careful effort of participating in an organization along with individual struggle. At the same time, the enormous risk of speaking out or upsetting the culture of segregation could lead to violence or death.

Reconstruction

At the conclusion of the Civil War, black labor was indispensable in the South and unwelcome in the industrial North. In the regional economic conflict between the North and the South both sides' interests were served by ensuring that ex-slaves remained in the South. The critical role played by cotton in the American economy helps us understand the post–Civil War economic and social structure. Cotton gradually emerged as king, not only of the Southern economy, but of the American export market as well. By 1860 cotton constituted 60 percent of American exports; by contrast, its nearest rivals, flour and tobacco, together accounted for less than 20 percent (Steinberg, 1989:28). Approximately 20 years earlier, Alexis de Tocqueville had written in *Democracy in America*, (1835–1840), "It is not for the good of the Negroes but for that of the whites that measures are taken to abolish slavery in the United States" (1954:360). It was in the interests of powerful economic and political forces in the North that after the Civil War cotton was restored as king in the Southern economy. Agricultural development in the South was dependent on the labor of blacks. Perhaps more than in the raising of other crops, cotton farming was extremely labor intensive. In the absence of slavery, other means were needed to maintain a class of agricultural laborers. Additionally, the North was apprehensive about blacks moving into its immigrant (white) labor markets.

The Reconstruction period of American history (1865–1877) was seen as a "splendid failure" (a phrase coined by W. E. B. Du Bois) because it offered former slaves a vision of a free society. Pointing out that the revisionist interpretation of Reconstruction that developed in the 1960s challenged the traditional historical portrait of the post–Civil War South as a society governed by corrupt black governments, historian Eric Foner (1983) demonstrates the uniqueness of Reconstruction in opening doors of opportunity. Psychologically, sociologically, and politically, blacks would begin a transformation process that was to become a social movement.

The chief instrument for the North's reorganization of Southern agriculture into a sharecropping system was the Freedman's Bureau. Created by Lincoln, in theory the Bureau was to distribute land to ex-slaves. In practice, however, the Freedman's Bureau was controversial from its inception. In 1866 President Andrew Johnson rescinded land distribution in favor of a contract labor program. Instead of the postbellum promise of "forty acres and a mule," the Bureau organized a system of contract labor thereby creating a dependent caste of workers. Indeed, rebuilding the South for the benefit of the North as well as the South took precedence over social reform. Thus, the most notable and enduring achievement of Reconstruction was the reconstruction of black servitude. Though the Civil War had ended slavery, the underlying economic functions that slavery had served were unchanged, and a surrogate system of compulsory paid labor developed in its place (Steinberg, 1989:199).

The Southern Caste System: The Culture of Segregation

A "separate but equal" division of the races formed a racial caste system in the South. Segregationist legislation made for segregated telephone booths, water fountains, transportation, parks, restaurants, and schools; most of those for blacks were poorly funded and inferior to those for whites. Florida and North Carolina segregated school textbooks. Mississippi banned whites and blacks from using the same taxis. Separation continued even in death—cemeteries too were segregated. Further, despite the Fifteenth Amendment to the U.S. Constitution, which was designed to protect black voting rights, few blacks in the South could vote. The denial of voting rights, known as disfranchisement, was accomplished by passing many state and local laws requiring literacy tests, property ownership, a poll tax, and white-only primaries. To most blacks over the voting age of 21, paying a poll tax was impossible. Unfair and unaffordable, the tax was often tallied on a fee per year of eligibility.

The two races interacted in conformity to custom, law, and "place." In *Trouble in Mind, Black Southerners in the Age of Jim Crow,* Leon Litwack describes the limits to racial interaction during the post-Reconstruction years. A violent history, it was also a period of extraordinary resourcefulness shown by black men and women, a period when an institutional infrastructure within black communities developed from the separate black and white worlds. Under severe constraints, black Southerners created a world of their own "behind the veil," as W. E. B. Du Bois described it, and found ways to respond to their situation. This interior life, largely unknown and incomprehensible to whites, permitted black Southerners to survive and endure (Litwack, 1998).

Segregation grew in a compost of the old racial order. The paradoxically personalized but state-backed racial power that grounded slavery survived emancipation and Reconstruction, and segregation was the law of the land for the states that so chose. The Supreme Court *Plessy v. Ferguson* decision in 1896 ruled that "separate but equal" accommodations were constitutional. Denied access to the "all-white" train car, Homer Plessy, who was one-eighth black, unsuccessfully challenged Louisiana's railroad car segregation law. *Plessy* provided the constitutional protection for segregation until it was overthrown with the 1954 *Brown v. Board of Education* decision. The Constitution reinforced state and local segregation laws. Segregation meant inferior schools and political disfranchisement, low-paying jobs, and second-class citizenship anchored in the caste system.

The custom and culture of segregation in the South developed with a violent, fearsome side. By the end of the nineteenth century, Southern whites burned, hanged, or otherwise brutalized African Americans with savage regularity. When black men violated the code of the caste system they often met with lynching. Viewing lynching as a proper response to crimes committed against "neighborhood values," the white press associated it with black crime. Black journalist Ida B. Wells attacked the white press for promoting blacks as rapists and fought racial stereotyping using statistics. The antilynching fund and antilynching campaigns indicate early forms of organized resistance. Archives at Tuskegee University in Alabama contain records of over 4,700 lynchings that occurred in this country between 1882 and 1944. During those years, Southern senators successfully blocked antilynching legislation. The violent side of Jim Crow contributed mightily to "keeping the Negro in his place." Kellogg's "Lynching and Mob Violence" (Reading 1.3) details lynching and the role it played in the early twentieth-century South. Indeed, the most dramatic method by which the white community reaffirmed its title to power—its dominant caste position—was by hanging blacks who were out of "place."

Most notorious of the hate groups was the Ku Klux Klan, organized in Tennessee in 1865. Founded to fight Reconstruction through harassment and intimidation, Klan members wore white robes, masks, and hoods to disguise their identities. The Klan terrorized blacks and white sympathizers with a burning cross, which was a warning of future assaults. The drive for white supremacy was undertaken by any means that would keep blacks in their place. Intimidation, harassment, and lynching worked one side of society, while the segregation laws worked the other. The result was an ordered racial caste system that associated blackness with inferiority. At the same time that white children were taught that "Negroes must be kept in their place," the law cast a blind eye on lynching.

Life in communities of the Deep South followed an ordered pattern. The inhabitants lived in a social world clearly divided into two ranks, the white caste and the black caste. The castes shared disproportionately in the privileges and obligations of labor, school, and government, and participated in separate family activities, associations, cliques, and churches. Only in the economic sphere did the caste sanctions relax, and then but for a few persons and in limited relationships. Within the caste were social classes, not so rigidly defined as the castes. During this time the black community turned increasingly inward (Davis, Gardner & Gardner, 1972:539).

The cultural stigma of slavery was not likely to disappear in this system. Caste replaced slavery as a means of maintaining the essence of the old social order of the South. The momentum of the culture of segregation continued, in large part, because of the structure of the caste system. Caste members tended to develop a distinctive psychology. Inferior caste resulted in social isolation for the individuals concerned and limited their personal development, so that it was more difficult for them to compete for the highest social rewards (Dollard, 1957:63).

The somber tale of decline and repression for blacks after Reconstruction and into the first part of the twentieth century was defined by full-scale segregation. It was the low-water mark in the history of African Americans since the time of slavery itself. Fittingly, the pioneering black historian Rayford Logan described this as the nadir of black life in America. In 1899 rural Georgia was the scene of the lynching of a black man who in self-defense accidentally killed his employer, a white landlord. The sensationalized lynching captures the violent side of segregation's last resort to keeping blacks in their place:

Some two thousand men and women witnessed it on Sunday afternoon, April 23, 1899, near Newman, Georgia, some of them arriving from Atlanta on a special excursion train. After stripping Hose of his clothes and chaining him to a tree, the self-appointed executioners stacked kerosene-soaked wood high around him. Before saturating Hose with oil and applying the torch, they cut off his ears, fingers, and genitals, and skinned his face. While some in the crowd plunged knives into the victim's flesh, others watched "with unfeigned satisfaction" (as one reporter noted) the contortions on Sam Hose's body as the flames rose, distorting the features, causing his eyes to bulge out of their sockets, and rupturing his veins. When in Hose's agony he almost managed to unloosen his bonds, the executioners quenched the flames, retied him, and applied more oil to the body before relighting the fire. . . . Before Hose's body had even cooled, his heart and liver were removed and cut into several pieces and his bones were crushed into small particles. The crowd fought over these souvenirs, and the "more fortunate possessors" made some handsome profits on the sales. Shortly after the lynching, one of the participants reportedly left for the state capitol, hoping to deliver to the governor of Georgia a slice of Sam Hose's heart (Litwack, 1998:281).

Incredibly, in this fearful, oppressive environment, early forms of black resistance emerged. The "hidden transcript" of the black community highlights the daily acts of resistance and survival—the infrapolitics of the oppressed—in the oppositional culture constructed in and around segregation. For example, public transportation became a source of conflict. Public norms within the constraints of Jim Crow were often challenged by blacks, but at a cost. Many times black women argued with white bus drivers over seating arrangements. Typically, the black woman was sent to the back of the bus or thrown off violently. This example, with countless other such acts, shows how unorganized working people resisted the strong arm of segregation. A pervasive tone of resistance eventually became an important part of the culture of protest from which the civil rights movement evolved (Kelley, 1993, Reading 2.1).

The Church

The black Baptist Church became the center of African American life in the South. By virtue of its internal structure, the church provided an organizational vehicle for balancing survival with dignity. In the closed society of Jim Crow, the church afforded African Americans an interstitial space in which to critique and contest white America's racial domination (Higgenbotham, 1993:10). Black sociologist E. Franklin Frazier described the black church as a "nation within a nation." Frazier's metaphor of the black church as a nation suggests a public distinct from and in conflict with the dominant white society and its racist institutions. (Higgenbotham, 1993:11).

The Double Self

The psychological consequence of segregation, the identity question, was described as a "twoness" haunting and defining African Americans. Historian and sociologist W. E. B. Du Bois, who was one of the founders and early leader of the NAACP, described in *Souls of Black Folk* the experience of race. "It is a peculiar sensation this double-consciousness, this sense of always looking at one's self through the eyes of others, of measuring one's soul by the tape of a world that looks on in amused contempt and pity. One ever feels his twoness,—an American, a Negro; two souls, two thoughts, two unreconciled strivings; two warring ideas in one dark body, whose dogged strength alone keeps it from being torn asunder." The title, *Souls of Black Folk,* means precisely two souls, one self. Du Bois wrote of the double-consciousness of blacks in America constantly forced to live beyond the veil of racial degradations.

This struggle for identity, a duality or paradox of black life in America, is graphically revealed in Ralph Ellison's portrayal of the black odyssey in *Invisible Man.* In the opening scene, the nameless hero is deeply moved by the words of his dying grandfather. After emancipation, his grandfather had stayed on at the same place. He worked hard, and he had brought up his children in the etiquette of accommodation and survival. On his deathbed, however, the grandfather confessed to having a more complex life (Litwack, 1998):

> "Son, after I'm gone I want you to keep up the good fight. I never told you, but our life is a war and I have been a traitor all my born days, a spy in the enemy's country ever since I give up my gun back in the Reconstruction. Live with your head in the lion's mouth. I want you to overcome 'em with yeses, undermine 'em with grins, agree 'em to death and destruction, let 'em swoller you till they vomit or bust wide open." (Ellison, 1952).

Resistance became social and political when the masses were involved, but at its heart it was individual. The complex personal reaction to Jim Crow, often burning on the conscience of blacks, would provide the drive to survive and succeed in unique ways. Balancing on one hand the threat of mob violence, on the other a strong sense of personal integrity, blacks throughout the segregation period developed forms of resistance while inching toward the road to reform. George Lipsitz, in *The Possessive Investment of Whiteness,* calls this the dialectical interplay of accommodation and resistance.

Accommodation and Agitation

Divided over strategies of accommodation and resistance, the black community carefully considered the two positions. Booker T. Washington, who earned a national reputation for furthering the cause of black education, became a leading spokesman for civil rights. Washington was one of the most influential black Americans of the early twentieth century. The 1895 Atlanta Exposition was the site for his address on the progress of the American Negro (Reading 1.1). In his view, the most productive course for black Americans was to work at self-betterment through agriculture and industry. Advocating a policy of accommodation on civil rights issues, Washington became a national black leader who advised Presidents Theodore Roosevelt and William Taft on race issues. He became the principal of Tuskeegee Institute, an industrial school in Alabama, and there he constructed a comprehensive social and economic program for black development from 1880 to 1915. The Atlanta Exposition selection offers a firsthand account of his position.

In contrast, W. E. B. Du Bois's idea of agitation frames the turn-of-the-century–African American debate. He proposed "a forward movement" whereby Negroes "must strive for the rights which the world accords to men." In his essay "Of Mr. Booker T. Washington and Others" (Reading 1.2), Du Bois praised Washington and the progress he had gained for blacks. Du Bois, however, thought Washington's program would make it difficult to gain equality. Calling Washington's speech the "Atlanta Compromise," Du Bois's critique suggested that it ensured the continuance of segregation while creating a lower, dependent working class of blacks. The key issue in the Washington-Du Bois debate was how blacks could most effectively change their segregated society—in the mainstream as Washington argued, or outside it, as Du Bois implored.

In spite of Washington's accommodationist public persona, behind the scenes he was actively engaged in lawsuits challenging Jim Crow. Du Bois took the more publicly activist route along with prominent blacks such as Ida B. Wells and William Monroe Trotter. Whites such as Mary White Ovington and Oswald Garrison Villard launched the interracial NAACP in 1909. Founded in part as a response to a series of antiblack race riots, the NAACP soon emerged as the leading black civil rights organization (Martin, 1998:7).

In 1905, Du Bois was elected secretary of the newly formed Niagara Movement, the earliest black organization to develop a program for gaining civil rights. This first civil rights organization provided blacks a more radical policy of protest compared to the conservatism of Washington. Seeking "civil rights and first class citizenship for blacks," the Niagara Movement faltered, falling short of its goals. Many who were involved with the Niagara Movement, however, joined the new NAACP, which became a formal civil rights organization. Du Bois was the only black among the five incorporators of the NAACP and editor of its official publication, the *Crisis*. The NAACP adopted many principles of the Niagara Movement, especially those that criticized Washington's accommodation policies.

Civil rights in America at the turn of the century were severely restricted for African Americans. Legal challenges to segregation and denial of basic rights were, for the most part, not successful. The *Plessy* decision in 1896 became the legislative standard for keeping the races separate and, in fact, unequal. The separate but equal notion stemming from the Louisiana public transportation case legitimized segregation, enabling the Southern states to continue designing a Jim Crow society. Threatened by lynching and other intimidating tactics, African Americans in the South as well as the North turned to subtle and sophisticated forms of resistance. They combined survival techniques with dignity and simultaneously adjusted to and resisted segregation in every arena of life.

World War I

The war experience gave hope to veterans who had encountered visions of freedom while fighting in other parts of the world. Their return to civilian life, however, was a cruel reminder of the absence of justice and of segregated restrictions on their freedom, causes for which they had fought abroad. In July 1917, ten thousand blacks marched down New York's Fifth Avenue in a silent protest parade. Protesting the violence of race riots and lynching, blacks began to demonstrate in public for civil rights. The end of World War I brought an improvement in the economy along with a cultural explosion in America's largest black community, Harlem. The Harlem Renaissance celebrated black culture at a national level.

In spite of federal endorsement of white supremacy in the South, the traditions of freedom and citizenship sustained "communities of resistance." These communities included the black church, Republican Party politics, and the NAACP. They became hosts for black community activism. Industrialization and urbanization of the South reflected the changing economy. Nevertheless, racial discrimination was part of the newly emerging economic form. The bleak economic depression that followed gave rise to a change on the federal level with Franklin Roosevelt's election in 1932. Promising a New Deal recovery program, the Roosevelt years would usher a new role for the federal government in public policy. With the passage of the Social Security Act of 1935 and other recovery acts, the federal government was enhancing its role in American life. Although African Americans who were employed in domestic and agricultural settings were excluded from receiving social security benefits, the New Deal would prove to be an important step in the future of civil rights. An encouraging development, for example, was the appointment of Clark Foreman, a white Southern liberal to serve as Special Adviser on the Economic Status of Negroes. Robert Weaver, a black economist, was appointed as Foreman's assistant. Of particular importance during the New Deal period is the switch of African American voters from the Republican (the party of Lincoln) to the Democratic Party.

The emergence of civil rights as a national issue during the 1930s New Deal political environment is highlighted by A. Philip Randolph's call for an all-black march on Washington. Randolph sought to pressure the Roosevelt administration by demanding equal opportunities for blacks in the military and in defense industries. His agenda is presented in "Civil Rights Can Be Secured by Mass Action" (Reading 1.5). Randolph called off the planned 1941 march when President Roosevelt issued an executive order desegregating defense industries and creating the Fair Employment Practices Commission. Twenty-two years later, Randolph was a prime organizer of the historic 1963 March on Washington. As a labor organizer and president of the Brotherhood of Sleeping Car Porters, Randolph believed that mass demonstrations would pressure the federal government into legislative action (Sullivan, 1996, Reading 1.4). This primary source selection offers an early example of civil rights demands directed at the federal government.

Urbanization: The Great Migration

In the 1930s most American blacks lived in the South. However, the demand for labor in the war industries of the North would lead to major demographic changes. With no vote and a rigid caste system to live in, many blacks cast a hopeful eye northward to the so-called promised land. Some blacks had relatives from Chicago who visited, spreading word of a different life, where there was employment and opportunity. During the decade of the 1940s over 1 million blacks migrated to Chicago. By 1950 over 9 million blacks lived in urban areas, marking the first decade in American history that more blacks lived in cities than in rural areas (see Table 1). Black newspapers including the *Chicago Defender* encouraged blacks to "Come North." Often distributed by Pullman porters despite bans in some Southern

Table 1

9

Introduction

Urbanization of the African American Population

Year	Rural	Urban
1890	6,171,614	1,317,062
1900	7,023,744	2,004,121
1910	7,138,534	2,689,229
1920	6,903,658	3,559,473
1930	6,697,230	5,193,913
1940	6,611,930	6,253,588
1950	5,649,678	9,392,608
1960	5,064,191	13,807,640
1970	4,212,971	18,367,318

Source: Ben J. Wattenberg, *The Statistical History of the United States* (New York: Basic Books, 1976) p. 12.

states, copies of the *Chicago Defender* became an important source of alternative news to the African American community in the South. The *Defender* printed train schedules for points from the South to Chicago.

The black migration to the North accelerated in 1944. The invention of the rust cotton reaper, a machine that could pick cotton at the rate of 50 pickers, doomed the livelihood of the Southern sharecropper. Factories in the industrial North wanted Southern blacks because they were good workers. Despite the mechanization of farming, Southern whites were angry that blacks were moving North. The influx of Southern blacks to work in Northern defense industries resulted in conflict. There was racial violence in the summer of 1943 when whites attacked unarmed blacks, who retaliated with rioting.

The increasing urbanization of African Americans leads some historians to argue that the civil rights era began in the early 1940s. Robert Korstad and Nelson Lichtenstein (1988) suggest that increasing unionization and a high-employment economy together with increasing federal presence established the framework for a potentially autonomous, labor-orientated civil rights movement. The civil rights struggle of the post-*Brown* years, however, had a different social and political agenda; issues of economic inequality and working class empowerment would not be addressed until after 1965.

World War II

Both major twentieth-century wars proved significant in changing conditions for blacks in segregated America. World War II ushered in an economic expansion that ended the Great Depression; millions of new jobs opened. But black soldiers were restricted mainly to all-black units commanded by white officers. Even though segregation persisted in all branches of the services throughout the war, thousands of blacks volunteered and fought courageously. From 1939 to 1945 African Americans conducted the "Double V Campaign." This called for a victory over fascism and Nazism overseas and victory over racism at home. The demand for democracy at home as well as abroad was part of the consciousness that would develop into the protest movements of the next two decades. De jure segregation was still the law of the land in the South, while de facto segregation was the norm in the North. John Dittmer's "Rising Expectations, 1946–54" (Reading 1.8), portrays Southern segregation in the workplace, public accommodations, movies, schools, and churches. In keeping with two earlier selections (Sullivan, Bloom, Readings 1.4 and 1.6) dealing with the role of national politics and the federal government, Dittmer offers the experiences of returning war veterans in Mississippi. These veterans inspired increased membership in the Mississippi branch of the NAACP. Their priority was voter registration. One of them was Medgar Evers.

Following World War I, the caste system and culture of segregation prevailed in the Mississippi delta counties, and white supremacy was enforced by lynching and economic inequality. World War II brought change to Mississippi in the form of defense industries. Although more than 85,000 Mississippi blacks served in the armed forces, public statements from James Eastland, Mississippi's junior senator, demeaned black soldiers and charged that the Negro race was inferior to the white race. This proclamation in the Senate came near the end of a war against Hitler's Germany.

In 1948 for the first time in a presidential election the treatment of blacks was a central issue. Jack Bloom's essay, "Nineteen Forty-Eight: The Opening of the Breach" (Reading 1.6), focuses on the nomination, campaign, and election of Harry Truman. Bloom shows the potential of black voting power to determine the outcome of the presidential election and many local offices. He cites a major demographic shift of blacks, who left the South to find jobs. In the North, 90 percent of the black population was concentrated in cities, and this urbanization represented potential political power. Truman balances the pressure from liberals on the race issue with the states' rights position of Southerners, reasoning that civil rights at home were necessary to fight the cold war. Blacks voted 69 percent for Truman and the black vote was instrumental in carrying the key states of Ohio, California, and Illinois for the Democrats. The 1948 election opened a breach in the Democratic Party. Further, it showed how isolated the South's culture of segregation and racism was from the political trends in the nation.

Popular Culture

Segregation was reinforced with popular racial stereotypes, but serious discussion of the race issue was absent in the popular media. The subject was considered too volatile for national public broadcast, until persistent efforts of NBC radio programmers resulted in *University of Chicago Round Table* and *America's Town Meeting of the Air,* which addressed issues of Jim Crow and race. The selection by Barbara Dianne Savage, "Radio and the Political Discourse of Racial Equality" (Reading 1.9), explores the history of introducing the race question on the public airwaves. She points out that the mere act of discussing the issue on the air was a rite of legitimization for African American arguments for freedom, and that fear and extreme caution among whites accompanied this change (Savage, 1999:243). Radio played an important role in providing a public forum for issues of freedom and civil rights, paving the way for more media exposure in the decades to follow.

Another area of popular culture, professional sports, remained segregated until 1947 when Jackie Robinson "broke the color barrier" in baseball. One year earlier the Brooklyn Dodgers chose Robinson, a college graduate and outstanding athlete, as a test case. Counseled by the owners about turning both cheeks to insult or injury, Robinson spent a year with the Dodgers' minor league team in Montreal. He became an immediate success blazing the trail for other "selected" blacks of superstar quality. Baseball great Willie Mays, another pioneer black to integrate the game, said of Robinson, "Someone like Jackie needed to do it, he was respected because he was a college man, he was someone we all looked up to." In spite of Robinson's success on the field and in sports' pages, he endured several years of vicious insults from fans and players. Because of housing segregation in Florida, the Dodgers had to move their spring training headquarters from that state to Cuba. Eventually, the presence of African American players on most teams, together with antidiscrimination laws forced Southern cities to accommodate baseball's integration.

Key Figures, Terms, and Concepts

Birth of a Nation
Black Shirts
carpetbaggers,
The *Chicago Defender*
The *Crisis*
W. E. Burghardt Du Bois
Dunning School of History
Clark Foreman
Freedman's Bureau
Aaron Henry
"intrapolitics"

Jim Crow
Mississippi Plan
the Niagara Movement
Plessy v. Ferguson
radical history
Asa Philip Randolph
revisionist history
scalawags
Henry Wallace
Booker T. Washington

Important Questions to Consider

1. What was the significance of Roosevelt's New Deal policy in the emergence of civil rights as a national issue? Compare the Roosevelt and Truman administrations in terms of changing race relations.

2. How can unorganized daily acts of black resistance to segregation be seen as precursors of an organized movement?

3. How did national political issues in the 1930s and 1940s break from previous presidential election campaigns?

The Atlanta Exposition Address

Booker T. Washington (1856–1915) was an educator and reformer who became an important spokesman for African Americans after the turn of the century. He was the founder of Tuskegee Institute, an industrial school for blacks in Alabama.

Cast down your bucket where you are.

One-third of the population of the South is of the Negro race. No enterprise seeking the material, civil, or moral welfare of this section can disregard this element of our population and reach the highest success. I but convey to you, Mr. President and Directors, the sentiment of the masses of my race when I say that in no way have the value and manhood of the American Negro been more fittingly and generously recognized than by the managers of this magnificent Exposition at every stage of its progress. It is a recognition that will do more to cement the friendship of the two races than any occurrence since the dawn of freedom.

Not only this, but the opportunity here afforded will awaken among us a new era of industrial progress. Ignorant and inexperienced, it is not strange that in the first years of our new life we began at the top instead of at the bottom; that a seat in Congress or the State Legislature was more sought than real estate or industrial skill; that the political convention or stump speaking had more attractions than starting a dairy farm or truck garden.

A ship lost at sea for many days suddenly sighted a friendly vessel. From the mast of the unfortunate vessel was seen a signal: "Water, water, we die of thirst." The answer from the friendly vessel at once came back, "Cast down your bucket where you are." A second time the signal, "Water, water, send us water," ran up from the distressed vessel and was answered, "Cast down your bucket where you are." And a third and fourth signal for water was answered "Cast down your bucket where you are." The captain of the distressed vessel, at last heeding the injunction, cast down his bucket and it came up full of fresh, sparkling water from the mouth of the Amazon River.

To those of my race who depend on bettering their condition in a foreign land, or who underestimate the importance of cultivating friendly relations with the Southern white man who is their next-door neighbor, I would say: Cast down your bucket where you are; cast it down in making friends, in every manly way, of the people of all races by whom we are surrounded. Cast it down in agriculture, mechanics, in commerce, in domestic service, and in the professions. And in this connection it is well to bear in mind that whatever other sins the South may be called upon to bear, when it comes to business pure and simple, it is in the South that the Negro is given a man's chance in the commercial world, and in nothing is this Exposition more eloquent than in emphasizing this chance. Our greatest danger is that, in the great leap from slavery to freedom, we may overlook the fact that the masses of us are to live by the productions of our hands and fail to keep in mind that we shall prosper in the proportion as we learn to dignify and glorify common labor, and put brains and skill into the common occupations of life; shall prosper in proportion as we learn to draw the line between the superficial and the substantial, the ornamental gewgaws of life and the useful. No race can prosper till it learns that there is as much dignity in tilling a field as in writing a poem. It is at the bottom of life we must begin, and not at the top. Nor should we permit our grievances to overshadow our opportunities.

To those of the white race who look to the incoming of those of foreign birth and strange tongue and habits for the prosperity of the South, were I permitted I would repeat what I say to my own race, "Cast down your bucket where you are." Cast it down among the 8,000,000 Negroes whose habits you know, whose fidelity and love you have tested in days when to have proved treacherous meant the ruin of your firesides. Cast down your bucket among these people who have, without strikes and labor wars, tilled your fields, cleared your forests, builded your railroads and cities, and brought forth treasures from the bowels of the earth and helped make possible this magnificent representation of the progress of the South. Casting down your bucket among my people, helping and encouraging them as you are doing on these grounds, and, with education of head, hand and heart, you will find that they will buy your surplus land, make blossom the waste places in your fields, and run your factories.

While doing this, you can be sure in the future, as in the past, that you and your families will be surrounded by the most patient, faithful, law-abiding, and unresentful people that the world has seen. As we have proved our loyalty to you in the past, in nursing your children, watching by the sickbed of your mothers and fathers, and often following them with tear-dimmed eyes to their graves, so in the future, in our humble way, we shall stand by you with a devotion that no foreigner can approach, ready to lay down our lives, if need be, in defense of yours; interlacing our industrial, commercial, civil, and religious life with yours in a way that shall make the interests of both races one. In all things that are purely social we can be as separate as the fingers, yet one as the hand in all things essential to mutual progress.

There is no defense or security for any of us except in the highest intelligence and development of all. If anywhere there are efforts tending to curtail the fullest growth of the Negro, let these efforts be turned into stimulating, encouraging and making him the most useful and intelligent citizen. Effort or means so invested will pay a thousand percent interest. These efforts will be twice blessed—"blessing him that gives and him that takes."

There is no escape, through law of man or God, from the inevitable:

> The laws of changeless justice bind
> Oppressor with oppressed,
> And close as sin and suffering joined
> We march to fate abreast.

Nearly sixteen million hands will aid you in pulling the load upward, or they will pull against you the load downward. We shall constitute one-third and more of the ignorance and crime of the South, or one-third its intelligence and progress; we shall contribute one-third to the business and industrial prosperity of the South, or we shall prove a veritable body of death, stagnating, depressing, retarding every effort to advance the body politic.

14

*The Architecture
of Segregation*

Gentlemen of the Exposition: As we present to you our humble effort at an exhibition of our progress, you must not expect overmuch. Starting thirty years ago with ownership here and there in a few quilts and pumpkins and chickens (gathered from miscellaneous sources), remember: the path that has led us from these to the invention and production of agricultural implements, buggies, steam engines, newspapers, books, statuary, carving, paintings, the management of drugstores and banks, has not been trodden without contact with thorns and thistles. While we take pride in what we exhibit as a result of our independent efforts, we do not for a moment forget that our part in this exhibition would fall far short of your expectations but for the constant help that has come to our educational life, not only from the Southern states, but especially from Northern philanthropists who have made their gifts a constant stream of blessing and encouragement.

The wisest among my race understand that the agitation of questions of social equality is the extremest folly, and that progress in the enjoyment of all the privileges that will come to us must be the result of severe and constant struggle rather than of artificial forcing. No race that has anything to contribute to the markets of the world is long in any degree ostracized. It is important and right that all privileges of the laws be ours, but it is vastly more important that we be prepared for the exercise of those privileges. The opportunity to earn a dollar in a factory just now is worth infinitely more than the opportunity to spend a dollar in an opera house.

In conclusion, may I repeat that nothing in thirty years has given us more hope and encouragement and drawn us so near to you of the white race as this opportunity offered by the Exposition; and here bending, as it were, over the altar that represents the results of the struggles of your race and mine, both starting practically empty-handed three decades ago, I pledge that, in your effort to work out the great and intricate problem which God has laid at the doors of the South, you shall have at all times the patient, sympathetic help of my race. Only let this be constantly in mind that, while from representations in these buildings of the product of field, of forest, of mine, of factory, letters and art, much good will come—yet by far above and beyond material benefits, will be that higher good, that let us pray God will come, in a blotting out of sectional differences and racial animosities and suspicions, in a determination to administer absolute justice, in a willing obedience among all classes to the mandates of law. This, coupled with material prosperity, will bring into our beloved South a new heaven and a new earth.

Of Mr. Booker T. Washington and Others

W. E. Burghardt Du Bois (1868–1963), author of The Souls of Black Folk, *was a sociologist, writer, scholar, and civil rights activist. He was one of the founders of the NAACP and editor of its publication, the* Crisis.

> *From birth till death enslaved; in word, in deed, unmanned!*
> *Hereditary bondsmen! Know ye not*
> *Who would be free themselves must strike the blow?*
>
> Byron

Easily the most striking thing in the history of the American Negro since 1876 is the ascendancy of Mr. Booker T. Washington. It began at the time when war memories and ideals were rapidly passing; a day of astonishing commercial development was dawning; a sense of doubt and hesitation overtook the freedmen's sons,—then it was that his leading began. Mr. Washington came, with a simple definite programme, at the psychological moment when the nation was a little ashamed of having bestowed so much sentiment on Negroes, and was concentrating its energies on Dollars. His programme of industrial education, conciliation of the South, and submission and silence as to civil and political rights, was not wholly original; the Free Negroes from 1830 up to wartime had striven to build industrial schools, and the American Missionary Association had from the first taught various trades; and Price and others had sought a way of honorable alliance with the best of the Southerners. But Mr. Washington first indissolubly linked these things; he put enthusiasm, unlimited energy, and perfect faith into this programme, and changed it from a by-path into a veritable Way of Life. And the tale of the methods by which he did this is a fascinating study of human life.

It startled the nation to hear a Negro advocating such a programme after many decades of bitter complaint; it startled and won the applause of the South, it interested and won the admiration of the North; and after a confused murmur of protest, it silenced if it did not convert the Negroes themselves.

To gain the sympathy and coöperation of the various elements comprising the white South was Mr. Washington's first task; and this, at the time Tuskegee was founded, seemed, for a black man, well-nigh impossible. And yet ten years later it was done in the word spoken at Atlanta: "In all things purely social we can be as separate as the five fingers, and yet one as the hand in all things essential to mutual progress." This "Atlanta Compromise" is by all odds the most notable thing in Mr. Washington's career. The South interpreted it in different ways: the radicals received it as a complete surrender of the demand for civil and political equality; the conservatives, as a generously conceived working basis for mutual understanding. So both approved it, and to-day its author is certainly the most distinguished Southerner since Jefferson Davis, and the one with the largest personal following.

Next to this achievement comes Mr. Washington's work in gaining place and consideration in the North. Others less shrewd and tactful had formerly essayed to sit on these two stools and had fallen between them; but as Mr. Washington knew the heart of the South from birth and training, so by singular insight he intuitively grasped the spirit of the age which was dominating the North. And so thoroughly did he learn the speech and thought of triumphant commercialism, and the ideas of material prosperity, that the picture of a lone black boy poring over a French grammar amid the weeds and dirt of a neglected home soon seemed to him the acme of absurdities. One wonders what Socrates and St. Francis of Assisi would say to this.

And yet this very singleness of vision and thorough oneness with his age is a mark of the successful man. It is as though Nature must needs make men narrow in order to give them force. So Mr. Washington's cult has gained unquestioning followers, his work has wonderfully prospered, his friends are legion, and his enemies are confounded. To-day he stands as the one recognized spokesman of his ten million fellows, and one of the most notable figures in a nation of seventy millions. One hesitates, therefore, to criticise a life which, beginning with so little, has done so much. And yet the time is come when one may speak in all sincerity and utter courtesy of the mistakes and shortcomings of Mr. Washington's career, as well as of his triumphs, without being thought captious or envious, and without forgetting that it is easier to do ill than well in the world.

The criticism that has hitherto met Mr. Washington has not always been of this broad character. In the South especially has he had to walk warily to avoid the harshest judgments,—and naturally so, for he is dealing with the one subject of deepest sensitiveness to that section. Twice—once when at the Chicago celebration of the Spanish-American War he alluded to the color-prejudice that is "eating away the vitals of the South," and once when he dined with President Roosevelt—has the resulting Southern criticism been violent enough to threaten seriously his popularity. In the North the feeling has several times forced itself into words, that Mr. Washington's counsels of submission overlooked certain elements of true manhood, and that his educational programme was unnecessarily narrow. Usually, however, such criticism has not found open expression, although, too, the spiritual sons of the Abolitionists have not been prepared to acknowledge that the schools founded before Tuskegee, by men of broad ideals and self-sacrificing spirit, were wholly failures or worthy of ridicule. While, then, criticism has not failed to follow Mr. Washington, yet the prevailing public opinion of the land has been but too willing to deliver the solution of a wearisome problem into his hands, and say, "If that is all you and your race ask, take it."

Among his own people, however, Mr. Washington has encountered the strongest and most lasting opposition, amounting at times to bitterness, and even to-day continuing strong and insistent even though largely silenced in outward expression by the public opinion of the nation. Some of this opposition is, of course, mere envy; the disappointment of displaced demagogues and the spite of narrow minds. But aside from this, there is among educated and thoughtful colored men in all parts of the land a feeling of deep regret, sorrow, and apprehension at the wide currency and ascendancy which some of Mr. Washington's theories have gained. These same men admire his sincerity of purpose, and are willing to forgive much to honest endeavor which is doing something worth the doing. They coöperate with Mr. Washington as far as they conscientiously can; and, indeed, it is no ordinary tribute to this man's tact and power that, steering as he must between so many diverse interests and opinions, he so largely retains the respect of all. . . .

Mr. Washington represents in Negro thought the old attitude of adjustment and submission; but adjustment at such a peculiar time as to make his programme unique. This is an age of unusual economic development, and Mr. Washington's programme naturally takes an economic cast, becoming a gospel of Work and Money to such an extent as apparently almost completely to overshadow the higher aims of life. Moreover, this is an age when the more advanced races are coming in closer contact with the less developed races, and the race-feeling is therefore intensified; and Mr. Washington's programme practically accepts the alleged inferiority of the Negro races. Again, in our own land, the reaction from the sentiment of war time has given impetus to race-prejudice against Negroes, and Mr. Washington withdraws many of the high demands of Negroes as men and American citizens. In other periods of intensified prejudice all the Negro's tendency to self-assertion has been called forth; at this period a policy of submission is advocated. In the history of nearly all other races and peoples the doctrine preached at such crises has been that manly self-respect is worth more than lands and houses, and that a people who voluntarily surrender such respect, or cease striving for it, are not worth civilizing.

In answer to this, it has been claimed that the Negro can survive only through submission. Mr. Washington distinctly asks that black people give up, at least for the present, three things,—

- First, political power,
- Second, insistence on civil rights,
- Third, higher education of Negro youth,—

and concentrate all their energies on industrial education, the accumulation of wealth, and the conciliation of the South. This policy has been courageously and insistently advocated for over fifteen years, and has been triumphant for perhaps ten years. As a result of this tender of the palm-branch, what has been the return? In these years there have occurred:

1. The disfranchisement of the Negro.
2. The legal creation of a distinct status of civil inferiority for the Negro.
3. The steady withdrawal of aid from institutions for the higher training of the Negro.

These movements are not, to be sure, direct results of Mr. Washington's teachings; but his propaganda has, without a shadow of doubt, helped their speedier accomplishment. The question then comes: Is it possible, and probable, that nine millions of men can make effective progress in economic lines if they are deprived of political rights, made of servile caste, and allowed only the most meagre chance for developing their exceptional men? If history and reason give any distinct answer to these questions, it is an emphatic *No*. And Mr. Washington thus faces the triple paradox of his career:

1. He is striving nobly to make Negro artisans business men and property-owners; but it is utterly impossible, under modern competitive

methods, for workingmen and property-owners to defend their rights and exist without the right of suffrage.

2. He insists on thrift and self-respect, but at the same time counsels a silent submission to civic inferiority such as is bound to sap the manhood of any race in the long run.

3. He advocates common-school and industrial training, and depreciates institutions of higher-learning; but neither the Negro common-schools, nor Tuskegee itself, could remain open a day were it not for teachers trained in Negro colleges, or trained by their graduates.

This triple paradox in Mr. Washington's position is the object of criticism by two classes of colored Americans. One class is spiritually descended from Toussaint the Savior, through Gabriel, Vesey, and Turner, and they represent the attitude of revolt and revenge; they hate the white South blindly and distrust the white race generally, and so far as they agree on definite action, think that the Negro's only hope lies in emigration beyond the borders of the United States. And yet, by the irony of fate, nothing has more effectually made this programme seem hopeless than the recent course of the United States toward weaker and darker peoples in the West Indies, Hawaii, and the Philippines,—for where in the world may we go and be safe from lying and brute force?

The other class of Negroes who cannot agree with Mr. Washington has hitherto said little aloud. They deprecate the sight of scattered counsels, of internal disagreement; and especially they dislike making their just criticism of a useful and earnest man an excuse for a general discharge of venom from small-minded opponents. Nevertheless, the questions involved are so fundamental and serious that it is difficult to see how men like the Grimkes, Kelly Miller, J. W. E. Bowen, and other representatives of this group, can much longer be silent. Such men feel in conscience bound to ask of this nation three things:

1. The right to vote.
2. Civic equality.
3. The education of youth according to ability.

They acknowledge Mr. Washington's invaluable service in counselling patience and courtesy in such demands; they do not ask that ignorant black men vote when ignorant whites are debarred, or that any reasonable restrictions in the suffrage should not be applied; they know that the low social level of the mass of the race is responsible for much discrimination against it, but they also know, and the nation knows, that relentless color-prejudice is more often a cause than a result of the Negro's degradation; they seek the abatement of this relic of barbarism, and not its systematic encouragement and pampering by all agencies of social power from the Associated Press to the Church of Christ. They advocate, with Mr. Washington, a broad system of Negro common schools supplemented by thorough industrial training; but they are surprised that a man of Mr. Washington's insight cannot see that no such educational system ever has rested or can rest on any other basis than that of the well-equipped college and university, and they insist that there is a demand for a few such institutions throughout the South to train the best of the Negro youth as teachers, professional men, and leaders.

This group of men honor Mr. Washington for his attitude of conciliation toward the white South; they accept the "Atlanta Compromise" in its broadest interpretation; they recognize, with him, many signs of promise, many men of high purpose and fair judgment, in this section; they know that no easy task has been laid upon a region already tottering under heavy burdens. But, nevertheless, they insist that the way to truth and right lies in straightforward honesty, not in indiscriminate flattery; in praising those of the South who do well and criticising uncompromisingly those who do ill; in taking advantage of the opportunities at hand and urging their fellows to do the same, but at the same time in remembering that only a firm adherence to their higher ideals and aspirations will ever keep those ideals within the realm of possibility. They do not expect that the free right to vote, to enjoy civic rights, and to be educated, will come in a moment; they do not expect to see the bias and prejudices of years disappear at the blast of a trumpet; but they are absolutely certain that the way for a people to gain their reasonable rights is not by voluntarily throwing them away and insisting that they do not want them; that the way for a people to gain respect is not by continually belittling and ridiculing themselves; that, on the contrary, Negroes must insist continually, in season and out of season, that voting is necessary to modern manhood, that color discrimination is barbarism, and that black boys need education as well as white boys. . . .

The South ought to be led, by candid and honest criticism, to assert her better self and do her full duty to the race she has cruelly wronged and is still wronging. The North—her co-partner in guilt—cannot salve her conscience by plastering it with gold. We cannot settle this problem by diplomacy and suaveness, by "policy" alone. If worse come to worst, can the moral fibre of this country survive the slow throttling and murder of nine millions of men?

The black men of America have a duty to perform, a duty stern and delicate,—a forward movement to oppose a part of the work of their greatest leader. So far as Mr. Washington preaches Thrift, Patience, and Industrial Training for the masses, we must hold up his hands and strive with him, rejoicing in his honors and glorying in the strength of this Joshua called of God and of man to lead the headless host. But so far as Mr. Washington apologizes for injustice, North or South, does not rightly value the privilege and duty of voting, belittles the emasculating effects of caste distinctions, and opposes the higher training and ambition of our brighter minds,—so far as he, the South, or the Nation, does this,—we must unceasingly and firmly oppose them. By every civilized and peaceful method we must strive for the rights which the world accords to men, clinging unwaveringly to those great words which the sons of the Fathers would fain forget: "We hold these truths to be self-evident: That all men are created equal; that they are endowed by their Creator with certain unalienable rights; that among these are life, liberty, and the pursuit of happiness."

Lynching and Mob Violence

Charles Flint Kellogg, author of NAACP, A History of the National Association for the Advancement of Colored People, Vols. 1 & 2, *was chairman of the Department of History at Dickinson College, Carlisle, Pennsylvania.*

The NAACP was founded in response to an incident of mob violence. The crusade against similar horrors continued to be a motivating force behind the Association's work. The violence was a conspicuous manifestation of the degradation of the Negro brought about by various forms of discrimination, segregation, and Jim Crow. In the early days of the Association much energy was expended in the attempt to prevent the spread and increase of these extreme manifestations of racial conflict. Calling public attention to the shamefulness of mob violence in modern society was the foremost task of the NAACP. Sensationalism in the press distorted the role of the Negro and was in large measure responsible for many of the race riots and other forms of mob violence which took with increasing frequency and savagery and reached a climax in 1919.

The most hideous form of mob violence was lynching. *The Crisis* published the lynching toll annually, although accurate statistics were difficult to obtain. *The Crisis* claimed that at least one hundred persons were lynched in 1911, but the Chicago Tribune reported only sixty-three. In 1912, according to *The Crisis*, sixty-three persons were lynched and in 1913, seventy-nine. The *Chicago Tribune* reported fifty-four in 1914; Tuskegee Institute, which also collected lynching statistics, reported fifty-two, and *The Crisis,* seventy-five, including four Negro women and five white persons.

Lynchings occurred in twelve Southern and Border states. The largest number took place in Mississippi (fifteen), Louisiana (thirteen), and Kentucky (eleven). Thirty persons were lynched for the alleged crime of murder; eight for rape, attempted rape, or presence in a woman's room; five for theft; two for arson; and one for resistance to search. Thirteen were killed by rioters and night riders. Mob violence often took the form of dynamitings and incendiary fires.

A study of available records from 1889 to 1918, published by the NAACP, reveal that in this thirty-year period 3,224 persons, including 61 women, were lynched. Walter White some years later pointed out that each decade from 1900 through 1927 had shown a decline in lynching but that with the decline came greatly aggravated brutality, and the victims suffered almost unbelievable tortures. He held that fundamentalist religious sects in the South contributed to violence by releasing dangerous passions and contributing to the emotional instability which played a part in lynching.

In the fight against lynching and mob violence, the Association tried to help the unjustly accused. They tried to see that lynchers were punished and attempted to prevent lynching by bringing about a change in public opinion. To accomplish this they did research for objective information, brought pressure to bear on national and state governments, and tried (but failed) to mobilize Southern white leadership. They fought for legislation to make lynching a crime punishable by the federal government, and in so doing achieved not the legislation, but the publicity they desired.

Five Years of Mob Violence, 1911–15

The spring and summer of 1911 were marked by a series of especially brutal lynchings. In May a barbarous lynching in Livermore, Kentucky, galvanized the Association into action. Newspapers reported that a Negro charged with the murder of a white man was taken to the so-called opera house and tied on the stage. Regular admission fees were charged for those who wished to witness the lynching, the receipts going to the family of the murdered man. Those who purchased orchestra seats were allowed to empty their revolvers into the swaying body. Holders of gallery tickets were limited to a single shot.

The horrified NAACP Executive Committee appealed to government officials for action. A memorial, presented to the President of the United States, the Vice-President, the Speaker of the House, and the chairmen of the Judiciary Committees of the Senate and House, was released to the Associated Press and the newspapers. The resolution of protest implored the President to send a special message to Congress, asking for action against the "foul blot" and "intolerable conditions of Lynch Law."

A committee of ten citizens of Washington, D.C., headed by Archibald Grimke, presented the resolution to President Taft, who replied that he was powerless to take any action, since this was a matter for the individual states. Oswald Garrison Villard, as chairman of the NAACP Executive Committee, wrote to the governor of Kentucky and spoke before the Ethical Culture Society in Philadelphia about the lynching and the unsuccessful attempt to move the President to action.

Booker T. Washington worked quietly until his death in 1915, using his influence against extension of lynching. He was more outspoken on this subject than on problems of civil rights. Typically he saw the brighter side, emphasizing any gesture of a Southern white to punish crimes against Negroes. In May, 1911, he wrote to Villard, Robert R. Moton, and Lyman Abbott of *The Outlook,* calling their attention to a decision of the Supreme Court of Alabama, which resulted in the removal of a sheriff from office for permitting the lynching of a Negro committed to his custody. The action of the court brought unstinting praise from Washington. "Nothing could be better or braver," he wrote. Alabama Governor Emmett O'Neal, who later became associated with NAACP efforts to eliminate lynching, also received an accolade for dismissing the sheriff. It was doubtless due to Washington's influence that *The Outlook* in 1911 published what Miss Ovington called a fine article regarding the lynching of six Negro men taken from the jail by a mob at Lake City, Florida.

One approach of the NAACP to bring an end to mob violence was to put pressure on state officials and to give publicity to their activities. Villard wrote Governor Albert W. Gilchrist about the Lake City lynchings. He also communicated with seventy-five prominent members of the Association, urging them to write the governor as well as their local newspapers. He confirmed the facts of the case from an instructor at Florida Institute at Tallahassee and sent an accurate account to forty newspapers throughout the country.

Governor Gilchrist answered all who wrote to him with an identical letter, which appeared to lack hostility or antagonism. He explained that, although he had limited funds at his disposal, he would offer a reward and employ such detective force as he could with the money at hand. Miss Ovington was sure the governor was insincere since he did not have a good record for administering justice.

A third case concerned the lynching of a mother and daughter by an Oklahoma mob. Protests sent to the governor of Oklahoma were ignored.

In the summer of 1911, the terrorism spread to the North. Like the Springfield riot of 1908, the Coatesville, Pennsylvania, lynching shocked and aroused NAACP leaders even more than the lynchings in the Southern and Border states. Zach Walker, a Negro, was wounded in a fight with a Coatesville policeman, whom he killed. He pleaded self-defense. At a prearranged signal, on August 12, 1911, Walker was taken from the hospital by a mob, dragged through the streets of the town, and burned alive. The NAACP Executive Committee at once began a prolonged and costly investigation, for the first time making use of professional detectives in the hope of providing evidence for a conviction.

The Association kept a close watch over the investigation and legal proceedings. One Board member, William Sinclair, who had followed the case daily, believed that the prosecuting attorney had done his duty. Serious doubts were aroused among other Board members. Mrs. Maclean went to Coatesville to investigate. She reported as incorrect the impression that the prosecuting attorney had done everything in his power to bring the lynchers to justice. She found that the trial had not been completed, that important witnesses for the prosecution had never been called to testify, and that several suspects had not been brought to trial. She was convinced there was enough new evidence to reopen the case. As a result of her report, the NAACP Executive Committee voted to guarantee one-half of a lawyer's fee to reopen the case. The remaining portion of the fee was to be raised by citizens who had promised Mrs. Maclean cooperation.

The Association employed the William J. Burns detective agency to secure evidence against the lynchers, and agents were sent to Coatesville, where they opened a restaurant as a screen for their activities. Villard assumed personal liability for the initial fee. The Burns agency reported that the district attorney had been in league with the lynchers from the beginning and that the state had given up the prosecution of the case.

In September, 1912, Wherry, the Association's attorney, Albert J. Nock of the *American Magazine,* Villard, and William J. Burns traveled to Harrisburg to present their findings to the governor of Pennsylvania, John K. Tener. The governor was sincere and straightforward, according to Villard, and promised to further the prosecution of the ringleaders.

The trip to Harrisburg convinced Nock that the *American Magazine* should print the Association's story, and he went to Coatesville to gather local color. He made a public indictment of the community in his article, "What We All Stand for: The Significance of the Behavior of a Community Toward Its Citizens Who Burned a Man Alive." Because of the conspiracy of silence, wrote Nock, even the detectives failed to ferret out the ringleaders, and the verdict of not guilty for the accused brought forth an ovation. To Nock both the lynching and the attitudes condoning it were the result of a community life lacking elements of civilization. Like so many other industrial communities, Coatesville had produced *"an upper class materialized, a middle class vulgarized, a lower class brutalized."*

Meanwhile, on the first anniversary of the lynching, John Jay Chapman, grandson of an abolitionist, and himself called a belated abolitionist, held a prayer meeting of three in a vacant store in Coatesville. When Francis Garrison learned that no resident of Coatesville had attended the prayer meeting he wrote that "the earth should yawn and swallow the whole community."

The Association held an anti-lynching rally in New York to raise money to continue the investigation and the prosecution of the lynchers. To link the old abolitionist movement with the new, Villard asked John Lovejoy Elliot to preside.

Although it proved impossible to reopen the case, the NAACP scored a partial victory when Governor Tener recommended to the legislature that the charter of Coatesville be revoked, because the inhabitants had been "consorting with and shielding murderers." Villard attributed the warmth of his message to NAACP activity in Coatesville.

The Philadelphia branch, assisted by friends of the Association in the Pennsylvania State Legislature, made energetic efforts to secure the adoption of a law similar to that of Ohio's, which made a county liable for damage inflicted by mob violence. Under the Ohio law a sheriff whose prisoner fell into the hands of a mob was immediately relieved of office. Similar legislation failed to pass in Pennsylvania. An anti-lynching bill was drawn up by J. C. Brinsmade at the national office, on laws in force in Ohio, Illinois, Kansas, and Indiana. It also failed to pass.

Publicity following investigation was the most frequently used weapon in the fight against lynching. Villard wrote editorials for publications such as *Century Illustrated Monthly Magazine,* and was instrumental in getting Albert J. Nock and John Jay Chapman to publicize the Coatesville crime. When Anne Bostwick, a Negro woman, was lynched at Cordele, Georgia, Villard gave publicity to the investigator's report in the *New York Evening Post,* and the story was sent to the Associated Press for national distribution. Joel Spingarn was also active in calling attention to the wave of lynchings and the work the Association was doing in behalf of the Negro. He persuaded James Oppenheim to visit Bluefield, West Virginia, and to write an article on the lynching of Robert Johnson, which took place in that town in September, 1912.

Sometimes publicity was denied. The state of Georgia was the scene of large-scale efforts in several counties to drive out Negroes and seize their property. In 1912 it was reported that in Forsyth and Dawson Counties the entire colored population was displaced. At the suggestion of William English Walling, Du Bois investigated and discovered that white farmers throughout Cobb County had received anonymous letters demanding that their Negro tenants be dismissed. When a storekeeper ignored a threatening note, his store was burned to the ground. Although Joseph Pulitzer's *New York World* supported most major reform movements of the period, Miss Nerney reported that Pulitzer had informed her that a series of articles on conditions in northern Georgia would not be of sufficient news value to warrant space in his paper.

In 1916, before he became the Association's secretary, Royal Nash, formerly a forester, was sent by Spingarn to investigate suspected acts of arson in Cherokee County, Georgia, said to be aimed at driving out Negroes. Assuming the role of a forester looking for timber, Nash was able to travel through the back country and talk to the natives without divulging his true purpose. In Forsyth County he found that a mob had lynched a Negro accused of rape and had then attacked Negroes throughout the county to drive them from the area. Nash concluded that the Forsyth County disturbances were based on competition between "crackers" and Negroes known to be industrious, law-abiding, and reliable. He claimed that, as a result of threatening letters, malicious burnings, and reprisals against employers, 2,100 Negroes out of a total population of 13,000 had fled the county, leaving the whites secure in their monopoly of the labor market. Many of these Negroes settled in adjacent counties, one of which was Cherokee County, where the fires of December, 1915, had started. There, unsettled conditions and the spreading of fear among the Negro population had an adverse effect on the economics of the county. Finding their chief labor supply affected and made more expensive, the white middle class appealed to the governor. The sheriff then took decisive action and within twenty-four hours the violence subsided.

The lynching of a white man in the summer of 1915 called attention to a significant court decision which the Association was instrumental in eventually having overruled. Leo Frank was removed from the Georgia state prison and lynched by a mob following the commutation of his death sentence to life imprisonment by the governor. Frank, a Jew and a New Yorker, had been convicted of the rape-murder of a white girl who worked in his factory in Atlanta. He had been tried and condemned to death in a court intimidated by an armed mob in which anti-Semitic and anti-Northern prejudices were clearly evident. His case was appealed to the United States Supreme Court, which upheld the verdict on grounds that "as long as a state court observed the form of a trial the federal government had no right to go beyond the form and inquire into the spirit which animated the trial." The Court thus opened the door for what Walling called legal lynching.

Shocked by Frank's murder, Villard wrote James Dillard that the report of this outrage was a summons to public duty and that the time had come for Southern men like Dillard to assume leadership of the struggle for law and order. Admitting that the North could be just as brutal as the South, Villard pointed out the difference: In the North people protested openly, organized, and tried for better things. He urged Dillard to lead and organize those in the South who did not care to act alone.

NAACP leaders had tried at other times to persuade their liberal Southern friends to speak out. Attending a session of the Commission on the Negro in Athens, Georgia, in 1912, Joel Spingarn met J. D. Hammond, president of Paine College. This college, in Augusta, Georgia, was according to Mrs. Hammond one of few colleges for Negroes owned and operated by Southern whites. Following the meeting, at which problems of the South were openly discussed, Mrs. Hammond warned Spingarn that all that had been said had been said in confidence and that in public she spoke "differently" on the Negro question.

Spingarn remarked that the Bleases and Vardamans were permitted to utter their thoughts freely, while those who represented the best thought of the South were forced to be silent, to which Mrs. Hammond replied that they were not cowards but would "speak out when the time comes—soon." Nevertheless, according to Villard, the Hammonds were driven out of Paine College by reason of their convictions.

The Anti-Lynching Campaign

In February, 1916, Philip G. Peabody of Boston startled and electrified the Association by offering the NAACP $10,000, provided it could evolve an effective program to stamp out lynching. A committee of five was appointed to draw up a program for Peabody's consideration. Villard thought the money could be used as rewards for the apprehension and conviction of lynchers, but he later decided that this would instantly raise the cry of Northern interference.

William English Walling, chairman of the Anti-Lynching Committee, reported the opinions of its members to the Board. Mrs. Kelley thought there would be little value in engaging Southerners to participate in anti-lynching work. She was in favor of continuing legal action, driving for federal anti-lynching legislation and reduction of Southern representation in Congress, and using the presidential campaign of 1916 to publicize the breakdown of democracy in the South.

Du Bois proposed that the fund be used for a study of lynching, in which lynchings would be investigated as they occurred, public opinion in the South would be mobilized, and suits would be brought against negligent officials under existing laws. Dr. Owen M. Waller, however, felt that legal action had no chance of success anywhere in the South. He advocated that the Association seek to reach and mold the opinion of Southern student bodies. Walling proposed enlisting the aid of the Southern Sociological Congress and similar organizations. Paul Kennaday agreed with Mrs. Kelley that neither persuasion nor an appeal to sentiment would in any way influence the South. He pressed for a program that would appeal to economic motives, arousing Chambers of Commerce to the costliness of lynching and to the hurt done to the labor market.

Consensus of the meeting of the Anti-Lynching Committee was that the program should concern itself with three fields of activity: the gathering and compiling of facts; investigation of specific cases as they occurred; and, most important, organizing Southern business and political leaders who would speak out against lynching. The first step was to be the printing and distribution in the South of 50,000 copies of W. D. Weatherford's strong paper against lynching, prepared for the Southern Sociological Congress.

Peabody, however, was not won over to the Association's program. Their study convinced him that $10,000 was too small a sum to accomplish the desired results. Because so-called outside interference in Southern affairs would not be tolerated, the NAACP would have to keep itself in the background of any work that was undertaken, and Peabody did not like the idea of working in the dark. He wanted the Association to act in a direct open way, utilizing the Northern press to its fullest extent. He gave $1,000, promising that, if another $9,000 could be raised before August from people who were convinced he was wrong, he would then give another $1,000.

In spite of this setback, Storey urged the Association not to abandon the program, and promised an additional $1,000 when the NAACP had raised $8,000. Villard agreed to be chairman of a committee of three to raise the money. By the fifteenth of August, Peabody's deadline, they were still short of the goal. They asked for an extension of time and by October 7 had raised more than $10,000. Every group responded except the churches; both races contributed about equally.

Three particularly savage lynchings in 1916 gave impetus to the campaign. The first was the case of Jesse Washington, a mentally retarded adolescent. Seized by a mob in a Waco, Texas, courtroom, where he had been found guilty and sentenced to death for murder of a white woman, he was taken to the public square, tortured, and burned alive before a crowd of 15,000 persons.

To verify the facts, the committee called on Elizabeth Freeman, who was in Dallas on a speaking tour for the suffragists. She went immediately to Waco, where she spent ten days investigating the crime. Her report and photographs were used in an eight-page supplement to *The Crisis*. Entitled "The Waco Horror," this highly sensational supplement was used as the opening wedge in the drive for the Anti-Lynching Fund. It was distributed to 42,000 *Crisis* subscribers, to 700 white newspapers and fifty Negro weeklies, to all members of Congress, and to a list of 500 "moneyed men" in New York, who were asked to aid the campaign. Villard wrote personally to thirty prominent editors. To raise additional funds, the NAACP sent Miss Freeman on a lecture tour to report on what she had seen and heard at Waco.

In the midst of the campaign, in August, 1916, a mass lynching took place near Gainesville, Florida. Five Negroes were murdered, two of them women. The trouble began with a quarrel between a Negro and a white man over a pig. The local sheriff was called in, and the arrest took the form of a raid. The sheriff was shot. The mob then lynched the five Negroes, all of whom were innocent according to the editors of *The New Republic,* who called this atrocity to the attention of the Association and urged an investigation.

In its editorial, *The New Republic* termed the psychological motive in lynching a mere hunger for blood. In no sense was it the rough-and-ready justice of a frontier community, where courts of justice had not yet been established. It was rather a social orgy of cruelty, in which certain classes in the community expressed their hatred of a race they consider inferior, their contempt for the law, and their sense of Anglo-Saxon superiority. The editorial was good publicity for the NAACP's drive to marshal public opinion, not in a bitter or sectional spirit, but in a spirit of scientific investigation and diagnosis.

Resentment of Negroes who acquired wealth and property was behind the lynching of Anthony Crawford at Abbeville, South Carolina, in November, 1916. Roy Nash investigated the case and found that Crawford, a well-to-do Negro farmer, had been jailed as a result of a dispute in which he had cursed a white man who had tried to defraud him. A mob broke into the jail and lynched Crawford. In this case, however, the "good citizens" of the town stepped in and prevented the lynching of the victim's family—nor was the family forced to abandon its property.

Nash, in an article in *The Independent,* pointed out the significant aspects of the case: the fine character of Crawford (the "embodiment of the things that Booker T. Washington stood for"); the triviality of his offense; the fact that the Governor of South Carolina, Richard I. Manning, had demanded that the lynchers be tried; and the unanimous condemnation of the act by the South Carolina press. National attention was focused on the lynching and on the work of the Association when Nash's article was copied by Southern papers and received considerable editorial comment in the North. The lynchers never came to trial, however; the grand jury refused to indict them.

Another technique used by the Association was to praise and reward those who averted lynching. At Lima, Ohio, the sheriff prevented a mob from seizing a Negro prisoner on September 30, 1916. In honor of his courage and devotion to duty the Association arranged a mass meeting at Columbus, where the Governor of Ohio on behalf of the NAACP presented a silver trophy to Sheriff Sherman Eley before an audience of 1,200 persons.

At the end of 1916, the chairman of the NAACP Board said in his annual report that the injection of lynching into the public conscience as a national problem was the most striking achievement of the year.

With the conclusion of the drive, a committee of five was appointed to draw up plans for administering the Anti-Lynching Fund. Storey took an active part in the work of this committee, stressing the importance of persuading Southerners to organize themselves to fight lynching. The experience of the Coatesville trial had proved that no criminal prosecution could successfully be brought if such outrages were upheld by the community. Storey hoped the committee could arouse those Southerners who were ashamed of their "barbarous communities." He thought a conference of Southerners and people from Border states, plus a fair infusion of Northerners, would be able to air the subject and form an organization against it.

When the Anti-Lynching Committee met in October, 1916, they agreed to continue the work already started. In an attempt to inject the lynching issue into the presidential campaign, they drew up an anti-lynching pamphlet which was distributed throughout the branches. Milholland arranged for additional distribution through Republican state headquarters.

Next, the committee decided to engage an agent to travel through the South to enlist friends of the Association, to determine their strength, and to sponsor a conference of Southern leaders. Mrs. J. D. Hammond agreed to visit the principal cities to learn how many leaders of Southern opinion could be persuaded to attend the Conference. James Dillard assured Walling that he would call the conference as soon as the preliminary conversations were completed.

In February, 1917, the Anti-Lynching Committee reported to the Board that Mrs. Hammond's trip had yielded unexpectedly favorable results, but in spite of this encouragement the hoped-for conference of Southern leaders did not materialize. The United States soon became involved in the World War, and it was two years before an anti-lynching conference could be held. By that time the climate of opinion toward the Negro had worsened, and the conference, held in the North, was composed largely of Northerners.

The East St. Louis Riot and the Great Migrations

On June 11, 1917, the Director of Publications and Research reported to the Board that he planned to go to East St. Louis, Illinois, to study conditions in a community typical of those which were attracting migration from the South. Before a month had passed, however, a riot occurred in that "typical" city, during which hundreds of Negroes were shot or burned alive in their homes. A large amount of property was destroyed, and nearly 6,000 were made homeless. Negroes were blamed for the outbreak, and a number were charged with inciting the riot and with murder.

The exodus of Negroes from the South to Northern cities, accepted as the underlying cause of the riot and of unrest in other urban areas, was greatly accelerated by the outbreak of World War I. Increased demand for labor in the prospering war industries of the North and dissatisfaction with conditions in the South led to a migration of such magnitude that observers both North and South were concerned.

Disasters in the South, such as the floods of 1915 and the devastation of the cotton fields by the boll weevil, were the principal economic causes. Added to these were the fact that the flow of European immigrant labor had been cut to a trickle with the coming of the war, and the agents of Northern industry were active in the South. The abuse and degradation of Negroes by Southern whites had made life intolerable for thousands, who readily responded to the enticements of better jobs, higher pay, and more satisfactory living conditions in the North.

Earlier, Booker T. Washington had tried to encourage Southern Negroes to stay in the country and on the farm. White Southern business was not alone in feeling the pinch caused by the migrations. Negro professional men and Negro businesses, such as insurance companies, were also hurt, But the advice of the conservative Negro preacher, teacher and professional man could not stop the flood, which neared its peak in 1916.

The editor of *The New Republic* saw, however, that the dissemination of the Negro throughout the United States, by bringing him economic and political power, would serve as an antidote to his nearly defenseless position in the South. *The Crisis* took issue with colored leaders who were urging Negroes to stay in the South. Instead, mass exodus was encouraged as the only effective protest the Negro could make against lynching and disfranchisement in that "devilish country."

Robert Moton echoed Booker T. Washington at a biracial conference on migration held at Tuskegee in January, 1917. Villard, on the other hand, criticized the conference for playing into the hands of the white South—the planters and employers of labor. He approved of the migration and regretted only the lack of organization behind it. Though he was aware that the migration would intensify the race problem in the North, he recognized the fact that the problem would eventually have to be faced in the North as well as in the South.

In the same month the Urban League held a conference on migration in New York City, where all schools of thought were represented. Present at the conference were experts on migration and immigration, including the Commissioner of Immigration, and representatives of railroads and industries which were employing large numbers of Southern Negroes. Villard, Joel Spingarn, and Butler Wilson represented the NAACP.

Hollis B. Frissell, spokesman for Hampton and Tuskegee, was convinced that the best place for the mass of Negroes was in the South. He acknowledged that some migrants would prosper in the North and that this would make the South realize the economic value of the colored man, but he feared that many would be subjected to competition in the labor market and exposed to the struggle of city life.

Dissension broke out on the floor of the conference when Butler Wilson proposed that Negroes should be encouraged to migrate "until the South shall accord them their political rights . . . protect them from mob violence, open to them school advantages and protect their women and children from intolerable persecution." Realizing that a bitter floor fight between the conservative and radical wings of the Negro movement would threaten the newly established harmony and good will engendered by the Amenia Conference, Spingarn offered a substitute proposal which Wilson refused to accept. The conservatives, however, defeated the radical measures. The resolutions adopted protested the exploitation and abuse of migrant labor by industrial employers. It was proposed that organizations be formed in the South to improve conditions and to encourage a fair attitude toward Negro labor. Other organizations were proposed for instructing migrants in regard to the dress and habits of living necessary in a Northern climate, the demands of Northern employers, and the dangers and opportunities of city life.

At the same time, in Wilmington, Delaware, a meeting was called by whites disturbed by the exodus. The Negroes were asked if better schools, churches, and other facilities would be sufficient inducement for them to stay in the South. When the Negroes indicated they wanted the vote, the meeting broke up in confusion, according to Miss Ovington, who was pleased that *The Crisis* and the NAACP had had something to do with this vigorous stand.

The NAACP authorized an investigation of the facts concerning the migration. Du Bois visited six Southern states and secured additional information through agents in nearly all parts of the South. To the surprise of the Board, the data showed the movement to be much larger in scope than they had believed possible. Du Bois estimated that 250,000 colored workmen had gone northward, and declared that the United States was witnessing a social change of great moment among American Negroes.

The problems of the Northern Negro were compounded by the migrations. Industry hired Negroes only when they could not obtain other labor. Frequently Negroes were brought in as strikebreakers, which earned them the enmity of white workers who feared competition. Moreover, the opportunities for employment nowhere equaled the number of migrants flooding the cities in search of economic and social betterment and greater freedom. This led to the concentration of masses of Negroes in slums, with all the attendant poverty, disintegration of family life, and delinquency that slum life entails. Some Negroes became tools of corrupt politicians. All these factors led to increased prejudice and increased racial tension in the cities.

Thus the violence that broke out in East St. Louis on July 2, 1917, was not entirely unexpected. The city was Southern in its racial attitudes. It was a center for heavy industry, a major railroad junction, and the site of stockyards and meatpacking plants. Workers lived in slums adjacent to the factories. During 1916 the industries waged war on unionization, using Negro labor to prevent the organization of labor. Public opinion was inflamed with stories, deliberately circulated, of Negro crime and with the claim of the local Democratic machine that the Republicans had imported Negroes to vote in the 1916 election. It was rumored that Dr. Le Roy Bundy, a dentist and Negro Republican leader, was organizing Negro migrants to vote both in East St. Louis and in Chicago. As Illinois was considered by the Wilson Administration to be a doubtful state in the coming election, the President himself, the Department of Justice, and the Office of the Attorney General warned of a conspiracy, predicting that fraudulent voting might result from the transportation of Negroes from the South to doubtful Midwestern states in order to secure a Republican victory.

Martha Gruening and Du Bois went to East St. Louis to investigate the riot. Their reports brought to light the nature of the community where the riot took place, an area friendly to the criminal element of both races, where because of political corruption both could get protection.

When trouble started, city officials were ineffectual in coping with the situation and the militia was called in. There was evidence that some of the militia forced escaping Negroes into the hands of the mob.

When news of the trouble reached the NAACP, the Board authorized Arthur Spingarn's legal committee to take appropriate action. The St. Louis branch cooperated by handling the investigation and the Chicago branch took charge of the legal action. At St. Louis, Du Bois organized a volunteer committee of twenty-five to take testimony. The NAACP took steps to bring suit against the city and county governments., and petitioned the governor of Illinois to remove the Sheriff of East St. Louis for failure to do his duty. Charles Nagel, former Secretary of Commerce under Taft, was engaged to supervise the defense of the ten Negroes indicted, but their trial led to their conviction for murder. Upon appeal, their conviction was upheld by the Supreme Court of Illinois.

In the course of the testimony, Dr. Le Roy Bundy was implicated in the murders. He was then brought to trial. To the white community he was an aggressive type of Negro and an outspoken champion of the cause of equal rights. Moreover he had won the enmity of union leaders by criticizing the exclusion of Negroes from labor unions.

Bundy alienated NAACP support when he refused to allow the national office to direct the conduct of his case. The Association became particularly concerned when Bundy, released on bail, went on tour, addressing Negro audiences and collecting funds for which he refused to give the NAACP adequate accounting. The Association therefore withdrew from the case. Bundy's trial resulted in his conviction, but upon appeal to the Illinois Supreme Court the judgment was reversed and the case was sent back to the lower court for a new trial. The state, recognizing the weakness of its case, never retried Bundy.

To finance the defense and provide for Negroes in East St. Louis left destitute, the Association raised a special fund, and broadened the scope of the Anti-Lynching Fund, which now became the Anti-Lynching and Mob Violence Fund. Peabody agreed to a more liberal interpretation of the word lynching in connection with the fund, and as a result lynching was defined as "not only the illegal killing of an accused person, but also the killing of an accused person by mob violence."

One significant reaction in the Negro world to the East St. Louis riot was the financial aid given to the NAACP for the first time by several of the great Negro secret and fraternal organizations, which had previously held aloof from the NAACP. Though the amounts were not large, contributions from these fraternal bodies later became an important element of support.

In the early summer of 1917, a Negro named Ell Persons, suspected of being an "ax murderer," was burned alive in Memphis. James Weldon Johnson spent ten days in Memphis but found no direct evidence that Persons was guilty. Following the investigation, Johnson attended a meeting at St. Philip's Church in New York, called jointly by a number of organizations planning a public protest against the lynching.

In the meantime, the East St. Louis riot erupted and the protest developed into a demonstration against the mass murders as well. Johnson credits Villard with the idea of a silent protest parade instead of a mass meeting. The group accepted this idea and evolved as a nonpartisan citizens' movement—the "Silent Protest Parade." The NAACP claimed a good share of the credit for its success. Between eight and ten thousand men, women, and children took part in the parade on Saturday, July 28, 1917. The march was accompanied only by the sound of muffled drums. Marchers carried banners and signs protesting lynching and mob violence. Circulars protesting discrimination, segregation, Jim Crow, and disfranchisement were distributed to the twenty thousand persons along the line of march.

Because of Johnson's skill, tact, and diplomacy, the Silent Protest Parade organization did not adjourn when its work was done, but merged with the New York branch of the NAACP. Some prominent New York Negroes were thus drawn into the Association for the first time.

Because of the widespread publicity given to the East St. Louis riots, Congress appointed an investigating committee which determined that interstate commerce and travel had been disrupted by the rioting. An inquiry into details of labor and race conflict was then authorized. Congressman L. C. Dyer of Missouri was helpful in preventing suppression of the report and told Spingarn that he intended to introduce a bill before Congress making lynching a Federal offense.

Protests and Legislation

John Shillady tried to bring lynchings to the attention of the federal government. When Jim McIllheron was tortured with red-hot irons and burned alive on Lincoln's birthday in 1918 at Estill Springs, Tennessee, Shillady sent a telegram of protest to President Wilson. The President's secretary referred the telegram to the Attorney General, who replied that the federal government had no jurisdiction because the crime was in no way connected with the war effort. Shillady again wrote Wilson, urging him to make a public statement condemning lynching for the sake of the tremendously stimulating effect this would have on the morale of colored people.

In spite of Shillady's messages, Wilson did not hear of the Estill Springs affair until James Weldon Johnson mentioned it at a White House interview. The Association had already tried to persuade Wilson to mention lynching in his second inaugural address, but without success. Johnson again pressed this point and after much urging Wilson finally promised that he would "seek an opportunity" to say something on the subject.

To increase the pressure on the President, Shillady sent letters and telegrams to forty-four of the most active NAACP branches, urging members to write or telegraph Wilson, asking that he condemn lynching in his Fourth of July address to the nation. In West Virginia, Mordecai W. Johnson, head of the Charleston branch of the NAACP and later president of Howard University, succeeded in persuading the governor and two judges of the West Virginia Supreme Court and other influential white and colored citizens to send telegrams. Again the President ignored the pleas.

Wilson finally made a public statement on July 26, 1918, asking the governors of all states, law officers, and, above all, the men and women of every community to cooperate "not passively merely, but actively and watchfully" to bring an end to lynching, which could not "live where the community does not countenance it." The Board rejoiced in the President's message, and ordered 50,000 copies to be printed and distributed.

In a letter written by Du Bois, the Association also sought to bring pressure to bear on the Attorney General of the United States, Thomas W. Gregory, calling his attention to the relationship between the number of lynchings that had taken place since he assumed office and his attitude that the federal government had no jurisdiction in cases of lynching. Why, Du Bois asked, was the federal government able to take action when a German, Robert Prager, was lynched on April 4, 1918, in Collinsville, Illinois, but unable to intervene in the case of colored American citizens? Gregory's only response came in an address to the Executive Committee of the American Bar Association in May, 1918, recommending an educational campaign against lynching and mob violence.

A month later lynching and mob violence was once more forcefully brought to the attention of the legal profession by Moorfield Storey in an address to the Wisconsin Bar Association entitled 'The Negro Question." Referring to the conspiracy of silence, he asked: "What college president, what orator at Commencement, takes the evil of lynching as his subject?" In response to Storey's eloquence, the Wisconsin Bar Association passed a resolution expressing unqualified condemnation of mob violence toward the colored race and calling upon the profession to invoke the law and suppress the rule of the mob.

Shillady also took strenuous action to bring lynching before state officials. The Estill Springs atrocity was only one of three burnings in Tennessee within a nine-month period. Shillady not only sent Governor Tom C. Rye a telegram of protest but wrote him that the Association could, if necessary, make funds available to the state for an investigation at Estill Springs. This was followed by telegrams to the two United States Senators from Tennessee, to the Representative of the Third District, and to six Chambers of Commerce in Tennessee cities. After inquiring what Tennessee proposed to do to vindicate her law and clear her name in regard to the torturing and burning at Estill Springs, Shillady asked bluntly, "Do you stand for law or do you approve mob violence?" The governor responded, deploring the murder; the Chamber of Commerce of Chattanooga answered with a resolution censuring mob violence; and the *Nashville Banner* printed an editorial condemning the burning.

In addition, a citizens' group organized the Tennessee Law and Order League to suppress lynching and encourage similar movements in all Southern states. Here, finally, was a manifestation of the Anti-Lynching Committee's constructive publicity program, which had envisaged the use of Southern agencies to fight lynching without involving the NAACP by name.

The harsh glare of publicity was focused upon Governor Hugh M. Dorsey and the state of Georgia following a five-day "orgy" in Brooks and Lowndes Counties which resulted in the lynching of eight Negroes. The reign of terror began with the fatal shooting of a white landlord and the wounding of his wife by a Negro they had held in **peonage**. Mob vengeance resulted in the deaths of several innocent Negroes, one of whom was Haynes Turner. Mary White Ovington described the scene:

> His wife Mary, after her husband's death, mourned and loudly proclaimed his innocence. For this she was slowly burned to death, watched by a crowd of men and women. She was pregnant, and as she burned, the infant fell to the ground and was trampled under a white man's heel.

Walter White and James Weldon Johnson carried out separate investigations for the Association. John Shillady sent the findings to Governor Dorsey, naming the two ringleaders and fifteen participants in the murders. Dorsey had risen to the governorship of Georgia as the result of his prosecution of Leo Frank, whose trial had been dominated by an armed mob. His answer to Shillady, stating that no definite results had been obtained in efforts to apprehend the guilty parties, bore a rubber-stamp signature.

Shortly after Governor Dorsey's letter was dispatched, a seventeen-year-old Negro, Sandy Reeves, was taken from peace officers and lynched near Blackshear, Georgia. He had been accused of assaulting a three-year-old child. The Waycross, Georgia, branch investigated and claimed that no assault had been committed or attempted. The child, a daughter of Reeves's employer, had been playing near Reeves while he was picking grapes. A five-cent piece dropped from his pocket and she picked it up. When he tried to take the coin from her, she made a scene and an outcry. For this Reeves was lynched.

There were nineteen verified and twelve probable lynchings in Georgia in 1918. The only effect of Wilson's public statement against such violence was an apparently concerted agreement between the press and the authorities to keep all news regarding lynchings out of the Georgia press. No account of the NAACP investigation of the Brooks and Lowndes County massacres appeared in the Georgia papers, although the governor knew the names of the leaders of the mob and there was considerable comment in the press of other states.

The administration of Governor William P. Hobby of Texas was also subject to criticism and unfavorable publicity by the NAACP. Shillady made public a telegram sent to the governor protesting the lynching of Mrs. Sarah Cabiness and her five sons at Huntsville, Texas, on June 1, 1918. There were three more lynchings in Texas that year. NAACP branches united to press for a state anti-lynching bill. They urged Governor Hobby to back appropriate legislation and offered to engage a prominent white lawyer to draft a bill. They proposed that all lynching trials should be held in the state capital, that the attorney general should prosecute all such cases, that the state should offer rewards for information leading to arrest and conviction in lynchings, that an indemnity should be paid to dependents of persons lynched, and that the crime of lynching should be legally defined, so as to include cases where three or more persons take the life of another without due process of law.

In spite of all the discouraging news from the South there were some efforts to curb mob violence. A few incidents occurred in which state executives, local officials, and newspapers were willing to take a stand for law and order. Tennessee's governor and attorney general asked John Shillady for assistance in drafting a state anti-lynching bill.

Governor Thomas W. Bickett of North Carolina requested federal authorities to assist the mayor and the home guard of Winston-Salem to prevent a mob from breaking into the jail and lynching a Negro prisoner. The local officials were given the support of a tank corps of 250 federal soldiers. The prisoner was successfully protected, "at the cost of the lives of some of the 'Home Guards.' " The Association publicly commended the governor and mayor for their stand. Fifteen persons were convicted and sentenced to terms ranging from fourteen months to six years.

Governor Stanley of Kentucky personally defied a mob at Murray, Kentucky, and saved from lynching a Negro who was later legally tried and condemned to death. The Anti-Lynching Committee engaged a writer from the *Louisville Courier-Journal* to secure complete details for a story about the incident, which was published in *The Independent*. The Constitution of Kentucky was later amended to permit the removal from office of any sheriff, jailer, constable or peace officer for neglect of duty.

The South was not the sole target of NAACP protests. In Wyoming, the lynching of Edward Woodson at Green River in December, 1918, brought publicized protests to the governor of that state against the lynchings and the driving from their homes of Negro residents of the community. In 1919, Wyoming enacted a law against mob violence.

By mid-1918, the Association was sending out press stories to nearly four hundred newspapers. Some responded by giving editorial support to the anti-lynching campaign. In Texas, the *San Antonio Express* offered a $500 reward for the conviction and punishment of lynchers of a white person—$1,000 if the victim were a Negro. Although no one came forward to claim the reward, the offer served to call attention to the spread of mob violence in the South. Nevertheless, it was usually difficult to get Southern newspapers to print NAACP press releases, and response from state officials and civic groups was discouraging. Upon receiving a letter of protest from the NAACP, signed by Shillady, following the lynching of four Negroes at Shubata, Mississippi, Governor Theodore G. Bilbo was reported by the *Washington Bee* to have given a state official "Advance information to the effect that I will tell them, in effect, to go to h____."

Efforts to introduce and secure passage of legislation providing penalties against participants in lynchings became a major project of the Association on the national as well as the state level. Two anti-lynching bills were introduced in Congress in 1918, one by Dyer of Missouri and the other by Merrill Moore of Indiana. Neither of these seemed to fulfill the requirements of the NAACP, however, and the Anti-Lynching Committee attempted to have another bill introduced. At the same time they decided to participate in the hearing on Dyer's bill for publicity purposes. Joel Spingarn, then in the intelligence service of the army, enlisted the help of a fellow officer, a lawyer, Captain George S. Hornblower, who drew up a third bill. On June 6, 1918, it was introduced by Warren Gard of Ohio at the hearing before the House Committee on the Judiciary as a substitute for Dyer's bill.

Storey examined the three bills. He held the Dyer bill to be unconstitutional because it assumed that an *individual* could be punished for depriving United States citizens of the privileges or immunities granted them under the Fourteenth Amendment. This intrepretation had already been invalidated by the Supreme Court which held that the Fourteenth Amendment was concerned only with "encroachment by the states" against the rights of citizens. The Moore bill proposed to give the right to appeal directly to a federal court to every citizen who felt he was likely to be denied equal protection of the laws. This Storey also held to be unconstitutional. He did not believe the bills could be rewritten and declined to appear before the House Judiciary Committee on behalf of either the Dyer or the Moore bill.

He thought the Gard bill, with some modification, would pass the test of constitutionality. It was aimed primarily at protecting persons of draft age for the duration of the war. Two factors would aid its passage, said Storey—first, it had been prepared and introduced by army officers with the approval of the War Department; second, there was no indication that it was especially designed to protect Negroes. Storey strongly advised the Association not to play a prominent role in pressing for the bill, so as not to arouse undue opposition by Congress. The ending of the war in November, 1918, made the Gard bill obsolete. Dyer continued to reintroduce his own bill, however, and Storey eventually changed his mind and supported Dyer.

The Anti-Lynching Conference

Efforts of the Anti-Lynching Committee to organize a conference of Southern leaders failed in spite of the early encouraging reports. At the end of 1918 the Committee decided to work for a national conference, calling on "the most substantial and influential leaders of public opinion" to endorse it. They even hoped to persuade a number of state governors, particularly of the Southern states, to attend the conference. The increasing number of incidents of mob violence against the Negro was clearly evident. During the year, sixty-four Negroes (five of them women) and four white men were lynched. These figures did not include the victims of the East St. Louis riots in July nor the Chester, Pennsylvania, riot in September. In eight Southern states thirteen victims were taken from jails or from the custody of law enforcement officers. In Dewey, Oklahoma, when a mob was frustrated in its efforts to lynch a Negro, it retaliated by burning the town. A discouraging sign was that in the stress of wartime, mob violence began to menace communities heretofore relatively immune. There were lynchings in California, Wyoming, and Illinois, and race riots in Brooklyn, New York, Philadelphia, and New Jersey.

During the first four months of 1919, nine known lynchings took place in five Southern states. In each case the victims were taken from jails or seized from officers of the law. The Hillsboro, Texas, lynching was reminiscent of the Waco atrocity where the victim was burned alive in the public square. An NAACP wire of protest to Governor Hobby was met with silence, as were those sent to the Chambers of Commerce in Dallas, Galveston, and Fort Worth. The Austin Chamber of Commerce sent a token reply: The situation was being investigated.

At this time the NAACP was frequently referred to in the South as the Advancement Association, or Negro Advancement Society. In response to an inquiry by the Association concerning the lynching of Eugene Green at Belzoni, Mississippi, Governor Bilbo was said to have answered with an ironic play on words, "He was 'advanced' all right from the end of a rope, and in order to save burial expenses his body was thrown into the Yazoo River." In spite of Bilbo's attitude, the sheriff from whom Green was taken was arraigned for neglect of duty, and an NAACP member in Mississippi reported that the judge had made a sincere effort to have the lynchers punished.

The governor of Florida, in answer to a protest, replied that the NAACP was upholding lawlessness among Florida's Negroes and advised the Association to concentrate its efforts on educating and otherwise uplifting the colored people.

The NAACP Anti-Lynching conference was held the first week in May, 1919. About 120 signatures were on the "call" which went out in April, including such notables as Attorney General A. Mitchell Palmer, former Secretary of State Elihu Root, Henry Van Dyke, Minister to the Netherlands, Charles Evans Hughes, and the president of the American Bar Association. Also included were four governors, three former governors (among whom was ex-governor O'Neal of Alabama), and seventeen signers from Southern states. To insure that the appeal would be biracial, representative colored men and women were among the signers.

Some who were asked declined to endorse the call. Robert R. Moton was unwilling to discuss lynching in the North. Emmett Scott agreed with Moton. Among the friends of the Negro of the so-called philanthropic wing who refused to sign was George Foster Peabody, whose reason for declining was that attempts by the NAACP to arouse public opinion against lynching would inflame the South and result in more lynchings. He believed the only true policy was that of gradually educating Southerners until they recognized their duties as civilized people. In a letter to Peabody, Storey pointed out that, though lynching had been the practice for many years, in very few cases had anyone been punished, and no substantial movement to put an end to lynching had ever originated in the South; toleration of lynching was itself an educational force.

The Anti-Lynching Conference opened at Carnegie Hall with an attendance of 2,500. Charles Evans Hughes, Governor Emmet O'Neal, Anna Howard Shaw of the woman's suffrage movement, Brigadier General John H. Sherburne of the 92nd (Negro) Division, and James Weldon Johnson were speakers. Walter White in his autobiography described the looks of astonishment that crossed the faces of the liberal-minded whites seated on the platform when Johnson gave voice to his conviction that the race problem was not only one of saving black men's bodies but of saving white men's souls.

Three resolutions were adopted by the conference: that efforts should be made to secure legislation making lynching a federal crime; that the NAACP should organize state committees to create a climate of favorable public opinion and work for legislation at the state level; and that the Anti-Lynching Committee should carry on a systematic fund-raising and advertising campaign against lynching.

The New York City Bar Association adopted resolutions calling for a congressional investigation of lynching and federal legislation for its prevention. NAACP members were disappointed that so few New York lawyers attended the session conducted by Storey on the legal aspect of lynching.

Following the Anti-Lynching Conference, Shillady and the Anti-Lynching Committee drew up "An Address to the Nation on Lynching," signed by 130 prominent citizens including those who had signed the call and several important new sponsors—former President William Howard Taft, William Dean Howells, President John Grier Hibben of Princeton, Theodore D. Bratton, Episcopal Bishop of Mississippi, and the governor of Tennessee. This manifesto was used for further publicity, and exerted additional pressure for a congressional investigation.

Red Summer

In 1919, the NAACP sent Herbert Seligmann on a trip to Tennessee and Mississippi to investigate increased racial tension. From his talks with leading Negroes and whites, Seligmann learned that the shortage of cheap labor in rural regions of the South was deeply resented by plantation owners. Southerners complained that the drafting of Negroes for the army tended to put them on an equal footing with white men. An additional cause of antagonism was the widespread belief that Negro soldiers were "recognized on equal terms by white women in France." These indications that Negroes were gaining status as citizens gave rise to what Du Bois called "the sex motive, the brutal sadism into which race hate always falls." Colored soldiers were lynched in Georgia and Mississippi for having appeared on the streets in uniform.

Seligmann found that Southern whites universally condemned what they termed a campaign or agitation from outsiders for equal rights for Negroes. Most considered the Negro inherently inferior, forever unsuited to political, economic, and social equality. Finally, white and Negro intellectuals alike recognized that tensions were heightened by the press and by politicians such as Vardaman, who, in his weekly political paper, the *Issue,* promoted race hatred in default of other issues. One politician, candidate for the Louisiana State Legislature, told Seligmann that lynching was necessary, and that no Negro should ever be allowed to vote or acquire an education—because education made confidence men of the males and prostitutes of the females. Some professional and business people deplored lynching, but only in a half-hearted fashion, and predicted the resurrection of the Ku Klux Klan among "the best people" of the South.

Seligmann reported that practically all intelligent Southerners believed that federal legislation was the only way to stop lynching, but extremists claimed they would punish offenders against Southern womanhood, regardless of the consequences. A leading Negro of Memphis, Robert Church, told Seligmann that antagonism between races in the South was mounting, that Negroes were arming, and that federal action was the only hope of averting serious conflict.

In mid-summer, 1919, in the midst of violence, restlessness, tension, and crisis, the NAACP resumed the pattern of holding its annual conference. In 1915 there had been no conference because of the financial condition of the Association. In 1916, Booker T. Washington's death had led to the Amenia Conference rather than an all-NAACP conference. In 1917 and 1918 there were no regular conferences because of wartime restrictions on travel.

The 1919 conference, held in Cleveland, was different from any of the previous annual meetings. It was the largest and the longest. The dramatically expanded membership was represented by delegates from thirty-four states. Also notable was the absence of white leadership, which had been so obvious a feature of the earlier conferences. The Association, organized by whites ten years before, was now being organized all over the United States by Negroes.

Bishop John Hurst set the tone of the conference in his address to the delegates. Negroes, he told them, had been lulled to sleep under the delusion that if they quit crying out so loudly for their rights and kept on working, justice would eventually he meted out to them. But the South renewed its assaults upon the black man with every forward step, and he called on the delegates to die if need be in the fight for their rights.

The race riots of the summer and fall of 1919 were violent and bloody. As if in response to the new note of defiance sounded at the conference, the Negro fought back. The fighting spirit of the new abolitionism, the fighting words of *The Crisis,* the yearning for better economic and citizenship status, and the Negro's wartime experiences—all were reflected in the incidents that took place in Washington, Chicago, Omaha, Knoxville, and Indianapolis, and in Phillips County, Arkansas, where the worst of the many riots of that year occurred.

The curtain raiser was the riot at Longview, Texas, in June, 1919, between whites and returning Negro soldiers, in which a number of both races lost their lives. The clash, typical of the lawlessness stalking restlessly through the nation, showed that Negroes were ready to resist. "Negroes are not planning anything," stated an Associated Press report in a Longview newspaper, "but will defend themselves if attacked."

In Washington, D.C., the rioting lasted three days; as in Longview, the Negro fought back. Investigating the riots, James Weldon Johnson observed a new spirit of determination among Negroes, a resolve "not to run, but to fight—fight in defense of their lives and their homes." He blamed the press of Washington for carrying on mob violence propaganda in the form of daily stories of attacks on white women. He claimed that this propaganda was in fact an attempt to discredit the Washington police department and to convince the public that crime in Washington had increased with the advent of Prohibition.

Johnson conferred with the District Commissioners, the chief of police, the editors of the *Post,* the *Times,* and the *Evening Star,* giving them NAACP literature on lynching and discussing with them the responsibility of the press for the riots. The *Evening Star* printed three editorials which the editor claimed had been influenced by the interview. In one editorial, the *Star* called for a congressional investigation, commenting that "every time the white mob runs amuck against the Negroes, the latter grow more bitter and defensive in their retaliatory measures."

Johnson interviewed a number of Senators, and the NAACP launched a campaign for an investigation. As a result of this pressure, Charles Curtis of Kansas introduced a resolution in the Senate on September 22, 1919, calling for an inquiry into the causes of the race riots in Washington and other cities and an investigation of the wave of lynchings throughout the country. The resolution was referred to the Senate Committee on the Judiciary. Curtis asked the Association to send him a brief to present to the committee, setting forth reasons why there should be an investigation, what might be revealed by such an inquiry, and what remedies could be recommended. Curtis also urged the Association to have persons of influence write the chairman of the Judiciary Committee, endorsing the resolution and urging its adoption. Dyer introduced a similar resolution in the House, but both resolutions died in committee.

The violence continued. Sixteen lynchings, including two burnings, took place in September. There were two whippings and two incidents in which mobs seized prisoners from peace officers; the victims were presumed dead. With the end of the war, unemployment and an unprecedented number of strikes accompanied by violence swept the country, further aggravating race relations. Political radicals and members of other ethnic groups were also victims in the postwar reaction against Wilsonian idealism and internationalism. Two Mexicans were lynched in Colorado. A member of the Industrial Workers of the World was taken from the jail and lynched at Centralia, Washington. In Stafford, Kansas, a member of the Non-Partisan League was lynched; the fate of two other members of the League seized by the mob was unknown.

In spite of the violence of the summer, Robert Moton, following in the steps of Booker T. Washington, whom he had succeeded at Tuskegee, wrote optimistically that lynching was on the wane. Incensed, Villard objected to the glaring untruth and the positive harm done by the reports from Tuskegee, which "lull people's consciences to sleep." In *The Crisis,* Du Bois urged Negroes to prepare for attack with bricks, clubs, and guns, yet he cautioned against angry retaliation or seeking reform by violence; in the same issue Johnson wrote that the riots in Washington and Chicago marked a turning point in the psychology of the nation regarding the Negro problem.

The Chicago riots followed closely on the violence in Washington. Twenty-three Negroes and fifteen whites were killed, and many Negroes were arrested, indicted, and tried for participating and inciting to riot. Walter White, John Shillady, and Herbert Seligmann went to Chicago to investigate for the NAACP and reported that again the newspapers were to blame for the eruption of violence because of their distorted reports of Negro crime. White listed other factors playing a part in the Chicago outbreak—racial prejudice, economic rivalry, political corruption and exploitation of Negro voters, police inefficiency (leading to many unpublished crimes against Negroes), the problem of Negro housing, and the moral letdown that follows every war.

Joel Spingarn conferred with the Chicago branch, and as a result of the deliberations, a delegation called on Mayor William Hale Thompson and Governor Frank O. Lowden of Illinois. The mayor took no action, but the governor, who had refused to call out the state militia, appointed a commission to study the riots and prepare a plan for preventing them in the future. The NAACP Board made $5,000 immediately available for the legal defense of the victims of the Chicago riots, and Arthur Spingarn went to Chicago to confer with the legal committee of the branch concerning their defense.

The race riots in the North had repercussions in the South. Two lynchings in Georgia were the result of fear of a Negro uprising aimed at wiping out the white population. In Georgia a man was lynched because he was supposed to have said that the Negroes of Georgia were going to do what Negroes had done in Chicago. In Mississippi a Negro was lynched for "expressing his views too freely" concerning another lynching in that state.

The NAACP investigations and the new fighting spirit among Negroes led to efforts to curtail activities of the Association. Early in August, 1919, the Austin, Texas, branch informed the national office that the state attorney general had subpoenaed the branch president to bring all NAACP books, papers, and correspondence to court. Texas seemed determined to close down all branches operating in the state on the grounds that the Association was not chartered to do business in Texas. The national office advised the Austin branch that the NAACP was not a business but a membership corporation, whose purposes were civic and educational. If Texas could stop the operation of the NAACP within its borders, other Southern states might follow suit. At that time there were 31 branches and 7,046 members in Texas. According to Miss Ovington, the subpeona had been issued because copies of *The Crisis,* containing resolutions adopted at the 1919 annual conference urging the end of segregation in public transportation, had come into the hands of Texas officials.

In response to this situation, John Shillady wired Governor Hobby and the Texas attorney general asking for an opportunity to explain the aims and purposes of the Association and immediately left for Texas. In Austin, he was unable to meet either the governor or the attorney general but talked with the acting attorney general and tried to explain that the NAACP was not engaged in organizing Negro uprisings against whites. When Shillady left the attorney general's office, he was haled before a secret session of what purported to be a court of inquiry, where the county attorney asked legitimate as well as insultingly personal questions. The following morning Shillady was set upon and beaten unconscious by a group of men who had been seen loitering about the building the night before. Six or eight men took part in the assault, while "an auto full of tough-looking men" stood by. Among the assailants were a judge and a constable, both of whom frankly admitted their part in the attack, claiming that Shillady was inciting Negroes against whites and had been warned to leave Austin.

Upon receiving news of the attack on Shillady through an Associated Press dispatch, the national office telegraphed Governor Hobby demanding that the assailants be punished. Hobby replied that Shillady was the only offender and that he had already been punished. When Miss Ovington wrote to police officials at Austin, the deputy sheriff answered that Shillady had been "received by redblooded white men," who did not want "Negro-loving white men" in Texas. They had sent him back home with the admonition: "We attend to our own affairs down here, and suggest that you do the same up there."

James Weldon Johnson was able to verify the rumor that a prominent Negro clergyman of Austin had brought about the attack on Shillady by informing a Texas Ranger that the NAACP was banding together to excite sedition and race riots. Johnson exposed the clergyman in the Negro press and urged the severest, most complete ostracism for such Negroes. At about the same time Richard Carroll, the Negro lecturer from Columbia, South Carolina, who had helped the NAACP with the Pink Franklin case, wrote in the *New York Age* that "fully half the outrages and lynchings and brutality were caused by 'Judas Iscariots' among Negroes."

At a special meeting of the Board, an appeal was sent to President Wilson asking him to appoint a "responsible commission" to investigate and report on the

Shillady attack. Resolutions were drafted, calling for congressional investigation on the grounds that the governor of Texas had approved and condoned a criminal assault by public officials. The Board requested Governor Hobby to remove from office the judge who took part in the assault, and the Governor of New York was urged to demand protection for citizens of New York visiting Texas. Mass meetings throughout the country and in New York protested the attack on Shillady.

A committee of lawyers, Moorfield Storey, Arthur B. Spingarn, Charles Studin, George Crawford, and Butler Wilson, was appointed to investigate the legal aspects of the case. They determined to secure only counsel of high standing, the inference being that if such counsel proved unavailable, the publication of this fact would itself constitute a severe indictment of the Texas authorities. The committee agreed that if Shillady returned to Austin to testify, he must first be given guarantees of protection from physical violence.

Shillady's experience in Austin was not without grave physical and psychological after effects. Years later, Johnson wrote that Shillady never fully recovered spiritually from the experience. A. B. Spingarn was more harsh in his judgment, claiming that the secretary had shown the white feather and quit the Association out of fear of returning to Austin. Walter White was more sympathetic. Miss Ovington compared Shillady to a shell-shocked soldier. By November the secretary's health was so obviously failing that he was given a vacation on full pay for six weeks to recuperate. The Board agreed to reimburse him for medical and other expenses resulting from the ordeal. Shillady returned to his duties as executive officer of the Association for a time, but resigned in August, 1920. His resignation brought an end to the possibility of a trial in Austin. It is doubtful that it would ever have been held, for the NAACP was unable to secure a local lawyer willing to argue the case.

In his letter of resignation, Shillady expressed his disillusionment. "I am less confident than heretofore of the speedy success of the Association's full program, and of the probability of overcoming, within a reasonable period, the forces opposed to Negro equality by the means and methods which are within the Association's power to employ."

To Du Bois, Shillady's conclusion was not news. The American Negro knew that his problem could not be solved quickly, that there were strong forces opposed to equality, and that the methods of combating these forces were limited. But white people, warned Du Bois, especially white social workers, must learn that the problem could not be avoided. The 90,000 members of the Association had banded together in an attempt to solve it. Shillady had tried to talk quietly and reasonably to Texans but "the haters of black folk beat him and maltreated him and scarred him like a dog." If peaceful, legal, reasonable methods were not adequate, what else, asked Du Bois, did America propose, and what were white men going to do about it? . . .

The Atlanta Conference

Throughout the fall and winter of 1919, the question of whether to hold the 1920 annual conference in Atlanta or in a Northern city divided both membership and Board. In the light of a campaign designed to intimidate members and stamp out the organization in Southern communities, there was justifiable fear that the Atlanta riots of 1906 might be repeated. In the attack on Shillady, Texas had shown the attitude of the South toward the NAACP and all "outsiders." Would Atlanta do the same? These fears were allayed, however, when invitations came from the Mayor of Atlanta, the Chamber of Commerce, and even from Governor Dorsey, indicating that the Association's convention would be welcome.

It was a shorter conference than the 1919 meeting at Cleveland, lasting only four days, and there were fewer participants, but the Atlanta conference marked another epoch. The Association was at last able to meet openly in the deep South and to express freely and frankly its radical aims. To Du Bois this was an announcement to the whole country that there was "no difference of aim and desire" between Negroes of the South and those of the North. James Weldon Johnson was moved to observe more than the wonted public courtesy in the city of Atlanta and a noticeable elasticity in the traditional racial bounds. So encouraged were the Board members by the Atlanta meeting that the following year they invited Governor Dorsey of Georgia to speak at the Detroit conference.

Racial violence was now a national problem. The protests and the publicity had focused public attention on the evil. Efforts to obtain passage of a federal anti-lynching law had been unsuccessful, but fear of federal interference and public awareness of the economic effects of the ill-treatment of Negroes in the South eventually brought about a decrease in the number of lynchings and a lessening of mob violence. Negroes had responded to the tension of the war years and their aftermath by aligning themselves with the NAACP and by subscribing to *The Crisis* as never before in the history of the organization.

1.4   Patricia Sullivan

On the Eve of the New Deal

Patricia Sullivan is author of Days of Hope: Race and Democracy in the New Deal Era. *She is a fellow at the W. E. B. Du Bois Institute for Afro-American Research at Harvard University.*

In 1932, as the nation sank deeper into the depression, an official of the Hoover administration told Congress, "My sober and considered judgement is that . . . federal aid would be a disservice to the unemployed." The promotion of self-reliance rang hollow, however, as the number of farm foreclosures multiplied and as people from all levels of society fattened the ranks of the unemployed. Even southern Democrats abandoned what had been an uncompromising opposition to federal intervention in southern affairs, the cardinal principle of post-Reconstruction state governments. As the presidential campaign approached, they pressed for government action and rallied behind the candidacy of the governor of New York, Franklin D. Roosevelt.

The South's retreat from a dogmatic adherence to states' rights showed the region's desperation. The *Atlanta Constitution*'s confident promotion of the Democratic Party as the guardian of "equal rights," however, reflected the extent to which national and regional sensibilities regarding race and citizenship were one. Except for the Reconstruction period, the federal courts and the nation's political institutions had accommodated the white supremacist order in the South. Woodrow Wilson, the last Democrat in the White House, had extended racial segregation to include all federal facilities in the nation's capital.

Yet, as Lester Granger and other young black leaders anticipated, the political upheaval spawned by the depression created new opportunities for African Americans to assert their citizenship. Black voters in northern cities, fed by the wave of war-induced migration from the South, earned strategic positions among the urban coalitions that transformed the national political landscape during the 1930s. The great majority of black Americans, however, remained in the South, where they were barred from politics. But even there, the nationalizing trends and democratic activism surrounding the New Deal stirred efforts among the disfranchised to find a way out of what one contemporary called the "economic and political wilderness."

On the eve of the New Deal, Horace Mann Bond, a young black scholar and educator, explored the schizophrenic contours of southern life in an essay for *Harper's* magazine. He began by noting the widely popular "cult of the South." Here, "The white man is the Southerner, the Negro—well, a Negro." Drawing on family memory and on his extensive travels throughout the region, Bond looked beneath this veneer and inquired into the nature of the South as a "geographical portion, a psychological entity." He wove a textured portrait of black and white life and of the transparent boundaries of the caste system. "Customs, politics, society, all of the deeper and more extensive ramifications of culture," Bond observed, "bear the imprint of those of us who, being Southerners, are also Negroes."

Regional identity, however, often failed to embrace the richness and complexity of southern life and culture. Bond explained that for whites and many blacks, the idea of the South was corrupted by the habitual celebration of a "white" South in which the Negro was a mere shadow "deepen[ing] the effect of the leading silhouette." It was this South that captured the national imagination. Although it had no basis in material reality, it reflected a political reality whereby "the accolade of Southern citizenship, of participation in the fate of the region," had been "appropriated by white persons." When Bond wrote in 1931, amid widespread economic despair, the South's deeply racialized civic life appeared to be unyielding, thus obstructing his effort to articulate a vision of the region's future.

Black exclusion was emblematic of the political order established at the turn of the century with the final triumph of the Democratic Party. In a relentless campaign of fraud and violence, Democrats had navigated the tumultuous electoral contests of the late nineteenth century under the mantra of white liberty and home rule, appealing to the white South's abiding mistrust of politics and government. The contentious politics of the era crested with the Populist challenge of the 1890s, along with a growing movement to restrict the franchise. Democrats adroitly manipulated the economic unrest and anxieties that fed the Populist movement, pinning the region's woes on the newly enfranchised black voters and promising their complete removal from public life. By the first decade of the twentieth century, suffrage restrictions were in place in all southern states, segregation laws penetrated every facet of southern life, and Democratic Party hegemony—or what North Carolina newspaperman Josephus Daniels hailed as "permanent good government by the Party of the white man"—had been secured.

The South's new order, which virtually nullified the constitutional amendments enacted during Reconstruction, won the approval of the Supreme Court and the sympathetic support of northern white sentiment. Reconciliation of northern and southern whites advanced on the battlefield of the Spanish-American War in 1898, a war that reinforced white racial arrogance. Meanwhile, the widely popular tenets of social Darwinism, offering "scientific" validation of Anglo-Saxon superiority, seasoned the politics of the **Progressive Era**. In the north, reformers blamed immigrants for labor turmoil and the corruption of urban politics and supported suffrage restrictions as essential to the smooth functioning of democracy. The history of Reconstruction, as it was written early in the twentieth century, offered a powerful lesson in the perils of enfranchising the ignorant and socially inferior. William A. Dunning and his graduate students at Columbia University provided scholarly legitimacy for the white South's indictment of Reconstruction as a horrific time, a fatally flawed experiment. D. W. Griffith further popularized this view in his 1915 celluloid testimonial to sectional reconciliation and white supremacy, *The Birth of a Nation*.

Having prevailed as the party of white solidarity and regional self-determination, the Democratic Party offered the South "a politics of balance, inertia and drift." Disfranchisement barred many whites as well as virtually all blacks from the electoral process. The party represented a diverse range of potentially conflicting economic interests, from Black Belt planters to New South boosters, with all kinds of state variations. A type of negative politics, committed to maintaining the fundamental principles of the racial and economic status quo, provided some coherence. As historian Michael Perman has explained, in the state constitutional and legislative battles to "redeem" the South, the Democrats "saddled the region with a constricted governmental apparatus and a repressive system of land and labor" that doomed the region to decades of static and adaptive economic development.

Federal endorsement of white hegemony had robbed black southerners of their last defenses against the usurpation of their civil and political rights. But traditions of freedom and citizenship, born in the crucible of Reconstruction, sustained communities of resistance. Black southerners developed an expansive vision of democracy in their efforts to secure the fruits of emancipation. The black church, as Elsa Barkley Brown has explained, was the site of mass meetings where the newly freed "enacted their understanding of democratic political discourse." During the tumultuous decades of the 1880s and 1890s, black men and women met white terrorism at the polls with a group presence on election day. As an organized and articulate body of citizens, black communities throughout the region took an active part in Republican Party politics and explored alliances with independent groups such as the Farmers' Alliance and the **Populist Party**. Indeed, the persistence and endurance of African Americans in an increasingly hostile political environment was used by proponents of disfranchisement to rally white support.

By the dawn of the new century, government and politics had become "inaccessible and unaccountable to Americans who happened to be black." African Americans continued to develop strategies for social and political development within a separate public sphere. This was dominated, in large part, by the church but also included fraternal organizations, the black press, and other institutions. Churches often focused the mobilization of community resources to provide educational and social welfare services, leadership training, and organizational networks. The church, notes Evelyn Brooks Higginbotham, served as a vehicle of collective identity and empowerment and provided a place "to critique and contest America's racial domination."

While the rudiments of citizenship expired, formative developments shaped possibilities for future change. Resistance to new laws segregating streetcars erupted in locally organized boycotts in at least twenty-five southern cities from 1900 to 1906. These failed to stem the tide of segregation, however, demonstrating the futility of such actions. Black leaders and intellectuals continued to debate a broad range of political thought and strategies, framed by the accommodationism of Booker T. Washington, the civil rights protests of Ida B. Wells, W. E. B. Du Bois, and others, and the legal activism of the National Association for the Advancement of Colored People (NAACP), founded in 1909. Ideological divisions and tactical differences were enhanced by the daunting nature of the struggle, namely to sustain black communities amid the crushing environment of white racism while envisioning a way forward.

Black migration, confined largely within the South, had been a vehicle of freedom, self-determination, and survival since the earliest days of emancipation. Starting in 1914, however, the "Great Migration" of the World War I era stimulated a steady and ultimately transforming movement of black southerners to the North. Black migration continued even after wartime demands ceased and jobs became scarce. The boll weevil and growing pressures of surplus labor pushed increasing numbers of blacks off the land during the twenties. Nearly one and a half million southern blacks went north from 1915 to 1929, an internal migration of vast proportions and significance. (At emancipation in 1863, the total population of freed blacks in the South has been estimated at four million.)

The North hardly resembled "the promised land." During the "Red summer" of 1919 racial violence erupted in riots in northern urban centers as well as in the South; the worst outbreak was in Chicago. But discrimination and segregation in northern cities lacked the relentless brutality seen in the southern system. In the North, blacks responded to white violence with a militancy that was refracted in the "New Negro" movement of the twenties, while the Garvey movement stirred mass demonstrations of racial pride. During the twenties, black communities in the North nurtured the outpouring of cultural, literary, and musical creativity that flowered in the Harlem Renaissance. And, in the North, black citizens had free access to the ballot. As their numbers increased, black participation in northern urban politics gradually became a factor of national consequence.

For the great majority of blacks remaining in the South, however, industrialization and urbanization extended the grip of segregation. During the war and postwar years, mechanization and upward pressure on unskilled wage earners sharpened racial dualism within the southern labor market. Black jobs and white jobs, with few exceptions, became increasingly noncompeting. Black men and women continued to dominate the tobacco industry, but white employees worked the machine-tended jobs in separate buildings. A similar trend of racial distinction emerged in the iron and steel industry, also dominated by blacks, who held both skilled and semiskilled positions. The textile industry had excluded blacks from the start; by the 1920s, its white workers were paid well above black wage earners. Unionization of skilled crafts increased during the 1920s, and these unions, such as the building trades, were among the most racially exclusive. In seeking to explain these developments, some historians have suggested that by the 1920s, black and white southerners were entering the work force with increasingly dissimilar educational backgrounds. But for most industrial jobs in the South, education bore little relevance to the job requirements. As historian Gavin Wright has explained, job classifications became primarily a function of caste and were "symptoms of the larger process of creating a segregated society."

Southern industrialists proudly presided over an abundant supply of "native" white labor—"thrifty, industrious, and one hundred percent American." They advertised a cheap and inexhaustible supply of nonunion labor as the region's greatest resource. A flurry of union activity among segments of the textile, mining, and tobacco industries met severe postwar wage cutbacks in 1919, but it quickly dissipated. Ten years later, worker opposition to the **stretch-out system** in the textile industry erupted in a series of strikes and unionization activities in the Carolinas. The most notorious and least typical confrontation came in Gastonia, where the Communist Party embarked on its preliminary effort to promote class struggle in the South. But Gastonia provided a lightning rod for antiunion sentiment. All efforts toward unionization ultimately yielded to combinations of employer intimidation, police force, and deep-rooted community hostility toward unions and "outsiders." Yet the most effective deterrent to unionization remained the vast pool of cheap white labor, desperate for work, and the army of black labor at the extreme margins of subsistence.

Black southerners were the first to absorb the economic downturn of the 1920s. The ravages of the boll weevil and the post–World War I economic slump stimulated a mass exodus of people "fleeing from hunger and exposure" in the countryside. African Americans dominated the rural movement to southern cities during 1922–24. In the latter part of the decade, whites began to follow in growing numbers. Rural refugees crowded into growing slums, where work was often irregular or nonexistent. As the economic squeeze tightened, white workers steadily took away what had been traditionally black jobs. Some towns passed municipal ordinances restricting black employment. But in most cases, intimidation and appeals to racial loyalty were most effective in securing jobs for whites.

In several cities, white terrorist organizations mobilized the frustration and helplessness of unemployed whites into sporadic drives to claim jobs held by blacks. In 1930, the Black Shirts marched up Peachtree Street in Atlanta with banners demanding, "Niggers, back to the cotton fields—city jobs are for white folks." They forced Atlanta hotels to replace black bellhops with whites and pressured for the employment of white domestics, street cleaners, and garbage collectors. Future Governor Eugene Talmadge and the Georgia commissioner of agriculture were among the prominent members of the association. Although such extremist organizations were short-lived, black displacement by whites was widespread. In 1932, a New Orleans city ordinance that would have reserved jobs on publicly owned docks for "eligible electors," costing thousands of black dockworkers their jobs, was blocked by the U.S. Court of Appeals. By then, however, the unemployment rate for black males in New Orleans, Atlanta, and Birmingham was twice the rate for whites.

By 1930, economic desperation enveloped the entire society. The depression issued the final, devastating blow to the plantation economy and unhinged its commercial and industrial dependencies. Thousands of landowners who had participated in the brief cotton boom of the mid-1920s through land speculation and increased production now faced foreclosures when the price of cotton plummeted. Between 1929 and 1930 farm income was cut in half. The urban boosterism of Atlanta, Birmingham, and other oases of New South prosperity fizzled with the collapse of the agrarian economy. Manufacturing dropped by a third nationally during the depression, but the South fared even worse. Total manufacturing dropped by 50 percent in Atlanta and New Orleans from 1929 to 1933; Birmingham, hailed as the "Pittsburgh of the South" in the early twenties, saw manufacturing plummet by more than 70 percent. Jobless rates in southern cities also surpassed the national average, which in 1932 was estimated at 25 percent. Among the hardest-hit urban areas, southern cities lacked the funds to provide emergency relief for the masses of unemployed. Birmingham, the only city that had a Department of Public Welfare, abandoned it in 1924.

The depression stood as the worst crisis the United States had endured since the Civil War. The dilemma was unprecedented: growing poverty and unemployment in the midst of the abundance produced by modern methods of agriculture and industry. But during 1930 and 1931, local, state, and national political leaders relied on traditional remedies, assuming and hoping that the cycle would run its course. Herbert Hoover's blend of progressive conservatism, with its emphasis on volunteerism and a limited role for the federal government, framed the government's initial response to national economic collapse. The failure of Hoover's efforts to stem the rapid downward plunge stiffened his resolve against more aggressive measures. This only compounded the fatalism and desperation that gripped the country and prepared the ground for a dramatic departure from old certainties and values.

The limited vision in Washington was matched at the state level. Political leaders relied on the old formulas of retrenchment, a balanced budget, and regressive taxation. During 1930 and 1931, southern politicians and businessmen reiterated the sanctity of states' rights, along with their opposition to federal intervention and any suggestion of a national dole. At the same time, localities proved increasingly unable to meet the mushrooming demand for unemployment relief and often engaged in futile efforts to shift the burden to black men and women and, in some cases, to white women. From 1929 to 1932, white men replaced white women in six thousand manufacturing positions in Memphis. Several states established emergency welfare commissions, but these were dominated by businessmen and distributed no funds to the cities. Commenting on the performance of the Georgia legislature, historian James Patterson concluded that no other legislature could "compare in stupidity, selfishness, and lack of purpose with the body which twiddled its thumbs while the fires of hope died to ashes in the hearts of its citizens."

By 1932, the failure of these limited measures forced a sobering confrontation with the destitution and despair that blanketed the nation. "A creeping paralysis had taken hold of the people," an Alabamian observed, "and everything was falling apart." Individual self-reliance, a cultural bedrock, proved to be completely ineffectual in countering personal misfortune. "People were losing homes like ripe fruit falling from a tree; farmers were being foreclosed off their lands and homes by the thousands." The transient populations had multiplied; tens of thousands of people wandered "aimlessly, hopelessly over the country," noted one observer. They included members of every class: "businessmen, salesmen, lawyers, doctors, . . . and ex-convicts." A New Orleans businessman cautioned: "The whole white collar class . . . [is] taking an awful beating. . . . They're whipped, that's all. And it's bad.

Edward O'Neal, a northern Alabama planter and chairman of the conservative American Farm Bureau Federation, was among the chorus of voices demanding aggressive and imaginative action by the federal government. Late in 1932 he warned, "Unless something is done for the American farmer, we will have revolution in the countryside in less than twelve months." In their enthusiastic embrace of Franklin D. Roosevelt and his amorphous plan for a New Deal, the South's political leaders could not know that Roosevelt's reforms would invite a bold new challenge to the South's economic and political order.

Franklin Roosevelt's boundless confidence, his infectious good cheer, and his commitment to positive action revived the national mood almost instantly. The collapse of the nation's banking system on the eve of his inauguration did not break his stride. Rather, it served to level the playing field bequeathed by his predecessor, leaving no question that "the bottom had dropped out of everything." The outworn economic verities of the 1920s were spent, and the way was clear for the thorough restructuring that Roosevelt was prepared to orchestrate. Political action and leadership, long thought to be the handmaidens of "natural" economic forces, moved to center stage. "Public discussion, public criticism and public agitation" fueled the collective enterprise of the New Deal.

There was no master plan, no promised panacea. Roosevelt was the "Great Experimenter," "Master of Ceremonies," "Chief Croupier" of the New Deal. He energized the political process, giving full play to a wide range of ideas, personalities, and interests. Ever eager for information, Roosevelt "cast a net as wide as possible." His cabinet included fiscal conservatives, progressive agrarians, and social welfare liberals, Democrats, Republicans, and Independents, and with the appointment of Frances Perkins as secretary of labor, the first woman cabinet chief. New Deal agencies were staffed with professors, financiers, labor leaders, social workers, and politicos and included an unprecedented number of black professional appointments. From the beginning, Roosevelt included the American people in the New Deal through his radio "fireside" chats. "The wildest radical in America can win a hearing for his idea just as well as the most powerful banker," a contemporary observed. In addition to oiling the wheels of the country's political machinery, Roosevelt was engaged in "sinking tap roots into the whole American experience."

Although the rhetoric and dazzling momentum of the Roosevelt team heralded a new departure, historians have emphasized the basic conservatism of the early New Deal recovery program. The National Recovery Industrial Act and the Agricultural Adjustment Act stood as the crowning achievements of the whirl of legislation that marked the first hundred days. Both were tailored to the traditional constituent interests of industry and large farmers and easily enjoyed the support of conservative southern Democrats, with several notable exceptions. Senators Harry Byrd and Carter Glass of Virginia and Senator Josiah Bailey of North Carolina clung stubbornly to their belief in the unhampered workings of the free enterprise system and opposed federally sponsored price supports and minimum wages as a dangerous intrusion. According to Senator Bailey, "The accepted doctrine for one hundred and fifty years is that fundamental economic laws are natural laws, having the same source as physical laws."

But from the beginning of the Roosevelt administration, there was a deep, abiding awareness that a sea change in American politics was under way. Byrd, Glass, and Bailey possibly sensed it and tried to nip it in the bud. Secretary of Agriculture Henry Wallace was among those who welcomed and nurtured the potential inherent in the New Deal. "We are children of the transition," he told a group in 1934. "We have left Egypt, but we have not yet arrived in the promised land." After the depression had eroded old confidences, Roosevelt's election stirred the expectations of people and constituencies who had never completely secured representation in the national political arena. The pragmatic, open spirit of the

New Deal, along with Roosevelt's promotion of government as a vehicle for advancing human betterment, provided a focus for the political currents released by the depression.

Will Alexander, founder and director of the Atlanta-based Commission on Interracial Cooperation (CIC), sensed that the Roosevelt administration would have a profound effect on the southern United States. "I had a hunch," Alexander later recalled, "that Washington was going to become the center of the country and that perhaps the next stage of race relations in this country . . . would center around what happened in Washington." Alexander wanted someone in Washington who could monitor national initiatives for their effects on American race relations and who could make federal officials aware of the special problems faced by black Americans. Alexander and Edwin Embree, director of the Rosenwald Fund, went to Washington early in 1933 to lobby for the creation of such a position, to be subsidized by the Rosenwald Fund. After contacting the White House and several government agencies, they arranged for a "Special Adviser on the Economic Status of Negroes" to serve under Harold Ickes, secretary of the interior. Ickes selected Clark Foreman, a Georgian and one of Alexander's young protégés.

The appointment of a white man from Georgia to the newly created post drew a storm of opposition from the black press, the NAACP, and other black leaders. The protest was not directed against Foreman personally but against "the idea of a white advisor for Negroes." Foreman agreed and advised Ickes to fill the post with a black person. Ickes insisted, however, that a white person be appointed, at least initially, whether or not Foreman took the job. He approved Foreman's suggestion that Robert Weaver, a young black economist and Harvard Ph.D. candidate, be hired as Foreman's assistant and potential successor in the post.

Clark Foreman was part of a new generation of white southern liberals who passed under the tutelage of Will Alexander and the CIC but who had outgrown the constraints of that pioneering organization. Foreman demonstrated an impatience with southern racial mores, an impatience that even Alexander considered unwise. When Alexander had submitted a list of names for Ickes to consider for the position of special adviser, he had added Foreman's name as an afterthought, with qualifications. Foreman was "a man of highest motives," Alexander told Ickes, "but he leaned over backwards to be on the liberal side and had a feeling that the way you got things done was to get at the billy-goat—just butt right into them and keep butting until you're through." He was "a young man of great charm, a very keen mind, but a very impatient lad who didn't pick any counsel of caution but went straight ahead into anything he chose." Alexander later recalled Ickes's response. Foreman was just the kind of person he wanted, "the only one who [could] do any good in a job like this."

Clark Howell Foreman was born to privilege in Atlanta, Georgia, at the turn of the century. His worldview was shaped by an inherited sense of noblesse oblige and energized by a strong dose of Wilsonian idealism. On graduating from the University of Georgia in 1921, Foreman embarked on a wide-ranging pursuit of education and experience, searching for a way to participate in advancing "the good of humanity." Cambridge, Massachusetts, Europe, the southern United States, New York, and the Soviet Union were home to Foreman for stretches of time between 1921 and 1933. His abiding interest in America's racial mores evolved as he experienced the dynamic intellectual and political ferment in postwar Europe and the new Union of Soviet Socialist Republics. By the late 1920s, Foreman had become keenly aware of the ways the caste system dominated all of southern life and enforced a sterile conformity even among its most "enlightened" white citizens. Not until the New Deal, however, was he able to envision a way to challenge the seemingly intractable color line.

Foreman's ancestry was rooted in the pre-Revolutionary South, marrying slaveholding aristocracy to sturdy yeoman stock. His immediate family were among the leading citizens of Atlanta. His mother's father, Evan P. Howell, purchased the *Atlanta Constitution* in 1876 and made it the leading promoter of a "New South" under the editorship of Henry Grady. Clark Howell, the son of Evan P., succeeded Grady as managing editor in 1889, a position he held until his death in 1936. The *Constitution* reflected Howell's paternalistic views toward blacks, but his views contrasted with the more virulent racism of the time, such as that promoted by the former Populist leader Tom Watson. Clark Howell ran unsuccessfully against Hoke Smith, who had the enthusiastic support of Watson, in the 1906 gubernatorial campaign that led to the notorious Atlanta race riot.

Robert Foreman, Clark's father, was a successful businessman who tended to be more of a progressive liberal than a New South booster. He had, Clark later recalled, "a great sense of justice" and was a fiercely independent individual, who taught his four sons "not to bend [a] knee to any man." Robert and Effie Howell Foreman held no organizational religious affiliation. They encouraged their sons to think freely and develop their own ideas about religion, but they imbued Clark with a deeply felt obligation "to leave the world a better place for having lived." All of the Foreman brothers pursued college and postgraduate study, acting on their father's counsel to train their minds "for the duties and possibilities of life."

In the fall of 1917, Clark Foreman entered the University of Georgia at the age of sixteen. He pursued a classical course of study and engaged contemporary issues and ideas through participation on the debating team and in speaking contests. The Great War stimulated much discussion on the pastoral Athens campus and caused the university to eliminate German from the curriculum. It did not challenge the personal expectations of Clark and his contemporaries, nor intrude on the carefree spirit that dominated student life at Georgia. For Clark, another event shook the sense of security and privilege that he shared with most of his classmates. In February 1921 a black man was lynched in Athens, one of Georgia's "oldest and most enlightened communities."

Clark wrote to his parents describing the day's events in great detail. Talk about an alleged rape and murder of a pregnant white woman by a black man spread among the students, along with rumors that a lynch mob was gathering. Clark and other students looked on as a crowd collected outside the "mob-proof" courthouse in Athens from early afternoon on. An estimated three thousand people had assembled by early evening when several men forced their way into the courthouse with sledgehammers and blowtorches. Two county sheriffs and their deputies were in another part of the courthouse at the time but later said they were unaware of the mob's visit. The group crowded into the jail on the fifth floor and "burned and hammered their way" into the cell where John Lee Eberhardt was confined. They chained and dragged Eberhardt from the jail, put him in one of the automobiles, and led the mob back to the scene of the crime five miles outside of the city. Clark jumped onto the running board of an automobile and followed along to see what was going on. In the letter to his parents, he described what happened next:

> The negro was carried to the place of the murder. He was shown the lady he was supposed to have murdered in the hopes that he would confess. The lady was about 23, fair and beautiful. She had a baby eighteen months old and was expecting another in June. The negro would not confess. He was brought out in the yard and tied to a pine tree, about a hundred yards from the house. The crowd of about three thousand people gathered around the tree in a large circle. A leader made a speech forbidding any shooting on account of the danger of onlookers. Strict order was preserved. Everyone was made to sit down, so that the ones behind them might see with ease the ghastly spectacle that was about to take place. A fire was built about the negro's feet and lit. Neither gasoline nor kerosene was used, in order that the job might not be done too fast. The family was brought to the center of the ring so that the negro might have one more chance to confess. He pleaded to God to testify his innocence. More wood was thrown on the fire. The negro yelled for mercy.
>
> The fire leaps up and seems to burn him too fast. Some hardened onlooker smolders it so that the negro might suffer longer. He tries to choke himself, his hands tied behind him. Finally with a monster effort he bends over far enough to swallow some flame. He dies amid the jeers of the crowd.
>
> The people . . . grab souvenirs from the branches of the guilty tree. Even the dead negro is not spared. Fingers and toes are pulled from the scorched corpse to remind the participants of the deed. At this juncture a woman comes forth with a pistol and asks to be allowed to shoot the negro. The request is granted. More wood is piled on, and the funeral pyre flares up and lights the faces of the watchers. The mob disperses each to his home, with an air of conquest and satisfaction rather than horror and condemnation.

This "sadistic orgy," Foreman later recalled, brought him "face to face with the barbarism" underlying race relations in the South and made an "indelible impression" on his mind. But he was not yet capable of connecting it to the core issue of racial discrimination in the South. "About that," he reflected, "I was still almost completely ignorant." He was a young man of nineteen, and his framework still reflected the racial liberalism and paternalism of his father. Robert Foreman was repulsed by the barbaric nature of the mob action and shamed by the duplicity of law enforcement officials. Such a complete breakdown of law and civility reflected on the entire society. In the valedictorian address to his graduating class, Clark echoed these sensibilities in an appeal to his classmates. "It is our solemn duty to uphold the laws of our state and see that they are enforced fearlessly by the constituted authorities, and not by cowardly mobs of night-riding ruffians—an unspeakable example of which was recently perpetrated at the very doors of this University."

Following a family tradition, Clark took a year of study at Harvard after his graduation from Georgia. The Harvard experience inaugurated a personal odyssey that took Clark far from his southern moorings. Living among northerners for the first time, he was a proud and sometimes chauvinistic ambassador for his region and frequently sought refuge at the Southern Club, where he met Virginia Foster of Birmingham, Alabama, then a student at Wellesley. (Foreman's friendship with Virginia Foster Durr blossomed in Washington more than a decade later.) But he delighted in the collection of companions he quickly became associated with, which included several young men from New York and Boston. Gradually, he became more questioning about the South. Foreman's first break from southern tradition came when he joined a group of students for dinner with W. E. B. Du Bois before a talk Du Bois delivered to the Liberal Club. Foreman had planned to attend the talk but did not know that a dinner was involved. At first he refused to go. He had never sat down to a meal with a black person before and said he could not do it. But his friends and roommates argued with him "until [he] had no rational defense." . . .

In the course of his studies, and through continuing work on interracial concerns, Foreman consulted with Charles S. Johnson, editor of *Opportunity* magazine and benefactor of the Harlem Renaissance. Foreman assisted Johnson with a major interracial conference, held in Washington, D.C., in the fall of 1928. This was his first introduction to segregation in the nation's capital. As the person responsible for local arrangements, Foreman confronted a policy that prohibited American blacks from staying in Washington hotels but that welcomed "colored people" from other countries. After much persistence, Foreman persuaded several hotels, including the Willard Hotel, to make an exception and to admit black American guests. But the change was only temporary.

The Julius F. Rosenwald Fund provided Foreman with an ideal opportunity for pursuing his doctoral research on "Environmental Factors in Negro Education." Established in 1917 by the founder of Sears & Roebuck, the Rosenwald Fund was the major patron of black education in the South. When Edwin Embree, the fund's director, hired Foreman late in 1928, the stock market was cresting, and the foundation was earning money faster than it could spend it. Julius Rosenwald had stipulated that the foundation should not be perpetual, requiring that the endowment be spent within twenty-five years. As associate for the Southern Program, Foreman's job was to travel throughout the South and devise more ways for quickly distributing the Rosenwald money.

Working out of the fund's Nashville office, Foreman developed a plan for supporting public libraries in the South. At a time when no southern county had a library that served all of the people, the Rosenwald Fund offered generous assistance to counties that would extend library services to all of its citizens—black and white, rural and urban. The fund supported programs in eleven counties in seven southern states. This project broke from the Rosenwald Fund's almost exclusive concern with black schools and health programs. Foreman found that several board members were hostile toward providing any assistance for southern whites, reflecting a common northern attitude that "the white people of the South were really all slaveholders at heart." The project, however, had Embree's enthusiastic support. It was supplemented by an infusion of money into library schools in the South to support the training of black and white librarians. Tommie Dora Barker, of Atlanta, worked with Foreman as the primary coordinator of this program, which was later continued with support from the Carnegie Foundation.

With the collapse of the stock market in October 1929, the Rosenwald Fund adopted a conservative approach to spending its shrinking resources in the South, enabling Foreman to devote most of his time to his dissertation research. Foreman worked with Horace Mann Bond pursuing a study of "Environmental Factors in Negro Education." Bond, then an instructor at Fisk University, had taken his Ph.D. at the University of Chicago under Robert E. Park and had written his dissertation on black education in Alabama. Bond and Foreman developed and implemented a research design to measure the ways in which environmental factors influenced the achievement of black students in the South, documenting a high correlation between expenditures and achievement. They worked from a representative sample drawn from North Carolina, Alabama, and Louisiana.

From October 1929 to May 1931, the team visited 569 schools and administered the new Stanford Achievement Test to ten thousand students in the third and sixth grades. In each place, they examined the wide range of factors shaping a child's educational environment: school facilities, the presence or absence of textbooks, term length, teacher qualifications and salaries, health and community organizations, and the local school superintendent. Since blacks had no political influence in any of the counties tested, the attitude of the local school superintendent proved to be an important factor in determining the quality of black education. Of the schools visited, they found 61 percent of them to be "unsatisfactory for school purposes." Their report noted: "If the schoolhouse is bad enough it can almost completely stop the educational process, as may be illustrated by one very small and dilapidated shack without windows, in which the investigators on opening the door found the school in absolute darkness and the teacher and pupils asleep. The teacher [who] faced the alternative of light and cold air through the open door and darkness and relative warmth with the door closed, chose the latter despite the soporific effect."

Fieldwork with Horace Mann Bond in the South introduced Foreman to the daily indignities and insults endured by black people, regardless of their class or achievement. The two men worked closely throughout the course of the study. Foreman recalled, "The difficulties in the way of our working together were so great that it made me appreciate more than ever the conditions which Negroes have to face in this country." When Foreman tried to ride with Bond in the Jim Crow coach on the train, the conductor forced him to move. When they traveled together by automobile, "there was always a great problem as to where he could find food and lodging." In many of the small southern communities they visited, the accommodations for white people were often far from comfortable. "But I always knew," Foreman recalled, "that Mr. Bond was having to put up with much worse."

Foreman's travels throughout the South during 1929–31 also confirmed his belief that southern whites were incapable of providing a solution to the racial injustice that permeated southern society. He was "greatly depressed" by the static, repressed condition of southern intellectuals. The Nashville Agrarians were reigning over the only intellectual movement of note, in the wake of the publication of their manifesto, *I'll Take My Stand,* in 1930. With the possible exception of Robert Penn Warren, Foreman concluded that these so-called fugitives were leading the retreat from reality, pining for an agrarian utopia that was built on the backs of a cheap, inexhaustible supply of black labor. He dubbed them "Neo-Confederates."

Liberal and humane sympathies were isolated or repressed in the South. An unspoken code of self-censorship seemed to prevail at private and public colleges; it was clearly understood that any questioning of the racial status quo would probably bring dismissal. Foreman admired the efforts of southern liberal journalists like Josephus Daniels, Mark Ethridge, and Julian Harris and found them to be enthusiastic supporters of the Rosenwald Fund. But none of them publicly endorsed fair treatment for black people, and it seemed unlikely that they would. After Julia Collier Harris and Julian Harris, editors of the *Columbus Enquirer-Sun,* won a Pulitzer Prize for their courageous campaign against the Ku Klux Klan, local opposition to the pair was so great that they finally left Columbus.

Foreman returned to Columbia University in the fall of 1931, wiser about the ways of the South but uncertain how to find a path forward. As the country sank deeper into the depression, the Rosenwald Fund continued to pay his salary while he completed his dissertation. He was awarded a Ph.D. in the spring of 1932. Since Foreman had no job prospects, Embree decided to keep him on for another year. The Rosenwald Fund sent him to Europe to broaden his education and suggested that he study rural organization in preparation for further work in the South. While visiting with his family in Highlands, North Carolina, before his departure, Clark listened to Franklin Roosevelt accept the Democratic Party's nomination in Chicago, pledging a "new deal."

1.5   Asa Philip Randolph

Civil Rights Can Be Secured by Mass Action

Asa Philip Randolph (1889–1979) was a labor and civil rights leader. He was president of the Brotherhood of Sleeping Car Porters, the largest black union in America.

We call upon you to fight for jobs in National Defense.

We call upon you to struggle for the integration of Negroes in the armed forces, such as the Air Corps, Navy, Army and Marine Corps of the Nation.

We call upon you to demonstrate for the abolition of Jim-Crowism in all Government departments and defense employment.

An Hour of Crisis

This is an hour of crisis. It is a crisis of democracy. It is a crisis of minority groups. It is a crisis of Negro Americans.

What is this crisis?

To American Negroes, it is the denial of jobs in Government defense projects. It is racial discrimination in Government departments. It is widespread Jim-Crowism in the armed forces of the Nation.

While billions of the taxpayers' money are being spent for war weapons, Negro workers are being turned away from the gates of factories, mines and mills— being flatly told, "NOTHING DOING." Some employers refuse to give Negroes jobs when they are without "union cards," and some unions refuse Negro workers union cards when they are "without jobs."

What shall we do?

What a dilemma!

What a runaround!

What a disgrace!

What a blow below the belt!

'Though dark, doubtful and discouraging, all is not lost, all is not hopeless. 'Though battered and bruised, we are not beaten, broken or bewildered.

Verily, the Negroes' deepest disappointments and direst defeats, their tragic trials and outrageous oppressions in these dreadful days of destruction and disaster to democracy and freedom, and the rights of minority peoples, and the dignity and independence of the human spirit, is the Negroes' greatest opportunity to rise to the highest heights of struggle for freedom and justice in Government, in industry, in labor unions, education, social service, religion and culture.

Self-Liberation

With faith and confidence of the Negro people in their own power for self-liberation, Negroes can break down the barriers of discrimination against employment in National Defense. Negroes can kill the deadly serpent of race hatred in the Army, Navy, Air and Marine Corps, and smash through and blast the Government, business and labor-union red tape to win the right to equal opportunity in vocational training and re-training in defense employment.

Most important and vital to all, Negroes, by the mobilization and coordination of their mass power, can cause PRESIDENT ROOSEVELT TO ISSUE AN EXECUTIVE ORDER ABOLISHING DISCRIMINATIONS IN ALL GOVERNMENT DEPARTMENTS, ARMY, NAVY, AIR CORPS AND NATIONAL DEFENSE JOBS.

Of course, the task is not easy. In very truth, it is big, tremendous and difficult.

It will cost money.

It will require sacrifice.

It will tax the Negroes' courage, determination and will to struggle. But we can, must and will triumph.

The Negroes' stake in national defense is big. It consists of jobs, thousands of jobs. It may represent millions, yes, hundreds of millions of dollars in wages. It consists of new industrial opportunities and hope. This is worth fighting for.

But to win our stakes, it will require an "all-out," bold and total effort and demonstration of colossal proportions.

Negroes can build a mammoth machine of mass action with a terrific and tremendous driving and striking power that can shatter and crush the evil fortress of race prejudice and hate, if they will only resolve to do so and never stop, until victory comes.

Dear fellow Negro Americans, be not dismayed in these terrible times. You possess power, great power. Our problem is to harness and hitch it up for action on the broadest, daring and most gigantic scale.

Aggressive Mass Action

In this period of power politics, nothing counts but pressure, more pressure, and still more pressure, through the tactic and strategy of broad, organized, aggressive mass action behind the vital and important issues of the Negro. To this end, we propose that ten thousand Negroes MARCH ON WASHINGTON FOR JOBS IN NATIONAL DEFENSE AND EQUAL INTEGRATION IN THE FIGHTING FORCES OF THE UNITED STATES.

An "all-out" thundering march on Washington, ending in a monster and huge demonstration at Lincoln's Monument will shake up white America.

It will shake up official Washington.

It will give encouragement to our white friends to fight all the harder by our side, with us, for our righteous cause.

It will gain respect for the Negro people.

It will create a new sense of sell-respect among Negroes.

But what of national unity?

We believe in national unity which recognizes equal opportunity of black and white citizens to jobs in national defense and the armed forces, and in all other institutions and endeavors in America. We condemn all dictatorships, Fascist, Nazi and Communist. We are loyal, patriotic Americans, all.

But, if American democracy will not defend its defenders; if American democracy will not protect its protectors; if American democracy will not give jobs to its toilers because of race or color; if American democracy will not insure equality of opportunity, freedom and justice to its citizens, black and white, it is a hollow mockery and belies the principles for which it is supposed to stand.

To the hard, difficult and trying problem of securing equal participation in national defense, we summon all Negro Americans to march on Washington. We summon Negro Americans to form committees in various cities to recruit and register marchers and raise funds through the sale of buttons and other legitimate means for the expenses of marchers to Washington by buses, train, private automobiles, trucks, and on foot.

We summon Negro Americans to stage marches on their City Halls and Councils in their respective cities and urge them to memorialize the President to issue an executive order to abolish discrimination in the Government and national defense.

However, we sternly counsel against violence and ill-considered and intemperate action and the abuse of power. Mass power, like physical power, when misdirected is more harmful than helpful.

We summon you to mass action that is orderly and lawful, but aggressive and militant, for justice, equality and freedom.

Crispus Attucks marched and died as a martyr for American independence. Nat Turner, Denmark Vesey, Gabriel Prosser, Harriet Tubman and Frederick Douglass fought, bled and died for the emancipation of Negro slaves and the preservation of American democracy.

Abraham Lincoln, in times of the grave emergency of the Civil War, issued the Proclamation of Emancipation for the freedom of Negro slaves and the preservation of American democracy.

Freedom from Stigma

Today, we call upon President Roosevelt, a great humanitarian and idealist, to follow in the footsteps of his noble and illustrious predecessor and take the second decisive step in this world and national emergency and free American Negro citizens of the stigma, humiliation and insult of discrimination and Jim-Crowism in Government departments and national defense.

The Federal Government cannot with clear conscience call upon private industry and labor unions to abolish discrimination based upon race and color as long as it practices discrimination itself against Negro Americans.

Nineteen Forty-Eight: The Opening of the Breach

Jack M. Bloom, author of Class, Race, and the Civil Rights Movement, *is a professor of sociology at Indiana University/Northwest. He was a movement activist in the 1970s.*

On Tuesday, July 13, 1948, George Vaughan rose to speak to the nominating convention of the Democratic party. Vaughan, a black attorney from St. Louis, was a member of the convention credentials committee. He was delivering a minority report, urging that Mississippi be excluded from the convention because of her commitment not to support Truman if he was nominated and his proposed civil rights platform plank adopted. After making the case, he raised his fist and spoke angrily into the microphone: "Three million Negroes have left the South since the outbreak of World War II to escape this thing. I ask the convention to give consideration. . . ." Vaughan's voice was drowned out in the shouts and screams coming from the Southern delegations. The chair called for a voice vote, and although several Northern delegations were demanding a roll call, they were ignored. The motion was declared defeated, and the session was quickly adjourned for the night.

This incident was remarkable in that it showed the Democratic party, the party of slavery and white supremacy, at war with itself over racial issues. The Northern and Southern Democratic parties were clearly bound in different directions. Tuesday was just a prelude to the tumultuous Wednesday session, when the platform was debated. After the party adopted a more militant plank than even President Truman wanted, the Mississippi delegation walked out, along with half of the Alabama delegation. They left calling for an all-Southern meeting of the "true Democratic Party." Within a few days they and others joined in a meeting in Birmingham to launch a new party, the States' Rights party, to run against Truman.

This party was the second split-off from the Democratic party that year. Earlier, Henry Wallace, Roosevelt's vice-president from 1940 to 1944, had announced that he would run against Truman on the new Progressive party ticket. Wallace's was a left-wing split. So, in 1948 the Democratic party split into three parties. Nothing like that had happened since the election of 1860—the prelude to Civil War.

The treatment of blacks emerged as a central issue for the first time ever in a presidential election in 1948. It did so for a variety of reasons, but most particularly because blacks perceived that they had an opportunity to exert political pressure and to reap some important political gains. Seeing that opportunity, they acted.

The experience of the Great Depression—the worst depression in history, and of World War II—the most destructive and expensive war in history, also had profound and lasting effects. These began to make themselves felt seriously in 1948.

This election was the first since 1928 in which Franklin Roosevelt had not headed the Democratic ticket. The 1928 election had split the Democratic party in the South, with many Southerners voting for Hoover and against the Catholic candidate, Al Smith. The Depression had ended that episode, and the South had flocked home to the Democrats, but Roosevelt's economic policies had met with bitter opposition from the Southern leadership. In 1944 the South had led the effort at the Democratic convention to ditch Henry Wallace as the vice-presidential candidate. Wallace had become identified with the New Deal liberal economic and racial policies and the left wing of the administration. Many felt Roosevelt's victories to be his *personal* victories and that once he was gone his policies would be repudiated by the voters. The New Deal and the changes it had made in politics and economics were being fought over in 1948. That was one of the reasons the nation was seriously divided.

The United States had emerged from the war deeply involved in international affairs. As the most powerful nation in the world, it was busily involved in the reconstruction of that world. That effort ranged from transferring control of much of the oil in the Middle East from Britain to America to refashioning the international monetary system to make the dollar the preeminent currency in the world, and to reforming the world trade system to greatly diminish trade barriers and therefore to give U.S. products access to all world markets. What became most significant was the competition with Russia—the **cold war**. This issue was central in the election.

Splits and dislocations as the nation and the world came to grips with reconstructing political, economic, and social life were only natural. Structural changes in the world and within the United States brought about these splits, which in their turn provided new opportunities for blacks to influence the federal government, and through it to affect the South.

Black Political Power

But these were opportunities that blacks could take advantage of only from a position of strength. In 1948 they had potential power such as they had never before had—voting power, power to determine the outcome of the presidential election and of many local offices. Moreover, blacks were conscious of their power, militant, and better organized than they ever had been.

The simple movement of population is part of what created this new black political power. If Vaughan exaggerated in his claim that 3 million blacks had fled the South during the war, the number was still huge. Between 1940 and 1950, 1.5 million blacks left the South in search of jobs. These numbers increased the Northern black population of 2.8 million by over half. Moreover, this population movement was focused: in 1940, 90 percent of the black population outside the South was concentrated in urban areas; 47 percent of these lived in New York, Chicago, Philadelphia, Detroit, Cleveland, and Pittsburgh. The new migration continued and even accentuated that trend. In the Portland-Vancouver area, the increase of blacks was 437 percent; in San Francisco it was 227 percent; in Detroit it was 60 percent.

The political division in 1948 gave blacks a potential importance in the election that their numbers alone could still not account for. In the 1944 election, with Roosevelt at the head of the ticket, four Northern industrial states were decided by less than a 1 percent vote: Wisconsin, Ohio, New Jersey, and Michigan. Another three were carried by less than 2 percent: Pennsylvania, Missouri, and Illinois; and four more had less than a 3 percent margin: Indiana, Massachusetts, and New York. In virtually all of these states, blacks were a greater percentage of the electorate than was needed to shift the results. By 1940 blacks were 4 to 5 percent of the electorate in New York, New Jersey, Pennsylvania, Ohio, Michigan, and Illinois. However, in that year Roosevelt was a sure winner and had no opposition organized in the Democratic party. In 1948 blacks were in a better position to demand that the piper be paid. Estimates of voting strength in 1948 saw blacks holding the balance of power in sixteen states with a total of 278 electoral votes, compared to 127 electoral votes controlled by the South. This fact alone was sufficient to suggest an important shift in the American political structure.

It didn't take long for this political potential to begin to be translated into actuality. In 1942, Democrat William Dawson was elected to Congress from Chicago. He was joined by Adam Clayton Powell from Harlem in 1944. In 1946, black candidates ran credible campaigns in Los Angeles, Philadelphia, and the Bronx. In that same year, thirty blacks won seats in ten state legislatures. By 1947 there were black judges in Cleveland, Chicago, Los Angeles, Washington, D.C., and seven in New York City, some elected and some appointed. "An alert, well-organized Negro electorate can be an effective factor in at least seventy-five congressional districts in eighteen Northern and border states," argued an observer in 1948. Clearly, black political power was becoming something to contend with.

Blacks and the Cold War

But politics is more than just numbers and votes. Conscious action and organization helped to make blacks into a cohesive and important political force. This strengthening occurred at the same time that changes were taking place in world politics that gave increasing prominence to black concerns and added to the pressures on the American government to do something about black treatment. America's increasing importance in world politics provided new leverage, which blacks were quick to take advantage of.

In 1942, a brutal racial lynching was picked up immediately by Japanese propaganda. The Japanese broadcast the news to the Dutch East Indies and India. It was presented as evidence of how those nations could expect to be treated under United States dominion. As the cold war took shape, Russia naturally picked up where the Japanese left off. The State Department estimated that almost half of all Russian propaganda against the United States at that time concerned racism. Secretary of State James Byrnes told of how the Soviet foreign minister had countered his attacks on Russia's activities in Eastern Europe with stories about racism and racist treatment in the United States.

What gave this matter particular urgency was the emerging revolution against colonialism. The war had hastened the process of the disintegration of the vast colonial empires. Shortly after the war's conclusion, India and Pakistan attained independence, as did several colonies in Africa. By the late forties, the Communist forces in China were clearly approaching victory. The United States was about to be deprived of vast markets, natural resources, and opportunities for investment, not to mention an important element in the world struggle for power. This movement toward self-determination meant that a great deal of the American competition with the Soviet Union focused on gaining the allegiance of the former colonies. In these circumstances, American treatment of blacks in their own country could not help but be weighed by these emerging countries and create serious difficulties for the United States.

Truman openly admitted the problem. Clark Clifford, Truman's special campaign strategist and advisor, recalled the president's feeling that failure to assure equal rights to blacks was one of the nation's weakest points in the struggle with Communism. As Truman delicately phrased it when speaking to the Black Press in 1947:

> More and more we are learning how closely our democracy is under observation. We are learning what loud echoes both our successes and our failures have in every corner of the world. That is one of the pressing reasons why we cannot afford failures. When we fail to live together in peace the failure touches not us, as Americans alone, but the cause of democracy itself in the whole world. That we must never forget.

Blacks could not help but be aware of the changing circumstances and their growing political importance. The NAACP not only saw the changes going on around the organization but directly experienced rapid growth. The association went from a membership of 50,000 before the war to 350,000 after. This change, naturally, provided the organization with many more resources, both finances and personnel. By the middle of the decade, a new mood was clearly sweeping the black communities across the nation. It was fueled by an increasing sense of power that blacks now had and an increased indignation concerning treatment they felt they no longer had to endure. The growth and conscious use of the black vote in the forties was part of a larger process of motion in the black community.

In the early forties, blacks received few of the jobs that were created in the first part of the war boom. They were hardly inclined to submerge their struggle for equality during the war. Instead, they called for "Victory at Home as well as Abroad." In 1941 A. Philip Randolph had upped the ante by organizing the March on Washington movement to pressure Roosevelt to establish a Fair Employment Practices Committee in order to provide jobs for blacks. Randolph's statement was militant:

> The Negro's stake in national defense is big. It consists of jobs, thousands of jobs. It may represent millions, yes hundreds of millions of dollars in wages. It consists of new industrial opportunities and hope. This is worth fighting for. Most important and vital of all, Negroes by the mobilization and coordination of their mass power, can cause PRESIDENT ROOSEVELT TO ISSUE AN EXECUTIVE ORDER ABOLISHING DISCRIMINATION IN ALL GOVERNMENT DEPARTMENTS, ARMY, NAVY, AIR CORPS AND NATIONAL DEFENSE JOBS. (emphasis in original)

Randolph threatened to bring thousands of blacks to march on the capital demanding action. In the midst of the war, the movement organized mass rallies of tens of thousands of blacks in New York, Chicago, and St. Louis. They won their committee.

Militancy continued after the war. Walter White, leader of the NAACP, testified before the Senate in 1945: "Throughout the Pacific I was told with grim pessimism by Negro troops that 'we know that our fight for democracy will really begin when we reach San Francisco on our way home.'" Black veterans in the South began to organize protests against their conditions. In January of 1946, over a hundred black veterans marched to the Birmingham courthouse to demand their right to register to vote. They were turned away, but their demonstration helped to unite black pressure on Truman. He responded by establishing the President's Committee on Civil Rights. The committee was told to prepare recommendations for government action to protect civil rights.

The NAACP submitted a petition of grievances to the United Nations Committee on Human Rights. "This protest," it read, "is to induce the nations of the world to persuade this nation to be just to its own people." Though the petition was rejected, it caused great embarrassment to the United States government, especially when the Soviet Union used it as an opportunity to score propaganda points against the United States. The Soviets proposed making a crime of the "advocacy of national, racial and religious hostility or of national exclusiveness or hatred and contempt as well as of any action establishing privilege or discrimination based on distinction of race, nationality or religion."

These acts were minor compared with the organization of the Committee against Jim Crow in Military Service and Training in late 1947, when, because of the developing cold war, the government was preparing to reintroduce the draft. A. Philip Randolph, once again in the lead, threatened to organize refusal among blacks to be drafted into a segregated army:

> I personally will advise Negroes to refuse to fight as slaves for a democracy they cannot possess and cannot enjoy. . . . I personally pledge myself to openly counsel and abet youth, both white and Negro, to quarantine a Jim Crow conscription system.

When reminded during his testimony at a Senate hearing that such an act would be treason in time of war, Randolph responded that

> the Government now has time to change its policy on segregation and discrimination and if the government does not change its policy . . . in the interests of the very democracy it is fighting for, I would advocate that Negroes take no part in the army.

"I am prepared," he said, "to oppose a Jim Crow army 'til I rot in jail." Randolph led a picket line outside the Democratic Convention in 1948 demanding an end to segregation in the military. A poll of black youth in Harlem found 71 percent favoring refusal to be drafted into a segregated army. *Newsweek* reported that among Negro college students "there were indications of strong sympathy and support for Randolph."

These were serious actions that indicated that blacks were ready and able to organize to pressure the government for equal rights. They were obviously aware of and willing to use the increased leverage provided by the pressures of the developing cold war. As Truman had indicated, with the United States trying to present itself as the leader of the free world as against the totalitarian Communists, the condition of blacks was the country's weak point. Henry Moon, voting analyst for the NAACP, wryly observed:

> Culturally and economically he [the Southern Negro] today surpasses the masses of the Rumanians, Bulgars and Poles for whom, ironically, former Secretary of State James F. Byrnes of South Carolina demanded "free and unfettered elections" at a time when this right was being denied to millions of Americans.

Truman, heading the Democratic ticket for the first time, was in trouble with liberals who had been discontent with him for some time. In 1944 he had been a conservative replacement for the enormously popular Henry Wallace, and he was then strongly supported by the South, whose leaders felt that Truman would be more sympathetic to their problems. Wallace's support had been from labor, blacks, liberals, and the left. It was not long after Truman succeeded Roosevelt that liberals began to be unhappy with his policies. The most crucial of these was the issue of relations with Russia. The two countries had enjoyed a close working relationship during the war. But six weeks after Roosevelt's death, when two leading liberals went to visit the new president, they were shocked to hear him say: "We have got to get tough with the Russians. They don't know how to behave. They're like bulls in a china shop. . . . We've got to teach them to behave." He replaced a number of liberal Roosevelt appointees, which upset many. He appeared sufficiently antilabor that the president of the Brotherhood of Railway Trainmen promised to spend the whole union treasury, if necessary, to defeat him for reelection after Truman urged the drafting of strikers during a railroad strike. Other labor leaders were unhappy enough with Truman that they tried to replace him as the Democratic party candidate. Blacks were so discontented with his policies that many voted Republican or simply did not vote in 1946. Many liberals saw Wallace as the rightful heir to Roosevelt. The 1946 election debacle, which brought about a Republican-dominated legislature for the first time since 1930, shook up the left and sent it casting in new directions. A third party was widely discussed.

At the time Wallace was considering running against Truman, he had reason to believe that he would get some substantial labor support. Many unions had indicated their interest. But by the time he declared, at the end of December 1947, that support had disappeared. In part, labor's desertion of Wallace was due to a left turn that Truman had made after the 1946 mid-term elections. That election had brought serious losses to the Democrats in Congress, and it illustrated how far the president was from prevailing attitudes. In particular, his veto of the Taft-Hartley antilabor law was important in helping Truman to regain labor's support. But more fundamental were the cold war and the domestic **red-baiting** that went with it, both of which had a big impact on American politics.

Truman was very conscious about his use of red-baiting to increase his popularity. His strategy was to use the antagonism with Russia that was growing as American and Soviet interests collided in order to create anti-Communist hysteria at home, and to use that hysteria against his opposition. This strategy was part of the overall election "game plan" developed for the president by Clark Clifford.

In 1947, Truman had already instituted a loyalty program for federal employees. While it was ostensibly for the purposes of national security, in the program's implementation the division between espionage and political radicalism was obliterated. The president called opposition to his foreign policy an effort to "sabotage the foreign policy of the United States [which] is just as bad in this Cold War as it would be to shoot our soldiers in the back in a hot war." Although this particular barb was aimed at congressional opposition, it helped to create a general atmosphere that labeled dissent as being disloyal. He even suggested that the Republican party was soft on Communism because Republicans had expressed differences on foreign policy.

Truman's rhetoric raised the level of hysteria. He rejected the support of "Wallace and his Communists." The Democratic National Committee labeled the Progressive party as "Communist-influenced." Jack Redding, Truman's publicity director, wrote concerning the 1948 campaign: "Wallace was smarting as we pinned red labels on him and his followers. Through every avenue we were pointing out that Wallace and his third party were following the Kremlin line slavishly." The formation of another liberal anti-Communist organization, the Americans for Democratic Action, was very helpful in the effort; these liberals served as frontmen for the president in the attack on Wallace. Indeed, as other support dropped away, virtually the only organized backing Wallace had was from the Communist party and the organizations it controlled.

But if Wallace's campaign was weakened by this activity, it was certainly not destroyed. Although Wallace had few hopes of winning now, his political base could still affect the issues. In November of 1947, a Wallacite had garnered 40 percent of the vote in a Chicago judicial election. On February 17, a special congressional election in New York City produced a victory for the American Labor party candidate, who was backed by Wallace. The candidate, Leo Isaacson, took 56 percent of the vote and defeated the Democratic candidate by about two to one. A *New York Times* survey found that after the election, Wallace had increased support in the crucial states of Michigan, Pennsylvania, Illinois, and California. The *Times* argued that Wallace was a sufficient threat that it would be hard for Truman to win any of these states now. Polls taken before the convention showed the same trend. In Pennsylvania, Truman got 41 percent, Dewey 49 percent, Wallace 7 percent; in Illinois, it was Truman 44 percent, Dewey 43 percent, Wallace 13 percent; in New York, results were similar.

Wallace's main issue was opposition to the **Truman Doctrine**, which defined Communism and Russia as America's main enemies—Wallace was for recognizing Russia's sphere of influence in Eastern Europe and maintaining a cooperative relationship with her. Nonetheless, he waged a hard-hitting campaign on other issues. He made serious efforts to woo labor and black support. Paul Robeson was made vice-chairman of the Progressive party; Joe Louis was a public contributor to the Wallace campaign fund; and W. E. B. DuBois and other blacks played a prominent role at the party convention in July.

Indeed, because of his previous record and his campaign, Wallace's most important single source of strength was in the black community. The Associated Negro Press reported that in Los Angeles, "thousands of Negro voters here began lining up behind Henry A. Wallace the day after he announced that he would run for the Presidency." Wallace deliberately went after the black vote. He and his vice-presidential candidate, Senator Glen Taylor, held election rallies in several cities in the South, including Little Rock, Memphis, Asheville, Greenville, Knoxville, and Chattanooga. At these rallies they verbally assaulted the segregation system and physically challenged it by refusing to hold segregated meetings. In doing so, they courted arrest and violence. Taylor was arrested in Birmingham by Eugene "Bull" Connor, who became nationally infamous in 1963 because of his treatment of civil rights demonstrators. Wallace and Taylor had to endure eggs, tomatoes, peach stones, and other sundries being hurled at them as they attempted to speak. Wallace was several times forced to cancel meetings.

These efforts paid off. Though Wallace failed to win the support of the national black leadership, he gained the endorsement of the president of the Indiana

NAACP and of officials in many of the large cities, including San Francisco and Philadelphia. Ward leaders in Brooklyn and Harlem thought that Wallace might get as much as 75 percent of the vote in their wards. Even as late as October 2, a poll taken in Baltimore indicated that Wallace was drawing a substantial percentage of the black vote—perhaps enough to hand the election to Dewey. The Chicago *Defender* was the only important black newspaper to endorse Truman, a fact that made the situation more worrisome for the president.

The Liberals Respond

It was the very strength of the Wallace campaign that made the liberal opposition within the Democratic party important. Many liberals who refused to follow Wallace were still quite unhappy with Truman. They organized the Americans for Democratic Action early in 1947 with a double aim: to exclude Communists from the liberal movement ("a reconstruction of the liberal movement free of totalitarian influence from either the Left or the Right") and to strengthen their own position within the Democratic party ("All our efforts, all our own ingenuity must be thrown into the struggle to establish liberal control of the Democratic Party"). The content of liberalism came very largely to be shaped in the course of the campaign itself.

The ADA was solidly behind the anti-Communist direction of Truman's policies at home and abroad. It was locked in battle against the Communists and their supporters for liberal supremacy in America. Nonetheless, the ADA was very much in opposition to Truman, because they felt he was not really a liberal, because of his antilabor policy, and because they felt he was a sure loser and would take the Democratic party and labor and the liberals down to defeat with him. Until shortly before the convention, the organization was engaged in a serious effort to deny the nomination to Truman. It was forced to abandon the effort when its candidate, General Eisenhower, announced that he would not accept the nomination.

Responding to the pressure of the Wallace campaign, the ADA now sought to shore up the Democratic party's weakest flank by turning to civil rights, which blacks had made an issue before Wallace began his campaign. The Civil Rights Committee that blacks had pressured the president to appoint in 1946 had produced a report of its findings in 1947. Truman had delivered a civil rights message to Congress in early 1948 that was largely based on this report. This act caused the white South to respond in anger, and Truman soon backed off. He refrained from sending legislation to Congress and from issuing any executive orders concerning the matter.

But it was impossible simply to placate the white South and ignore blacks. Truman himself had created expectations with his civil rights address to Congress; he had even had it broadcast over the Voice of America to make sure it would be used as a weapon in the cold war. Blacks were not letting the matter rest—Randolph was in the midst of campaigning against the segregated armed forces. And the Wallace threat continued.

Truman tried to respond to both pressures by resurrecting for the platform a rewritten version of the civil rights plank from 1944, which was an innocuous statement that read:

> We believe that racial and religious minorities have the right to live, develop and vote equally with all citizens and share the rights that are guaranteed by

our Constitution. Congress should exert its full constitutional powers to protect those rights.

Even the Republican party platform was stronger than this statement. It included a call for abolition of the poll tax and for ending segregation in the armed forces.

Truman's proposal pleased no one. It certainly did not please the South, which wanted its own plank assuring states' rights. Nor did it please blacks, who felt it insufficient. Walter White, head of the NAACP, appeared before the convention platform representing not only the association but twenty other black organizations as well, with a combined membership of over six million. White said the plank was totally unsatisfactory and reminded the committee of the voting power of blacks, who, he said, would vote on issues, not party labels. The Truman forces continued to press on with their planned position, hoping to keep support of the South with it.

But the ADA was unwilling to let things stand and determined to challenge the president on the civil rights plank, if necessary, in order to strengthen it. They took their proposal, which included the following points, to the floor of the convention after they failed to get it through the platform committee:

> The right to full and equal political participation, the right to equal opportunity of employment, the right of security of persons [referring to lynchings in particular], and the right of equal treatment in the services and defense of our nation.

They were backed in their efforts by several big-city-machine bosses, including those from Chicago, Pittsburgh, the Bronx, San Francisco, and Minneapolis, who were concerned about losing not only the presidential election but the local elections in which Wallace was giving them a hard time in competition for black votes. Hubert Humphrey, who was facing a strong Republican opponent in his bid to be elected senator of Minnesota, and who was threatened by the Wallacites, was the public leader of the fight. He presented the case eloquently:

> There are those who say this issue of civil rights is an infringement on states' rights. The time has come for the Democratic Party to get out of the shadow of states' rights and walk forthrightly into the bright sunshine of human rights.

What was most instructive was his clear explanation of the issue in terms of world politics:

> Yes, this is far more than a party matter. Every citizen has a stake in the emergence of the United States as the leader of the free world. That world is being challenged by the world of slavery. For us to play our part effectively we must be in a morally sound position. We cannot use a double standard for measuring our own and other people's policies. Our demands for democratic practices in other lands will be no more effective than the guarantee of those practiced in our own country.

Humphrey made the point clearly. He and his coworkers had set the liberal and the Democratic party agenda. In order to be able to wage the cold war effectively, they had to espouse civil rights at home. The pressures of international politics together with changes in domestic politics gave civil rights their day—at least in rhetoric.

The amendment carried, and the states' rights advocates walked out. The ADA and their allies had carried off a remarkable feat. They had challenged a sitting president and defeated him within the party. They, rather than he, had determined one of the principal issues on which the campaign would be run. But it was black organization, activity, and power that had made it imperative to do and possible to accomplish. "Never since 1932," said the *New York Times,* "had there been such a material change in a party platform after it had reached the convention floor."

Campaign and Election

Truman had little choice but to run on the platform, especially after the loss of the right-wing Southerners. Less than two weeks after the convention, he issued two executive orders that he had been sitting on for six months or more. He barred discrimination in federal employment and established a review board in each government department. Employees who felt discriminated against could appeal to this board.

Truman further announced a policy of "equality of treatment and opportunity for all persons in the armed services without regard to race, color, religion or national origin." It was unclear, however, if that meant a policy of desegregation in the armed forces, especially when he further announced that he would appoint a committee to study the problem. Two days later, General Bradley, army chief of staff, announced that the army would not be a laboratory for social reforms and that it would change "when the Nation as a whole changes." The president responded at a press conference that the policy indeed was to integrate the armed forces. In mid-August, when the civil disobedience campaign against the new draft was to have begun, Randolph terminated it, satisfied that the point had been won.

In the end, Truman felt compelled to pursue the black vote openly. At the end of October, he toured the black ghetto in Philadelphia; and on October 29 he became the first president to speak in Harlem. On the anniversary of his receipt of the report of his Civil Rights Committee, he addressed some 65,000 people and affirmed his commitment to civil rights: "Our determination to attain the goal of equal rights and equal opportunity must be resolute and unwavering."

Truman, of course, won. "Labor did it," said Truman. And it was true that labor had played a crucial role in his victory. But it was a very close election. The president beat Dewey by 2,000,000 votes, but he won three crucial states—Ohio, California, and Illinois—by a total of only 58,584 votes. If he had lost those states, he would have lost the election; if he had lost two of them, it would have been thrown into the House of Representatives. Blacks, who voted 69 percent for Truman overall, carried those states for him. The black vote in Los Angeles, Chicago and Cleveland and Akron provided the margin of victory in those key states.

Truman's strategy with regard to blacks was successful. He won their vote and appears to have gotten a better percentage of it than had Roosevelt. So was the black strategy a success. For the first time blacks forced the issue of race into the very center of national politics.

The election was very much focused around the developing cold war, and Truman's strategy called for intensifying the emphasis on the competition with

Russia. The emerging colonial revolution put extraordinary new pressures on the United States to develop an acceptable racial policy, while at the same time blacks were beginning to gain some power. Their activity and muscle forced the issue to public attention, thus making it a matter of international concern. These pressures persisted after 1948. As more colonies became independent, their presence encouraged American blacks to oppose their own conditions. The 1948 election demonstrated the new power and position that blacks had attained after depression and war. In that sense, it was a reflection of change, as well as a turning point that quickened the pace of events.

The election struggle had opened a breach in the Democratic party and in the nation. The country was becoming divided again. The strength of blacks in the North was pitted against the racists in the South, and the latter lost. Truman's appeal to blacks was a success, despite the States' Rights party, which carried four Southern states. That was an important lesson. It showed that it was possible for a Democrat to win by ignoring Southern racism and courting blacks. It was a lesson that would figure significantly in Senator John F. Kennedy's bid for the presidency in 1960. It illustrated, furthermore, how isolated the South's racist culture and political structure had become from the prevailing sentiments and political trends in the nation. Both of these perceptions would have an impact on the black community and, as they were reinforced in the fifties, would encourage black activism.

The breach was not to close before it was wrenched open much further. The events of 1948 were the beginning of the struggle that was to burst into open battle in the 1960s. Blacks were encouraged by what happened and became more self-confident and more demanding in the South as well as the North.

Black demands for equality were given legitimacy in the campaign. Three of the four candidates for president, including the nominees of the two major parties, announced themselves as being for civil rights and black equality. This new attitude among political leaders, in addition to the rising tide of black militancy, created an atmosphere that helped to propel the Supreme Court into rendering decisions that struck at the whole structure of racial politics. The Court had begun changing its decisions from endorsing segregation to finding it unacceptable in the late thirties, and had quickened the pace in the forties. But the most important judicial decisions were issued from 1948 to 1954, culminating in the famous *Brown v. Board of Education* case that caused such an uproar in the South. These decisions, in their turn, played an important role in creating the conditions that led to the civil rights explosion of the 1960s. Thus, this exercise of black political power, and the resulting realignment of the federal government, would have a major impact on the civil rights struggles of the coming decade.

This process assured the continued alienation of those sections of the South that had led and supported the **Dixiecrat** revolt. The States' Rights movement of 1948 was the first step down the road to what became known as "massive resistance" in the 1950s, and to violent, brutal attacks on black and white integrationists in the 1960s. "The Dixiecrat movement . . . fixed the broad aims and many of the programs that were to carry over into massive resistance," said Numan Bartley in his study of the massive resistance movement.

The election of 1948 illustrated the new strength blacks had attained, but it came before the massive and powerful struggles of the sixties, in which blacks sought to reap the gains their new power entitled them to. Because of the peculiar juncture of circumstances in the political arena during the first postwar election, new opportunities became suddenly available to blacks. It was as though a curtain had temporarily been drawn aside to provide a preview of the struggle that was yet to come, and to reveal the great historical changes that had already taken place.

1.7   John Dittmer

We Return Fighting

John Dittmer, professor of history at DePauw University, is author of Local People: The Struggle for Civil Rights in Mississippi *and* Black Georgia in the Progressive Era, 1900–1920.

> *We return from the slavery of the uniform which the world's madness demanded us to don to the freedom of civilian garb. . . . We sing: This country of ours, despite all its better souls have done and dreamed, is yet a shameful land. It lynches. . . . It* disfranchises *its own citizens. . . . It* encourages ignorance. . . . *It steals from us. . . . It insults us. . . . We return. We return from fighting. We return fighting.*
>
> W. E. B. Du Bois, *Crisis,* 19 (May 1919), 13–14

On July 2, 1946, Medgar Wylie Evers celebrated his twenty-first birthday by leading a group of World War II veterans, including his brother Charles, through the nearly abandoned streets of Decatur, Mississippi. Their destination was the county courthouse, where they intended to vote in the Democratic primary election. Medgar had seen combat in both France and Germany, but he and the other GIs were unprepared for the scene that greeted them in their hometown. When the group arrived at the courthouse, "some 15 or 20 armed white men surged in behind us, men I had grown up with, had played with. . . . We stood there for a minute. We were bluffing. We knew we weren't going to get by this mob." As the veterans retreated down the street, Evers looked up to see a black Ford cruising alongside, and "a guy leaned out with a shotgun, keeping a bead on us all the time."

Angered and humiliated, the men went home and returned with their guns. Leaving the weapons hidden in their car, they again attempted to enter the polling place, but once more the mob turned them away. After that, "We didn't pursue it. We drove back." Years later Medgar Evers, now the Mississippi NAACP state field secretary, ruefully observed that "I was born in Decatur, was raised there, but I never in my life was permitted to vote there."

The 1946 election was the first statewide Mississippi contest since *Smith* v. *Allwright,* the 1944 U.S. Supreme Court decision that had outlawed the white primary. (The Democratic primary was the only election of importance in the Deep South.) National attention had focused on the Magnolia State, for Theodore "The Man" Bilbo was seeking a third U.S. Senate term in a hotly contested race. A political force in Mississippi for four decades, Bilbo was the champion of the state's poor whites and an ardent white supremacist. His solution to the nation's race problems was to deport black Americans to Africa. Along with his Mississippi colleague Senator James O. Eastland, Bilbo had fought the repeal of the poll tax, antilynching legislation, and a bill to establish a permanent Fair Employment Practices Committee (FEPC). In this reelection campaign, however, he focused on the immediate threat posed by *Smith* v. *Allwright.*

In towns and hamlets across the state, Bilbo urged his white audiences to prevent blacks from voting in the primary, predicting that "if you let a handful go to the polls in July there will be two handfuls in 1947, and from there on it will grow into a mighty surge." He warned that "the white people of Mississippi are sleeping on a volcano, and it is left up to you red-blooded men to do something about it." Then, dramatically lowering his voice, the senator would confide, "But you and I know what's the best way to keep the nigger from voting. You do it the night before the election. I don't have to tell you any more than that. Red-blooded men know what I mean." Bilbo was not alone in his determination to keep blacks from the polls. The *Jackson Daily News* gave this advice to Negro voters under the headline "DON'T TRY IT! Don't attempt to participate in the Democratic primaries anywhere in Mississippi on July 2nd. Staying away from the polls on that date will be the best way to prevent unhealthy and unhappy results." Nevertheless, on primary day several thousand blacks turned out to vote, among them the Reverend William Albert Bender.

A chaplain at Tougaloo College, the sixty-year-old Bender had been the leading spiritual force at that American Missionary Association school, founded in the aftermath of the Civil War on a cotton plantation just north of the state capital at Jackson. Proud, courageous, and combative, Bender embodied the democratic principles set forth in the college's charter and transmitted to generations of black Mississippi students trapped along the color line. On primary day Bender enlisted two Tougaloo students to drive him to his voting precinct in Ridgeland, a small community a few miles from the campus. As he approached the schoolhouse where the voting was underway, three white men stopped him, bluntly stating that they were not permitting blacks to vote. When Bender replied that he was registered and asked what right they had to "prevent a citizen from voting," one of the whites retorted, "This is a Democratic primary, this is a white man's primary, and niggers haven't any business voting in a Democratic primary." The Tougaloo chaplain calmly told the men, "I came here to vote, and I guess I will attend to my business." As he pushed past them and climbed the steps he found his path blocked by a deputy sheriff who, with his pistol drawn, cursed Bender and dared him to enter the polls. Bender called to the two students to come over and act as witnesses. Terrified, they remained in the car. A short time later the minister rejoined the students, assuring them that "we will have a chance to come back in the next election." On returning home Bender filed a complaint with U.S. Attorney General Tom Clark. It was futile. Later, a cross burned on the Tougaloo campus. The experiences of William Bender and Medgar Evers were typical on that election day.

Bilbo easily won the primary. Of 5,000 black registrants, approximately half were permitted to cast their ballots. Even if all registered blacks had voted against Bilbo, the results would have been the same. But these figures beg the question. Almost 350,000 black Mississippians were of voting age in 1946, and blacks believed that Bilbo's intimidating speeches frightened away thousands of potential registrants. On September 19, fifty Mississippians (including several whites) filed a complaint with the U.S. Senate Committee to Investigate Campaign Expenditures, claiming that Bilbo had subjected blacks to a "reign of terror" during the campaign and urging the full Senate to impeach Bilbo and remove him from office. Leading the anti-Bilbo campaign were local NAACP branches and the Progressive Voters' League, a new middle-class black civic organization that had chapters in several cities and towns.

Although the committee agreed to hold hearings in Jackson during the first week in December, the deck was already stacked against the petitioners. Three of the five senators on the committee—Democrats Burnett Maybank of South Carolina, Elmer Thomas of Oklahoma, and Chairman Allen Ellender of Louisiana—represented states with long histories of discrimination against black voters. The two Republican members, Styles Bridges of New Hampshire and Burton Hickenlooper of Iowa, were conservatives not known for their advocacy of civil rights. Ellender, a close friend of Bilbo, rejected a request that NAACP lawyers serve as formal counsel for the witnesses; declined to subpoena blacks to testify, thereby leaving "volunteer" witnesses more vulnerable to reprisal; and refused to summon reporters covering the campaign to verify their stories describing Bilbo's inflammatory rhetoric. Blacks received some support from the national office of the NAACP and from attorney Emanuel Bloch of the leftist Civil Rights Congress. Still, few observers believed that blacks would turn out to testify in significant numbers. NAACP attorney Charles Houston reported from Jackson that "everybody on our side was afraid that only a few witnesses would show up," and Senator Ellender told the press that he expected only about twenty-five people to agree to testify under oath.

When the hearings opened at the Federal Building courtroom in Jackson on December 2, nearly 200 blacks from all parts of the state were packing the corridors, registering to testify. Included in the group were farmers, day laborers, doctors, ministers, and college students. A majority were World War II veterans. Ellender was not the only person "taken aback by the numbers who appeared." Although civil rights attorneys had counseled a few key people, they had not met with most of the witnesses, a failure Houston immediately regretted. To begin with, there was no mistaking the fact that the deliberations were taking place deep in the Jim Crow South. The federal courtroom was strictly segregated, with the first seventeen of the twenty rows of seats reserved for white spectators. Court officials at first refused attorney Houston admittance to the chamber and then denied him a seat with the other attorneys inside the bar. At the end of each day's session, a court attendant stationed himself at the huge rear door to make sure that all white spectators had cleared the hall before blacks were permitted to leave.

Chairman Ellender made his biases clear early on. He stated that the election officials were within their legal rights in barring black voters from the white primary. In his view, *Smith* v. *Allwright,* a Texas case, was not binding on Mississippi. He charged that the entire challenge had developed through the machinations of outsiders from New York. Throughout the four days of the hearings Ellender acted informally as Bilbo's counsel, badgering witnesses, anticipating and asking questions handed up by Bilbo's attorneys, and exchanging winks with the senator as black victims testified. Ellender made no effort to mask his sympathies for Bilbo's position. "You know, I am sure," he lectured one black witness, "that only white folks should vote in the Democratic primaries."

Still, despite their inadequate briefing, the partisanship of the committee's Democratic majority, and the intimidating presence of several hundred unfriendly white Mississippians in the audience, the witnesses acquitted themselves admirably.

Victor Bernstein of *PM* newspaper, one of about twenty reporters on the scene, recorded his impressions of the first day of the hearing: "More than a score of Negro witnesses, dressed carefully in their Sunday best, dignified in manner but by no means servile, calmly laid bare some of the less appetizing aspects of American democracy." Their testimony revealed a pattern of discrimination throughout the state, ranging from paternalistic coercion to kidnapping and beating, all designed to prevent blacks from voting in the Democratic primary, the only election that counted.

Among those giving testimony was Vernando R. Collier, a thirty-six-year-old army veteran and president of the NAACP's Gulfport branch. On primary day he and his wife, a local schoolteacher, arrived at city hall to vote. A police officer accompanied them into the building, and as they approached the polls "about fifteen poor-looking white men" blocked their way. Collier told the Senate investigators what happened next: "They knocked me down, dragged me to the front of the porch and threw me out—and at the same time assaulted and struck my wife, who was constantly screaming and pleading to the officer to stop them from beating me. The officer ignored us completely and kept walking as though nothing had happened." The Colliers fled city hall, and after receiving treatment from a local black physician, V. R. Collier called the FBI in Jackson, requesting federal protection so that he might return to cast his ballot. The FBI agent's reply would become a familiar litany to civil rights workers over the next two decades: "It is not our job to give protection, only to investigate." Collier next called the U.S. attorney in Jackson, who said that this was the FBI's jurisdiction. The Colliers did not vote in the primary.

Etoy Fletcher of Rankin County testified as one of the hundreds of thousands of unregistered black voters in Mississippi. Fletcher told the committee that shortly after his army discharge he had unsuccessfully attempted to get his name on the books, and as he was waiting for a bus, four white men abducted him, took him to a woods four miles away, forced him to strip, and then flogged him with large cable wire.

Such acts of violence created the climate of fear that intimidated potential black voters, but subtler methods often achieved the same results. Perhaps the most bizarre story to come out of the hearings was that of J. D. Collins, a black businessman from the Delta town of Greenwood and third district chairman of the Progressive Voters' League. In the spring of 1946 Collins had encouraged black veterans to register for the primary, but shortly before the election the mayor and several white businessmen advised him to contact the veterans and tell them not to vote. Although Collins protested that he "didn't want the job," he and another black man made the rounds and persuaded the veterans to stay at home on election day. For performing their civic duty each man was paid twenty-five dollars. A bemused Senator Hickenlooper observed that "usually up our way it costs money to get the vote out. Here it apparently costs money to keep the vote away."

The most effective way to keep blacks from voting had been to prevent them from registering in the first place. Mississippi's two-year residency requirement and two-dollar poll tax were the most exacting in the South. Beyond that, registrars administered the law selectively, as was made clear during the Bilbo hearings. The Mississippi voting statute was the product of the 1890 constitutional convention, which was called for the express purpose of eliminating the Negro vote. Residency requirements and the poll tax were written into the constitution, but the heart of the electoral provision was the "understanding clause," which stated that a prospective voter must be able to read any section of the constitution, *or,* as an alternative, be able to understand it when read to him, *or* to give "a reasonable interpretation of it." The registrar (the circuit clerk) usually insisted that black applicants be able to read *and* interpret the constitution. So widespread was this practice that some registrars might even have believed it to be valid. When committee counsel reminded Leflore County circuit clerk C. E. Cocke that "it is not necessary to question a man on the constitution if that man is able to read," Cocke innocently replied, "Doesn't it go further to state that he must understand the Constitution when read to him?"

In choosing questions for black applicants, registrars often looked beyond the state constitution. Nathaniel Lewis, a black veteran from McComb, told the committee that after he had correctly answered all questions, the Pike County circuit clerk asked him to describe what was on the ballot. Because he had had no opportunity to see the ballot, he could not answer the question, whereupon the clerk dismissed him with "You brush up on your civics and come back." When the clerk in question, Wendell Holmes, later took the stand and was asked whether he had in fact required Lewis to describe the ballot, Holmes replied, "I am sure I did." An incredulous Senator Bridges then inquired whether Holmes believed he could "make up questions at your own convenience . . . rather than confining yourself to the Constitution?" "Well, I thought I was following the procedure of the law," Holmes responded. When another circuit clerk was asked why he made it more difficult for blacks to register than for whites, he truthfully answered, "I have no other reason than that they were colored."

Witnesses recounted other examples of intimidation and fraud, including the common practice of challenging black ballots at the polls. The election official might place the ballot in an envelope, telling the voter that the election commission would decide later whether to count the ballot. Although black voters faced little harassment in a few communities, such as Greenville and Jackson, and in the all-black town of Mound Bayou, the testimony demonstrated a pervasive pattern of unlawful behavior.

However, the issue before the Senate investigating committee was whether *Bilbo* was responsible for the election-day travesty, an allegation that proved more difficult to substantiate. Although politically sophisticated witnesses like Reverend Bender made the connection between black intimidation and Bilbo's campaign rhetoric, others were less successful. Here Chairman Ellender was most effective, leading witnesses into admitting that Bilbo's speeches had not deterred *them* from going to the polls and hammering home the point that the vast majority of white Mississippians shared Bilbo's obsession that blacks should not vote. There is truth in the Senate investigators' conclusion that blacks would have faced the same obstacles attempting to vote in the primary "regardless of who the senatorial candidates may have been, and what they may have said in campaign speeches." The larger point, that Mississippi was making a mockery of the Fifteenth Amendment, was largely ignored by the politicians and press.

On the fourth and final day of the hearings Bilbo himself took the stand, playing to a packed house of white supporters. Although still sporting his flashy tie and diamond horseshoe stickpin, Bilbo looked old and ill as he read his prepared statement. But the senator was not at all chastened by the preceding testimony. (A *Pittsburgh Courier* reporter calculated that Bilbo had used the word *nigger* no fewer than seventy-nine times during his appearance.) Bilbo's defense was simply to deny all charges of wrongdoing. Although he admitted that the newspaper and magazine accounts of his speeches were essentially accurate, he noted one important exception: every time the press made reference to his call for whites to use "every means" to keep blacks from the polls on July 2, reporters had omitted his use of the word *lawful*. He had never advocated illegal methods to prevent blacks from voting. To accept this explanation stretches the limits of credulity; whether they represented the *New York Times* or Mississippi's white supremacist press, reporters to a person failed to pick up the word *lawful* in any of his speeches. As to his oft-repeated observation that "the best way to keep a nigger from the polls is to visit him the night before," the senator assured his colleagues that he meant only a peaceful, persuasive visit. At the close of his remarks, which lasted nearly two hours, Bilbo fielded questions from committee members, but there were no spirited exchanges. As Bernstein observed, the committee appeared "in a hurry to get the thing over with."

Back in Washington the committee divided along partisan lines: the Democratic majority exonerated Bilbo; the Republican minority condemned him. Yet sentiment was building in Washington to deny Bilbo his seat when the Senate reorganized in January. Republicans had taken control of the Senate for the first time in nearly two decades, and, led by Senator Robert A. Taft, they saw in the Bilbo case an excellent opportunity to score points with black voters while embarrassing Democratic liberals. Bilbo, however, was determined to keep his job. As the Republicans attempted to organize the Senate, minus Bilbo, southern Democrats led by Ellender began a filibuster to prevent the full Senate from taking action against their Mississippi colleague. A protracted debate was avoided when Bilbo agreed to step aside temporarily. He needed another operation, and under the terms of the Senate compromise, his credentials would lie on the table until he recovered his health. Bilbo left the capitol on January 5, never to return. After two more operations, Bilbo deteriorated rapidly. He died in New Orleans on August 21, 1947, succumbing (ironically, as numerous observers pointed out) to cancer of the mouth.

Bilbo's death did not herald a new day in race relations for Mississippi. His successor, Judge John Stennis, though no race-baiter, was also dedicated to preserving white supremacy in the Magnolia State. Still, the 1946 primary election and the subsequent challenge to Bilbo is a significant event in the history of the black struggle for freedom. For four days that December, sixty-eight courageous black men and women publicly served notice that they would no longer accept the denial of their basic human rights. World War II veterans had led the way, along with older activists such as the Reverend William A. Bender. Few would predict in the winter of 1946 that victory was in sight, but in that crowded federal courtroom in Jackson the shock troops of the modern civil rights movement had fired their opening salvo. . . .

* * * *

The Delta was Mississippi's last frontier. This football-shaped expanse, which lies "flat as a tabletop" over the northwestern quadrant of the state, extends 200 miles from Memphis to Vicksburg and contains some of the richest soil in the nation. Blacks were a majority of this region's population. Prior to the Civil War most of the Delta was swampland and thick forests. There were no towns except for a few river settlements, and the regular flooding of the Mississippi made cotton cultivation an unacceptable risk. Between Reconstruction and World War I, settlers had the lands drained, levees built, and the forests cleared. A relatively small number of whites owned the land; tens of thousands of poor black families worked it. A "Delta aristocracy" soon emerged that dominated the state politically and economically for nearly a half century, maintaining its hegemony by exploiting the racial phobias of the poor whites from the hill counties to the east.

The Delta is both a clearly defined geographical area and a state of mind. It is the birthplace of the blues, which was created by resilient black sharecroppers who labored on the plantations under conditons reminiscent of the old regime. The region is also home to the Percy family, who were representative of the small group of wealthy planters who regarded the Delta as their fiefdom and who pictured themselves as the embodiment of southern civility and gentility, Mississippi's natural aristocracy of wealth and talent surrounded by ignorant blacks and venal rednecks. The Delta carries special meaning for the black freedom struggle. From Dr. T. R. M. Howard and Amzie Moore in the early 1950s to Fannie Lou Hamer, Aaron Henry, and Charles McLaurin in the 1960s, the Delta supplied much of the movement's leadership. Here key battles were fought, with names like "Greenwood" and "Ruleville" evoking the same bitter-proud-sacred memories in the new abolitionists as did "Shiloh" and "Gettysburg" for their forebears.

Mississippi blacks had fought for their freedom during the Civil War. Confederate troops put down slave revolts in two parts of the state, and when the Union army marched into Mississippi, blacks proved their worth as spies, guides, and combat troops. With the coming of freedom the state's 437,000 former slaves looked forward to full citizenship rights, including the economic opportunity provided by "forty acres and a mule." There followed instead a turbulent decade of Reconstruction that set the course of Mississippi history for the next century.

The stereotype of Reconstruction has died hard in Mississippi. Most whites today view that period as a tragic era of chaos, corruption, and—above all—Negro rule, an interpretation drilled into the minds of generations of school children. Reconstruction was in fact far more complex. Although blacks never controlled any branch of state government, many served with distinction in elective offices ranging from constable to United States senator. Corruption did exist (although it paled in comparison with that of the "Redeemer" regime that followed it), and some officials were unprepared to meet their responsibilities. Nevertheless, in a land devastated by war, the Reconstruction government rebuilt railroads and bridges, constructed hospitals and other health facilities, expanded the range of government services to the people, established Mississippi's first public school system, and wrote the most progressive constitution the state has had. When white conservatives brought an end to Reconstruction in 1875 through a campaign of intimidation and violence euphemistically called the "Mississippi Plan," it was not because black political participation had been a failure. Indeed, the progress of the Radical Reconstructionists in rebuilding Mississippi and in fostering a climate of democracy convinced privileged whites they had to act quickly—and brutally—if they were to regain political control.

Events in the late nineteenth century set the pattern for the twentieth. Racial segregation, which had not been rigidly observed even in the aftermath of Reconstruction, became a Mississippi "folkway" with passage of a series of Jim Crow statutes, beginning with an 1888 law segregating railroad passengers. Although for a time blacks continued to vote and hold minor offices, it was usually in alliance with conservative Democrats, who used the black vote to put down attempts by white insurgents to break the stranglehold that wealthy planters had on state government. Such "coalition" politics was risky—it could cut both ways—so in 1890 conservatives decided to eliminate forever the "threat" of Negro voting, enacting a new constitution with black disfranchisement as its centerpiece. By the turn of the century almost all white Mississippians agreed that the Negro was now in his proper place and must be kept there, whatever the cost.

Over the next four decades blacks struggled against the forces of white supremacy with limited success. In his definitive *Dark Journey: Black Missisippians in the Age of Jim Crow,* Neil R. McMillen shows that by 1940 many of the gains made by blacks in the post–Civil War years had been swept away. Most major black businesses—particularly banks, insurance companies, and newspapers, which emerged in the post–Civil War era—had collapsed by World War I. Blacks owned less farmland in 1940 than they had in 1920, and during this period the value of their total farm holdings declined by more than 50 percent. Sharecropping and the crop-lien system, together with a racist judicial system, fostered on the vast majority of blacks a new slavery almost as pernicious and effective as the old. For blacks, racial violence was a daily reality. Between 1880 and 1940 nearly 600 Mississippi blacks were lynched, and no jury would convict a white man for killing a Negro. On the eve of World War II, then, it appeared that the caste system, in place for more than half a century, would continue to dominate the lives of Mississippians, black and white, well into the future.

World War II brought change to Mississippi. Training camps and defense contracts poured money into the state. Thousands of Mississippians left the farm to work in defense industries or at military bases. Biloxi and Hattiesburg became boom towns, facing for the first time modern urban problems created by uncontrolled growth. Not since Reconstruction had outside forces intruded so dramatically. World War II was "a watershed for Mississippi," observed historian John Ray Skates, "before which there was basic historical continuity for a century, but after which nothing again was quite the same."

Black Mississippians made marginal economic gains. Wartime labor shortages forced plantation owners to pay more attention to their tenants, and wages and working conditions improved to a degree both in the countryside and in the cities. At the same time, however, the demand for labor accelerated the mechanization of cotton farming. Chemical weed killers and cotton-picking machines were no longer a curiosity, particularly in the Delta. Farm population declined during the war years, while total acreage actually showed a slight increase. Few blacks were able to find jobs in the new industries. As a result of these developments, thousands of blacks left the state during the war years. Net outmigration among blacks during the 1940s totaled nearly 300,000. Most headed due north to Chicago or other midwestern cities, drawn by the expectation that the doors of industrial opportunity would open for them there. Moreover, the war had not improved the state's racial climate, for though they were enjoying the benefits of Yankee capital and technology, white Mississippians still clung to a caste system that seemed to have served them well for nearly a century. Jim Crow would not be a casualty of World War II; in fact, the major short-term impact of wartime upheaval in Mississippi was an increased level of racial tension.

At first whites feared that the war would foster black militancy at home. Although blacks were not yet organized to demand their rights, rumors spread across the state that they were stockpiling weapons—guns, ammunition, even ice picks—for use in a race war now that so many white men were away in uniform. The wartime economy offered new opportunities to black women, but white house-wives saw instead a conspiracy: Mrs. Franklin D. Roosevelt was sponsoring "Eleanor Clubs" among cooks and maids, designed to "put a white woman in every kitchen." In this atmosphere of fear and uncertainty the historical pattern of white violence against blacks continued unabated.

Lynching had always been the ultimate form of social control, and neither youth, old age, nor social class offered protection to Negroes who did not stay in their place. In 1942 Charlie Lang and Ernest Green were both fourteen and lived in Shubuta, a small town near the Alabama border. The two black youths were playmates with a young white girl, and on an early October day of that year a passing motorist saw the two boys run out from under a bridge, chasing the girl. A short time later Lang and Green found themselves in the Quitman jail on charges of attempted assault. A mob stormed the jail and took the boys. Their bodies were found hanging from a river bridge. Less than a week later, a few miles away in Jones County, a mob lynched Howard Wash, forty-five, of Laurel. A jury had con-victed Wash of killing his dairyman employer but had not recommended the death penalty. The U.S. attorney general ordered the FBI to investigate the lynchings, promising that if the investigation developed a case, "relentless prosecution will follow." No one was convicted.

Six white men abducted the Reverend Isaac Simmons in Amite County in early 1944 and killed him with three shots into the back. When relatives found his body, they saw that Simmons's tongue had been cut out. He had not been charged with murder or with the "unmentionable crime." The sixty-six-year-old minister was lynched because he was a successful black man intent on keeping his property. Simmons owned 220 acres of debt-free land. When word got out that oil might be on the property, a local white man named Noble Ryder tried to take possession. Simmons then hired a white attorney from Jackson to protect his land. On the morning of March 26 Simmons and his son Eldridge were forced into a car and beaten. Eldridge Simmons later recalled that "they kept telling me that my father and I were 'smart niggers' for going to see a lawyer." The son witnessed the execution of his father. Before releasing him, one of the killers told the younger Simmons that "if this comes up again you had better not know anything about it" and gave him ten days to "get off the place." Simmons did leave, but he also brought charges against Noble Ryder, Ryder's brother, and four other men. The case did go to trial, and the prosecuting attorney urged the jury to disregard "all appeals to prejudice." None of the accused was found guilty. These events transpired in and around a Mississippi town called Liberty.

White leaders were also concerned over the consequences of stationing thou-sands of black troops in segregated units in military camps across the state. To be a black soldier in Mississippi was to face daily abuse and humiliation. Strict seg-regation was the rule on all bases, and white officers went to ridiculous lengths to enforce it. Second Lieutenant Lowry Wright was one of the few black officers at Camp Shelby, which was located outside Hattiesburg. Wright reported that he and another black lieutenant were assigned their own latrine, consisting of four urinals, seven sinks, ten showers, and sixteen commodes, enough to bathe and flush an entire company. Black officers at Shelby had few responsibilities. Both white enlisted men and officers refused to recognize their rank. The army provided blacks with few recreational facilities on base and limited their access to Hattiesburg out of deference to local sentiment. Black soldiers were beaten by whites in the camp, and two black GIs were wounded in an altercation with the Mississippi Highway Patrol.

The most serious racial trouble occurred at Camp Van Dorn, located near the small town of Centreville in an isolated section of southwest Mississippi. Clyde Blue, a Detroit native, was drafted in 1941 and assigned to the black 518th Quartermaster (Truck) Battalion at Camp Van Dorn. Blue recalled that when the 518th arrived, the camp was still under construction, "and the grounds would qualify for a massive mud puddle." Blue quickly learned that there was a black PX and a white PX, the latter out of bounds for black troops. Camp shows were also off limits: "Entertainers came and entertainers went; I guess they didn't know we were there since we never saw them." Although the men of the 518th resented these restrictions, they did not strongly protest against them. On the whole, the camp ran "smoothly"—until that day in May 1943 when the black 364th Infantry Regiment marched and rode through the gates of Van Dorn.

Insofar as the United States Army was concerned, the 364th was a regiment of troublemakers. While stationed in Phoenix, Arizona, the unit became involved in two serious disturbances. As punishment—or so the men believed—the 364th was shipped to Mississippi. For Clyde Blue, the sudden appearance of the infantry regiment was like the cavalry coming to the rescue: "They had mounted guns, artillery, the works. . . . The real thrill for us was when we saw our first black officers; they were mostly lieutenants, but they were officers. With the coming of the 364th a whole new ballgame began." The men of the 364th had barely disembarked when they attacked Jim Crow head on, desegregating a whites-only USO show and invading the off-limits PX. On their first Saturday night in Mississippi about seventy-five men checked out Centreville and confronted its chief of police and nervous white townspeople, who were armed with shotguns. A military police officer intervened to prevent further trouble. The following night a private from the regiment became involved in a dispute with an MP just outside the base lines. On hand to assist the MP was the county sheriff, who shot and killed the private. When word of the killing reached the barracks a race riot broke out. "That night I saw black hatred," recalled Private Blue. "I saw two or three black soldiers jump one white and give him a brutal beating." Whites retaliated in kind, and at one point the rumor surfaced that they were going to attack the black barracks with tanks. Sergeant Jeffries Bassett Jones was at the scene: "One of the officers from the 364th went into the white area and warned them that if this were true not to do it because the men of the 364th anti-tank company had sworn they would blow to hell any tank they saw coming near this area. All kinds of rumors were flying, along with fists, feet, cudgels, everything. It was a small war."

Tensions remained high in the aftermath of the riot. Whites in the Centreville area armed themselves and demanded the regiment's immediate transfer. The War Department kept word of the riot out of the papers and eventually shipped the 364th to the Aleutian Islands to perform garrison duty for the rest of the war. Looking back on his basic training in Mississippi, Sergeant Jones remembers Camp Van Dorn as "the backside of hell," where "I saw and participated in more fighting than I experienced in all my days overseas."

More than 85,000 Mississippi blacks served in the armed forces during World War II, and each felt the sting of racial discrimination. Whether they trained at Van Dorn, Shelby, or in camps in the North, they were always second-class citizens. Nonetheless, black Mississippians served their country well, whether on the battlefield or as support troops. Black GIs were not as naive in 1945 as their doughboy counterparts had been in 1918, when they had hoped that the war to make the world safe for democracy might make Mississippi a decent home for all its citizens. Still, blacks in Mississippi and across the land experienced shock mixed with outrage when James Eastland, a Delta planter and the state's junior senator, rose before his colleagues on June 29, 1945, and delivered an incredible speech on the performance of black troops in the war against Hitler's Germany.

Eastland began his harangue by posing a rhetorical question: "What is the history of the Negro soldier in the American army?" His answer: "The Negro was an utter and dismal failure in combat in Europe." Black troops were lazy, irresponsible, and "of very low intelligence." At crucial times they deserted their posts and refused to fight. Eastland dwelt at length on another familiar stereotype, charging that black soldiers raped white women in areas that the Allies occupied in Europe. His final judgment was that "Negro soldiers disgraced the flag of their country." Included in the senator's remarks was a personal plea for white supremacy. "I assert that the Negro race is an inferior race," the Mississippi statesman began. "I say quite frankly that I am proud of the white race. I am proud that the purest of white blood flows through my veins. I know that the white race is a superior race. It has ruled the world. It has given us civilization. It is responsible for all the progress on earth." Two weeks later, on the floor of the Senate, Robert Wagner of New York set the record straight. Where the Mississippi senator claimed that his information on the performance of black troops came from American generals in the field, Wagner quoted their denials, reading into the record numerous examples of individual and collective acts of black heroism in the European theater. But Senator Eastland had made his point—for the folks back home whose votes were counted.

When World War II ended a month later, all Mississippians joined in celebrating the Allied victory over Japan. Beneath the surface, however, there lay a profound uneasiness over the uncertain period ahead. The war *had* brought change to Mississippi, yet it remained to be seen whether, in the critical area of race relations, the state would move forward with the times or continue to cling to the vestiges of the Jim Crow society that had for so long retarded the advancement of the majority of its citizens, black and white.

Rising Expectations, 1946–54

John Dittmer, professor of history at DePauw University, is author of Local People: The Struggle for Civil Rights in Mississippi *and* Black Georgia in the Progressive Era, 1900–1920.

The decade following World War II was one of intensifying black activism in Mississippi, beginning with modest voter registration efforts and culminating in an attack on the color line in the state's public schools. Although local people did obtain some assistance from the National Association for the Advancement of Colored People and the NAACP Legal Defense Fund, the drive for political and educational equality was indigenous, receiving no support or encouragement from the federal government or from the labor movement, an ally of black activists in other southern states. The World War II veterans and traditional black leaders were facing a seemingly impossible task in Mississippi, for despite the wartime upheavals, whites were determined to maintain their supremacy by denying blacks political, educational, and economic opportunity and by maintaining racial segregation in all walks of life.

In postwar Mississippi most blacks were still working at jobs associated with slavery. Nearly two-thirds of the black male labor force engaged in some form of agriculture-related activity; more than 80 percent of these men were sharecroppers or day laborers on white-owned plantations. Few blacks held jobs in factories, and most of these were in the lowest-paying janitorial positions. For black women the designated place was still the white woman's kitchen. Of the 58,000 black women employed in nonagricultural jobs in 1950, two-thirds worked as domestics.

Median annual family income for blacks in 1949 was $601; it was $1,614 for whites. More than a third of black families reported incomes under $500. The black professional class was small and concentrated in the larger towns and cities. In 1950 only five black attorneys, thirty dentists, and sixty-four physicians were practicing in the state. There were nearly 1,000 preachers and some 5,500 teachers, the largest professional group. Given their limited economic opportunity, blacks continued to leave the state in large numbers. Between 1940 and 1950 Mississippi's black population declined by nearly 300,000. Blacks now constituted 45.3 percent of the state's population, down from 54 percent in 1940. Contributing to the continuing black migration was the caste system, which had proscribed black freedom for generations.

From drinking fountains and movie houses to schools and churches, Jim Crow dictated the pace of Mississippi life, and "keeping the Negro in his place" was the duty of every white citizen. That place might vary, depending on circumstance. When delivering the mail, letter-carrier Carsie Hall walked through the front door of the Heidelberg, Jackson's leading hotel, and rode the main elevator while making his rounds. Yet attorney Carsie Hall, at the Heidelberg to take the state bar exam, had to use the rear entrance and take the freight elevator to the floor where the test was given. Whites maintained their racial integrity on the playing fields, too, as when Mississippi State canceled its 1946 football game with the

University of Nevada because of Nevada's "use of Negro players." A year later city officials in Jackson and Hattiesburg barred the Freedom Train, a government-sponsored "rolling showcase of democracy," rather than permit nonsegregated viewing of such documents as the Declaration of Independence.

Mississippi's courts were the arbiters of the color line, and any number of judicial decisions illustrate the nature of justice, Jim Crow style. Consider the case of Davis Knight, who believed he was a white man, enlisted in the navy as a white man, and married a white woman. The state of Mississippi later charged Knight with violating the 1890 miscegenation law. At issue here was the ancestry of Knight's great-grandmother, a woman known as Rachel. The state contended that she was a Negro; Knight argued that she was a Cherokee Indian. The judge ruled that Rachel was black, and Knight drew a five-year sentence at Parchman penitentiary. Equally bizarre was the Mississippi State Supreme Court decision upholding an Adams County jury award of $5,000 to Mary Dunningham. It seems that the *Natchez Times* had incorrectly identified Mrs. Dunningham as "a negro," and that, in the eyes of the court, was "libel, *per se.*"

The courts were especially cruel in cases involving sex crimes alledgedly committed by black men against white women. On the morning of November 3, 1945, a Laurel housewife named Wilmetta Hawkins reported to the police that she had been raped by a Negro. Thirty-two-year-old Willie McGee, married and the father of four children, was arrested and charged with the crime. His trial lasted less than a day. The Laurel jury deliberated only a few minutes before finding him guilty; the judge sentenced McGee to die in the electric chair. This was to be the first of three trials. The Mississippi Supreme Court threw out the first verdict by ruling that McGee should have had a change of venue, overturned the second on grounds that blacks had been systematically excluded from the juries, and then upheld the third conviction. The case dragged on for over five years. After the first trial McGee turned his defense over to the Civil Rights Congress (CRC); his chief counsel was a young New York attorney named Bella Abzug. The Communist party took an interest in the McGee case and transformed it into a *cause célèbre*. Rallies and protests took place around the world. Governor Fielding Wright received thousands of letters, including petitions signed by such notables as Josephine Baker, Jean-Paul Sartre, and Albert Einstein.

McGee's lawyers had originally argued that the penalty was unfair because no white man had ever received a death sentence for rape, but in their final appeal the CRC attorneys exploded a bombshell: McGee and his wife Rosalee presented sworn statements that the alleged victim had been having an affair with McGee for a number of years before she claimed to have been raped. Although this new evidence smacked of desperation, the revelation did not come as a shock to a number of Laurel citizens who had long suspected such a relationship. The Mississippi Supreme Court rejected the new evidence as a "revolting insinuation and plainly not supported." The U.S. Supreme Court refused to review the case. Both Governor Wright and President Harry S. Truman denied appeals for clemency. Late in the evening of May 7, 1951, a crowd of some 700 whites gathered outside the Laurel courtroom, where the state's portable electric chair was now in place. At 12:07 A.M. they let out a loud, piercing rebel yell when word came that Willie McGee was dead.

In addition to facing a discriminatory judiciary, blacks attempting to bring change to Mississippi had to deal with political institutions that were corrupt as well as racist. When the political scientist Alexander Heard toured the state in 1947, interviewing scores of elected and appointed officials, he uncovered a sordid picture of wheeling and dealing at all levels of government. Money changed hands at the polls during every election. The going rate per vote ranged from $1.00 to $2.50, depending on the closeness of the contest. The Delta was an exception. There, according to longtime political operative Wilbur Buckley, "the big planters merely call in their people and tell them who they are going to vote for."

A major reason for such pervasive political corruption was the absence of ideological conflict within the white electorate. "In Mississippi," observed editor Hodding Carter II, "everybody more or less agrees on everything anyway." When asked to explain why poor whites did not rally around pocketbook issues that would ally them against planter and business interests, Carter pointed to the "common anti-black attitude" as a barrier to class politics, particularly "the campaign uses to which the Negro could be put by the 'rich' elements." The Delta still exercised disproportionate power in the affairs of state. George McLean, editor of the *Tupelo Daily Journal,* observed privately that "part and parcel of this control is the fact that the Delta returns the same old evil men again and again to the legislature and therefore gets seniority and influence out of proportion to the rest of the state." Delta lawmakers were strongly influenced by the Delta Council, a conservative organization established in 1935 to promote the interests of the planter class. Poor whites had no significant voice in government. With the death of Bilbo they had lost their champion, but even "The Man" had posed no real threat to corporate interests, no matter how much he railed against them on the stump.

White voters gave overwhelming support to Franklin D. Roosevelt in each of his four election campaigns. Angered by federal programs assisting southern blacks, however, Mississippi Democrats had turned against the New Deal by the 1940s. Using the race issue to keep the white lower classes in their place, the men who ran Mississippi unabashedly proclaimed an economic conservatism that would preserve and widen the gap between rich and poor. Nowhere is there a better example of the privileged class at work protecting its privileges than in the campaign against the Congress of Industrial Organizations (CIO) in the years surrounding World War II.

Mississippi seemed overdue for a labor organization drive. By World War II only the Magnolia State had no worker's compensation law and no department of labor. One-third of the state's 71,400 factory workers were making less than thirty cents an hour, the lowest rate in the South. As late as 1947, a ten-hour day and a sixty-hour week was the norm for women workers, again the worst record in the region. Given such conditions, the CIO moved into Mississippi in 1946 as part of its "Operation Dixie" campaign to organize workers across the South.

Resistance developed quickly. Although it was not an industrial state, Mississippi was attempting to attract factories from the North, and an abundant labor supply and an absence of unions were the state's best selling points. The American Federation of Labor (AFL) had established craft unions in the state, but these skilled white workers posed little threat to the status quo. The Congress of Industrial Organizations was another matter. The Mississippi establishment was paranoid about the CIO, linking it with racial integration and the international communist conspiracy. Jackson editor Fred Sullens labeled CIO organizers "strife breeders . . . more dangerous than rattlesnakes." In an open letter opposing the CIO, a group of citizens asked, "Do you want to be ruled from Russia by the Communists?" White opinion makers went to such extremes in attacking the CIO because they believed the stakes were high. A unionized work force in Mississippi, so the argument ran, would be unattractive to northern capital. Moreover, the CIO policy of organizing across racial lines would, if successful, present Mississippi with a class movement threatening conservative rule. Thus, Delta planters joined with small-town editors in meeting the CIO challenge. The battle was primarily for the mind of the white worker, and while the union offered a vision of higher wages and better working conditions, CIO opponents dusted off the tried-and-true race-baiting arguments that had historically kept poor whites in line (and also poor).

Experience had taught the CIO to step gingerly around the race question. During the war years integrated teams of organizers had worked in the state. When Frank Davis, black, and Claude Welch, white, attempted to organize woodworkers in Vicksburg, the chief of police locked them up without charges for twenty-four hours and then turned the two men over to a mob, which handcuffed them to a tree and whipped them. In the postwar campaign most of the organizers in Mississippi were white, and they tried to finesse the race issue.

The CIO enjoyed some success in Mississippi, winning fifty-seven union elections between 1946 and 1949 involving approximately 11,000 workers. The union did best in predominantly white counties in the southern half of the state, faring poorly in the north and in the Delta. The CIO base in the state was in Jones County, where the union won several elections, including a big victory against the AFL in the large Masonite plant in Laurel. Yet the Laurel success also demonstrated that Jim Crow held sway even in a union town.

State CIO director Robert W. Starnes, a native white who had graduated from Mississippi College, told Alexander Heard in 1947 that union gatherings in Laurel were "segregated according to color" because whites refused to participate in integrated events. The Laurel CIO Political Action Committee worked to register white workers and see that they paid their poll taxes, but "they . . . made no effort among the Negroes." Heard expressed surprise that CIO leader Starnes was "not acquainted with Negro political activities in Mississippi."

The CIO called off its Mississippi organizing drive in 1949, concluding that the campaign was too expensive for the results achieved. CIO (and AFL) locals survived into the 1950s, but the union movement was not a force for social change. Many union members supported the racist Citizens' Council and in the 1960s joined the Ku Klux Klan. Their leaders denounced the NAACP as a "communist-infiltrated organization." State CIO vice president J. W. Webb spoke for the rank and file when, in 1956, he vowed that "we'll support no movement that's opposed to segregation. We're very much a part of the national union, but we'll have nothing to do with integration." As black activists began to put together a program in the postwar years, they had no more friends in the House of Labor than in other elements of white society.

That program centered on voter registration, the focus of the civil rights struggle in Mississippi for the next two decades. Desegregation of public facilities, including schools, was not as compelling an issue in Mississippi as in other southern states. White repression made direct action projects more dangerous, and endemic black poverty meant that the right to spend the night at the Heidelberg Hotel was not a high priority for most black citizens. Although the desegregation movement later took hold in the larger cities, the appeal of the ballot was statewide. Robert Moses, who directed the voter registration drive of the early 1960s, observed later that obtaining the franchise was a program behind which everyone in the community could unite: "There was almost universal agreement. Almost everyone you went to, whether they would go to register or not, believed that registration would help."

Until the New Deal years, what black vote there was in Mississippi had gone to the party of Lincoln. The so-called Black and Tan Republican party was the political plaything of Perry W. Howard, a black Washington, D.C., lawyer and longtime Republican national committeeman from Mississippi. Howard, who made only occasional trips back to his home state to look after party interests, did not impress the younger blacks now becoming involved in the suffrage campaign. R. L. T. Smith, who would run for Congress in 1962, recalls that in the 1930s and 1940s the Republicans "had a rotten setup here. They had a group of blacks who were part of the apparatus to keep us down." Howard had a reputation as a wheeler-dealer and denied local blacks political participation and patronage. Nathaniel Lewis, the McComb resident who testified at the Bilbo hearings, said that the handful of "Negroes that ran the Republican Party in Mississippi . . . never said anything about getting more Negroes to vote. They didn't help one bit." Howard and his associates appeared content to dispense (or sell, as many claimed) patronage when the Republicans were in power and to handpick the Mississippi delegation to the national convention every four years. Neither Howard nor the Republican party played a role in the civil rights movement, and what influence Howard enjoyed in national Republican circles had ended by 1960.

The organizational base for the postwar voter registration drive was the newly organized Mississippi Progressive Voters' League, which claimed approximately 5,000 members by 1947. With its headquarters in Jackson and with major branches in Clarksdale and Hattiesburg, the league mounted a nonpartisan effort to educate and motivate potential black voters. League president T. B. Wilson stressed the nonthreatening, cooperative character of the movement. By adopting a moderate position, Wilson told Alexander Heard, the league had an easier time attracting church and lodge support and recruiting members than did local NAACP branches, which drew bitter opposition from whites.

Dr. T. W. Hill, chairman of the league's Clarksdale branch, epitomized the organization's middle-class orientation. A successful dentist in his fifties, Hill impressed Alexander Heard as "a very canny man with the ability to understand and get along with people." Hill described the Clarksdale league's function as primarily that of voter registration. He urged members to register, to pay their poll taxes, and to "work individually to get other blacks to do the same." Yet Hill opposed any systematic block-by-block, door-to-door canvassing "for any purpose." Although other members urged Hill to send people into adjoining counties to stimulate interest in voting, he refused, explaining that "the Negroes who live in these nearby counties know their white people best and know best how to handle them." Hill also resisted efforts to organize an NAACP branch in Clarksdale, for though he supported the NAACP program, white opposition "was simply too strong. . . . Clarksdale cannot handle it yet." (The Clarksdale branch of the NAACP was organized in 1953 with Aaron Henry as president.)

Despite efforts by people like Hill and Wilson to portray black political participation in positive, nonthreatening terms, whites took home a different message. "White Supremacy Is in Peril," screamed a *Jackson Daily News* headline early in 1947. Fred Sullens informed his readers that "Negroes in large numbers are paying their poll taxes down at the courthouse" and asked whether "you want a white man's government, or will you take the risk of being governed by Negroes?" White officials took a series of steps to ensure that such a calamity did not occur. First, in the spring of 1947, several months before the gubernatorial primary, the legislature passed a law stating that persons could vote in party primaries only if they were "in accord with" principles set forth by the party. Next, the state Democratic executive committee enumerated those "principles," including opposition to federal antilynching laws, anti–poll tax legislation, and the Fair Employment Practices Committee (FEPC). Blacks challenged at the polls in the primary, then, had to disavow their own beliefs in order to vote. In a move that surprised some observers, T. B. Wilson advised members of the voters' league to agree to the party principles because "we believe, as the party believes, in states' rights." Privately, Wilson said that blacks should go along because the Democratic primary was the only game in town.

Reports of large numbers of blacks registering and voting had been exaggerated. Despite front-page stories and display ads in the Negro weekly newspapers urging blacks to register and vote, the rallies in major cities, and the unanimous endorsement of the most important black social, religious, and political organizations, turnout was disappointingly low for the 1947 primary. The *New York Times* reported that "only a comparative handful of Negroes" showed up to vote, and thus it was not necessary for white Democrats to challenge the "loyalty" of black voters. Only in the Delta's Washington County were a number of blacks denied the ballot because they refused to adhere to party principles. Other tactics of fraud and intimidation were reported in Jackson, where the few blacks registered had previously voted without incident.

Having turned back this latest effort by blacks to play a political role, Mississippi whites soon faced another challenge, this time from the nation's capital. In 1946 President Harry S. Truman, under pressure from blacks and white Democratic liberals, had appointed a commission to study the race problem in America. Its report, *To Secure These Rights,* issued in October 1947, called for an ambitious federal effort to bring about "the elimination of segregation, based on race, color, creed, or national origin, from American life." Truman then sent a civil rights package to Congress that included a bill to strengthen voting rights. This was too much for Mississippi's governor, Fielding Wright, who early in 1948 set in motion the "Dixiecrat" movement. First, Wright called a meeting in Jackson, where 5,000 Mississippi Democrats attacked the president and his civil rights program and called for a convention of "true white Jeffersonian Democrats." Ten days later Democrats from Mississippi and nine other southern states convened in Jackson and unanimously agreed that unless the national convention adopted a states' rights plank, the southern delegates would walk out and nominate their own ticket. When the national Democratic party instead passed a strong civil rights plank at its convention, the Mississippi delegates and half of the Alabama delegation did walk out, while other southerners remained to wage a futile battle against the nomination of Truman. After the convention the **Dixiecrats** met to nominate South Carolina governor Strom Thurmond for president and Fielding Wright for vice president, a ticket that swept Mississippi in November, with Truman getting only 10 percent of the vote. Nationally, of course, Harry Truman pulled off the biggest upset in American political history.

The estimated 7,000 black voters in Mississippi split three ways in this election. A few blacks joined with a handful of whites to support the **Progressive party** crusade of former vice president Henry Wallace, whose platform called for improved relations with the Soviet Union and for full equality for Negro Americans. Wallace had taken his campaign to Mississippi, speaking at Southern Christian Institute, a black college, and delivering a statewide radio speech in which he castigated Governor Wright for his racial views. The Black and Tan Republicans delivered some 2,500 votes for the Republican nominee, Governor Thomas E. Dewey of New York. President Truman had the support of most black Mississippians, whether they could vote or not. Percy Greene, the editor of the black *Jackson Advocate,* took charge of the Truman campaign in the black community, and from this effort emerged the Mississippi State Democratic Association, with Greene as its president. This organization, along with the Progressive Voters' League and local NAACP branches, led the effort to register blacks over the next few years. By 1952 the number of black voters had increased to 20,000, no small achievement, but this figure represented less than 6 percent of the eligible black electorate, and activists remained aware of the immense task that lay ahead.

A number of factors accounted for the failure to register large numbers of black voters. As noted, tactics of intimidation did not die with Bilbo. Most blacks were afraid to try to register and vote, and with reason. Moreover, with all state and local candidates for office pledged to maintain white supremacy, there was simply no one to vote for. (At least Bilbo had been someone to vote *against.*) No candidate dared seek the black vote, and blacks realized that their numbers were too small to make a difference, even if they voted as a bloc. Finally, the registration campaigns of the late 1940s and early 1950s centered on the small black middle class. Not until the civil rights movement of the 1960s would activists attempt to register and organize the hundreds of thousands of black sharecroppers and unskilled urban workers.

With the voter registration drive making but limited progress, younger activists searched for other avenues to advance the cause and sensed that outside support would be necessary if meaningful change were to come to Mississippi. It was natural, then, that they would turn to the National Association for the Advancement of Colored People for help.

For three decades civil rights activity in Mississippi had been closely identified with the NAACP. Vicksburg blacks had organized the first branch in 1918. Mound Bayou followed in 1919, and Jackson, Meridian, and Natchez started branches in the 1920s. These branches all subsequently folded, only to be reorganized later. Several other cities received charters in the 1930s and early 1940s, but the NAACP did not become a viable presence in Mississippi until after World War II. Primarily a legalistic organization, the national NAACP had filed suits against the discriminatory laws and practices that violated the constitutional rights of blacks and lobbied Congress to enact federal antilynching legislation, abolish the poll tax, and establish a permanent FEPC. Although black Mississippians endorsed these goals, the world of Washington was far removed from that of Washington County. The New York national NAACP office, in return, gave low priority to work in Mississippi, believing that change must first come to the border states before the Deep South could be breached. National officials visited the state during the Depression years, but aside from legal advice and assistance in several court cases, the organization's work in Mississippi consisted mainly of limited solicitation of memberships.

Simply belonging to the NAACP in Mississippi was risky business. Most whites accepted without question the false accusation that the NAACP was a communist organization, and thus any card-carrying member was by definition a traitor.

The problem was most severe in the smaller towns. The Reverend R. G. Gilchrist of Aberdeen told the national office, "We have got to figure out some safe and effective way to get members. It is a dangerous risk for anyone to try to set up a branch of the NAACP in small towns or counties." Until the end of World War II, then, the NAACP maintained a holding operation in Mississippi. NAACP director of branches Ella Baker reported "with regret" that in 1944 there were only 129 members in the state's six branches.

Jackson had the only branch to operate with any degree of regularity during this period. Living in the state's capital and largest city afforded black activists a degree of protection, but here too they took precautions, seldom meeting in the same place twice in succession. Examination of the Jackson branch's leadership is instructive, for these people were representative of the small group of Mississippi blacks who placed themselves at risk during the darkest days of Jim Crow.

A trait that all Jackson NAACP leaders shared was their relative economic independence from whites. A. W. Wells, who "kept alive" the Jackson branch in the 1930s, was a federal railway postal clerk, as was A. J. Noel. Other postal employees active in the NAACP were John Dixon, R. L. T. Smith, Percy Greene, Carsie Hall, and Jack Young. Greene became editor of the *Jackson Advocate,* a black weekly, while Hall and Young later distinguished themselves as the state's first civil rights lawyers. A. H. McCoy was a dentist and businessman, M. C. Collins owned a funeral home, and William A. Bender was the chaplain at Tougaloo. All these men were "protected" from direct economic retaliation by whites, either through federal civil service laws or by providing services directly to the black community. As political activity expanded in the 1940s and 1950s, leaders throughout the state came from the thin ranks of small business owners, doctors, dentists, lawyers, government workers, and land-owning farmers.

An even more apparent characteristic was that the leadership was overwhelmingly male. In this the black community reflected the mores dominant in American society, as well as the tradition of the black church, which next to the family was the most important institution in the black community. Women did hold important positions in the NAACP hierarchy: Ella Baker was director of branches during the war years, and Ruby Hurley later provided distinctive leadership as southeast regional secretary. Within Mississippi several women were influential in the larger black community, most notably Mrs. Ruby Stutts Lyells. An educator, forceful orator, and president of the Negro State Federation of Women's Clubs, Lyells was a well-known Republican. A strong advocate of black rights, she was an independent force for social change for more than four decades.

Nonetheless, leadership in the NAACP and in the black community as a whole remained a male prerogative through the decade of the 1950s. Among the officers of the Mississippi State Conference of the NAACP in 1953, for example, Mary E. Holmes, the assistant secretary, was the only woman. Only two of the twenty-seven members of the board of directors were women. As late as 1959 no women headed local branches, though thirteen branches had elected women to the traditional post of secretary. That emphasis began to shift over the years, and the daughters and wives of the NAACP's "founding fathers," women like Gladys Noel Bates, Claire Collins Harvey, and Aurelia Young, later emerged as leaders in their own right.

Inspired by the militancy of the war veterans and influenced by the civil rights agenda of the Truman administration, blacks in the late 1940s intensified their efforts to expand the NAACP presence in the state. Ten new branches in Mississippi were established between 1945 and 1947, and thirteen had the minimum fifty members needed to send delegates to the 1947 national NAACP convention. NAACP members had been active in the fight to unseat Bilbo, and the Jackson branch initiated a suit to equalize teachers' salaries in the public schools. Voter registration was a priority for Mississippi branches, which worked with the existing suffrage organizations.

Because of the growth in membership activities, in 1946 the Mississippi State Conference of Branches was organized to coordinate efforts of local branches and to act as liaison with the national office. There was no paid fieldworker, a shortcoming that hampered efforts to expand the organization's influence in the black community. The national office's failure to provide adequate resources for work in Mississippi disturbed NAACP attorney Thurgood Marshall, who in August 1950 wrote director of branches Gloster Current, "We have never done a good job in Mississippi. . . . The only way to do a good job in Mississippi is to have someone there who knows Mississippi and who knows the people." Marshall recommended that the Reverend William A. Bender be "placed on the field staff and assigned to work there as our local representative," praising Bender as "the one contact we can rely upon in Mississippi."

Current opposed the appointment, questioning Bender's leadership as president of the State Conference of Branches and citing the need to find "young men who can . . . develop into good field workers and fundraisers." Part of the problem was that Current disapproved of the Tougaloo chaplain's personality and style. Current was a bureaucrat very much at home in the NAACP's hierarchical structure. He demanded loyalty and obedience from his people in the field and regarded Bender as something of a loose cannon. Bender was his own man and possessed an explosive temper. When several members of the Yazoo City branch wrote the national office criticizing the manner in which Bender was mediating a local factional dispute, the chaplain fired back that "I felt like taking my .38 and walking to Yazoo City to do what ought to be done to the one or two scoundrels that got up that letter." This combativeness served Bender well as an organizer in a state where most blacks were afraid to get near the NAACP. Despite Current's objections, however, NAACP executive secretary Walter White agreed with Marshall that Bender was the best candidate, and the Tougaloo chaplain got the job. He was to be the first Mississippi NAACP official to organize branches across the state.

Just as the NAACP was becoming more directly involved in Mississippi, there arose a new organization for racial advancement. The Regional Council of Negro Leadership (RCNL) was founded in Cleveland, Mississippi, in late 1951 by Dr. T. R. M. Howard, a prosperous Mound Bayou physician and businessman. The guiding force in the RCNL for the next six years, Howard became the state's most charismatic advocate of black rights. Howard was a native of Kentucky who moved to Mound Bayou in the early 1940s as chief surgeon at the Knights and Daughters of Tabor hospital. Within a short time he had set up his own medical clinic, bought a large plantation, and organized the Magnolia Mutual Life Insurance Company.

At first glance the Delta physician did not appear to fit the image of a dedicated activist. A tall, powerful man in his early forties, Howard enjoyed life in the fast lane. His home on the outskirts of town was a showplace, replete with a staff of servants and chauffeurs, where he entertained in the finest tradition of a Delta planter. He raised pheasant, quail, and hunting dogs for sport; played the horses;

and loved flashy cars. Myrlie Evers, whose husband, Medgar, began his career in Mound Bayou as a Magnolia Mutual agent, recalls seeing "Doc" Howard "sailing down the highway in a red Buick convertible on the way to visit a patient." She also remembers his "friendly smile, and a hearty handshake. . . . One look told you he was a leader: kind, affluent, and intelligent, that rare Negro in Mississippi who had somehow beaten the system."

The national office of the NAACP was not so taken by this flamboyant upstart and believed that Howard had put together the RCNL for reasons of "self-aggrandizement." Always protective of its turf, the NAACP regarded Mississippi as its **bailiwick** and saw Howard as a potential rival. The RCNL, on the other hand, was more **ecumenical**, welcoming state and local NAACP people into its leadership. Aaron Henry has described the council as a "homegrown NAACP"; the young Clarksdale pharmacist served on the RCNL board at the same time that he was president of his local NAACP branch. Concerned by Howard's success in attracting much of the NAACP leadership into his organization, Ruby Hurley told Walter White that "the Council is a threat which I have recognized and tried to combat on my several visits to the state." Although its actual membership was never large—one source reported it had 500 members in twenty-nine counties—the RCNL knew how to attract a crowd. In May 1952 more than 7,000 blacks gathered in the comfortable surroundings of Mound Bayou to eat Doc Howard's barbecue and listen to a speech by Chicago Democratic congressman William Dawson, with additional entertainment provided by gospel singer Mahalia Jackson. Two years later 10,000 people showed up to hear Thurgood Marshall. T. R. M. Howard, Hurley realized, was a force to be reckoned with.

The program of the RCNL was similar to that of the NAACP. The council was active in voter registration and stood for "first class citizenship for Negroes in Mississippi." Howard campaigned against police brutality, arranging an unprecedented meeting with state police commissioner Colonel T. B. Birdsong to air grievances against the Mississippi Highway Patrol. As a local group the RCNL avoided the stigma attached to the national NAACP and thus had more freedom to operate.

National NAACP leaders saw more substantive differences. Current characterized the RCNL's program as "midway between that of the NAACP and the Urban League," and Hurley claimed that the RCNL accepted the doctrine of "separate but equal." There was some truth to the latter charge, at least in the council's early days. One of its first actions was a boycott against filling station owners who did not provide rest rooms for black patrons. The "Don't Buy Gas Where You Can't Use the Rest Room" campaign did not challenge segregation and would have accepted "separate but equal" facilities. Still, the differences between the national NAACP and the RCNL were more territorial than ideological. Howard's organization was not accommodationist, as future events would prove. Both Howard and the NAACP members who supported the RCNL knew they were all facing a common enemy and could not afford the luxury of destructive interorganizational warfare.

Although the early 1950s was certainly no golden age of race relations in Mississippi—Jim Crow and everything it stood for remained firmly in place—there were signs of gradual improvement in the racial climate. The NAACP was experiencing slow but steady growth, with local branches becoming bolder in communicating their message to the general public. In urban areas several thousand blacks had added their names to the registration books, a development white politicians for the most part ignored. Younger men taking seats in the Mississippi legislature appeared to be more forward-looking than their hidebound predecessors. A racial moderate, Frank Smith, was now representing the Delta in the U.S. House of Representatives. After the black Natchez Business and Civic League urged its members to register and vote, an unprecedented 400 blacks did so in a special 1954 election, with "the calm acceptance of the white community." For the first time since Reconstruction, blacks served on a Natchez grand jury, and two blacks were jurors in a Greenville case. Indianola and Biloxi each quietly employed a Negro policeman to patrol black areas of town.

Whites had not been aroused by these developments because they had become convinced that the racial status quo was no longer threatened. The dire predictions of masses of blacks registering and voting had proven false. At the current rate of registration, blacks would pose no political threat until well into the twenty-first century. Congress had failed to take action on Truman's civil rights measures. Now Ike was in the White House, the Korean War was over, and many white Mississippians were sharing in the returning prosperity. And yet, unobserved by most Mississippians, a number of school desegregation cases had been slowly working their way up through the courts. With *Brown* v. *Board of Education* the tranquility of the Eisenhower years would vanish overnight, plunging Mississippi into a period of violent interracial conflict unmatched since the bloody years of the 1870s.

Even the most ardent segregationist would admit that under the principle of "separate but equal," black children in Mississippi had been denied educational opportunity. As late as 1950, 70 percent of blacks twenty-five years of age and older had less than a seventh-grade education. Only 10,250, or 2.3 percent, had completed high school. During that year the state spent $122.93 per pupil for the education of whites and $32.55 for blacks. No less a champion of white supremacy than Fred Sullens had written in a 1949 *Jackson Daily News* editorial that "in the matter of education we have for many years been treating Negroes most outrageously. The type of education we have been providing for them is nothing short of a disgrace. It might well be called a public scandal." Sullens advised his readers to "go into any rural school building for Negroes and see for yourself . . . Negro schools are poorly equipped, shabby, delapidated, and unsightly. . . . Almost without exception they are one-room structures, rickety stoves are propped up on brickbats, blackboards are absent or worn to the point of uselessness, sanitation is sadly lacking." Conditions in city schools were often no better. Where city and county governments refused to appropriate funds, blacks had to provide their own school buildings while paying taxes to support white schools.

The needs of white students always took priority. Their school year was nearly two months longer, their buildings were better, they had libraries—most black schools did not—and they received free bus transportation. The scholar J. Lewis Henderson, a white Mississippian, observed that "few southerners seem to resent it when the son of a millionaire cotton planter in Coahoma County rides to school in a free bus, while the Negro sharecropper's son must pay three dollars a month." Also blatant was the discrepancy in teachers' salaries. In 1948 the average yearly salary for white teachers was $1,861; for blacks, $711.

In the spring of 1948 Gladys Noel Bates, a black science teacher at the Smith Robinson School in Jackson, filed suit in U.S. District Court charging that the local school board had denied her and all other black teachers and administrators salaries equal to those paid to white teachers with similar education and experience. A graduate of Tougaloo College, Bates had also done graduate work at the University of West Virginia. Her father, A. J. Noel, was a Jackson NAACP leader, and NAACP Legal Defense Fund attorneys Constance Baker Motley and Robert Carter represented her. The case dragged on for nearly three years. The Jackson school board had immediately fired Bates and her husband, also a teacher, and then argued in court that the case was moot since the plaintiff was no longer employed in the system. At that point R. Jess Brown, a teacher at Lanier High School, entered the case as an intervening plaintiff. (Brown, too, lost his job and went on to a career as an attorney.) Bates and Brown lost the case on a technicality. Taking his cue from a similar case in Georgia, Judge Sidney Mize ruled that the plaintiffs had not exhausted their administrative remedies before filing suit. In a significant footnote, Mize wrote that had he been forced to hand down a decision, he would have sided with the plaintiffs, as the weight of evidence was on their side.

White political leaders had seen the handwriting on the wall. They came to believe that the only way to maintain their dual school system was to make separate-but-equal more of a reality, even though the economic costs would be substantial. A short time after the Bates decision, Governor Fielding Wright persuaded the legislature to allocate funds to begin equalizing teacher salaries. However, many local and county school boards, which were responsible for distributing the money equally, either refused to do so or engaged in subterfuges such as raising the monthly salaries of black teachers and then shortening the school year. Wright's successor, Hugh L. White, pursued equalization more vigorously. Starting from the premise that all Mississippi schools were underfinanced, White proposed an ambitious program of school consolidation and reorganization that would also allocate funds to build black schools, provide bus transportation for black students, and equalize the salaries of black and white teachers. The legislators were ambivalent; many members rejected the argument that they must take remedial action under threat of federal action. At a special session of the legislature called in November 1953 to deal with the educational budget, the Mississippi House passed a constitutional amendment permitting the abolition of the public school system if the U.S. Supreme Court required desegregation. The Senate voted down the amendment—this time.

Both the special session and the regular January 1954 meeting of the legislature convened under the shadow of *Brown*. The U.S. Supreme Court was now hearing the cases, with a decision expected in late spring. Taking the easy way out, the legislature adopted a wait-and-see attitude. If the Court upheld the separate-but-equal principle, then Mississippi would spend millions of dollars to upgrade black education. If the decision called for desegregating the schools, more drastic measures would be in order.

Black Mississippians were not of one mind about the school court cases. The state NAACP had consistently opposed segregation. At its sixth annual convention delegates passed a resolution calling on branches "to take any and all necessary legal steps to end segregation in public education." In January 1954 the NAACP assisted Medgar Evers in his unsuccessful bid to enroll at Ole Miss law school. Black principals and teachers, on the other hand, were understandably ambivalent about the prospect of school desegregation. With no tenure, and under the direct control of white school boards, they could be fired for taking any position opposed by the white establishment.

A number of black educators, especially administrators, had an economic interest in maintaining the status quo. The segregated environment had provided them both with a livelihood and with status in the community. They feared—in many cases appropriately, as it turned out—that they would not fare well in an integrated system. Moreover, after they had worked for years at low wages in dilapidated buildings with meager facilities, now white officials seemed prepared to raise their salaries and build new schools in the black community. Privately, and later publicly, leading black educators sided with the segregationists to preserve Mississippi's dual school system.

On May 17, 1954, Chief Justice Earl Warren spoke for a unanimous U.S. Supreme Court when he said, "Separate educational facilities are inherently unequal. . . . Segregation is a denial of equal protection of the laws." White Mississippi at first did not respond to the *Brown* decision with a single voice. Predictably, Senator Eastland breathed defiance: "The South will not abide by nor obey this legislative decision of a political court. . . . We will take whatever steps are necessary to retain segregation in education. . . . We are about to embark on a great crusade to restore Americanism." Other voices were at first more cautious. Senator John Stennis observed that "there is plenty of time, and I believe there are even years to seek a solution." Hodding Carter of the *Delta Democrat-Times* pleaded for moderation: "Let's keep our shirts on. The decision has been made. It is a momentous one. . . . And in the South it gives us the challenge to replace trickery and subterfuge with the honest realization that every child has the right to an equal education." And in the Delta town of Cleveland, a young Episcopal priest named Duncan Gray called on Mississippians to comply with the Court's decision—and kept his job.

Most white Mississippians opposed *Brown,* but it was by no means immediately apparent that the state would defy the decision if the Eisenhower administration demonstrated a commitment to enforce it. (In the immediate aftermath of the decision, Duncan Gray talked with the Cleveland superintendent of schools and the president of the local school board, and both men said that they believed that Cleveland schools would be desegregated within a relatively short time.) At the state level, most discussion centered on strategies to avoid compliance without provoking a direct confrontation with the federal government. Attorney General James P. Coleman, whose apparent moderation made him the state's most effective segregationist, asked every white lawyer to sign up as a "Special Assistant Attorney General" to represent local school districts should blacks file desegregation suits, as they were threatening to do. Walter Sillers, the powerful Speaker of the House— and an opponent of Governor White's equalization plan—said he would reintroduce the constitutional amendment giving the legislature the authority to abolish the public schools rather than desegregate them. The unstated assumption here was that Mississippi would fund a private school system for white children. As for Governor White, who appeared to be genuinely committed to upgrading black schools, his plan was the most interesting of all: he would persuade the leaders of the Mississippi black community to endorse what he called "voluntary segregation."

On July 1 the governor met with seven black men whom he believed to be key leaders in their community. Among those present were J. D. Boyd, the president of Alcorn College; J. H. White, president of Mississippi Vocational College; the Reverend H. H. Humes, a Delta minister, editor, and president of the 400,000-member General Missionary Baptist Convention; and Percy Greene of the *Jackson Advocate.* (Greene had by this time discarded the militancy of his earlier years and was currying favor with important whites.) Most of these men had previously gone on record against school desegregation, with Reverend Humes the most outspoken in his advocacy of all-black schools. They responded enthusiastically to the governor's pledge that if blacks supported voluntary segregation, then the legislature would begin allocating millions of dollars to improve black education.

The group urged the governor to invite nearly 100 black leaders from across the state to meet with him in Jackson to discuss his plan, assuring him that 95 percent of those in attendance would endorse continued school segregation, provided that funds were immediately made available for equalization. The seven men were so confident of their position that they persuaded White to include representatives from the NAACP and the Regional Council of Negro Leadership on his guest list, arguing that if these spokespersons were excluded, any ensuing agreement would lack credibility in the black community.

White sent out approximately ninety letters on July 13, inviting the representatives to meet with him and his newly appointed Legal Educational Advisory Committee on July 30. Among those on the list was Emmett J. Stringer, a young dentist from Columbus and the new state president of the NAACP. Stringer accepted and used the NAACP network to learn the names of the other guests, calling them to a meeting at Farish Street Baptist Church in Jackson the night before they were to see the governor.

The "meeting the night before," as it would later be known, was a stormy one. Boyd, J. H. White, and the other members of the conservative faction soon realized they had miscalculated: they would not be able to persuade this group to go along with the governor. At one point during the meeting, Stringer recalled, the argument became so heated that Humes and T. R. M. Howard almost came to blows. After hours of debate, the group agreed to present a united front. They voted to select speakers to convey the message that black Mississippians expected the governor to enforce the *Brown* decision.

When the black delegation and Governor White and his entourage assembled at the State Office Building at 10:00 A.M., the atmosphere was tense. After a few opening remarks about the long history of good race relations in the Magnolia State, the governor turned the meeting over to House Speaker Walter Sillers to chair. The first black to get the floor was E. W. "Charlie" Banks of Jackson, who read a statement endorsed by the black delegation calling for "strict observance of the Supreme Court's integration order [through] consolidation and integration of the present schools on all levels." Subsequent speakers reiterated the theme. Howard minced no words. Although the governor had not yet introduced his plan, the Delta activist warned him that "the Negroes who have come here today have not come to help work out any trick plan to circumvent the decision of the Supreme Court outlawing segregation in the public schools. We believe that the decision is a just and humane decision."

Finally, in a desperate effort to salvage the situation, Speaker Sillers looked around for a friendly face and said, "I am going to call on Reverend Humes now." Humes strolled lazily to the floor and told the white leaders that "the real trouble is that for too long you have given us schools in which we could study the earth through the floor and the stars through the roof." At that, the governor hurriedly adjourned the meeting. Afterward, a visibly shaken Hugh White told reporters, "I am stunned." It was evident, he contended, that those blacks he had counted on for support had bowed "under pressure from members of their own race." "I have believed that a certain element representing a vast majority of the Negroes would go along," he said. "Now I am definitely of the conclusion that you can't put any faith in any one of them on this proposition."

Aaron Henry left the meeting with a different feeling. As the black delegation prepared to leave, "we shook hands, congratulating each other on what appeared to be a major triumph." It was an occasion, he recalled, "when I was really proud to be a Negro in Mississippi."

1.9   Barbara Dianne Savage

Radio and the Political Discourse of Racial Equality

Barbara Dianne Savage, assistant professor of history at the University of Pennsylvania, is author of Broadcast Freedom: Radio, War, and the Politics of Race, 1938–1948.

Popular national political forums were among radio's most prominent features in the war era and one of its many gifts to television. All of the networks had some version of this public affairs format, and of these, the *University of Chicago Round Table* and *America's Town Meeting of the Air* were the most popular, respected, and influential. Because of their continuity, these two shows are particularly valuable sites for observing how over the course of a decade the political subject of race, first deemed unspeakable, came to be aired and then rose to prominence as a national issue. Quite literally, these broadcasts chart the evolution of a permissible political discourse about racial oppression, a development that provides insights into the fashioning and limitations of the white liberal response to the emergence of the civil rights movement.

African Americans waged a mind war against the shameful paradox of a segregated democracy during this period, although it would take two decades of mass protests, litigation, and deaths to overcome virulent white resistance to dismantling its edifice. On a rhetorical level, the discourse of racial equality was challenged by a discourse of white resistance, a fight played out before a national listening audience. The concerted assault by African Americans on the conceptual world of racial segregation and the airing of a new political narrative on race have been overshadowed by their legacy: the dramatic battles and victories of the 1950s and 1960s that would be carried not on radio but on television.

Airing the Race Problem

NBC's *University of Chicago Round Table* began in the early 1930s as a local program broadcast from the campus of the University of Chicago. In 1937, the university hired William Benton to fill the new post of vice president for public relations, whose responsibilities included oversight of radio operations. Benton was the premier practitioner of radio advertising and founder of the advertising firm Benton and Bowles. *Round Table* pioneered a format in which faculty members engaged national political figures and journalists in discussions about pressing national political and economic issues. The program built up a loyal nationwide listenership that it reinforced by distributing printed transcriptions and bibliographies for each of the weekly Sunday shows. *Round Table's* audience grew rapidly, rising from 1.5 million in the 1930s to approximately 10 million by 1941. Although other programs competed with it, *Round Table* under Benton's leadership earned a reputation as the most stately of the panel discussion shows, becoming recognized as the "intellectual's radio paradise."

Attempts to introduce the race question into this paradise repeatedly met with defeat, and the resistance to those attempts offers valuable insights into the volatility of the race question over the course of the decade. Sherman Dryer, director of radio for the university, believed that the program had a public responsibility to confront the race issue and that if it did not do so it would risk accusations that it was afraid to take on controversial contemporary topics. Under Dryer's leadership, the program staff approved, scheduled, and publicly announced a broadcast in 1939 with the provocatively simple title "Is the Negro Oppressed?" Answering that question would not be easy. A black newspaper announced the upcoming broadcast with a description of the show's conflicted intentions: "Lynchings, Jim Crow laws, and other evidence of discrimination against the Negro in the United States will be compared with the advances made by the American Negro with the assistance of government and individuals interested in more than legal emancipation of the Negro." Walter White of the National Association for the Advancement of Colored People (NAACP) and University of Chicago sociologist Louis Wirth were expected to appear on the show. Wirth would argue, according to this report, that "Hitler has accused America of ignoring its own minority problem" but that progress for blacks had been made "principally by the efforts of the Negro himself." This meant, according to Wirth, that "the Negro is not one of our greatest problems." The show never aired and was replaced by a special on the coal miners' strike.

Dryer persisted in trying to get a show about blacks on the air. After the cancellation, Dryer argued to Benton that, "purely from a public relations angle," the series had to include a show about blacks or it would become the target of a protest campaign from the "left-wingers." He explained: "Influences will begin seeping out from New York, through the Daily Record–Daily Worker on the one hand and through the National Association for the Advancement of Colored People on the other, the net effect of which will be to undermine the prestige of the Round Table. When I say undermine, I mean not only with the so-called liberals but the academic conservatives as well. If once our own Faculty feel (as some of them do already) that the Round Table had cut off a program because of external influences, even the most conservative members would tend to look at it askance." Dryer suggested ways that such a broadcast could be kept "innocuous," such as adding a white southerner to the show or limiting the discussion to "the economic position of the Negro in the Northern cities." He advised that the title be changed to the more neutral "Today's American Negro" instead of "Is the Negro Oppressed?," although he confessed that he liked the drawing power of the more controversial title, which "would have a million dials twisting our way."

Benton's work as an advertising executive made him quite cautious about risking negative audience reaction to any direct discussion of blacks, a point of view shared by officials at NBC. This is richly ironic because Benton had been the person who had convinced Pepsodent to sponsor the local show *Amos 'n' Andy* for national broadcast on NBC, a decision that brought enormous profit to NBC and the two white men who played the black characters on the show. But there was a difference between depicting African Americans and airing a show that actually discussed their place in American political life. Benton asked NBC president Niles Trammell for advice on the idea of airing a "Negro show," letting him know that the university had received quite a few letters protesting the cancellation and that "the Communist papers and other left wing papers have been nipping a bit at our heels."

Judging by their reaction, NBC officials had been unaware that any show on blacks was even under consideration. NBC vice president John Royal advised Trammell to prevent the show from being broadcast: "Today's American Negro, Today's American Jew, Today's American Catholic, Today's American Irish, would all be difficult and dangerous subjects to be discussed by the Round Table. The fact that the Communist papers and other left-wing papers have been nipping at his heels is not reason why it should be done, but perhaps a very good reason why it shouldn't be. Anyone who knows what's going on in this country realizes that the Communists are making a very strong play to arouse the Negroes in America." Royal disparaged Dryer, describing him as "a young man with radical or at least 'broad minded' tendencies," and vowed to keep him from maneuvering "us into some embarrassing positions." The question of "the Negro," Royal told Trammell, simply had to be left alone: "They would *like* to have a Southerner on, but you, as a Southerner, know more than anyone else that you cannot *discuss* the nigger question." Royal recommended that the network cancel *Round Table* altogether if it decided to go forward with the show. Trammell agreed with Royal's assessment. He called Benton directly to make the network's position clear, later informing Royal that Benton "understands our position and I don't think you will hear from this matter again."

Silence on the race matter was enforced for another three years until American entry into the war emboldened Dryer in May 1942 to raise once again the idea of a "Negro Round Table." Dryer explained that Archibald MacLeish at the Office of Facts and Figures "now smiles upon a discussion of the Negro." Indeed, MacLeish had made a closed-circuit address to the radio industry in which he spoke of his fears of the dangers to national security of continued low black morale. Taking MacLeish's remarks as federal imprimatur for radio to act, Dryer argued that as the most popular show of its type, *Round Table* had "a patriotic obligation to treat this topic" because "we can do more with one broadcast on 'The Negro' than probably a score of certain other 'national' programs, more than a hundred local programs." Dryer emphasized that the declaration of war had changed everything: "[T]he Negro problem today is not, as it was before December 7, a Southern problem. It is now a nationwide problem, which the government has officially recognized." Certain precautions and "practical considerations" would be necessary, he warned. One participant had to be a white southerner, and no panelist should be black, "for if a Negro is on the program, whatever good things we have to say about the Negro race will be construed by a lot of people as something we couldn't avoid because of the Negro's presence." Implicit here is Dryer's fear that plans to include an African American panelist would automatically doom the broadcast just as surely as ignoring the southern white perspective would.

Encapsulated here once again was the struggle about who was to speak on the "Negro problem," who was to serve as an expert at a time when African Americans were excluded from the symbolically equalizing formality of political discourse. Southern politicians and journalists still claimed sole legitimate authority concerning "the Negro" and most other white Americans deferred to this claim. When fears had surfaced among federal officials at the Office of War Information (OWI) and the War Department about their broadcasts about race relations, the specific object of concern was southern congressional control of key appropriations committees. But the immediate concern of *Round Table* was to avoid offending southern white listeners' sensibilities, to which it ceded veto powers.

Dryer sought advice from federal officials on how to proceed with his proposed show in June 1942. He turned to his liberal friend, Charles Siepman, in the Radio Division of the Office of Facts and Figures at the OWI. . . . Siepman was battling to convince his agency to sponsor broadcasts on the race question. Although he and Dryer were in agreement on the need for radio to act, he cautioned Dryer about the risks of talking about a problem that had no political solution:

> It is obviously a delicate subject, the action necessary to the solution of the problem being as yet absent. An airing of the issues involved may prove the most helpful contribution that can be made over the radio as long as this is done in terms that do not provoke hotter feelings than at present exist. Any decent person will sympathize with the negroes [*sic*] aspirations. Many will recognize and with distress, the anomaly of his position under the law and in a free democracy. But many too, will realize what deep seated prejudice and what a long tradition lies behind this unhappy story. . . . To arouse false hopes would be as dangerous as to inflame violent passions.

Siepman's warning was unnecessary since Dryer's efforts to bring a show on African Americans to the air were for naught. Benton again had sent a copy of Dryer's suggestions to Trammell, asking him once more for guidance but without taking any position himself: "Does Dryer make his case or is it your feeling that we'd better pass up this subject?" Two months later, Benton reported to Dryer that Trammell had told him that "he doesn't want to face this issue. He doesn't want us to face it." Trammell feared "all kinds of trouble and tribulation in the future around this issue." Benton asked Dryer, for the sake of the series, to "drop the matter," predicting that "if we decide to press this further, we'll have a major issue with NBC."

The subject might have been dropped, but it would not go away. In August, Edwin Embree of the Chicago-based Rosenwald Fund called Benton to suggest that the series include a show about the poll tax, with Senator Claude Pepper as a participant. Benton replied that the subject would need to be broadened to include all "interferences with the democratic franchise," presumably to keep its focus away from the South and the race question. When he passed the information on to his colleagues at *Round Table,* the reaction was negative, based on the realization that "any broadcast on this subject will be in substantial part a discussion of the Negro question," which remained an issue to be avoided.

Finally, after four years of internal conflict and delay, *Round Table* could no longer ignore the continued escalation of white fears concerning black activism and the steady migration of African Americans out of the Deep South. In 1943, faced with the eruption of racial violence in several major cities, the show publicly acknowledged the existence of African Americans, albeit only as a problem. Within a four-month period, *Round Table* broadcast two discussions on the "Negro question," the first in April and the second in July. Despite the decision to go forward, there was still serious trepidation about how to frame the issue and how it would be received. For example, to be on the safe side and to avoid any preshow objections, Benton cleverly suggested that the announcement for the first show include no reference to blacks but that it be given the covert title "Minorities," even though, as Dryer would later point out, "two-thirds of this program was devoted to the Negroes."

The broadcast on minorities featured none, having as its guests Avery Craven of the university's history department; Robert Redfield, an anthropologist and the school's dean of social sciences; and Ralph McGill, editor of the *Atlanta Constitution*. In many ways, the discussion played itself out as representational performance, with each panelist speaking on behalf of an imagined constituency. Although he was chosen to represent the South, McGill took on the role of the southern race moderate. A more conservative southern position on race was expressed by Craven, who was a southerner by birth as well as a historian of the South and the Civil War. That left Redfield to advocate more liberal views. What was missing from the performance, although not yet noticeable to the actors, was the voice of the subject itself.

Although they knew the show's purpose was to raise the race issue, the three men alternately approached and avoided the subject. They began with vague introductory comments about the importance of "minorities" to the country's development, with brief mention of Jews, Mexican Americans, Japanese Americans, and "the Negro." After the discussion skirted specifics, Redfield boldly suggested the obvious—that "the Negro" was the "number-one minority" problem and the one they needed most to discuss. Craven agreed and described the "problem" this way: "The Negro does . . . represent the minority group to the nth degree. . . . If ever there is a problem under the sun that had something of history and tradition back of it, it is the Negro problem. If I can judge, there are the other two things—restlessness on the part of the Negro as never before, demanding his rights and recognition as an individual, and there is also a stimulation of fears on the part of the dominant group. The majority, in other words, are as much disturbed over the race question as the Negro himself."

It was this duality—black restlessness and white fear—that had finally rendered the issue of race too urgent to be ignored. McGill confirmed Craven's definition, but he added that African Americans were dissatisfied because they wanted their rights and that they should have them. Craven and McGill quickly agreed that the "Negro problem" was a national matter and no longer simply a southern concern, as if to protect themselves (and the show) from charges that they were "interfering" in the South's business. Furthermore, Redfield added that "what we do with reference to the Negro is attended to by persons in all parts of the world today, including our own allies of a different color." This laying claim to the race problem marked a shift in thinking among some whites as they embraced the idea long advanced by African Americans that the national deference that had been accorded the South on the race issue was harmful to national interests, both domestic and foreign.

Redfield dared to raise the obvious question: "[S]omething has to be done about the Negro—is this the time to do it, and what is it we are to do?" When Craven argued that the war's needs came first, Redfield countered that the two problems—the war and "the Negro"—were intertwined and that solving the "Negro problem" was "also a strong step toward winning the war and the peace to come after." Redfield concluded that "the race problem has now become so important to the security of the nation that the national government must, in some form or another, declare its interest in solving it and implement that interest by appropriate legislation." But when Redfield suggested that enforcement of such legislation be left to the localities, both Craven and McGill predicted failure, with Craven citing Reconstruction as a particularly strong case in point.

The show concluded with agreement that progress on the issue in the South would be most likely to come from the leadership of southern race moderates. In summation, Redfield laid out this consensus statement: "We seem to agree that this racial discrimination is a great evil; that it is in conflict with our democratic principles; that that conflict was never more dangerous, perhaps, than it is today when we are so seriously at war; and that some solution must be found. The difficulty we have is that difficulty of making a reasonable-enough progress in the direction of granting to the minority groups the rights which they should have without, at the same time, endangering public safety by stirring up reactionary resentment and perhaps violence.

The consensus then, it seemed, was that this was a moral and political problem for the nation as a whole and that the war required that something *might* need to be done, perhaps by the federal government, provided it did not create reactionary violence among whites. That, of course, was the crux of the political problem of "the Negro"— what should be done, under whose leadership, at what pace, and with what resistance. The long-avoided *Round Table* discussion about "the Negro," mounted under the rubric of "minorities," had reached the heart of the racial dilemma in 1943.

Even with all of its limitations, this representational drama captured well certain shifts in white thinking on race relations that occurred during the war, in large part because of the increasing political visibility of African Americans. One was the idea that the war itself had nationalized the issue of race relations, especially in the eyes of the international community. The other was the notion that the federal government, and not just white southern leaders, had the authority and obligation to address the race issue. The political narrative on the race question was being reopened, although its ending was still far from being rewritten. On this broadcast, the solution to the question was represented as resting in the hands of southern white moderates; the power of Supreme Court intervention or the potential force of white resistance or that of the "Negro" race itself was missing both from this drama and from its expected denouement.

Round Table staff members had not misjudged the amount of interest a program about racial matters would draw, even one masked under the bland title "Minorities." Dryer reported that the volume of mail sent in response to the broadcast had been extraordinarily heavy, about 500 letters a day. To reassure his superiors, he emphasized that "only an infinitesimal percentage of the letters" had been critical. Most listeners had voiced enthusiastic approval, he explained, and he noted with some surprise that a number of the letters had come from black listeners.

The idea that African Americans also were listening to a political discussion show had not occurred to many people at *Round Table,* and this broadcast about the "Negro problem" had the ironic effect of making black listeners visible and enlarging the scope of the show's "imagined community" of listeners. Two prominent African Americans, Ira De A. Reid of Atlanta University and Claude Barnett of the Chicago-based Associated Negro Publishers, contacted McGill directly. Both recognized the political significance of the broadcast, but neither was satisfied with its content. Barnett thanked McGill for saying as much as he could to a broad national audience: "You must have known that many Negroes, as well as whites, north and south, some of whom are inclined to be apprehensive of the southern liberal's attitudes these days, were vitally interested in your pronunciations. On the other hand, they must have known that southern conservatives and demagogs were listening with equal attention and appreciated the necessity for careful statement on your part." Reid was more blunt about the show's weaknesses, concluding that the discussion about a remedy was "not very fruitful" because it was so limited, both in content and in duration. He urged McGill to "give this thing further 'airing' " in his daily *Atlanta Constitution* column. As Siepman at the OWI had warned Dryer, discussing a problem that had no current solution carried the risk of criticism, in this case from African Americans who found the program lacking in that regard.

The eruption of racial violence later in 1943 helped propel *Round Table's* return to the issue of race on a July 4 broadcast. Efforts to avoid controversy for fear of inciting racial tensions seemed moot at that point, so this discussion, unlike the earlier one, was more urgent and, as a result, more daring in tone and content. Under the title "Race Tensions," the show featured as panelists black sociologist E. Franklin Frazier and Carey McWilliams, a leading activist writer on issues of race and ethnicity. Robert Redfield, who had espoused the most liberal views on the previous program, made a return appearance, this time in company more in line with his own views.

Despite the generally favorable reactions to the earlier show on the "Negro question," officials at NBC were no less nervous about airing this second broadcast. Indeed, they were more anxious because of the decision to include a black panelist. On the Friday before the scheduled Sunday broadcast, Judith Waller, director of public service for NBC's Central Division in Chicago, phoned Dryer to warn him that many stations, mostly southern, had notified the network in New York City that they would not carry the program because they objected to the topic or "the participation of a Negro" or both. Waller said that "the South was 'irrational,' " but she insisted that a white southerner be added to the program or that the program be canceled. Dryer suggested that a southerner "introduce" the panel and the topic, an arrangement that was acceptable to NBC. NBC also approved the choice of University of North Carolina sociologist Howard Odum for that role.

Once again the white South was represented on *Round Table* by a racial moderate. In brief remarks broadcast from North Carolina, Odum opened the show by asserting "that our problem of the Negro in America is a southern and national problem." Odum urged "that America, and the South in particular, declare a moratorium on all violence." He ended with this plea: "[O]ur immediate problem here now is to covenant together for some new high morale on the part of all the people everywhere and for a master strategy for the better ordering of race relations in the war and the post-war period." It is difficult to imagine how Odum's remarks about a "better ordering of race relations" could have been intended to achieve the show's goal of appeasing the imagined southern listener. Presumably Odum's representational status as a southerner slurred the starker political implications of his words.

The discussion in Chicago then began in the same way that other shows that reacted to the race riots had begun: by tantalizingly drawing attention to the fact that the subject matter was considered "hot" and taboo. Redfield opened by admitting that some *Round Table* listeners had advised against broaching the topic, saying it was "too dangerous" to discuss (avoiding any reference to the fact that NBC held a similar view). Thus cued, McWilliams and Frazier reassuringly responded that the times demanded the attention and that, in Frazier's words, "an intelligent understanding of the situation is necessary for intelligent action." Redfield insisted that the "objective atmosphere of a university group" was indeed the best place for that discussion, laying claim to the show's special qualifications as an objective site and protecting it from attacks for broadcasting the issue.

McWilliams and Frazier both came prepared with demographic data about various minority groups, including their relative poverty in terms of health care, education, employment, and housing. Both also emphasized the impediments of the color line and, as Frazier described it, a "melting pot" that had "excluded the dark ingredients." McWilliams sought to set the record straight on the "**zoot-suit** riots," stressing that they were the result of attacks by white soldiers and sailors on Mexican Americans and African Americans and not the reverse. All of the panelists agreed that small steps toward advancement had come with the war but that it was that progress—and the potential for more—that was stirring up racial violence against blacks.

The panel advanced the idea that changes were necessary to address the problem of racial inequality. Frazier insisted that an end to segregation and the sanctioned inferior status of blacks was the first step. McWilliams and Redfield quickly agreed, and McWilliams argued that the Fair Employment Practices Commission (FEPC) be strengthened and a new federal civil rights statute be passed. But the question of how to bring about the changes in public attitudes necessary for federal action to end segregation stumped and silenced this panel of opinionated men. Indeed, this silence was telling, as the issue of segregation would continue to be an issue that divided blacks and white race liberals, especially southern moderate whites. Although most blacks, like Frazier, saw segregation as the primary issue, whites who considered themselves southern race liberals did not follow suit.

After the show had aired, officials at *Round Table* congratulated themselves for having balanced the concerns of network officials and "southerners" sufficiently to get the show on the air. But as Judith Waller had feared, some local stations had refused to broadcast the show: only 86 of the 100 to 120 affiliate stations that normally carried *Round Table* aired the "Race Tensions" show. Like the response to the earlier broadcast on minorities, however, the volume of mail sent in response to the show was heavy, about 1,700 letters, and again Dryer reported that most letters were approving. Dryer as usual tried to cast as positive a spin as possible on the overall response, but even he admitted that many less supportive listeners also had written in, almost all of whom were from the South. After reading a random selection of these letters, Dryer was shocked to find that almost all criticized "the Negro" because "he was a menace to white women." That topic certainly had not been discussed or alluded to in any way, but it was clearly on many southerners' minds as the unspoken and unspeakable implication of the changes in the racial order envisioned by the panelists. The mere advocacy of ending segregation was heard by these listeners as the equivalent to arguing for intermarriage.

This reading of sexual transgression was related to the political transgression of having a black man on the show as an equal participant with white men in advancing political solutions to the race problem. Indeed, the Tennessee father of one of Benton's neighbors registered a protest about the broadcast that captured just that sentiment. The man objected vehemently because "the colored participant addressed the other two participants by their last names without a 'Mr.' " Southern racial etiquette had been violated not only by Frazier but also by the two white men who allied themselves with him as coequals.

Frazier's presence on the show was as much an affront to prevailing racial etiquette as it was a divergence from familiar aural representations of African Americans; he was, after all, no Amos, Andy, or Rochester. Vigilant white listeners, ever on the lookout for blacks' assertions of social equality, heard such a claim in Frazier's voice, his erudition, and the assumption of his authority to speak forcefully on behalf of African Americans against segregation and discrimination. This was not a misreading or an overreaction on the part of those listeners, for they understood well that Frazier's presence represented a powerful symbolic shift. His arguments signaled that the prevailing political narrative about race was losing some of its potency and that African Americans, although long rendered voiceless, were laying claim to a place in that process. One supportive listener wrote Frazier that he had been listening to the show for many years, hoping to hear just such a discussion. He thanked Frazier for being such a "capable representative" and for his "profound and enlightening presentation," sentiments he also expressed in a letter to *Round Table*.

Dryer tried to protect Frazier from the racist remarks in some listeners' letters about the show. He thanked Frazier for his "excellent participation," but he was purposely vague in describing listener reaction, telling him only that the response had been extraordinary and that "most" listeners agreed that the show was among the most "stimulating and socially important." Dryer shared with Frazier his hope that "not too long a time will pass before you'll face our microphone again."

This hope would go unrealized. After these two shows in 1943, *Round Table* was almost completely silent on the subject of American race relations, despite the extraordinary public attention the subject received in this period. Indeed even the appearance of Gunnar Myrdal's *American Dilemma* in 1944 failed to motivate this "intellectual's radio paradise" to revisit the questions that had been so eloquently raised by panelists on its two broadcasts in 1943 and that were now encapsulated in Myrdal's encyclopedic treatise. Myrdal's book, like the two shows, had the effect of airing, describing, and validating the race problem, but both the book and the shows faltered when the discussion shifted to solutions.

Although it was no longer taboo or controversial to admit that race was a national political issue, the question of remedy or intervention remained as elusive and volatile as ever. Only when the federal government acknowledged in 1947 the need for a remedy would this series be drawn back to search for solutions in the political minefield of American race relations.

America's Town Meeting of the Air

America's Town Meeting of the Air, a New York City–based town hall–style political discussion program, had a much livelier and less pretentious tone than the staid academic atmosphere of *Round Table*. A descendent of the suffragist-founded League for Political Education, the town hall discussion meeting originated in 1921 and was brought to radio in 1935. Hosted by George Denny, a former drama teacher and professional actor, *Town Meeting* was intended to be a nationwide version of the old New England town meeting. Guests on the show debated controversial issues in front of audiences of over 1,000 people who were allowed to ask the panelists questions. As in *Round Table*, listeners could obtain weekly transcriptions of the program, which *Town Meeting* used in an aggressive public outreach campaign, actively promoting the use of its broadcasts and transcriptions in schools and the hundreds of listening and discussion clubs that gathered during the show's weekly broadcasts. The show also took to the road for half of the year, broadcasting live from cities around the nation. Although both *Round Table* and *Town Meeting* were broadcast initially on NBC, *Town Meeting* seemed to have enjoyed far greater independence from the network than *Round Table*, and for that reason, it followed a different path to the racial issue.

Panelists first debated the issue of racial inequality in 1941 on a show broadcast live from Birmingham, Alabama, on southern economic problems. Although Mark Ethridge, the moderate editor of the *Louisville Courier-Journal,* appeared on the show to cast the North as a colonizer of the South and to blame northern economic oppression for part of the South's problems, he also emphasized that he refused to defend the South for "the KKK, lynchings, floggings of union organizers, violations of civil rights," for poll taxes and white primaries, or for "imitating" Hitler. Columnist John Temple Graves admitted that the South had "sinned against the Negro," but he argued that the "number one problem of the Negro" was the "man across the sea," whom he called "the greatest race hater in history, the Jim Crow of all ages." This was as aptly ironic a description of Hitler as any. As argued earlier, Hitler's brand of white supremacy conjured up resonating visions of American white supremacy—for African Americans and here some southerners as well. Ethridge's reference to "imitating" Hitler and Graves's attempt to compare Hitler to Jim Crow only begged the question of why this American referent was so fitting in the first place.

An editorial in a Birmingham newspaper pointed to the broadcast with pride, calling it a "bloodless battle" of free expression and apparently attaching much significance to the fact that southern whites were willing to disagree with each other in front of a national listening audience. Similar conclusions were reached in an editorial in the newspaper at Birmingham Southern College, where the debate was held. In its extolling of the value of free debate, it barely hinted at the discussion of the economic plight of southern blacks, referred to obliquely as a "few local ills." The on-air discussion and these editorials showed how narrow the southern views on the race question were, even if they alluded to differences of opinion. That narrowness and those differences would drive southern political responses to the questions of racial inequality for the duration of the war and decades to follow. Most significant by its absence, however, was the voice of African Americans themselves, a point lost entirely on the editorial writers in their rush to celebrate the value to democracy of southern white free speech.

Attempts to move *Town Meeting* into a more direct confrontation with the race issue met with little success, and as on *Round Table*, radio officials looked to the federal government for guidance. In 1942, Denny proposed to Archibald MacLeish at the OWI that *Town Meeting* broadcast a program on "the Negro in the defense problem." Theodore Berry, the black lawyer working inside the agency to get radio programming about African Americans on the air, strongly advised MacLeish to encourage Denny. But *Town Meeting* never presented an episode on that subject, and indeed it is difficult to imagine how the series could have addressed such a volatile issue. Fairness would have required the presence of an African American and a government representative, and the broadcast could not have avoided confronting the paradox of fighting a segregated war for democracy. This was too much too soon for *Town Meeting*, as we have seen was the case for the duration of the war for the OWI.

Figuring out how to openly confront the race issue was a puzzle for *Town Meeting*, as it had been for *Round Table*. *Town Meeting*'s initial foray into the question of race also relied on the tactic of exploring a seemingly neutral subject, but the show was set in a more daring symbolic space. In May 1942, *Town Meeting* aired a show from the chapel of the premier black academic institution of the day, Howard

University. The show's guests were all black Howard faculty members: philosopher Alain Locke; Howard's president Mordecai Johnson; Leon Ransom, dean of the Law School; and Doxey Wilkerson, professor of education. In introducing these representatives of the black intelligentsia, Denny hastened to emphasize that although the panelists were all African Americans, they had been asked to deal not with the "race problem" but with the broader philosophical question, "Is there a basis for spiritual unity in the world today?" Despite the designated topic, to those eager to hear the race question aired, the site selection alone served as clue and cue enough, as it did for the panelists.

Locke and his colleagues took the show as an opportunity not only to discuss the philosophy of religion, which they did with vigor, but also to portray racism as an international ethical problem. Locke, for example, characterized as "poor seedbeds for world unity and world order" what he called the "superciliously self-appointed superior races aspiring to impose their preferred culture, self-righteous creeds and religions expounding monopolies on ways of life and salvation." Wilkerson was even more blunt, noting that "in this war in which colonial people play such an important role, the traditional relations of master and subject peoples are being altered. The chain of imperialist slavery tends definitely to weaken." Taking the point further, Ransom asked, "[H]ave we, Negroes and whites in this country, for instance, achieved any sort of spiritual unity? Are we not still enslaved by the idea that one must be dominant and the other the subservient group?"

The audience's questions generated responses from the panelists that were more wide-ranging than the initial discussion. One person asked: "[D]o you agree that the Negro has made his progress in America because of cooperation rather than through his opposed struggles?" Ransom's answer drew hearty applause: "[B]eing a realist, I am afraid that I must say that the Negro has made his progress in America *in spite* of the majority group."

The broadcast from Howard put African American intellectuals on display, where they embraced a cultural and political role, not just through the logic of their arguments but also through their aural presence as articulate, thoughtful representatives of the race. Operating in an educational forum, they could engage in a relatively free and protected level of political discourse. One paradoxical characteristic of the broadcasts from Birmingham and Howard was that the subject of race was being discussed by a group of whites and a group of blacks separately, although both groups were speaking to an integrated radio listening audience. Segregated arguments were being made but with no dialogue or dialectic. For *Town Meeting*, the subject still remained too volatile to be discussed by a mixed-race panel in any setting.

Although it had not yet broadcast a show devoted solely to the race question, *Town Meeting* had not shied away entirely from related controversial issues. For example, whereas *Round Table* resisted a request to deal with the poll tax issue, *Town Meeting* broadcast not one but two shows on the issue, including one with Claude Pepper, whom *Round Table* officials had specifically rejected. The series also aired discussions about problems facing other minority groups, such as the detention of Japanese Americans, the continued restrictions on Chinese immigration, and the prospect of Japanese assimilation. Plainly, the creators of this series viewed controversy as a way to sustain and build audience interest. Taboo subjects stir listener interest, and racial equality was still at the top of the list of such subjects, although that fact alone was not enough to overcome deep fears about how to address the issue more directly.

As was the case with *Round Table*, the escalation of racial tensions and growing political attention directed at African Americans finally drove *Town Meeting* to abandon its caution. Departing from its usual practice of presenting the week's debate topic in the form of a question, *Town Meeting* aired a show from New York City in early 1944 with the imperative title: "Let's Face the Race Question." Following the seemingly standard format for introducing shows on race at the time, Denny opened the broadcast by warning that "[t]onight we're going to discuss a question that is considered by some timid souls to be dangerous—the race question, more specifically, the Negro question." He predicted that there would be "no disagreement among our speakers that we have a race problem. The difference in opinion lies in the way it should be approached." Adding to the air of danger, Denny took the very unusual cautionary step of asking the audience "to refrain from applause or demonstrations of any kind during the program." Special care had also been taken to balance the presentation and debate. The show's panelists were well-known African American poet and writer Langston Hughes; Carey McWilliams, an effective progressive radio presence throughout the decade; John Temple Graves, again representing a white southern point of view; and James Shepard, the president of North Carolina College for Negroes, who expressed a more conservative black southern stance.

E. Franklin Frazier had broken the race barrier on *Round Table* the year before, but on the more relaxed and freewheeling *Town Meeting*, Langston Hughes launched a frontal attack on the race problem unlike anything heard on national radio before. He accused the country of treating black soldiers shabbily, of being "unwilling to provide more than inadequate Jim Crow cars or back seats in buses south of Washington for our own colored soldiers," and of undermining "the morale of Negro soldiers by segregating them in our armed forces and by continuing to Jim Crow them and their civilian brothers in public places." Hughes blasted opposition to social equality as a smoke screen for a profound fear of intermarriage, "as if permitting Negroes to vote in the poll-tax states would immediately cause Whites and Negroes to rush to the altar." That conception of equality, he concluded, had "nothing to do with the broad problem of civil, legal, labor, and suffrage rights for all Americans." What was needed was an "over-all federal program protecting the rights of all minorities and educating all Americans to that effect."

The voice of the South then rose to answer Hughes. John Temple Graves began his rebuttal of Hughes's performance with some drama of his own, silencing the audience to offer a prayer "that nothing tonight will increase the sum total of race hate in America." Graves argued again, as he had on the 1941 broadcast from Birmingham, that states should be left alone to deal with the race problem because "not all the laws this nation can pass, not all the excitement this Nation's race leaders can create, not all the federal bureaus laid end to end, can force 30 million white people in the South to do what they are passionately and deeply resolved not to do in race relationships."

Carey McWilliams took on Graves, countering that Americans "cannot solve this question even in their own communities until it is solved nationally, for the question has now become national in scope and effect, and it now falls full square within the field of federal action." His reading of the war's import contrasted starkly with Graves's plea for the status quo. McWilliams used Popular Front rhetoric to argue that the war was a "world revolution" that had "profoundly altered the relationships and factors involved in what we call the race question."

Members of the live audience eagerly pushed this frank discussion even further. One person asked Graves, "How can you expect the states down south to handle the Negro problem when these states are in the hands of men who don't represent the people?" Denny called that question unfair and excused Graves from answering it, but the very vocal New York City audience insisted on an answer. Graves did not deny that democracy had historically been restrained by race in the South, but he said that such restraints were necessary because blacks so outnumbered whites. McWilliams pointed out that "the Negro minority in the South is declining decade by decade" and asked Graves how much it would have to decrease to satisfy southern whites.

The broadcast generated a large volume of letters and would remain among *Town Meeting*'s most popular shows ever by that measure. The staff seemed relieved that there were so few negative responses to the program, credit for which rested with McWilliams and Hughes, both of whom had amicable styles that softened the political meanings of their arguments for some white listeners. After all, radio listeners heard tone as well as content in these discussions, and one could override the other. Hughes and McWilliams both had managed to project a nonthreatening tone even as they made fairly radical arguments in substance. Indeed, most listeners complimented the show for its fair discussion and the absence of bitterness.

Hughes's appearance sparked an outpouring of personal support from many listeners who valued his message and his tone. They wrote him directly rather than through the network to thank him and to commend his political courage. "Not only did you ably tell how and why Federal action would be more effective than the states in attacking the race problem, but you so intelligently discussed that delicate aspect of the problem 'social equality,'" one listener wrote; "[u]nlike some Negroes would have done, you did not evade that issue, you faced it and upheld it." Perhaps the letter that best captured the meaning of the broadcast for many black listeners came from a group of students at Spelman College: "Thousands and thousands of thanks. . . . As all of us students . . . huddled around the radio in our various dormitories here on campus tonight, we rallied and cheered you as you so frankly and beautifully spoke the truth on the 'race question.' Thanks a million for your wisdom in treating and combing out the kinks in our dear Mr. Graves' approach. . . . The questions of the audience certainly did 'stick him up'—It was so amusing." The managing editor of a black newspaper in Kansas City wrote him that "you did a swell job and I just wanted you to know that we out here in the Middle West enjoyed it very much." She also asked the question that may have been on many minds: "What percentage of the audience was colored and how many of those who asked questions were colored? We couldn't tell over the air."

Several white listeners also commended Hughes, one of whom thanked him for his "fine contribution towards a better understanding of one of America's greatest problems." A recent white immigrant from England congratulated Hughes and observed "that towards the negro question the Southerners have a blind spot, to overcome which nothing avails, neither argument nor logic, neither appeal to Christian principles nor appeal to national or self interest."

Hughes knew the power of radio and had repeatedly sought access to it, although with much disappointment. He had written poems and dramatic plays for radio but as a black writer had faced difficulties in getting his work aired. Indeed, in a 1943 *Chicago Defender* column, Hughes wrote a letter to "Southern White Folks" in which he subverted the usual "Negro problem" imagery to make a point about radio's refusal to broadcast more of his work: "I tell you, you are really a problem to me. I, as a writer, might have had many scripts performed on the radio if it were not for you. The radio stations look at a script about Negro life that I write and tell me, 'Well, you see, our programs are heard down South, and the South might not like this.' You keep big Negro stars like Ethel Waters and Duke Ellington off commercial programs, because the sponsors are afraid the South might not buy their products if Negro artists appear regularly on their series." Hughes recognized that the imagined southern listener was not the only reason or perhaps even the real reason radio executives were so reluctant to air more serious programming about race. Several weeks after his *Defender* column, he observed that during the war radio had become "fairly receptive" to presenting material about the "positive achievement" of particular African Americans, like George Washington Carver and navy hero Dorie Miller, but was still unwilling to air anything "setting forth the difficulties of the Jim Crow military set-up, segregation in war in-dustries, etc., and what people of good will can do about it." The fact that radio had "censored out any real dramatic approach to the actual problems of the Negro people" rendered the radio industry "almost as bad as Hollywood." African Americans, he wrote, continued to hold a deep disdain for radio's presentation of what he called "'handkerchief head' sketches" in which black stars usually were featured.

Fueled by his anger over radio's failure to treat the race issue, Hughes seized the opportunity to appear on *Town Meeting* to present his own political views. His appear-ance on this national broadcast also opened the way for him to undertake an extremely successful speaking tour that included sizable white audiences. As a result of the broad-cast, he became the first African American to be booked on a national tour by Feakins, the country's most well respected speakers' bureau. On tour for three months after the show, Hughes made over fifty appearances throughout the Midwest and the Southwest, addressing a variety of enthusiastic audiences, black and white.

Hughes's experience with the power of radio only fed his anger and disap-pointment over radio's failures on the race issue. "Considering the seriousness of the race problem in our country," he wrote in 1945, "I do not feel that radio is serving the public interest in that regard very well. And it continues to keep alive the stereotype of the dialect-speaking amiably-moronic Negro servant as the chief representative of our racial group on the air." Recounting that "liberal" network executives lacked the political resolve to air a dramatic series about African Ameri-cans that he had repeatedly proposed to them, Hughes concluded: "I DO NOT LIKE RADIO, and I feel that it is almost as far from being a free medium of expression for Negro writers as Hitler's airlanes are for the Jews."

Despite Hughes's continued disappointment in radio's treatment of the race issue, his appearance on *Town Meeting* had brought listeners face to face with the race ques-tion. The scarcity of listener protest eased the way for *Town Meeting* to tackle the more difficult issue of what to do about racial inequality. A discussion of the provocative question, "[S]hould government guarantee job equality for all races?," was aired in reaction to the ongoing campaign to make the FEPC a permanent agency.

What remains most remarkable about this 1944 debate is the fact that point for point the arguments made against a government role in helping African Ameri-cans obtain fair access to employment were exactly the same as those directed at federal affirmative action programs decades later. Opponents blamed affirmative intervention for creating the very bitterness and racial hatred that mandated the measures in the first place, as if race prejudice, discrimination, and segregation had no prior independent or enduring existence. For example, Texas congressman Clark Fisher claimed to support equal opportunity in principle but said he opposed any federal role in furthering it because it will "stir up race consciousness, bitterness, and intolerance." He preferred the current system, which allowed "the poorest boy in the poorest family if he will work, if he has the ability and the initiative, to lift himself to the very top." Journalist Ray Thomas Tucker made a corollary and very creative argument that the creation of a permanent FEPC would prevent African Americans from following the traditional difficult path to success of immigrants and therefore "will breed bitterness and racial hatred." Lillian Smith, the controversial writer and liberal activist, appeared in support of the FEPC, arguing that "it is the Government's job to protect the individual against those people who would endanger his basic right to work, just as the Government protects our safety on the streets and our health in epidemics."

This exchange captured well public disagreement about the role the federal government should play in protecting and furthering the access of African Americans to employment. But as in many of the *Town Meeting* broadcasts, the debate expanded when questions were taken from the 1,500 people in the audience and telegrams sent in anticipation of the broadcast. One leading question came from Mary McLeod Bethune, who wrote, "[C]onsidering the increased industrialization of the USSR, China, and India, will the U.S. be able to successfully compete for the postwar world trade without guaranteeing job equality for Americans of every race?" A person in the studio audience pointed out that blacks had already proven themselves capable of hard and ardent labor and yet they were still discriminated against in employment and therefore needed government help. Once again, *Town Meeting* staff were surprised by the degree to which white listeners wrote long "dissertations on their personal feelings about the Negro question," exhibiting "emotional reactions" that far exceeded the issue of employment.

Having faced one aspect of racial discrimination, *Town Meeting* turned to the broader question of racial injustice in a May 1945 broadcast entitled "Are We Solving America's Race Problem?" This topic generated passionate expressions of white resistance to the very idea of raising it for public discussion. Indeed, this would be one of *Town Meeting*'s most controversial and tumultuous broadcasts. The mere announcement of the topic drew letters of protest from white listeners, even before the show was aired. Many fear-filled letters came from outside the South, evidence in part that wartime migrations of African Americans had nationalized the race problem in many whites' minds.

These fears may have been amplified by Franklin Roosevelt's death and the growing anticipation that the war would soon end, although such concerns were not given direct voice in the letters. Several writers warned that the show was "playing with dynamite" and would only encourage more racial strife. Some listeners earnestly suggested remedies to the race problem, including the often-repeated idea that all blacks be relocated to reservations or separate cities, regions, or states of their own, with one writer suggesting that this be done "in the same spirit as Zionism." Another wanted blacks to have completely equal opportunities with whites in employment, education, and housing, provided that this could be done in away that would keep "ALL OF THOSE THINGS SEPARATE." The most colorful description of the race problem came from a man in Seattle who may have mixed metaphors but captured well the fears held to some degree by many people outside the South: "The Negro population, is like the Sahara Desert, advancing every year about a mile, with overwhelming and irresistible force. Only one thing can stop the Desert, by drowning or letting in the sea. . . . But you cannot drown America's

TOWN HALL
AND
THE BLUE NETWORK

PRESENT THE 371ST BROADCAST OF

America's Town Meeting

MAY 24, 1945

SUBJECT:

Are We Solving America's Race Problem?

SPEAKERS:

Affirmative:

IRVING IVES
*Majority leader of N.Y. State Assembly
and co-author of the Ives-Quinn Anti-
Discrimination Bill*

ELMER CARTER
*Former editor of the magazine "Opportunity"
and member of N.Y. State Unemployment
Appeal Board*

Negative:

Representative JERRY VOORHIS
Democrat of California

RICHARD WRIGHT
Author of "Native Son" and "Black Boy"

Moderator: **GEORGE V. DENNY, JR.**

PRE-MEETING: 8:00 P.M.   BROADCAST: 8:30 TO 9:30 P.M.

Announcement of an America's Town Meeting of the Air *broadcast, "Are We Solving America's
Race Problem?"* (America's Town Meeting of the Air *Collection, New York Public Library*)

no. 1 problem, the negro. We are saturated with an incurable cancer. It has been
allowed to go on so long, to operate now is impossible."

When the show was aired, these prebroadcast responses prompted Denny to
spread the responsibility for the choice of the topic, reminding his listeners that
their votes and letters "had put this subject near the top of the list of America's
major domestic problems." Richard Wright, one of the country's most powerful
black writers, and Elmer Carter, the black former editor of the National Urban
League's *Opportunity* magazine, took opposing points of view on whether the race
problem was being solved. Carter was paired with Irving Ives, the majority leader
of the New York State Assembly; on Wright's side was liberal congressman Jerry
Voorhis of California. Carter offered the more conservative black position that the
country was making progress toward racial equality, contrasting the record of the
treatment of blacks in World War I with that in World War II and also noting that
"the lynching record has almost been eradicated."

In sharp contrast to Carter's voice of moderation, Wright launched an aggressive and unrelenting attack on racism and its effects, overstepping the bounds of
politically acceptable discourse much further than had Langston Hughes the year
before. Wright's extraordinary use of language not only overpowered Carter's argu-

ments but also allowed him to dominate the program in a way that was utterly beyond the moderator's ability to control. Wright essentially reframed the entire debate and took over the show by asking:

> What do we mean by a solution of the race problem? It means a nation in which there will exist no residential segregation, no Jim Crow Army, no Jim Crow Navy, no Jim Crow Red Cross Blood Bank, no Negro institutions, no laws prohibiting intermarriage, no customs assigning Negroes to inferior positions. . . . Racial segregation is our national policy, a part of our culture, tradition, and morality. . . . We see reflections of it in our films and hear it over our radios. . . . Gradual solutions are out of date. . . . [H]ere is the truth, whites can no longer regard Negroes as a passive, obedient minority. Whether we have a violent or peaceful solution of this problem depends upon the degree to which white Americans can purge their minds of the illusions that they own and know Negroes.

Taking his argument a step further, Wright told his listeners that the "Negro has a sacred obligation and a moral duty to bring before the people of this country again and again and again the meaning of his problem," but, he added, "the fundamental problem rests upon whites and I believe that Negro protests, Negro agitation, should increase and become intense." In replying to a question about intermarriage prohibitions, Wright insisted that such laws should be abandoned because they were meaningless: "I was down in Mississippi in 1940 and I saw the streets thronged with Mulattoes in a state where you have an airtight anti-intermarriage law."

Wright's call for black agitation and his comments on intermarriage jolted white listeners across the country. Denny, who had been unable to harness Wright on the air, feared that a negative response might ensue. In an unusual step, the day after the broadcast he asked for daily verbal reports on letters received rather than waiting for the normal weekly written tabulation and summary. His fears were well founded. Not only did the show generate an extraordinary volume of mail, but it drew long, passionate letters from well-educated white listeners who heard Wright's spirited argument as a threat to the racial world as they knew it, regardless of whether they lived inside or outside the South. According to an internal report, listeners were "highly critical of Richard Wright's attitude" and deplored the airing of the discussion of intermarriage. A closer look at a sample of the mail reveals that this was an understated summary of the audience's reaction. Furthermore, these letters demonstrate the high levels to which white preoccupation with and fears about the race problem had risen nationwide by 1945. Again, this was a time when many whites were eager for normalcy after a war period marked both by southern black migration into areas previously without a visible black presence and by increasing expressions of black bitterness and anger, whether in city streets or under the sanction of radio forums like *Town Meeting*.

Wright's remarks about intermarriage sparked outrage, especially among white women. The year before, when Hughes had raised the issue, he had reassured whites that blacks did not want intermarriage but just wanted equal rights and equal opportunity. Wright inverted the entire question and ridiculed white men for their hypocrisy by citing his Mississippi example. White women attacked Wright for his obvious implication that mulattoes were the result of liaisons between white men and black women. One woman referred to the show as "revolting," and another reported that she had been "appalled" by what she described as Wright's demand for a "hybrid cesspool." Other women called Wright's comments a "disgrace" and warned that they would lead to lynchings and encourage the resurgence of the Ku Klux Klan. Indeed, white women listeners who wrote in seemed most concerned about defending the honor of their husbands, brothers, and fathers. Moreover, these women apparently did not oppose intermarriage as a way of defending themselves from imagined black suitors, as white men felt compelled to do on their behalf. Rather, in criticizing Wright's accusation that mulattoes were evidence of white male desire for black women, these white women revealed deep fears of sexual competition from black females, which might increase, they believed, if unions between white men and black women were sanctioned by law. In defense of white men, one woman from Detroit asserted that "I have never heard yet of a white man raping a colored woman." White men, of course, also had been angered by Wright's comments, and their letters were even less polite. One particularly vehement man from Houston accused all black men of wanting to rape white women and referred to Wright repeatedly as "that buck negro" or "that ignorant negro buck."

Many listeners, like those who had written letters before the show aired, offered as a solution to the race problem the idea of sending blacks away or somehow physically roping them off from whites. Some people earnestly suggested that African Americans be granted a homeland in the United States, be given a portion of the Pacific Northwest to settle, or be returned to Africa. One anonymous writer thought the only solution was to send all black Americans to Europe and to "exchange them for whites who would appreciate the advantage given them here, and eliminate these eternal race riots." Many whites still searched for a solution to the "Negro problem" that would not upset the racial status quo; they simply wanted the problem to go away, as had whites who had embraced similar schemes throughout American history.

While some listeners offered solutions to the race problem, others eagerly denied that there was a problem. One writer from Chicago explained, without intended irony, that the only problem was that African Americans had been exposed to too much "propaganda employing such words as freedom and equality." More predictably, some white southerners insisted that the problem was northern agitators themselves, dubbed by one person as "noisy mouthed reformers in the North" who were "broadcasting their views" and "trying to stir up unhappiness and discontent among our colored citizens."

Among the most interesting letters about the broadcast were those that revealed whites' anxieties that many blacks were no longer as deferential in their interactions with them as they used to be or ought to be. Some writers offered specific examples of increasing black arrogance and transgressions of racial etiquette, especially in southern border states and midwestern cities. One of the most telling letters came from a listener in Oklahoma who detailed what he called the "overbearing" ways in which blacks had begun to "push white people around." He complained that there was an "organized effort" among blacks "to make one day of the week a sort of 'push day,' on which the colored women of the town throng the places of business, and the sidewalks, just to shove white folks about." He warned that "once the war is over," blacks would be forced to "desist" from all such activities. A writer from Chicago reported that he saw blacks on streetcars and buses acting as if "they are better than the white." Another listener from Cincinnati complained of blacks' new "overbearing attitude toward white people."

These reactions of white Americans mirror descriptions of everyday acts of resistance waged by black working-class men and women in crowded and contested public spaces and in other interactions with white people during this period. They also represent white fears about any acts that appeared to be out of line with white expectations of black positionality, as was apparent in the spate of rumors of organized black resistance. "Race rebels" like Wright employed discursive and ideological tactics with the same effect in their intellectual encounters with white audiences. Wright's arguments on the broadcast served as further confirmation for whites that these acts of racial rebellion were not isolated but were likely to increase, and Wright himself provided a frightful personification of this change, all adding further fuel to white fears.

Many white listeners channeled their fury about Wright's arguments into an attack on *Town Meeting* for allowing him to be on a "nation-wide radio hook-up," permitting him such free expression, and not having a southerner to defend the "white" point of view or at least "some one well acquainted with the negro faults and shortcomings." One California woman complained that "the white man's mistreatment of the negro" was "not good material for radio comment," chiding Wright for even mentioning intermarriage, which she thought only worked to close the minds of the "millions of people" who were listening. One listener chastised Denny for his polite handling of Wright: "He should have been cut off the air—with apology to the listening audience."

Some considered Denny personally complicit in Wright's racial transgressions, specifically the fact that he referred to Wright as "MISTER"—a complaint similar to the one lodged against *Round Table* because Frazier addressed the white panelists without calling them "mister." When an established radio forum lent its credibility, respect, and reach to black intellectuals like Frazier, Hughes, and now Wright, many white listeners deeply resented the division in white ranks it represented and the breach in the sanctioned silence on racial inequalities they desperately desired.

On the other hand, some listeners, mostly black, wrote in support of airing the issue in such a forthright manner, many writing to Wright directly or through his publisher rather than through the network. The president of a black women's club in Mt. Vernon, New York, wrote: "I have never heard anything as well done as your expressions of last night at Town Hall. It was amazing and very much to the point." Among the most emphatic responses was a letter written to Wright on behalf of the black men assigned to the army air force's 477th Bombardment Group stationed in Kentucky: "All radios of this group were tuned in on the program, so keen is the interest. Especially did we enjoy the way you handled the $64 question. It always comes up and we were glad to hear you handle it as you did. From all of us thanks a million. That personifies our outlook. We do not *ask* for democracy we *demand* it. In order to make democracy work it must work for all not just a few 'Uncle Tom' leaders."

Other listeners also allied themselves with the thrust of Wright's overall views, often basing their arguments on contemporary examples. A black listener in Richmond asked: "[W]hy do Americans go 1,000 miles across the ocean to defend Democracy against the same evils as they are tolerating here upon our race?" The writer attached clippings about the police beating of a black soldier in Mississippi, inquiring, "[W]hy is it that the Secretary of War does not give our Negro in uniform the protection from white police officers and civilians wherever they may be?" Another particularly poignant letter asked: "How can we fight for the minorities abroad and keep our own in virtual slavery? If it is not corrected our boys will have died in vain." This writer recounted an incident in which Tuskegee airmen had to be partitioned off by a screen before they were allowed to eat in a public space shared by whites.

Others who agreed with Wright made their case on moral grounds. "In every important event in our American History," one listener wrote, "the negro has been present, taking part regardless of danger for his white countryman and country—and you can't overlook a people like that and still think you are right in doing so." A few white listeners wrote in asking how they could support African Americans in their struggle for racial justice. One writer wanted to know what groups she could join to help, and another asked, "[What] is there that we can do?"

Wright's controversial appearance on *Town Meeting* demonstrates once again the crucial cultural and political role African American intellectuals played in this period. Wright, Locke, and Hughes used their limited guest privileges on these political discussion shows to advance arguments too daring for most political figures to make, especially politicians who would have been featured on these programs. They offered a new representation of African Americans and their abilities, arguing point for point with whites and sparring as equals in the arena of political debate. On a medium that was ideal for the skilled use of language and oratory, these accomplished African American writers took on the duty of becoming public intellectuals, serving the race by fighting the battle of ideas that was essential to bringing about shifts in public opinion.

These men and others argued eloquently for an end to discrimination and segregation, but that goal was still not even rhetorically acceptable to the majority of white Americans in 1945. For that majority, the solution was to simply send the problem away or to continue to cordon it off. Until that view changed, there was little more that was politically safe to say. Silence on the issue of racial inequality set in again at *America's Town Meeting of the Air,* just as it had at the *University of Chicago Round Table.* Both of these important national political forums would confront the question of fashioning a remedy for racial discrimination and segregation only after the end of the war and after the insertion of a federal voice on the issue.

Additional Resources

Suggested Readings

Allen, James. *Without Sanctuary, Lynching Photography in America.* Sante Fe, New Mexico: Twin Palms, 2000. Stunning and horrifying photographs of lynchings collected by an antiques dealer along with essays by John Lewis and Leon Litwack.

Egerton, John. *Speak Now against the Day: The Generation before the Civil Rights Movement in the South.* New York: Knopf, 1994. A social and political history of the South in the 1930s and 1940s and of the Southerners who were active on human rights and civil rights issues.

Franklin, John Hope, and Alfred A. Moss Jr. *From Slavery to Freedom: A History of Negro Americans,* 7th ed. New York: McGraw-Hill, 1994. A comprehensive historical account of the African American freedom struggle to the present.

Foner, Eric. *A Short History of Reconstruction.* New York: Harper & Row, 1990. A first-rate history of the Reconstruction period.

Hale, Grace Elizabeth. *Making Whiteness: The Culture of Segregation in the South, 1890–1940.* New York: Vintage Books, 1998. A nuanced picture of segregation. It shows how the culture of the Reconstructionist South contributed to current racial attitudes.

Litwack, Leon. *Trouble in Mind: Black Southerners in the Age of Jim Crow.* New York: Knopf, 1998. A portrayal of the American South between Reconstruction and World War I.

Pfeffer, Paula. *A. Philip Randolph, Pioneer of the Civil Rights Movement.* Baton Rouge: Louisiana State University, 1990. A biography of the civil rights and labor leader who founded the Brotherhood of Sleeping Car Porters in 1925.

Sullivan, Patricia. *Days of Hope: Race and Democracy in the New Deal Era.* Chapel Hill: University of North Carolina Press, 1996. Illuminates the decades of the 1930s and 1940s that preceded the modern civil rights movement of the 1950s and 1960s, with an account of activists who brought the New Deal to the Old South.

Woodward, C. Vann. *The Strange Career of Jim Crow.* 3d ed. New York: Oxford University Press, 1974. A description of race and caste segregationist customs in the South before the modern civil rights movement.

Web Sites

www.search-beat.com/civilrights.htm

This Web site offers a comprehensive overview of the civil rights movement. It contains many links to civil rights organizations, museums, and college and university history departments with primary resource materials.

www.nps.gov/bowa/home.htm

This Web site created by the National Parks Service centers around the life of Booker T. Washington. Notes about a current archeological dig and research on Washington's life as a slave on a Hardy, Virginia, plantation make this site interesting. There is information about Tuskegee Institute.

www.blackbaseball.com

In the area of popular culture, segregation was nowhere more apparent than in professional baseball. Two parallel major leagues coexisted from the nineteenth century until well into the 1950s. This site demonstrates the separate and unequal culture of segregation through information about the Negro Baseball Leagues.

www.duke.edu/doubletake/cds/btv/

This site is part of a project of the Center of Documentary Studies at Duke University. The oral history project, "Behind the Veil" captures the experience of living in the segregated American South during the first two-thirds of the twentieth century.

http://memory.loc.gov/ammem/aap/timeline.html

The Library of Congress Web site presents a comprehensive timeline of nineteenth- and early twentieth-century African American history. Its African American perspective section offers a year-by-year documentation of significant events up to 1925.

Chapter 2

From Resistance to a Social Movement

Long before the African American struggle for rights became a mass movement, local resistance in black communities took many forms. Individual acts of resistance were common during the period of segregation. This chapter looks at some of the early twentieth-century civil rights efforts through individual acts, local organizations such as church groups, national organizations such as the National Association for the Advancement of Colored People (NAACP), and emerging leaders of these organizations. The first selection, Robin Kelley's " 'We Are Not What We Seem': Rethinking Black Working-Class Opposition in the Jim Crow South" (Reading 2.1) describes the daily acts of resistance and survival in the Jim Crow South. Living in a caste system that required conformity in the form of subservience presented a complex challenge for blacks. The Southern behavioral norms of obsequiousness along with unwritten race and gender "guidelines" made public organizing against Jim Crow difficult if not nearly impossible. Lynching was a reality black families had to recognize. Other reprisals such as losing one's home or one's only means of economic support succeeded in "keeping blacks in their place." Outward signs of consent and approval on the part of blacks were often balanced with individual acts of resistance. Beneath the "veil of consent" lay the hidden history of unorganized, everyday conflict waged by African American working people (Kelley 1993:76). Given the day-to-day struggle of life in a segregated society, black opposition to segregation took on creative and heroic forms.

The Growth of Organizations

Social movements are organized, collective activities aimed at changing or reforming institutions or the social order itself. Some promote change while others resist social change. Social movements—the environmental or women's or civil rights movement—involve many organizations, coordination, and mass appeal. All the participants tend to share the goals of change, although they may differ on strategies to accomplish those goals. Leadership emerges and a dynamic builds over time. The longevity of a movement, however, depends on many factors, including its rate of change and the ability of its participants to mobilize and organize. Furthermore, movement success is measured by the effectiveness of its opposition, be it open resistance or covert political maneuvering.

Formal or informal, organizations may have individual objectives and goals. For example, the NAACP, with its general goal of equality and specific legal strategy of attacking the separate-but-equal laws of segregation, is an example of an organization. Devoted to equality and civil rights, the NAACP was one of the first and most significant organizations in what would eventually become a mass movement. There were other organizations concerned with the civil rights of African Americans. In 1911 an interracial group from New York City formed the National Urban League (NUL) to aid black migrants moving to Northern cities. Primarily concerned with social work, the NUL was involved with student activism and the modern phase of the civil rights movement under the leadership of Whitney M. Young. The Congress of Racial Equality (CORE) was formed in the early 1940s by a group of pacifist graduate students at the University of Chicago. Led by James Farmer, this interracial group was committed to the tactic of nonviolent direct action to achieve racial equality. Another civil rights organization active from the late 1930s into the 1940s, the Southern Negro Youth Congress (SNYC), headed by Esther Cooper Jackson and James E. Jackson, did not survive past 1949. After the Montgomery bus boycott of 1955–56, a group of young Southern ministers formed an organization in Atlanta, Georgia, to foster a role for the black church in the civil rights movement. This organization, the Southern Christian Leadership Conference (SCLC), headed by Martin Luther King Jr., served as a regional coordinating group for a coalition of churches, civic leagues, and small, local civil rights organizations. College students founded the Student Nonviolent Coordinating Committee (SNCC) in 1960 at historically black Shaw University.

Organizations themselves, however, do not constitute a movement. The leap from individual resistance and specific organizational functions into a national mass movement did not occur until the 1950s. Elements commonly identified with the struggle for civil rights, including mass protest, legal action, and media coverage, apply to the modern phase of the African American fight for civil rights beginning in 1955. The notion of a movement—expanding, emotional, and attracting more and more attention—crystallized in the early 1960s. Nevertheless, the period preceding the modern phase is relevant to the history of civil rights and social change not simply as a precursor but as the early beginning of change.

NAACP (National Association for the Advancement of Colored People)

Most historians argue that the major organizational effort to fight racism and discrimination in the twentieth century centers on the efforts of the NAACP, the oldest and largest civil rights organization in America. Growing out of the principles of W. E. B. Du Bois's Niagara Movement, the NAACP was formed in 1909 by white progressives and blacks jointly. Some of the white founders included a wealthy Northerner, Mary White Ovington, a liberal Southern journalist, William Walling, and a grandson of William Lloyd Garrison, Oswald Garrison Villard. One year earlier, in 1908, a brutal race riot erupted in Springfield, Illinois, the home of Abraham Lincoln. For two days, a mob looted and burned homes of African Americans, lynching two blacks and driving hundreds from the city. The incident shocked Ovington, Garrison, and others into forming an organization to secure the basic rights to life and liberty.

Initially called the National Negro Committee, the NAACP and its workers were interracial. Whites, however, never ran the organization. Although it began as an elite group and continued to have the reputation of being an elite organization, the association reached out to thousands of blacks and liberal whites. The official newspaper, the *Crisis,* became the voice of the organization's goals.

Under the editorship of W. E. B. Du Bois, the *Crisis* became a leading publication devoted to African Americans. In the first issue, Du Bois stated that the *Crisis* would stand for "the highest ideals of American democracy, and for reasonable but earnest and persistent attempts to gain these rights and realize these ideals." One of the first objectives was an antilynching law campaign.

With the creation of a national office, the organization grew by establishing local branches around the country. The NAACP's goal of complete equality for blacks met with opposition in conservative white circles as well as with some blacks. The *Crisis* was denounced and banned in some cities in the South, and the organizing of NAACP branches in those cities carried the risk of violent reprisals.

The NAACP assault on racism and discrimination was directed at the legal system under the direction of Charles Hamilton Houston. While A. Philip Randolph and black labor advocated mass protest demonstrations, the NAACP pursued its work through legal channels. The key role of NAACP attorney Charles Houston as a social engineer in the assault on segregated public education is described by historian Genna Rae McNeil in "Charles Hamilton Houston: Social Engineer for Civil Rights" (Reading 2.4). Houston formulated a three-pronged strategy: (1) de-segregation of public graduate and professional schools, (2) equalization of white and black teachers' salaries, and lastly, (3) equalization of elementary and secondary school facilities. He and other NAACP lawyers developed a plan to attack segregation in the South; first in the border states, then, moving into the deep South, legal challenges to segregated education were initiated.

Two important legal decisions, one in 1938, *Missouri ex. Rel. Gaines v. Canada,* and the other in 1944, *Smith v. Allwright,* were significant victories for the NAACP's civil rights lawyers. In the *Missouri* case, the U.S. Supreme Court ruled that Lloyd Gaines, an African American, must be admitted to the University of Missouri Law School. *Smith v. Allwright* was an important civil rights victory. The decision overturned the use of the "white primary" by Southern states to deny blacks voting rights. Establishing primary elections from which blacks were barred virtually ensured that they were effectively disfranchised. Thurgood Marshall argued the *Smith* case, brought by a Houston, Texas, dentist. The legal victories in the high court culminating in the *Brown* decision of 1954 established a place for the NAACP in changing civil rights. *Brown* was to be followed by legislative successes leading to the Civil Rights Act of 1964 and the Voting Rights Act of 1965 (see chapters 3, 4, and 5).

The selection by Thurgood Marshall, "The Legal Attack to Secure Civil Rights" (Reading 2.5), is from a speech he made in 1944 outlining the legal strategies of the NAACP and the philosophies behind them. Citing the Thirteenth, Fourteenth, and Fifteenth Amendments, Marshall describes the legal basis of civil rights for all Americans. Furthermore, he calls for action to ensure that the few existing civil rights statutes be enforced and new laws be passed.

In the selection "The NAACP as a Reform Movement, 1909–1965: 'To Reach the Conscience of America' " (Reading 2.3), August Meier and John H. Bracey Jr. argue that although the NAACP reflected ideas of mainstream pro-gressivism, it was marginal to the Progressive movement (1890–1917). Relying on a moral appeal "to reach the conscience of America," the NAACP devoted enormous resources to gain the passage of a federal antilynching bill. The organization sought legal redress and legislative reform while protecting basic rights of blacks and bringing justice to whites guilty of mob violence.

Meier and Bracey explore a sociological question of how a reform organization interacts over a long period of time with its changing environment, to analyze the history of the NAACP. From the beginning, the NAACP established a goal of securing basic citizenship rights guaranteed under the Fourteenth and Fifteenth Amendments of the Constitution. Its tactics and strategies were flexible enough to meet the changing political and economic environment. For example, during the 1920s, the organization linked to the Harlem Renaissance by presenting awards to black writers. Incorporating cultural issues enabled the NAACP to expand its base and support in New York. The Great Depression shifted the focus to economic issues, throwing the organization into conflict with the Communist Party. Supporting organized labor and labor leaders such as A. Philip Randolph, the NAACP continued to expand its base in the North and in the South. Growth during the 1940s reflected postwar hope as well as support from the progressive community.

Nineteen fifty-four is a key year because after the *Brown* decision blacks felt they had achieved a legal standing in many areas. There was tremendous psychic energy stemming from the decision. "Free by '63" became a slogan to mobilize civil rights volunteers when Thurgood Marshall argued the Clarendon County case (see chapter 3).

The Church

In "Domination, Church and the NAACP" (Reading 2.2), Aldon Morris discusses a tripartite system of domination of white society over blacks in the South. In the areas of the economy, state and local politics, and personal life, state governments in the South dominated blacks. The racial caste system of the South was structured around segregation. Morris argues that, ironically, segregation facilitated the development of black institutions. In this context, "the black church functioned as the institutional center of the modern civil rights movement." It provided support and direction in all areas of black life. The growth in urban churches in the South reflected the rural-to-urban population movement beginning at the time of World War I. Consequently urban churches became organizations with emerging power. At the center of this emerging power is the black minister. Indeed, King himself is a major example of the local black leadership that emerged from the segregated cities of the South.

The black church and the NAACP both functioned as early institutional centers of the movement. Most of the early civil rights leaders were ministers and church officials. The public's association of the civil rights movement with leaders such as Martin Luther King results from a top-down approach to its history. King's charismatic speaking style and the media's response fitted together to offer structured news coverage and, until recently, a history that revolved largely around King. August Meier, in "On the Role of Martin Luther King" (Reading 2.6), challenges the top-down historical approach that portrays King as charismatic leader and others as mere followers.

Social Movement Theory

Classical collective behavioral theory maintains that collective behavior differs from everyday institutional behavior in that it arises in response to unusual situations. Collective behavior theorists recognize that organizations and planning occur in social movements, but these are by-products of movements emerging only in their later stages (Morris 1984:276). The figure below illustrates the collective behavior model.

Structural strain → Disruptive psychological state → Social movement

Although it helps in creating a paradigm to understand social change, this model falls short of explaining the civil rights movement. In *The Origins of the Civil Rights Movement: Black Communities Organizing for Change,* Aldon Morris writes that the civil rights movement was essentially a political phenomenon in that blacks were engaged in a struggle for power against whites. In this context, movement centers, strategic planning, organizing, charisma, and preexisting institutions were central to the civil rights movement in that they enabled the black community to effectively confront an entrenched opposition dedicated to keeping them subservient (Morris, 1984:277).

The theory of charismatic movements, developed by turn-of-the-century German sociologist Max Weber, suggests that at certain periods in history a charismatic leader and followers will emerge to challenge the existing legal-rational or bureaucratic functioning of society. The extraordinary personality of such leaders offers an unwritten appeal to followers (Weber, 1947:361). People follow charismatic leaders because of their vision, and such leaders emerge during periods of stress and crisis. This is relevant to analyzing the modern civil rights movement in that King fits this ideal personality type described by Weber. Morris argues, however, that King and other leaders facilitated the mobilization of the movement because they had both organizational backing and charisma. Hence, Weber's theory is useful in understanding the civil rights movement but only up to a point. Arguing that charisma as a social form already existed in the black church before the movement, Morris demonstrates that the civil rights struggle provided a larger stage for the further development of preexisting charismatic relationships (Morris, 1984:279). The potential for black churches to get involved with the movement was always there. Nevertheless, it was the task of the minister to make it happen. In this context, charismatic relationships had an effect on the emergence of a social movement. As for Martin Luther King, the issue is not whether or not he was a charismatic leader, but the effect that his charismatic qualities had on mobilizing and sustaining movement activities.

Drawing heavily on the resource mobilization model along with Weber's theory of charisma as an independent quality, Aldon Morris employs the indigenous perspective, which is concerned with movements by dominated groups. Resource mobilization theory emphasizes the resources necessary for initiation and development of social movements. A dominated group works to create and take advantage of social conditions to engage in power struggles with the dominant group. From this perspective, nonbureaucratic but formal organizations are often the most appropriate for wide-scale social protest because they facilitate mass participation, tactical innovations, and rapid decision-making. Both SCLC and SNCC are examples of these nonbureaucratic but formal organizations (Morris, 1984:285).

A Look at Two Leaders

A brief overview of the leadership styles of Martin Luther King Jr. and Ella Baker illustrates the complexities that emerged as the movement for equal rights gathered momentum.

Martin Luther King Jr.

At the center of the historical struggle is the potent symbol of Martin Luther King Jr. as the leader of the SCLC, the nonviolent direct action movement. The successful Montgomery bus boycott thrust King onto the national political scene. The direct action method of fighting segregation became identified with King in spite of the fact that the Congress of Racial Equality (CORE) developed it in 1942. In "On the Role of Martin Luther King" (Reading 2.6), August Meier adds that the idea of mass direct action by Negroes must be ascribed to A. Philip Randolph, the labor leader who first planned a March on Washington in 1941. Less well known were CORE's early beginnings, which, when considered along with Randolph's role, play a critical historical role. King's extraordinary appeal to blacks and whites combined with his sudden popularity placed him in the forefront of the movement. Moreover, King was able to raise money from sources outside the South.

The direct action method, however, became identified with the youthful Student Nonviolent Coordinating Committee (SNCC) after their sit-ins in 1960. More impatient and uncompromising, SNCC's rhetoric and actions reinforced King's image as a responsible, moderate leader on the national scene. King occupied a position as the "vital center" of the movement. This became apparent during the militant period of the 1960s. With younger, outspoken activists employing threatening rhetoric, King's moral tone gained him respect and stature with politicians and mainstream Americans. The critical role played by King was determined in large part by the events of the movement. For example, the Montgomery bus boycott thrust King onto the national picture as a young, highly educated minister. Identified as the leader of the boycott, King's speeches were persuasive in making arguments about strategies as well as in raising money. When he was arrested in Georgia during the 1960 sit-in protests, national press coverage blew it into a presidential election issue. Local civil rights leaders, who from time to time called on King for speeches to galvanize the black community, continued the movement in many Southern states. Increasingly, on the national scene, civil rights protest was identified with King.

Clayborne Carson's selection, "Martin Luther King, Jr.: Charismatic Leadership in a Mass Struggle" (Reading 2.7), points out that the King myth portrayed in the mass media departs from historical reality because far too much attention is focused on the exceptional qualities of a leader at the expense of social structural factors. Carson concludes that the movement depended on mass activism and not on the actions of a single leader.

Ella Baker

Largely overlooked by the media, Ella Baker is nevertheless an important civil rights activist. Traveling across the segregated South in the 1940s, she became director of branches for the NAACP in 1943. Her invaluable contribution to the civil rights movement was an organizing style that propelled ordinary people to seek solutions to their problems. She urged local people to explore their own resources to resolve the issues they faced and to create grassroots leadership. Her notion of "group-centered leadership, rather than leadership-centered group," consistently challenged the bureaucratic decision-making structure of organizations like the NAACP and SCLC. With a relentless emphasis on democracy, Baker urged the NAACP to recruit more low-income members. Charles Payne writes in "Ella Baker and Models of Social Change" (Reading 2.8) that in contrast to the more traditional form of leadership as moving people and directing events, hers was a conception of leadership as teaching.

She tried to avoid exerting too much influence on the young people of SNCC. The selection "Organization without Dictatorship" (Reading 2.9) recalls her adamant refusal to sanction the SCLC's attempt to influence students to become part of that organization.

Summary

Four factors: (1) NAACP legal attacks on segregated schools, (2) local Southern black resistance, (3) emerging hope and organizational activity among African Americans and, (4) the growing role of the federal government—all simultaneously cast an eye toward segregation and discrimination, aiming at institutional change of American society. The movement resulted from the mobilization of the black community, its institutions, financial resources, and grassroots leaders. The modern civil rights movement emerged from the overlapping interests of the national organization of the NAACP, local organizations throughout the South, regional organizations that coordinated attacks against segregation, such as SCLC, and Northern-based organizations including the Congress of Racial Equality and the National Urban League. The movement became locally and regionally based, not led by one national leader but by many, representing different organizations and working together to overcome racial inequality. Ideas for change—strategies, objectives, and goals—came from the bottom up as well as from the top down.

Key Figures, Terms, and Concepts

charismatic leadership
Garland Fund
Herbert Hill
Niagara Movement
Mary White Ovington
Progressive Era

reform movement
Julius Rosenwald
Scottsboro Boys
Joel Spingarn
Oswald Garrison Villard
Max Weber

Important Questions to Consider

1. How has the NAACP grown throughout the twentieth century? What goals and objectives were carried out in the early period?

2. Why did the NAACP fail in its attempt to get national antilynching legislation passed?

3. What makes Ella Baker's philosophy of organizing different from that of established bureaucratic organizations?

4. Why was the NAACP in the South closely tied to the black church?

5. The emergence of charismatic leaders within the black church proved beneficial to the modern civil rights movement. Discuss.

6. Many major civil rights campaigns were not successful locally but contributed to federal legislation. Describe this pattern of local failure and national victory.

"We Are Not What We Seem": Rethinking Black Working-Class Opposition in the Jim Crow South

Robin D. G. Kelley, professor of history at New York University, is author of Yo' Mama's Dysfunktional! Fighting the Culture Wars in Urban America.

Each day when you see us black folk upon the dusty land of the farms or upon the hard pavement of the city streets, you usually take us for granted and think you know us, but our history is far stranger than you suspect, and we are not what we seem.

> —Richard Wright, *Twelve Million Black Voices,* 1940

The Negro, in spite of his open-faced laughter, his seeming acquiescence, is particularly evasive. You see we are a polite people and we do not say to our questioner, "Get out of here!" We smile and tell him or her something that satisfies the white person because, knowing so little about us, he doesn't know what he is missing.

> —Zora Neale Hurston, *Mules and Men,* 1935

On the factory floor in North Carolina tobacco factories, where women stemmers were generally not allowed to sit or to talk with one another, it was not uncommon for them to break out in song. Singing in unison not only reinforced a sense of collective identity in these black workers but the songs themselves—most often religious hymns—ranged from veiled protests against the daily indignities of the factory to utopian visions of a life free of difficult wage work.

Throughout the urban South in the early twentieth century, black women household workers were accustomed to staging so-called incipient strikes, quitting or threatening to quit just before important social affairs to be hosted by their employers. The strategy's success often depended on a collective refusal on the part of other household workers to fill in.

In August 1943, on the College Hills bus line in Birmingham, Alabama, black riders grew impatient with a particularly racist bus driver who within minutes twice drew his gun on black passengers, intentionally passed one black woman's stop, and ejected a black man who complained on the woman's behalf. According to a bus company report, "the negroes then started ringing bell for the entire block and no one would alight when he stopped."

These daily, unorganized, evasive, seemingly spontaneous actions form an important yet neglected part of African-American political history. By ignoring or belittling such everyday acts of resistance and privileging the public utterances of black elites, several historians of southern race relations concluded, as Lester C. Lamon did in his study of Tennessee, that black working people "remained silent, either taking the line of least resistance or implicitly adopting the American faith in hard work and individual effort." But as Richard Wright, Zora Neale Hurston, and countless cases like those recounted above suggest, the appearance of silence and accommodation was not only deceiving but frequently intended to deceive. Beneath the veil of consent lies a hidden history of unorganized, everyday conflict waged by African-American working people. Once we explore in greater detail those daily conflicts and the social and cultural spaces where ordinary people felt free to articulate their opposition, we can begin to ask the questions that will enable us to rewrite the political history of the Jim Crow South to incorporate such actions and actors.

Drawing examples from recent studies of African Americans in the urban South, mostly in the 1930s and 1940s, I would like to sketch out a research agenda that might allow us to render visible hidden forms of resistance; to examine how class, gender, and race shape working-class consciousness; and to bridge the gulf between the social and cultural world of the "everyday" and political struggles. First and foremost, my thoughts grow out of rereading Herbert Aptheker's *American Negro Slave Revolts,* a pioneering study that is celebrating its fiftieth anniversary this year. In it Aptheker gave us a framework to study the hidden and disguised, not only locating acts of resistance and plans for rebellion among slaves but also showing how their opposition shaped all of antebellum southern society, politics, and daily life. Second, I am indebted to scholars who work on South Asia, especially the political anthropologist James C. Scott. Scott and other proponents of subaltern studies maintain that, despite appearances of consent, oppressed groups challenge those in power by constructing a "hidden transcript," a dissident political culture that manifests itself in daily conversations, folklore, jokes, songs, and other cultural practices. One also finds the hidden transcript emerging "on stage" in spaces controlled by the powerful, though almost always in disguised forms. The submerged social and cultural worlds of oppressed people frequently surface in everyday forms of resistance—theft, footdragging, the destruction of property—or, more rarely, in open attacks on individuals, institutions, or symbols of domination. Together, the "hidden transcripts" that are created in aggrieved communities and expressed through culture and the daily acts of resistance and survival constitute what Scott calls "infrapolitics." As he puts it, "the circumspect struggle waged daily by subordinate groups is, like infrared rays, beyond the visible end of the spectrum. That it should be invisible . . . is in large part by design—a tactical choice born of a prudent awareness of the balance of power."

Like Scott, I use the concept of **infrapolitics** to describe the daily confrontations, evasive actions, and stifled thoughts that often inform organized political movements. I am not suggesting that the realm of infrapolitics is any more or less important or effective than what we traditionally consider politics. Instead, I want to suggest that the political history of oppressed people cannot be understood *without* reference to infrapolitics, for these daily acts have a cumulative effect on power relations. While the meaning and effectiveness of acts differ according to circumstances, they make a difference, whether they were intended to or not. Thus, one measure of the power and historical importance of the informal infrapolitics of the oppressed is the response of those who dominate traditional politics. Daily acts of resistance and survival have had consequences for existing power relations, and the powerful have deployed immense resources in response. Knowing how the powerful interpret, redefine, and respond to the thoughts and actions of the oppressed is just as important as identifying and analyzing opposition. The policies, strategies, or symbolic representations of those in power—what Scott calls the "official" or "public" transcript—cannot be understood without examining the infrapolitics of oppressed groups. The approach I am proposing will help illuminate how power operates, how effective the southern power structure was in maintaining social order, and how seemingly innocuous, individualistic acts of survival and opposition shaped southern urban politics, workplace struggles, and the social order generally. I take the lead of the ethnographer Lila Abu-Lughod, who argues that everyday forms of resistance ought to be "diagnostic" of power. Instead of seeing these practices primarily as examples of the "dignity and heroism of resistors," she argues that they can "teach us about the complex interworkings of historically changing structures of power."

An infrapolitical approach requires that we substantially redefine our understanding of politics. Too often politics is defined by *how* people participate rather than *why*; by traditional definition the question of what is political hinges on whether or not groups are involved in elections, political parties, grass-roots social movements. Yet, the how seems far less important than the why since many of the so-called real political institutions have not proved effective for, or even accessible to, oppressed people. By shifting our focus to what motivated disenfranchised black working people to struggle and what strategies they developed, we may discover that their participation in "mainstream" politics—including their battle for the franchise—grew out of the very circumstances, experiences, and memories that impelled many to steal from an employer, to join a mutual benefit association, or to spit in a bus driver's face. In other words, those actions all reflect, to varying degrees, larger political struggles. For southern blacks in the age of Jim Crow, politics was not separate from lived experience or the imagined world of what is possible. It was the many battles to roll back constraints, to exercise power over, or create space within, the institutions and social relationships that dominated their lives.

Using this revised framework for understanding power, resistance, and politics, the following explores three sites of urban black working-class opposition in the American South in the early twentieth century: the semiprivate/semipublic spaces of community and household, the workplace, and public space. My remarks are intended to be interrogations that may lead to new ways of understanding working-class politics.

At Home, at Play, at Prayer

Several southern labor and urban historians have begun to unveil the hidden social and cultural world of black working people and to assess its political significance. They have established that during the era of Jim Crow, black working people carved out social space and constructed what George Lipsitz calls a "culture of opposition" through which to articulate the hidden transcript free from the watchful eye of white authority or the moralizing of the black middle class. Those social spaces constituted a partial refuge from the humiliations and indignities of racism, class pretensions, and waged work. African-American communities often created an alternative culture emphasizing collectivist values, mutuality, and fellowship. There were vicious, exploitative relationships within southern black communities, particularly across class and gender lines, and the tentacles of Jim Crow touched even black institutions. But the social and cultural institutions and ideologies that ultimately informed black opposition placed more emphasis on communal values and collective uplift than the prevailing class-conscious, individualist ideology of the white ruling classes. As Earl Lewis so aptly put it, African Americans turned segregation into "congregation."

Ironically, segregation facilitated the creation and maintenance of the unmonitored, unauthorized social sites in which black workers could freely articulate the hidden transcript. Jim Crow ordinances ensured that churches, bars, social clubs, barbershops, beauty salons, even alleys, remained "black" space. When southern white ruling groups suspected dissident activities among African Americans, they tried to monitor and sometimes to shut down black social spaces—usually swiftly and violently. During World War II, as Howard Odum observed, mere rumors of black uprisings made any black gathering place fair game for extralegal, often brutal invasions. More significantly, employers and police officials actively cultivated black **stool pigeons** to maintain tabs on the black community. Clearly, even if historians have underestimated the potential threat that rests within black-controlled spaces, the southern rulers did not.

Grass-roots black community organizations such as mutual benefit societies, church groups, and gospel quartets were crucial to black people's survival. Through them, African Americans created and sustained bonds of community, mutual support networks, and a collectivist ethos that shaped black working-class political struggle. As Elsa Barkley Brown points out in her work on Richmond, Virginia, mutual benefit societies, like many other black organizations, "institutionalized a vision of community based on notions of collectivity and mutuality even as [they] struggled with the practical problems of implementing and sustaining such a vision." Although the balance of power in these organizations was not always equal, with males and the middle class sometimes dominant, Brown demonstrates that within benevolent societies all members played some role in constructing a vision of the community.

Yet we need to acknowledge intraracial class tensions. Mutual disdain, disappointment, and even fear occasionally found their way into the public transcript. Some middle-class blacks, for example, regarded the black poor as lazy, self-destructive, and prone to criminal behavior. Geraldine Moore, a black middle-class resident of Birmingham, Alabama, wrote that many poor blacks in her city knew "nothing but waiting for a handout of some kind, drinking, cursing, fighting and prostitution." On the other hand, in his study of a small Mississippi town, the sociologist Allison Davis found that "lower class" blacks often "accused upper-class persons (the 'big shots,' the 'Big Negroes') of snobbishness, color preference, extreme selfishness, disloyalty in caste leadership, ('sellin' out to white folks'), and economic exploitation of their patients and customers."

To understand the significance of class conflict among African Americans, we need to examine how specific communities are constructed and sustained rather than to presume the existence (until recently) of a tight-knit, harmonious black community. This romantic view of a "golden age" of black community—an age when any elder could beat a misbehaving child, when the black middle class mingled with the poor and offered themselves as "role models," when black professionals cared more about their downtrodden race than about their bank accounts—is not just disingenuous; it has deterred serious historical research on class relations within African-American communities. As a dominant **trope** in the popular social science literature on the so-called underclass, it has hindered explanations of the contemporary crisis in the urban United States by presuming a direct causal relationship between the disappearance of middle-class role models as a result of desegregation and the so-called moral degeneration of the black jobless and underemployed working class left behind in the cities.

Such a reassessment of African-American communities would also require us to rethink the role of black working-class families in shaping ideology and strategies of resistance. Social historians and feminist theorists have made critical contributions to our understanding of the role of women's (and, to a lesser degree, children's) unpaid work in reproducing the labor power of male industrial workers and maintaining capitalism. Nevertheless, we still know very little about power relations and conflicts within black working-class families, the role of family life in the development of class consciousness (especially among children), and how these things shape oppositional strategies at the workplace and in neighborhoods. For instance, if patriarchal families enabled exploited male wage earners to control and exploit the labor of women and children, then one might find a material basis to much intrafamily conflict, as well as hidden transcripts and resistance strategies framed within an ideology that justifies the subordinate status of women and children. We might, therefore, ask how conflicts and the exploitation of labor power in the family and household shape larger working-class politics.

Indeed, in part because most scholarship privileges the workplace and production over the household and reproduction, the role of families in the formation of class consciousness and in developing strategies of resistance has not been sufficiently explored. The British women's historian Carolyn Steedman, for example, points out that radical histories of working people have been slow "to discuss the *development* of class consciousness (as opposed to its expression)" and to explore "it as a learned position, *learned* in childhood, and often through the exigencies of difficult and lonely lives." Likewise, Elizabeth Faue asks us to look more carefully at the formation of class, race, and gender identities long before young people enter the wage labor force. She adds that "focusing on reproduction would give meaning to the relationship between working class family organization and behavior and working class collective action and labor organization."

Such a reexamination of black working-class families should provide insights into how the hidden transcript informs public, collective action. We might return, for example, to the common claim that black mothers and grandmothers in the age of Jim Crow raised their boys to show deference to white people. Were black working-class parents "emasculating" potential militants, as several black male writers argued in the 1960s, or were they arming their boys with a sophisticated understanding of the political and cultural terrain of struggle? And what about black women's testimony that their mothers taught them values and strategies that helped them survive and resist race, class, and gender oppression? Once we begin to look at the family as a central (if not *the* central) institution where political ideologies are formed and reproduced, we may discover that households hold the key to understanding particular episodes of black working-class resistance. Elsa Barkley Brown has begun to search for the sources of opposition in black working-class households. In an essay on African-American families and political activism during Reconstruction, she not only demonstrates the central role of black women (and even children) in Republican party politics, despite the restriction of suffrage to adult males, but also persuasively argues that newly emancipated African Americans viewed the franchise as the collective property of the whole family. Men who did not vote according to the family's wishes were severely disciplined or ostracized from community institutions.

Black workers, therefore, participated in or witnessed oppositional politics—whether in community institutions or households—before they entered the workplace or the labor movement. Average black workers probably experienced greater participatory democracy in community- and neighborhood-based institutions than in the interracial trade unions that claimed to speak for them. Anchored in a prophetic religious ideology, these collectivist institutions and practices took root and flourished in a profoundly undemocratic society. For instance, Tera Hunter demonstrates that benevolent and secret societies constituted the organizational structures through which black washerwomen organized strikes. In separate studies, Michael Honey and Robert Korstad suggest that black religious ideology and even some churches were key factors in the success of the Food, Tobacco, Agricultural, and Allied Workers union in Memphis, Tennessee, and Winston-Salem, North Carolina. Brenda McCallum illustrates that black gospel quartet circuits were crucial to the expansion and legitimation of the Congress of Industrial Organizations (CIO) in Birmingham, Alabama. My book argues that black working people enveloped the Alabama Communist party with a prophetic religious ideology and collectivist values that had grown out of black communities. The subcultures of working people do not always or automatically suffuse formal working-class organizations. The relationship is **dialectical**; the political culture that permeated labor organizations, including radical left-wing movements, often conflicted with aspects of working-class culture. The question historians might explore is whether certain interracial labor organizations were unable to mobilize sufficient black support because they failed to work through black community institutions or to acknowledge, if not to embrace, the cultural values of the African-American working class.

Much of southern black working-class culture falls outside "conventional" labor history, in part because historians have limited their scope to public action and formal organization. Part of the problem is that those who frequented the places of rest, relaxation, recreation, and restoration rarely maintained archives or recorded the everyday conversations and noises that filled the bars, dance halls, blues clubs, barbershops, beauty salons, and street corners of the black community. Nevertheless, folklorists, anthropologists, oral historians, musicians, and writers fascinated by "Negro life" preserved cultural texts that allow scholars access to the hidden transcript. Using those texts, pioneering scholars and critics, including Amiri Baraka, Lawrence Levine, and Sterling Stuckey, have demonstrated that African-American working people created an oppositional culture that represents at least a partial rejection of the dominant ideology and that was forged in the struggle against class and racial domination. The challenge for southern labor historians is to determine how this rich expressive culture—which was frequently at odds with formal working-class institutions—shaped and reflected black working-class opposition.

Even modes of leisure could undergird opposition. Of course, black working-class popular culture was created more to give pleasure than to challenge or explain domination. But people thought before they acted, and what they thought shaped, and was shaped by, cultural production and consumption. Moreover, for members of a class whose long workdays were spent in backbreaking, low-paid wage work in settings pervaded by racism, the places where they played were more than relatively free spaces in which to articulate grievances and dreams. They were places that enabled African Americans to take back their bodies, to recuperate, to be together. Two of the most popular sites were dance halls and blues clubs. Despite opposition from black religious leaders and segments of the black middle class, as well as many white employers, black working people of both sexes shook, twisted, and flaunted their overworked bodies, drank, talked, flirted and—in spite of occasional fights—reinforced their sense of community. Whether it was the call and response of a blues man's lyrics or the sight of hundreds moving in unison on a hardwood dance floor, the form and content of such leisure activities were unmistakably collective.

Much African-American popular culture can be characterized as alternative rather than oppositional. Most people went to parties, dances, and clubs to escape from the world of assembly lines, relief lines, and color lines and to leave momentarily the individual and collective battles against racism, sexism, and material deprivation. But their search for the sonic, visceral pleasures of music and fellowship, for the sensual pleasures of food, drink, and dancing was not just about escaping the vicissitudes of southern life. They went with people who had a shared knowledge of cultural forms, people with whom they felt kinship, people with whom they shared stories about the day or the latest joke, people who shared a vernacular whose grammar and vocabulary struggled to articulate the beauty and burden of their lives. Places of leisure allowed freer sexual expression, particularly for women, whose sexuality was often circumscribed by employers, family members, the law, and the fear of sexual assault in a society with few protections for black women. Knowing what happens in these spaces of pleasure can help us understand the solidarity black people have shown at political mass meetings, illuminate the bonds of fellowship one finds in churches and voluntary associations, and unveil the *conflicts* across class and gender lines that shape and constrain these collective struggles.

When we consider the needs of employers and the dominance of the Protestant work ethic in American culture, these events were resistive, though not consciously. Speaking of the African diaspora in general, and that in Britain in particular, cultural critic Paul Gilroy argues that black working people who spent time and precious scarce money at the dance halls, blues clubs, and house parties "see waged work as itself a form of servitude. At best, it is viewed as a necessary evil and is sharply counterposed to the more authentic freedoms that can only be enjoyed in nonwork time. The black body is here celebrated as an instrument of pleasure rather than an instrument of labor. The nighttime becomes the right time and the space allocated for recovery and recuperation is assertively and provocatively occupied by the pursuit of leisure and pleasure."

In southern cities where working-class blacks set Friday and Saturday nights aside for the "pursuit of leisure and pleasure," some of the most intense skirmishes between such blacks and authority erupted during and after weekend gatherings. During World War II in Birmingham, for example, racial conflicts on public transportation on Friday and Saturday nights were commonplace; many of the incidents involved black youths returning from dances and parties. The young men and women who rode public transportation in groups were energized by a sense of social solidarity rooted in a shared culture, common friends, and generational identity, not to mention naïveté as to the possible consequences of "acting up" in white-dominated public space. Leaving social sites that had reinforced a sense of collectivity, sometimes feeling the effects of alcohol and reefer, many young black passengers were emboldened. On the South Bessemer line, which passed some of the popular black dance halls, white passengers and operators dreaded the "unbearable" presence of large numbers of African Americans who "pushed and shoved" white riders at will. As one conductor noted, "negroes are rough and boisterous when leaving down town dances at this time of night."

The nighttime also afforded black working people the opportunity to become something other than workers. In a world where clothes signified identity and status, "dressing up" was a way of shedding the degradation of work and collapsing status distinctions between themselves and their oppressors. As one Atlanta domestic worker remembers, the black business district of Auburn Avenue was "where we dressed up, because we couldn't dress up during the day. . . . We'd dress up and put on our good clothes and go to the show on Auburn Avenue. And you were going places. It was like white folks' Peachtree." Seeing oneself and others "dressed up" was important to constructing a collective identity based on something other than wage work, presenting a public challenge to the dominant stereotypes of the black body, and shoring up a sense of dignity that was perpetually under assault. In these efforts to re-present the body through dress, African Americans wielded a double-edged sword, since the styles they adopted to combat racism all too frequently reinforced, rather than challenged, bourgeois notions of respectability. Yet, by their dress as by their leisure, black people took back their bodies.

Clothing, as a badge of oppression or an act of transgression, is crucial to understanding opposition by subordinate groups. Thus black veterans were beaten and lynched for insisting on wearing their military uniforms in public. A less-known but equally potent example is the **zoot suit**, which became popular during World War II. While the suit itself was not created and worn as a direct political statement, the language and culture of zoot suiters emphasized ethnic identity and rejected subservience. Young black males created a fast-paced, improvisational language that sharply contrasted with the passive stereotype of the stuttering, tongue-tied Sambo, and whereas whites commonly addressed them as "boy," zoot suiters made a fetish of calling each other "man." The zoot suiters constructed an identity in which their gendered and racial meanings were inseparable; they opposed racist oppression through public displays of masculinity. Moreover, because fabric rationing regulations instituted by the War Productions Board forbade the sale and manufacturing of zoot suits, wearing the suit (which had to be purchased through informal networks) was seen by white servicemen as a pernicious act of anti-Americanism—a view compounded by the fact that most zoot suiters were able-bodied men who refused to enlist or found ways to dodge the draft. A Harlem zoot suiter interviewed by black social psychologist Kenneth Clark declared to the scholarly audience for whom Clark's research was intended: "By [the] time you read this I will be fighting for Uncle Sam, the bitches, and I do not like it worth a dam. I'm not a spy or a saboteur, but I don't like goin' over there fightin' for the white man—so be it." It is not a coincidence that whites who assaulted black and Chicano zoot suiters across the country during the fateful summer of 1943 took great pains to strip the men or mutilate the suits.

While no one, to my knowledge, has investigated zoot suiters in the South, they undoubtedly were a presence on the wartime urban landscape. As Howard Odum observed during the early 1940s, the mere image of these draped-shape-clad hipsters struck fear into the hearts of many white southerners. On Birmingham's already overcrowded buses and streetcars during World War II, some of these zooted "baaad niggers" put on outrageous public displays of resistance that left witnesses in awe, though their transgressive acts did not lead directly to improvements in conditions, nor were they intended to. Some boldly sat down next to white female passengers and challenged operators to move them, often with knife in hand. Others refused to pay their fares or simply picked fights with bus drivers or white passengers. Nevertheless, like the folk hero himself, the Stagolee-type rebel was not always admired by other working-class black passengers. Some were embarrassed by his actions; the more sympathetic feared for his life. Black passengers on the Pratt-Ensley streetcar in 1943, for example, told a rebellious young man who was about to challenge the conductor to a fight "to hush before he got killed." Besides, black hipsters were hardly social bandits. Some were professional hustlers whose search for pleasure and avoidance of waged labor often meant exploiting the exploited. Black hustlers took pride in their ability to establish parasitical relationships with women wage earners or sex workers, and those former hipsters who recorded memories in print wrote quite often of living off women, in many cases by outright pimping. The black male hipsters of the zoot suit generation remind us that the creation of an alternative culture can simultaneously challenge *and* reinforce existing power relations.

Lastly, I want to briefly leap from the "bad," lawless, secular world to the sacred—a realm of practice to which historians have paid great attention. Despite the almost axiomatic way the church becomes central to black working-class culture and politics, religion is almost always treated simply as culture, ideology, and organization. We need to recognize that the sacred and the spirit world were also often understood and invoked by African Americans as weapons to protect themselves or to attack others. How do historians make sense of, say, conjure as a strategy of resistance, retaliation, or defense in the daily lives of some working-class African Americans? How do we interpret divine intervention, especially when one's prayers are *answered?* How does the belief that God is by one's side affect one's willingness to fight with police, leave an abusive relationship, stand up to a foreman, participate in a strike, steal, or break tools? Can a sign from above, a conversation with a ghost, a spell cast by an enemy, or talking in tongues unveil the hidden transcript? If a worker turns to a root doctor or prayer rather than to a labor union to make an employer less evil, is that "false consciousness"? These are not idle questions. Most of the oral narratives and memoirs of southern black workers speak of such events or moments as having enormous material consequences. Of course, reliance on the divine or on the netherworlds of conjure was rarely, if ever, the only resistance or defense strategy used by black working people, but in their minds, bodies, and social relationships this was real power—power of which neither the CIO, the Populists, nor the National Association for the Advancement of Colored People (NAACP) could boast. With the exception of Vincent Harding, no historian that I know of since W. E. B. Du Bois has been bold enough to assert a connection between the spirit and spiritual world of African Americans and political struggle. Anticipating his critics, Du Bois in *Black Reconstruction* boldly considered freed people's narratives of divine intervention in their emancipation and, in doing so, gave future historians insight into an aspect of African-American life that cannot be reduced to "culture": "Foolish talk, all of this, you say, of course; and that is because no American now believes in his religion. Its facts are mere symbolism; its relevation vague generalities; its ethics a matter of carefully balanced gain. But to most of the four million black folk emancipated by civil war, God was real. They knew Him. They had met Him personally in many a wild orgy of religious frenzy, or in the black stillness of the night."

At the Point of Production

Nearly a quarter of a century ago, as Herbert Gutman was poised to lead a revolution in the study of labor in the United States, George Rawick published an obscure article that warned against treating the history of working-class opposition as merely the history of trade unions or other formal labor organizations. If we are to locate working-class resistance, Rawick insisted, we need to know "how many man hours were lost to production because of strikes, the amount of equipment and material destroyed by industrial sabotage and deliberate negligence, the amount of time lost by absenteeism, the hours gained by workers through the slowdown, the limiting of the speed-up of the productive apparatus through the working class's own initiative." Unfortunately, few southern labor historians have followed Rawick's advice. Missing from most accounts of southern labor struggles are the ways unorganized working people resisted the conditions of work, tried to control the pace and amount of work, and carved out a modicum of dignity at the workplace.

Not surprisingly, studies that seriously consider the sloppy, undetermined, everyday nature of workplace resistance have focused on workers who face considerable barriers to traditional trade union organization. Black domestic workers devised a whole array of creative strategies, including slowdowns, theft (or "pan-toting"), leaving work early, or quitting, in order to control the pace of work, increase wages, compensate for underpayment, reduce hours, and seize more personal autonomy. These individual acts often had a collective basis that remained hidden from their employers. Black women household workers in the urban South generally abided by a code of ethics or established a blacklist so they could collectively avoid employers who had proved unscrupulous, abusive, or unfair. In the factories, such strategies as feigning illness to get a day off, slowdowns, sometimes even sabotage often required the collective support of co-workers. Studies of black North Carolina tobacco workers by Dolores Janiewski and Robert Korstad reveal a wide range of clandestine, yet collective strategies to control the pace of work or to strike out against employers. When black women stemmers had trouble keeping up with the pace, black men responsible for supplying tobacco to them would pack the baskets more loosely than usual. Among black women who operated stemmer machines, when one worker was ill, other women would take up the slack rather than call attention to her inability to handle her job, which could result in lost wages or dismissal.

Theft at the workplace was a common form of working-class resistance, and yet the relationship between pilfering—whether of commodities or of time—and working-class opposition has escaped the attention of most historians of the African-

American working class, except in slavery studies and the growing literature on domestic workers. Any attempt to understand the relationship between theft and working-class opposition must begin by interrogating the dominant view of "theft" as deviant, criminal behavior. From the vantage point of workers, as several criminologists have pointed out, theft at the workplace is a strategy to recover unpaid wages or to compensate for low wages and mistreatment. Washerwomen in Atlanta and other southern cities, Hunter points out, occasionally kept their patrons' clothes "as a weapon against individual employers who perpetuated injustices or more randomly against an oppressive employing class." In the tobacco factories of North Carolina, black workers not only stole cigarettes and chewing tobacco (which they usually sold or bartered at the farmers' market) but, in Durham at least, also figured out a way to rig the clock in order to steal time. In the coal mines of Birmingham and Appalachia, miners pilfered large chunks of coke and coal for their home ovens. Black workers sometimes turned to theft as a means of contesting the power public utilities had over their lives. During the Great Depression, for example, jobless and underemployed working people whose essential utilities had been turned off for nonpayment stole fuel, water, and electricity: They appropriated coal, drew free electricity by tapping power lines with copper wires, illegally turned on water mains, and destroyed vacant homes for firewood.

Unfortunately, we know very little about black workplace theft in the twentieth-century South and even less about its relationship in working-class opposition. Historians might begin to explore, for example, what Michel de Certeau calls "wigging," employees' use of company time and materials for their own purposes (for example, repairing or making a toy for one's child or writing love letters). By using part of the workday in this manner, workers not only take back precious hours from their employers but resist being totally subordinated to the needs of capital. The worker takes some of that labor power and spends it on herself or her family. One might imagine a domestic who seizes time from work to read books from her employer's library. In a less creative, though more likely, scenario, washerwomen wash and iron their families' clothes along with their employers'.

A less elusive form of resistance is sabotage. Although the literature is nearly silent on industrial sabotage in the South, especially acts committed by black workers, it existed. Korstad's study of tobacco workers in Winston-Salem introduces us to black labor organizer Robert Black, who admitted using sabotage to counter speedups:

> These machines were more delicate, and all I had to do was feed them a little faster and overload it and the belts would break. When it split you had to run the tobacco in reverse to get it out, clean the whole machine out and then the mechanics would have to come and take all the broken links out of the belt. The machine would be down for two or three hours and I would end up running less tobacco than the old machines. We had to use all kind of techniques to protect ourselves and the other workers.

Historians provide ample evidence that domestic workers adopted sabotage techniques more frequently than industrial workers. There is evidence of household workers scorching or spitting in food, damaging kitchen utensils, and breaking household appliances, but employers and white contemporaries generally dismissed these acts as proof of black moral and intellectual inferiority. Testifying on the "servant problem" in the South, a frustrated employer remarked: "the washerwomen . . . badly damaged clothes they work on, iron-rusting them, tearing them, breaking off buttons, and burning them brown; and as for starch!—Colored cooks, too, generally abuse stoves, suffering them to get clogged with soot, and to 'burn out' in half the time they ought to last."

These examples are rare exceptions, however, for workplace theft and sabotage in the urban south has been all but ignored by labor historians. Given what we know of the pervasiveness of these strategies in other parts of the world and among slaves as well as rural African Americans in the postbellum period, the absence of accounts of similar clandestine activity by black industrial workers is surprising. Part of the reason, I think, lies in southern labor historians' noble quest to redeem the black working class from racist stereotypes. In addition, company personnel records, police reports, mainstream white newspaper accounts, and correspondence have left us with a somewhat serene portrait of black folks who only occasionally deviate from what I like to call the "cult of true Sambohood." The safety and ideological security of the South required that pilfering, slowdowns, absenteeism, tool breaking, and other acts of black working-class resistance be turned into ineptitude, laziness, shiftlessness, and immorality. But rather than reinterpret these descriptions of black working-class behavior, sympathetic labor historians are often too quick to invert the images, remaking the black proletariat into the hardest working, thriftiest, most efficient labor force around. Historians too readily naturalize the Protestant work ethic and project onto black working people as a whole the ideologies of middle-class and prominent working-class blacks. But if we regard most work as alienating, especially work done amid racist and sexist oppression, then a crucial aspect of black working-class struggle is to minimize labor with as little economic loss as possible. Let us recall one of Du Bois's many beautiful passages from *Black Reconstruction:* "All observers spoke of the fact that the slaves were slow and churlish; that they wasted material and malingered at their work. Of course they did. This was not racial but economic. It was the answer of any group of laborers forced down to the last ditch. They might be made to work continuously but no power could make them work well."

Traditional documents, if used imaginatively, can be especially useful for reconstructing the ways in which workers exploited racial stereotypes to control the pace of work. Materials that describe "unreliable," "shiftless," or "ignorant" black workers should be read as more than vicious, racist commentary on African Americans; in many instances these descriptions are employers', foremen's, and managers' social reconstruction of the meaning of working-class self-activity, which they not only misunderstood but were never supposed to understand. Fortunately, many southern black workers understood the cult of true Sambohood all too well, and at times they used the contradictions of racist ideology to their advantage. In certain circumstances, their inefficiency and penchant for not following directions created havoc and chaos for industrial production or the smooth running of a household. And all the while the appropriate grins, shuffles, and "yassums" served to mitigate potential punishment.

Among workers especially, the racial stereotypes associated with industrial disruption were also gendered. As David Roediger has demonstrated in a penetrating essay, Covington Hall and the Brotherhood of Timber Workers (BTW) in Louisiana understood sabotage as a direct, militant confrontation with the lumber companies rather than an evasive strategy. As a native southern white leader of the working class, born of privilege, Hall sought to use appeals to "manhood" to build biracial unity. His highly gendered rhetoric, which insisted that there were no "Niggers" or "white trash"—only MEN—had the effect of turning clandestine tactics into direct confrontation. Roediger writes, "it is hard to believe the zeal with which [sabotage] was propagandized was not intensified by the tremendous emphasis on manhood, in part as a way to disarm race, in BTW thinking. . . . Hall's publications came to identify sabotage with the improbable image of the rattlesnake, not the black cat symbolizing the tactic elsewhere."

Yet, despite Hall's efforts, employers and probably most workers continued to view what black male workers in the lumber industry were doing as less than manly—indeed, as proof of their inferiority at the workplace and evidence that they should be denied upward mobility and higher wages. Thus, for some black male industrial workers, efficiency and the work ethic were sometimes more effective as signifiers of manliness than sabotage and foot dragging. As Joe Trotter's powerful new book on African Americans in southern West Virginia reminds us, theft, sabotage, and slowdowns were two-edged weapons that, more often than not, reinforced the subordinate position of black coal miners in a racially determined occupational hierarchy. As he explains, "Job performance emerged as one of the black miners' most telling survival mechanisms. To secure their jobs, they resolved to provide cooperative, efficient, and productive labor." Their efficient labor was a logical response to a rather limited struggle for job security and advancement since their subordination to specific tasks and pay scales were based, at least ostensibly, on race alone. More than a few black workers seemed to believe that a solid work record would eventually topple the racial ceiling on occupational mobility. Obviously, efficiency did not always lead to improved work conditions, nor did sabotage and foot dragging always go unnoticed or unpunished. What we need to know is why certain occupations seemed more conducive to particular strategies. Was efficiency more prevalent in industries where active, interracial trade unions at least occasionally challenged racially determined occupational ceilings (for example, coal mining)? Did extensive workplace surveillance deter sabotage and theft? Were black workers less inclined toward sabotage when disruptions made working conditions more difficult or dangerous for fellow employees? Were evasive strategies more common in service occupations? These questions need to be explored in greater detail. They suggest, as British labor historian Richard Price has maintained, that to understand strategies of resistance thoroughly we need to explore with greater specificity the character of subordination at the workplace.

Nevertheless, the relative absence of resistance at the point of production does not mean that workers acquiesced or accommodated to the conditions of work. On the contrary, the most pervasive form of black protest was simply to leave. Central to black working-class infrapolitics was mobility, for it afforded workers relative freedom to escape oppressive living and working conditions and power to negotiate better working conditions. Of course, one could argue that in the competitive context of industrial capitalism—North and South—some companies clearly benefited from such migration since wages for blacks remained comparatively low no matter where black workers ended up. But the very magnitude of working-class mobility weakens any thesis that southern black working-class politics was characterized by accommodationist thinking. Besides, there is plenty of evidence to suggest that a significant portion of black migrants, especially black emigrants to Africa and the Caribbean, were motivated by a desire to vote, to provide a better education for their children, or to live in a setting in which Africans or African Americans exercised power. The ability to move represented a crucial step toward empowerment and self-determination; employers and landlords understood this, which explains why so much energy was expended limiting labor mobility and redefining migration as "shiftlessness," "indolence," or a childlike penchant to wander.

Gender, Race, Work, and the Politics of Location

Location plays a critical role in shaping workplace resistance, identity, and—broadly speaking—infrapolitics. By location I mean the racialized and gendered social spaces of work and community, as well as black workers' position in the hierarchy of power, the ensemble of social relations. Southern labor historians and race relations scholars have established the degree to which occupations and, in some cases, work spaces were segregated by race. But only recently has scholarship begun to move beyond staid discussions of such labor market segmentation and inequality to an analysis of how spatial and occupational distinctions helped create an oppositional consciousness and collective action. Feminist scholarship on the South and some community histories have begun to examine how the social spaces in which people work (in addition to the world beyond work, which was also divided by race and, at times, sex) shaped the character of everyday resistance, collective action, and domination.

Earl Lewis offers a poignant example of how the racialized social locations of work and community formed black working-class consciousness and oppositional strategies. During World War I, the all-black Transport Workers Association (TWA) of Norfolk, Virginia, began organizing African-American waterfront workers irrespective of skill. Soon thereafter, its leaders turned their attention to the ambitious task of organizing all black workers, most notably cigar stemmers, oyster shuckers, and domestics. The TWA resembled what might have happened if Garveyites had taken control of an Industrial Workers of the World (IWW) local: The ultimate goal seemed to be One Big Negro Union. What is important about the Norfolk story is the startling success of the TWA's efforts, particularly among workers who have been deemed unorganizable. Lewis is not satisfied with such simplistic explanations as the power of charismatic leadership or the primacy of race over class to account for the mass support for the TWA; rather, he makes it quite clear that the labor process, work spaces, intraclass power relations, communities and neighborhoods—indeed, class struggle itself—were all racialized. The result, therefore, was a "racialized" class consciousness. "In the world in which these workers lived," Lewis writes, "nearly everyone was black, except for a supervisor or employer. Even white workers who may have shared a similar class position enjoyed a superior social position because of their race. Thus, although it appears that some black workers manifested a semblance of worker consciousness, that consciousness was so embedded in the perspective of race that neither blacks nor whites saw themselves as equal partners in the same labor movement."

A racialized class consciousness shaped black workers' relations with interracial trade unions as well. Black workers did not always resist segregated union locals (although black union leaders often did). Indeed, in some instances African-American workers preferred segregated locals—if they maintained control over their own finances and played a leading role in the larger decision-making process. To cite one example, black members of the Brotherhood of Timber Workers in Louisiana, an IWW affiliate, found the idea of separate locals quite acceptable. However, at the 1912 BTW convention black delegates complained that they could not "suppress a feeling of taxation without representation" since their dues were in the control of whites, and demanded a "coloured executive board, elected by black union members and designed to work 'in harmony with its white counterpart.' "

Although gender undoubtedly shaped the experiences, work spaces, and collective consciousness of all southern black workers, historians of women have been the most forthright and consistent in employing gender as an analytical category. Recent work on black female tobacco workers, in particular, has opened up important lines of inquiry. Not only were the dirty and difficult tasks of sorting and stemming tobacco relegated to black women, but those women had to do the tasks in spaces that were unbearably hot, dry, dark, and poorly ventilated. The coughing and wheezing, the tragically common cases of workers succumbing to tuberculosis, the endless speculation as to the cause of miscarriages among co-workers, were constant reminders that these black women spent more than a third of the day toiling in a health hazard. If some compared their work space to a prison or a dungeon, then they could not help but notice that all of the inmates were black women like themselves. Moreover, foremen referred to them only by their first names or changed their names to "girl" or something more profane and regarded their bodies as perpetual motion machines as well as sexual objects. Thus bonds of gender as well as race were reinforced by the common experience of sexual harassment. Recalled one Reynolds worker, "I've seen [foremen] just walk up and pat women on their fannies and they'd better not say anything." Women, unlike their black male co-workers, had to devise a whole range of strategies to resist or mitigate the daily physical and verbal abuse of their bodies, ranging from putting forth an "asexual" persona to posturing as a "crazy" person to simply quitting. Although these acts seem individualized and isolated, the experience of, and opposition to, sexual exploitation probably reinforced bonds of solidarity. In the tobacco factories, these confrontations usually took place in a collective setting, the advances of lecherous foremen were discussed among the women, and strategies to deal with sexual assault were observed, learned from other workplaces, or passed down. (Former domestics, for example, had experience staving off the sexual advances of male employers.) Yet, to most male union leaders, such battles were private affairs that had no place among "important" collective bargaining issues. Unfortunately, most labor historians have accepted this view, unable to see resistance to sexual harassment as a primary struggle to transform everyday conditions at the workplace. Nevertheless, out of this common social space and experience of racism and sexual exploitation, black female tobacco workers constructed "networks of solidarity." They referred to each other as "sisters," shared the same neighborhoods and community institutions, attended the same churches, and displayed a deep sense of mutuality by collecting money for co-workers during sickness and death and celebrating each other's birthdays. In fact, those networks of solidarity were indispensable for organizing tobacco plants in Winston-Salem and elsewhere.

In rethinking workplace struggles, black women's work culture, and the politics of location, we must be careful not to assume that home and work were distinct. While much of this scholarship and the ideas I am proposing directly challenge the "separate spheres" formulation, there is an implicit assumption that working-class households are separate from spaces in which wage labor takes place. Recent studies of paid homework remind us that working women's homes were often extensions of the factory. For African-American women, in particular, Eileen Boris and Tera Hunter demonstrate that the decision to do piecework or to take in laundry grows out of a struggle for greater control over the labor process, out of a conscious effort to avoid workplace environments in which black women have historically confronted sexual harassment, and out of "the patriarchal desires of men to care for their women even when they barely could meet economic needs of their families or from women's own desires to care for their children under circumstances that demanded that they contribute to the family economy." The study of homework opens up numerous possibilities for rethinking black working-class opposition in the twentieth century. How do homeworkers resist unsatisfactory working conditions? How do they organize? Do community- and neighborhood-based organizations protect their interest as laborers? How does the extension of capital-labor relations into the home affect the use and meaning of household space, labor patterns, and the physical and psychological well-being of the worker and her family? How does the presumably isolated character of their work shape their consciousness? How critical is female homework as a survival strategy for households in which male wage earners are involved in strikes or other industrial conflicts? Thanks to the work of Boris and Hunter, many of these questions have been explored with regard to northern urban working women and southern laundry workers. But aside from washerwomen and occasional seamstresses, what do we really know about black homeworkers in the Jim Crow South?

For many African-American women homework was a way to avoid the indignities of household service, for as the experience of black tobacco workers suggests, much workplace resistance centered around issues of dignity, respect, and autonomy. White employers often required black domestics to don uniforms, which reduced them to their identities as employees and ultimately signified ownership—black workers literally became the property of whoever owned the uniform. As Elizabeth Clark-Lewis points out, household workers in Washington, D.C., resisted wearing uniforms because they were symbols of live-in service. Their insistence on wearing their own clothes was linked to a broader struggle to change the terms of employment from those of a "servant" (that is, a live-in maid) to those of a day worker. "As servants in uniform," Clark-Lewis writes, "the women felt, they took on the identity of the job—and the uniform seemed to assume a life of its own, separate from the person wearing it, beyond her control. As day workers, wearing their own clothes symbolized their new view of life as a series of personal choices rather than predetermined imperatives."

But struggles for dignity and autonomy often pitted workers against other workers. Black workers endured some of the most obnoxious verbal and physical insults from white workers, their supposed "natural allies." We are well aware of dramatic moments of white working-class violence—the armed attacks on Georgia's black railroad firemen in 1909, the lynching of a black strikebreaker in Fort Worth, Texas, in 1921, the racial pogroms in the shipyards of Mobile, Alabama, during World War II, to mention only three—but these were merely explosive, large-scale manifestations of the verbal and physical violence black workers experienced on a daily basis. Without compunction, racist whites in many of the South's mines, mills, factories and docks referred to their darker co-workers as "boy," "girl," "uncle," "aunt," and more commonly, just plain "nigger." Memphis United Auto Workers

(UAW) organizer Clarence Coe recalls, "I have seen the time when a young white boy came in and maybe I had been working at the plant longer than he had been living, but if he was white I had to tell him 'yes sir' or 'no sir.' That was degrading as hell [but] I had to live with it." Occasionally white workers kicked and slapped black workers just for fun or out of frustration. Without institutional structures to censure white workers for racist and sexist attacks, black workers took whatever opportunity they could to contest white insults and reaffirm their dignity, their indignation often exploding into fisticuffs at the workplace or after work. Black tobacco worker Charlie Decoda recalled working "with a cracker and they loved to put their foot in your tail and laugh. I told him once, 'You put your foot in my tail again ever and I'll break your leg.' " Even sabotage, a strategy usually employed against capital, was occasionally used in the most gruesome and reactionary intraclass conflicts. Michael Honey tells of George Holloway, a black UAW leader in Memphis, Tennessee, whose attempt to desegregate his local and make it more responsive to black workers' needs prompted white union members to tamper with his punch press. According to Honey, the sabotage "could have killed him if he had not examined his machine before turning it on." But as Honey also points out, personal indignities and individual acts of racist violence prompted black workers to take collective action, sometimes with the support of antiracist white workers. Black auto workers in Memphis, for example, staged a wildcat strike after a plant guard punched a black woman in the mouth.

Intraclass conflict was not merely a manifestation of false consciousness or a case of companies fostering an unwritten policy of divide and rule. Rather, white working-class consciousness was also racialized. The construction of a white working-class racial identity, as has been illustrated in the works of Alexander Saxton, David Roediger, and Eric Lott, registered the peculiar nature of class conflict where wage labor under capitalism and chattel slavery existed side by side. That work is especially important, for it maps the history of how Euro-American workers came to see themselves as white and to manifest that identity politically and culturally. What whiteness and blackness signified for antebellum white workers need not concern us here. We need to acknowledge, however, that while racism was not always in the interests of southern white workers, it was nonetheless a very "real" aspect of white working-class consciousness. Racist attacks by white workers did not need instigation from wily employers. Because they ultimately defined their own class interests in racial terms, white workers employed racist terror and intimidation to help secure a comparatively privileged position within the prevailing system of wage dependency, as well as what Du Bois and Roediger call a "psychological wage." A sense of superiority and security was gained by being white and *not* being black. White workers sometimes obtained very real material benefits by institutionalizing their strength through white-controlled unions that used their power to enforce ceilings on black mobility and wages. The limited privileges afforded white workers as whites meant a subordinate status for African-American workers. Hence even the division of labor was racialized—black workers had to perform "nigger work." And without the existence of "nigger work" and "nigger labor," whiteness to white workers would be meaningless.

Determining the social and political character of "nigger work" is therefore essential to understanding black working-class infrapolitics. First, by racializing the division of labor, it has the effect of turning dirty, physically difficult, and potentially dangerous work into humiliating work. To illustrate this point, we might examine how the meaning of tasks once relegated to black workers changed when they were done predominantly, if not exclusively, by whites. Among contemporary coal miners in Appalachia, where there are few black workers and racial ceilings have been largely (though not entirely) removed, difficult and dangerous tasks are charged with masculinity. Michael Yarrow found the miners believed that "being able to do hard work, to endure discomfort, and to brave danger" is an achievement of "manliness." While undeniably an important component of the miner's work culture, "the masculine meaning given to hard, dangerous work [obscures] its reality as class exploitation." On the other hand, the black miners in Trotter's study were far more judicious, choosing to leave a job rather than place themselves in undue danger. Those black miners took pride in their work; they often challenged dominant categories of skill and performed what had been designated as menial labor with the pride of skilled craftsmen. But once derogatory social meaning is inscribed upon the work (let alone the black bodies that perform the work), it undermines its potential dignity and worth—frequently rendering "nigger work" less manly.

Finally, because black men and women toiled in work spaces in which both bosses and white workers demanded deference, freely hurled insults and epithets at them, and occasionally brutalized their bodies, issues of dignity informed much of black infrapolitics in the urban South. Interracial conflicts between workers were not simply diversions from some idealized definition of class struggle; white working-class racism was sometimes as much a barrier to black workers' struggle for dignity and autonomy at the workplace as the racial division of labor imposed by employers. Thus episodes of interracial solidarity among working people and the fairly consistent opposition by most black labor leaders to Jim Crow locals are all the more remarkable. More important, for our purposes at least, the normative character of interracial conflict opens up another way to think about the function of public and hidden transcripts for *white* workers. For southern white workers openly to express solidarity with African Americans was a direct challenge to the public transcript of racial difference and domination. Indeed, throughout this period, leaders of southern biracial unions, with the exception of some left-wing organizers, tended to apologize for their actions, insisting that the union was driven by economic necessity or assuring the public of their opposition to "social equality" or "intermixing." Thus, even the hint of intimate, close relations between workers across the color line had consequences that cut both ways. Except for radicals and other bold individuals willing to accept ostracism, ridicule, and even violence, expressions of friendship and respect for African Americans had to remain part of the "hidden transcript" of white workers. White workers had to disguise and choke back acts and gestures of antiracism; when white workers were exposed as "nigger lovers" or when they took public stands on behalf of African Americans, the consequences could be fatal.

On Buses, Streetcars, and City Streets

African-American workers' struggle for dignity did not end at the workplace. For most white workers public space—after intense class struggle—eventually became a "democratic space," where people of different class backgrounds shared city theaters, public conveyances, streets, and parks. For black people, white-dominated public space was vigilantly undemocratic and potentially dangerous. Jim Crow signs, filthy and inoperable public toilets, white police officers, dark bodies standing in the aisles of half-empty buses, black pedestrians stepping off the sidewalk or walking with their eyes turned down or away, and other acts of interracial social "etiquette"—all reminded black people every day of their second-class citizenship. The sights, sounds, and experiences of African Americans in white-dominated public spaces challenge the notion that southern black working-class politics can be understood by merely examining labor organization, workplace resistance, culture, and the family.

While historians of the civil rights movement have exhaustively documented the organized movement to desegregate the South, the study of unorganized, day-to-day resistance to segregated public space remains undeveloped. We know very little about the everyday posing, discursive conflicts, and small-scale skirmishes that not only created the conditions for the success of organized, collective movements but also shaped segregation policies, policing, and punishment. By broadening our focus to include the daily confrontations and blatant acts of resistance—in other words, the realm of infrapolitics—we will find that black passengers, particularly working people, were concerned with much more than legalized segregation. A cursory examination of black working-class resistance on Birmingham buses and streetcars during World War II reveals that in most incidents the racial compartmentalization of existing space was not the primary issue. Rather, the most intense battles were fought over the deliberate humiliation of African Americans by operators and other passengers; shortchanging; the power of drivers to allocate or limit space for black passengers; and the practice of forcing blacks to pay at the front door and enter through the center doors. For example, half-empty buses or streetcars often passed up African Americans on the pretext of preserving space for potential white riders. It was not unusual for a black passenger who had paid at the front of the bus to be left standing while she or he attempted to board at the center door.

The design and function of buses and streetcars rendered them unique sites of contest. An especially useful metaphor for understanding the character of domination and resistance on public transportation might be to view the interior spaces as "moving theaters." Here I am using the word *theater* in two ways: as a site of performance and a site of military conflict. First, plays of conflict, repression, and resistance are performed in which passengers witness, or participate in, "skirmishes" that shape the collective memory of the passengers, illustrate the limits as well as the possibilities of resistance to domination, and draw more passengers into the "performance." The design of streetcars and buses—enclosed spaces with seats facing forward or toward the center aisle—gave everyday discursive and physical confrontations a dramaturgical quality. Second, theater as a military metaphor is particularly appropriate because all bus drivers and streetcar conductors in Birmingham carried guns and blackjacks and used them pretty regularly to maintain (the social) order. In August 1943, for example, when a black woman riding the South East Lake–Ensley line complained to the conductor that he had passed her stop, he followed her out of the streetcar and, in the words of the official report, "knocked her down with handle of gun. No further trouble." Violence was not a completely effective deterrent, however. In the twelve months beginning September 1941, there were at least 88 cases of blacks occupying "white" space on public transportation, 55 of which were open acts of defiance in which African-American passengers either refused to give up their seats or sat in the white section. But this is only part of the story; reported incidents and complaints of racial conflict totaled 176.

These cases included at least 18 interracial fights among passengers, 22 fights between black passengers and operators, and 13 incidents in which black passengers engaged in verbal or physical confrontations over being shortchanged.

Public transportation, unlike any other form of public space (for example, a waiting room or a water fountain), was an extension of the marketplace. Because transportation companies depend on profit, any action that might limit potential fares was economically detrimental. This explains why divisions between black and white space had to be relatively fluid and flexible. With no fixed dividing line, black and white riders continually contested readjustments that affected them. The fluidity of the color line meant that their protestations often fell within the proscribed boundaries of segregationist law, thus rendering public transportation especially vulnerable to everyday acts of resistance. Furthermore, for African Americans, public transportation—as an extension of the marketplace—was also a source of economic conflict. One source of frustration was the all too common cheating or shortchanging of black passengers. Unlike the workplace, where workers entered as disempowered producers dependent on wages for survival and beholden, ostensibly at least, to their superiors, public transportation gave passengers a sense of consumer entitlement. The notion that blacks and whites should pay the same for "separate but equal" facilities fell within the legal constraints of Jim Crow, although for black passengers to argue publicly with whites, especially those in positions of authority, fell outside the limits of acceptable behavior. When a College Hills line passenger thought she had been shortchanged, she initially approached the driver in a very civil manner but was quickly brushed off and told to take her seat. In the words of the official report, "She came up later and began cursing and could not be stopped and a white passenger came and knocked her down. Officer was called and made her show him the money which was .25 short, then asked her where the rest of the money was. She looked in her purse and produced the other quarter. She was taken to jail." The incident served as compelling theater, a performance that revealed the hidden transcript, the power of Jim Crow to crush public declarations swiftly and decisively, the role of white passengers as defenders of segregation, the degree to which white men—not even law enforcement officers—could assault black women without compunction. The play closes with the woman utterly humiliated, for all along, the report claims, she had miscounted her change.

Although the available records are incomplete, it seems that black women outnumbered black men in incidents of resistance on buses and streetcars. In 1941–1942, nearly twice as many black women were arrested as black men, most of them charged with either sitting in the white section or cursing. Indeed, there is a long tradition of militant opposition to Jim Crow public transportation by black women, a tradition that includes such celebrated figures as Sojourner Truth, Ida B. Wells-Barnett and, of course, Rosa Parks. More significantly, however, black working women in Birmingham generally rode public transportation more often than men. Male industrial workers tended to live in industrial suburbs within walking distance of their places of employment, while most black working women were domestics who had to travel to relatively wealthy and middle-class white neighborhoods on the other side of town.

Unlike the popular image of Parks's quiet resistance, most black women's opposition tended to be profane and militant. There were literally dozens of episodes of black women sitting in the white section, arguing with drivers or conductors, and fighting with white passengers. The "drama" usually ended with the woman being ejected, receiving a refund for her fare and leaving on her own accord, moving to the back of the vehicle, or being hauled off to jail. Indeed, throughout the war, dozens of black women were arrested for merely cursing at the operator or a white passenger. In October of 1943, for example, a teenager named Pauline Carth attempted to board the College Hills line around 8:00 P.M. When she was informed that there was no more room for colored passengers, she forced her way into the bus, threw her money at the driver, and cursed and spit on him. The driver responded by knocking her out of the bus, throwing her to the ground, and holding her down until police arrived. Fights between black women and white passengers were also fairly common. In March of 1943, a black woman and a white man boarding the East Lake–West End line apparently got into a shoving match, which angered the black woman to the point where she "cursed him all the way to Woodlawn." When they reached Woodlawn she was arrested, sentenced to thirty days in jail, and fined fifty dollars.

Although black women's actions were as violent or profane as men's, gender differences in power relations and occupation did shape black women's resistance. Household workers were in a unique position to contest racist practices on public transportation without significantly transgressing Jim Crow laws or social etiquette. First, transit company rules permitted domestics traveling with their white employers' children to sit in the section designated for whites. The idea, of course, was to spare white children from having to endure the Negro section. Although this was the official policy of the Birmingham Electric Company (owner of the city transit system), drivers and conductors did not always follow it. The rule enabled black women to challenge the indignity of being forced to move or stand while seats were available because their retaining or taking seats was sometimes permissible under Jim Crow. Second, employers intervened on behalf of their domestics, which had the effect of redirecting black protest into legitimate, "acceptable" avenues. Soon after a white employer complained that the Mountain Terrace bus regularly passed "colored maids and cooks" and therefore made them late to work, the company took action. According to the report, "Operators on this line [were] cautioned."

Among the majority of black domestics who had to travel alone at night, the fear of being passed or forced to wait for the next vehicle created a sense of danger. Standing at a poorly lit, relatively isolated bus stop left them prey to sexual and physical assault by white and black men. As the sociologist Carol Brooks Gardner reminds us, in many neighborhoods the streets, particularly at night, are perceived as belonging to men, and women without escorts are perceived as available or vulnerable. In the South, that perception applied mostly (though not exclusively) to black women, since the ideology of chivalry obligated white men to come to the defense of white women—though not always working-class white women. To argue that black women's open resistance on the buses is incompatible with their fear when on the streets misses the crucial point that buses and streetcars, though sites of vicious repression, were occupied, lighted public spaces where potential allies and witnesses might be found.

Such black resistance on Birmingham's public transit system conveyed a sense of dramatic opposition to Jim Crow before an audience. But discursive strategies, which may seem more evasive, also carry tremendous dramatic appeal. No matter how effective drivers, conductors, and signs were at keeping bodies separated, black voices flowed easily into the section designated for whites, constantly reminding riders that racially divided public space was contested terrain. Black passengers were routinely ejected and occasionally arrested for making too much noise, often by directing harsh words at a conductor or passenger or launching a monologue about racism in general. Such monologues or verbal attacks on racism make for excellent theater. Unlike passersby who can hurry by a lecturing street corner preacher, passengers were trapped until they reached their destination, the space silenced by the anonymity of the riders. The reports reveal a hypersensitivity to black voices rising from the back of the bus. Indeed, verbal protests or complaints registered by black passengers were frequently described as "loud"—an adjective almost never used to describe the way white passengers articulated their grievances. One morning in August 1943, during the peak hours, a black man boarded an Acipco line bus and immediately began "complaining about discrimination against negroes in a very loud voice." Black voices, especially the loud and profane, literally penetrated and occupied white spaces.

Cursing, a related discursive strategy, was among the crimes for which black passengers were most commonly arrested. Moreover, only black passengers were arrested for cursing. The act elicited police intervention, not because the state maintained strict moral standards and would not tolerate profanity, but because it represented a serious transgression of racial boundaries. While scholars might belittle the power of resistive, profane noise as opposition, Birmingham's policing structure did not. On the South Bessemer line in 1942, one black man was sentenced to six months in jail for cursing. In most instances, however, cursing was punishable by a ten-dollar fine and court costs, and jail sentences averaged about thirty days.

Some might argue that the hundreds of everyday acts of resistance in public spaces—from the most evasive to the blatantly confrontational—amount to very little since they were individualized, isolated events that almost always ended in defeat. Such an argument misses the unique, dramaturgical quality of these actions within the interior spaces of public conveyances; whenever passengers were present no act of defiance was isolated. Nor were acts of defiance isolating experiences. Because African-American passengers shared a collective memory of how they were treated on a daily basis, both within and without the "moving theaters," an act of resistance or repression sometimes drew other passengers into the fray. An interesting report from an Avenue F line bus driver in October 1943 illustrates such a moment of collective resistance: "Operator went to adjust the color boards, and negro woman sat down quickly just in front of board that operator was putting in place. She objected to moving and was not exactly disorderly but all the negroes took it up and none of [the] whites would sit in seat because they were afraid to, and negroes would not sit in vacant seats in rear of bus."

Most occupants sitting in the rear who witnessed or took part in the daily skirmishes learned that punishment was inevitable. The arrests, beatings, and ejections were intended as much for all the black passengers on board as for the individual transgressor. The authorities' fear of an incident escalating into collective opposition often meant that individuals who intervened in conflicts instigated by others received the harshest punishment. On the South Bessemer line one early evening in 1943, a young black man was arrested and fined twenty-five dollars for coming to the defense of a black woman who was told to move behind the color dividers. His crime was that he "complained and talked back to the officer." The fear of arrest or ejection could persuade individuals who had initially joined collective acts of resistance to retreat. Even when a single, dramatic act captured the imaginations of other black passengers and spurred them to take action, there was no guarantee that it would lead to sustained, collective opposition. To take one example, a black woman and man boarded the South East Lake–Ensley line one evening in 1943 and removed the color dividers, prompting all of the black passengers already on board and boarding to occupy the white section. When the conductor demanded that they move to their assigned area, all grudgingly complied except the couple who had initiated the rebellion. They were subsequently arrested.

Spontaneous collective protest did not always fizzle out at the site of contestation. Occasionally the passengers approached formal civil rights organizations asking them to intercede or to lead a campaign against city transit. Following the arrest of Pauline Carth in 1943, a group of witnesses brought the case to the attention of the Birmingham branch of the NAACP, but aside from a perfunctory investigation and an article in the black-owned *Birmingham World*, no action was taken. The Southern Negro Youth Congress (SNYC), a left-wing organization based in Birmingham, attempted a direct-action campaign on the Fairfield bus line after receiving numerous complaints from black youth about conditions on public transportation. Mildred McAdory and three other SNYC activists attempted to move the color boards on a Fairfield bus in 1942, for which she was beaten and arrested by Fairfield police. As a result of the incident, the SNYC formed a short-lived organization, the Citizens Committee for Equal Accommodations on Common Carriers. However, the treatment of African Americans on public transportation was not a high-priority issue for Birmingham's black protest organizations during the war, and very few middle-class blacks rode public transportation. Thus working people whose livelihood depended on city transit had to fend for themselves.

The critical point here is that the actions of black passengers forced mainstream black political organizations to pay some attention to conditions on Jim Crow buses and streetcars. Unorganized, seemingly powerless black working people brought these issues to the forefront by their resistance, which was shaped by relations of domination as well as the many confrontations they witnessed on the stage of the moving theater. Their very acts of insubordination challenged the system of segregation, whether they were intended to or not, and their defiance in most cases elicited a swift and decisive response. Even before the war ended, everyday acts of resistance on buses and streetcars declined for two reasons. First, resistance compelled the transit company to "re-instruct" the most blatantly discourteous drivers and conductors, who cost the company precious profits by passing up black passengers or initiating unwarranted violence. Second, and more important, the acts of defiance led to an increase in punitive measures and more vigorous enforcement of segregation laws. An internal study by the Birmingham Transportation Department concluded, "continued re-instruction of train men and bus operators, as well as additional vigilance on the part of our private police, has resulted in some improvement."

The bitter struggles waged by black working people on public transportation, though obviously exacerbated by wartime social, political, and economic transformations, should force labor historians to rethink the meaning of public space as a terrain of class, race, and gender conflict. The workplace and struggles to improve working conditions are fundamental to the study of labor history. For southern black workers, however, the most embattled sites of opposition were frequently public spaces, partly because policing proved far more difficult in public spaces than in places of work. Not only were employees constantly under the watchful eye of foremen, managers, and employers, but workers could also be dismissed, suspended, or have their pay docked on a whim. In the public spaces of the city, however, the anonymity and sheer numbers of the crowd, whose movement was not directed by the discipline of work (and therefore unpredictable), meant a more vigilant and violent system of maintaining social order. Arrests and beatings were always a possibility, but so was escape. Thus, for black workers public spaces both embodied the most repressive, violent aspects of race and gender oppression and, paradoxically, afforded more opportunities to engage in acts of resistance than the workplace itself.

Black Working-Class Infrapolitics and the Revision of Southern Political History

Shifting our focus from formal, organized politics to infrapolitics enables us to recover the oppositional practices of black working people who, until recently, have been presumed to be silent or inarticulate. Contrary to the image of an active black elite and a passive working class one generally finds in race relations scholarship, members of the most oppressed section of the black community always resisted, but often in a manner intended to cover their tracks. Given the incredibly violent and repressive forms of domination in the South, workers' dependence on wages, the benefits white workers derived from Jim Crow, the limited influence black working people exercised over white-dominated trade unions, and the complex and contradictory nature of human agency, evasive, clandestine forms of resistance should be expected. When thinking about the Jim Crow South, we need always to keep in mind that African Americans, the working class in particular, did not *experience* a liberal democracy. They lived and struggled in a world that resembled, at least from their vantage point, a fascist or, more appropriately, a colonial situation.

Whether or not battles were won or lost, everyday forms of opposition and the mere threat of open resistance elicited responses from the powerful that, in turn, shaped the nature of struggle. Opposition and containment, repression and resistance are inextricably linked. A pioneering study, Herbert Aptheker's *American Negro Slave Revolts,* illustrates the dynamic. The opening chapters, "The Fear of Rebellion" and "The Machinery of Control," show how slave actions and gestures and mere discussions of rebellion created social and political tensions for the master class and compelled southern rulers to erect a complex and expensive structure to maintain order. Furthermore, Aptheker shows us how resistance and the threat of resistance were inscribed in the law itself; thus, even when black opposition appeared invisible or was censored by the press, it still significantly shaped southern political and legal structures. The opening chapters of Aptheker's book (the chapters most of his harshest critics ignored) demonstrate what Stuart Hall means when he says "hegemonizing is hard work."

Hegemonizing was indeed hard work, in part because African-American resistance did make a difference. We know that southern rulers during this era devoted enormous financial and ideological resources to maintaining order. Police departments, vagrancy laws, extralegal terrorist organizations, the spectacle of mutilated black bodies—all were part of the landscape of domination surrounding African Americans. Widely publicized accounts of police homicides, beatings, and lynchings as well as of black protest against such acts of racist violence abound in the literature on the Jim Crow South. Yet, dramatic acts of racial violence and resistance represent only the tip of a gigantic iceberg. The attitudes of most working-class blacks toward the police were informed by an accumulation of daily indignities, whether experienced or witnessed. African Americans often endured illegal searches and seizures, detainment without charge, billy clubs, nightsticks, public humiliation, lewd remarks, loaded guns against their skulls. African-American women endured sexual innuendo, molestation during body searches, and outright rape. Although such incidents were repeated in public spaces on a daily basis, they are rarely a matter of public record. Nevertheless, everyday confrontations between African Americans and police not only were important sites of contestation but also help explain why the more dramatic cases carry such resonance in black communities.

We need to recognize that infrapolitics and organized resistance are not two distinct realms of opposition to be studied separately and then compared; they are two sides of the same coin that make up the history of working-class self-activity. As I have tried to illustrate, the historical relationships between the hidden transcript and organized political movements during the age of Jim Crow suggest that some trade unions and political organizations succeeded in mobilizing segments of the black working class because they at least partially articulated the grievances, aspirations, and dreams that remained hidden from public view. Yet we must not assume that all action that flowed from organized resistance was merely an articulation of a preexisting oppositional consciousness, thus underestimating collective struggle as a shaper of working-class consciousness. The relationship between black working-class infrapolitics and collective, open engagement with power is dialectical, not a **teleological** transformation from unconscious accommodation to conscious resistance. Hence, efforts by grass-roots unions to mobilize southern black workers, from the Knights of Labor and the Brotherhood of Sleeping Car Porters to the Communist party and the CIO, shaped or even transformed the hidden transcript. Successful struggles that depend on mutual support among working people and a clear knowledge of the "enemy" not only strengthen bonds of class (or race or gender) solidarity but also reveal to workers the vulnerability of the powerful and the potential strength of the weak. Furthermore, at the workplace as in public spaces, the daily humiliations of racism, sexism, and waged work embolden subordinate groups to take risks when opportunities arise. And their failures are as important as their victories, for they drive home the point that each act of transgression has its price. Black workers, like most aggrieved populations, do not decide to challenge dominant groups simply because of the lessons they have learned; rather, the very power relations that force them to resist covertly also make clear the terrible consequences of failed struggles.

In the end, whether or not African Americans chose to join working-class organizations, their daily experiences, articulated mainly in unmonitored social spaces, constituted the ideological and cultural foundations for constructing a collective identity. Their action, thoughts, conversations, and reflections were not always, or even primarily, concerned with work, nor did they abide well with formal working-class institutions, no matter how well these institutions articulated aspects of the hidden transcript. In other words, we cannot presume that trade unions and similar labor institutions were the "real" standard bearers of black working-class politics; even for organized black workers they were probably only a small part of an array of formal and informal strategies by which people struggled to improve or transform daily life. Thus for a worker to accept reformist trade union strategies while stealing from work, to fight streetcar conductors while voting down strike action in the local, to leave work early in order to participate in religious revival meetings or rendezvous with a lover, to attend a dance rather than a CIO mass meeting was not to manifest an "immature" class consciousness. Such actions reflect the multiple ways black working people live, experience, and interpret the world around them. To assume that politics is something separate from all these events and decisions is to **balkanize** people's lives and thus completely miss how struggles over power, autonomy, and pleasure take place in the daily lives of working people. People do not organize their lives around our disciplinary boundaries or analytical categories; they are, as Elsa Barkley Brown so aptly put it, "polyrhythmic."

Although the approach outlined above is still schematic and tentative (there is so much I have left out, including a crucial discussion of periodization), I am convinced that the realm of infrapolitics—from everyday resistance at work and in public spaces to the elusive hidden transcripts recorded in working-class discourses and cultures—holds rich insights into twentieth-century black political struggle. As recent scholarship in black working-class and community history has begun to demonstrate, to understand the political significance of these hidden transcripts and everyday oppositional strategies, we must think differently about politics and reject the artificial divisions between political history and social history. A "remapping" of the sites of opposition should bring us closer to "knowing" the people Richard Wright correctly insists are not what they seem.

2.2   Aldon Morris

Domination, Church, and the NAACP

Aldon Morris, author of The Origins of the Civil Rights Movement: Black Communities Organizing for Change, *is associate professor of sociology and faculty associate of the Center for African American and African Studies at the University of Michigan.*

The Tripartite System of Racial Domination

By the 1950's Southern whites had established a comprehensive system of domination over blacks. This system of domination protected the privileges of white society and generated tremendous human suffering for blacks. In the cities and rural areas of the South, blacks were controlled economically, politically, and personally. Those three dimensions were combined in what can be called a "tripartite system of domination."

Economic oppression emerged in the fact that blacks were heavily concentrated in the lowest-paying and dirtiest jobs the cities had to offer. In a typical Southern city during the 1950s at least 75 percent of black men in the labor force were employed in unskilled jobs. They were the janitors, porters, cooks, machine operators, and common laborers. By contrast, only about 25 percent of white males were employed in these menial occupations. In the typical Southern city approximately 50 percent of black women in the labor force were domestics, while slightly less than 1 percent of white women were employed as domestics. Another 20 percent of black women were lowly paid service workers, while less than 10 percent of white women were so employed. In 1950 social inequality in the work place meant that nonwhite families earned nationally only 54 percent of the median income of white families.

The negative impact of racial inequality in the work place was more than financial. In factories and other places of employment, workers with authority over other workers enjoyed greater freedom, status, and deference. Being at the bottom of the work hierarchy, blacks were controlled in the work place by whites. Positions vested with authority—managerial and supervisory—were almost always filled by whites.

Whites had the jobs that required white shirts and neckties. Whites decided who would be promoted, fired, and made to work the hardest. While black men in greasy work clothes labored in these conditions, their mothers, wives, and sisters cleaned the houses of white women and prepared their meals. Blacks entered into these exploitative economic relationships because the alternative was starvation or at least unemployment, which was usually much higher than average in the black community.

Southern urban black communities of this period were oppressed politically because blacks were systematically excluded from the political process. As a general rule there were no black officials in city and state governments, because such measures as the poll tax, all-white primaries, the "grandfather clause," intimidation, and violence disfranchised blacks as a group. Law and order were usually maintained in the black community by white police forces. It was common for law officials to use terror and brutality against blacks. Due process of law was virtually nonexistent because the courts were controlled by white judges and juries, which routinely decided in favor of whites. The white power structure made the decisions about how the public resources of the cities were to be divided. Blacks received far less than whites, because in practice blacks had few citizenship rights and were not members of the polity.

Compounding the economic and political oppression was the system of segregation that denied blacks personal freedoms routinely enjoyed by whites. Segregation was an arrangement that set blacks off from the rest of humanity and labeled them as an inferior race. Blacks were forced to use different toilets, drinking fountains, waiting rooms, parks, schools, and the like. These separate facilities forever reminded blacks of their low status by their wretched condition, which contrasted sharply with the well-kept facilities reserved for whites only. The "colored" and "white only" signs that dotted the buildings and public places of a typical Southern city expressed the reality of a social system committed to the subjugation of blacks and the denial of their human dignity and self-respect.

Segregation meant more than separation. To a considerable extent it determined behavior between the races. Blacks had to address whites in a tone that conveyed respect and use formal titles. Sexual relationships between black men and white women were viewed as the ultimate infraction against the system of segregation. Black males were therefore advised to stare downward when passing a white woman so that she would have no excuse to accuse him of rape and have his life snatched away. Indeed, segregation was a personal form of oppression that severely restricted the physical movement, behavioral choices, and experiences of the individual.

The tripartite system of racial domination—economic, political, and personal oppression—was backed by legislation and the iron fist of Southern governments. In the short run all members of the white group had a stake in racial domination, because they derived privileges from it. Poor and middle-class whites benefited because the segregated labor force prevented blacks from competing with them for better-paying jobs. The Southern white ruling class benefited because blacks supplied them with cheap labor and a weapon against the labor movement, the threat to use unemployed blacks as strikebreakers in labor disputes. Finally, most Southern whites benefited psychologically from the system's implicit assurance that no matter how poor or uneducated, they were always better than the niggers.

Meager incomes and the laws of segregation restricted city blacks to slum neighborhoods. In the black part of town housing was substandard, usually dilapidated, and extremely overcrowded. The black children of the Southern ghetto received fewer years of formal schooling than white children, and what they did receive was usually of poorer quality. On the black side of town life expectancy was lower because of poor sanitary conditions and too little income to pay for essential medical services. Adverse social conditions also gave rise to a "black-against-black" crime problem, which flourished, in part, because its elimination was not a high priority of the usually all-white police forces.

Ironically, urban segregation in the South had some positive consequences. It facilitated the development of black institutions and the building of close-knit communities when blacks, irrespective of education and income, were forced to live in close proximity and frequent the same social institutions. Maids and janitors came into close contact with clergy, schoolteachers, lawyers, and doctors. In the typical Southern city, the black professional stratum constituted only about 3 percent of the black community, and its services had no market outside the black community. Skin color alone, not class background or gender, locked blacks inside their segregated communities. Thus segregation itself ensured that the diverse skills and talents of individuals at all income and educational levels were concentrated within the black community. Cooperation between the various black strata was an important collective resource for survival.

Segregation provided the constraining yet nurturing environment out of which a complex urban black society developed. The influx of migrants from rural areas intensified the process of institution-building. The heavy concentration of blacks in small areas in the cities engendered efficient communication networks. In cities, white domination was not as direct as on the plantations, because urbanization tended to foster impersonal, formal relationships between the races. Within these compact segregated communities blacks began to sense their collective predicament as well as their collective strength. Growth in the black colleges and in the black church was especially pronounced. It was the church more than any other institution that provided an escape from the harsh realities associated with domination. Inside its walls blacks were temporarily free to forget oppression while singing, listening, praying, and shouting. The church also provided an institutional setting where oppression could be openly discussed and resources could be developed to organize collective resistance. By the 1950s the tripartite system of domination was firmly entrenched in Southern cities, but in those cities were born the social forces that would challenge the very foundations of Jim Crow.

The black church functioned as the institutional center of the modern civil rights movement. Churches provided the movement with an organized mass base; a leadership of clergymen largely economically independent of the larger white society and skilled in the art of managing people and resources; an institutionalized financial base through which protest was financed; and meeting places where the masses planned tactics and strategies and collectively committed themselves to the struggle.

Successful social movements usually comprise people who are willing to make great sacrifices in a single-minded pursuit of their goals. The black church supplied the civil rights movement with a collective enthusiasm generated through a rich culture consisting of songs, testimonies, oratory, and prayers that spoke directly to the needs of an oppressed group. Many black churches preached that oppression is sinful and that God sanctions protest aimed at eradicating social evils. Besides, the church gave the civil rights movement continuity with its antecedents in the long-standing religious traditions of black people. Finally, the black church served as a relatively autonomous force in the movement, being an indigenous institution owned and controlled by blacks.

Scholars of the black church have consistently argued that it is the dominant institution within black society. It has provided the organizational framework for most activities of the community—economic, political, and educational endeavors as well as religious ones. The black church was unique in that it was organized and developed by an oppressed group shut off from the institutional life of the larger society. Historically, the institutions of the larger society were of very little use to blacks. Blacks were never equal partners in those economic, political, and cultural institutions and in fact were systematically excluded from their decision-making processes. This institutional subordination naturally prevented blacks from identifying with the institutions of the larger society. In short, the larger society denied blacks the institutional access and outlets necessary to normal social existence.

The black church filled a large part of the institutional void by providing support and direction for the diverse activities of an oppressed group. It furnished outlets for social and artistic expression; a forum for the discussion of important issues; a social environment that developed, trained, and disciplined potential leaders from all walks of life; and meaningful symbols to engender hope, enthusiasm, and a resilient group spirit. The church was a place to observe, participate in, and experience the reality of owning and directing an institution free from the control of whites. The church was also an arena where group interests could be articulated and defended collectively. For all these reasons and a host of others, the black church has served as the organizational hub of black life.

The urban church, by virtue of its quality of religious services and potential for political action, developed into a more efficient organization than its rural counterpart. Even by the early 1930s urban churches had become significantly more powerful and resourceful than rural churches. Urban churches were better financed, more numerous, and larger in membership. Urban ministers usually received more formal education and earned higher salaries than their rural counterparts. Stable leadership emerged as higher salaries led to a lower turnover rate among ministers, allowing them to become full-time pastors. The urban church was able to offer its congregations more activities and programs, which meant more committees and other formal bodies to run them, and greater organized cooperation within the church.

The great migration of blacks from rural to urban areas between 1910 and 1960 was responsible for the tremendous growth of the urban church throughout that period. By 1930 Southern cities had so many black churches that Mays and Nicholson, in their pioneering study of the black church, asked whether Negroes were overchurched. They found that in 1930 the Negroes of Atlanta constituted 33 percent of the total population but owned 57.5 percent of the churches; in Birmingham Negroes constituted 38 percent of the population while having 53 percent of the total churches; in New Orleans, the black population was 28 percent but owned 52 percent of the churches; and in Richmond blacks constituted 29 percent of the population but owned 38 percent of the churches. They found similar ratios in Charleston, Richmond, and Memphis.

Between 1940 and 1960 the black population in Birmingham and Montgomery, Alabama, increased by 84 and 40 percent, respectively. In Baton Rouge, Louisiana, the black population increased by 453 percent over the same period, while in Tallahassee, Florida, it increased by 145 percent. Newly urbanized Southern blacks established close ties with the institution they knew best, the church. Numerous problems attended the major shift from rural to urban life, and the church facilitated the transition by offering valuable friendships and social networks through which the migrants could assimilate into urban life. Moreover, the Southern urban church was similar to its rural counterpart in that it provided an institutional alternative to, and an escape from, the racism and hostility of the larger society. Behind the church doors was a friendly and warm environment where black people could be temporarily at peace with themselves while displaying their talents and aspirations before an empathetic audience. For these reasons the urban church, like the rural church of the South, continued to function as the main community center. However, the great migration made it possible for the urban church to function on a scale unattainable in rural settings.

The urban churches of the South became organizations of considerable social power. The principal resource of the church was its organized mass base. The church not only organized the black masses but also commanded their allegiance. The fact that the church has been financially supported by its economically deprived parishioners clearly demonstrates that allegiance. Furthermore, the black community has always contributed the voluntary labor necessary to meet the church's considerable needs in its role as the main community center. W. E. B. DuBois, commenting on the large volume of church activity, stated, "so frequent are . . . church exercises that there are few Negro churches which are not open four to seven nights a week and sometimes one or two afternoons in addition." These activities emerged from an elaborate organizational structure.

The typical church had a well-defined **division of labor**, with numerous standing committees and organized groups. Each group was task-oriented and coordinated its activities through authority structures. Individuals were held accountable for their assigned duties, and important conflicts were resolved by the minister, who usually exercised ultimate authority over the congregation. A strong work ethic existed in the church, where individuals and groups were routinely singled out and applauded for their contributions. This practice promoted a strong group identification with the church as members were made to feel important and respected, an experience denied to blacks by the institutions of the larger society.

The black church is a complex organization but not a typical bureaucracy. Behavior within the church is organized, but much of it is not highly formalized. The personality of the minister plays a central role in structuring church activities. A striking feature of the church is the considerable loyalty and commitment usually displayed by church members toward the minister. The relationship between the minister and the congregation is often one of charismatic leader to followers rather than the formalized levels of command found in large corporations. In church people express their feelings and often mingle in informal groups long after service has ended. This fluid and informal quality of the church has led some to view the church erroneously as a nonorganization fueled by emotionalism. Consistent with this view is the notion that the church serves as a convenient safety valve for the emotional release of dangerous tensions. While there is some truth to this claim, it overlooks the extraordinary degree to which the church is a sound mass-based organization through which diverse goals are achieved.

The black minister presides over the church hierarchy. He is the individual ultimately responsible for the overall functioning of the diverse committees and groups. In DuBois's words, "The preacher is sure to be a man of executive ability, a leader of men, a shrewd and affable president of a large and intricate corporation." As a leader, the minister oversees the work force of the church and delegates authority throughout its organizational structure. The minister, more than anyone else, determines the goals of the church and identifies the causes to be supported by the congregation. The social power of the black minister stems from his personal persuasiveness and his considerable control over the collective resources of the church.

Charisma and the Black Church

Another source of the black minister's power is charisma. Max Weber, the eminent sociologist of charismatic movements, argued that charismatic leadership arose outside of established organizations and group norms. But in the civil rights movements the process worked differently. The black church, a well-established institution, produced and thrived on charismatic relationships between minister and followers. Churches, especially the prestigious or leading ones, demanded ministers who could command the respect, support, and allegiance of congregations through their strong, magnetic personalities. Furthermore, the majority of black ministers claimed to have been "called" to the ministry directly by God or at least by God's son through such agencies as dreams, personal revelation, or divine inspiration. Once such a call was accepted, a minister continued—in his own perception and, usually, that of his congregation—to have a personal relationship with God. Clearly, the congregation's belief that such individuals enjoyed a direct pipeline to the Divine served to set them off from the rest of the population.

Charisma, however, is based not so much on the beliefs held by charismatic individuals or their followers as on performance. Experience is often crucial to performance, and most ministers who became charismatic civil rights leaders brought a great deal of experience into the movement. Most of them had grown up in the church and understood its inner workings. They knew that the highly successful minister developed a strong, magnetic personality capable of attracting and holding a following. Many of the ministers were college graduates with considerable training in theological studies. It cannot be overemphasized that much of these ministers' training occurred in black colleges and universities under the direction of leading black educators and theologians of the day. They were taught and counseled by such men as Dr. Benjamin Mays, C. D. Hubert, and S. A. Archer. The Reverend C. K. Steele, one of the early leaders of the movement, remarked: "These are strong men and you could hardly sit under them seriously and sincerely, without being affected." He states further that these educators and theologians, who themselves had struggled to get an education, stressed such values as human dignity, personhood, manhood, and courage. These became core values of the civil rights movement.

During this period black universities and colleges were closely linked to the black church. Thus, a significant number of the leading professors were also ministers or closely attached to the ministerial profession. It was not unusual for the students to be required to attend daily or weekly chapel services, during which these influential cultural figures, expert in public speaking and the art of dramatic communication, attempted to imbue the students with certain values. In college as well as in the church, the future leaders of the movement were exposed to and taught the excitement and art of stimulating, persuading, and influencing crowds by individuals who had mastered the art of charisma.

The black church combines the mundane (finance of buildings, maintenance services, committee meetings, reports, choir rehearsals) and the charismatic (strong face-to-face personal relationships that foster allegiance, trust, and loyalty, and give rise to a shared symbolic world that provides an interpretation of earthly affairs and the anticipated after life). The charismatic element requires no allegiance to man, the government, the "city fathers," or traditional norms of behavior. For example, when Birmingham's blacks began to boycott buses, the Southern Conference Educational Fund reported:

> The city's famous police commissioner, Eugene "Bull" Connor, issued a decree that no Negro minister should urge his people to stay off the buses. Mr. Shuttlesworth's response was typical: Only God can tell me what to say in the pulpit. And I'm going to tell my people to stay off those buses if I have to go to Kilby prison.

But, of course, allegiance was conferred by the congregation on the earthly but charismatic minister. Such ministers had to be aware of the power of charisma and prepared to use it. The Reverend C. T. Vivian, a key activist and minister, was asked whether ministers were aware of charisma as a resource. He replied, "Of course. After all, we were preachers . . . remember we're Baptist preachers. We know who controls meetings and things. We know what kind of people make things happen and what kind of people who just sit around and preside over something." They therefore used their position, experience, and charisma to accomplish goals. The black Baptist church, in fact, encouraged the development of charisma through its ministerial recruiting procedures. The task of obtaining a pastorate confronted the ministerial candidate immediately upon finishing seminary training (or equivalent preparation). The first step in this occupational quest was usually to be invited to deliver a trial sermon to a congregation in need of a minister. The primary objectives of the candidate were to deliver a powerful sermon, to relate socially to the congregation members, and, above all, to impress them with his abilities. The Reverend Vivian explained that the black minister came up from the rank-and-file:

He had to be nominated to that post. He had to be voted in. He had to be made the pastor. Nobody sent him down. No bishop said here's who you're [the congregation] going to have whether you like it or not. That minister had to make it out of nothing, what we call the rough side of the mountain.

Vivian goes on to make the point that charisma is a central ingredient which heavily influences whether the candidate will be successful:

You don't make it simply by standing around and going yes, yes. Or by flashing your degree in front of people every fifteen minutes. They could care less. If you've got it, prove it. That's all folks are saying. "You know, don't tell me how many letters behind your name, just do it. We'll see what the letters mean." That's what folks say. "Can you really deal with us?" is what they're asking. "We have a bundle of needs and problems, and so on, out here. What you got to say to that? What can you do with it, and for it, in spite of it?" Lots of things you have to do as leaders in spite of all those problems. It takes charisma.

A statement by Martin Luther King, Jr., regarding his trial sermon at Dexter Avenue Baptist Church is illuminating. He confesses that although he had preached many times in churches, "I was very conscious that this time I was on trial. How could I best impress the congregation? Since the membership was educated and intelligent, should I attempt to interest it with a display of scholarship? Or should I preach just as I had always done, depending finally on the inspiration of the spirit of God? I decided to follow the latter course." It was the latter course that would allow him and the congregation the freedom to set in motion the dynamics of the charismatic relationship.

Students of charismatic leadership have persuasively argued that if individuals are to be recognized as charismatic leaders, they must personify, symbolize, and articulate the goals, aspirations, and strivings of the group they aspire to lead. The ministers who were to become the charismatic leaders of the movement occupied strategic community positions which enabled them to become extremely familiar with the needs and aspirations of blacks.

The black minister, because of his occupation, listened to and counseled people about their financial woes, family problems, and health problems, as well as problems stemming from discrimination, prejudice, and powerlessness. By the same token, the black preacher was the figure who witnessed the resiliency, pride, and dignity that resided in what Dr. W. E. B. DuBois had characterized as the "souls of black folk." The ministers listened to the educational and occupational aspirations of countless black children, along with the pleas of their parents that God and the white man give their offspring the chance to have it better than they had had. Part of the minister's job was to single out for praise those individuals in the congregation who landed impressive jobs, were admitted to colleges and universities, or made any other personal stride.

Thus the black ministers of the 1950s knew black people because they had shared their innermost secrets and turmoils. They were happy when blacks progressed, and, with their fellows, they recoiled in shock when a member of their race was tarred, feathered, and lynched while the white mob drank beer and assembled for "show time." The minister was firmly anchored in the center of the ebb and flow of the social and cultural forces of the black community.

Specifically, the words and actions of such leaders as Martin Luther King, Jr., Fred Shuttlesworth, and C. K. Steele seemed to radiate the qualities required to jar loose the tripartite system of domination that paralyzed the black community. Their displays of courage, dignity, integrity, and burning desire for freedom earned the approval of the black masses, because such values were deeply embedded in the social fabric of black society. Moreover, these ministers, with their oratorical talents and training, were able to instill in people a sense of mission and commitment to social change. The words they used were effective because they symbolized and simplified the complex yearnings of a dominated group. This is one of the reasons blacks in the movement showed little hesitation in accepting such personalities as their charismatic leaders.

The Collective Power of Churches

To some extent the large variety of churches represented social divisions within the black community. Conflict and competition among churches were not uncommon. At times conflict even arose between the minister and factions within a church, producing splinter groups. Yet the churches had many institutional commonalities. For one thing, they all had the responsibility of spiritually and emotionally soothing an oppressed group. Most of their congregations sang the same songs, were inspired by similar sermons, and recognized the importance of cooperation and of giving financially to their churches and other worthy causes. Therefore, it can be said that a common church culture existed in the black community. The church culture and even the churches themselves, however, could not provide the kind of social network that would be necessary to launch mass movements. That need was satisfied by formal and informal interaction among the clergymen who headed the various churches.

It was (and is) common for black ministers in a community and even in different communities to have personal relationships among themselves. They met at conventions, community gatherings, civic affairs, and the like. At times they exchanged pulpit duties and encouraged their choirs to sing at the churches of colleagues. Furthermore, black ministers in a community were linked formally by either a city ministerial alliance or an interdenominational alliance, through which they were able to debate and confer on issues important to the black community.

Within the ministerial alliances were to be found ministers of the poor, the educated, the unemployed, professionals, laborers, housemaids—indeed, the entire spectrum of black society. If these ministers, through their informal and formal bodies, could be persuaded to support protest activity, each could then mobilize his own slice of the community. The National Baptist Convention, one such body, operates on the national level with a membership of more than 5 million.

Scholars of the church have consistently noted how rapidly and efficiently information is transmitted to the black community from the pulpit. This reliable channel for disseminating information greatly enhances the possibility for mass action. The minister can deliver any type of message to the congregation; his salary is paid by the church, which frees him from white economic pressures. Moreover, with their disciplined work forces churches are able to act collectively. Once a plan of action is agreed on by a number of congregations it can be implemented systematically. Thousands of dollars can be raised by a number of churches in a short time to finance a concerted plan.

The impressive social power generated when black churches act collectively has been appreciated by astute members of the white power structure. Whites have sometimes dealt with the black community by first gaining the cooperation of certain clergymen, who have helped them elicit favorable action from blacks through use of the church's influence. On the other hand, the same social power is essential to the furtherance of black interests, particularly through the organization of collective protest and political action. Several prominent scholars of the church noted this possibility even before the civil rights movement. Gunnar Myrdal, for instance, perceptively wrote in 1944 that "potentially, the Negro church is undoubtedly a power institution. It has the Negro masses organized and, if the church bodies decided to do so, they could line the Negroes behind a program."

. . . A significant number of urban churches of the South and North acted collectively, and out of those efforts the first major battles of the modern civil rights movement emerged. However, another organization central to the black community kept the flames of protest alive long before the church became the vanguard. That organization was the NAACP.

The National Association for the Advancement of Colored People

Before the outbreak of the modern civil rights movement, the National Association for the Advancement of Colored People (NAACP) was clearly the dominant black protest organization. The NAACP, in contrast to the church, was organized specifically to fight for equal rights for black Americans. It was founded in 1909 and 1910 by a group of black and white intellectuals vehemently opposed to the racism that confronted the black community. From the beginning the NAACP was interracial and Northern-based, with headquarters in New York City. The white founders were highly educated and distinguished within their professions or businesses. A number of them were wealthy philanthropists, and all were influential in the larger society.

The black founders were also highly educated professionals. Significant in uniting them was their displeasure over the accommodationist politics of Booker T. Washington. The black organizers of the NAACP maintained that aggressive action was required if blacks were to attain their full citizenship rights. The majority of the black founders came to the NAACP from the militant Niagara Movement, which had been organized several years earlier by W. E. B. DuBois and Monroe Trotter to fight for goals similar to those embraced by the NAACP.

The NAACP evolved as a bureaucratic organization. It did not emerge within the black community, nor were the black masses involved in shaping the organization at the outset. The NAACP began as a small group of black and white intellectuals who intended to organize the black masses to struggle for their rights. With one important exception, all the top administrative positions of the NAACP—President, Chairman of the Executive Committee, Treasurer, Disbursing Treasurer, and Executive Secretary—were originally filled by whites. DuBois, who became the

Director of Publicity and Research, was the only black highly placed within the administrative hierarchy.

Decision-making within the NAACP was highly centralized. Most plans of action had to be cleared through the hierarchy in New York. Within a short time detailed rules, regulations, and standard operating procedures were formulated to guide the activities of the NAACP and its branches. Official policies were established by those at the top of the organization. The communication structure was formalized, and information flowed through the hierarchy via memoranda and other approved channels. Organizational protocol became an enduring feature of the NAACP.

The principal tactics through which the NAACP attempted to gain equality for blacks were persuasion and legal action. The early officials of the NAACP believed that much of American racism stemmed from the white man's ignorance of blacks. Early in the twentieth century, when the NAACP was founded, the belief that blacks were innately inferior was widespread. White newspapers and films promoted this view by portraying blacks in a demeaning light. NAACP officials attempted to enlighten white America through massive educational efforts aimed at depicting blacks in a realistic and nonstereotypical manner. NAACP founders, many of whom were versed in the arts and humanities, sought to change public opinion of blacks through press releases, speeches, lobbying, pamphlets, and *Crisis,* the official organ of the NAACP. Much of this effort was undertaken by the black scholar W. E. B. DuBois, who directed the NAACP's Publicity and Research Department and founded *Crisis.* DuBois sought to counteract the negative image by conducting studies of blacks and publishing the works of gifted black poets, artists, and writers in *Crisis.* The NAACP's tactic of educational persuasion, well suited to the intellectual background of its founders, was based on the premise that white Americans would treat blacks as equals once they overcame their own ignorance.

Legal action became the main tactic of the NAACP. Its preeminence was reflected at the outset when Moorfield Storey, a distinguished Boston lawyer, became the NAACP's first president. Storey quickly established a Legal Committee headed by Arthur Spingarn and composed largely of distinguished white attorneys. The NAACP immediately began attacking the system of segregation and racial inequality in the courts. Within a short time the NAACP scored some impressive legal victories. For example, in 1915 the NAACP won a Supreme Court suit that invalidated the "grandfather clause," which made it illegal for most Southern blacks to vote, and in 1927 the organization won a Supreme Court case that began the important legal battle against the all-white primary. Its efforts also led to Supreme Court decisions requiring that blacks be admitted to white universities because they were superior to black universities.

The early legal victories of the NAACP, coupled with educational persuasion, kept protest alive in the black community. Because of these successes the NAACP began spreading to cities outside the North. The organization of Southern branches did not get under way until eight years after the NAACP was organized, when James Weldon Johnson, a black man born and reared in the South, was hired by the NAACP as National Field Secretary and Organizer. Johnson's persistent organizational efforts resulted in the creation of NAACP branches in all the Southern states by the end of 1918. By 1919 Southern membership exceeded that of the North, 42,588 to 38,420. The increasing importance of Southern branches was apparent by 1921, when NAACP officials agreed to hold the annual Conference in the Southern city of Atlanta.

From the very beginning, some Southern black NAACP leaders wanted to move faster than the national office, which produced uneasiness and tensions between the Northern-based NAACP and its all-black Southern branches. However, racial oppression in the South was so deeply ingrained and powerful that in many places the NAACP was the only organized force pushing for change. Indeed, many of the legal cases originated in the South. They covered such varied aspects of oppression as political disfranchisement, segregated transportation, segregated education, lynchings, and so on. Southern whites immediately labeled the NAACP as an "outside agitator" seeking to "stir up trouble" between the races. Southern hostility toward the NAACP was formidable, because the economic and political life of the very people whom the NAACP attempted to organize was largely controlled by whites.

Out of necessity, the NAACP in the South was closely tied to the black church. The church, being independent of the white power structure, was often the only place where the NAACP could meet. Moreover, the NAACP in the South was largely financed through the church, and many of the local NAACP leaders were ministers. Membership exposed these ministers to the workings of an organizational structure outside of the church. Many gained the experience of building NAACP chapters from the ground up and shaping them into organized bodies consonant with the bylaws and rules of national NAACP. They had to learn the NAACP's organizational procedures and protocol, then to make the political trade-offs necessary to keep their local units in harmony with the national organization. Such activities enhanced the community status of local leaders by bringing them in contact with the famous lawyers and national leaders of NAACP. By the same token, the national NAACP had to cultivate working relationships with the Southern leaders because their local units were important sources of support for the national association.

Ministers were not the only community leaders brought together by the NAACP. Local lawyers, doctors, union organizers, and other professionals developed working relationships with each other by operating through the NAACP. Usually these leaders were already acquainted, and the presence of the NAACP further strengthened their ties.

For all the widespread sympathy and support it has enjoyed in the black community, the NAACP has never been able to organize a mass base. Its membership has seldom included more than 2 percent of the black population. White repression, the NAACP's bureaucratic structure, and the complexity of the legal procedures that absorbed its attention all discouraged mass participation. Individual involvement was often limited to making financial contributions and reporting incidents of racial injustice and discrimination to the local branch. Reports were passed along to the national office for decision on whether or not to litigate. These procedures discouraged mass participation. Local involvement was often confined to the actions of local leaders and a few litigants. Still, the black masses usually respected the NAACP as an organization fighting for their rights.

In summary, the NAACP became the dominant black protest organization for the first half of the twentieth century. Through agitation and legal action it presented an organized challenge to the rampant racism in America and to the racist regimes of the South in particular. The NAACP was particularly important in providing opportunities for local leaders to acquire organizing skills and develop networks through which resources could be pooled. The NAACP set the stage from which most of the leadership of the modern civil rights movement would emerge.

The NAACP as a Reform Movement, 1909–1965: "To Reach the Conscience of America"

August Meier is author of numerous books on the civil rights movement. He is a professor of history at Kent State University.

John Bracey Jr. is a professor in the W. E. B. Du Bois Department of African American Studies at the University of Massachusetts at Amherst.

The history of the National Association for the Advancement of Colored People (NAACP) from its origins in the **Progressive movement** to the victories achieved in the passage of the Civil Rights Act of 1964 and the Voting Rights Act of 1965 illuminates the history of American reform in the twentieth century. The focus of this essay will be on the development of the NAACP and its programs and the dynamics of their interrelationships with the changing social milieu in which the Association operated. Involved on the one hand are both the political and economic transformations that were taking place in U.S. society and the long-range shifts that were taking place in white attitudes toward racial minorities. On the other hand are the NAACP's responses to rivals and critics from within the black community. As in any organization there were also internal conflicts over program and strategy and intense rivalries between leading personalities. In contrast to the situation in many social movement organizations, however, these internal conflicts had scant impact on the basic direction of the NAACP's programs and goals.

The authors' interest in these particular issues stemmed from our attempts to address two broad questions. One was that posed some years ago by historians who were investigating the fate of the Progressive movement and the possible relationship of the Progressive movement to the New Deal. The other was the sociological one of how a reform organization interacts over time with its changing environment. Using this conceptual framework we have carried our analysis of the NAACP's history through to the climax of American liberalism and civil rights reform in the 1960s.

Born in 1909 on the fringes of Progressive Era reform, the Association singlemindedly kept to its original goal of securing the basic citizenship rights guaranteed by the **Fourteenth** and **Fifteenth Amendments** of the Constitution. However, the NAACP also proved to be a flexible organization, modifying its tactics and strategies to meet the challenges of the changing economic and political environment in which it operated. For example, beginning with the Great Depression and the New Deal, the NAACP was able to incorporate into its program new economic concerns without altering its basic goal. Amid the reform impulses unleashed during the depression and World War II, the NAACP flourished. The membership and staff grew to unprecedented size. Its legal arm, the NAACP Legal Defense and Educational Fund Inc., won a series of stunning victories before the Supreme Court in the space of ten years: from *Smith v. Allwright,* which outlawed the white primary in 1944, to the *Brown* decision of 1954. There then followed a decade of legislative successes culminating in the passage of the Civil Rights Act of 1964 and the Voting Rights Act of 1965, which together brought to a conclusion the struggle to achieve the original goals enunciated by the NAACP in 1909.

Given this long history and its relationship to American reform, it is interesting to note that the NAACP and its achievements are given scant attention in virtually all of the general studies of Progressivism and liberal reform. The early influential study of the Progressive movement, John Chamberlain's *Farewell to Reform: Being a History of the Rise, Life and Decay of the Progressive Mind in America* (1932), has no references to Negroes or to the NAACP. Twenty years later, another influential study, Richard Hofstadter's *The Age of Reform: From Bryan to F. D. R.* (1956) has only seven incidental references. Scholars such as Eric F. Goldman in *Rendezvous with Destiny* (1952) and Allen F. Davis in *Spearheads for Reform: The Social Settlements and the Progressive Movement, 1890–1914* (1967) do pay significant attention to racial matters. In *An Encore for Reform: The Old Progressives and the New Deal* (1967), Otis L. Graham, Jr., exhibits an awareness that support for the NAACP was a significant indicator of Progressive sentiments but otherwise ignores the question. And in his later volume, *Toward a Planned Society: From Roosevelt to Nixon* (1976), there is no reference at all to racial matters.

It is indeed surprising that even after the shift in racial consciousness brought about in the late 1950s and 1960s, most of the books on liberal reform either have omitted or have given only passing attention to the NAACP. Thus for example a symposium published by the Lyndon B. Johnson School of Public Affairs and edited by Wilbur J. Cohen, entitled *The Roosevelt New Deal: A Program Assessment Fifty Years After* (1986), has chapters on the New Deal and Jews, the New Deal and women, and the New Deal and labor, but none on the New Deal and blacks!

A survey that does pay attention to race and to the NAACP is Arthur S. Link and Richard L. McCormick, *Progressivism* (1983). This is in sharp contrast to Link's seminal 1959 article, "What Happened to the Progressive Movement in the 1920's?" in which race is not mentioned at all. On the other hand, Alonzo L. Hamby's *Liberalism and Its Challengers: FDR to Reagan* (1985), while uneven, does devote a full chapter to Martin Luther King, Jr., and the civil rights movement of the 1960s, but its references to the NAACP are generally inaccurate. Significant exceptions are two studies of Americans for Democratic Action (ADA), the leading predominantly white liberal reform organization of the post–World War II era, which made civil rights one of its central concerns. Thus Clifton Brock in *Americans for Democratic Action: Its Role in National Politics* (1962) does address this matter. Oddly enough, while devoting much attention to the ADA's civil rights activities, Steven M. Gillon's more recent study, *Politics and Vision: The ADA and American Liberalism, 1947–1985* (1987), does not use the NAACP papers nor does it contain any mention of the NAACP's interactions with the ADA. Moreover, the index contains no references to such prominent NAACP leaders as Clarence Mitchell, Jr., Walter Francis White, or Roy Wilkins. From the NAACP's point of view, Denton L. Watson's *Lion in the Lobby: Clarence Mitchell, Jr.'s Struggle for the Passage of Civil Rights Laws* (1990) contains numerous references to the ADA and to Joseph L. Rauh, the ADA's most notable civil rights advocate.

Given the extreme racism of the Progressive period, the discriminatory impact of some important Progressive reforms (*e.g.,* the way in which the new primary system served to disenfranchise black voters in the South) and the racist attitudes of many Progressive leaders and intellectuals from John R. Commons to Theodore Roosevelt, it is paradoxical that among the highly varied reform organizations originating at that time was one like the NAACP. Although some of its leaders were prominent in other reform activities (most notable perhaps was Oswald Garrison Villard, publisher of the New York *Evening Post* and editor of the *Nation,* whose interests ranged from pacifism to women's suffrage), the NAACP itself was marginal to the Progressive movement as a whole. But this is especially ironical in view of the NAACP's attempt to extend Progressive values, goals, and methods into the area of race relations. The Association's belief in investigation and exposure and in the importance of laws and of the state as a guarantor of social order, its faith in the assimilability of minority groups, its belief in progress and the essential rationality of human behavior, all reflect the ideas of mainstream Progressivism. But unlike most other Progressives who either ignored the race problem or considered blacks and Asians to be inferior, the NAACP was willing to carry the implications of Progressivism to their logical conclusions and in this regard was more progressive than most of the Progressives themselves. Above all the appeal of the NAACP like that of the Progressives was fundamentally a moral one, or as the NAACP said in its tenth annual report its goal was "to reach the conscience of America."

Like many of the organizations formed during the Progressive Era, the NAACP had links back to nineteenth-century reformism through the descendants of white abolitionists and a few veterans of the older black self-help organizations such as the Afro-American League. The leading founders among both the whites and the blacks ranged ideologically from socialist intellectuals like W. E. B. Du Bois to politically conservative Republicans like Moorfield Storey of Boston (a past president of the American Bar Association), who were united by their intense dislike of imperialism and racism and their skepticism as to the efficacy of the strategies of Booker T. Washington. This group, resolutely interracial in its outlook, virtually adopted the program of Du Bois's Niagara Movement (1905–1910) as its own. Both the Niagara Movement and the NAACP were united in their opposition to Booker T. Washington's policies and in their program of militant protest and litigation against the denial of constitutional rights guaranteed to black Americans by the Fourteenth and Fifteenth Amendments. Like the Afro-American League, the Niagara Movement was all black. Given conditions at the turn of the century this mode of organizing appeared at least to its adherents to be the only viable option. Du Bois and most of his colleagues in the Niagara Movement acted with little hesitation when given the opportunity to forge effective alliances with sympathetic whites. In fact, it was largely through Du Bois's efforts that people like Villard became convinced of the bankruptcy of Washington's approach and were willing to ally with blacks in posing an alternative.

This of course was a period of disfranchisement legislation, Jim Crow laws, **sharecropping** and **debt peonage**, lynchings and racial pogroms. Given these extreme manifestations of white racism, the indifference of even most enlightened northern opinion, and the reluctance of most black intellectuals to challenge the leadership of Booker T. Washington, the NAACP began as a frail organization. Except for Du Bois, the principal figures in the early years were leading white Progressives such as Villard and Joel Elias Spingarn, and for the first decade the executive secretaries of the NAACP were white reformers. Du Bois edited the *Crisis,* which served as an effective vehicle for keeping the organization's programs and activities before the black public. With its limited resources, the NAACP began its long-term strategy of undermining the legal foundations of the American race system by involving itself in court cases dealing with disfranchisement and residential segregation. In 1915 the Supreme Court declared Oklahoma's "grandfather clause" unconstitutional and two years later overturned the Louisville, Kentucky, municipal residential segregation ordinance. The Association also initiated public protests against Jim Crow arrangements being instituted in federal offices in Washington, D.C., and against showing D. W. Griffith's 1915 racist movie, *The Birth of a Nation*. In both the legal cases and the protests the NAACP achieved only limited results. Much more successful was its vigorous opposition to the rash of anti-Negro legislation that came before Congress and a number of northern state legislatures during Woodrow Wilson's presidency.

From its founding until past the middle of the century what highlighted the NAACP's activities and dramatized its work were its efforts to secure the protection for black Americans of the basic rights to life and liberty. Both rights were threatened by mob violence (lynchings and race riots) and by gross mistreatment in the area of criminal justice on the part of law enforcement authorities and the courts. This mistreatment took place in the South and in the North. In addition to its intrinsic importance, the attention to lynchings and criminal justice was sound strategy that enabled the Association to rally the broadest possible range of support and garner maximum publicity for its programs.

For nearly thirty years the NAACP devoted immeasurable amounts of energy and large amounts of money in the ultimately futile effort to achieve the passage of a federal antilynching bill, although lynchings did almost come to a halt by 1940. Similarly the NAACP devoted considerable efforts to cases involving injustice before the courts, especially in the South. The NAACP was involved in attempts to protect the lives of individual blacks and/or to bring to justice whites guilty of mob violence in such cases as the Coatesville, Pennsylvania, lynching of 1912; the railroading of soldiers in the all-black Twenty-fourth Infantry Regiment of the U.S. Army to death sentences and long prison terms because of their alleged involvement in the Houston riot of 1917; the East St. Louis riot of the same year; the Elaine, Arkansas, and Chicago riots of 1919; the Tulsa, Oklahoma, riot of 1921; the Ossian Sweet case in Detroit in 1925; the Scottsboro case, which began in 1930; the Detroit riot of 1943; the blinding of World War II veteran Isaac Woodward by two white South Carolina policemen in 1946; the assassination of Harry T. Moore, NAACP state coordinator of branches for Florida, and his wife in 1951; and the Emmett Till and Mack Charles Parker lynchings in 1955 and 1959, respectively.

A striking and unusual case that illustrates the strengths and limitations of the NAACP's approach to mob violence was the Aiken, South Carolina, lynchings in October 1926. What we know about the lynchings is due to the efforts of Walter White, the NAACP's assistant secretary who, able to pass for white, undertook an investigation that included interviews with members of the mob and the compilation of vivid eyewitness accounts. White, using his contacts with the press, persuaded the New York *World* to do a lengthy series of articles spotlighting these South Carolina lynchings. The gist of this case was that in April 1925 a family of sharecroppers named Lowman was accused of making and selling illegal liquor. During the attempt to arrest Sam Lowman, the father and head of the family, who was away at the time, a gunfight occurred in which the white sheriff and Mrs. Annie Lowman were killed. The three children, the oldest of whom was thirteen, were seriously wounded. The Lowman children were arrested, charged, tried hastily, and convicted of murder. The two males were sentenced to death, and the female received a life sentence. The father was subsequently charged with possession of liquor and given a two-year sentence on a chain gang.

The injustice of these proceedings outraged N. J. Frederick of Columbia, South Carolina, the only black lawyer in the state who took civil rights cases and had previously handled NAACP cases. Frederick initiated an appeal of his own, retaining at his own expense a white lawyer who was willing to assist him. They were successful in securing from the South Carolina Supreme Court a reversal of the convictions, resulting in a directed verdict of "not guilty" for one defendant and jury trials for the remaining two. The youth who had been acquitted was immediately rearrested on new charges and sent back to jail. Late that same night a mob of two thousand people stormed the jail where the three black children were being held, took them away, told them to run, and then shot them from behind until they were dead. Despite a quite vigorous publicity campaign that caused some South Carolina newspapers to condemn the lynchings, no members of the mob were ever brought to justice. The NAACP's annual report for 1926 seized upon this situation to make yet another appeal for a federal antilynching law.

Despite the unsatisfactory resolutions of many of the NAACP's legal cases, there were enough victories to warrant the observation by Ralph J. Bunche, a NAACP critic from Howard University, that in the first three decades of the NAACP's history "the most important of the tactics employed by the NAACP is that of legal redress. The outstanding victories of the Association have been in court."

Meanwhile during and following World War I there were major changes in race relations that affected the workings—both internal and external—of the NAACP. These tumultuous years witnessed extensive migration of blacks to northern cities, antiblack riots, the revival of the Ku Klux Klan, the rise of Marcus Garvey, the onset of the **Harlem Renaissance**, the introduction of varieties of Marxist thought among black intellectuals, and the emergence of a new breed of black politician in northern cities (that would in 1928 lead to the election of Oscar De Priest of Chicago as the first black congressman from a northern district and the first black in Congress since 1901). In short, the general atmosphere was one of heightened racial consciousness on all fronts, epitomized by the widespread usage among blacks of the term "the New Negro."

In this context the NAACP, while holding on to its basic program of seeking legal redress and legislative reform, underwent important changes in internal organization. Due in large part to wartime prosperity and the shift in black population to northern cities where it was safer to join the organization, NAACP membership grew among blacks so rapidly that by 1920 membership fees from blacks were supplying most of the organization's income. This development masked the failure of the deliberate attempt to attract large numbers of white members. But perhaps the most important internal consequence was the transfer of administrative power to the black secretariat. In 1916 James Weldon Johnson was employed as field secretary. This was followed in 1918 by the appointment of Walter White as assistant executive secretary. In 1921 Johnson was promoted to executive secretary on a permanent basis, a post he held for the next decade. The same rise in race consciousness that led to the success of Marcus Garvey's nationalist appeal also had an impact on the NAACP. This consciousness coupled with the hiring of black staff led to the increase in black membership, which in turn reaffirmed the strategy of hiring black staff. The stature and talent of these new staff members were further affirmations; both Johnson and White as well as Robert W. Bagnall, the director of branches, were men of considerable organizational skills with extensive contacts among black fraternal orders, churches, and business and civic leaders.

As editor of the *Crisis,* W. E. B. Du Bois was at the center of much of the ideological controversy that characterized the postwar period. Even though Du Bois had been fostering his own version of **Pan-Africanism** since the beginning of the century, that did not prevent Marcus Garvey from attacking Du Bois from Garvey's own nationalist point of view. The NAACP's interracial makeup, its politics of integration and assimilation, and even Du Bois's light skin color were anathema to Garvey who, in his speeches and in his newspaper the *Negro World,* ridiculed the NAACP and called Du Bois "purely and simply a white man's nigger." Although Du Bois had considered himself a socialist for some time, he was also attacked from the left by socialists such as A. Philip Randolph, the militant editor of the *Messenger.* In Randolph's view Du Bois and the NAACP had sold out to bourgeois interests and were not at all concerned with the problems facing the black working class. Despite all the attention that these polemics received, there was no discernible effect on the NAACP's programs or direction. At the end of the decade the *Crisis* was still the preeminent black journal while Randolph's *Messenger* was defunct and Garvey's *Negro World* had lost most of its influence.

The NAACP's relationship with the Harlem Renaissance can be best understood as "the politics of art," to use David Levering Lewis's phrase. Characteristic of this renaissance was the intricate interaction of racial advancement organizations with art and artists. From the point of view of NAACP strategy there was a widespread assumption that the work of black artists was an aspect of the struggle to advance the status of black Americans. The positive images flowing from their art were widely recognized as a cultural force capable of both undermining notions of white supremacy and encouraging self-esteem among Negroes.

From its founding the NAACP had among its leaders creative writers and literary critics. The writings of Du Bois of course are well known. Less known are the writings of Du Bois's closest NAACP associates during this period, Joel Spingarn and Mary White Ovington, both white liberals. Spingarn, a poet, leading literary critic, and a founder of the "new criticism," served for many years as treasurer or chairman of the board of directors of the NAACP. Mary White Ovington, a founder who was active in the NAACP for almost four decades, was a novelist and playwright.

When the NAACP began to expand the number of its black staff, the most prominent of its additions, James Weldon Johnson, had extensive literary and cultural interests and was appointed to the staff at Spingarn's insistence. It is easy to infer that one of the reasons that Spingarn found the multitalented Johnson so attractive was the quality of his literary work. Walter White, who came from an insurance background, did not begin to write until well after he joined the NAACP staff. Perhaps influenced by the number of writers around him, White wrote both novels and nonfiction. Beginning in the late 1910s and 1920s the *Crisis,* like the Urban League's *Opportunity* magazine later on, encouraged young writers to publish in its pages and to compete for a literary prize named for Amy Spingarn, Joel's wife. Also joining the staff during this period were the novelist Jessie Redmon Fauset, literary editor of the *Crisis,* and William Pickens, field secretary from 1919 to 1938.

Given this unparalleled collection of literary talent in one organization the NAACP was in an ideal position to exercise a major role in the creative flowering of the 1920s and to undertake a program of cultural advancement in conjunction with its legal and protest activities. The NAACP, in providing an outlet for some of the early writers of the Harlem Renaissance, both stimulated the cultural outpouring and benefited from this newly awakened consciousness.

During the 1920s, a period when Republicans dominated the White House and black voters remained overwhelmingly Republican, the black vote, such as it was, was essentially taken for granted. Conditions in the South were not improving for blacks, and conditions in the North in many respects were growing worse. The NAACP continued the fight for an antilynching bill and chipped away with minor successes against the white Democratic primaries in the South. The NAACP had less success opposing the **restrictive covenants** that hemmed the growing urban black populations into overcrowded ghettos.

The 1920s was neatly bracketed by two important legal battles: the Arkansas riot case that arose in 1919 and the opposition to the nomination to the U.S. Supreme Court of Judge John J. Parker of North Carolina, who had endorsed black disfranchisement. The Arkansas riot case had arisen from an incident in 1919 when, as a result of a racial altercation, eighty-nine blacks were convicted for their alleged involvement; twelve were sentenced to death. The NAACP took the case all the way to the Supreme Court, and after five years of litigation the defendants were freed on the grounds that an impartial trial had not been possible because of mob intimidation of the community and court. Then in 1930, emboldened by the increasing black voting power in the North, the NAACP made significant contributions to mobilizing senators to vote against the confirmation of Judge Parker. This political effort challenged President Herbert C. Hoover's "lily-white" policies and his indifference to the black electorate. After campaigning vigorously against the reelection of four of the senators who had voted for Parker, the Association could take considerable credit for the defeat of two of them.

Although the anti-Parker campaign was dramatic, it had no lasting impact on the NAACP. However, a tentative decision taken about the same time initiated a series of legal steps that would have an enormous impact on the NAACP's future course of litigation. By the end of the 1920s the Association was exploring the utility of exposing the blatant inequities between black and white schools in the South as an opening wedge in the long-range effort to overturn *Plessy v. Ferguson,* the 1896 court decision that based segregation on the doctrine of separate but equal facilities.

Building on the legal work of the 1920s the NAACP program of litigation continued to expand, even during the Great Depression. The deaths in 1929 of both Louis Marshall and Moorfield Storey, two whites who were among the country's leading constitutional lawyers and who had worked for the NAACP for years on a pro bono basis, compelled the Association to consider whether to develop its own paid legal staff and what role black lawyers would play. After discussing these issues for several years and weighing pressures from the black bar association, the NAACP by mid-1935 had employed Charles Hamilton Houston as its full-time special counsel. This decision would prove to be the beginning of the development of a black legal staff.

Houston played a critical role in this process. First, the move to hire a black counsel was facilitated by the emergence of a small group of black lawyers who had studied constitutional law under Felix Frankfurter of the Harvard Law School. Two of the most prominent of them were Houston himself and his close friend

William H. Hastie, both of whom were destined to play important roles in the future of the NAACP. Second, in its effort to improve black higher education in general, the Rockefeller Foundation's General Education Board decided to develop a first-rate law school at Howard University under Houston's leadership. Houston was committed to creating a cadre of skilled black lawyers who would be experts in civil rights law, and he firmly believed that such a cadre would then be able to undertake the litigation required to overturn discrimination in the South.

Houston was optimistic about what could be done through the use of the law, which he saw as a tool for **social engineering**. In this regard Houston's ideas undoubtedly reflected the more general ethos of New Deal social planning and anticipated Gunnar Myrdal's later application of this approach to the solution of the race problem. Although Houston resigned the post of special counsel in mid-1936, he was succeeded by his most brilliant law student, Thurgood Marshall.

During the 1930s the NAACP's litigation maintained a remarkable continuity with that of the 1920s. Much effort was still devoted to legal redress on behalf of individuals, with the NAACP selecting cases from the many received on the basis of two criteria: 1) an issue of citizenship rights had to be involved, and 2) the racial discrimination had to be clear. By 1940 the volume of this kind of litigation, most of it originating in the local branches, had grown to the point that the legal staff now decided to limit itself to cases that had the potential of establishing a new precedent of constitutional significance. NAACP lawyers also continued the earlier campaigns against restrictive covenants and white primaries. They won three Supreme Court victories against the Texas white primary system, although the Texas Democrats continued to find ways to circumvent the decisions. But legal victories in the restrictive covenant cases proved elusive.

The major new legal initiative, underwritten in part by the American Fund for Public Service, a philanthropy more commonly known as the Garland Fund, was the inauguration of the fight against educational discrimination in the South. A two-pronged strategy was involved: directly attacking the exclusion of blacks from the professional and graduate schools at state universities and indirectly attacking segregation in the primary and secondary grades with litigation calling for full equalization of salaries, length of school term, and physical facilities in the public schools. The rationale for this indirect approach was to make segregated public schooling so expensive that the choice would be desegregation or economic ruin. The plan adopted was to begin with the border states, then move into the upper South, and finally challenge the Deep South. A latent function of this strategy was to use these local cases as opportunities to raise funds for the NAACP and increase its membership.

While the legal program and the campaign for an antilynching law were characterized by significant continuity and were shaped independently of the Great Depression, it would be difficult to overestimate the impact of the economic collapse and the New Deal on other aspects of the NAACP's programs and activities. The NAACP was operating in a radically new environment, and a series of mutually reinforcing developments caused a number of changes. At the initiative of a strengthened executive branch led by Franklin D. Roosevelt, there was a proliferation of federal programs addressing the nation's economic problems. By the end of the 1930s the majority of black voters had shifted from the Republican to the Democratic party. The importance of this shift was heightened by the continued migration of blacks into urban centers generally controlled by Democratic political machines. There was also a general shift to the left on the part of substantial numbers of Americans. One manifestation of this leftward shift was a relatively large and extremely active Communist party that continually criticized the NAACP for its lack of radicalism. Another response to both the depression and government initiatives was the rise of the Congress of Industrial Organizations (CIO), which, while not free of discrimination, had made serious efforts to implement its official policy of organizing all workers. Finally, from within the black community itself came a range of challenges to the NAACP's traditional assumptions and programs.

In response to these circumstances and the accompanying pressures, the NAACP as early as 1930–1931 began to make economic issues more important to its agenda. Blacks were faced with obvious inequities in the implementation of New Deal programs: for example, wage differentials sanctioned by the National Recovery Administration; virtual exclusion of black sharecroppers from the benefits of the Agricultural Adjustment Act; the exclusion of certain occupations in which blacks were heavily represented, such as sharecropping and domestic work, from coverage by Social Security. Even those agencies that were most helpful to blacks—the Works Progress Administration, the National Youth Administration, and the United States Housing Authority—and did the most to attract blacks to the Democratic party also exhibited discriminatory practices. The NAACP monitored the patterns of such discrimination and lodged protests with the appropriate federal agencies. The Association established personal contacts with leaders in the New Deal administration, most notably with Eleanor Roosevelt, who in contrast to her husband was openly supportive of the NAACP. Her warm relationship with Walter White and sincere interest in the NAACP's goals epitomized the growing sensitivity of some left-wing New Dealers to racial discrimination.

Blacks suffered disproportionately from the economic devastation of the Great Depression, and one result was that NAACP members and other segments of the black community put increased pressure on the Association for assistance. Local branches began to entreat the national office for help as the full effects of the depression began to be felt. The majority of the protests that NAACP filed with New Deal agencies resulted from such complaints. The NAACP had responded as best it could to economic discrimination since its 1909 origin, when at its founding convention it was presented with a petition from a group of black firemen on the Georgia railroads being forced out of their jobs by racist white workers. In the absence of relevant federal law or a favorable legislative consensus, there was almost nothing the NAACP could do. However, after 1930 not only did the urgency and volume of the complaints escalate but the national government was committed to some sort of response.

The Association's most painful internal conflict, although it had negligible long-range consequences, was between Du Bois and Walter White. The contention was rooted in a long-simmering hostility between the two men. Among other reasons, the economic downturn of the 1930s had exacerbated their disagreement over the allocation of funds for the *Crisis,* an issue that had bedeviled Du Bois and other leaders of the Association for two decades. The particular confrontation that led to Du Bois's resignation in 1934 was his proposal, published in the *Crisis,* to solve the economic problems of the black masses by creating all-black cooperative enterprises while downplaying the struggle for integration. In fact Du Bois's willingness to accept a large degree of voluntary separation seemed to represent a repudiation of the founding principles and goals of the NAACP. To White and his colleagues, such a distinction between forced segregation and voluntary separation (a distinction made with much more success under different circumstances by Malcolm X thirty years later) was unacceptable. In the ensuing debate and struggle Du Bois was forced to resign from the organization that he had helped to found and played a leading role in for a quarter of a century.

At the same time a small group of radical intellectuals centered primarily at Howard University urged the NAACP to reorient its programs and approaches toward an alliance with the white working class. The most prominent of these radicals were economist Abram L. Harris, sociologist E. Franklin Frazier, and political scientist Ralph J. Bunche. Charles H. Houston, who in his own law practice represented southern black railway workers, also thought that the NAACP needed to pay greater attention to economic problems and privately nudged White in that direction. After some resistance, the NAACP leadership responded by commissioning Harris to head a committee for making specific recommendations. The so-called Harris Report in 1935 advocated such sweeping changes to the Association's organization that it foreclosed any possibility of being adopted. The report did, however, sensitize the NAACP leadership to the importance of the relationship between black and white workers. As a result, the Harris Report had long-range consequences for the organization.

Relations with the Communist party were predictably quite stormy, even during the period of the **Popular Front** (1935–1940). In addition to fundamental ideological differences, there was a bitter struggle over which of the two organizations would benefit from the increased militancy of black people. This discord became clear in the conflict between the NAACP and the Communist party over defense of the so-called Scottsboro Boys. Thus, long before the Cold War and McCarthyism, the resolutely liberal NAACP had its own reasons for opposing American Communists. That the NAACP saw fit to interact with American Communists at all was due to the Communist party's success among the black population with such militant tactics as picketing, holding marches, organizing unemployment councils, and fighting with landlords over evictions.

The National Negro Congress (NNC) emerged as a result of the intersecting concerns of the Howard radicals (especially Bunche) and the Communist party. The NNC was the outgrowth of a conference on the economic problems of blacks held at Howard University in 1935, underwritten by the Julius Rosenwald Fund and arranged by John P. Davis, a black Harvard graduate who was very close to the Communists. Projected as a broad coalition of racial advancement organizations, the NNC adopted a program quite similar to that of the NAACP but with the promise of more militant action and closer ties to white workers in the new industrial unions. Roy Wilkins, then assistant secretary to Walter White, attended the 1936 founding convention in Chicago as an observer and reported with obvious distaste on the number of Communists he saw active in the proceedings. But the following year black support for the NNC had grown to such an extent that even Walter White agreed to appear as one of the convention speakers. From the NAACP's point of view it was quite fortunate that the NNC and the Popular Front began to fall apart in 1939 over disagreements on Soviet foreign policy.

In contrast, the NAACP formed a lasting relationship with the CIO. The road to cooperation was complicated by mixed motives on both sides. The CIO policy of organizing black workers contrasted greatly with that of the craft unions in the American Federation of Labor (AFL), most of which had herded blacks into impotent Jim

Crow locals, excluded them altogether from jobs under AFL control, and even driven black workers from jobs they had already held. Many of the NAACP leaders were impressed by the positions taken by the CIO but were constrained from readily embracing the new union by two factors: the extent of Communist leadership among some unions and the justifiable skepticism many NAACP branch leaders and rank-and-file members felt about unions in general. This distrust was not confined only to the black elite but was widely shared by working-class blacks who had had a long history of bad experiences with racist white workers and their unions. The CIO unions themselves were anxious to capitalize on the militancy of black workers but had earlier turned to the NNC because it had a stronger and more consistently pro-CIO stance than the NAACP did. The collapse of the NNC and the successful collaboration of the United Automobile Workers with the NAACP in the Ford strike of 1941 prompted the NAACP to form an alliance with the CIO, a coalition with labor that continued even after the merger of the AFL and the CIO in 1955.

At the end of the 1930s like the end of the 1920s the NAACP had weathered the storms of both internal and external challenges and emerged as the strongest of all the race advancement organizations. In fact, the membership of the NAACP, although not equal to its earlier peak in 1918, doubled between 1929 and 1939. Surprisingly, membership figures during the Great Depression in the early 1930s held up remarkably well, and numerous branches were revitalized and others founded. The Association was now firmly under black control and direction, and effective power had passed from the board to the executive secretary. Thus the organization was prepared to shape actively the future of the black struggle for equal rights. In the crisis of the depression, blacks, especially those in urban areas outside the South, could be mobilized as never before, and the organization that they chose to join was the NAACP.

Much of the credit for building membership in the local branches should go to countless black women, whose activities have yet to be carefully examined. Women also served in a variety of leadership capacities in the branches, particularly as secretaries and treasurers, some as vice presidents, and, on occasion, as branch presidents or chairs of the executive board. More visible than local women officers were the unusual succession of talented black women on the national staff whose achievements have thus far been overlooked by most historians. In the aftermath of the elevation of James Weldon Johnson to executive secretary, Mary B. Talbert of Buffalo, a past president of the National Association of Colored Women's Clubs, was appointed field secretary. She was followed by Addie W. Hunton of Brooklyn and by Daisy Lampkin of Pittsburgh, who worked with extraordinary success even during the depths of the depression. In the mid-1930s the Association appointed Juanita E. Jackson of the powerful Baltimore branch to increase the involvement of black youth. Ella J. Baker, better known for her later work with the Southern Christian Leadership Conference (SCLC) and Student Nonviolent Coordinating Committee (SNCC), served both as a field secretary and during the 1940s a brief but vigorous term as director of branches. After the war came the appointment of individuals like Lucille Black and Ruby Hurley who served long terms as membership secretary and southeast regional secretary, respectively.

The outbreak of World War II in Europe, the subsequent mobilization of the American economy for war, and the creation of millions of new jobs solidified the NAACP's concern with economic matters. At first white workers were the main beneficiaries of the expanding economy, while black workers still found themselves in the depths of the depression. Protestations to Washington were decidedly unproductive. In this context A. Philip Randolph proposed a march of 100,000 blacks on Washington to take place in June 1941.

Randolph was no stranger to the NAACP. Although he had been one of its most outspoken critics early in his career, the Association had supported his efforts to organize the Pullman porters in the 1920s. Following the recognition of the Brotherhood of Sleeping Car Porters by the AFL in 1935 and the collective bargaining agreement with the Pullman Company in 1937, Randolph was widely hailed as the leading spokesman for black workers. He served as president of the National Negro Congress from 1936 until forced out by the Communists in 1939. Influenced by the success of mass action demonstrations to achieve economic goals, even the NAACP mounted a picket line outside the 1934 AFL convention in San Francisco while inside Randolph was giving a speech that addressed the practice of discrimination by the craft unions. It therefore is not surprising that the NAACP welcomed Randolph's call for a March on Washington and played a key role in helping him use this tactic to force President Roosevelt to establish a Fair Employment Practices Committee (FEPC) in 1941. An important factor in the calculations of both Roosevelt and the NAACP was the growing political strength of northern black voters as part of the Democratic coalition.

In short, the depression and the New Deal proved to be a watershed in the NAACP's history. Unlike many other reform organizations of the Progressive Era, the NAACP had been able to adapt successfully, taking on economic concerns without abandoning its traditional agenda.

World War II provided a more favorable environment for NAACP activism. The goal to defeat Nazi Germany, which expressed an openly racist ideology, promoted concern for domestic racial problems among some white Americans. Although there was much racial tension, even rioting, in wartime America, both official and popular attitudes were significantly different from those of the World War I period. Race riots no longer took the exclusive form of pogroms, for blacks were now better able to defend themselves, inflict casualties on whites, and even attack white property in predominantly black areas.

A telling indicator of the differences between the eras was the soaring NAACP membership, which for the first time surpassed the heights it had reached during World War I. As during the preceding decades, economic and demographic factors loomed large. Continuing job discrimination notwithstanding, wartime labor needs had encouraged a massive increase in black migration to cities in the North and West, which continued at the rate of one million per decade through the 1960s. Although there was some economic reversal following the war, basically blacks had been able to establish firm footholds in semiskilled positions outside southern agriculture.

The wartime gains in employment had stemmed in part from the embarrassing testimony at public hearings conducted by the FEPC, and also from the quiet work of regional FEPC and War Manpower Commission staff members negotiating with industry officials in the North and West. However, the FEPC lacked enforcement powers, was constantly attacked by southern congressmen, and ceased operations at the end of the war. In 1943 A. Philip Randolph created a coalition of organizations known as the National Council for a Permanent FEPC with which the NAACP at first cooperated on an ad hoc basis and eventually joined after the end of the war. For the next two decades the enactment of fair employment legislation would prove to be an elusive goal. But largely through the adroit machinations of Roy Wilkins the National Council evolved by 1952 into an influential lobby for civil rights legislation, the Leadership Conference on Civil Rights (LCCR). This coalition, however, was led not by Randolph but by the NAACP.

This particular development, which has escaped the notice of historians, marked a radical transformation of the NAACP's lobbying strategy from one based on personal contacts by a few top officers of the Association to one that mobilized the resources of scores of civic, labor, and religious organizations. This change was made possible by a significant shift in white public opinion toward accepting the necessity to confront the issue of racial inequality. This influx of support and the new climate of public opinion that it indicated in turn raised the expectations of the NAACP and encouraged it to press its agenda even more forcefully.

The nine years between the end of World War II and the *Brown* decision of 1954 coincided with the onset of the Cold War and the climax of McCarthyism. Although generally unrecognized by scholars, the anti-Communist atmosphere actually had a contradictory impact on the NAACP and the struggle for equal rights. On the one hand, for many white southerners and right-wing conservatives, civil rights for blacks was perceived to be part of an international Communist conspiracy, and the NAACP was attacked repeatedly as being Communist-inspired, -led, and -dominated. On the other hand, the NAACP, which like some other liberal organizations maintained its vigorous opposition to Communist influence, employed the threat posed by the Cold War and the influence of the Soviet Union among non-white peoples of the world to press its own agenda. The gist of the argument was that American racial practices played into the Soviet argument about the nature of capitalism, imperialism, and racism. In fact, as an organization, the NAACP entered its most prosperous period during the heyday of the Cold War. Through expanded and effective fund-raising mechanisms such as the Life Membership campaigns and the "Freedom Fund" banquets, it established a firm financial footing. This permitted an expansion of the NAACP staff, including maintaining a Washington bureau headed by a full-time lobbyist and the employment of a specialist to deal with organized labor on questions of discrimination.

Late in the war (1944–1945) and in the postwar era, labor and lobbying activities revolved around an alliance between the NAACP and the CIO. The NAACP lobbied in behalf of labor-sponsored social welfare legislation such as minimum wages, public housing, and expansion of unemployment compensation and campaigned against right-to-work laws and the Taft-Hartley Act. From the NAACP's perspective, labor's legislative agenda, if enacted, would also benefit blacks. For its part the CIO not only supported antilynching legislation but was also a vigorous proponent of bills for a permanent FEPC. In part this was a marriage of convenience because, as was frequently said, "both blacks and labor are facing identical enemies in Congress: Southern Democrats and conservative northern and western Republicans." With migration from the South continuing at a high level, blacks were more than ever an essential part of the New Deal–Fair Deal coalition. In 1948 civil rights policy became an important national political issue for the first time since Reconstruction, and black votes in the North and West were key to Harry S. Truman's victory in 1948.

During this period the NAACP also forged alliances with certain leading Jewish secular organizations including the Anti-Defamation League, the American Jewish Committee, and the American Jewish Congress. There has been a mythological tone about what has been called the "Black-Jewish Alliance." For more than three decades after the NAACP was founded, Jewish involvement was limited to the contributions of a handful of individuals. Among the few people of Jewish ancestry connected with the NAACP in the early years were Joel Spingarn and his brother Arthur Spingarn, a lawyer, who as chair of the legal committee played a major role in NAACP litigation until Houston and Thurgood Marshall were hired in the 1930s. Louis Marshall, a constitutional lawyer, was a founder and president of the American Jewish Committee, which played no role in the affairs of the NAACP during this period. Marshall's son-in-law Jacob Billikopf was active in Jewish philanthropic circles during the Great Depression. He arranged for substantial contributions from a few wealthy Jews like Lessing Rosenwald (whose father Julius Rosenwald had given some fairly large contributions to the NAACP during its early years), Joseph Fels of the Fels-Naptha Soap Company, and Herbert Lehman, the prominent Democratic politician. After mid-century, individuals of Jewish ancestry held important positions on the NAACP staff, including Herbert Hill as labor secretary and June Shagaloff as education secretary. However, cooperation between Jewish organizations and the NAACP began only with the campaign to establish a permanent FEPC. This particular alliance played a decisive role in the LCCR legislative coalition that lobbied for the passage of the civil rights acts in 1964 and 1965. In fact, Arnold Aronson, the executive secretary of the LCCR who had had a career in Jewish advancement organizations, became executive secretary Roy Wilkins's most trusted ally. Like most political alliances this one was based on a combination of self-interest, shared goals, and idealism.

President Truman's support for equal rights was not entirely consistent, and he had to be prodded. In 1946 he did appoint a Committee on Civil Rights that issued a report the following year entitled *To Secure These Rights*. Among other recommendations was "the elimination of segregation, based on race, color, creed, or national origin, from American life." In the aftermath Truman issued an order integrating the armed forces. This action illustrates something of the complex maneuvering required for even limited changes. A. Philip Randolph had dramatized the issue by calling for a civil disobedience campaign against the draft; the NAACP, like other race advancement organizations, disavowed the strategy but used the threat posed by Randolph to underline its own concern with the issue. Receiving private assurances that the president would act to integrate the armed forces, Randolph then withdrew his call, and after some delay Truman issued the appropriate executive order.

The NAACP abandoned the seemingly hopeless fight for an antilynching bill. The struggle for a permanent FEPC, which, after early 1949, became the NAACP's top legislative priority, also proved frustrating. The NAACP—unhappy with Randolph's direction of the National Council—had created the LCCR. Probably the most important gains made by the NAACP itself during the period from 1944 to 1954 came through its long-standing program of litigation in the federal courts. Not only had the Supreme Court overturned the system of white primary elections in 1944, but four years later it declared restrictive covenants unenforceable. In the early 1950s came a series of decisions banning the exclusion or segregation of blacks in publicly owned recreation facilities. The NAACP's campaign against Jim Crow schools was coming to a climax. In a series of decisions the Supreme Court required southern states to admit blacks to graduate and professional schools in public universities.

In 1948, possibly capitalizing on the recommendations in *To Secure These Rights,* the NAACP officially undertook a series of suits aimed directly at overthrowing the *Plessy* doctrine of separate but equal. Finally in 1954 in the combination of cases subsumed under *Brown v. Board of Education,* the Supreme Court accepted unanimously the NAACP argument that separate schools were inherently unequal. At the local level coalitions held chiefly by the NAACP and Jewish organizations succeeded in obtaining FEPC laws in a number of states and cities and, in a few places, fair housing laws as well.

During the years following the *Brown* decision, though the pace of change seemed to accelerate, federal court decisions were not self-enforcing and the NAACP had plenty of work to do. In fact, there was a notable expansion of NAACP activity on all fronts. In the southern states white resistance intensified, manifest in a resurgence of the Ku Klux Klan, the formation of white Citizens' Councils, and massive resistance to school desegregation (most notably in the violence at Little Rock that was quelled only when President Dwight D. Eisenhower reluctantly sent in federal troops). Three southern states, Texas, Louisiana, and Alabama, passed laws making it illegal for the NAACP to operate within their boundaries, and across the South violence and intimidation against the NAACP increased. For its part the Association continued to win victories before the courts. The LCCR, backed by a growing array of organizations and sympathetic figures in the Eisenhower administration, was able to secure passage of the civil rights acts of 1957 and 1960. Modest though their provisions were, having been diluted by the compromises of Senate majority leader Lyndon B. Johnson, they were nevertheless significant as the first national civil rights laws passed since 1875.

In retrospect, the policies of the Eisenhower administration could be characterized as moderate Republican. For example, the NAACP labor secretary Herbert Hill utilized well the machinery of the President's Committee on Government Contracts, which was charged with resolving incidents of discrimination practiced by both management and labor in cases involving contracts with the federal government. This sort of mechanism had first been put into place by Truman after the continued failure of the Congress to pass fair employment legislation. Headed by Vice President Richard M. Nixon, Eisenhower's committee performed with surprising efficacy. Acting on complaints from the NAACP and other groups, it resolved a number of the most egregious individual cases.

All of this was taking place against the background of the rise of anticolonial movements in Asia and Africa. Ghana's independence in 1957 prompted the view among black Americans that their brothers and sisters in Africa were achieving freedom at a more rapid pace than blacks in America.

Domestically the pace of events also quickened but at a slower rate. State FEPC laws, Supreme Court decisions, and congressional legislation seemed to promise so much but made only relatively small dents in basic patterns of discrimination. An example of the difficulties faced can be seen in the Supreme Court ruling in 1955, which blunted the thrust of the *Brown* decision by sanctioning "all deliberate speed" and thereby afforded the white South the encouragement and time to mobilize against the movement toward equal rights. Another example was the situation with regard to the franchise. By 1954, a decade after the white primary decision, black voter registration in the South had risen from 250,000 to 1,250,000, with increases chiefly in the upper South but also in repressive areas of the Deep South such as some of the Louisiana parishes. But an important aspect of the development of southern resistance to black advances was the increased use of intimidation and of technicalities such as literacy tests that actually reduced the number of blacks registered.

In this context there was what we may call a "revolution in expectations" among American blacks, a new sense of urgency to speed the dismantling of barriers to racial equality. The result was an outpouring of nonviolent direct action that by the early 1960s came to characterize this most recent phase of the civil rights movement. Tens of thousands of people—black and white—were mobilized for the first time, and the rise of new organizations such as SCLC, SNCC, and many local organizations ended the NAACP's hegemony over the civil rights movement. Ironically the NAACP's successful work in the courts and legislatures had created the impatience and dissatisfaction with its tactics and strategies.

The first organizational challenge to the NAACP came from the Montgomery bus boycott, which led to the rise of Martin Luther King, Jr., and the founding of SCLC in 1957. Unlike the situation with Randolph, the NAACP had had no knowledge of or working relationship with King before his appearance as a leader; King, for his part, did not need the NAACP. Therefore the NAACP leadership was unable to exert substantial influence over his activities. In this changing climate, and given King's personal magnetism, the founding of SCLC posed the most serious threat to the NAACP's leadership that it had faced since the founding of the National Negro Congress in 1936. Even though the Supreme Court case resulting from the Montgomery bus boycott was won by NAACP lawyers, King's charisma was such that this achievement—which effectively clinched the victory—went virtually unnoticed.

During the early 1960s, though vastly overshadowed in the mass media by King, by the southern student revolt and the rise of SNCC, by the resurgence of the Congress of Racial Equality (CORE) under James Farmer's leadership, and by the appearance of Malcolm X, the NAACP was more active and successful than ever before. The sixties was a period of especially intense conflict and competition among civil rights organizations partly over questions of strategy, tactics, and the pace of change but largely over organizational credit. The NAACP was criticized from both within and without the Association's ranks as being a conservative, bureaucratic organization that was out of touch with the new militancy. In the context of the early 1960s this lack of unity was actually quite helpful as civil rights organizations at both the national and local levels competed with one another in their quest for victories in the struggle for equality. Oddly enough its long-established structure enabled the NAACP to reap the benefits from the new racial consciousness, and by 1963 its membership crested at over 400,000, making it by far the largest civil rights organization. Moreover, it was the only civil rights organization that was funded primarily by the black community.

As could be expected in an organization of its age and size, there was an enormous range of attitudes and responses in the branches to the new wave of demonstrations. Some branches figuratively sat on their hands, while others embraced the new activism with enthusiasm. In fact, the NAACP branches were probably the major source of legal aid to the youthful activists of 1960 and 1961, and the Association's own youth councils and college chapters did much to make this phase of the movement effective. In South Carolina, for example, in 1963 and 1964 the NAACP State Conference of Branches led the direct action struggle. As Roy Wilkins said with some justice, "the NAACP branches put up the money and others get the credit." The NAACP was also deeply involved in litigation against de facto school segregation in northern cities and provided support for school boycotts in Boston, New York, and other cities in 1963 and 1964. Numerous NAACP members were also among the demonstrators at construction sites in northeastern cities protesting discrimination in the building trades and among the masses of protestors against job discrimination in such places as the cities in the San Francisco Bay area.

With regard to the issue of racial bias by many labor unions, beginning in the late 1950s the NAACP labor secretary Herbert Hill had adopted an innovative approach to job discrimination. Using a combination of litigation and publicity, Hill kept constant pressure on government, corporations, and labor unions to do their part in opening up more job opportunities for blacks. At the same time Hill was carrying out this aspect of the NAACP program, Clarence Mitchell, head of the Washington bureau, and the whole LCCR strategy were heavily dependent on the AFL-CIO legislative lobby for stronger civil rights legislation. In effect NAACP executive secretary Roy Wilkins was pursuing a skillful two-pronged strategy of confronting labor with specific examples of discrimination while continuing to maintain an alliance with labor on matters of joint legislative interest. This whole strategy depended upon the need for the AFL-CIO's leadership to maintain the liberal image of the labor movement and labor's role and influence in the New Deal coalition. Moreover, the AFL-CIO leadership admitted that on the question of union discrimination it could not clean its own house without the assistance of federal fair employment legislation.

The culmination of direct action North and South came during the year following the Birmingham demonstrations of spring 1963. The August 1963 March on Washington symbolized unprecedented national support for some form of civil rights legislation. In this context of dramatic confrontations displaying both racist repression and individual courage, the NAACP mobilized the LCCR for the successful lobbying for the passage of the Civil Rights Act of 1964 and the Voting Rights Act of 1965. The support of both the large AFL-CIO lobby in Washington and the representatives of the major religious faiths was vital as was the political pressure applied by President Johnson, but it was the NAACP's executive secretary who made the important decisions, including the one to incorporate a strong employment antidiscrimination clause that became Section 7 of the 1964 Act. One should not discount the role of the direct action organizations in awakening public opinion and exerting tremendous moral and political pressures. But it is important to emphasize the development of a symbiotic relationship between the campaigns led by new waves of demonstrators and the NAACP's skillful translation of their joint concerns into lasting legislative victories.

The civil rights legislation came during the apex of New Deal–style reformism that characterized the war on poverty. This legislation finally removed the legal barriers that had prevented blacks from exercising their basic rights under the Fourteenth and Fifteenth Amendments, which the NAACP had sought since its founding. This legislation also brought into being the legal sanctions against employment discrimination that the NAACP had first included in its national agenda during the Roosevelt era.

The enactment of the civil rights laws of 1964 and 1965 produced what A. Philip Randolph called a crisis of victory. It soon became apparent that the mere passage of legislation and the recognition of constitutional rights were not sufficient to redress three hundred years of racial oppression. The issues associated with economic inequality—widespread poverty, poor and inadequate housing, inferior schools, police brutality, and other inequities in the criminal justice system—proved to be virtually intractable. Much of the black power response consisted of attempts to deal with the difficulties and frustrations of this situation. Ideologically the NAACP resisted this tendency toward separatism, and the national leadership's success in this matter was probably due to the commitment, especially in the South, of its largely middle-aged membership to the struggle for integration. Yet at this point the national board for the first time became all black, and it has remained that way ever since.

Just as the New Deal–style economic and social programs of the **Great Society** were on the verge of decline, so also the NAACP, from an organizational point of view, was looking at a bleaker future. Finding that its traditional strategies of legal redress and legislative reform were not adequate to deal with problems of this magnitude and that there was no national consensus on how to deal with these matters, the Association began to drift and decline. The NAACP began to lose its membership and its leadership role.

The Voting Rights Act opened up the possibility of significant gains in the political system; consequently much of black leadership has gravitated toward electoral politics. Leadership began to develop from the local level through the Congressional Black Caucus. The irony is that it was the NAACP's success in lobbying for black voting rights that helped lay the groundwork for the drift away from the organization and toward political activism. However, the increase in black voting power caused many white southerners and northern white ethnics to shift to the Republican party, reinforcing the decline in liberalism associated with the Republican ascendancy since the end of the 1960s.

In short, the NAACP, which outlived many of the Progressive and New Deal organizations and had a successful post-World War II career, now appears to have suffered the general fate of liberal reform in the 1970s and 1980s.

2.4   Genna Rae McNeil

Charles Hamilton Houston: Social Engineer for Civil Rights

Genna Rae McNeil, *author of* Groundwork: Charles Hamilton Houston and the Struggle for Civil Rights, *is professor of African American history and U.S. social movements of the twentieth century at the University of North Carolina.*

On May 17, 1954, the U.S. Supreme Court announced a series of decisions in which the justices declared segregation in public schools unconstitutional. These landmark cases set the stage for massive legal and extralegal attacks on segregation in every phase of the nation's life. Addressing an audience at Amherst College in April 1978, Justice Thurgood Marshall recalled that "Charlie Houston" was the "engineer of it all." Marshall spoke at length in paying homage to his former law professor, mentor, and colleague, Charles Hamilton Houston. Because few knew of Houston's contribution to civil rights but most were well-acquainted with Marshall's important role in the 1954 cases, his assessment was telling. He explained that when *Brown* v. *Board of Education* (1954) and *Bolling* v. *Sharpe* (1954) were argued before the Supreme Court, "there were some two dozen lawyers on the side of the Negroes fighting for their schools.... Of those ... there were only two who hadn't been touched by Charlie Houston."

For over two decades, Houston taught and practiced law, championed civil rights for black Americans, defended black workers facing unfair, racist labor policies or practices, and expounded the use of the law as an instrument of fundamental social change—"**social engineering**"—that would promote justice and liberty in the United States for blacks as well as whites. Houston's intellect, skill, and ingenuity during an era of racist state policies, laws, and practices, severe economic depression, and heightened class and racial conflicts all served to place him in a high position among Afro-American leaders. Among Howard University Law School students, faculty, and alumni he was the respected and inspiring "Dean Houston." Among civil rights veterans, there is a consensus that he was the first "Mr. Civil Rights"—an expert in constitutional law and a strategist and litigator in education, labor, and housing rights cases. This examination of Houston focuses on his activities as an educator, lawyer, and civil rights leader from 1929 to 1950.

Houston was born in Washington, D.C., in 1895, the grandson of former slaves and son of a lawyer and a hairdresser. He attended the District of Columbia's segregated public schools and was graduated from the excellent M Street college-preparatory high school. After earning a Bachelor of Arts degree at Amherst, he served as an officer in the American Expeditionary Forces from 1917 to 1919. These were genuinely formative years. Observing the court martial of a black officer for following orders, being adjudged unfit to command white field artillery soldiers, and having his life capriciously threatened by a lynch mob of enlisted men etched the meaning of racism on his mind. Houston left the "war to save democracy" and America's army with fiery determination. "I made up my mind that I would never get caught ... without knowing ... my rights, that I would study law and use my time fighting for men who could not strike back."

Houston attended Harvard Law School from September 1919 to June 1923, specializing in the study of constitutional law under the noted future Supreme Court Justice Felix Frankfurter. He absorbed much of the philosophy of "sociological jurisprudence" then in its ascendancy at Harvard under the influence of the celebrated Dean Roscoe Pound and attained the distinction of being the first black to serve on the editorial board of the *Harvard Law Review.* After winning a fellowship for a year of foreign study, Houston returned to Washington in the summer of 1924, where he joined his father, William L. Houston, in private practice and accepted a professorship at Howard University's Law School.

When Houston began teaching at Howard's Law School, its curriculum was typical of most successful evening law schools, which students could attend part-time, and its alumni had distinguished themselves in various areas of law and politics. Many of them, especially in the border states, had provided the backbone of the legal work of local branches for the National Association for the Advancement of Colored People. Nonetheless, Howard's standing in the field of legal education was in jeopardy. Like all schools for part-time students, it was suspect due to a confluence of factors. Legal authorities insisted that part-time law schools were not comparable in quality to full-time institutions and ought to be improved. The American Bar Association (ABA), which excluded black lawyers from membership, had set standards that Howard University Law School could hardly meet. Howard was ineligible for membership in the Association of American Law Schools (AALS), the key agency for establishing or maintaining credibility in legal education, because it could not meet the AALS's standards for law libraries, faculty, or admissions policies.

177

*2.4 Charles
Hamilton
Houston: Social
Engineer for
Civil Rights*

Houston replaced the last white dean of Howard's Law School in 1929. Already, cautious steps had been taken to insure its upgrading. In 1927–28, supported by a grant from the Laura Spelman Rockefeller Memorial, Houston had undertaken a study of black lawyers. His findings revealed a striking shortage of black lawyers and, in particular, only a negligible number, in the North or South, with training and experience in constitutional law and thus equipped to handle effectively civil rights cases in the federal courts. Houston believed—and he convinced Howard University President Mordecai Johnson—that Howard should offer a fully accredited program of legal education to students attending classes on a full-time basis and that Howard's formal legal training should include preparation for civil rights litigation. Johnson, the university's first black president, was intrigued with the possibility of producing outstanding lawyers whose work could benefit the entire race. Consequently, he authorized Houston to take charge of a new program for full-time day students and a law school accreditation drive.

Under Houston the school became fully accredited by the ABA and the AALS. It was no small accomplishment, nor was it easily achieved. The requisite approvals were obtained between 1929 and 1931, in part, because Houston relished the challenge and knew how to stay on top of a variety of projects.

The law school's reorganization during Houston's leadership transformed the institution into one committed to excellence in both the study of law and in the defense of Afro-Americans' civil rights. Houston repeatedly pointed out that the future required what he was attempting to do. Already, "Howard University School of Law is performing an indispensable social function," he stressed, but the black lawyer must be especially "trained . . . [and] prepared to anticipate, guide and interpret his group's advancement." He expressed his views with an intensity that could frequently move to passion: "I believe that the race problem is one of the most fundamental problems in American life today. . . . The orderly process of the solution of this problem depends largely upon the prompt, just and efficient administration of the law." Under Houston, self-conscious racial advancement and the pursuit of full freedom and justice became central to the work of the school. In the university setting Houston developed and expounded his philosophy of "social engineering." This view that law could be used to effect social change imbued the law students and faculty as well as the civil libertarians who would participate in the decades of civil rights struggles after 1935.

Houston's philosophy was grounded in two beliefs about law: that law could be used to promote and secure fundamental social change for the betterment of society and that law was an instrument available to minority groups who were unable to achieve their rightful places in the nation through direct action. More specifically, Houston maintained that Afro-American lawyers were obliged to understand the Constitution and explore its uses, both in the solution of problems of local communities and in the improvement of conditions under which black and poor citizens lived. In 1932 he wrote that social engineering should ensure that "the course of change is . . . orderly, with a minimum of human loss and suffering." At the same time, it should also articulate the demands and expectations of the weak and oppressed.

As Houston directed the work of the law school and taught his courses, he challenged the law students to become "sentinels guarding against wrong." For the black lawyer–social engineer, Houston underscored commitment and skilled advocacy. Two of his high-ranking students readily admitted that Houston was "absolutely fair," but they recalled even more vividly that he was not one to equivocate—"a lawyer's either a social engineer or he's a parasite on society." Moreover, as the head of the law school, Houston seized every opportunity to dispel myths about the inferiority of black lawyers and to use black lawyers from Howard in the cause of civil rights. He recognized the important contribution that prominent white constitutional lawyers like Moorfield Storey and Louis Marshall had made in arguing important NAACP cases before the Supreme Court until they both died in 1929, but he felt strongly that the time had come for black lawyers to play the commanding role in defending and advancing the rights of the race. Securing the accreditation for Howard University's Law School and making it a major source of black attorneys highly competent in civil rights litigation were directed toward this end. He told an NAACP national convention that, "for its greatest effectiveness," it ought to be "of the Negroes, by the Negroes . . . for all the Negroes," committing itself to a program of "intelligent leadership plus intelligent mass action." He also expressed the belief that black Americans should attempt to "unite with the 'poor white' . . . [although] the minds of both . . . have been poisoned against each other" by the ruling class that exploited both groups. Houston's view that blacks and poor whites needed to work out common objectives brought a new perspective to the work of the NAACP.

Houston's close friend and fellow Harvard Law School alumnus, William H. Hastie, underscored the magnitude of Houston's achievement at Howard when he noted, after Houston's death, that "a transformation which ordinarily requires a generation in the history of an educational institution" Houston accomplished in less than six years. All subsequent objective assessments of Howard Law School's modern growth and development reveal that the years of Houston's administration were the era during which the law school moved into a sphere of larger usefulness and national prominence. Supreme Court Justice Marshall is the most famous illustration of the lawyer that Houston's reorganization of the Howard University Law School produced.

Houston's work at the law school and his philosophy of social engineering brought him to the attention of civil rights/civil libertarian groups. In the early 1930s, on matters of due process, equal protection of the laws, lynching, voting rights, and employment security, he became a leading activist. He marched for the freedom of the "Scottsboro Boys," who were accused of raping two white women in Alabama, and he filed a brief on their behalf in the U.S. Supreme Court. On another occasion, he enlisted a Howard colleague and an alumnus to prepare a special legal memorandum arguing against lynching and for prosecution of derelict or conspiring officials under federal law.

Recognizing Houston's potential contribution beyond Washington, leaders of both the NAACP and the Communist-oriented International Labor Defense (ILD), which was at the time very active in civil rights litigation, approached Houston about greater participation in nationwide civil rights advocacy. This was also the time when many groups, including the NAACP and the ILD, were seeking ways to help the vast numbers of blacks hit by the Great Depression. It was an appeal that Houston could not resist. Houston himself, deeply concerned with the economic problems of the black working class, did not flinch from cooperating with the Communists on occasion, but he opted to work within the framework of the black-controlled, reformist NAACP, even though that organization was being widely criticized for clinging too closely to its civil rights litigation program and not concerning itself enough with the economic problems of the masses. The first case he took for the NAACP involved an indigent Virginia black, accused of murder. Although Houston lost this case in 1933, it was a landmark for the NAACP, which used it to demonstrate that a black lawyer could handle a delicate, highly emotional case in a small southern town, with the respect and even admiration of local lawyers and judges. Two years later in the case of *Hollins v. State of Oklahoma,* Houston established an even more important precedent. Successfully defending a black man sentenced to death for criminal assault on a white girl, Houston—in the first case in which the NAACP employed exclusively black counsel before the Supreme Court—convinced the high tribunal to overturn the conviction because blacks had been illegally excluded from the jury panel.

Soon afterward Houston obtained a leave of absence from Howard University to serve as full-time special counsel for the NAACP. This position and title he retained from July 1935 until 1940, although beginning in 1938 he handled special legal projects from his Washington firm, leaving Marshall to work from the New York headquarters. For the rest of his life Houston remained deeply involved in a wide range of litigation affecting the rights and welfare of American blacks. The most notable civil rights cases resulting from this work were in the areas of education, labor, and housing. He argued civil rights cases before the Supreme Court, and he aided in the preparation of lower court suits. Between 1939 and 1950 he was the general counsel for the Association of Colored Railway Trainmen and for the International Association of Railway Employees. For nearly a decade he represented clients seeking relief from restrictive covenants (discriminatory agreements entered into by white homeowners to prevent movement of blacks into their neighborhoods).

The man who became head of the NAACP's first permanent salaried legal department in July 1935 was imposing—over six feet tall, roughly two hundred pounds, with features and bronze coloring that left no doubt about his Afro-American descent. An intense gaze, a steady baritone voice, and a confident demeanor worked together to create an aura of authority and immense competence. Both Walter White, the executive secretary, and Roy Wilkins, the assistant secretary, were optimistic about the man who was selected to take charge of the NAACP's legal program and develop a legal department that could effectively work for social change through law.

Among Houston's dozen or more legal defense inquiries in his first year with the NAACP were critical life and death matters. A telephone call or some papers left on his desk could place him in the middle of hearings for clients whom he had never met, but who required his help for successful appeals. Then there were requests for speeches about the new NAACP legal program. Sometimes traveling with White, other times with Eddie Lovett or Oliver Hill, both Howard graduates, and occasionally alone, Houston spoke at meetings and rallies of civic bodies, teachers' associations, interracial councils, church congregations, parents' groups, sororities, fraternities, and student organizations throughout black communities in the cities and rural areas of the South. He logged nearly 25,000 miles for the campaign against discrimination in education during his first year as special counsel.

Houston's reputation is undoubtedly most indelibly linked with his role in initiating the NAACP's long-range and ultimately successful campaign against segregation in southern public schools. Even before Houston joined its staff, the NAACP had decided to make its attack on this form of discrimination the central focus of its legal work. Houston was well aware that even under the more liberal climate of the New Deal, the conservative policies and cautious procedures of the American judicial system militated against judges entertaining an immediate direct attack on segregation that would force them to overrule an earlier court's decision on the constitutionality of segregation. Moreover, Houston knew that nothing in the history of the United States or the history of the Supreme Court justified the assumption that either would suddenly decide to promote racial equality. To secure both equal protection under the laws and justice for Afro-Americans required a protracted struggle, which would include successive legal battles (handled by lawyers working with black communities) that would be designed to undercut the legality of discrimination and segregation. Rather than waiting for cases to be referred to the NAACP's national office, Houston established not only a long range goal for the legal campaign—the elimination of segregation—but also limited objectives, priorities for blacks' civil rights, and criteria for suitable cases. Thereafter, Houston sought cases and test litigants that would effectively advance the NAACP's cause. Houston based the NAACP's legal strategy on his understanding of the United States, the American legal system, history, and racism. As a result the NAACP won a series of court battles that paved the way for successful attacks on the constitutionality of segregation itself.

Accordingly, Houston was careful not to move immediately against the separate-but-equal dictum, enunciated in 1896 in the case of *Plessy* v. *Ferguson,* which declared constitutional laws providing for segregation in public transportation. A carefully drawn, long-term assault on the citadel of southern school segregation was required. Houston developed a two-pronged strategy to topple the edifice of school segregation. On the one hand, the NAACP attacked the inequities, especially in teachers' salaries, that characterized the southern elementary and high school systems; on the other hand, Houston and his associates conducted litigation against the exclusion of blacks from the graduate and professional courses offered in state-owned white universities but not in the black colleges. In addition to the purely legal aspects of this work, Houston believed that the development of "a sustaining mass interest behind the program . . . along with or before litigation" was essential. Houston's message was clearly and simply expressed. If ignorance prevails among the masses of any race, they are bound to become "the tools of a small exploiting class," he explained to one gathering. And on the matter of racially segregated schools and inequities, Houston repeatedly told black Americans: "The mass of Negroes . . . are a part of the public which owns and controls the schools. . . . Both schools belong to one and the same system and the system belongs to the public."

Parents, teachers, and black community leaders in Maryland, Virginia, Tennessee, and Missouri took action to achieve equality of educational opportunities and to equalize the salaries of teachers. In Virginia and Maryland Houston consulted with local leaders and by 1936 launched a successful attack on racial discrimination in the appropriation of funds affecting black students and teachers in elementary and secondary schools. In Tennessee and Missouri the focus was on exclusion from graduate-professional public education. Interested adults and students with good academic records came forward to volunteer for court battles. As part of his overall strategy, Houston planned for every situation and consequence he could anticipate, including when to accept or reject volunteers. Each case had to be measured against exacting standards, so that funds would not be expended unless there were some reasonable expectation of success on the appellate level.

As special counsel and chief legal officer of the NAACP, Houston developed test case requirements. Plaintiffs had to be "proper parties," representing "the discrimination which we desire to attack," and the situation had to represent "a sharply defined issue . . . support[able] . . . by auxiliary legal proceedings," and it should "present key discriminations," thereby furnishing "a focus or springboard for extending the attacks on a larger front."

With his eye on the Supreme Court, Houston took the situation of one Lloyd Lionel Gaines of Missouri under advisement. Gaines, a young college graduate, wanted to be a lawyer and did not want to wait until the state black institution, Lincoln University, had been voted sufficient appropriations to offer a legal education equal to that offered to white students. He therefore asked the St. Louis local chapter and the national office of the NAACP to handle his case against the white university. Using a complaint similar to a Maryland law school admissions case (in which Marshall and Houston had earlier prevailed on the state appellate level), the NAACP filed suit in 1936 on behalf of Gaines against the University of Missouri.

Houston's decision to handle the Gaines case was a tactical maneuver in the long-range plan to secure a favorable U.S. Supreme Court ruling against racial discrimination. Test cases that would systematically eviscerate the separate-but-equal principle of *Plessy* v. *Ferguson* were to be planned deliberately and prosecuted. Each case would progressively establish both a precedent for equality where segregation existed and the prerogative of the Supreme Court to determine what constituted equality consistent with the Constitution. (Concurrently, the NAACP through its magazine *Crisis* and in press releases provided interpretation of the significance of each case.) Houston targeted state-supported legal education because he reasoned that judges were qualified to compare legal education at various institutions and certainly, when they were asked to rule on the equality of law school offerings, they could not demur on the basis of lack of expertise or experience.

Everywhere Houston involved local black lawyers and community institutions in the law suits. In St. Louis Sidney Redmond and Henry Espy of the Mound City Bar Association worked on the case. The black press reported regularly on each step of the litigation, and black residents attended the hearings. One of the highlights of the case was the reaction of the dean of the Missouri Law School, William Edward Masterson, who not only had a "complete lapse of memory" when Houston asked him telling a question, but who also "wiggled like an earthworm" on the stand.

As Houston had anticipated, the case was lost in Missouri's Supreme Court. (An understanding of jurisdiction necessitated that lawyers present in state courts claims regarding a state's obligation to its black citizens, but rarely had southern or border states ruled in favor of blacks.) Houston, with the assistance of his former students and colleagues at Howard University—Leon Ransom, NAACP Assistant Special Counsel Marshall, and Lovett, as well as Redmond and Epsy—prepared to appeal. Houston appeared before the Supreme Court in 1938 for the oral arguments in the Gaines case. On trial was more than Gaines's individual claim. Houston challenged white supremacy as illegal, immoral, and inequitable when he made assertions about myths and biased interpretations of *Plessy v. Ferguson.* Was it not true that equal protection of the laws meant that if white Missourians were entitled to legal education by the state, then black citizens were entitled to legal education of the same quality? The contention was unambiguous: Missouri had denied Gaines equal protection by excluding him from the law school of the tax-supported University of Missouri for no reason other than his race; further, the university had failed to prove its out-of-state scholarships for blacks provided an equal opportunity for legal training.

Hardly had one month elapsed before the Supreme Court held that Missouri's Supreme Court had erred in denying the petitioner, Gaines, his federal rights. Chief Justice Charles Evans Hughes delivered the opinion that vindicated the NAACP's position, and he enunciated the new controlling precedent: the "obligation of the State to give the protection of equal laws" is imposed upon the state by the Constitution and must be "performed . . . within its own jurisdiction. . . . Here the petitioner's right was a personal one . . . and the State was bound to furnish him within its borders facilities for legal education substantially equal to those which the State . . . afforded for persons of the white race."

The implications of the decision were far-reaching, as the precedent inevitably extended beyond tax-supported law schools. It outlawed out-of-state scholarships and regional university programs for blacks as a means by which states might maintain segregation and shirk constitutional duties within their borders. Houston's success in the case of Gaines ushered in a period of widespread influence among NAACP-affiliated lawyers. The results of the Gaines case also provided a basis for changes in his personal life.

Ideally Houston should have been directing legal affairs for the NAACP from its Manhattan headquarters, but in mid-1938 he had responded to other responsibilities. In order to keep the firm, Houston, Houston & Hastie, out of jeopardy while his father served as special assistant to the U.S. attorney general and his colleague Hastie served as U.S. district court judge in the Virgin Islands, Houston had moved back to Washington, D.C. From here he supervised the education cases; his protégé Marshall—elevated to co-special counsel—worked in New York City. Whatever doubts might have existed about the arrangement were quieted by the impact of the Gaines's victory and the momentum it provided. No one presented a formidable challenge to Houston's NAACP strategy, which aimed at laying a social and legal foundation for direct attacks on racial discrimination and segregation.

Though he relinquished the title "special counsel" in 1940, Houston continued to cooperate with the NAACP Legal Department and its tax-exempt arm (which was established by the NAACP in 1939), the NAACP Legal Defense and Educational Fund, Incorporated (Inc. Fund) until his death in 1950. The Inc. Fund concentrated on racial discrimination in public education, while the NAACP's own legal work was concerned with a wide variety of litigation on other civil rights matters. Under Houston's leadership as member and later chairman of the NAACP's National Legal Committee, the NAACP's policy and practice were to support and promote the activities of the Inc. Fund. Due to Houston's unusual interpersonal skills, the NAACP board and staff, its legal committee, and the Inc. Fund all worked together and in effect spoke with one voice.

Houston remained the greatly admired and heavily leaned-upon philosopher-teacher, legal strategist, and tactician. His propensity for entertaining a broad range of views regarding the civil rights struggle and for arriving at sound approaches through careful analysis and discussion was striking. Marshall himself was accustomed to writing Houston for "suggestions as to [a NAACP lawyers'] meeting ... [and] working together between the National Legal Committee, the legal staff of the national office [Inc. Fund] and ... branch lawyers." In the years between Houston's death and the 1954 school segregation decision, Marshall and others at the Inc. Fund continued to ask, "What would Charlie say?"

For both Houston and the NAACP the goal of complete elimination of segregation remained compelling. As Houston had expressed it initially, "Equality of education is not enough. ... No segregation operates fairly on a minority group unless it is a dominant minority." By the late 1940s the impressive series of successful NAACP cases had turned the attack from an indirect one into a direct one. In 1947 Houston wrote in a major black newspaper that "one of the most interesting developments in the entire campaign is the change in the way the issue of segregation has been handled. ... The NAACP lawyers in order to get the campaign underway accepted the doctrine that the state could segregate ... provided equal accommodations were afforded. Now the NAACP is making a direct, open, all-out fight against segregation. ... There is no such thing as 'separate but equal.' ... Segregation itself imports inequality." Gradually, however, as his health failed, he withdrew from direct participation. As he wrote one of the NAACP's chief new leaders in the campaign in 1949: "These education cases are now tight sufficiently so that anyone familiar with the course of the decisions should be able to guide the cases through. You and Thurgood can proceed without any fear of crossing any plans I might have."

Houston had been interested in the problems of the black workers, and after returning to private practice in 1938 much of his attention was given to pioneering litigation on their behalf. No philanthropist or national civil rights organization offered funds with which to fight racial discrimination and injustice in employment when Houston decided to turn his attention to labor law and inequities affecting black workers. Samuel Clark and J. A. Reynolds, members of the Association of Colored Railway Trainmen and Locomotive Firemen (ACR) of Virginia, an all-black union, had come to Houston, Houston & Hastie because of Houston's reputation with the NAACP. Clark recalled, "I wanted to go to Washington to go before Congress or anybody that I could to find out what we should do to protect our rights." The workers felt virtually helpless in the face of large racist unions, unsympathetic employers, and the new collective-bargaining procedures of the amended National Railway Labor Act of 1934. Under the law only bargaining agents chosen by the majority of members in a union could be statutory representatives in collective-bargaining negotiations. Invariably this seemed to work to the detriment of the minority black workers, since all of the railroad brotherhood excluded blacks from membership. In 1940 Houston became the general counsel for both the ACR and a sister organization, the International Association of Railway Employees (IARE). The pace for pursuing the rights of these black railroad workers was less cautious than that of the NAACP's education campaign. Nonetheless, it was a carefully designed assault on bastions of white supremacy in the world of labor. Houston, with a young Howard law graduate, Joseph Waddy, assisting him, expressed the militancy and urgency of the workers in legal papers fashioned for judges.

In another important respect this fight differed from the campaign against discrimination in education. Minor skirmishes and battles to invalidate a particularly unfavorable precedent gradually would not be acceptable "positionary tactics." In the case of black workers' rights, a direct attack was imperative. There was virtual silence from both Congress and the Supreme Court on the issue at hand, and in the one significant precedent (*Hodges v. United States,* 1906) the Supreme Court had held that even though they were covered by union contract, black workers dismissed from their jobs had no federally protected rights under which they could sue. Houston summarized the situation for Clark: "You don't have any laws to protect you, but I'm going to make some laws that will."

Two primary concerns dictated how forcefully and how uncompromisingly the attack was to be launched. First, the well-being of Houston's clients and their unions had to be considered. Acts of hostility toward blacks by national unions dated back to 1863 and included the removal of blacks from upwardly mobile or steady jobs by exclusion from craft unions, secret union-management agreements, and even murder. Second, the lawyers needed to establish as soon as possible, through a test case, that there was a constitutional principle of fair representation regardless of race. Houston and Waddy sued on behalf of the ACR and IARE, articulating grievances that ranged from loss of wages, destruction of seniority rights, breach of contract, and fraud to the federal question of breach of duty under the Railway Labor Act.

Recognizing that the success and the credibility of his leadership in any battle for workers' employment rights hinged on more than legal expertise, Houston came to know the black union people and to move in their circles. The ACR and IARE were independent unions of men who operated trains—i.e., operating workers—therefore, he went to where they were meeting in their locals and on their jobs, climbing piers and examining tracks to "find out how the work was, what they had to do."

In *Steele v. Louisville & Nashville* and *Tunstall v. Brotherhood of Locomotive Firemen* (1944), Houston first clarified for the courts the relation of fairness and freedom under the Constitution to the racially discriminatory activities of railway labor unions acting under federal law. Houston planned and with the aid of Waddy and an Alabama attorney, Arthur Shores, promptly prosecuted Bester William Steele's case through the Alabama state court system while petitioning the federal court system for relief on behalf of Tom Tunstall. Carefully constructed arguments and strong records in both cases won the workers a hearing before the U.S. Supreme Court after the Alabama Supreme Court and the U.S. Court of Appeals ruled against Steele and Tunstall, respectively.

Arguing both cases before the U.S. Supreme Court, Houston declared that an agent designated under federal law as the exclusive bargaining agent had a good faith duty to the minority workers. That duty minimally included representing the minority equally with the majority, which had selected the agent, and seeking no profit for union members in the majority over the non-union or minority union members. "An opposite interpretation," Houston insisted, "would legitimize a federal law permitting the denial of equal protection and due process."

The Court's decision in December 1944 vindicating Houston's position was a signal constitutional achievement. It established a precedent for fair representation of all workers regardless of race or union affiliation. Nevertheless, Houston perceived it as no final victory. The Supreme Court extended to the men the opportunity to sue for their rights in accordance with the principle established in the cases, but the principle would have to be developed further to "make sure that [the cases] give our people real protection," Houston reported to the ACR and IARE. Moreover, consistent with his view of judges and other public officers—whom he labelled generally "servants of the class which places them in office and maintains them there"—Houston quickly reminded a friend the mass "agitation . . . over the plight of the Negro [locomotive] firemen" and "the work of the President's Committee on Fair Employment Practices. . . . served as the background" for the high court's action. Subsequently Houston and Waddy handled a series of cases for railroad workers. The practical benefits of their legal victories proved limited, given the context of the times, but they were of utmost importance in establishing the precedents on which A. Philip Randolph's Brotherhood of Sleeping Car Porters and others succeeded in fashioning a body of labor law that eventually proved highly effective in breaking down barriers of discrimination by both industry and unions.

Convinced that all the questions about workers' rights and fairness "cannot be fought out in . . . courts because the courts are too slow and litigation . . . too expensive," Houston had supported the wartime Fair Employment Practices Committee (FEPC) since its inception in 1941. The FEPC had been created under pressure by Franklin D. Roosevelt's executive order in response to Randolph's threatened March on Washington during 1941. Houston's vocal and persistent advocacy of black workers' rights had led to his appointment to the FEPC by Roosevelt in February 1944. The Norfolk *Journal & Guide* reporter remarked then, "Mr. Houston's appointment, because of his militancy and ability will undoubtedly meet with . . . hearty approval from the Negro and other liberal organizations."

Hard-working, outspoken, and unyielding in his demand for fairness regardless of race, Houston personally investigated workers' complaints against corporations across the country, but especially on the West Coast. In late 1945 he became a spokesman for the committee, focusing on the problem of employment discrimination in the urban transit industry. This problem had a low priority in the view of the executive branch of the federal government, and Houston voiced his discontent. Subsequently he made public his criticism of President Harry Truman's alleged commitment to racially fair employment practices when the president's office blocked, on the basis of specious logic, the FEPC's directive to Capital Transit of the District of Columbia that it cease discriminatory hiring and promotion practices. At first evasive and finally unresponsive, White House aides flaunted their lack of respect for the FEPC and Houston during the entire transit controversy.

The refusal of Truman to meet with the FEPC, despite the committee's urgent request, compelled Houston to conclude that the president was both repudiating the committee and nullifying the executive orders that created the administrative body. In a letter to Truman, in December 1945, which received wide press coverage, Houston resigned from FEPC. Telling Truman that "the effect of your intervention in the Capital Transit case is not to eliminate the discrimination but to condone it," Houston could not see himself remaining a part of an administration marked by its "failure to enforce democratic practices and to protect minorities."

Houston had not sought greater recognition and acclaim from civil libertarian lawyers and Afro-Americans in connection with his challenges to racially discriminatory employment practices and policies, but he had gained it anyway. Although he fell out of favor with the Truman administration, Houston managed to move in and out of a presidential appointment with his militancy and integrity intact. According to Houston, it was the duty of the lawyers to "find a way to make the United State Supreme Court change" rulings that permitted denials of liberty.

It would have sounded self-serving if Houston had hinted to anyone except Henrietta, his wife of eight years, how responsible for blacks and America he felt. Sometimes he felt driven. He really believed what he so often told his Howard students and colleagues—"no tea for the feeble, no crepe for the dead." Although Houston wanted to be with his family and he was quite attached to his son, he could not be satisfied with less than superior effort in any professional undertaking, so he was often absent from his family. Getting the job done right was one of the important attributes that all of his students, colleagues, family, and friends remembered about Houston. So when Henrietta Houston heard him explain, before he left for an NAACP conference on restrictive covenants, that "the test of character is the amount of strain it can bear," she was not surprised.

The NAACP had decided upon a full-fledged attack on racially restrictive covenants, and at this planning conference Houston was undoubtedly the most respected lawyer present. Contracts that contained restrictions on the buying and selling of houses to a particular race or ethnic group were major impediments to equal housing opportunities. Since 1940 Houston had been handling restrictive covenant cases in the District of Columbia through his firm. He had spent years on strategy and tactics because he was unalterably opposed to infringements on the rights to convey property and to live in a house of one's choice in the land of one's birth.

As in the education and the employee-rights cases, there existed a negative precedent from the Supreme Court. The Court, in an NAACP-supported case, *Corrigan* v. *Buckley* (1926), had refused to rule against the practice. Now in the fall of 1947 a new NAACP-supported case, the Missouri case of *Shelley* v. *Kraemer*, had been certified for review by the Supreme Court. Houston, with his acute sense of timing, was anxious that a District of Columbia case, *Hurd* v. *Hodge*, for which he was attorney, should be considered by the Court at the same time. In the litigation concerning Houston's clients, lower court judgments had restricted the Hurds' purchase and occupancy of a covenanted house. The U.S. District Court and the U.S. Court of Appeals ruled against them. Even a motion for rehearing at the Court of Appeals level had been denied. Their attorney's last resort was to petition the U.S. Supreme Court. Timing was critical to Houston, because he was certain that the attack on this restrictive covenant would be most effective if heard in conjunction with the NAACP cases.

Working with Howard law alumnus and future judge of the U.S. Court of Appeals, Spottswood Robinson III, and a white civil libertarian attorney, Phineas Indritz, who volunteered his services without fee, Houston worked on the case in his usual intensive way. Robinson recalled that "long hours, incessant toil and meticulous attention to each element of the problem were the keys. . . . And at no time when I worked with him did I see any 'tea for the feeble.' " As they worked on the request for a hearing in the U.S. Supreme Court, Houston returned drafts to Robinson for refinement with regularity and, as Robinson remembered, Houston's "wide advice, accompanied by explanation of the analysis and synthesis forerunning it, was a revelation in itself." The three men researched and wrote painstakingly in order to show the applicability of the Fifth Amendement and the federal Civil

Rights Act of 1866 to their clients' claim. Conrad Harper writes that "*Hurd,* in which Houston's richly comprehensive presentation drew on constitutional, statutory, common law, public policy and social science materials, was one of his most extensively prepared cases." The central question of the brief was also a challenge to the justices and the system of which they were a part: "Shall we in the United States have ghettoes for racial, religious and other minorities, or even exclude such minorities entirely from whole areas of our country, by a system of judicially enforced restrictions based on private prejudices and made effective through the use of government authority and power?"

As in all of his civil rights cases, Houston considered public support a necessity. He and the NAACP lawyers invited organizations interested in the battle to file briefs as friends of the court. He was most gratified, for obvious reasons, by such a brief filed by the office of the U.S. attorney general. And Houston created his own propaganda. In the *Afro-American,* he publicized the housing rights cases during 1947 and January 1948.

In oral argument before the Supreme Court, Houston called the attention of the Court to the meaninglessness of the right to own property without the right to be protected from judicially enforced discrimination. Houston stressed the racism inherent in the right his opponents claimed, discussed the legal propositions that clarified federal duty, and pointed out the record of facts pertaining to race relations. After his opponents confidently reminded the Court of its precedent in *Corrigan* v. *Buckley,* Houston forced the issue out of its private-agreement vacuum. In rebuttal he asked how such privacy could be reconciled with participation in World War II and with national security concerns. Robinson allowed that "just to watch him in action was to witness a demonstration of the way it ought to be done," as others in attendance remembered Houston exhibiting an intrepidity not frequently witnessed in the U.S. Supreme Court. To be certain that the justices understood the fundamental matter before them, Houston concluded with startling clarity, "Racism must go!"

Hurd v. *Hodge* and *Shelley* v. *Kraemer* settled the issues of judicial enforcement of restrictive covenants. Delivering opinions on both of these cases in May 1948, the justices declared such contracts unenforceable in the courts of the land. The equal protection clause of the Fourteenth Amendment prohibited such state action and the U.S. Code invalidated federal court enforcement of such agreements.

By the last years of the 1940s, Houston had enormous influence among civil rights and civil liberties proponents, but his court arguments did not reach the masses of black people as he had hoped. He was litigating education, labor, and housing cases. He was in demand throughout the United States to speak in defense of the rights of black Americans in every area of life. His legal advice was often coveted. Supporting the National Negro Congress's appeal to the United Nations, Houston told the readers of his weekly newspaper column that "discrimination and denial of human and civil rights [had] reach[ed] a national level" and the national government was not protecting black Americans against "local aggression." Houston encouraged Afro-Americans to see themselves a part of the non-white majority in a world that included Africans and Asians intent upon freeing themselves from the bonds of Western imperialism and colonialism. Regarding white America, he added, we have a "spiritual responsibility to lead . . . white United States brethren into the real fellowship of nations."

In Houston's last years, black people saw him as part of black leadership delegations in the White House protesting segregation or as a keynote speaker for rallies on the rights of blacks and he was. In 1950, when both the black and white press prominently reported his death from a heart attack, blacks of all classes knew that they had lost a champion in Houston. Mourners at his funeral included five U.S. Supreme Court justices, federal judges, the secretary of the Department of the Interior, journalists who had covered Houston's many activities, colleagues such as Marshall, Wilkins, and White of the NAACP, Waddy, and Robinson as well as a score of other lawyers who identified themselves as "social engineers" and civil rights lawyers. As Hastie reminded those present, Houston engaged in struggle with full knowledge of its risks, yet he believed that "every battle must be fought until it is won . . . without pause to take account of those stricken in the fray."

Charles Hamilton Houston, as an educator and civil rights lawyer/activist, played a principal role in defining and pacing the legal phase of the Afro-American struggle for freedom from 1935 until his death. He always tried to take into account not only racial and class violence and exploitation, but also the *modus operandi* of the judicial system, limited minority access to law-making branches of government, and an historically racist, undemocratic, non-egalitarian society. In the context of this legal struggle he operated primarily in the judicial arena. Nevertheless, Houston also worked through other arms of the legal system because he recognized that "courts [were] too slow." He believed, however, that disfranchisement and racial repression militated against the immediately successful use of Congress, state legislatures, or executive agencies with no enforcement power as weapons in the struggle. Convinced that mass agitation and protest were essential, Houston supported direct action and participated in demonstrations, although his own major contribution lay in working through the courts.

Houston consistently held a position of leadership among Afro-Americans between 1935 and 1950. His legal accomplishments were the consequence of carefully considered, well-developed legal strategies and skillful arguments. Justice William 0. Douglas of the U.S. Supreme Court, who was appointed in 1939 and had occasion to assess Houston as a litigator, noted: "I knew Charles H. Houston; and I sincerely believe he was one of the top ten advocates to appear before this court in my 35 years." His philosophy of social engineering—using the law to secure fundamental social change for the improvement of society and to establish and protect minority rights—had wide acceptance among civil rights lawyers. Moreover Houston maintained a strong leadership position among black people because of his skill at interpersonal relationships. His successes in the Supreme Court were shared accomplishments. They resulted from the cooperation of many legal associates throughout the nation and even the active efforts of communities, individuals, and protest organizations. He was a respected leader because people could sense that he was neither arrogant nor manipulative. He regarded himself as a "technician probing in the courts . . . how far the existing system will permit the exercise of freedom," and therefore he openly entertained a wide range of views pertaining to the struggle for freedom and justice. Finally, his legal strategy for promoting judicial recognition of the Afro-Americans' rights was successful. Not only did his work have some immediate impact on the opportunities for blacks to explore or exercise rights in some areas of American life, but his Supreme Court victories had far-reaching significance for the future progress of blacks in American society.

The Legal Attack to Secure Civil Rights

Thurgood Marshall (1908–1993) became an attorney with the NAACP's Legal Defense Fund in 1936. He headed the legal attack on segregated education culminating in the landmark Brown v. Board of Education *decision, in which the Supreme Court found segregated schools to be inherently unequal. In 1967 he became the first African American to serve on the Supreme Court.*

The struggle for full citizenship rights can be speeded by enforcement of existing statutory provisions protecting our civil rights. The attack on discrimination by use of legal machinery has only scratched the surface. An understanding of the existing statutes protecting our civil rights is necessary if we are to work toward enforcement of these statutes.

Defining Civil Rights

The titles "civil rights" and "civil liberties" have grown to include large numbers of subjects, some of which are properly included under these titles and others which should not be included. One legal treatise has defined the subject of civil rights as follows: "In its broadest sense, the term civil rights includes those rights which are the outgrowth of civilization, the existence and exercise of which necessarily follow from the rights that repose in the subjects of a country exercising self-government."

The Fourteenth and Fifteenth Amendments to the Constitution are prohibitions against action by the states and state officers violating civil rights. In addition to these provisions of the United States Constitution and a few others, there are several statutes of the United States which also attempt to protect the rights of individual citizens against private persons as well as public officers. Whether these provisions are included under the title of "civil rights" or "civil liberties" or any other subject is more or less unimportant as long as we bear in mind the provisions themselves.

All of the statutes, both federal and state, which protect the individual rights of Americans are important to Negroes as well as other citizens. Many of these provisions, however, are of peculiar significance to Negroes because of the fact that in many instances these statutes are the only protection to which Negroes can look for redress. It should also be pointed out that many officials of both state and federal governments are reluctant to protect the rights of Negroes. It is often difficult to enforce our rights when they are perfectly clear. It is practically impossible to secure enforcement of any of our rights if there is any doubt whatsoever as to whether or not a particular statute applies to the particular state of facts.

As to law enforcement itself, the rule as to most American citizens is that if there is any way possible to prosecute individuals who have willfully interfered with the rights of other individuals such prosecution is attempted. However, when the complaining party is a Negro, the rule is usually to look for any possible grounds for *not* prosecuting. It is therefore imperative that Negroes be thoroughly familiar with the rights guaranteed them by law in order that they may be in a position to insist that all of their fundamental rights as American citizens be protected.

The Thirteenth Amendment to the Constitution, abolishing slavery, the Fourteenth Amendment, prohibiting any action of state officials denying due process or the equal protection of its laws, and the Fifteenth Amendment, prohibiting discrimination by the states in voting are well-known to all of us. In addition to these provisions of the Constitution, there are the so-called Federal "Civil Rights Statutes" which include several Acts of Congress such as the Civil Rights Act and other statutes which have been amended from time to time and are now grouped together in several sections of the United States Code. The original Civil Rights Act was passed in Congress in 1866, but was vetoed by President Andrew Johnson the same year. It was, however, passed over the veto. It was reintroduced and passed in 1870 because there was some doubt as to its constitutionality, having been passed before the Fourteenth Amendment was ratified. The second bill has been construed several times and has been held constitutional by the United States Supreme Court, which in one case stated that "the plain objects of these statutes, as of the Constitution which authorized them, was to place the colored race, in respect to civil rights, upon a level with the whites. They made the rights and responsibilities, civil and criminal, of the two races exactly the same." (*Virginia v. Rives,* 100 U.S. 313 [1879])

The Thirteenth and Fourteenth and Fifteenth Amendments, along with the civil rights statutes, protect the following rights:

1. Slavery is abolished and peonage is punishable as a federal crime. (13th amendment)
2. All persons born or naturalized in the U.S. are citizens and no state shall make or enforce any law abridging their privileges or immunities, or deny them equal protection of the law. (14th amendment)
3. The right of citizens to vote cannot be abridged by the United States or by any state on account of race or color. (15th amendment)
4. All persons within the jurisdiction of the United States shall have the same right to enforce contracts, or sue, be parties, give evidence, and to the full and equal benefit of all laws and proceedings as is enjoyed by white citizens.
5. All persons shall be subject to like punishment, pains, penalties, taxes, licenses, and extractions of every kind, and to no other.
6. All citizens shall have the same right in every state and territory, as is enjoyed by white citizens to inherit, purchase, lease, sell, hold and convey property.
7. Every person who, under color of statutes, custom or usage, subjects any citizen of the United States or person within the jurisdiction thereof to the deprivation of any rights, privileges, or immunities secured by the Constitution and laws is liable in an action at law, suit in equity, or other proper proceedings for redress.
8. Citizens possessing all other qualifications may not be disqualified from jury service in federal or state courts on account of race or color; any officer charged with the duty of selection or summoning of jurors who shall exclude citizens for reasons of race or color shall be guilty of a misdemeanor.
9. A conspiracy of two or more persons to deprive any person or class of persons of any rights guaranteed by constitution and laws is punishable as a crime and the conspirators are also liable in damages.

Most of these provisions only protect the citizen against wrongdoing by public officials, although the peonage statutes and one or two others protect against wrongs by private persons.

Despite the purposes of these Acts which the United States Supreme Court insisted in 1879 "made the rights and responsibilities, civil and criminal, of the two races exactly the same," the experience of all of us points to the fact that this purpose has not as yet been accomplished. There are several reasons for this. In the first place, in certain sections of this country, especially in the deep south, judges, prosecutors and members of grand and petit juries, have simply refused to follow the letter or spirit of these provisions. Very often it happens that although the judge and prosecutor are anxious to enforce the laws, members of the jury are reluctant to protect the rights of Negroes. A third reason is that many Negroes themselves for one reason or another hesitate to avail themselves of the protection afforded by the United States Constitution and statutes.

These statutes protecting our civil rights in several instances provide for both criminal and civil redress. Some are criminal only and others are for civil action only. Criminal prosecution for violation of the federal statutes can be obtained only through the United States Department of Justice.

Up through and including the administration of Attorney General Homer S. Cummings, Negroes were unable to persuade the U.S. Department of Justice to enforce any of the civil rights statutes where Negroes were the complaining parties. The NAACP and its staff made repeated requests and in many instances filed detailed statements and briefs requesting prosecution for lynch mobs, persons guilty of peonage and other apparent violations of the federal statutes. It was not until the [1939–1940] administration of Attorney General Frank Murphy that any substantial efforts were made to enforce the civil rights statutes as they apply to Negroes. Attorney General Murphy established a Civil Rights Section in the Department of Justice.

During the present [1944] administration of Attorney General Francis Biddle there have been several instances of prosecution of members of lynch mobs for the first time in the history of the United States Department of Justice. There have also been numerous successful prosecutions of persons guilty of peonage and slavery. However, other cases involving the question of the beating and killing of Negro soldiers by local police officers, the case involving the action of Sheriff Tip Hunter, of Brownsville, Tennessee, who killed at least one Negro citizen and forced several others to leave town, the several cases of refusal to permit qualified Negroes to vote, as well as other cases, have received the attention of the Department of Justice only to the extent of "investigating." Our civil rights as guaranteed by the federal statutes will never become a reality until the U.S. Department of Justice decides that it represents the entire United States and is not required to fear offending any section of the country which believes that it has the God-given right to be above the laws of the United States and the United States Supreme Court. . . .

There are, however, certain bright spots in the enforcement of the federal statutes. In addition to the lynching and peonage cases handled by the Washington office of the Department of Justice, there have been a few instances of courageous United States Attorneys in such places as Georgia who have vigorously prosecuted police officers who have used the power of their office as a cloak for beating up Negro citizens.

An Example of Civil Rights Enforcement

As a result of the recent decision in the Texas Primary Case [*Smith v. Allwright*], it is possible to use an example of criminal prosecution under the civil rights statutes by taking a typical case of the refusal to permit the Negroes to vote in the Democratic Primary elections. Let us see how a prosecution is started: In Waycross, Georgia, for example, we will suppose a Negro elector on July 4, 1944, went to the polls with his tax receipt and demanded to vote in the Democratic Primary. He should, of course, have witnesses with him. Let us also assume that the election officials refused to let him vote solely because of his race or color.

As a matter of law, the election officials violated a federal criminal law and are subject to fine and imprisonment. But how should the voter or the organized Negro citizens, or the local NAACP Branch go about trying to get the machinery of criminal justice in motion? Of course, the details of what happens must be put in writing and sworn to by the person who tried to vote and also by his witnesses. Then the matter must be placed before the United States Attorney. This is the *federal* district attorney.

I wonder how many of the delegates here know who is the United States Attorney for their district, or even where his office is. Every Branch should know the United States Attorney for that area, even if a delegation goes in just to get acquainted and let him know that we expect him to enforce the civil rights laws with the same vigor as used in enforcing other criminal statutes.

But back to the voting case. The affidavits must be presented to the United States Attorney with a demand that he investigate and place the evidence before the Federal Grand Jury. At the same time copies of the affidavits and statements in the case should be sent to the National Office. We will see that they get to the Attorney General in Washington. I wish that I could guarantee you that the Attorney General would put pressure on local United States Attorneys who seem reluctant to prosecute. At least we can assure you that we will give the Attorney General no rest unless he gets behind these reluctant United States Attorneys throughout the south.

There is no reason why a hundred clear cases of this sort should not be placed before the United States Attorneys and the Attorney General every year until the election officials discover that it is both wiser and safer to follow the United States laws than to violate them. It is up to us to see that these officials of the Department of Justice are called upon to act again and again wherever there are violations of the civil rights statutes. Unfortunately, there are plenty of such cases. It is equally unfortunate that there are not enough individuals and groups presenting these cases and demanding action.

Neglected Civil Rights Statutes

The responsibility for enforcement of the civil provisions of the civil rights statutes rests solely with the individual. In the past we have neglected to make full use of these statutes. Although they have been on the books since 1870, there were very few cases under these statutes until recent years. Whereas in the field of general law there are many, many precedents for all other types of action, there are very few precedents for the protection of civil liberties.

The most important of the civil rights provisions is the one which provides that "every person who, under color of any statute, ordinance, regulation, custom or usage of any state or territory, subjects or causes to be subjected any citizen of the United States or person within the jurisdiction thereof to the deprivation of any rights, privileges or immunities secured by the Constitution and laws shall be liable to the party injured in an action at law, suit in equity or other proper proceeding for redress." Under this statute any officer of a state, county or municipality who while acting in an official capacity, denies to any citizen or person within the state any of the rights guaranteed by the Constitution or laws is subject to a civil action. This statute has been used to equalize teachers' salaries and to obtain bus transportation for Negro schoolchildren. It can be used to attack *every* form of discrimination against Negroes by public school systems. . . .

This statute, along with other of the civil rights statutes, can be used to enforce the right to register and vote throughout the country. The threats of many of the bigots in the south to disregard the ruling of the Supreme Court of the United States in the recent Texas Primary decision has not intimidated a single person. The United States Supreme Court remains the highest court in this land. Election officials in states affected by this decision will either let Negroes vote in the Democratic Primaries, or they will be subjected to both criminal and civil prosecution under the civil rights statutes. In every state in the deep south Negroes have this year attempted to vote in the primary elections. Affidavits concerning the refusal to permit them to vote in Alabama, Florida and Georgia have already been sent to the United States Department of Justice. We will insist that these election officials be prosecuted and will also file civil suits against the guilty officials.

It can be seen from these examples that we have just begun to scratch the surface in the fight for full enforcement of these statutes. The NAACP can move no faster than the individuals who have been discriminated against. We only take up cases where we are requested to do so by persons who have been discriminated against.

Another crucial problem is the ever-present problem of segregation. Whereas the principle has been established by cases handled by the NAACP that neither states nor municipalities can pass ordinances segregating residences by race, the growing problem today is the problem of segregation by means of restrictive covenants, whereby private owners band together to prevent Negro occupancy of particular neighborhoods. Although this problem is particularly acute in Chicago, it is at the same time growing in intensity throughout the country. It has the full support of the real estate boards in the several cities, as well as most of the banks and other leading agencies. The legal attack on this problem has met with spotty success. In several instances restrictive covenants have been declared invalid because the neighborhood has changed, or for other reasons. Other cases have been lost. However, the NAACP is in the process of preparing a detailed memorandum and will establish procedure which will lead to an all-out legal attack on restrictive covenants. Whether or not this attack will be successful cannot be determined at this time.

The National Housing Agency and the Federal Public Housing Authority have established a policy of segregation in federal public housing projects. A test case has been filed in Detroit, Mich., and is still pending in the local federal courts. The Detroit situation is the same as in other sections of the country. Despite the fact that the Housing Authority and other agencies insist that they will maintain separate but equal facilities, it never develops that the separate facilities are equal in all respects. In Detroit separate projects were built and it developed that by the first of this year every single

white family in the area eligible for public housing had been accommodated and
there were still some 800 "white" units vacant with "no takers." At the same time
there were some 45,000 Negroes inadequately housed and with no units open to
them. This is the inevitable result of "separate but equal" treatment. . . .

State Laws

We should also be mindful of the several so-called civil rights statutes in the several
states. There are civil rights acts in at least 18 states, all of which are in the north and
middle west. These statutes are in California, Colorado, Connecticut, Illinois, Indiana,
Iowa, Kansas, Massachusetts, Michigan, Minnesota, Nebraska, New Jersey, New York,
Ohio, Pennsylvania, Rhode Island and Washington. California provides only for civil
action. Illinois, Kansas, Minnesota, New York and Ohio have both civil and criminal
provisions. In New Jersey the only action is a criminal action, or an action for penalty
in the name of the state, the amount of the penalty going to the state.

In those states not having civil rights statutes it is necessary that every effort
be made to secure passage of one. In states having weak civil rights statutes efforts
should be made to have them strengthened. In states with reasonably strong civil
rights statutes, like Illinois and New York, it is necessary that every effort be made
to enforce them. . . .

Outside of New York City there are very few successful cases against the civil
rights statutes because of the fact that members of the jury are usually reluctant
to enforce the statutes. I understand the same is true for Illinois. The only method
of counteracting this vicious practice is by means of educating the general public,
from which juries are chosen, to the plight of the Negro.

It should also be pointed out that many of our friends of other races are not
as loud and vociferous as the enemies of our race. In northern and mid-western
cities it repeatedly happens that a prejudiced southerner on entering a hotel or
restaurant, seeing Negroes present makes an immediate and loud protest to the
manager. It is very seldom that any of our friends go to the managers of places
where Negroes are excluded and complain to them of this fact. Quite a job can be
done if our friends of other races will only realize the importance of this problem
and get up from their comfortable chairs and actually go to work on the problem.

Bring Civil Rights Violators to Justice

Thus it seems clear that although it is necessary and vital to all of us that we continue
our program for additional legislation to guarantee and enforce certain of our rights,
at the same time we must continue with ever-increasing vigor to enforce those few
statutes, both federal and state, which are now on the statute books. We must not be
delayed by people who say "the time is not ripe," nor should we proceed with caution
for fear of destroying the "status quo." Persons who deny to us our civil rights should
be brought to justice now. Many people believe the time is always "ripe" to discriminate
against Negroes. All right then—the time is always "ripe" to bring them to justice.
The responsibility for the enforcement of these statutes rests with every American
citizen regardless of race or color. However, the real job has to be done by the Negro
population with whatever friends of the other races are willing to join in.

On the Role of Martin Luther King

August Meier is author of numerous books on the civil rights movement. He is a professor of history at Kent State University.

The phenomenon that is Martin Luther King consists of a number of striking paradoxes. The Nobel Prize winner is accepted by the outside world as *the* leader of the nonviolent direct action movement, but he is criticized by many activists within the movement. He is criticized for what appears, at times, as indecisiveness, and is more often denounced for a tendency to accept compromise. Yet in the eyes of most Americans, both black and white, he remains the symbol of militant direct action. So potent is this symbol of King as direct actionist that a new myth is arising about his historic role. The real credit for developing and projecting the techniques and philosophy of nonviolent direct action in the civil rights arena must be given to the Congress of Racial Equality [CORE], which was founded in 1942—more than a dozen years before the Montgomery bus boycott projected King into international fame. And the idea of mass action by Negroes themselves to secure redress of their grievances must, in large part, be ascribed to the vision of A. Philip Randolph, architect of the March on Washington Movement during World War II. Yet, as we were told in Montgomery on March 25, 1965, King and his followers now assert, apparently without serious contradiction, that a new type of civil rights strategy was born at Montgomery in 1955 under King's auspices.

In a movement in which respect is accorded in direct proportion to the number of times one has been arrested, King appears to keep the number of times he goes to jail to a minimum. In a movement in which successful leaders are those who share in the hardships of their followers, in the risks they take, in the beatings they receive, in the length of time they spend in jail, King tends to leave prison for other important engagements, rather than remaining there and suffering with his followers. In a movement in which leadership ordinarily devolves upon persons who mix democratically with their followers, King remains isolated and aloof. In a movement which prides itself on militancy and "no compromise" with racial discrimination or with the white "power structure," King maintains close relationships with, and appears to be influenced by, Democratic presidents and their emissaries, seems amenable to compromises considered by some half a loaf or less, and often appears willing to postpone or avoid a direct confrontation in the streets.

King's career has been characterized by failures that, in the larger sense, must be accounted triumphs. The buses in Montgomery were desegregated only after lengthy judicial proceedings conducted by the NAACP [National Association for the Advancement of Colored People] Legal Defense Fund secured a favorable decision from the U.S. Supreme Court. Nevertheless, the events in Montgomery were a triumph for direct action and gave this tactic a popularity unknown when identified solely with CORE. King's subsequent major campaigns—in Albany, Georgia; Danville, Virginia; Birmingham, Alabama; and St. Augustine, Florida—ended as failures or with only token accomplishments. But each of them, chiefly because of his presence, dramatically focused national and international attention on the plight of the southern Negro, thereby facilitating overall progress. In Birmingham in particular, demonstrations which fell short of their local goals were directly responsible for a major Federal Civil Rights Act. Essentially, this pattern of local failure and national victory was recently enacted at Selma, Alabama.

King is ideologically committed to disobeying unjust laws and court orders, in the Gandhian tradition, but generally he follows a policy of not disobeying federal court orders. In his recent Montgomery speech he expressed a crude, neo-Marxist interpretation of history romanticizing the Populist movement as a genuine Union of black and white common people, ascribing race prejudice to capitalists playing white workers against black. Yet, in practice, he is amenable to compromise with the white bourgeois political and economic establishment. More important, King enunciates a superficial and eclectic philosophy, and by virtue of it he has profoundly awakened the moral conscience of America.

In short, King can be described as a "conservative militant." In this combination of militancy with conservatism and caution, of righteousness with respectability, lies the secret of King's enormous success.

Certain important civil rights leaders have dismissed King's position as the product of publicity generated by the mass communications media. But this can be said of the successes of the civil rights nonviolent action movement generally. Without publicity it is hard to conceive that much progress would have been made. In fact, contrary to the official nonviolent direct action philosophy, demonstrations have secured their results not by changing the hearts of the oppressors through a display of nonviolent love, but through the national and international pressures generated by the publicity arising from mass arrests and incidents of violence. And no one has employed this strategy of securing publicity through mass arrests and precipitating violence from white hoodlums and law enforcement officers more than King himself. King abhors violence; as at Selma, for example, he constantly retreats from situations that might result in the deaths of his followers. But he is precisely most successful when, contrary to his deepest wishes, his demonstrations precipitate violence from southern whites against Negro and white demonstrators. We need only cite Birmingham and Selma to illustrate this point.

Publicity alone does not explain the durability of King's image, or why he remains, for the rank and file of whites and blacks alike, the symbol of the direct action movement, the nearest thing to a charismatic leader that the civil rights movement has ever had. At the heart of King's continuing influence and popularity are two facts. First, better than anyone else, he articulates the aspirations of Negroes who respond to the cadence of his addresses, his religious phraseology and manner of speaking, and the vision of his dream for them and for America. King has intuitively adopted the style of the old-fashioned Negro Baptist preacher and transformed it into a new art form; he has, indeed, restored oratory to its place among the arts. Second, he communicates Negro aspirations to white America more effectively than anyone else. His religious terminology and manipulation of the Christian symbols of love and nonresistance are partly responsible for his appeal among whites. To talk in terms of Christianity, love, and nonviolence is reassuring to the mentality of white America. At the same time, the very superficialities of his philosophy—that rich and eclectic amalgam of Jesus, Hegel, Gandhi, and others as outlined in his *Stride Toward Freedom*—make him appear intellectually profound to the superficially educated middle-class white American. Actually if he were a truly profound religious thinker, like Tillich or Niebuhr, his influence would of necessity be limited to a select audience. But by uttering moral clichés, the Christian pieties, in a magnificent display of oratory, King becomes enormously effective.

If his success with Negroes is largely due to the style of his utterance, his success with whites is a much more complicated matter. For one thing, he unerringly knows how to exploit with maximum effectiveness their growing feeling of guilt. King, of course, is not unique in attaining fame and popularity among whites through playing upon their guilt feelings. James Baldwin is the most conspicuous example of a man who has achieved success with this formula. The incredible fascination which the Black Muslims have for white people, and the posthumous near-sanctification of Malcolm X by many naive whites (in addition to many Negroes whose motivations are, of course, very different), must in large part be attributed to the same source. But King goes beyond this. With intuitive but extraordinary skill he not only castigates whites for their sins but, in contrast to angry young writers like Baldwin, he explicity states his belief in their salvation. Not only will direct action bring fulfillment of the "American Dream" to Negroes, but the Negroes' use of direct action will also help whites to live up to their Christian and democratic values; it will purify, cleanse, and heal the sickness in white society. Whites will benefit as well as Negroes. He has faith that the white man will redeem himself. Negroes must not hate whites, but love them. In this manner King first arouses the guilt feelings of whites, and then relieves them—though always leaving the lingering feeling in his white listeners that they should support his nonviolent crusade. Like a Greek tragedy, King's performance provides an extraordinary catharsis for the white listener.

King thus gives white men the feeling that he is their good friend, that he poses no threat to them. It is interesting to note that this was the same feeling that white men received from Booker T. Washington, the noted early twentieth century accommodator. Both men stressed their faith in the white man; both expressed the belief that the white man could be brought to accord Negroes their rights. Both stressed the importance of whites recognizing the rights of Negroes for the moral health and well-being of white society. Like King, Washington had an extraordinary following among whites. Like King, Washington symbolized for most whites the whole program of Negro advancement. While there are important similarities in the functioning of both men vis-à-vis the community, needless to say, in most respects, their philosophies are in disagreement.

It is not surprising, therefore, to find that King is the recipient of contributions from organizations and individuals who fail to eradicate evidence of prejudice in their own backyards. For example, certain liberal trade union leaders who are philosophically committed to full racial equality, who feel the need to identify their organizations with the cause of militant civil rights, although they are unable to defeat racist elements in their unions, contribute hundreds of thousands of dollars to King's Southern Christian Leadership Conference (SCLC). One might attribute this phenomenon to the fact that SCLC works in the South rather than the North, but this is true also for SNCC [Student Nonviolent Coordinating Committee], which does not benefit similarly from union treasuries. And the fact is that ever since the college students started their sit-ins in 1960, it is SNCC which has been the real spearhead of direct action in most of the South and has performed the lion's share of work in the local communities, while SCLC has received most of the publicity and most of the money. However, while King provides a verbal catharsis for whites, leaving them feeling purified and comfortable, SNCC's uncompromising militancy makes whites feel less comfortable and less beneficent.

The above is not to suggest that SNCC and SCLC are responsible for all, or nearly all, the direct action in the South. The NAACP has actively engaged in direct action, especially in Savannah under the leadership of W. W. Law, in South Carolina under I. DeQuincy Newman, and in Clarksdale, Mississippi, under Aaron Henry. The work of CORE—including most of the direct action in Louisiana, much of the non-violent work in Florida and Mississippi, and the famous Freedom Ride of 1961—has been most important. In addition, one should note the work of SCLC affiliates, such as those in Lynchburg, Virginia, led by the Reverend Virgil Wood; in Birmingham, by the Reverend Fred Shuttlesworth; and in Savannah, by Hosea Williams.

(There are other reasons for SNCC's lesser popularity with whites. These are connected with the great changes that have occurred in SNCC since it was founded in 1960, changes reflected in the half-jocular epigram circulating in SNCC circles that the Student Nonviolent Coordinating Committee has now become the "Non-Student Violent Non-Coordinating Committee." The point is, however, that even when SNCC thrilled the nation in 1960–61 with the student sit-ins that swept the South, it did not enjoy the popularity and financial support accorded to King.)

King's very tendencies toward compromise and caution, his willingness to negotiate and bargain with White House emissaries, and his hesitancy to risk the precipitation of mass violence upon demonstrators further endear him to whites. He appears to them a "responsible" and "moderate" man. To militant activists, King's failure to march past the state police on that famous Tuesday morning outside Selma indicated either a lack of courage or a desire to advance himself by currying presidential favor. But King's shrinking from a possible bloodbath, his accession to the entreaties of the political establishment, his acceptance of face-saving compromise in this, as in other instances, are fundamental to the particular role he is playing and essential for achieving and sustaining his image as a leader of heroic moral stature in the eyes of white men. His caution and compromise keep open the channels of communication between the activists and the majority of the white community. In brief: King makes the nonviolent direct action movement respectable.

Of course, many, if not most, activists reject the notion that the movement should be made respectable. Yet American history shows that for any reform movement to succeed, it must attain respectability. It must attract moderates, even conservatives, to its ranks. The March on Washington made direct action respectable; Selma made it fashionable. More than any other force, it is Martin Luther King who impressed the civil rights revolution on the American conscience and is attracting that great middle body of American public opinion to its support. It is this revolution of conscience that will undoubtedly lead fairly soon to the elimination of all violations of Negroes' constitutional rights, thereby creating the conditions for the economic and social changes that are necessary if we are to achieve full racial equality. This is not to deny the dangers to the civil rights movement in becoming respectable. Respectability for example, encourages the attempts of political machines to capture civil rights organizations. Respectability can also become an end in itself, thereby dulling the cutting edge of its protest activities. Indeed, the history of the labor movement reveals how attaining respectability can produce loss of original purpose and character. These perils, however, do not contradict the importance of achieving respectability—even a degree of modishness—if racial equality is ever to be realized.

There is another side to the picture: King would be neither respected nor respectable if there were not more militant activists on his left, engaged in more radical forms of direct action. Without CORE and, especially, SNCC, King would appear "radical" and "irresponsible," rather than "moderate" and "respectable."

King occupies a position of strategic importance as the "vital center" within the civil rights movement. Though he has lieutenants who are far more militant and "radical" than he is, SCLC acts, in effect, as the most cautious, deliberate and "conservative" of the direct action groups because of King's leadership. This permits King and the SCLC to function—almost certainly unintentionally—not only as an organ of communication with the establishment and majority white public opinion, but as something of a bridge between the activist and more traditionalist or "conservative" civil rights groups as well. For example, it appears unlikely that the Urban League and NAACP, which supplied most of the funds,* would have participated in the 1963 March on Washington if King had not done so. Because King agreed to go along with SNCC and CORE, the NAACP found it mandatory to join if it was to maintain its image as a protest organization. King's identification with the March was also essential for securing the support of large numbers of white clergymen and their moderate followers. The March was the brain child of the civil rights movement's ablest strategist and tactician, Bayard Rustin, and the call was issued by A. Philip Randolph. But it would have been a minor episode in the history of the civil rights movement without King's support.

Yet curiously enough, despite his charisma and international reputation, King thus far has been more a symbol than a power in the civil rights movement. Indeed, his strength in the movement has been derived less from an organizational base than from his symbolic role. Seven or eight years ago, one might have expected King to achieve an organizationally dominant position in the civil rights movement, at least in its direct action wing. The fact is that in the period after the Montgomery bus boycott King developed no program and, it is generally agreed, revealed himself as an ineffective administrator who failed to capitalize upon his popularity among Negroes. In 1957 he founded SCLC to coordinate the work of direct action groups that had sprung up in southern cities. Composed of autonomous units, usually led by Baptist ministers, SCLC does not appear to have developed an overall sense of direction or a program of real breadth and scope. Although the leaders of SCLC affiliates became the race leaders in their communities—displacing the established local conservative leadership of teachers, old-line ministers, businessmen—it is hard for an observer (who admittedly has not been close to SCLC) to perceive exactly what SCLC did before the 1960's except to advance the image and personality of King. King appeared not to direct but to float with the tide of militant direct action. For example, King did not supply the initiative for the bus boycott in Montgomery, but was pushed into the leadership by others, as he himself records in *Stride Toward Freedom*. Similarly, in the late 1950's and early 1960's, he appeared to let events shape his course. In the last two years this has changed, but until the Birmingham demonstrations of 1963 King epitomized conservative militancy.

SCLC under King's leadership called the Raleigh Conference of April, 1960, which gave birth to SNCC. Incredibly, within a year the SNCC youth had lost their

---

*Actually the March on Washington was financed largely through the philanthropist Stephen Currier, whose Taconic Foundation has also made possible the voter registration campaigns in the South in 1962–64.

faith in the man they now satirically call "De Lawd," and had struck out on their own independent path. By that time, the spring of 1961, King's power in the southern direct action movement had been further curtailed by CORE's stunning Freedom Ride to Alabama and Mississippi.

The limited extent of King's actual power in the civil rights movement was illustrated by the efforts made to invest King with the qualities of a messiah during the recent ceremonies at the state capitol in Montgomery. The Reverend Ralph Abernathy's constant iteration of the theme that King is "our Leader," the Moses of the race, chosen by God, and King's claim that he originated the nonviolent direct action movement at Montgomery a decade ago, are all assertions that would have been superfluous if King's power in the movement was very substantial.

It is, of course, no easier today than it has been in the past few years to predict the course of the Negro protest movement, and it is always possible that the current state of affairs may change quite abruptly. It is conceivable that the ambitious program that SCLC is now projecting—both in southern voter registration and in northern urban direct action programs—may give it a position of commanding importance in civil rights. As a result of the recent demonstrations in Selma and Montgomery, King's prestige is now higher than ever. At the same time, the nature of CORE and NAACP direct action activities at the moment has created a programmatic vacuum which SCLC may be able to exploit. Given this convergence of circumstances, SCLC leaders may be able to establish an organizational base upon which to build a power commensurate with the symbolic position of their president.

It is indeed fortunate that King has not obtained a predominance of power in the movement commensurate with his prestige. For today, as in the past, a diversity of approaches is necessary. Needed in the movement are those who view the struggle chiefly as a conflict situation, in which the power of demonstrations, the power of Negroes, will force recognition of the race's humanity and citizenship rights, and the achievement of equality. Equally needed are those who see the movement's strategy to be chiefly one of capitalizing on the basic consensus of values in American society by awakening the conscience of the white man to the contradiction between his professions and the facts of discrimination. And just as necessary to the movement as both of these are those who operate skillfully, recognizing and yet exploiting the deeply held American belief that compromise among competing interest groups is the best *modus operandi* in public life.

King is unique in that he maintains a delicate balance among all three of these basic strategy assumptions. The traditional approaches of the Urban League (conciliation of the white businessmen) and of the NAACP (most preeminently appeals to the courts and appeals to the sense of fair play in the American public) basically attempted to exploit the consensus in American values. It would of course be a gross oversimplification to say that the Urban League and NAACP strategies are based simply on attempting to capitalize on the consensus of values, while SNCC and CORE act simply as if the situation were purely a conflict situation. Implicit in the actions of all civil rights organizations are both sets of assumptions—even where people are not conscious of the theoretical assumptions under which, in effect, they operate. The NAACP especially encompasses a broad spectrum of strategies and types of activities, ranging from time-tested court procedures to militant direct action. Sophisticated CORE activists know very well when a judicious compromise is necessary or valuable. But I hold that King is in the middle, acting in effect as if he were basing his strategy upon all three assumptions described above. He maintains a delicate balance between a purely moral appeal and a militant display of power. He talks of the power of the bodies of Negro demonstrators in the streets, but, unlike CORE and SNCC activists, he accepts compromises at times that consist of token improvements and calls them impressive victories. More than any of the other groups, SCLC can, up to this point at least, be described as exploiting all three tactical assumptions to an approximately equal degree. King's continued success, I suspect, will depend to a considerable degree upon the difficult feat of maintaining his position at the "vital center" of the civil rights movement.

Viewed from another angle King's failure to achieve a position of power on a level with his prestige is fortunate, because rivalries between personalities and organizations remain an essential ingredient of the dynamics of the movement and a precondition for its success as each current tries to outdo the others in effectiveness and in maintaining a good public image. Without this competitive stimulus, the civil rights revolution would slow down.

I have already noted that one of King's functions is to serve as a bridge between the militant and conservative wings of the movement. In addition, by gathering support for SCLC, he generates wider support for CORE and SNCC as well. The most striking example is the recent series of demonstrations in Selma, where SNCC had been operating for nearly two years with only moderate amounts of publicity before King chose that city as his own target. As usual, it was King's presence that focused world attention on Selma. In the course of subsequent events, the rift between King and SNCC assumed the proportions of a serious conflict. Yet people who otherwise would have been hesitant to support SNCC's efforts, even people who had become disillusioned with certain aspects of SNCC's policies during the Mississippi Summer Project of 1964, were drawn to demonstrate in Selma and Montgomery. Moreover, although King received the major share of credit for the demonstrations, it seems likely that in the controversy between King and SNCC the latter emerged with more power and influence in the civil rights movement than ever before. It is now possible that the administration will, in the future, regard SNCC as more of a force to be reckoned with than it has heretofore.

Major dailies like the *New York Times* and the *Washington Post,* basically sympathetic to civil rights and racial equality though more gradualist than the activist organizations, have congratulated the nation upon its good fortune in having a "responsible and moderate" leader like King at the head of the nonviolent action movement (though they overestimate his power and underestimate the symbolic nature of his role). It would be more appropriate to congratulate the civil rights movement for *its* good fortune in having as its symbolic leader a man like King. The fact that he has more prestige than power; the fact that he not only criticizes whites but also explicitly believes in their redemption; his ability to arouse creative tension, combined with his inclination to shrink from carrying demonstrations to the point where major bloodshed might result; the intellectual simplicity of his philosophy; his tendency to compromise and exert caution, even his seeming indecisiveness on some occasions; the sparing use he makes of going to or staying in jail himself; his friendship with the man in the White House—all are essential to the role he plays, and invaluable for the success of the movement. It is fortunate, of course, that not all civil rights leaders are cut of the same cloth—that King is unique among them. Like Randolph, who functions very differently, King is really an institution. His most important function, I believe, is that of effectively communicating Negro aspirations to white people, of making nonviolent direct action respectable in the eyes of the white majority. In addition, he functions within the movement by occupying a vital center position between its conservative and radical wings, by symbolizing direct action and attracting people to participate in it without dominating either the civil rights movement or its activist wing. Viewed in this context, traits that many activists criticize in King actually function not as sources of weakness, but as the foundations of his strength.

2.7 Clayborne Carson

Martin Luther King, Jr.: Charismatic Leadership in a Mass Struggle

Clayborne Carson, a professor of history at Stanford University, is author of In Struggle: SNCC and the Black Awakening of the 1960s *and* Malcolm X: The FBI File. *He is senior editor of* The Papers of Martin Luther King Jr. *at the university's Martin Luther King Jr. Center for Nonviolent Social Change.*

The legislation to establish Martin Luther King, Jr.'s birthday as a federal holiday provided official recognition of King's greatness, but it remains the responsibility of those of us who study and carry on King's work to define his historical significance. Rather than engaging in officially approved nostalgia, our remembrance of King should reflect the reality of his complex and multifaceted life. Biographers, theologians, political scientists, sociologists, social psychologists, and historians have given us a sizable literature of King's place in Afro-American protest tradition, his role in the modern black freedom struggle, and his eclectic ideas regarding nonviolent activism. Although King scholars may benefit from and may stimulate the popular interest in King generated by the national holiday, many will find themselves uneasy participants in annual observances to honor an innocuous, carefully cultivated image of King as a black heroic figure.

The King depicted in serious scholarly works is far too interesting to be encased in such a didactic legend. King was a controversial leader who challenged authority and who once applauded what he called "creative maladjusted nonconformity." He should not be transformed into a simplistic image designed to offend no one—a black counterpart to the static, heroic myths that have embalmed George Washington as the Father of His Country and Abraham Lincoln as the Great Emancipator.

One aspect of the emerging King myth has been the depiction of him in the mass media, not only as the preeminent leader of the civil rights movement, but also as the initiator and sole indispensible element in the southern black struggles of the 1950s and 1960s. As in other historical myths, a Great Man is seen as the decisive factor in the process of social change, and the unique qualities of a leader are used to explain major historical events. The King myth departs from historical reality because it attributes too much to King's exceptional qualities as a leader and too little to the impersonal, large-scale social factors that made it possible for King to display his singular abilities on a national stage. Because the myth emphasizes the individual at the expense of the black movement, it not only exaggerates King's historical importance but also distorts his actual, considerable contribution to the movement.

A major example of this distortion has been the tendency to see King as a charismatic figure who single-handedly directed the course of the civil rights movement through the force of his oratory. The charismatic label, however, does not adequately define King's role in the southern black struggle. The term *charisma* has traditionally been used to describe the godlike, magical qualities possessed by certain leaders. Connotations of the term have changed, of course, over the years. In our more secular age, it has lost many of its religious connotations and now refers to a wide range of leadership styles that involve the capacity to inspire—usually through oratory—emotional bonds between leaders and followers. Arguing that King was not a charismatic leader, in the broadest sense of the term, becomes somewhat akin to arguing that he was not a Christian, but emphasis on King's charisma obscures other important aspects of his role in the black movement. To be sure, King's oratory was exceptional and many people saw King as a divinely inspired leader, but King did not receive and did not want the kind of unquestioning support that is often associated with charismatic leaders. Movement activists instead saw him as the most prominent among many outstanding movement strategists, tacticians, ideologues, and institutional leaders.

King undoubtedly recognized that charisma was one of many leadership qualities at his disposal, but he also recognized that charisma was not a sufficient basis for leadership in a modern political movement enlisting numerous self-reliant leaders. Moreover, he rejected aspects of the charismatic model that conflicted with his sense of his own limitations. Rather than exhibiting unwavering confidence in his power and wisdom, King was a leader full of self-doubts, keenly aware of his own limitations and human weaknesses. He was at times reluctant to take on the responsibilities suddenly and unexpectedly thrust upon him. During the Montgomery bus boycott, for example, when he worried about threats to his life and to the lives of his wife and child, he was overcome with fear rather than confident and secure in his leadership roles. He was able to carry on only after acquiring an enduring understanding of his dependence on a personal God who promised never to leave him alone.

Moreover, emphasis on King's charisma conveys the misleading notion of a movement held together by spellbinding speeches and blind faith rather than by a complex blend of rational and emotional bonds. King's charisma did not place him above criticism. Indeed, he was never able to gain mass support for his notion of nonviolent struggle as a way of life, rather than simply a tactic. Instead of viewing himself as the embodiment of widely held Afro-American racial views, he willingly risked his popularity among blacks through his steadfast advocacy of nonviolent strategies to achieve radical social change.

He was a profound and provocative public speaker as well as an emotionally powerful one. Only those unfamiliar with the Afro-American clergy would assume that his oratorical skills were unique, but King set himself apart from other black preachers through his use of traditional black Christian idiom to advocate unconventional political ideas. Early in his life King became disillusioned with the unbridled emotionalism associated with his father's religious fundamentalism, and, as a thirteen year old, he questioned the bodily resurrection of Jesus in his Sunday school class. His subsequent search for an intellectually satisifying religious faith conflicted with the emphasis on emotional expressiveness that pervades evangelical religion. His preaching manner was rooted in the traditions of the black church, while his subject matter, which often reflected his wide-ranging philosophical interests, distinguished him from other preachers who relied on rhetorical devices that manipulated the emotions of the listeners. King used charisma as a tool for mobilizing black communities, but he always used it in the context of other forms of intellectual and political leadership suited to a movement containing many strong leaders.

Recently, scholars have begun to examine the black struggle as a locally based mass movement, rather than simply a reform movement led by national civil rights leaders. The new orientation in scholarship indicates that King's role was different from that suggested in King-centered biographies and journalistic accounts. King was certainly not the only significant leader of the civil rights movement, for sustained protest movements arose in many southern communities in which King had little or no direct involvement.

In Montgomery, for example, local black leaders such as E. D. Nixon, Rosa Parks, and Jo Ann Robinson started the bus boycott before King became the leader of the Montgomery Improvement Association. Thus, although King inspired blacks in Montgomery and black residents recognized that they were fortunate to have such a spokesperson, talented local leaders other than King played decisive roles in initiating and sustaining the boycott movement.

Similarly, the black students who initiated the 1960 lunch counter sit-ins admired King, but they did not wait for him to act before launching their own movement. The sit-in leaders who founded the Student Nonviolent Coordinating Committee (SNCC) became increasingly critical of King's leadership style, linking it to the feelings of dependency that often characterize the followers of charismatic leaders. The essence of SNCC's approach to community organizing was to instill in local residents the confidence that they could lead their own struggles. A SNCC organizer failed if local residents became dependent on his or her presence; as the organizers put it, their job was to work themselves out of a job. Though King influenced the struggles that took place in the Black Belt regions of Mississippi, Alabama, and Georgia, those movements were also guided by self-reliant local leaders who occasionally called on King's oratorical skills to galvanize black protestors at mass meetings while refusing to depend on his presence.

If King had never lived, the black struggle would have followed a course of development similar to the one it did. The Montgomery bus boycott would have occurred, because King did not initiate it. Black students probably would have rebelled—even without King as a role model—for they had sources of tactical and ideological inspiration besides King. Mass activism in southern cities and voting rights efforts in the deep South were outgrowths of large-scale social and political forces, rather than simply consequences of the actions of a single leader. Though perhaps not as quickly and certainly not as peacefully nor with as universal a significance, the black movement would probably have achieved its major legislative victories without King's leadership, for the southern Jim Crow system was a regional anachronism, and the forces that undermined it were inexorable.

To what extent, then, did King's presence affect the movement? Answering that question requires us to look beyond the usual portrayal of the black struggle. Rather than seeing an amorphous mass of discontented blacks acting out strategies determined by a small group of leaders, we would recognize King as a major example of the local black leadership that emerged as black communities mobilized for sustained struggles. If not as dominant a figure as sometimes portrayed, the historical King was nevertheless a remarkable leader who acquired the respect and support of self-confident, grass-roots leaders, some of whom possessed charismatic qualities of their own. Directing attention to the other leaders who initiated and emerged from those struggles should not detract from our conception of King's historical significance; such movement-oriented research reveals King as a leader who stood out in a forest of tall trees.

King's major public speeches—particularly the "I Have a Dream" speech—have received much attention, but his exemplary qualities were also displayed in countless strategy sessions with other activists and in meetings with government officials. King's success as a leader was based on his intellectual and moral cogency and his skill as a conciliator among movement activists who refused to be simply King's "followers" or "lieutenants."

The success of the black movement required the mobilization of black communities as well as the transformation of attitudes in the surrounding society, and King's wide range of skills and attributes prepared him to meet the internal as well as the external demands of the movement. King understood the black world from a privileged position, having grown up in a stable family within a major black urban community; yet he also learned how to speak persuasively to the surrounding white world. Alone among the major civil rights leaders of his time, King could not only articulate black concerns to white audiences, but could also mobilize blacks through his day-to-day involvement in black community institutions and through his access to the regional institutional network of the black church. His advocacy of nonviolent activism gave the black movement invaluable positive press coverage, but his effectiveness as a protest leader derived mainly from his ability to mobilize black community resources.

Analyses of the southern movement that emphasize its nonrational aspects and expressive functions over its political character explain the black struggle as an emotional outburst by discontented blacks, rather than recognizing that the movement's strength and durability came from its mobilization of black community institutions, financial resources, and grass-roots leaders. The values of southern blacks were profoundly and permanently transformed not only by King, but also by involvement in sustained protest activity and community-organizing efforts, through thousands of mass meetings, workshops, citizenship classes, freedom schools, and informal discussions. Rather than merely accepting guidance from above, southern blacks were resocialized as a result of their movement experiences.

Although the literature of the black struggle has traditionally paid little attention to the intellectual content of black politics, movement activists of the 1960s made a profound, though often ignored, contribution to political thinking. King may have been born with rare potential, but his most significant leadership attributes were related to his immersion in, and contribution to, the intellectual ferment that has always been an essential part of Afro-American freedom struggles. Those who have written about King have too often assumed that his most important ideas were derived from outside the black struggle—from his academic training, his philosophical readings, or his acquaintance with Gandhian ideas. Scholars are only beginning to recognize the extent to which his attitudes and those of many other activists, white and black, were transformed through their involvement in a movement in which ideas disseminated from the bottom up as well as from the top down.

Although my assessment of King's role in the black struggles of his time reduces him to human scale, it also increases the possibility that others may recognize his qualities in themselves. Idolizing King lessens one's ability to exhibit some of his best attributes or, worse, encourages one to become a debunker, emphasizing King's flaws in order to lessen the inclination to exhibit his virtues. King himself undoubtedly feared that some who admired him would place too much faith in his ability to offer guidance and to overcome resistance, for he often publicly acknowledged his own limitations and mortality. Near the end of his life, King expressed his certainty that black people would reach the Promised Land whether or not he was with them. His faith was based on an awareness of the qualities that he knew he shared with all people. When he suggested his own epitaph, he asked not to be remembered for his exceptional achievements—his Nobel Prize and other awards, his academic accomplishments; instead, he wanted to be remembered for giving his life to serve others, for trying to be right on the war question, for trying to feed the hungry and clothe the naked, for trying to love and serve humanity. "I want you to say that I tried to love and serve humanity." Those aspects of King's life did not require charisma or other superhuman abilities.

If King were alive today, he would doubtless encourage those who celebrate his life to recognize their responsibility to struggle as he did for a more just and peaceful world. He would prefer that the black movement be remembered not only as the scene of his own achievements, but also as a setting that brought out extraordinary qualities in many people. If he were to return, his oratory would be unsettling and intellectually challenging rather than remembered diction and cadences. He would probably be the unpopular social critic he was on the eve of the Poor People's Campaign rather than the object of national homage he became after his death. His basic message would be the same as it was when he was alive, for he did not bend with the changing political winds. He would talk of ending poverty and war and of building a just social order that would avoid the pitfalls of competitive capitalism and repressive communism. He would give scant comfort to those who condition their activism upon the appearance of another King, for he recognized the extent to which he was a product of the movement that called him to leadership.

The notion that appearances by Great Men (or Great Women) are necessary preconditions for the emergence of major movements for social change reflects not only a poor understanding of history, but also a pessimistic view of the possibilities for future social change. Waiting for the Messiah is a human weakness that is unlikely to be rewarded more than once in a millennium. Studies of King's life offer support for an alternative optimistic belief that ordinary people can collectively improve their lives. Such studies demonstrate the capacity of social movements to transform participants for the better and to create leaders worthy of their followers.

Ella Baker and Models of Social Change

Charles Payne, author of I've Got the Light of Freedom: The Organizing Tradition and the Mississippi Freedom Struggle, *is a professor of African American studies, sociology, and urban affairs at Northwestern University and is the Charles Deering McCormick Professor of Teaching Excellence.*

Ella Jo Baker died in 1986. Her entire adult life was devoted to building organizations that worked for social change by encouraging individual growth and individual empowerment. Nonetheless, even among those generally knowledgeable about the modern history of the Afro-American struggle, neither her name nor her sense of how we make change are widely known. She worked during a time when few Americans were capable of taking a Black woman seriously as a political figure. Yet, Ella Baker was a central figure in Afro-American activism as an organizer and as an advocate of developing the extraordinary potential of ordinary people. Few activists can claim a depth and breadth of political experience comparable to Ella Baker's half-century of struggle. She was associated with whatever organization in the Black community was on the cutting edge of the era—the NAACP (National Association for the Advancement of Colored People) in the forties, the Southern Christian Leadership Conference (SCLC) in the fifties, and the Student Nonviolent Coordinating Committee (SNCC) in the sixties.

Miss Baker's activism—and she was always pointedly Miss Baker to the people she worked with, a mark of respect—was strongly influenced by her family and childhood community. Born in 1903, she grew up primarily in rural North Carolina. She took pride in being from a family with a tradition of social consciousness. Her grandparents bought part of the land they had worked as slaves. She grew up hearing stories of slave revolts from her grandmother, who as a slave had been whipped for refusing to marry the man selected for her by her master. She described her grandfather as a Reconstruction-era activist, a man who tried to create a model Black community and who mortgaged his farm after a flood so that he could buy food for other families. Similarly, her mother and grandmother were independent women, central to the lives of their communities, the people to whom others turned in time of need. Her mother was a talented public speaker and an ardent church worker active in local missionary societies. Ella later said, "I became active in things largely because my mother was active in the field of religion." Before she was out of grade school, Ella had acquired a local reputation herself as an effective public speaker.

She remembered the world of her childhood as a kind of "family socialism," a world in which food and tools and homes were shared, where informal adoption of children was taken for granted, a world with a minimal sense of social hierarchy "in terms of those who have, having the right to look down upon, or to evaluate as a lesser breed, those who didn't have. Your relationship to human beings was far more important than your relationship to the amount of money that you made."

As an activist she self-consciously saw herself as a bridge across the sharpening social class divisions in the Black community. By her own interpretation, having been raised where there was a pervasive sense of community among Blacks "helped to strengthen my concept about the need for people to have a sense of their own value and *their* strengths and it became accentuated when I began to travel in the forties for the National Association for the Advancement of Colored People.... As people moved to towns and cities, the sense of community diminished." Looking for ways to reestablish among Blacks and other dispossessed groups the self-sufficiency and community of her youth was to be an important element in her thinking all of her life.

She was valedictorian of her class at Shaw University in 1922, and the administration was probably glad to see her leave; she had been protesting the school's restrictive dress code for students and its policy of having students sing Negro spirituals for visitors. She wanted to go to graduate school to study sociology or to become a medical missionary, but the family's financial situation would allow neither. Instead, she moved to New York where she could find only factory or domestic work. She refused to go into teaching since that was just what a Black woman with a degree was expected to do. Exactly how she first became involved in organizing is not clear—she says she left college with conventional notions of personal success—but it is clear that the smorgasbord political environment of New York intrigued her. "And so wherever there was a discussion, I'd go. It didn't matter if it was all men.... You see, New York was the hotbed of—let's call it radical thinking.... Boy, it was *good,* stimulating." Subsequently, the economic dislocations of the Depression played an important part in her rejection of "the American illusion that anyone who is determined and persistent can get ahead."

Between 1929 and 1932, she was on the editorial staffs of at least two newspapers, the *American West Indian News* and *Negro National News.* During the Depression, she became national director of the Young Negroes' Cooperative League, which established stores, buying clubs that encouraged poor people to pool their purchasing power, and other cooperative economic ventures in Black neighborhoods. During the same period, she worked with a variety of labor organizations in Harlem, including the Women's Day Workers and Industrial League, which focused on the problems of domestic workers. In 1935 Miss Baker herself pretended to be a domestic worker in order to investigate the employment conditions of Black domestics.

Her organizing work in Harlem brought her to the attention of some people active in NAACP circles, and in 1941 she applied to the NAACP for a job as an assistant field secretary. The job involved extensive travel throughout her native South, raising funds, memberships, and consciousness, trying to get people to see the relevance of the organization to their lives and trying to help them work through their very real fears about being associated with the NAACP. She spent about half of each year organizing membership drives and new chapters in the South—Florida, Alabama, Georgia, and Virginia—thus becoming exposed to a wide variety of leadership styles and organizational structures while making innumerable contacts with grassroots leadership, contacts that would become important in her work with the SCLC and SNCC.

In 1943 she became the NAACP's National Director of Branches. In what seems to be the pattern of her life, she was more in the organization than of it. She was a critic—not always a gentle one—of that organization's style of work. By 1941, she was calling the program "stale and uninteresting." She thought the leadership was overly concerned with recognition from whites, overly oriented to a middle-class agenda, unaware of the value of mass-based, confrontational politics, not nearly aggressive enough on economic issues, and too much in the hands of the New York office. She was particularly critical of the organization's tendency to stress membership size without attempting to involve those members more meaningfully in its program. She saw the organization as the victim of its own success. It was successful enough with its program of attacking the legal bases of racial oppression that its very success blinded the organization to its shortcomings. The legal emphasis meant that the huge mass base of the NAACP—400,000 by 1944—could not play a meaningful role in the development of policy and strategy.

She urged the organization to recruit more low-income members by, for example, sending organizers into pool rooms and taverns; her experience had been that some people would join up out of sheer surprise. The branches, she argued, not the national office, should be the focal point of struggle. "Any branch which says it has nothing around which it can build a program," she wrote, "is simply too lazy to concern itself with things on its own doorstep." While many of her recommendations were ignored, she was able in 1944 to initiate a series of regional leadership conferences. The conferences, one of which was attended by Rosa Parks, were intended to help local leaders search for more effective ways to attack local problems and at the same time see how local issues were, inevitably, expressions of broader social issues.

She left the national office in 1946, partly as a result of having accepted responsibility for raising a niece and partly as a result of her conflicts with the organization's viewpoint. She worked for a while as a fund-raiser for the National Urban League and continued to work with the NAACP at the local level, becoming president of the New York City branch which, in her phrase, she tried to "bring back to the people" by moving the office to a location where it would be more visible to the Harlem community and by developing a program in which Black and Hispanic parents actively worked on issues involving school desegregation and the quality of education. For her, the point was that the parents work on the issues themselves rather than having civil rights professionals work on their behalf.

In the mid-1950s, with Bayard Rustin and Stanley Levison, she helped organize In Friendship, an organization that offered economic support for Blacks suffering reprisals for political activism in the South. This same group helped develop the idea of a mass-based organization to continue the momentum that came out of the Montgomery bus boycott. From that idea, developed by several groups almost simultaneously, grew the Southern Christian Leadership Conference. The initial meeting of the embryonic SCLC was called by the Reverend C. K. Steele, one of the contacts Baker had made in the South, and it was the In Friendship group that encouraged Steele to call the meeting.

Levison and Rustin felt that the fledgling SCLC needed an experienced organizer and were able to talk a reluctant Ella Baker into taking the job. In 1957, she went south, intending to stay only a few weeks. She wound up staying two and a half years, becoming the first full-time executive director. At the beginning, she used to joke, SCLC's "office" was her purse and the nearest phone booth. She was responsible for organizing the voter registration and citizenship training drives that constituted the SCLC program during this period. She did this largely by exploiting the network of personal contacts she had developed while with the NAACP.

As with the NAACP, she had trouble getting her own thinking reflected in the programs of the SCLC. She tried to get the leadership to go into some of the rural counties where Blacks were not voting at all. Prophetically, she tried, also without success, to get the organization to place more emphasis on women and young people, the constituencies that would soon carry much of the movement. Miss Baker's emphasis on women reflected her sense of how southern Black organizations worked. "All of the churches depended, in terms of things taking place, on women not men. Men didn't do the things that had to be done and you had a large number of women who were involved in the bus boycott. They were the people who kept the spirit going [the women] and the young people." Being ignored was hardly a surprise to her: "I had known . . . that there would never be any role for me in a leadership capacity with SCLC. Why? First, I'm a woman. Also, I'm not a minister. . . . The basic attitude of men and especially ministers, as to . . . the role of women in their church setups is that of taking orders, not providing leadership."

Despite the difficulties, her association with SCLC put her in a position to help create and shape one of the most significant organizations of the sixties, the Student Nonviolent Coordinating Committee (SNCC). When the sit-in movement among Black college students first began, Ella Baker, like several other adult activists, used her extensive contact list to help it spread. The sit-in phenomenon at the time was essentially a series of disconnected local actions. Feeling that the movement might be more effective with some coordination, Ella talked SCLC into sponsoring a meeting of activist students on the campus of her alma mater, Shaw University. From that meeting, held Easter weekend, 1960, evolved SNCC.

Adult civil rights organizations sent representatives to the organizing meeting with hopes of co-opting all that youthful energy. Three organizations—SCLC, the NAACP, and the Congress of Racial Equality (CORE)—wanted in on the action. The SCLC felt it had the inside track, since many SCLC leaders had worked with the student leaders and, after all, one of the SCLC staff members was in charge of the organizing meeting. They should have consulted with the staff member.

Miss Baker preferred that the students remain independent. Indeed, at one point she walked out of a staff meeting where strategies to bring the students into the SCLC were discussed. In Raleigh, she reinforced the feelings of those students who saw traditional adult leadership as too accommodating and unimaginative; and SNCC remained independent.

By this time, Miss Baker had been working in the South on and off for almost twenty years. In its early years SNCC, like SCLC previously, had her contact network at its disposal. Thus, when SNCC's Bob Moses first ventured into Mississippi she was able to send him to Amzie Moore, a courageous older activist whom Baker had met years before, probably through In Friendship. Much of what would happen in that state for the next four years was predicated on the relationship between these two strangers whom she brought together.

By 1961 SNCC had become the kind of organization that Ella Baker had been trying to create for some years. It went into the rural areas that other groups were reluctant to enter, it was far more open to the participation of women and young people than the established civil rights groups, and it disdained centralization and bureaucracy and insisted that leadership had to be discovered and developed at the local level. Clay Carson notes that "Baker's notion of 'group-centered leadership' had taken hold among student activists, and they strongly opposed any hierarchy of authority such as existed in other civil rights organizations."

Baker was key in preventing an internal dispute from splintering the organization. By 1961 a split had developed between those who wanted the organization involved in voter registration work and those who wanted it to continue in the direct-action tradition in which it had been born. Ella Baker's advice was ordinarily couched in questions, but this time she interceded more directly, suggesting that the students compromise by developing programs in both areas.

Thus, she played a crucial role in creating and shaping a movement organization that set much of the direction and pace of struggle in the early sixties. Bernice Reagan notes that the struggle for civil rights was the "borning" struggle of the decade, the struggle that helped generate and give form to many of the era's battles for social justice. In the same sense SNCC, even more directly than the other civil rights organizations, may be regarded as the "borning" organization, and it is difficult to see how SNCC as we knew it could have come into existence without Ella Baker.

Miss Baker continued to work with a variety of groups through the sixties and well into the seventies. With SNCC, she helped organize the Mississippi Freedom Democratic Party (FDP), a vehicle to give the poor of that state some political voice. She also helped organize the challenge FDP made at the 1964 Democratic National Convention. She had a significant influence on the early leaders of SDS (Students for a Democratic Society), which in its early years adopted a style of work that duplicated the style she encouraged SNCC to adopt. Aldon Morris says she was the "mother" of the activist phase of both organizations. She also influenced the political development of some young women, including Mary King and Casey Hayden, who were later influential in shaping the growth of the contemporary feminist movement. She was involved with attempts to reform urban schools, with South African support groups, with Third World women's organizations, and attempts to organize poor whites in the South. Hers was a wonderfully eclectic style. Whatever the form of the injustice, she was willing to oppose it.

The ideas which undergirded her long activist career do not seem to have changed substantially since the 1930s. If there is one idea that seems central to her approach, it may be the idea of group-centered leadership rather than leader-centered groups. "I have always thought what is needed is the development of people who are interested not in being leaders as much as in developing leadership among other people." In contrast to the more traditional conception of leadership as moving people and directing events, hers was a conception of leadership as teaching, a conception that changes the nature of what it means to be successful. How many people show up for a rally may matter less than how much the people who organize the rally learn from doing so. If the attempt to organize the rally taught them anything about the mechanics of organizing, if the mere act of trying caused them to grow in self-confidence, if the organizers developed stronger bonds among themselves from striving together, then the rally may have been a success even if no one showed up for it. As she said, "You're organizing people to be self-sufficient rather than to be dependent upon the charismatic leader." If growth toward self-sufficiency is the point, then there may be times when people will have to be allowed to make "wrong" decisions, since making decisions and learning from the consequences are necessary to such growth. That was why Ella Baker tried to avoid exerting too much influence on the decision making in SNCC, for example. "Most of the youngsters had been trained to believe in or to follow adults.

. . . I felt they ought to have a chance to learn to think things through and to make the decisions."

It follows that she had a poor opinion of centralized leadership, even if skillful and well intentioned.

> I have always felt it was a handicap for oppressed people to depend so largely on a leader, because unfortunately in our culture, the charismatic leader usually becomes a leader because he has found a spot in the public limelight. It usually means that the media made him, and the media may undo him. There is also the danger in our culture that, because a person is called upon to give public statements and is acclaimed by the establishment, such a person gets to the point of believing that he *is* the movement. Such people get so involved with playing the game of being important that they exhaust themselves and their time and they don't do the work of actually organizing people.

From her perspective, the very idea of leading people to freedom is a contradiction in terms. Freedom requires that people be able to analyze their own social position and understand their collective ability to do something about it without relying on leaders. "Strong people," she said in one interview, "don't need strong leaders." "My basic sense of it has always been to get people to understand that in the long run they themselves are the only protection they have against violence or injustice. . . . People have to be made to understand that they cannot look for salvation anywhere but to themselves."

Whether people develop a sense of their own strength depends partly on the organizational context in which they are working. Ella Baker had misgivings about the common assumption that the bigger the political organization, the better, as well as the parallel assumption that rapid growth is always a sign of organizational vitality. Large organizations more easily become antidemocratic, are not as likely to offer the kind of nurturing of individual growth that smaller ones can provide, and may be especially off-putting to members of low-income communities, where the predominant style of relating to individuals is still prebureaucratic. It is easy to forget that during most of the time when SNCC was at the forefront of the southern movement, the organization had only a few hundred very dedicated members. Part of what made that dedication possible, no doubt, was the organization's ability to generate a strong sense of community among its members in the early years. Its scale helped make that community possible, just as it helped each member of the organization to feel that his or her contribution mattered. It also seems that the decline of the organization was related to the sudden growth in the size of its membership after 1964. According to SNCC members like Cleveland Sellers and Mary King, the rapid growth led to the development of political factions and a general deterioration in the quality of relationships within the organization.

Mary King writes about how Ella Baker encouraged her political growth: "Periodically, Miss Baker would stop whatever Bobbi or I was doing and probe with a series of questions. With Socratic persistence, in her resonant and commanding voice, she would query, 'Now let me ask this again, what is our purpose here? What are we trying to accomplish?' Again and again, she would force us to articulate our assumptions. Sometimes I felt intimidated by her scrutiny."

Baker could be very intimidating indeed when she chose to be. That her persistent questioning could have such positive impact on so many young people is probably partly a reflection of her ability to appear nonjudgmental. Though it is not impossible for such detailed attention to the intellectual growth of the individual to take place in large organizations, their scale certainly militates against it. On the other hand, if part of progressive politics is helping other people grow, no organization can be too small for that.

Ella Baker was much impressed by cell structures, including that of the Communist party. "I don't think we had any more effective demonstration of organizing people for whatever purpose." She thought that one of the most sensible structures for change-oriented organizations would have small groups of people maintaining effective working relationships among themselves but also retaining contact in some form with other such cells, so that coordinated action would be possible whenever large numbers really were necessary.

Her awareness of the value of small organizations is part of a larger theme, a consistent concern for the well-being of particular individuals—not just the "community," or "Black people," or some other abstraction. Before a meeting she habitually tried to find out if anyone had a personal problem that needed attention. Her sensitivity to this kind of question may be partly a reflection of the fact that she was a woman, and quite self-consciously so, or a reflection of her rootedness in the highly personal culture of the South.

Her concern extended to the quality of relationships among activists themselves. Conflicts over the direction of the movement as well as purely personal conflicts were ongoing, of course, but Ella Baker was concerned that some of them were more destructive than they had to be. One of the reasons for this, she suggested more than once, was "the old business of groups that are better prepared to advocate their position sometimes engendering a defensiveness on the part of those who are less prepared." The real issues involved are then submerged under the resentment, and the losing side may withdraw or bide its time for revenge.

While not committed to nonviolence herself, she seems to have appreciated its value as a force for regulating behavior within the movement. Referring to the young people of early SNCC, she spoke approvingly of the fact that "they were so keen about the concept of nonviolence that they were trying to exercise a degree of consciousness and care about not being violent in their manner of judgement of others."

How shall we deal with the differences and disagreements among ourselves, real or imagined, without alienating one another? That question crops up repeatedly in Ella Baker's thinking, but it has received far too little attention from those concerned with social change, with the exception of some feminists. Products of the society we wish to change, we carry within ourselves some of its worst tendencies, including tendencies that will lead to self-aggrandizing and exploitative relationships. Once, in the context of an argument within SNCC over who had the right to participate in the movement, Baker said, "We need to penetrate the mystery of life and perfect the mastery of life and the latter requires understanding that human beings are human beings." Unless we do a better job of responding to the human contradictions and weaknesses of the people we work with, we are likely to continue to create politics that are progressive in the ideas expressed but disempowering in the way individuals expressing those ideas relate to one another.

Group-centered leadership is leadership in which the ego needs of leaders are placed beneath the developmental needs of the group. It requires leaders who can deal nondestructively with their own need for recognition. Ella Baker held a special fear of the need of leaders for some sort of recognition from the larger society, seeing it as part of the pattern by which initially progressive American movements have traditionally been routinized.

Among Blacks she saw it as a distorting factor across several generations of leadership and across various ideological lines. Black radicals as well as Black moderates have allowed the desire to be recognized to blunt the thrust of their activism. Thus, in the NAACP of the forties and fifties, Ella Baker thought the thirst for recognition was one of the factors leading to accommodationist politics at a time when many of the members were ready for a more militant program. The thirst for recognition was also a problem for the radicals of the late 1960s, some of whom became so enamored of the coverage they were receiving from the press that they began performing for the press. As she saw it: "I think they got caught up in their own rhetoric. . . . To me, it is a part of our system which says that success is registered in terms of, if not money, then how much prestige and how much recognition you have. . . . So these youngsters with their own need for recognition began to respond to the press." It is not difficult to imagine what media recognition must have done to the egos of the leaders involved or how it must have poisoned their relationships with other, less-recognized activists who were working just as hard, risking just as much, as the handful of media celebrities.

The distorting potential of media recognition underscores again the case for groups not being too dependent upon leaders. Part of the reason Ella Baker is not a household name is her conviction that political organizers lose a certain kind of effectiveness when they allow themselves to become media stars. Typically, at the conference at which SNCC was organized, she was at pains to put some distance between the students and the press, and in its early years none of SNCC's leading figures became media celebrities. We do not know whether that pattern was due in any measure to the influence of Ella Baker, but it is certainly consistent with what she advocated.

Miss Baker seems to have viewed the press as more useful in the process of mobilizing than in the process of organizing. The distinction between mobilizing and organizing was crucial for her. Organizing, according to Ella Baker, involves creating ongoing groups that are mass-based in the sense that the people a group purports to represent have real impact on the group's direction. Mobilizing is more sporadic, involving large numbers of people for relatively short periods of time and probably for relatively dramatic activities. What SNCC did in rural Mississippi, Alabama, and Georgia was organizing. Activists went into a community committed to staying there for a period of time, trying to identify local leadership, strengthen it, and help it find ways to create organizations and programs that would help local people reach a point of development where they would no longer need to rely on SNCC or anything similar. The intention was to leave behind enduring organizations led by the people in whose name they were created, organizations like the Freedom Democratic Party in Mississippi and the Lowndes County Freedom Organization in Alabama. At least, organizing under this conception involves the creation of stable, ongoing relationships and of ongoing attempts at political education.

By way of contrast, what the SCLC did in Birmingham and Albany and elsewhere was mobilizing—going in for a matter of weeks or months, leading massive demonstrations aimed at bettering the conditions under which people lived, and then moving on. By its nature, mobilizing is more likely to be public and to be dependent upon generating appropriate publicity. The point is not that one or the other is more important historically—both are clearly necessary—but that they are two different political activities.

The distinction between organizing and mobilizing has become increasingly muddled. Young people looking back at the movement tend to see the mobilizing but not the organizing. They see the great demonstrations and the rallies and take that to be the movement. They do not see the organizing effort, often years of such effort, that made the grand moments possible. They do not see organizers going door to door for months on end trying to win trust, overcome fear, and educate people to the ways the movement might connect with their lives. Cordell Reagon, one of the young SNCC organizers in the Albany, Georgia, movement remembers the early phase of organizing in that city as largely hanging around the student union talking to students, hanging around playgrounds, visiting people in their homes. In general, Deep South organizing was a process of trying to become a part of the lives of the people one was trying to work with, and there was frequently nothing very dramatic about it.

Ella Baker understood the failure of the radical thrust of the late sixties as being partly a failure to continue the undramatic work of organizing. She thought that much of what Stokely Carmichael, for instance, was saying around 1968 was thoughtful and grounded in his many years of working to change the system. Then his ideas became a slogan for people who were less thoughtful and had done less work. The rhetoric, as Ella Baker said, got far ahead of the organization. At least a part of what was missing was "a greater degree of real concentration on organizing people. I keep bringing this up. I'm sorry, but it's part of me. I just don't see anything to be substituted for having people understand their position and understand their potential power and how to use it. This can only be done, as I see it, through the long route, almost, of actually organizing people in small groups and parlaying those into larger groups." She was always dubious about the real value of demonstrations. Lobbying and demonstrations may produce some gains from the powers that be relatively quickly but the same powers may retract those gains as soon as the political winds shift. What Miss Baker called "real organizing" might mean that results would take longer to achieve, but it might also mean these results would be better protected.

My purpose in writing this essay was to introduce the Grand Lady, as her grandfather used to call her, to people who may not have heard much about her way of working and thinking. That Ella Baker could have lived the life she did and remain so little known even among the politically knowledgeable is important in itself. It reminds us once more of how much our collective past has been distorted—and distorted in disempowering ways. What I know of Ella Baker's thinking does not strike me, and never struck her, as offering any complete set of answers, but I think it does offer a more promising way to begin framing questions about where we are and how we get to the next stage than the ideas of many activists who did become media figures.

One has to wonder how she sustained her involvement for so long. It is not difficult to imagine how much frustration was built into the work she chose for herself. Nowadays we tend to think that anyone who works for social change for a year or two has made an enormous sacrifice. In the few places I know of where she comments on this, there is a suggestion that she was sustained by the faith that her work was a part of something on-going:

Every time I see a young person who has come through the system to a stage where he could profit from the system and identify with it, but who identifies more with the struggle of black people who have not had his chance, every time I find such a person I take new hope. I feel new life as a result.

It isn't impossible that what those who came along with me went through, might stimulate others to continue to fight for a society that does not have those kinds of problems. Somewhere down the line the numbers increase, the tribe increases. So how do you keep on? I can't help it. I don't claim to have any corner on an answer, but I believe that the struggle is eternal. Somebody else carries on.

2.9   Ella Baker

Organization without Dictatorship

Ella Baker (1903–1986) was an early civil rights worker from the 1940s to the 1960s. She shunned the spotlight and is credited with motivating and inspiring young college students to form the Student Nonviolent Coordinating Committee (SNCC).

New York City, December 27, 1966.

[Ella Baker is a middle-aged woman, a graduate of Shaw University in Raleigh, North Carolina. She has worked for the NAACP and SCLC and it was she who called the conference at which SNCC was founded. She was a strong influence over it in its early years.]

Q. What is the basic goal of SNCC?

A. To change society so that the have-nots can share in it.

Q. Could you discuss in detail SNCC's move from the sit-ins to other things?

A. In the early days, there was little communication, except on a highly personal basis, as between friends and relatives, in the sit-in movement. I had originally thought of pulling together 120–125 sit-in leaders for a leadership training conference—but the rate of speed of the sit-ins was so rapid and the response so electrifying, both North and South, that the meeting ended up with 300 people. Many colleges sent representatives; there was a great thrust of human desire and effort. The first sit-in took place February 1, 1960; the meeting in Raleigh was around April 17, 1960, for three days. Nineteen colleges above the Mason-Dixie Line sent representatives, most of them white. There were so many Northerners that at the meeting it was decided that Northerners could not participate in decision-making. This decision was made sort of by mutual agreement after discussion, because the Northerners recognized that the thrust of the action came from the South. They had been drawn magnetically to the movement because of their great admiration for the wonderful, brave Southerners. The Southerners wanted it that way, at that meeting, because of the divergent levels of political thinking both within the Northern group and between the North and the politically unsophisticated Deep South. (There were many representatives from Georgia, Louisiana, Alabama, although only token representation from Mississippi.) There was an outstanding leadership group from Nashville. It was a basic insecurity that caused the South to keep the North out of decision-making. The North and South used different terminology, had trouble communicating. This has cropped up again in SNCC. It became more subdued in the summer of '64 when there was a real program to be carried out.

Q. What else was decided on at the meeting?

A. That the coordinating group (SNCC) was not to be part of any other organization. Some tried to make it the student arm of SCLC, which had put up the few dollars to hold the meeting. They decided that it was too early to fix the structure of the organization, but the feeling was that it ought to be independent from adults.

Moreover, some of those who took part (I realize in retrospect) saw a basic difference in the role of leadership in the two organizations. In SCLC, the organization revolved around King; in SNCC, the leadership was group-centered (although I may have had some influence). Southern members of the movement were somewhat in awe of each other. There was a feeling that it was the "dawn of a new era," that something new and great was happening and that only they could chart the course of history. A strong equalitarian philosophy prevailed. There was a belief you could just go into an area and organize if you had had no leadership experience. SNCC rejected the idea of a God-sent leader. A basic goal was to make it unnecessary for the people to depend on a leader, for them to be strong themselves. SNCC hoped to spread into a big movement, to develop leadership from among the people. . . .

Q. What is SNCC's basic goal, that makes it unique?

A. The NAACP, Urban League, etc., do not *change* society, they want to get in. It's a combination of concern with the black goal for itself and, beyond that, with the whole society, because this is the acid test of whether the outs can get in and share in equality and worth. By worth, I mean creativity, a contribution to society. SNCC defines itself in terms of the blacks but is concerned with all excluded people.

Q. Has there been a change in SNCC's goal over time?

A. During the sit-in movement, we were concerned with segregation of public accommodations. But even then we recognized that that was only a surface goal. These obvious "irritants" had to be removed first; this was natural. Some people probably thought this in itself would change race relations; others saw deeper.

Q. Would you tell in detail how SNCC's policy changed after the sit-ins?

A. From the start, there were those who knew sitting-in would not bring basic changes. Youngsters who had not thought it through had not bargained with the intractable resistance of the power structure. The notion of "appeals to the conscience" assumed that there *is* a conscience, and after a while the question began to be raised, *is* there a conscience? Students, because they were most out front in the movement, began to see this and its political connotations. People began asking who *really* controlled things. The realization arose in Georgia that the rural areas had control because of the county unit system and that change had to be in the direction of political action. The NAACP had long been conducting voter action through the courts. In the process of internal communications, the question of the vote arose. SNCC people began to go to Washington to talk to the attorney general, at first about Interstate Commerce [Commission rulings]. Kennedy [Attorney General] tried to sell them on the idea of voter registration. . . .

Some people in SNCC thought voter registration was it; others liked the nonviolent resistance effort and feared that it would be sacrificed to voter registration. It was later decided that you couldn't possibly have voter registration without demonstrations. . . .

Q. How were whites in SNCC dealt with before the summer of '64?

A. It was not a major problem. Anybody who wanted to help was welcomed. After '64 the problem arose not in terms of whites but in terms of the right of the individual to make his own decisions in SNCC (this was Freedom High).

At a staff meeting in November '64, the issue of structure versus non-structure arose. Some wanted structure; others thought the real genius of SNCC was in the scope given to the original organizer. Some people said nobody should ever be fired. I thought this was unrealistic, that people were thinking in terms of a small closed society. It was a tragedy . . . people finding their personal need was not SNCC's purpose.

Old radicals have a saying: "You can't make the new world and live in it too." The young people in SNCC wanted to live in it too. This was all part of a general thing about young people not conforming. At first we dressed in work clothes in order to identify with those with whom we were working, but later this became a part of our *right* to identity.

Q. Was the Freedom High connected with the white-black problem?

A. I'm not sure. I think maybe it was—because there were more whites in Freedom High, especially whites who felt their talents hadn't been well used, for reasons of their philosophy or their psychological problems. In those days, resentment against whites came not from black nationalism but from a feeling that it was the whites who brought in these ideas (Freedom High) and who perhaps had trouble accepting leadership.

Freedom High was an effort to develop a nucleus of the "pure" in which you could disregard the outside world.

* * * *

The sense of community was pervasive in the black community as a whole, I mean especially the community that had a sense of roots. This community had been composed to a large extent by relatives. Over the hill was my grandfather's sister who was married to my Uncle Carter, and up the grove was another relative who had a place. So it was a deep sense of community. I think these are the things that helped to strengthen my concept about the need for people to have a sense of their own value, and *their* strengths, and it became accentuated when I began to travel in the forties for the National Association for the Advancement of Colored People. Because during that period, in the forties, racial segregation and discrimination were very harsh. As people moved to towns and cities, the sense of community diminished. A given area was made up of people from various and sundry other areas. They didn't come from the same place. So they had to *learn* each other, and they came into patterns of living that they had not been accustomed to. And so whatever deep sense of community that may have been developed in that little place that I spoke of, didn't always carry over to the city when they migrated. They lost their roots. When you lose that, what will you do next? You *hope* that you begin to think in terms of the *wider* brotherhood. . . .

I guess revolutionary is relative to the situations that people find themselves in, and whatever their goals are, and how many people are in agreement that this is a desired goal. The original four kids who sat down in Greensboro, North Carolina, I'm confident that they had little or no knowledge of the revolutionary background that people talk about when they speak of changing the society by way of socialism or communism. They were youngsters who had a very simple reaction to an inequity. When you're a student with no money, and you go buy what you need like your paper or your pencils, where do you go? The five-and-ten-cent-store. At least you could then, because the prices were not quite as disproportionate as they are now. These two had been talking with a dentist, a black dentist who apparently had some experience with the earlier days of the formation of the Congress of Racial Equality (CORE). They were able to talk with him about their frustrations, going in there, spending all their little money, and yet not being able to sit and buy a five-cent Coke. That was a rather simple challenge as you look back. They decided they were going to do something about it, and so they sat down. Then some others followed their actions. A sister who had a brother in school in another town, her town had already sat in. She might call and ask, why doesn't his school sit in? This was the communication link, plus the media. They sat, and the others came and sat, and it spread. I guess one of the reasons it spread was because it was simple, and it struck home to a lot of young people who were in school.

It hadn't gone on so long before I suggested that we call a conference of the sit-inners to be held in Raleigh. It was very obvious to the Southern Christian Leadership Conference that there was little or no communication between those who sat in, say, in Charlotte, North Carolina, and those who eventually sat in at some other place in Virginia or Alabama. They were motivated by what the North Carolina four had started, but they were not in contact with each other, which meant that you couldn't build a sustaining force just based on spontaneity.

My estimate was that the conference would bring together a couple hundred of the young leadership. I had not hoped for such large numbers of adults who came. These adults were part and parcel of groups such as the Montgomery bus boycott. They also may have been relating to the organizing first steps of SCLC, which had been officially established but had not expanded very much.

We ended up with about three hundred people. We had insisted that the young people be left to make their own decisions. Also, we provided for those who came from outside the South to meet separately from those who came from the sit-in areas, because the persons who came from say, New York, frequently had had wider experience in organizing and were too articulate. In the initial portion of the conference, the southern students had the right to meet, to discuss, and to determine where they wanted to go. It wasn't my idea to separate the northern and southern students. I hesitated to project ideas as pointedly as that, but those who had worked closely with me knew that I believed very firmly in the right of the people who were under the heel to be the ones to decide what action they were going to take to get from under their oppression. As a group, basically, they were the black students from the South. The heritage of the South was theirs, and it was one of oppression. Those who came from the other nineteen schools and colleges and universities up North didn't have the same oppression, and they were white. They were much more erudite and articulate, farther advanced in the theoretical concepts of social change. This can become overwhelming for those who don't even understand what you're talking about and feel put down.

The Southern Christian Leadership Conference felt that they could influence how things went. They were interested in having the students become an arm of SCLC. They were most confident that this would be their baby, because I was their functionary and I had called the meeting. At a discussion called by the Reverend Dr. King, the SCLC leadership made decisions who would speak to whom to influence the students to become part of SCLC. Well, I disagreed. There was no student at Dr. King's meeting. I was the nearest thing to a student, being the advocate, you see. I also knew from the beginning that having a woman be an executive of SCLC was not something that would go over with the male-dominated leadership. And then, of course, my personality wasn't right, in the sense I was not afraid to disagree with the higher authorities. I wasn't one to say, yes, because it came from the Reverend King. So when it was proposed that the leadership could influence the direction by speaking to, let's say, the man from Virginia, he could speak to the leadership of the Virginia student group, and the assumption was that having spoken to so-and-so, so-and-so would do what they wanted done, I was outraged. I walked out.

Additional Resources

Suggested Readings

Fairclough, Adam. *Martin Luther King, Jr.* Athens: University of Georgia Press, 1990. Chronicles the major events in King's life with an assessment of his legacy to America.

Grant, Joanne. *Ella Baker, Freedom Bound.* New York: John Wiley, 1998. A biography of the little-known civil rights activist who influenced many radicals of the civil rights era.

Howard, John R., *The Shifting Wind, The Supreme Court and Civil Rights from Reconstruction to Brown.* Albany: State University of New York Press, 1999. Explores the relationship between race and rights in terms of policy making from the Civil War to 1954.

McAdam, Doug. *Political Process and the Development of Black Insurgency, 1930–1970,* 2d ed. Chicago: University of Chicago Press, 1999. Explains the rise and decline of black protest movements in the United States. Shows that the civil rights movement was the culmination of a long process of building institutions in the black community.

Meier, August, and Elliot Rudwick. *CORE: A Study in the Civil Rights Movement, 1942–1968.* New York: Oxford University Press, 1973. A complete history of the Congress of Racial Equality, a civil rights organization.

Morris, Aldon. *The Origins of the Civil Rights Movement: Black Communities Organizing for Change.* New York: Free Press, 1984. A comprehensive background history of black organizations.

Robnett, Belinda. *How Long? How Long? African American Women in the Struggle for Civil Rights.* New York: Oxford University Press, 1997. Demonstrates the role of race, class, and especially gender in the civil rights movement.

Web Sites

www.stanford.edu/group/King/

This is the Web site for the Martin Luther King, Jr. Papers Project at Stanford University headed by Clayborne Carson. It contains extensive historical information about King's life including his Nobel Prize acceptance speech. The site offers many links to related sites.

www.fordham.edu/halsall/mod/modsbook56.html

Social movements, including the women's movement and the civil rights movement, are available to explore with readings and references. The sections on "Black Power" and "The U.S. Civil Rights Movement" are informative.

www.naacp.org

This is an active and daily updated Web site of the National Association for the Advancement of Colored People. Visit the history section for a brief overview of the formation and development of the organization. The site also serves as a news source for current civil rights issues.

www.southerncouncil.org

This Web site contains issues pertinent to racial equality and complete details of an audio series, "Will the Circle Be Unbroken?" Further, available on the site, is a list of civil and human rights organizations.

www.unc.edu/depts/sohp/

This is the Web site of the Southern Oral History Program at the University of North Carolina. It contains information on the Southern civil rights movement key figures, as well as links to other social movements. Photographs and freedom songs highlight this site.

Chapter 3

Brown and Beyond: Rising Expectations, 1953–1959

The modern period of the civil rights movement begins with the early 1950s and the landmark Supreme Court *Brown v. Board of Education, Topeka, Kansas* decision, which declared that separate-but-equal facilities were unconstitutional. The historic 1954 decision was followed one year later by the Court's attempt to remedy the segregated school problem with what has become known as *Brown II*. Chief Justice Earl Warren, having secured a unanimous decision in *Brown*, sought to find a middle ground that simultaneously addressed Southern blocs while making definite strides toward desegregation. The phrase "with all deliberate speed" was chosen as a benchmark. Despite the controversy over the wording of *Brown II*, the landmark decision became a symbol of optimism for African Americans. Blacks and their allies in the liberation struggle were pleased and hopeful, but often cautious (Martin, 1998:32). The different civil rights groups and organizations coordinated a mass movement protesting bus segregation in Montgomery, Alabama, using the *Brown* victory for motivation and eventually to make a legal argument.

In the late 1890s, when Homer Plessy challenged the constitutionality of Louisiana's segregated railroad cars, the Supreme Court, by a vote of seven to one, found that separating the races was legal. Moreover, the Court in 1896 found that "equal" accommodations for passengers in railroad transportation were, indeed, provided. The separate-but-equal legal interpretation of the Constitution became the law of the land. The one dissenting voice of the *Plessy* case was Justice John Marshall Harlan, who wrote:

> The white race deems itself to be the dominant race in this country. And so it is, in prestige, in achievements, in education, in wealth and in power. . . . But in view of the Constitution, in the eye of the law, there is in this country no superior, dominant, ruling class of citizens. There is no caste here. Our Constitution is color-blind, and neither knows nor tolerates classes among its citizens. In respect of civil rights, all citizens are equal before the law. The humblest is the peer of the most powerful. The law regards man as man, and takes no account of his surroundings or of his color when his civil rights as guaranteed by the supreme law of the land are involved (Kluger, 1975:82).

In this dissent, Harlan employed the Fourteenth Amendment citing that "all citizens are equal before the law."

There are several legal cases preceding the 1954 *Brown* decision that challenged state-endorsed racial discrimination. NAACP lawyers argued these cases. The evolution of the *Brown* case began approximately 20 years earlier with the case of *Pearson v. Murray* (1936). Donald Murray, a black graduate of Amherst College, won a decision by the Maryland Court of Appeals that he had been denied equal opportunity when he was refused admission to the University of Maryland Law School. The court judged that, "We cannot find the remedy to be that of ordering a separate school for Negroes. . . . And as in Maryland now the equal treatment can be furnished only in the one existing law school the petitioner in our opinion, must be admitted there."

In 1938 the Supreme Court, in *Missouri ex rel. Gaines v. Canada,* ruled that Missouri must provide legal education within its boundaries for a black, Lloyd Gaines. The ruling required states to make equal provisions for blacks or to admit them to state-supported universities for whites. The Court, however, was deeply divided in judgment, casting doubt on *Plessy.*

The NAACP played a major role in the case of *Sipuel v. Board of Regents of University of Oklahoma* (1948). The Court upheld the right of black plaintiffs to equal educational opportunity, although possibly under separate circumstances. The ruling that denial of the applicant's admission to the university violated the equal protection clause of the Fourteenth Amendment represented the NAACP's first real victory in the campaign against segregated facilities.

In the Texas case, *Sweatt v. Painter* (1949), the Supreme Court held that the black law school at the University of Texas did not provide "a truly equal education in law." Hence, Sweatt's exclusion from the law school at the university violated the equal protection clause of the Fourteenth Amendment. This decision gave support to the admission of blacks to previously all-white graduate or professional schools.

Another significant ruling was *McLaurin v. Oklahoma State Regents* (1950). The black plaintiff, George McLaurin, was admitted to the University of Oklahoma Graduate School and permitted to use the same facilities as white students, but he had to sit in a separate section of the classroom. During lunch he was required to sit a table away from the white students and in using the library to study, McLaurin was restricted to the mezzanine section. Initially, McClaurin lost his case but upon appeal the Court ruled in his favor. This case is important in leading up to *Brown* in that NAACP lawyers used psychosocial data to show that segregation inflicted harm on victims.

In *Sweatt* and *McLaurin,* the Supreme Court ruled that blacks have the right to attend state graduate schools and receive full educational benefits from such schools. In 1950, after these two decisions, the NAACP Legal Defense Fund, led by Thurgood Marshall, decided on a new legal strategy: to argue for schooling on a nonsegregated basis. Marshall's argument was crafted to establish that segregation stigmatized an entire race and therefore denied blacks "equal protection under the law" as guaranteed by the Fourteenth Amendment.

Brown I: Brown, Briggs, Davis, Belton, and *Bolling*

Collectively known as *Brown v. Topeka Board of Education,* five separate cases became part of a consolidated challenge to overturn the *Plessy* decision. At the time, segregation was required in 17 states and the District of Columbia. The cases charged that (1) local schools for blacks were inferior to white schools, and (2) the separate-but-equal rule was unconstitutional because it violated the equal protection clause of the Fourteenth Amendment.

The selection "Shades of *Brown*: Black Freedom, White Supremacy, and the Law," by Waldo Martin (Reading 3.1), examines the cultural context in which the NAACP launched and completed a legal assault on segregated education throughout the country. The NAACP's legal strategy, though challenged by many, was to focus initially on cases dealing with graduate education and law schools in Missouri, Texas, and Oklahoma. In the late 1940s the emphasis was shifted to public education. In late 1952, the Court consolidated and first heard the cases under the rubric of *Brown*: *Brown v. Board of Education of Topeka, Kansas*; *Briggs v. Elliot* (South Carolina); *Davis v. County School Board of Prince Edward County* (Virginia); *Belton v. Gebhart* (Delaware); and *Bolling v. Sharpe* (District of Columbia).

The case out of Topeka, Kansas, involved a black third grader, Linda Brown. Oliver Brown, her father, tried to get her enrolled in the white elementary school nearest her home. When Linda was denied admission, Oliver Brown went to the state NAACP for help. Long awaiting an opportunity to challenge public school segregation, the NAACP encouraged other parents to join Brown and, in 1951, requested an injunction to forbid public school segregation in Topeka. Using the precedent of *Plessy* the district court ruled in favor of the Board of Education. The Court, however, accepted the argument that segregated schools had a detrimental effect on black children. This was documented by the use of social and psychological studies. The judges wrote that "a sense of inferiority affects the motivation of a child to learn." The NAACP appealed to the Supreme Court in 1951. Soon their case would be combined with other cases that challenged school segregation in South Carolina, Virginia, Delaware, and Washington, D.C.

In Clarendon County, South Carolina, Thurgood Marshall and state NAACP leaders met with parents in an attempt to get them to join a lawsuit against the school board. For blacks this entailed risking their jobs or residences, or losing bank loans on their farms. The first name on the list of plaintiffs was Harry Briggs, a gas station attendant.

Marshall and the Legal Defense lawyers in the *Briggs* case applied a novel strategy that further challenged the very premise of segregation, using data from psychology and related sociological arguments. They engaged a black psychologist, Kenneth Clark, who had been using an interesting methodology in studying the effects of segregation. Clark and his wife used black and white dolls in their interviews with children. Testing 16 children in Clarendon County, Clark showed that the results were the same as in other parts of the South. The psychological evidence demonstrated that many of the black children selected the white doll as "good' and the black doll as "bad." Some of the children picked the white doll as the one most like themselves. Overall the tests indicated that segregation and racial discrimination severely affected the self-esteem of black children. Although the court found that the study was unrelated to the case, Clark's work would reappear later in the *Brown* argument.

The plaintiffs lost at the state level. The dissenting judge, J. Waties Waring, who had for years urged Marshall to challenge the constitutionality of segregation, requested that Marshall rewrite his brief twice, reinforcing his Fourteenth Amendment argument. Waring's dissent stated that "segregation in education can never produce equality." This was cause for some optimism in the larger school desegregation battle.

In the spring of 1951, as the *Brown* and *Briggs* cases were pending before the Supreme Court, a black student walkout took place in the Prince Edward County town of Farmville, Virginia. A Moton High School student assembly led by a high school junior, Barbara Johns, called for a protest strike. Taylor Branch (1988:20) describes the incident:

> [S]he reminded her fellow students of the sorry history since 1947, when the county had built three temporary tar-paper shacks to house the overflow at the school—how the students had to sit in shacks with coats on through the winter; how her history teacher, who doubled as the bus driver, was obliged to gather wood and start fires in the shacks in the mornings after driving a bus that was a hand-me-down from the white school and didn't have much heat either, when it was running; how the county had been promising the Negro principal a new school for a long time but had discarded those promises. . . . With that she called for a strike and the entire student body marched out of the school behind with her.

This grassroots beginning grew into a legal challenge argued by the NAACP. *Davis v. County School Board of Prince Edward County* was filed in May 1951 on behalf of 117 Moton High School students. Dorothy Davis, the daughter of a farmer, was the first name on the list. The NAACP lawyers argued for abolishing the Virginia state law mandating segregated schools. One year later, the court unanimously upheld the separate-but-equal doctrine stating that separate schools were the result not of racism but of the long tradition of the Southern way of life. The case was appealed to the U. S. Supreme Court and eventually became part of the historic *Brown* case.

In the Delaware case of *Belton v. Gebhart,* the Supreme Court ruled that the plaintiffs were entitled to immediate admission to the white schools in their communities.

The postwar demographic trends of whites moving to nearby suburbs and blacks moving into the city affected the District of Columbia. A situation of overcrowding developed in the black public schools, and many students attended school in double and triple shifts. One such school, Browne Junior High School, hosted a double shift. At a neighboring white junior high school, however, there were about 150 open spaces. Some of the parents of children attending Browne went to court demanding that their children be admitted to the all-white school. In response the court eliminated the double shift at all black schools, and in 1950, the D.C. Court of Appeals ruled against the Browne parents. One of the black students, Spottswood Bolling Jr., appealed. This case went before the Supreme Court, which ruled in his favor. *Bolling v. Sharpe* was decided at the same time as *Brown*.

Ruling in favor of the plaintiffs on May 17, 1954, the Supreme Court struck down the separate-but-equal doctrine of *Plessy* for public education. The Court decided unanimously in all of the five cases that school segregation violated the Constitution. *Brown,* however, did not abolish segregation in other public areas. Nor did it require school desegregation by a specific time. The goal of the Legal Defense Fund lawyers—the total and unconditional abolition of Jim Crow schools—was accomplished legally, though enforcement of the desegregation ruling would become another matter.

Brown II

The landmark decision to end segregation did not set a deadline for the accomplishment of this goal in public schools. Desegregation began quickly in the District of Columbia, but in few other places. The NAACP argued for immediate desegregation—by September 1955. Opposition lawyers representing the school boards argued that given the complex problems of race relations in the South, desegregation should proceed slowly. On May 31, 1955, the Court issued its guidelines for local school boards to desegregate "with all deliberate speed." With this wording, Southern school boards could delay desegregation and not violate the order. The vague language of *Brown II* was a concession to more conservative justices, so that a unanimous decision could be reached.

Southern Reaction

Despite the carefully worded *Brown II* remedy issued in 1955, whites began to form private resistance groups throughout the South. These groups, including the Southern Gentlemen, White Brotherhood, Christian Civic League, and the National Association of White People, organized and resisted under the banner of states' rights and protectors of the white race. In contrast to the violence associated with some resistance groups, the White Citizens' Councils, which included respectable citizens, favored subtle forms of intimidation.

"The Southern Manifesto" (Reading 3.2) demonstrates the deep concern that Southern elected officials had with the *Brown* ruling. In March 1956 Southern congressmen attacked the *Brown* decision as "judicial encroachment" that destroyed the Southern way of life, which had existed for 90 years since the Civil War. The "Manifesto," or "Declaration of Constitutional Principles," pledged to reverse the *Brown* decision and prevent its enforcement. Eighty-one members of the House of Representatives and nineteen senators with the exception of Lyndon Johnson, Albert Gore, and Estes Kefauver, signed the "Manifesto" on March 12, 1956, during the middle of the Montgomery bus boycott. This extended legitimacy to the Southern resistance to public school desegregation.

Baton Rouge Bus Boycott

A Jim Crow bus was one of the few places in the South where blacks and whites were segregated under the same roof and in full view of each other (Morris, 1984:17). Recognizing that the Baton Rouge bus system was mostly financed by black riders, local black leaders petitioned the City Council to pass an ordinance permitting blacks to be seated on a first-come-first-served basis. The white bus drivers, however, refused to accept the ordinance. In June 1953 the black community of Baton Rouge, Louisiana, began a mass boycott against segregated buses. Morris (1984:25) writes:

The Baton Rouge boycott occurred before the famous 1954 school desegregation decision won by the NAACP and also predated the more celebrated 1955–56 Montgomery bus boycott. But it was the Baton Rouge movement, largely without assistance from outside elites, that opened the direct action phase of the modern civil rights movement. Its impact was temporarily overshadowed, however, by the 1954 Supreme Court decision in *Brown v. Board of Education of Topeka,* which thrust the NAACP into the limelight and crystallized the emerging massive resistance movement dedicated to systematically destroying the NAACP across the South.

Martin Luther King would eventually consult the Reverend T. J. Jemison, the official leader of the Baton Rouge boycott and an old college friend, in matters concerning the Montgomery bus boycott.

Montgomery Bus Boycott

Planned nonviolent mass action was born on December 1, 1955, when a middle-aged seamstress and civil rights volunteer Rosa Parks refused to give up her seat upon request of a white passenger and the bus driver. Jim Crow norms required black riders to sit in the rear of the bus or in "no-man's-land," a middle seating area often separating blacks from whites, if white riders didn't want those seats. Parks was not sitting in the white section of the bus but in no-man's-land. The bus driver was firm in asking her and three other blacks to move: "You better make it light on yourselves and let me have those seats." Parks violated Jim Crow custom and law. She was arrested, beginning a series of events culminating in the Montgomery bus boycott. Parks phoned her mother, who in turn phoned NAACP leader, E. D. Nixon. Unable to get information from the police, Nixon phoned Clifford Durr, a Southern white liberal who once worked in Roosevelt's New Deal. Durr found out from the police that Parks was charged with violating the Alabama bus segregation laws. Both Nixon and Durr went to the jail to bail her out. Clifford Durr's wife, Virginia, had known Rosa Parks and earlier in 1955 had recommended her for an interracial workshop on desegregation at the Highlander Folk School in Monteagle, Tennessee. Together with the Durrs, Nixon, and her family, Rosa Parks decided to fight the segregation law. The selection in this chapter, " . . . I Tried Not to Think about What Might Happen" (Reading 3.4), reflects the careful thought and inner strength of Parks.

The bus boycott became a mass civil rights protest with E. D. Nixon arranging a meeting with black ministers. At the same time, JoAnn Robinson, president of the Women's Political Council, a black professional organization, began to plan a one-day bus boycott in support of Parks. The boycott of December 5th was almost completely observed by Montgomery's black citizens. That evening a meeting was held at the Holt Street Baptist Church where blacks proclaimed they would stay off the buses as long as necessary. Nixon selected Martin Luther King, who was relatively new to Montgomery, to give the keynote speech. King was elected president of the boycott committee of the Montgomery Improvement Association (MIA), the organization that would hold talks with Montgomery city officials to negotiate an end to the boycott. Nixon's key role in the boycott is presented in John White's selection, "Nixon *Was* the One: Edgar Daniel Nixon, the MIA and the Montgomery Bus Boycott" (Reading 3.3).

The boycott strategy worked and, after more than one year of protest, the buses in Montgomery were integrated. Martin Luther King gained national attention and broad appeal from this year-long protest. King's philosophy of nonviolent resistance and strategy of nonviolent direct action gained the attention and respect of the nation. The Montgomery boycott is considered the event that began the modern civil rights movement. Its success and positive media coverage had an effect on other Southern cities. Similar bus boycotts followed in Birmingham, Alabama, and Tallahassee, Florida.

Central High School: Little Rock, Arkansas

In a plan to comply with the *Brown* decision, the Little Rock school board provided for the limited integration of one of its high schools. Nine black students, selected because of their good grades, attempted to integrate the school in September 1957. The night before the opening day of school, however, the governor of Arkansas, Orval Faubus, stated that it would be difficult to maintain order if "forcible integration" took place. He ordered the National Guard to surround the school building. The black students stayed home. The next morning the guardsmen blocked the entrance to the school when the nine black students tried to enter. Elizabeth Eckford, a 15-year-old black student, narrowly escaped mob violence. Her reflections, "Don't Let Them See You Cry," appear in this chapter (Reading 3.5).

The Little Rock Nine accompanied by Daisy Bates, president of the Arkansas NAACP chapter, entered the school through a side entrance. The crowd of whites outside the school became hysterical when they learned that the black students were inside. Soon the mayor of Little Rock, fearing violence, ordered the black students out. Daisy Bates appealed to President Eisenhower to protect the nine black students. Finally, on September 24, 1957, Eisenhower federalized the Arkansas National Guard and sent troops from the 101st Airborne Division to Little Rock to protect the students.

With federal troop protection, the integration began. Under the leadership of Bates, the nine students went through the school year being escorted from class to class by the National Guardsmen.

In June, however, after one of the black students, Ernest Green, graduated from Central High School, the Little Rock school board asked a federal judge to suspend the integration plan because of an "unfavorable community attitude." The suspension was granted. Immediately, the NAACP appealed to the U.S. Supreme Court. The case, *Cooper v. Aaron*, was argued in a special session late in August 1958. The Court decided that the *Brown* case could not be directly or indirectly nullified "through evasive schemes for segregation." Before the Court reached a decision, Governor Faubus ordered all public schools closed in Little Rock. They remained closed for the entire school year.

David Kirp's selection, "Retreat to Legalism: The Little Rock School Desegregation Case in Historic Perspective" (Reading 3.6), offers a hindsight look at school desegregation. The events at Little Rock squarely placed the federal government on the side of public school integration. It was a federal-versus-state authority conflict in which blacks would have an ally in the U.S. government. The Little Rock crisis attracted national attention and focused on the difficulties of enforcement of the 1954 *Brown* decision.

Key Figures, Terms, and Concepts

Daisy Bates
Virginia Durr
Highlander Folk School
Montgomery Improvement Association
nonviolent direct action

JoAnn Robinson
rule of law
Southern Christian Leadership Conference
 (SCLC)
"Southern Manifesto"

Important Questions to Consider

1. In *Brown v. Board of Education,* the Supreme Court unanimously overturned local school district regulations concluding that "separate educational facilities are inherently unequal." On what argument is this conclusion based?

2. How did the *Brown* decision become reason for hope and optimism among blacks in the 1950s? In contrast, what was the Southern white reaction to the decision?

3. What was the NAACP's strategy in challenging segregated public schools in America?

4. What makes the *Brown* decision so important in American history? Why was the *Brown II* remedy so controversial?

5. When U.S. president Dwight Eisenhower ordered federal troops into Little Rock, Arkansas, he did so using what laws? Explain.

6. What organizational factors enabled the bus boycott in Montgomery to take place? Discuss the role of religious organizations in organizing and sustaining the boycott.

Shades of Brown: Black Freedom, White Supremacy, and the Law

Waldo Martin, author of Brown v. Board of Education, A Brief History with Documents, *is a professor of history at the University of California at Berkeley.*

Arguably the most important Supreme Court ruling in United States history, the *Brown* decision in 1954 not only overturned the doctrine of separate but equal schools as unconstitutional, but it also put other forms of antiblack discrimination on the road to extinction. The unanimous decision reversed the Court's 1896 decision in *Plessy v. Ferguson,* which had upheld the concept and practice of state-endorsed racial discrimination—Jim Crow—the chimera of separate but equal public accommodations and institutions for blacks and whites. The *Brown* decision was the culmination of countless interrelated collective and personal battles waged by blacks and of a series of legal efforts by the National Association for the Advancement of Colored People (NAACP) from the early days of its existence in the 1910s and 1920s.

Indeed, the legal cases that have influenced the status of African Americans historically have come out of the day-to-day struggles of regular people, such as those in Clarendon County, South Carolina, whose fight for better black schools in the late 1940s became one of five cases to be ultimately joined as *Brown v. Board of Education.* The segregated schools for blacks in Clarendon County at the time were a disgrace, clearly worse than most all-black schools in the South. Black life in the county was extremely hard. In his definitive work *Simple Justice: The History of* Brown v. Board of Education *and Black America's Struggle for Equality,* Richard Kluger notes that "if you had set out to find the place in America in . . . 1947 where life among black folk had changed the least since the end of slavery, Clarendon County is where you might have come." In 1950, more than two-thirds of the county's black households earned less than $1,000. The county maintained twelve schools for whites and sixty-one for blacks. Over half of the black schools were shanties with a teacher or two and a student body ranging widely in age and educational level. In 1950, the total value of the black schools was $194,575; that of the white schools was $673,850. For the 1949–50 school term, the county school board spent $43 per black child, $179 per white child. Black teachers earned two-thirds less than their white counterparts.

In 1947, black parents, led by Reverend J. A. DeLaine and Hugh Pearson, a local farmer, began pressing the county to provide buses for black students as it already did for white students. By the following year, with the help of local black lawyer Harold W. Boulware and the local and national branches of the NAACP, the struggle had escalated dramatically, with a lawsuit in federal court. Argued by Thurgood Marshall, the head of the NAACP legal defense team, the lawsuit demanded that the county go beyond equalizing its black and white schools and fully integrate its public school system. The plaintiffs in the suit, Liza and Harry Briggs, lost their jobs as maid and service station attendant, respectively; despite other instances of white repression of local blacks, the legal battle went forward.

Briggs v. Elliott soon joined four similar cases argued by the NAACP's legal team before the Supreme Court: *Brown v. Board of Education of Topeka, Kansas; Davis v. County School Board of Prince Edward County* (Virginia); *Belton v. Gebhart* (Delaware); and *Bolling v. Sharpe* (District of Columbia). In late 1952, the Court consolidated and first heard these cases under the rubric of *Brown*. Public school segregation, according to the NAACP's legal brief, was a violation of the Fourteenth Amendment's equal protection clause. An integral element of the effort to make blacks part of the nation during the Reconstruction period (1863–77), this 1867 amendment clearly defined U.S. citizenship to encompass all blacks. Furthermore, it stated that all citizens were equal under the law. Consequently, the NAACP lawyers argued, the blatantly unequal racially segregated schools were unconstitutional and had to be integrated. In each case, local lawyers in conjunction with NAACP lawyers sought the immediate end of Jim Crow schools as intrinsically separate and unequal. The lawyers also argued that state-sanctioned segregation stamped blacks with a stigma of inferiority that undermined their self-esteem. In effect the aim in *Brown*—the total and unconditional abolition of Jim Crow schools—represented a critical move in the black freedom struggle. . . .

The Evolution of the NAACP Legal Campaign against Jim Crow

. . . The NAACP pursued several lines of attack in its assault on the "color line." Lobbying for favorable legislative, judicial, and executive action; waging a publicity war through the media, most effectively in the *Crisis* magazine, initially edited by Du Bois; and working with grassroots chapters on specific issues of local concern such as discriminatory ordinances, the organization endeavored to advance a black civil rights agenda. Intensely fought battles against antiblack discrimination in jobs, housing, voting, public accommodations, and education demanded functional knowledge, savvy, and flexibility. Given its limited resources and the awesome power of the racist status quo, the NAACP favored significant yet workable battle-grounds where its members could realistically achieve the upper hand. Victories with far-reaching impact were thus highly desirable.

From the beginning, litigation proved to be a particularly important and effective tool in the organization's armament. The legal struggle against segregated schools in mid-nineteenth-century Boston and Jim Crow railway cars at the turn of the century clearly presaged the NAACP legal campaigns. In the Boston school integration (1849), *Dred Scott* (1857), and *Plessy* (1896) cases, the decisions went against the individual black claimants and the collective aspirations of blacks. Nevertheless, hope remained that the rule of law would eventually be squared with constitutional claims for full black equality, especially following the enactment of the Fourteenth Amendment.

The legal endorsement of equality in *Brown* was a capstone to an extraordinary series of battles against de jure (legal) and de facto (actual) Jim Crow. The Fourteenth Amendment's guarantee of equal protection under the law epitomized the legal tradition undergirding *Brown*. Early American legal tradition (1787–1830) was built on English common law and emphasized freedom, equality, and justice for all citizens as framed in the Constitution (1787) and Bill of Rights (1791). With its powerful Enlightenment grounding, this compelling vision of constitutional law stressed reason, order, and progress as inseparable from freedom, equality, and justice. The United States ideologically embraced a republican form of government that deepened the young nation's commitment to these tenets.

This libertarian, or pro-freedom, reading of the Constitution and the law is fundamentally antithetical to the slavery and racism the nation's founders embraced. In fact, the founding patriarchs countenanced freedom for whites fully predicated upon black slavery and black debasement This haunting paradox has decisively shaped the American nation since its founding. However, the libertarian view of the Declaration of Independence (1776) and the Constitution, along with the radical egalitarianism of the former, provided indispensable ideological bases for the black freedom struggle from the beginning until now. . . .

A deep-seated belief in the prospects for advancing black civil rights through the legal system earmarked the highly influential career of Charles Hamilton Houston, who was most responsible for charting the various legal paths that led to *Brown*. In 1983, Judge A. Leon Higginbotham Jr. wrote that "Houston was the chief engineer and the first major architect of the twentieth-century civil rights legal scene." He "almost single-handedly . . . organized and led the legal battalion in the critical early battles seeking equality for black Americans."

Harvard-trained and the first black elected to *Harvard Law Review,* Houston left a private practice he shared with his father in Washington, D.C., to become dean of Howard University's law school (1924–35). Houston put that institution on sound academic footing, making changes that led to the school's full accreditation and greatly enhanced its prestige. Among his numerous accomplishments, several bear mentioning. First, he trained many talented black lawyers at a time when there were precious few. Besides Thurgood Marshall, who would be instrumental in *Brown* and later would be a Supreme Court justice, Houston taught a number of prominent attorneys who would distinguish themselves in civil rights litigation, including Edward P. Lovett, James G. Tyson, Oliver W. Hill, Coyness L. Ennix, and Leslie S. Perry. Second, he pioneered in two fields of legal study and practice: civil rights law and public interest law. Third, he engaged in a whirlwind of civil liberties, civil rights, and antidiscrimination activities, beyond his university duties, including the defense in the highly publicized Scottsboro case in which nine young Alabama blacks were accused of raping two white women on a freight train. By 1935, Houston had emerged as the most influential black lawyer in the United States.

In light of that status, it is not surprising that when the NAACP sought a new special counsel in 1934, Houston was chosen. Having taught law and litigated a variety of cases, he was now charged with the responsibility of directing the litigation activities of the most important black civil rights organization in the country. Houston stressed that the law was a potentially useful means to promote social change, especially in the context of a complicated social struggle. Why the judicial system? As historian Genna Rae McNeil has noted: "With little power to compel congressional or presidential concessions and with virulent racism ever a possible consequence of direct action, blacks were in a better position to seek redress through the courts."

Limitations of the judiciary tempered the optimism of Houston and other civil rights lawyers, however. They fully understood that historically the law had been principally a conservative and at times reactionary force. They were deeply aware of what historian Mary Frances Berry has aptly referred to as "constitutionally sanctioned violence against blacks and violent suppression of black resistance—the outgrowth of a government policy based on essentially racist, not legal, concerns—throughout the American experience." In other words, whites used "the Constitution in such a way as to make law the instrument for maintaining a racist status quo."

Houston's view of the lawyer as a **social engineer** owed heavily to his fervent commitment to the black freedom struggle and his belief in the integral relationship between that social insurgency and legal activism. The black lawyer, according to Houston, had to envision and to practice law as a mechanism for progressive social change. A modern "race man" he fully understood that black lawyers had a special mission to fight their own people's battles. They could not depend on the white-dominated legal guild—given its historic support for white supremacy—to fight for black rights. It was imperative, according to Houston, that the black lawyer embrace

> . . . the social service he can render the race as an interpreter and proponent of its rights and aspirations. . . . Experience has proved that the average white lawyer, especially in the south, cannot be relied upon to wage an uncompromising fight for equal rights for Negroes. He has too many conflicting interests, and usually himself profits as an individual by that very exploitation of the Negro, which, as a lawyer he would be called upon to attack and destroy.

Houston's adherence to the legal realism of his Harvard mentors Roscoe Pound and Felix Frankfurter provided a powerful intellectual framework for his activist legal philosophy. According to the sociological **jurisprudence** of legal realism, law served particular social interests; it reflected the biases and predilections of those who made and interpreted it. Legal realism, a view first fully enunciated by the eminent Supreme Court Justice Oliver Wendell Holmes Jr. (1841–1935) earlier in his legal scholarship, rejected the dominant and traditional view of the law as a set of formal rules deducible from abstract concepts like justice. Whereas legal tradition inspired judicial restraint, **legal realism**—especially as articulated by Houston—inspired judicial activism.

Houston's legal realism complemented and energized his view that black lawyers had to be social engineers. These interlocking philosophies had an enormous impact on the Howard law curriculum, the lawyers he trained and influenced, the legal philosophy of the NAACP, and the activism of those engaged in black rights litigation. In effect, social engineering through law meant the use of the law itself wherever possible to solve the problems confronting blacks.

Houston's legal reasoning authenticated the use of sociological evidence when arguing against segregation. A key example was the use of social psychological data to argue the harmful effects of racism on whites and blacks. Persuasive challenges to public and social policies which braced Jim Crow became an important objective of this brand of sociological jurisprudence. These kinds of legal arguments also gave focus and shape to the burgeoning field of civil rights law. As legal scholar Mark Tushnet notes, "The constitutional argument against segregation could be keyed to facts and policy." Tushnet concludes that "the sociological argument was Realist to the core. Law, even constitutional law, was social policy. Social policy had to be understood as it actually operated."

Houston, Marshall, and the many other lawyers and activists engaged in the war against segregation understood that victory could not be won solely in the courts, but only through a broad-based attack. Marshall, who succeeded Houston as NAACP general counsel in 1939, relied on his mentor's counsel until Houston's untimely death in 1950. He continued to elaborate on his mentor's social engineering framework throughout his distinguished legal career. Both men envisioned litigation as a tool to educate and politicize the public, white and black, about the black freedom struggle and the role of the judiciary in advancing that cause. The NAACP's legal campaign, therefore, was not a series of uncoordinated court battles, but an integral part of a much broader philosophy of social insurgency. In part, this legal campaign functioned as a mechanism to publicize the work of the NAACP and in turn to recruit members for the organization and the black freedom struggle generally.

Believing that carefully executed litigation could contribute to local grassroots activism and the development of a mass movement, the NAACP and its legal staff supported local legal struggles. NAACP lawyers worked hand in glove with local lawyers, whether the issue was black political exclusion, disparities between white and black teachers' salaries, a black falsely accused or convicted of a crime, or some other miscarriage of racial justice. The NAACP also mounted a vigorous legal and educational campaign against the most virulent forms of legal racism, such as the highly visible terrorism of state-sanctioned white rule through mob action and lynch law. In far too many instances in the first half of the twentieth century, a black accused of a crime—especially a black man accused of raping a white woman—was murdered publicly by angry white lynch mobs with no concern for niceties like court trials or convictions. Although the NAACP had waged an unrelenting and highly public battle against white lynch law since 1919, the group—like others struggling against this heinous injustice—was unable to persuade the federal government to pass an antilynching law. Southern white opposition, notably in the Congress, effectively blocked all such efforts.

Battered but undaunted, the NAACP went forward. The seemingly impregnable state-sanctioned world of Jim Crow fueled extensive debate within the organization around what tactics to use to dismantle institutionalized racism. Two related debates in the 1930s illuminate the nature and impact of this spirited discourse: (1) the kind of legal strategy to pursue and (2) more broadly considered, legalism versus alternative strategies.

The first debate was over whether the NAACP lawyers should attack the entire edifice of Jim Crow forthrightly by seeking a ruling nullifying *Plessy*—a direct attack strategy—or, whether they should work incrementally, building a series of legal victories that paved the way for the eventual dismantling of *Plessy*—a developmental strategy. A principal goal of the developmental strategy was to force the South to equalize its separate black and white worlds through litigation by making Jim Crow fiscally and politically unworkable. Given the relative poverty of the South and the declining respectability of Jim Crow, equalization would undermine American apartheid.

Nathan Margold, Houston's predecessor as head of the NAACP legal team, had pushed for the direct attack strategy. Like Houston, Margold was a protégé of Felix Frankfurter and was committed to both legal realism and judicial activism. In 1931, a year after his hiring, Margold issued a bold report strategically arguing for a direct attack on segregation, leaving open the issue of equalization. A frontal assault would cut immediately to the heart of the issue—cogent legal demonstration of the fundamental wrong of state-sanctioned racial segregation—and would require an immediate end to Jim Crow. Margold preferred that the issue of equalization be treated as a related but subordinate concern.

Margold maintained that a direct attack was preferable as it required fewer suits and the NAACP's legal staff could devote its attention to precedent-setting cases. Similarly, this approach avoided litigating overlapping suits at the state and local levels and thus the often confusing and conflicting welter of federal, state, and local statutes. Also, as the Margold report explained, a direct attack was a better use of the NAACP's limited fiscal resources and its small legal staff.

Houston and Marshall after him firmly believed that the Margold report put forth a position which the NAACP and the larger black freedom struggle should support in theory; however, in reality, they realized that the times were inauspicious for such an aggressive strategy. In the Depression years, economic hardships intensified among blacks and spread among whites. Economic turmoil further exacerbated racial tensions and did not provide the most supportive setting to battle Jim Crow. In addition, the NAACP lacked sufficient mass black support and progressive white support on the one hand and the necessary strategic support within the legal establishment on the other. In the 1930s in particular, many blacks still had to be convinced that legal assault against Jim Crow was viable. Otherwise, local blacks facing the extraordinary pressures brought to bear against those who filed anti–Jim Crow suits might not have the uncommon courage and the black community support necessary to proceed. Another important impediment which had to be overcome was the widespread lack of trained black lawyers. Therefore, Houston decided to employ a more moderate strategy of equalization as a way to build support for a direct attack later. Cultivating a network of popular and professional support became a vital tactical goal.

Houston chose to focus the legal assault on education because of its centrality to advancement and fulfillment within American culture. As such, the blatant denial of equal educational opportunities to black youth touched a powerful nerve in the American psyche. The terrible realities of segregated education in the South offered compelling evidence of gross racial disparities in facilities, budgets, and salaries. Also, Houston contended, "discrimination in education is symbolic of all the more drastic discriminations," such as lynch law. Furthermore, Jim Crow education represented the deeply ingrained stigma of innate black racial inferiority.

Houston's strategy featured three related aspects. Desegregation of public graduate and professional schools was one. Here the battle was fought at a less contentious level than that of elementary and secondary schools. Equalization of white and black teachers' salaries was the next aspect. The NAACP legal team achieved a number of important victories in salary cases. As a result, many southern school boards masked salary differentials through the use of so-called merit criteria, and the cases became much harder to argue. It was not until the late 1940s that the next level of the legal plan—equalization of elementary and secondary school facilities—became feasible. Until then, overcoming the local and tactical obstacles hindering these cases proved too difficult.

Another challenge was finding and sustaining the morale of litigants whose character and resources would have to withstand intense public scrutiny and white reprisals—typically economic, sometimes physical and violent. The prolongation of many cases caused litigants to lose enthusiasm and even drop out. Racist southern school districts used various legal strategies to tie up the proceedings and to exhaust black litigants financially and emotionally. Often these districts admitted to the disparities in their educational offerings but exaggerated or lied about efforts under way to ameliorate them. The defense used this tactic in the South Carolina district court case of *Briggs v. Elliott.*

Other obstacles faced the legal team. First, the fact that the states and local school districts themselves were primarily responsible for public school education policy and funding inhibited litigation at the federal level. Second, with the awesome weight of tradition and social custom, *Plessy* was the precedent upon which pro–Jim Crow rulings rested. Third, it followed that courts did not consider state-sanctioned Jim Crow to violate the Fourteenth Amendment right of blacks to equal protection under the law and therefore left Jim Crow intact. Fourth, the defendants and courts alike variously ignored, trivialized, masked, neutralized, explained away, and accepted the pervasive reality of separate and unequal. All of these tactics naturalized Jim Crow as fundamental to a "higher law" of white supremacy, or integral to the organic order of society. According to Mary Frances Berry, the controlling factor in legal decisions was the ubiquity of constitutional racism. Ultimately, as Derrick Bell maintains, the law functioned to sustain white supremacy.

The NAACP's Legal Strategy Challenged

It is not surprising, then, that searching questions were raised about the NAACP's growing commitment to legalism as a primary strategy: the group's second pivotal 1930s controversy. Many committed to the black freedom struggle called for greater emphasis on economic issues because of the Depression's ravaging effects. As one would expect, economic critique was widespread: it could easily be found on the street, in colleges and universities, and among radicals and progressives. Bluesman Carl Martin observed:

> Everybody's crying: "Let's have a New Deal,"
> 'Cause I've got to make a living,
> If I have to rob and steal.

At the same time, economist Abram Harris and political scientist and future United Nations stalwart Ralph Bunche, both young professors at Howard University, called for interracial labor unity and an understanding of the centrality of economics, or material forces, to the historic oppression of blacks. They maintained that the oppression of blacks was not merely a problem of race but was a question of class as well. Broadly speaking, the struggle had to be one of ameliorating capitalism's most flagrant abuses. Far more oppositional, albeit less influential, voices like black Alabama Communist Party activist Hosea Hudson found capitalism itself to be the problem, socialist revolution the solution.

The venerable W. E. B. Du Bois was the most provocative and powerful voice questioning the NAACP's focus in the 1930s. His perceptive critique cut two ways. First, harking back to the ideas of Booker T. Washington at the turn of the century, Du Bois now wanted the fiercely interracialist and integrationist NAACP to promote black economic development—and in turn black elevation—through aggressive support of a separate black economic world. Du Bois's Marxist-socialist-inspired critique of capitalism, calling for greater workers' control over the economy, spoke more and more of the necessity for black networks like consumer cooperatives. This message did not sit well with the intensely pro-capitalist NAACP.

Du Bois and others emphasized that legalism had to be prefaced by the redistribution of wealth and across-the-board leveling of power and influence. Reliance on legalism as a remedy for the problems confronting black Americans signaled a reformist agenda at best, they felt, certainly not a revolutionary one. After leaving the association in 1934, once the ideological rift became irreparable, Du Bois continued to offer an increasingly militant socialist and internationalist approach. The "road to *Brown*," however, was clearly being plotted through capitalism, not socialism.

Du Bois's call for black economic nationalism vividly exposed the tensions between voluntary and imposed segregation, between separatism and integrationism, between black nationalism and American nationalism. Seeking to get beyond these tensions, he stressed that blacks had to strengthen the institutional infrastructure and social fabric of their own communities. The critical issue was to forge more effective forms of collective organization and action aimed at intraracial uplift. In this vision, integration assumed a decidedly secondary, even ancillary, position. He emphasized the importance of black institutions and black culture in structuring and propelling the black freedom struggle and in nurturing the black psyche. The thrust of NAACP politics, from this point of view, increasingly now collided with rather than meshed with black needs and aspirations.

The historical and rhetorical development of *Brown* reflected a profound discomfort with racial separatism. Essential to the social-scientific discourse behind *Brown* was the argument that racial segregation, even voluntary segregation, was responsible for the psychological damage and sociocultural pathology among blacks. Du Bois clearly perceived that this negative characterization of a distinctive black life and culture as well as of blacks as victims was one-sided and misleading. This potentially baneful argument, increasingly vital to the NAACP's liberal indictment of Jim Crow, failed to make the crucial distinction between what Du Bois saw as the benefits of voluntary segregation—autonomy and psychic health—and the harm of state-imposed segregation—dependency and dehumanization. The point was not that white racism had deformed black life and culture, but rather that it had deformed the American experience.

Du Bois stressed in his 1935 discussion "Does the Negro Need Separate Schools?" that the fundamental issue was equality of educational opportunity: making available to black students the best education possible, whether that be in segregated or integrated schools. He explained that

> . . . the Negro needs neither segregated nor mixed schools. What he needs is education. What he must remember is that there is no magic, in either mixed schools or in segregated schools. A mixed school with poor and unsympathetic teachers, with hostile public opinion, and no teaching of truth concerning black folk, is bad. A segregated school with ignorant placeholders, inadequate equipment, poor salaries, and wretched housing, is equally bad. Other things being equal, the mixed school is the broader, more natural basis for the education of all youth. It gives wider contacts; it inspires greater self-confidence; and suppresses the inferiority complex. But other things are seldom equal, and in that case, Sympathy, Knowledge, and the Truth, outweigh all that the mixed school can offer.

Du Bois also reiterated that the problem was white racism, not the cruel hoax of innate black inferiority. Structurally speaking, he maintained, the crux of the issue was the **symbiosis** between racism and capitalism. In terms of education in particular, the problem went in two directions: racist constraints on black educational opportunity, and black as well as white devaluation of black institutions and culture. In this case, the denigration of black schools and black educators, in spite of their noteworthy achievements against all odds, was common even among blacks. The brainwashing of blacks, what historian Carter G. Woodson referred to as "The Mis-Education of the Negro," was indispensable to the propaganda of white supremacy. Du Bois countered, however:

> If the American Negro really believed in himself; if he believed that Negro teachers can educate children according to the best standards of modern training; if he believed that Negro colleges transmit and add to science, as well as or better than other colleges, then he would bend his energies, not to escaping inescapable association with his own group, but to seeing that his group had every opportunity for its best and highest development. He would insist that his teachers be decently paid; that his schools were properly housed and equipped; that his colleges be supplied with scholarship and research funds; and he would be far more interested in the efficiency of these institutions of learning, than in forcing himself into other institutions where he is not wanted.

Whereas Du Bois's economic and cultural nationalism did not find favor with the NAACP leadership, Du Bois and his opponents within the NAACP did agree upon the necessity of strengthening the organization's grassroots constituencies. Ordinary black folk had to be brought into the organization; they had to be made to feel that this was *their* civil rights organization. Otherwise, a black freedom struggle guided in large measure by the NAACP stood no real chance of success. Local and state branches had to be strengthened. Black politicization during the Depression and war years, especially the latter, was the seedbed of the concurrent flowering of the NAACP's membership rolls. Growing black movement toward the Democrats, the party of FDR, most notably in the North, marked this politicization. A more important signal of this trend, especially in the South where the "lily white" Democratic Party moderated the ultimately pivotal black shift toward the Democrats, was the phenomenal expansion of the NAACP.

Historian Patricia Sullivan has shrewdly observed:

> Black identification with the party of Roosevelt and the revival of the NAACP were primary mediating forces in the emerging civil rights movement. The NAACP provided the essential vehicle for meeting the escalation of black expectations and militancy that accompanied the war. NAACP membership in the South by the late 1930s was slightly more than 18,000. By the end of the war it approached 156,000.

That jump in the association's membership owed heavily to the good work of the group, including its legal defense work, its efforts to remove impediments to the black vote, and its southern speaking and recruitment tours featuring prominent national spokesmen like Houston and Marshall. It likewise owed significantly to the indefatigable efforts of Ella Baker, wartime southern field secretary for the NAACP.

While the national office paid much lip service to the notion of making the NAACP relevant to the masses of black people, within the upper echelon an elitist and top-down vision of black liberation dominated. The NAACP leaders firmly believed that they would lead their people to freedom. Baker, however, advanced a far more democratic and participatory vision of black insurgency. She saw herself as a facilitator of local-based movements, working with a broad spectrum in local communities to articulate clearly both common goals and viable strategies for effective collective struggle. In other words, she advanced a bottom-up approach to organization. Baker "spent six months of each year in the South, taking the NAACP to churches, schools, barbershops, bars, and pool halls," writes Sullivan, adding that Baker "helped to build chapters around the needs and concerns of individual communities and encouraged cooperation with labor unions and other progressive organizations."

Baker's emphasis on alliances constituted another article of faith within the NAACP. For example, there was the Southern Negro Youth Congress (1937–48), a group committed to forging links between workers and southern black youth. Similarly, the 1940s South Carolina Progressive Democratic Party constituted another element of the growing black insurgency. Organized labor, notably CIO unions and the Highlander School, with its commitment to working toward interracial labor activism in the South, played crucial roles in fostering support for the black struggle. So did the Communist Party—especially prior to the widespread postwar anti-Communist hysteria and repression. Also important were many New Deal–inspired southerners and white-dominated interracial organizations like the Southern Conference for Human Welfare. In various and sundry ways, these organizations and many other groups and individuals contributed to the groundwork for *Brown*. These were often difficult yet heady times; the 1930s and the pre–cold war 1940s were ultimately, as Sullivan demonstrates, "days of hope." *Brown* was clearly a product of that hope.

The Growing Anti-Racist Offensive: *An American Dilemma* Confronts World War II

Another vital development fueling the NAACP's crusade was the declining intellectual and cultural respectability of racism. In *Brown* and the various cases the NAACP lawyers argued leading up to it, the growing scientific and humanistic consensus in favor of egalitarianism was crucial. Nowhere was this point more effectively put forward to national and worldwide audiences than in Gunnar Myrdal's magisterial study of race relations in the United States, *An American Dilemma* (1944). The Swedish economist directed a large staff in an exhaustive study, four years in the making, of the evidence and significance of the discrepancy between the American creed and the American reality for African Americans. The awesome final product consisted of more than 1,000 pages of text, ten appendices, and more than 250 pages of notes.

For 1950s America and beyond, the *Brown* decision and *An American Dilemma* constitute twin pillars in the evolving liberal racial orthodoxy: America had no choice but to live up to the American creed in its treatment of its black citizens. Evidence of the impact of *An American Dilemma* can be seen in its extensive use in the theory and practice of civil rights law—where its findings became crucial— and its influence on the Supreme Court that decided *Brown*. It became the authoritative work on black-white race relations until the mid-1960s when its assimilationist and integrationist approach came under attack (notably within the black insurgency) as being too liberal, too reformist, and complicitous in the negative construction of black life and culture. From World War II up to the radical Black Power movement beginning in 1966, *An American Dilemma* defined the liberal orthodoxy on American race relations. The *Brown* decision experienced a similar path.

As the antisegregation documents for the period after 1944 . . . make clear, the authority of *An American Dilemma* was constantly invoked implicitly as well as explicitly. . . . [and] an understanding of the basic problem discussed in *An American Dilemma*—the disjunction between the American creed and the white oppression of African Americans—goes back to the nation's founding. Of course it can be traced back even further to the European enslavement of Africans in the New World. Even the related emphasis in Myrdal's text on the baneful impact of white racism on whites as well as on blacks is a recurrent historical theme. . . .

As a social scientist committed to moral exhortation and social engineering, Myrdal emphasized both vigorous government leadership and strong government intervention to resolve the problems among blacks engendered by racial prejudice and discrimination. Those engaged in the black freedom struggle—including antebellum abolitionists, postbellum supporters of Reconstruction, and New Deal–inspired racial activists—have shared Myrdal's faith in an activist government committed to racial equality. Unfortunately, at midcentury this activist approach had not found enough public support.

While there was much new and original material in *An American Dilemma,* what was particularly striking then and now is how well the text captured the evolving liberal support of racial egalitarianism and integrationism among the lay public and scholars, especially sociologists and anthropologists. Myrdal employed many of the best available black and white minds for his study and distilled the results of their contributions through his own perspective as a relative outsider to the American scene. The fact that extraordinary national effort had to be undertaken to ameliorate the inequalities African Americans experienced was patently clear. In line with its scholarly and objective goals, though, Myrdal's text was very long on description and analysis and short on policy prescriptions.

As in *Brown,* the argument and the remedy in *An American Dilemma*—like most American efforts to deal with racial inequality—did not go far enough. What became increasingly clear in the period from *An American Dilemma* to *Brown* was a growing yet insufficient national will to tackle this thorny problem. In spite of brief moments to the contrary, such as the noteworthy government efforts spawned by black insurgency between 1954 and 1974, the national will has proven insufficient to the challenge.

Even the explosive wartime economy that brought the nation out of the Depression and the subsequent thirty years of sustained economic growth were insufficient to create racial equality. Neither was postwar U.S. global supremacy. Nonetheless, in this broad context of sustained economic growth and "Pax Americana," or worldwide U.S. dominance, the black freedom struggle surged. *Brown* represented a turning point in its building momentum.

The pulsating wartime economy transformed the American landscape. Streams of rural blacks leaving the South during the Depression reached flood proportions during the war as job opportunities and prospects for a better life proliferated in northern and western cities. Heightened black political consciousness engendered by the Depression continued to grow during the war. Increasingly, the race problem became a national issue, not merely a southern one. As Pax Americana demanded that the United States assume the awesome pressures and glaring spotlight of international center stage, African Americans and their allies fully understood that from a geopolitical perspective, state-enforced white supremacy was indefensible. In this radically altered context, with its local southern black membership base expanding and energized, the NAACP shifted its strategic attack from equalization to direct attack.

This significant shift reflected several developmental and organizational factors as well. In the South, there were increasing numbers of blacks willing to file civil rights cases and black lawyers able to argue those cases. The NAACP legal staff had grown in size and maturity, reaching the point where by the war's end it had become a well-oiled and flexible machine. In 1939 the NAACP created the NAACP Legal Defense and Educational Fund as a functionally autonomous wing. This streamlined and enhanced the association's legal enterprise. By 1945 the staff had coalesced around the move from equalization to direct attack and in 1948 the board of directors and the Annual Conference issued a full-fledged statement in support of the direct attack strategy.

Recent court successes by the NAACP legal team and its cohorts, especially the 1944 Supreme Court ruling in *Smith v. Allwright* outlawing the white primary in the South spurred that support. This racially exclusionary device had functioned as a critical prop of white, one-party, Democratic rule in the South. In a related vein, a significant measure of the success of NAACP organizing in the 1940s owed to increasing black political mobilization around voting, particularly in the South. Growing black political power in the North enhanced the national impact of black politicization in general. Chicago's South Side and New York City's Harlem, where recently elected black congressmen were beginning to flex their political muscles—most notably Harlem's Reverend Adam Clayton Powell Jr.—signaled this important trend. In the overall domestic and international context, an all-out legal assault against Jim Crow and *Plessy* became a viable enterprise.

Continuity and Change in the Legal Struggle: Equality, Equalization, and Direct Attack

The creation of legal precedents was absolutely essential to the NAACP's overall strategy against Jim Crow. Reverses as well as victories thus proved to be invaluable learning tools. Indeed the long-term "road to *Brown*" had many ups and downs. . . . Two key legal setbacks in the nineteenth century [were] *Roberts v. City of Boston* (1849), which dealt with equal educational opportunity; and *Plessy v. Ferguson* (1896), which legitimized separate but equal railway accommodations. The former case painfully revealed that the prejudice and discrimination endured by free blacks in the antebellum slave South had clear parallels in the free states of the antebellum North. White supremacy was a national dilemma, not a regional one.

Roberts was a Supreme Judicial Court of Massachusetts decision that separate common or public schools for Boston's black schoolchildren did not deny them their legal rights and did not expose them to undue logistical difficulties or degradation. In addition, Massachusetts' highest court agreed with the defendant, the Boston School Committee, that it was within its constitutionally delegated power to separate black schoolchildren from white schoolchildren, given the committee's statutory authority over the ways and means of local public education. If in the committee's judgment racially segregated schools served reasonable educational and sociopolitical objectives, the ruling maintained, then this particular form of racial discrimination was legal. While a state law in 1855 overturned the original decision, the resonances between the *Roberts* and *Plessy* cases and the significance of both cases in the history of American apartheid are revealing.

An even more stunning and influential constitutional setback was *Plessy v. Ferguson.* The majority opinion cited *Roberts v. City of Boston* as one among several key precedents. The legal logic in *Plessy,* as in *Roberts,* owed heavily to social customs rooted in white supremacy. It also relied on an interpretation of the Fourteenth Amendment's guarantee of each citizen's right to equal protection under the law as consistent with racially separate but equal public accommodations and institutions. In later cases, *Plessy* was at times interpreted narrowly as affirming segregation in transportation and comparable kinds of public accommodations, while *Roberts* affirmed segregated education. As the documents demonstrate, prosegregation legal cases relied extensively on these distinctions and related arguments and rulings.

In the case for the black plaintiff in *Roberts,* the venerable Massachusetts abolitionist and senator Charles Sumner eloquently articulated an elaborate and powerful brief for the concept of racial equality as well as the policy of integrated public schools in "enlightened" Boston. Again, the pro-egalitarian and pro-integration documents . . . demonstrate that the twentieth-century "road to *Brown*" made extensive use of Sumner's stirring and ultimately compelling nineteenth-century brief. In many ways, the antebellum abolitionist crusade that gave rise to Sumner's brief later reconfigured itself into a neo-abolitionist crusade against Jim Crow. The NAACP's legal campaign exemplified this transition.

Justice John Marshall Harlan's famous dissent in *Plessy* is best known for its articulation of the Constitution as color-blind. He wrote that "in view of the Constitution, in the eye of the law, there is in this country no superior, dominant, ruling class of citizens. There is no caste here. Our Constitution is color-blind, and neither knows nor tolerates classes among citizens. In respect of civil rights, all citizens are equal before the law." This inspiring and idealistic vision was eventually enshrined in *Brown,* furnishing the egalitarian and integrationist forces with a powerful endorsement.

Less well known and less often discussed was Harlan's embrace of de facto white supremacy and his opposition to any kind of social equality between the races. . . . Jim Crow's legal partisans often quoted Harlan on these points as a way of undercutting his assertion that the Constitution is color-blind. Harlan's acceptance of segregated public school education as consistent with state power likewise curried favor with advocates of Jim Crow education and incurred the opprobrium of its opponents. His dissent proved to be very influential in large measure precisely because of its double edge.

Until direct attack became the NAACP's guiding strategy in the late 1940s, both sides accepted the *Plessy*-defined terms of the debate—separate and equal—as the controlling issue. *Gong Lum v. Rice* (1927) illustrates how *Plessy* carried the day. The father of nine-year-old Martha Lum sought admission for his daughter to a local white school in Mississippi on the grounds that his family was of Chinese descent. He argued that it was wrong for Martha to be compelled to attend the black school, given the stigma attached to blacks and their separate schools, especially as his daughter was not black. Neither was she white, the Supreme Court argued, as it upheld the power of the state to categorize and place students as it saw fit. The issue here was not the right of the state to maintain segregated schools, which the plaintiff accepted. Rather, the issue was both legal and categorical: the state of Mississippi could compel the girl to go to a black school when she was neither black nor white, but of Chinese descent.

This case is also instructive in its erasure of Chinese racial identity and its conflation of that identity with a black racial identity. Two points, among others, are critical to this discussion. First, the dualistic construction of race in America obscures both powerful cultural differences among nonwhites, in this case blacks and Chinese, and critical differences in their historical experiences in the United States. This racial dualism also misrepresents and thus devalues the integrity of their group-based identities. In turn, it buttresses white supremacy.

Second, it is worth thinking critically about the power of the state, or the government, to determine racial identities or to define who belongs to which race. That power did not reside ultimately with the oppressed, nonwhite minorities themselves, in this instance with the black and Chinese citizens. Indeed, a vital aspect of the Asian American movement, particularly between the late 1960s and early 1980s, and the black civil rights and Black Power movements (1955–75) was the same. Both fought to wrest the ultimate power of group definition from the state and federal governments and to reassert control over their identity: to define on their terms who they are.

In the years before *Brown*, the search for precedential decisions undermining *Plessy* proceeded. In the area of equal educational opportunity for blacks, particularly in the Upper South, the NAACP carved out a series of important victories in salary equalization cases in the 1930s. The larger strategic problem, of course, had been anticipated: the process was piecemeal, gradual, and very time-consuming because each separate school jurisdiction had to be challenged separately. In addition, the tactical move among southern school districts to mask racial disparities in salaries through the introduction of merit criteria exposed a serious flaw in the salary equalization strategy and pushed the NAACP lawyers toward the direct attack strategy.

Similarly, a series of "victories" in graduate and professional school cases— *Pearson v. Murray* (1936), *Missouri ex rel. Gaines v. Canada* (1938), *Sipuel v. Oklahoma State Regents* (1948)—nibbled away at *Plessy*.

Taken together and over time, these cases played out the equalization approach to the point where the direct attack approach became imperative. In *Pearson v. Murray*, the Maryland Court of Appeals ruled that Donald Murray, a black Amherst College graduate, had been denied equality of educational opportunity when he was refused admission to the University of Maryland's law school. The state's alternative of providing scholarships for blacks to attend out-of-state schools was viewed as a violation of Murray's Fourteenth Amendment right to equal treatment under the law. Because the constitutional injury to Murray was "present and personal," the remedy had to be immediate. Murray either had to be admitted at once to Maryland's School of Law or a separate and equal school of law for Maryland blacks had to be created forthwith. Since a comparable black law school could not be created overnight, he had to be admitted to Maryland's School of Law.

Nevertheless, with the possibility that a separate black law school might satisfy the letter of the ruling, *Plessy* clearly remained intact. In the *Gaines* and *Sipuel* cases, similar circumstances resulted in similar rulings, this time in the Supreme Court. The decisions in these cases turned on the issue of the inequality between the reputable all-white state-supported law schools in Missouri and Oklahoma and the makeshift all-black arrangements those states scrambled to provide to avoid admitting blacks to their all-white law schools. Notwithstanding the impact of the sociological arguments on the behind-the-scenes discussions of these cases, the Court was deeply divided on the issue of overruling *Plessy* and thus did not go that far.

For the NAACP, the *Gaines* decision was a moment to be savored, however; it was the first favorable Supreme Court judgment casting doubt on the legality of *Plessy.* In a comparable decision in *Sipuel,* the Supreme Court upheld the right of the black plaintiffs to equal educational opportunity, although possibly under separate circumstances. The limits of equalization as a strategy were becoming patently clear, particularly in light of fallacious defense arguments claiming the comparability as against the actual equality of separate schools. By the late 1940s, the NAACP legal trust was working on a Texas case, *Sweatt v. Painter* (1949), where the direct attack strategy was being readied.

The strategy employed in *Sweatt v. Painter* and a related case, *McLaurin v. Oklahoma State Regents* (1949), failed to get the Supreme Court to overturn *Plessy.* Even so, that same strategy would soon prove effective in *Brown.* In the *Sweatt* and *McLaurin* cases, the NAACP lawyers used a two-pronged approach. First, they focused on how separate black law schools, especially quickly contrived ones created to forestall integration, lacked the many advantages of the traditional all-white law schools and were thus a blatant denial of equal educational opportunity. Second, in a tactical innovation, the NAACP lawyers utilized psychosocial evidence on the harm segregation inflicted on its victims. This kind of argument had been used in a 1945 friend-of-the-court brief filed in support of a lawsuit against Orange County, California, for its practice of segregating Mexican American schoolchildren from white schoolchildren. In *Sweatt* and *McLaurin,* this tactic foreshadowed the increasingly influential emphasis in postwar America on the psychological damage that segregation inflicted on blacks.

In *Henderson v. United States* (1949), a case coupled with *Sweatt* and *McLaurin,* the federal government issued a friend-of-the-court brief vigorously condemning segregated railroad dining cars, which the Court subsequently declared illegal. Earlier, in *Shelley v. Kraemer* (1947) and *Sipes v. McGhee* (1947), the Supreme Court outlawed **restrictive covenants** (contracts forbidding the sale of property to blacks and other "stigmatized" groups and individuals) as invidious and unconstitutional forms of racial discrimination. Charles Houston himself, in concert with his NAACP colleagues, argued this series of cases. In its friend-of-the-court brief to support the government's opposition to restrictive covenants, the Department of Justice revealed the growing importance of cold war concerns. That brief made it clear that Jim Crow was a very serious problem for the United States in its propaganda war with the Soviets for the hearts and minds of the Third World, especially in Africa. Indeed, this was an issue that the NAACP legal team and its cohorts increasingly exploited to good effect.

In *Henderson,* Attorney General Howard McGrath maintained before the Supreme Court that "segregation signifies and is intended to signify that a member of the colored race is not equal to the white race." Jim Crow, McGrath further explained, represented "an anachronism which a half-century of history and experience has shown to be a departure from the basic constitutional principle that all Americans, regardless of their race or color or religion or national origin, stand equal and alike in the sight of the law." This ringing endorsement of constitutional egalitarianism by the nation's number one lawyer meshed well with the Justice Department's earlier argument for desegregation on cold war grounds. This kind of ammunition, including President Harry Truman's official initiation of desegregation of the armed forces, verified strong opposition within the government to state-sanctioned racial segregation. The stage was now set for a full-fledged direct attack against *Plessy*-sanctioned segregation: the "road to *Brown*" was taking shape.

Politics, Social Change, and Decisionmaking within the Supreme Court: The Crafting of *Brown*

Brown v. Board of Education of Topeka, Kansas, as well as *Briggs v. Elliott, Davis v. County School Board of Prince Edward County, Belton v. Gebhart,* and *Bolling v. Sharpe*—the cases eventually argued collectively as *Brown v. Board of Education*—all wound their separate ways toward the Supreme Court in the early 1950s. In each case, and in spite of anticipated lower court setbacks, the NAACP legal staff remained hopeful about a positive Supreme Court ruling in favor of equal educational opportunity. Third World nationalist struggles, most importantly growing assertiveness within America's own communities of color, pervaded the international community, which was reeling from the Holocaust, the dropping of the atomic bomb on Hiroshima and Nagasaki, and an escalating cold war. Worldwide as well as at home, white supremacy was under furious assault. Even though the "Red scare" repressed left-progressive forces in this country, seriously undermining the most radical elements within the black struggle, that insurgency soon reinvigorated itself via the civil rights movement. *Brown* contributed significantly to the ethos and spirit of this revitalized social movement, which was fast becoming a mass movement.

. . . [B]oth sides in *Brown* mounted strong cases. From the lower courts, *Briggs v. Elliott* is included because the case featured two legal titans: the celebrated establishment lawyer John W. Davis for the defense and Thurgood Marshall for the plaintiffs. In oral arguments, they both provided high drama as well as astute argumentation. In their legal briefs, they compellingly presented their cases. *Briggs v. Elliott* encapsulated the twin battles in the NAACP's all-out war on segregated schools. First was the clear-cut evidence of the denial of equal educational opportunity owing to gross physical and funding disparities between white and black schools. Second was the interrelated argument of psychosocial harm inflicted on black schoolchildren as a result of Jim Crow schools. Although only the lower court dissent of Judge J. Waties J. Waring responded favorably to the second argument, it clearly made an impact on both sides.

Indeed, the sociological argument figured in all of the component cases in *Brown* except *Bolling v. Sharpe*. The NAACP lawyers relied heavily on the social-scientific work of many influential scholars such as Otto Klineberg and Gordon Allport. The most important of these experts, however, were social psychologists Kenneth and Mamie Clark. The Clarks had devised a doll test as a way to gauge evidence of personality dysfunction among black children under Jim Crow. When shown two dolls—one white and one black—the children were asked which one they preferred. The fact that a preponderance of the black children expressed a preference for the white doll was most revealing for the Clarks. From this finding, they extrapolated that the damage done to the self-esteem of these children reinforced notions of black inferiority and white superiority. Racial segregation did indeed damage the black psyche. The issue was not, as the majority opinion in *Plessy* had contended, that the antiblack stigma was all in the minds of blacks. Rather, the stigma was all too real, for whites as well as blacks.

In the lower court opposition, only in *Davis v. County School Board of Prince Edward County* did the defendants use experts to rebut the sociological argument. Throughout the lower court litigation in these cases, however, the sociological argument forced the opposition at least to seek to diffuse it. In the Topeka case, the defendants questioned the social-scientific viability of the sociological evidence and its specific applicability to the children under consideration as opposed to black schoolchildren in Jim Crow schools generally. In other words, except for the Clarendon County data offered by the Clarks, the evidence in these cases was often drawn from studies conducted outside the community in question.

At the time and subsequently, this sociological jurisprudence spawned innumerable critics as well as supporters. Many in both camps bemoaned the sociological incursion into legal argumentation. Supporters have stressed that the evidence of the deleterious impact of racial caste on the American psyche, in particular the black psyche, could not be diminished by reference to the methodological and interpretive limitations of the social psychological evidence—especially the Clarks' doll test. Instead, they have argued, on balance the Clarks' study was persuasive. Furthermore, for many, the gravity of the constitutional and moral issues involved overrode considerations of both scholarly detachment and judicial restraint, compelling intellectual and legal activism.

The right-wing conservative opposition blasted what they saw as blatant social engineering. They strongly decried liberal and integrationist bias masquerading as legal reasoning and reiterated their opposition to sociological jurisprudence and their support for judicial restraint and scholarly detachment. Other opponents, among them racial moderates and liberals, criticized the social-scientific evidence as more faddish than substantive, more ambiguous and contested than clear-cut and persuasive. Some pointed out problems in research design, methodology, and assessment of evidence.

Some critics of the Clarks' doll test highlighted the need to disentangle the influence of the broader environment from that of the school. It was also argued that black children might identify with nonblack, even white, images without being imprisoned by self-hate. Some argued that especially outside the South, similar kinds of tests have shown that close proximity to whites, or integration, yielded comparable evidence of black self-hate. For some, it was a question of what was worse for black self-esteem, integration or segregation? In fact, social science experts from 1919 to 1941 downplayed the argument of lowered black self-esteem as a principal consequence of segregation, notably of all-black institutions like schools. These experts saw the problem of black self-esteem as a more complex phenomenon. Nevertheless, between the *Brown* decision and the late 1960s black challenge to integrationism, an expanding social-scientific consensus about the negative effects of segregation on the black psyche became increasingly important to the argument for integration.

Chief Justice Earl Warren's reference to the persuasiveness of this sociological evidence in the very text of the 1954 decision touched off a vigorous debate.

Footnote 11 of the decision lists seven authorities—an address by Kenneth Clark leads off—and draws directly from the NAACP brief. This famous footnote further heightened the controversy around that evidence and the decision itself.

Many, particularly judicial conservatives and pro-segregationists, saw this use of sociological evidence as deeply threatening. They viewed the decision as a judicial usurpation of states' rights and of federal legislative and executive powers. It represented a flagrant abuse of judicial review: the right of the Supreme Court to rule on the constitutionality of the acts of the other branches of government.

They also saw the decision as part of an all-out assault on white supremacy, or, euphemistically speaking, southern mores. This kind of thinking led to an extremist southern white backlash to *Brown* and integrationism: a movement identified as "massive resistance." . . . The "Southern Manifesto" [Reading 3.2] was the foundational document of this racist and reactionary white counterinsurgency. Signed by ninety-six southern white leaders, this document pledged unyielding opposition to judicial usurpation and dedication to overturning the decision.

This kind of response had been feared by the justices, several of whom were southerners, because they clearly perceived the depth of white racist attachment to Jim Crow. In fact, by the time *Brown* reached the high court in December 1952, a majority of the justices were predisposed to striking down *Plessy*. Under the failed leadership of Chief Justice Fred Vinson, however, the Supreme Court had been deeply fractured and unable to forge a consensus about overturning *Plessy*. Changes in court personnel, the most important of which was the death of Vinson in September 1953 and the selection of Earl Warren as chief justice, proved critical. Warren and his colleagues understood that the enormity of overruling a precedent of *Plessy*'s magnitude demanded that the decision be unanimous. A divided ruling would dilute its impact.

The arguments in *Brown* proceeded in three stages. First, the initial presentation of the case did not give the justices all the time and evidence they needed to decide definitively. To gain more time to sift through the evidence and try to sway one another on various points, the justices called for a second stage to the proceedings: reargument on the intentions of the Fourteenth Amendment's framers. Had the framers created that amendment as opposing or supporting segregated public school education? The third and final stage, after the decision to strike down *Plessy* on the merits of the case was reached—often called *Brown I*—the court called for arguments about the remedy, or how to enforce the ruling. That decision regarding implementation is often referred to as *Brown II*.

During the first stage of deliberations, a consensus emerged that overall the claimants' case was powerful enough to be sustained and in turn to be used as a platform to overrule *Plessy*. Speaking to the sociological argument, Justice Tom Clark privately observed that "we need no modern psychologist to tell us that 'enforced separation of the two races stamp[s] the colored race with a badge of inferiority,' contrary to [the argument in] *Plessy v. Ferguson*." Agreement on racial equality and the related imperative of equality of educational opportunity emerged early on. Two other issues loomed as more contentious. In spite of much debate, the evidence of the intentions of the Fourteenth Amendment's framers was not very convincing. A modest preponderance of the evidence suggested that they saw the amendment as favoring segregated public school education. Ultimately, however, the justices found the evidence inconclusive and wholly insufficient to sustain a judgment one way or the other.

There was also much interesting behind-the-scenes debate about whether the case could be decided principally on its legal merits or whether political and social considerations were primary. Once the focus shifted away from the traditional issues of original intent and reliance on precedent to considerations of the impact or consequences of an admitted error—*Plessy*—the die was cast. As Mark Tushnet demonstrates in the reasoning of Justice Robert Jackson, "an appropriate premise for overruling *Plessy*" did not necessitate compelling explanations of either "the failure of the representative branches [Congress and the president] or the intentions of the framers." Instead, the appropriate legal premise was a profound mid-twentieth-century global paradigm shift: an emerging and increasingly powerful consensus regarding racial equality. Within a legal framework based on this premise rather than the fallacy of white racial superiority, the view of racial equality as a fundamental principle of law as well as of society and culture meant that state-sanctioned racial segregation in education, and beyond, was a dead constitutional letter.

A consensus within the Court about overruling *Plessy* was easier to reach than an agreement regarding remedy. Indeed, much of the debate among the justices about overturning *Plessy* pivoted around how, in effect, to implement such a potentially cataclysmic decision. This deeply felt sensitivity about how the nation, especially the white South, would react clearly circumscribed the whole of the Court's lengthy deliberations, not just the third stage where remedy was the explicit subject. The justices, like many Americans, feared what Justice Clark prophetically referred to as "subversion or even defiance of our mandates in many communities." In an early closed conference of the justices on the case, Alabama-born Justice Hugo Black had pointed to the issue agitating all of the justices: the extraordinary depth of racial caste in the South, the "deep seated antagonism to commingling" across racial boundaries. He argued that many southern school districts would shut down "rather than mix races at grade and high school levels." Ultimately, however, the issue of the differences between desegregating at the level of colleges and universities as opposed to the primary and secondary levels, where social intercourse between the races was seen as far more explosive, did not prove determinative.

What did prove compelling was agreement that the remedy had to be gradual. Without this commitment to incrementalism, the commitment to overturning *Plessy* weakened. The contending briefs on this issue fully aired both sides: immediatism and gradualism. Fears of an extremely volatile southern white response to an immediate implementation decree rendered gradualism the only viable option. At the point of remedy, therefore, legal concerns were plainly secondary. The NAACP brief argued strongly for immediate relief given that egregious violations of constitutional rights had been established. But the Court wanted to weigh the effects of immediate or gradual implementation. This delicate situation led to the ambiguous and in many ways ill-fated compromise of the eventual relief decree: implementation "with all deliberate speed."

The Court's fundamental lack of nerve and will mirrored that of the executive and congressional leadership as well as of the vast majority of white Americans. As Tushnet has shown, "It was not so much that the Justices understood that it would be difficult for courts to accomplish what they wanted through judicial decrees: the more acute problem was that they never truly decided what they wanted the courts to accomplish."

While they hoped and prayed for the best, the NAACP lawyers and perceptive observers everywhere were fully aware that the relief decree lacked muscle. A less radical and perhaps more effective decree might have been the middle ground option—immediate desegregation tempered by modifications sensitive to local conditions. On the cusp of the twenty-first century, the continuing national scandal of separate and unequal schools for children of color is a tragedy of epic proportions. The same is true of the persistence of racial apartheid in many areas of American life, including housing and employment. Tushnet has provocatively offered in retrospect that "had the Court followed through on the promises of *Brown*, political resistance to desegregation might have been smaller, the courts might not have had to develop intrusive remedies, and the reaction against 'judicial activism' ... might not have occurred." Perhaps the "shock therapy" of immediatism would have served the short-term future better. It is hard to imagine it serving worse than "all deliberate speed."

The *Brown* Decision: Immediate Responses and Immediate Consequences

As soon as Chief Justice Warren announced the decision on May 17, 1954, the reaction was swift and predictable. Most commentators did not emphasize the exceedingly moderate and measured language of the decision. The legal rhetoric neither soared nor inspired. The text stressed that segregation is wrong and had damaged all Americans, especially blacks. It also emphasized that in midcentury America, Jim Crow was morally and intellectually indefensible. There was no ringing rejection of segregation as a profound legal error in *Plessy*. There was no pointed legal argument against race as an arbitrary and thus indefensible category or for a color-blind society. The egalitarianism of the decision's text was dutiful and restrained.

Far more important than the modest substance of the text of the decision has been its awesome symbolic resonance—what Americans have read into the decision, how they have interpreted it. Blacks and their allies in the black liberation struggle were pleased and hopeful, but often cautious. Pro-segregationists and their allies were deeply alarmed. Both camps fretted about the immediate and long-term consequences of this momentous decision. In particular, racial liberals and supporters of the black freedom struggle felt vindicated. Richard Kluger writes that the decision "represented nothing short of a reconsecration of American ideals. . . . The Court had restored to the American people a measure of humanity that had been drained away in their climb to worldwide ascent." Not surprisingly, therefore, within an hour of the decision's announcement, "the Voice of America would begin beaming word to the world in thirty-four languages: In the United States, schoolchildren could no longer be segregated by race."

Nationwide editorial comment reflected a predictable range of opinion. Notwithstanding an undercurrent of caution, black newspapers throughout the country lauded the decision as heralding a new age in race relations. The white press more clearly reflected local and regional perspectives. Northern and western newspapers saw the ruling as positive and hopeful. Pro-segregationist southern papers uniformly condemned the decision, while the liberal southern white press summoned up a guarded hope for the best.

Black response ran the gamut from elation to occasional opposition. Cleophus Brown, a labor and civil rights leader in Richmond, California, remembered that moment as "the point at which 'black folks in Richmond saw the light' and really began to believe they could break through." Black cultural racialists like anthropologist and writer Zora Neale Hurston rejected the logic of *Brown* as self-defeating at best, antiblack at worst. Reflecting a tactical position uncommon among blacks, she chose to emphasize the strengths of all-black institutions rather than the inequities under which they labored. From Hurston's perspective, the decision plainly reiterated notions of black inferiority, with its insinuation that black schoolchildren could learn best under the tutelage of white teachers, sitting next to white students. For Hurston, this was a brutal slap in the face of black teachers and administrators as well as black schoolchildren. She charged: "How much satisfaction can I get from a court order for somebody to associate with me who does not wish to be near me?" In fact, a critical failure of the egalitarianism of the liberal and social-scientific consensus undergirding *Brown* was its devaluation of black culture and black institutions and, ultimately, of blacks themselves.

While W. E. B. Du Bois lauded *Brown*, he shared Hurston's concern about its limitations and possible consequences. He was especially troubled by the decision's blindness both to the potential for the mistreatment of black children in integrated schools and to the strengths of a distinctive black culture. Still, on balance, he viewed *Brown I* and *II* as important but imperfect steps along freedom's bumpy journey.

Nevertheless, the legacy of *Brown* rightly looms large in interpretations of the modern American experience. *Brown* is peerless as a moral touchstone in the legal struggle for African American rights. H. M. Levin contends that *Brown* "was central to eliciting the moral outrage that both blacks and whites were to feel and express about segregation, and this new awareness set the stage for the changes that were to follow." In 1957 Albert Blaustein and Clarence C. Ferguson characterized *Brown* as "the most controversial and far-reaching decision of the Twentieth Century." *Brown* "has had a greater impact upon American life than any other legal decision in our history," they wrote, "and it will remain a source of contention and commentary for generations to come."

Brown's jurisprudential legacy is equally impressive, albeit a bit more contested. As Tushnet observed in 1991, "for nearly forty years, *Brown v. Board of Education* has defined the central values of constitutional adjudication in the United States." More specifically, it has contributed enormously to subsequent civil rights battles and social movements on behalf of the marginalized, including other peoples of color, women, gays and lesbians, and the disabled. Likewise, the decision has profoundly influenced the evolution of "rights consciousness" within American society—that is, "judicial activism on behalf of human rights," notably the rights of oppressed groups and individuals. It constitutes a precedential bulwark in the burgeoning legal fields of human rights law, public interest law, and civil rights law.

The pro-egalitarian and antiracist minority on both the right and the left who question *Brown's* impact largely pursue two lines of argument. Some, like Du Bois, question the effectiveness of the law and the courts as a central arena for the pursuit of social reform. They interpret the post-*Brown* realities of continuing segregation in schools (and beyond) and the related persistence of white supremacy in many forms as proof of the weaknesses of *Brown*. Conservatives use this evidence to underscore their opposition to judicial activism and social change, especially legally mandated. Radicals use the same evidence to call for more effective kinds of judicial activism, as well as social change via law as well as other avenues.

It should be clear by now, however, that neither *Brown* nor the judiciary can be summoned to resolve America's complex and persistent race problems. As this discussion has emphasized, amelioration of this national dilemma has demanded yet failed to generate national will, commitment, and action. The courts are particularly impotent in this regard as they constitute the nonrepresentative branch of government. They have no real power to institutionalize racial equality, not to mention racial integration. Seeking to achieve racial equality principally through legal as opposed to economic, political, and social means has contributed to what the legal scholar Morton J. Horwitz terms a "distortion" in "the battle against racial discrimination." He explains: "The schools—the weakest and most vulnerable of American institutions—have been forced to bear the brunt of the social change required in the battle against racial discrimination, even though school segregation is now largely a function of discriminatory housing patterns which are, in turn, related to job discrimination."

The distortion engendered by the "legalization of the problem of racial discrimination" is largely a post-*Brown* phenomenon. Horwitz astutely observes that "our legal system is overwhelmingly geared to a conception of redressing individual grievances, not of vindicating group rights or of correcting generalized patterns of injustice. This perspective does not easily encourage judges to focus on the burdens, stigmas, and scars produced by history." This bias favoring the individual has undercut the courts' limited ability to alleviate group-based patterns of racial inequality.

In a related vein, the courts' conservative, at times reactionary, refusal to grapple with the clear-cut links between economic and racial inequality exacerbates the disparity between *Brown's* promise of equal opportunity and the post-*Brown* reality of unequal opportunity for blacks. In the end, the salient issue remains that courts view socioeconomic inequality and racial inequality as separable and in crucial ways unrelated.

In 1979 Horwitz outlined an extensive and telling series of basic dilemmas *Brown* has presented over time. At that point, twenty-five years after the decision, these dilemmas remained unresolved.

> Does it stand simply for color blindness—for the principle that it is constitutionally impermissible for the state to take race into account even for benign purposes—or instead does it stand as a barrier only to the use of racial classifications for the purpose of oppressing minorities? Should the principle of *Brown* continue to be directed only at governmental discrimination—so-called state action—or should it apply to private action as well? Does *Brown* require only that racial minorities be provided equality of opportunity? But what happens when even after all of the formal barriers of exclusion are dropped, the intangible culture of racism or the scars of a history of deprivation continue to produce racially unequal consequences? Is a racially discriminatory program one that is intended to produce unequal results or one that actually produces such results regardless of the intentions or motivations of its creators? Do such programs interfere with the constitutional rights of non-minority members who may be excluded because of minority preference for jobs, housing, or admission?

At the end of the twentieth century, almost fifty years after *Brown*, these questions are still pressing. Horwitz's structural critique of liberal jurisprudence recalls Du Bois's critique of the NAACP's legalism in the 1930s. At that time Du Bois had come to embrace black economic nationalism within the confines of voluntary segregation. The key point of both arguments is compelling: legal change can obviously accomplish only so much without fundamental economic change.

Similarly, the radical 1930s politics of Du Bois and the conservative 1950s politics of Hurston converged around a shared critique of the cultural politics shaping the road to and beyond *Brown*. Both Hurston and Du Bois saw the negative views of black culture in the liberal **assimilationism** driving the NAACP legal assault against Jim Crow as wrongheaded and dangerous. Unsuccessfully, they furiously argued against it. The NAACP legal campaign had pushed black integration into the white American mainstream, a norm against which African American culture was measured and found woefully wanting.

The assimilationist view of African American culture as defective was deeply political. In fact, it was far more political than anthropological. Those like Thurgood Marshall and highly influential black sociologist E. Franklin Frazier who argued that black culture was in crucial ways flawed and dysfunctional did so in large part because they wanted to place all of the onus for the African American situation on white oppression of blacks. From their point of view, the issue was black powerlessness: Africans had been stripped of their African cultures. They had lost their Africanness. They were Americans, yet racially oppressed and therefore marginalized.

This blatantly political view of black culture thus had a pointed goal. Its proponents, black and white, wanted none of the blame for the "black condition" to be loaded off onto the "Africanness," or blackness, of black people. White Americans had to be made to feel responsible for their racist oppression of blacks and galvanized in the process to alleviate it. If the responsibility for the "black condition" could be foisted onto the racial and cultural distinctiveness of blacks, then whites might be able to blame black problems on those differences, not on white racism.

Unfortunately, as Du Bois and Hurston argued, in its erasure of both the enduring Africanness and related strengths of black cultural uniqueness, this brand of liberal racial politics demeans blackness. Indeed, in a related and revealing context, historian Daryl Michael Scott has demonstrated that the modern political manipulation of "the image of the damaged black psyche" has been both invidious and widespread. He shows that what he characterizes as

> damage imagery has been the product of liberals and conservatives, of racists and antiracists. Often playing on white contempt towards blacks, racial conservatives have sought to use findings of black pathology to justify exclusionary policies and to explain the dire conditions under which black people live. Often seeking to manipulate white pity, racial liberals have used damage imagery primarily to justify policies of inclusion and rehabilitation. Even when relatively devoid of emotional appeals or damage, the social science image of black personality has historically been sketched by experts motivated or heavily influenced by racial ideologies and politics.

A cultural analogue of the "damaged black psyche" has been the concept of black cultural inferiority. The false and misleading linkage of psychological damage with cultural deficiency has reinforced the notion of black inferiority as both innate, or biological, and improvable, or environmental. Even though biological concepts of race are scientifically indefensible and cultural concepts of race are often equally erroneous and misleading, both persist. Indeed, the tenacious myth of black inferiority typically blurs the distinction between biology and culture. In the popular American imagination, cultural and racial inferiority are seen as synonymous, playing into the notion of black inferiority as natural. Regrettably, these (mis)understandings obscure the fundamental fact of egalitarianism—we are all far more alike than different—and continue to haunt post-*Brown* America.

Nevertheless, *Brown* deserves to be recognized for its enormously liberating impact on America and the world. Post-*Brown* American society was forced to look deep within itself and confront the fundamental problem of white racism and its impact on whites and blacks alike. As the great African American leader Frederick Douglass observed in the nineteenth century, the American race problem is essentially a white problem. Structural inequalities bracing white privilege in concert with white racist notions of black social pathology, black cultural inadequacy, and black biological inferiority have fueled America's historic refusal to grapple with the real problem: white racism. *Brown* was a wake-up call America continues to struggle with.

Reflecting unconditional faith in the best of the founding American ideals, *Brown* signifies hope for America's future. It stands for a better America: a humane, inclusive, and free America. The profundity of that vision propelled the black freedom struggle of which *Brown* was a vital part. In 1965 Martin Luther King Jr. paid homage to the centrality of the legal campaign against American apartheid. "The road to freedom," King observed, "is now a highway because lawyers throughout the land, yesterday and today, have helped clear the obstructions, have helped eliminate roadblocks, by their selfless, courageous espousal of difficult and unpopular causes."

White resistance to black equality and empowerment has historically been fierce, and the reaction to *Brown* was no different. In August 1955, three months after *Brown II* had been announced, Emmet Till, a fourteen-year-old black teenager visiting relatives in Mississippi, was lynched for allegedly whistling at a white woman. In December of that year blacks in Montgomery, Alabama, launched the successful year-long Montgomery bus boycott. In September 1957 President Dwight D. Eisenhower was forced to send federal troops to Little Rock, Arkansas, to protect black schoolchildren integrating previously all-white Central High. The conclusion of Cyrus Cassell's poem "Soul Make a Path Through Shouting" poignantly captures the riveting drama and complex historical context of that most revealing moment:

> I have never seen the likes of you,
> Pioneer in dark glasses:
> You won't show the mob your eyes,
> But I know your gaze,
> Steady-on-the-North-Star, burning—
>
> With their jerry-rigged faith,
> Their spear of the American flag,
> How could they dare to believe
> You're someone scared?;
> *Nigger, burr-headed girl,*
> *Where are you going?*
>
> *I'm just going to school.*

Brown gave us that heroic moment and infinite others. Most important, the struggle to realize the promise of *Brown* endures.

The Southern Manifesto

This pronouncement, signed by most Senators and Representatives from eleven southern states and reflecting a widespread determination to resist the Supreme Court's Brown decision of 1954, was introduced into the Congressional Record on March 12, 1956. The Manifesto carries ninety-six signatures, nineteen from the Senate and seventy-seven from the House of Representatives. Five more Representatives signed later.

Declaration of Constitutional Principles

The unwarranted decision of the Supreme Court in the public school cases is now bearing the fruit always produced when men substitute naked power for established law.

The Founding Fathers gave us a Constitution of checks and balances because they realized the inescapable lesson of history that no man or group of men can be safely entrusted with unlimited power. They framed this Constitution with its provisions for change by amendment in order to secure the fundamentals of government against the dangers of temporary popular passion or the personal predilections of public officeholders.

We regard the decision of the Supreme Court in the school cases as a clear abuse of judicial power. It climaxes a trend in the Federal Judiciary undertaking to legislate, in derogation of the authority of Congress, and to encroach upon the reserved rights of the States and the people.

The original Constitution does not mention education. Neither does the 14th amendment nor any other amendment. The debates preceding the submission of the 14th amendment clearly show that there was no intent that it should affect the system of education maintained by the States.

The very Congress which proposed the amendment subsequently provided for segregated schools in the District of Columbia.

When the amendment was adopted in 1868, there were 37 States of the Union. Every one of the 26 States that had any substantial racial differences among its people, either approved the operation of segregated schools already in existence or subsequently established such schools by action of the same law-making body which considered the 14th amendment.

As admitted by the Supreme Court in the public school case (*Brown v. Board of Education*), the doctrine of separate but equal schools "apparently originated in *Roberts v. City of Boston* (1849), upholding school segregation against attack as being violative of a State constitutional guarantee of equality." This constitutional doctrine began in the North, not in the South, and it was followed not only in Massachusetts, but in Connecticut, New York, Illinois, Indiana, Michigan, Minnesota, New Jersey, Ohio, Pennsylvania and other northern States until they, exercising their rights as States through the constitutional processes of local self-government, changed their school systems.

In the case of *Plessy v. Ferguson* in 1896 the Supreme Court expressly declared that under the 14th amendment no person was denied any of his rights if the States provided separate but equal public facilities. This decision has been followed in many other cases. It is notable that the Supreme Court, speaking through Chief Justice Taft, a former President of the United States, unanimously declared in 1927 in *Lum v. Rice* that the "separate but equal" principle is "within the discretion of the State in regulating its public schools and does not conflict with the 14th amendment."

This interpretation, restated time and again, became a part of the life of the people of many of the States and confirmed their habits, customs, traditions, and way of life. It is founded on elemental humanity and common sense, for parents should not be deprived by Government of the right to direct the lives and education of their own children.

Though there has been no constitutional amendment or act of Congress changing this established legal principle almost a century old, the Supreme Court of the United States, with no legal basis for such action, undertook to exercise their naked judicial power and substituted their personal political and social ideas for the established law of the land.

This unwarranted exercise of power by the Court, contrary to the Constitution, is creating chaos and confusion in the States principally affected. It is destroying the amicable relations between the white and Negro races that have been created through 90 years of patient effort by the good people of both races. It has planted hatred and suspicion where there has been heretofore friendship and understanding.

Without regard to the consent of the governed, outside agitators are threatening immediate and revolutionary changes in our public-school systems. If done, this is certain to destroy the system of public education in some of the States.

With the gravest concern for the explosive and dangerous condition created by this decision and inflamed by outside meddlers:

We reaffirm our reliance on the Constitution as the fundamental law of the land.

We decry the Supreme Court's encroachments on rights reserved to the States and to the people, contrary to established law, and to the Constitution.

We commend the motives of those States which have declared the intention to resist forced integration by any lawful means.

We appeal to the States and people who are not directly affected by those decisions to consider the constitutional principles involved against the time when they too, on issues vital to them, may be the victims of judicial encroachment.

Even though we constitute a minority in the present Congress, we have full faith that a majority of the American people believe in the dual system of government which has enabled us to achieve our greatness and will in time demand that the reserved rights of the States and of the people be made secure against judicial usurpation.

We pledge ourselves to use all lawful means to bring about a reversal of this decision which is contrary to the Constitution and to prevent the use of force in its implementation.

In this trying period, as we all seek to right this wrong, we appeal to our people not to be provoked by the agitators and troublemakers invading our States and to scrupulously refrain from disorder and lawless acts.

Nixon Was *the One: Edgar Daniel Nixon, the MIA and the Montgomery Bus Boycott*

John White is author of Black Leadership in America: From Booker T. Washington to Jesse Jackson *and* Billie Holiday: Her Life and Times. *He is a reader in American history at the University of Hull.*

In 1948, the distinguished French socialist Daniel Guerin travelled across the United States, and in his later published account of American race relations commented on an encounter in Montgomery, Alabama, with

> a vigorous colored union militant who was the leading spirit in his city both of the local union of Sleeping Car Porters and the local branch of the NAACP. What a difference from other branches of the Association, which are controlled by dentists, pastors and undertakers. [This man] has both feet on the ground. He is linked to the masses, he speaks their language. He has organized the work of race defence with the precision and method of a trade unionist. Men like E. D. Nixon . . . incarnate the alliance which has at last been consummated between the race and labor.

Guerin's 'colored union militant' himself once remarked, 'The labor movement gave black people the opportunity to do things that the civil rights movement gave [them] the right to do.'

Edgar Daniel Nixon had been a notable figure in Montgomery twenty years before the creation of the Montgomery Improvement Association (MIA) and the subsequent bus boycott. By 1955 his long-standing connections with organized labour, friendships with such prominent liberal white Montgomerians as Joe Azbell, Aubrey Williams, Clifford and Virginia Durr, and in the African-American community with Mrs Rosa Parks, Jo Ann Gibson Robinson, and the lawyer, Fred Gray, had placed Nixon in a unique and commanding position. Not least, it was E. D. Nixon who early recognized the charismatic qualities of a recently-arrived young African-American preacher who was to achieve national and international fame when he assumed (with Nixon's endorsement) leadership of the MIA. Unhappily, Nixon, well before his death in 1987, believed (with some justification) that his own contributions to the boycott, the MIA and racial progress in Montgomery had been eclipsed in both popular and scholarly accounts by Martin Luther King's towering reputation. In June, 1957, Nixon resigned as Treasurer of the MIA, informing Dr King 'Since I have only been treasurer in name and not in reality, it will not be hard to find someone to do what I have been doing, even a schoolboy.' Although Nixon's belief that the MIA was mis-handling its funds was the occasion of his resignation, his accompanying statement—'I resent being treated as a newcomer to the MIA. It is my dream, hope and hard work since 1932 and I do not expect to be treated as a child'—suggests divisions within the MIA and Montgomery's black community which also deserve consideration.

E. D. Nixon was born in Montgomery on 12 July 1899, the fifth of eight children. His father was a tenant farmer and an untrained Primitive Baptist preacher. Nixon's mother, a maid and cook, died when he was eight and he was brought up by his paternal aunt, Winnie Bates, a laundress. By his own accounts, Nixon had little more than a third-grade education, and left home in 1911. In 1923, after working briefly in a meat-packing plant, a store in Birmingham, and on a streetcar line, Nixon was a baggage-room porter in Montgomery, and in 1925 became a Pullman porter, taking regular runs from Montgomery to Florida. Although they were regarded as among the elite of the African-American working class, Nixon deeply resented the treatment of Pullman porters—by white passengers and the Pullman Company. But his experiences on the railroad literally (and metaphysically) widened Nixon's horizons. As he declared on many occasions: 'I was over 20 years old before I knew the whole world wasn't like Montgomery'. Already convinced of the necessity of a union for porters, Nixon's **Road to Damascus** came in 1929 when he heard A. Philip Randolph speak in St Louis and immediately joined the Brotherhood of Sleeping Car Porters. In 1937, twelve years after the first meeting of the BSCP in New York, the Pullman Company recognized the union and signed a labour contract that improved the working conditions of black porters.

This recognition undoubtedly increased Nixon's standing and influence in Montgomery's African-American community—where he had already organized the Montgomery Welfare League to assist blacks who needed relief during the Depression—and in 1938 he was elected as president of the new union's Montgomery local, an office he held for 25 years. During the 1930s, Nixon was involved with Myles Horton's Highlander Folk School in Tennessee in an attempt to secure union organization of cucumber pickers in Alabama. The young labour militant had also been attracted to the NAACP—which formed a Montgomery chapter in 1918—because of its record in securing black rights through legislation, litigation and lobbying. Defeated in his bid for branch president in 1944, he was elected in 1945, re-elected the following year, and served as president from 1946 to 1950, when he was replaced by Robert L. Mathews—the man he had defeated in 1945. In 1947 Nixon became president of the Alabama Conference of NAACP chapters, after defeating the incumbent, Emory O. Jackson, a Birmingham newspaper editor. But with national and local NAACP officials hostile to Nixon's lack of formal education and his allegedly dictatorial tendencies, he was not reelected to the state post in 1949.

A summary of Nixon's other activities in the 1940s and 1950s would include his involvement in Randolph's March on Washington Movement, the securing of a water fountain and toilet facilities for blacks (provided by Sears Roebuck) in Montgomery's train station, and the construction during World War II of a United Services Organizations Club for black military personnel stationed near Montgomery. This last achievement was gained with the help of Eleanor Roosevelt. Earlier, when the First Lady had been a passenger on Nixon's train, he had requested (and received) an audience, which marked the beginning of their life-long friendship.

In 1940, Nixon organized the Montgomery Voter's League—to register black voters—and on 13 June 1944, led 750 African-Americans to the board of registrars, demanding to be allowed to qualify to vote. Less than 50 blacks were registered.

Nixon himself had paid the $36.00 poll tax in Montgomery and tried to register to vote for ten years—and then had to file one lawsuit and threaten another—before being registered in 1945. From May to October, 1944, Nixon took leave from his porter's job and travelled through Alabama to organize black voters—the number of black voters in the state increased from 25 000 in 1940 to 600 000 by 1948. In 1948 Nixon described himself as being 'very busy in this fight for the right to vote for Negroes', and stated, 'I wish I could sell the people on this one idea of full citizenship . . . but these crackers here have did [*sic*] a good job of keeping the Negro afraid and also keeping him unlearned.'

As president of the Montgomery NAACP, Nixon handled many cases involving police brutality, the rape of black women, murder and lynchings. In one instance, he managed to persuade Alabama Governor Chauncey Sparks to commute the death sentences of three African-American men found guilty of raping a white woman to terms of life imprisonment. A man of undoubted personal courage, Nixon was openly contemptuous of southern white liberals who confined their ostensible concern for African-Americans to armchair discussion. When Amanda Baker, a Negro schoolgirl was raped and murdered near Montgomery, Nixon went to see Governor Sparks, and later recounted:

> I was walking to the Capitol [and] passed a church where the Southern Conference for Human Welfare was having a meeting, talking about the terrible things going on. I went in . . . and was sitting in the back, when the chairman, [an] elderly white woman, seen me and said, 'I see we got a new face here this morning, and I'm going to let the gentleman come up and identify himself.' So I walked up and said, 'Good morning—I'm E. D. Nixon, president of the NAACP, and I'm on my way up to Governor Sparks to ask for a reward for the arrest and conviction of the guilty party who committed the crime against Amanda Baker, and all I want to ask is if there is one man or woman here, white or black, that has the courage to go with me, because if you do, I'd be glad to have you.' I stood there a few minutes, and not a word did I get out of them. Finally, I said, 'Madam chairman, I'm sorry I've taken up your time, and I see now that nobody here really believes in what you are talking about'.

In March 1947, the Montgomery chapter celebrated the twenty-fifth anniversary of the founding of the NAACP with a rally at Holt Street Baptist Church. The programme carried a short entry on Nixon, its president, in which he was described as 'well versed on the problems confronting Negroes in Montgomery', and as having 'spent long hours working toward the time when the two races will have a better understanding as regards each other. He is respected by all who know him and many members of our race rely upon his judgement'. In 1952, Nixon won election to the presidency of the Montgomery chapter of the Progressive Democratic Association, the organization of Alabama's African-American Democrats. During the 1950s, Nixon pressured the city and county commissioners into hiring black policemen, creating a food stamp programme for poor blacks and whites, and after the 1954 *Brown* decision, attempted (unsuccessfully) to integrate the William Harrison High School in Montgomery. The minutes of a special Executive Committee meeting of the Montgomery chapter of the NAACP for 17 May 1955, celebrating the first anniversary of the Supreme Court's *Brown* decision recorded that: 'Mr E. D. Nixon said that we had not done very much about implementing the May 17 Supreme Court decision . . . The NAACP and other organizations should join in letting it be known in Washington that segregation in public schools must be abolished.'

When Davis Lee, African-American publisher of the Newark, New Jersey *Telegraph*, who opposed school desegregation—on the grounds that it would result in the loss of many Negro teaching posts—was scheduled to speak in Montgomery in July 1953, Nixon as leader of the Montgomery Progressive Democrats and the BSCP, joined the Women's Political Council, Bethel Baptist Church and Association of Women's Clubs in placing 'An Open Letter to the People of Montgomery' in the *Advertizer*, protesting the visit. As a consequence of the 'Open Letter' and pickets outside the City Auditorium when Lee appeared, he addressed a sparse gathering. An estimated 75 spectators, of whom only 25 were Negroes, attended.

In May 1954, Nixon filed as candidate in the Montgomery Democratic primary for membership of the county Democratic Executive Committee, the first black to seek public office in the state since Reconstruction, and lost by only 97 votes (with some white support). He was also chosen by Montgomery's blacks as the *Alabama Journal's* 'Man of the Year'—the prize included a free haircut and shoe shine, dry cleaning vouchers, theatre tickets, two turkey dinners, a shirt and tie, a large family photograph, presentation during the half-time period at the Tuskegee State game, and a certificate from the management of the *Journal*. The accompanying profile stated that Nixon was 'very unassuming, yet militant . . . aggressive, yet not a radical'.

Nixon again made headlines in the local press when in 1955 he tried to purchase a ticket to the Democratic party Jefferson-Jackson Day dinner in Birmingham, Alabama. Refused admission on the grounds of race, Nixon (now characterized by the *Montgomery Advertiser* as 'the NAACP Mau Mau chief') protested against his exclusion and in response, the principal scheduled speaker, Governor G. Mennen Williams of Michigan, cancelled his appearance. (Always sensitive to policies of racial exclusion/segregation, Nixon in the 1950s went three years without a telephone in Montgomery rather than accept one on a four-party 'all colored' line).

Three weeks before Rosa Parks's historic refusal to give up her seat to a white passenger, New York Congressman Adam Clayton Powell, at Nixon's request, visited Alabama State College in Montgomery to speak to the city's chapter of the Progressive Democratic Association. The flamboyant Powell, who stayed overnight with Nixon in Montgomery, caused a double sensation. Governor James E. Folsom sent the state limousine to Montgomery airport to meet Powell and to convey him to the governor's mansion for a drink—a gesture which severely tarnished Folsom's political image in the state. In private, Folsom declared: 'Adam Clayton Powell is one son of a bitch I wish I'd never seen'. In his address to the Progressive Democrats, Powell asserted that the economic pressures of the racist White Citizens' Council 'can be counter met with our own [black] economic pressure'. Given that Powell had organized a bus boycott by African-Americans in New York City in 1941 and that blacks in nearby Selma had recently staged a boycott of white-owned businesses following the firing of black petitioners seeking school integration, the African-American leadership in Montgomery—and almost certainly E. D. Nixon—doubtless drew the appropriate conclusions.

The WPC in Montgomery, organized in 1949 to urge African-American women to register to vote, had lodged several complaints with the City Commission about the mistreatment and humiliation of black female passengers on the city's busline, but had achieved little amelioration of conditions. Several incidents (all involving African-American women) had aroused the black community—the most notable being the arrest on 2 March 1955 of a teenager, Claudette Colvin, who had refused to vacate her seat when ordered to do so by the bus driver, Robert W. Cleere. After Colvin pleaded not guilty to violating Alabama's segregation law (and to assault and disorderly conduct), E. D. Nixon (who initially consulted Clifford Durr and Fred Gray on using the Colvin incident as a test case) decided—to the anger of some members of the WPC—that Colvin, an unmarried pregnant teenager, was hardly the ideal choice for lengthy, expensive and uncertain litigation.

The arrest of Rosa Parks, a known activist and a respectable member of the black community, on 1 December 1955, however, provided Nixon—and Jo Ann Robinson, the most active member of the WPC—with an ideal opportunity to mount a protest against continuing discrimination on the city's buses. Rosa Parks, who became chapter secretary of the NAACP in 1943 and was later an adviser to its youth auxiliary, recalled that when she first met E. D. Nixon (in 1943), he had urged her to become a registered voter: 'Mr Nixon explained to me very fully the qualifications of being a voter, and the necessity of getting registered.'

After Nixon lost the presidency of the NAACP, Mrs Parks worked for him at his union office, and it was Nixon who introduced her to Mrs Virginia Durr. It was Mrs Durr (for whom she worked on a part-time basis as a seamstress) who arranged for Rosa Parks to attend Highlander Folk School in the summer of 1955. On her return to Montgomery, and to the great satisfaction of Nixon, Mrs Parks presented a report to the NAACP on her attendance at a workshop on desegregation.

It was also E. D. Nixon (with Clifford and Virginia Durr in attendance) who paid Rosa Parks's bail bond, and gained her permission to use her arrest as a test case of the segregation laws. Again it was Nixon (and the WPC) who decided that the protest would take the form of a one-day boycott by Montgomery's blacks of the Montgomery City Lines. As he liked to relate, on the day following Mrs Parks's arrest, Nixon began to call the city's black civic leaders and ministers (beginning with Ralph Abernathy) informing them of the decision, and soliciting their support. According to Nixon, when he called Dr King, he was told, 'Brother Nixon, let me think about it a while and call me back.' When Nixon called again, King said that he would support the protest and elicited from Nixon the riposte, 'I'm glad you agreed because I have already set the meeting up to meet at your church.'

Because of his railroad commitments, Nixon could not be present at the Dexter Avenue Baptist Church meeting, but before leaving town for his Chicago run, called *Montgomery Advertizer* reporter Joe Azbell and alerted him to the proposed boycott and the pamphlets printed and about to be circulated by Jo Ann Robinson and the WPC, advising blacks: 'Please stay off all buses [on] Monday.' As Nixon anticipated, the *Advertizer*, in its Sunday edition, carried the headline 'Negro Groups Ready Boycott of City Lines'. Following the successful one-day boycott, a meeting was held at Mt. Zion AME Baptist Church at which it was decided that a permanent organization, the MIA headed by Dr King, would continue and coordinate the protest already launched by the actions of the WPC. The initial demands of the MIA—reflecting earlier proposals by Nixon's Progressive Democratic Association—were for more courtesy from bus drivers, the hiring of black drivers on predominantly black routes, and the seating of blacks towards the front and of whites from the front towards the back (without a section being assigned for each race). The decision was to be put to a mass meeting at Holt Street Baptist Church, later that

261

3.3 Nixon Was
*the One: Edgar
Daniel Nixon,
the MIA and the
Montgomery Bus
Boycott*

day. Sensing that some black ministers favoured a return to the buses, while others, aware of the press photographers present, were reluctant to speak and favoured mimeographing and distributing the MIA's recommendations secretly at the planned meeting, Nixon angrily upbraided them and later recalled:

> I got up and said 'Let me tell you gentlemen one thing. You ministers have lived off of these washwomen for the last 100 years and never done anything for them. Now you have a chance to pay them back for some of the things they've done for you. If this program isn't accepted and brought out into the open tonight (and there will be over 1000 people at that church), I'll take the microphone and tell the people that the reason we don't have a program is because you are all too cowardly to stand on your feet and be counted . . . We ought to be men enough to stand on our feet and be counted or admit to ourselves that we are a bunch of scared boys'.

This outburst—whether calculated or spontaneous—had the desired effect. As Martin Luther King observed: 'With this forthright statement the air was cleared. Nobody would again suggest that we try to conceal our identity or avoid the issue head on. Nixon's courageous affirmation had given new heart to those who were about to be crippled by fear.'

Again, it would seem that although Nixon informed the local chapter of the NAACP of the decision to extend the boycott, he decided that a new organization should lead the protest, since

> the man who was president of the NAACP at that time said 'Bro Nixon, I'll have to wait until I talk to New York to find out what they think about it.' I said, man we ain't got time for that. He believed in doing everything by the book. And the book stated that you were suppose[d] to notify New York before you take a step like that.

Nixon can also claim some credit for the MIA's decision, in February 1956, to file a civil case in federal court testing the legality of Alabama's segregation ordinance, rather than awaiting the outcome of its appeal against Mrs. Parks's conviction. Attorney Fred Gray (who cites Nixon as being instrumental in finding five black lawyers who sponsored his original application to law school) accordingly filed suit on behalf of five black women—Aurelia S. Browder (40), Susie McDonald (77), Jeanetta Reese (64), Claudette Colvin (16), and Mary Louise Smith (19)—all of whom had experienced discrimination on municipal transportation during the preceding year. In *Browder v. Gayle,* a Federal district court ruled that bus segregation violated the Fourteenth Amendment, and the Supreme Court upheld the ruling in November 1956, bringing the Montgomery boycott to its ultimate and 'legal' conclusion. Although Dr King later asserted that the decision to file suit in federal court was a response to the intransigence of the Montgomery City Commission and the bombing of his own and Nixon's homes, Nixon relates that in January 1956, and after conferring with Clifford Durr, he proposed such a measure to King and Abernathy. He reminded them of the Viola White episode, a similar case to Rosa Parks's in the mid-1940s, and pointed out that ten years later, it was still pending in the courts. In Nixon's retelling:

I came in from my run on the second Sunday in January 1956 and I called
Reverend King and Reverend Abernathy, and I told them, I got news for you
boys. I said I can call you 'boys' because I got a son that's older than either of
you. I said, you all think we goin' to the Supreme Court in Mrs Parks's case.
The city fathers knows we feels that the only outlet we got is that case, and
they goin' to freeze us out. I told them what we would have to do.

Nixon's repeated accounts of his role in the events immediately preceding and
following Rosa Parks's arrest and the formation of the MIA are in some respects
contradictory, and have been variously interpreted. His activities *during* the 381-day
boycott, as Treasurer and fund-raiser for the MIA—which have never received adequate scholarly recognition—were undoubtedly crucial to its success.

The first collection for MIA funds was taken at Holt Street Baptist Church
and approximately $500 was raised. Nixon, as Treasurer, left the meeting with the
money, and pointedly asked the local police in attendance to escort him home for
protection. They complied and drove him in a patrol car, in what was to be the
only gesture of cooperation between the MIA and the Montgomery Police Department. Nixon also proposed that the MIA should use its capital surplus, together
with a loan from the federal government, to establish a Negro bank, which would
also contain office space for African-American professional men. Such an enterprise,
Nixon argued, would provide much-needed capital for the development of the
Negro section of the city, but his suggestion was never taken up.

From the inception of the boycott, Nixon was acutely aware that the MIA
needed substantial funds to mount its operations. On one occasion, when he
phoned a labour leader in Los Angeles and explained the MIA's financial needs,
'the man replied that he had no authority as a union president to commit his group
for any sum of $100.00 or over, without getting authorization from the member-
ship. He did promise, though, to send along a check for   every week for ten
weeks'.

In March, 1956, Nixon was the guest speaker at a BSCP-sponsored Meeting
of the National Committee for Rural Schools, in New York City. His topic was the
Montgomery Bus Boycott, and he began his address by announcing:

I am from the heart of Dixie, but sometimes I wonder whether Dixie has a
heart . . . I would like to say that . . . Rosa Parks's case was not the sole foundation for this mass protest . . . the papers named it a boycott. But over a period
of years, we have had different things happen on the buses and in the streets
[and] police brutality . . . we have called on the city's commissioners and the
bus company with reference to these situations . . . but we found that we were
not able to get anywhere.

Nixon then recounted his role in calling Montgomery ministers after Rosa Parks's
arrest, and the *Montgomery Advertiser*'s notice of the proposed boycott. 'They gave
us a two-page column down the front page . . . we could not have bought this as
an advertizement for $500.00. Aside from giving us two pages in the paper, they
gave us radio and television, and thousands of people who would have never known
about what we was trying to do was able to read about it in the paper and hear
about it on radio and television.'

Nixon also stated the 'many objectives' of the MIA as of March 1956. 'Our
prime interest right now is to adjust the seating arrangements on the bus, and

we're trying to do that within the existing law. We knew that we'd eventually have to go to court and we is hoping to renew the Rosa Parks case. But ... we have filed a case [*Browder* v. *Gayle*] in federal court in the name of five people who was a party to that.' Nixon then explained the organisation and operation of the MIA's transportation committee and its car pool, with 47 pick-up stations and 300 cars—which now provided 'a better job ... than the Montgomery bus line has done in 20 years'. After describing to a northern audience the etiquette of Jim Crow on southern buses, and his own activities in providing car transportation, Nixon claimed, 'I think I'm more involved in this thing than most peoples, and ... I have contributed 25 years of my life to this thing, and I believe if I'd died two, three years ago, without living to see this thing, I'd say to the Lord, "Jesus, you've already discriminated against me once." I wouldn't have missed it for nothing'.

He also stressed that if and when the MIA achieved its immediate objective, it would remain in existence to fight police brutality and other forms of racial discrimination. He ended by retelling a favourite joke about a small boy going down the street with a basket, selling puppies. Asked their price by a lady, the boy replied '25 cents'. The lady was tempted, but decided not to buy a puppy. The next day, she saw the boy again, and asked him if he had any more puppies. The boy said he had, and the lady was about to ask him for one when he said that a puppy cost 50 cents. Lady: 'Why are they 50 cents today and only a quarter yesterday?' Boy: 'Their eyes are open.' Nixon: 'I'd like to leave this with you people here tonight—that the Negroes' eyes are open in Montgomery and they aren't being sold for 25 cents anymore.'

Nixon also addressed the National Committee on the following day when he was introduced by A. Philip Randolph as 'the foundation of this spirit being expressed in this protest against the Jim Crow bus'. On Nixon's behalf, Randolph appealed to delegates to support the boycott. 'Brother Nixon tells me that it costs $3,500 a week to keep the automobile pool rolling that carries the people to and fro, from work, from day to day ... the porters in Chicago sent him a hundred dollars. The porters in Jacksonville sent him $25, and I believe that the porters here have the same sort of devotion that they have all over the country.' Nixon began his second address by bringing greetings to the delegates from Montgomery, Alabama, 'The cradle of the Confederacy that has stood still for a long, long time, prior to December 1st, but is now being rocked by 50 000 Negroes in Montgomery.'

After paying a warm tribute to his hero and mentor, Randolph, Nixon again recounted the events surrounding Rosa Parks's arrest, and stressed the importance of the mass meetings in Montgomery in maintaining the impetus of the boycott and the donations which the MIA was receiving from across the country. In an aside, he observed that the Montgomery city fathers that 'tried to say that Reverend King came from up North, so we had to let them know if Atlanta, Georgia, was "up North," then we were guilty'.

He ended on both a rhetorical and an entrepreneurial note. 'The Negroes in Montgomery is tired of being kicked around ... of being Jim-Crowed on the Montgomery City Line or any other form of transportation ... They have made up their mind that they're going to fight it until the court says they don't have to do it.' But the need was for funds—to pay for court costs, oil and gasoline and all the expenses incurred by the car pool. 'I still believe in prayer,' Nixon concluded, 'had I not believed in it, I wouldn't have come here. So one thing, you can pray for us, and the next thing ... you can put your hand in your pocket and make a contribution. Whether it's large or small, the MIA will be eternally grateful.'

In April 1956, a press release by the International Union of United Automobile, Aircraft and Agricultural Implement Workers of America announced that 'an attentive, and at times demonstrative, audience of more than 1500 UAW members' had attended a Civil Rights Rally, sponsored by UAW Region 1 (Detroit's East Side) to hear E. D. Nixon, treasurer of the MIA 'tell how his home was bombed by terrorists after he had led a "No Ride" protest of Negroes against racial segregation and inhuman treatment on the Montgomery buses'. Nixon had informed the audience: 'They couldn't find the man who bombed my house, so, they arrested me.' Among those present at the Detroit rally were UAW Secretary Treasurer Emil Mazey and Vice-Presidents Norman Matthews and Pat Greenhouse. Acting Chairman George Merrelli opened the rally with a review of current civil rights injustices and the need for organized labour to support the Montgomery struggle both morally and financially. Mazey presented Nixon with a cheque for $500 from the International UAW, and the financial secretary of Chrysler Local 7 'presented a check for $50 from his Local plus a membership collection of $483.71'. The press release also noted that: 'Local 212 President Pat Caruso gave Nixon a check for $500 from the Local and a cash donation of $110 from third shift members.' Local 208 reported that it had raised $379 in cash 'and were pledging an additional $100 per month for the duration of the bus stoppage'. Local 410 indicated that it was pledging $100 a month, while a pledge of $500 was received from Local 351. In addition, 'a total of $326.25 was donated by those attending the rally, as they left the hall'.

Nixon, the release observed, had 'roused the audience to a great shout when he asserted that "I don't believe the people of Montgomery will ever accept Jim Crow travel again" '. After expressing his gratitude to the ministers for the 'job they have done in Montgomery', Nixon—'the fighting Negro leader'—had declared: 'We've got to win not only for the people of Montgomery but for the people everywhere who believe in freedom and justice.'

The following month, Nixon made a great impression when he appeared at a NAACP/BSCP/AFL–CIO civil rights rally in Madison Square Garden, together with Eleanor Roosevelt, A. Philip Randolph, Tallulah Bankhead, Martin Luther King and Adam Clayton Powell Jr. As the last scheduled speaker, Nixon brought the audience of 16 000 people to its feet when he stood up and announced:

> I'm E. D. Nixon from Montgomery, Alabama, a city that is known as the Cradle of the Confederacy and the city that stood still for more than ninety-three years until Rosa Parks was arrested and thrown in jail like a common criminal, and 50,000 Negroes rose up and caught hold of the cradle and began to rock it until the Jim Crow rocker began to reel and the segregated slats began to fall. I'm from that city.

Roy Wilkins remembered that 'People began to shout and yell and thump one another on the back, and the Garden resonated with enough joy and hope to keep all of us going for months afterward.'

From the outset of the bus boycott, Nixon's activities were extensively covered in the BSCP newspaper, *The Black Worker.* In its December 1955 issue, the paper announced: 'Bro. Nixon Steps Up the Fight For Civil Rights', and recounted how following Rosa Parks's arrest, Nixon, together with Fred Gray had posted $100 bond to have her released from custody. The resulting bus boycott was now almost

265

3.3 *Nixon* Was
the One: Edgar
Daniel Nixon,
the MIA and the
Montgomery Bus
Boycott

100 per cent successful and 'our hats are doffed to you once again, Brother Nixon'. Three months later, A. Philip Randolph prefaced a *Black Worker* profile of Nixon with the comment that he was a leading member of the BSCP and 'particularly, and unquestionably . . . a leader of the citizens of Montgomery'. In February 1956 the paper carried the headline 'Nixon Helps Lead Bus Boycott' and in the accompanying article observed that:

> This notable exhibition of courage, determination, unity and intelligence by the boycott of jim crow buses in Montgomery ought to serve as a source of inspiration and hope to the Negroes not only in Dixie, but throughout the country . . . We salute the Rev. L. M. [*sic*] King, Jr., and E. D. Nixon, president of the Montgomery Division of the Brotherhood of Sleeping Car Porters, whose homes were bombed, upon their integrity, courage and devotion in this great and significant struggle for human dignity for black citizens.

A separate feature carried a full account of the bombing of Nixon's home in Montgomery, and noted that it followed the earlier bombing of 'the home of a Negro minister, Rev. L. M. [sic] King, Jr., who like Nixon is also a leader in the boycott of the Montgomery buses'. But the paper's focus was definitely on Nixon who, readers were reminded, 'has for more than a score of years given an enlightened and aggressive type of leadership in Montgomery', and, 'Brother Nixon seems not disturbed or deterred by the bombing but on the contrary, with his wife, he is more determined to play his part with other Negroes in Montgomery in all efforts to eliminate racial inequities and other undemocratic practices.'

Nixon was reported as having said that black Montgomerians 'are madder than ever' and that 'whoever is responsible for these bombings isn't going to end the boycott that way. We are all in this to the end'. The *Black Worker* concluded that Nixon was a credit to the BSCP, and deserving of its support. 'Brother Nixon is one of the Brotherhood's most aggressive, courageous and forward looking leaders. A man of great ability, forthrightness and integrity, he is well prepared to lend leadership in this historic period when the walls of racial segregation are beginning to crumble.'

Nixon's response to the bombing (and its aftermath) was also revealed in a personal 'note' to A. P. Randolph:

> Well bom [*sic*] missed my house about 12 ft. No police protection here as the whole city force mayor and all are members of the white Citizens Council. They have made every effort to intimidate me but I dont scare easy. I get about 50 threatening [*sic*] calls every 24 hours, (smile) but they wont come out in the open, a bunch of cowards. I was not home but they tell me in 20 minutes after the bom went off there was 2,000 people and shortly after there was 5,000 including most of the porters.

In reply, Randolph applauded 'the reaction which resulted in thousands of your admirers gathering around the home to give you protection. This shows that the people believe in your sound and courageous leadership.'

Aubrey Williams, publisher of the *Southern Farmer,* and himself a supporter of the Montgomery boycott, wrote to Randolph in May, 1956—while the boycott was still in progress—concerning Nixon 'your great admirer and I am proud to say, I think my good friend'. Nixon, Williams asserted 'is and has been the real leader of the bus protest', and had devoted his time to it 'in an amount which must have been very hard on his earnings'. Reporting as 'one on the scene who can and does testify to his indispensibility,' Williams believed that: 'this magnificent show of strength, character and power would never have happened but for his leadership. It is the fruit of a lifetime of courage and single-purposed pursuit of an ideal.' Responding to this encomium, Randolph expressed himself 'in complete accord with your thinking that this great spirit of Negroes in Montgomery in the boycott of the jim-crow buses is the outgrowth and expression of a long, courageous and unselfish struggle on the part of Brother Nixon for freedom and manhood rights for Negroes in Montgomery'. And, Randolph informed Williams: 'Knowing of his [Nixon's] dedication to this cause of civil rights, I have sought to involve him in various meetings and conferences here in the North, in order that his position in the struggle may be better known.'

Two months later, Randolph wrote to Nixon 'to congratulate you and the Montgomery Improvement Association upon the great fight being made to abolish jim crow transportation on buses in Montgomery'.

In April 1956 the Chicago Division of the BSCP hosted 'A Salute to A. Philip Randolph' in the Grand Ballroom at the Midland Hotel. E. D. Nixon was the key-note speaker before the 600 guests and as the *Black Worker* duly reported, 'The address presented by Brother E. D. Nixon gave the people present a ringside view of the important undertaking being carried on successfully by the Negroes in Alabama. Brother Nixon detailed the origin and purpose of the Montgomery Improvement Association, of which he is treasurer and which is the group behind the bus boycott in Montgomery. Brother Nixon's address was most inspiring.'

Nixon's contributions to the bus boycott were also reported in *The Militant,* the newspaper of the Workers Party of America. In 1956, reporter William Bundy characterized Nixon as 'an old time civil rights and union fighter in Montgomery', and cited an anonymous Montgomery source as saying: ' . . . if it hadn't been for E. D. Nixon this movement wouldn't be where it is today'. The article also quoted Nixon to good effect: 'Some of us tried to get something done about the buses long before this protest. We tried to talk to the city officials, but they wouldn't even listen. When Mrs Parks got arrested that was the last straw.' Nixon also informed Bundy that: 'We could have settled this thing long ago if the white leaders had just sat down and talked to us, but after that first day it was too late. We had to go on. Our people just insisted. They voted to go on with the protest until we got something definite, and we organized the association [MIA] right there on the spot.'

The Militant also reviewed Daniel Guerin's *Negroes on the March,* with its mention of Nixon, and noted that his 'current role as one of the most prominent boycott organizers and treasurer of the Montgomery Improvement Association bears out the author's foresight of seven years before'. In a later article on 'The Civil Rights Fight and the White Worker', Nixon was described as a 'symbolic figure' who 'epitomized the necessity of an alliance between the labor movement and the Negro freedom fighters'.

On the occasion of the tenth anniversary of the Montgomery bus boycott, Nixon was guest of honour at a dinner sponsored by the socialist Militant Labor Forum in New York City. Noting that Nixon had not been invited to the anniversary celebrations in Montgomery, Farrell Dobbs, National Secretary of the Socialist Workers Party, observed to the assembled guests that: 'We of the Militant Labor Forum felt that he should be included, that he before all others should be recognized as the pioneer, the founding father, the initiator, the spark plug and principal man of the hour in the battle.' In his address, Nixon—described in the *Militant's* report of the proceedings 'an authentic spokesman who emerges from the ranks of a working class movement'—observed that the MIA 'was not started just because someone came to town or someone felt it was the proper thing to do at this time. It was started because there had been a struggle of the people for long years'. In a lightly-veiled reference to his disagreements with the middle-class leadership of the MIA, Nixon had asserted that:

267

3.3 *Nixon* Was
the One: Edgar
Daniel Nixon,
the MIA and the
Montgomery Bus
Boycott

> in every organization there are people who get carried away by big words. There are sometimes people who get carried away by how the words are said. But . . . there are two things that are important in dealing with organizations. One of them is not how much you say but how much you do. The other thing is not just to say things but to tell the truth about the things you deal with. And that's what I have tried to contribute to the Montgomery Improvement Association and to any other organization I have dealt with.

On the twentieth anniversary of the boycott, in a letter to Mrs Johnny Carr, president of the MIA, Nixon rejected an overture from that organization 'after twenty years' and asserted:

> . . . it was I that bonded Mrs Parks out of jail, it was I who called the people together to organize the MIA, it was I who wrote the 3 recommendations, it was I who selected Rev. King to be the spokesman, and during the early part of the MIA, it was I who made contact with organized labor, and politicians across the country, and during this period that I served as Treasurer of the MIA, and I cut checks for $415,000.00 . . . I personally raised $97,000.00 myself, and I had $68,000.00 that came to my house in letters from across the country, and I begged 5 automobiles, and no one brought back an automobile except me, and when they arrested the 90 odd of us, and Fred Gray was out of town, everybody was all excited and didn't know what to do . . . and I personally called Attorney Thurgood Marshall, who advised us the next step to take. In view of these things, and other contributions that I made to help serve the community through the MIA, and to find for 20 years that I have been completely left out of the picture of the MIA . . . I feel as a Christian and a dedicated worker who are [*sic*] really sincere, I'm forced to decline your invitation.

E. D. Nixon had always claimed that he was a 'founding father' of the MIA, and a major contributor to the Montgomery bus boycott. In certain crucial respects this was true: Nixon was the one who (with Martin Luther King) brought a grassroots protest to national attention. As the late Alex Haley observed, Nixon, through his affiliation with organized labour and left-wing protest groups, helped to nationalize the Montgomery movement, while these same connections 'gave him the foresight and the organizational skills to impress and mobilize Montgomery's black community'. That he was not impressed by and did not appeal to the college-educated, middle-class and largely clerical leadership of the MIA is revealed in Mrs Johnny Carr's comment: 'Mr. Nixon was a hardworking man, a fine leader and everything, but he [didn't] have that thing that could weld people together in a movement like ours . . . I have heard Mr. Nixon say that "When I walk into an

MIA meeting, don't nobody clap or say anything, but when Dr. King walks in, everybody stands up and claps." Now he [Nixon] had been working down through the years and all, but it was just one of those things.'

Although he was conspicuously absent from the civil rights protests which followed after the Montgomery boycott, Nixon continued to work for the city's working-class community. Ironically, in his last years E. D. Nixon began to receive belated recognition—including celebratory newspaper articles by Joe Azbell and an honorary doctorate from Alabama State University—by the city's white and black establishments as 'A Forgotten Hero'.

In 1986, Nixon's home on Clinton Street, Montgomery, was registered as 'a significant landmark' by the Alabama Historical Commission, with the endorsement of Governor George Wallace. A historical marker in front of the now dilapidated house (still lived in by Nixon's widow, Arlet), accurately records that:

> Edgar D. Nixon, Sr., posted bail for segregation law violator Rosa Parks. In her defense, Nixon gathered the support of Montgomery blacks in implementing the successful 1955–56 Montgomery Bus Boycott. His commitment and active involvement as a grassroots organizer, civic leader and founder of the Montgomery NAACP chapter has paralleled local movement for the advancement of blacks . . . As chief strategist of the Montgomery Bus Boycott, Nixon spearheaded a local protest which launched a massive movement of social reform and earned him local recognition as "The Father of the Civil Rights Movement".

3.4   Rosa Parks

" . . . *I Tried Not to Think about What Might Happen*"

Rosa Parks was a black seamstress and civil rights worker in Montgomery, Alabama, who refused to give up her bus seat to a white man on December 1, 1955. This incident triggered the Montgomery bus boycott that led to desegregation of that city's public transportation system.

I knew [the opponents of the bus rules] needed a plaintiff who was beyond reproach, because I was in on the discussions about the possible court cases. But that is not why I refused to give up my bus seat to a white man on Thursday, December 1, 1955. I did not intend to get arrested. If I had been paying attention, I wouldn't even have gotten on that bus.

I was very busy at that particular time. I was getting an NAACP workshop together for the 3rd or 4th of December, and I was trying to get the consent of Mr. H. Council Trenholm at Alabama State to have the Saturday meeting at the college. He did give permission, but I had a hard time getting to him to get permission to use the building. I was also getting notices in the mail for the election of officers of the Senior Branch of the NAACP, which would be the next week.

When I got off from work that evening of December 1, I went to Court Square as usual to catch the Cleveland Avenue bus home. I didn't look to see who was driving when I got on, and by the time I recognized him, I had already paid my fare. It was the same driver who had put me off the bus back in 1943, twelve years earlier. He was still tall and heavy, with red, rough-looking skin. And he was still mean-looking. I didn't know if he had been on that route before—they switched the drivers around sometimes. I do know that most of the time if I saw him on a bus, I wouldn't get on it.

I saw a vacant seat in the middle section of the bus and took it. I didn't even question why there was a vacant seat even though there were quite a few people standing in the back. If I had thought about it at all, I would probably have figured maybe someone saw me get on and did not take the seat but left it vacant for me. There was a man sitting next to the window and two women across the aisle.

The next stop was the Empire Theater, and some whites got on. They filled up the white seats, and one man was left standing. The driver looked back and noticed the man standing. Then he looked back at us. He said, "Let me have those front seats," because they were the front seats of the black section. Didn't anybody move. We just sat right where we were, the four of us. Then he spoke a second time: "Y'all better make it light on yourselves and let me have those seats."

The man in the window seat next to me stood up, and I moved to let him pass me, and then I looked across the aisle and saw the two women were also standing. I moved over to the window seat. I could not see how standing up was going to "make it light" for me. The more we gave in and complied, the worse they treated us. . . .

The driver of the bus saw me still sitting there, and he asked was I going to stand up. I said, "No." He said, "Well, I'm going to have you arrested." Then I said, "You may do that." These were the only words we said to each other. . . .

As I sat there, I tried not to think about what might happen. I knew anything was possible. I could be manhandled or beaten. I could be arrested. People have asked me if it occurred to me then that I could be the test case the NAACP had been looking for. I did not think that at all. In fact if I had let myself think too deeply about what might happen to me, I might have gotten off the bus. But I chose to remain.

3.5   Elizabeth Eckford

"Don't Let Them See You Cry"

Elizabeth Eckford was one of the "Little Rock Nine," a group of black honors students chosen to integrate Central High School, Little Rock, Arkansas, in 1957.

That night I was so excited I couldn't sleep. The next morning I was about the first one up. While I was pressing my black-and-white dress—I had made it to wear on the first day of school—my little brother turned on the TV set. They started telling about a large crowd gathered at the school. The man on TV said he wondered if we were going to show up that morning. Mother called from the kitchen, where she was fixing breakfast, "Turn that TV off!" She was so upset and worried. I wanted to comfort her, so I said, "Mother, don't worry."

Dad was walking back and forth, from room to room, with a sad expression. He was chewing on his pipe and he had a cigar in his hand, but he didn't light either one. It would have been funny, only he was so nervous.

Before I left home Mother called us into the living room. She said we should have a word of prayer. Then I caught the bus and got off a block from the school. I saw a large crowd of people standing across the street from the soldiers guarding Central. As I walked on, the crowd suddenly got very quiet. Superintendent Blossom had told us to enter by the front door. I looked at all the people and thought, "Maybe I will be safer if I walk down the block to the front entrance behind the guards."

At the corner I tried to pass through the long line of guards around the school so as to enter the grounds behind them. One of the guards pointed across the street. So I pointed in the same direction and asked whether he meant for me to cross the street and walk down. He nodded "yes." So, I walked across the street conscious of the crowd that stood there, but they moved away from me.

For a moment all I could hear was the shuffling of their feet. Then someone shouted, "Here she comes, get ready!" I moved away from the crowd on the sidewalk and into the street. If the mob came at me I could then cross back over so the guards could protect me.

The crowd moved in closer and then began to follow me, calling me names. I still wasn't afraid. Just a little bit nervous. Then my knees started to shake all of a sudden and I wondered whether I could make it to the center entrance a block away. It was the longest block I ever walked in my whole life.

Even so, I still wasn't too scared because all the time I kept thinking that the guards would protect me.

When I got in front of the school, I went up to a guard again. But this time he just looked straight ahead and didn't move to let me pass him. I didn't know what to do. Then I looked and saw that the path leading to the front entrance was a little further ahead. So I walked until I was right in front of the path to the front door.

I stood looking at the school—it looked so big! Just then the guards let some white students through.

The crowd was quiet. I guess they were waiting to see what was going to happen. When I was able to steady my knees, I walked up to the guard who had let the white students in. He too didn't move. When I tried to squeeze past him, he raised his bayonet and then the other guards moved in and raised their bayonets.

They glared at me with a mean look and I was very frightened and didn't know what to do. I turned around and the crowd came toward me.

They moved closer and closer. Somebody started yelling, "Lynch her! Lynch her!"

I tried to see a friendly face somewhere in the mob—someone who maybe would help. I looked into the face of an old woman and it seemed a kind face, but when I looked at her again, she spat on me.

They came closer, shouting, "No nigger bitch is going to get in our school. Get out of here!"

I turned back to the guards but their faces told me I wouldn't get any help from them. Then I looked down the block and saw a bench at the bus stop. I thought, "If I can only get there I will be safe. I don't know why the bench seemed a safe place to me, but I started walking toward it. I tried to close my mind to what they were shouting, and kept saying to myself, "If I can only make it to the bench I will be safe."

When I finally got there, I don't think I could have gone another step. I sat down and the mob crowded up and began shouting all over again. Someone hollered, "Drag her over to this tree! Let's take care of that nigger." Just then a white man sat down beside me, put his arm around me and patted my shoulder. He raised my chin and said, "Don't let them see you cry."

3.6   David L. Kirp

Retreat into Legalism: The Little Rock School Desegregation Case in Historic Perspective

David Kirp is a professor of public policy at the School of Public Policy, University of California at Berkeley. Author of two recent books, Our Town: Race, Housing and the Soul of Suburbia *and* Learning by Heart: AIDS and School Children in America's Communities, *he is a policy-oriented lawyer who deals with the connections between law, policy, and social justice.*

> *Law and order are not here to be preserved by depriving the Negro children of their constitutional rights. . . . The right of a student not to be segregated on racial grounds is indeed so fundamental and pervasive that it is embraced in the concept of due process of law.*
>
> —Cooper v. Aaron *(1958)*

> *During the 1970s and 1980s, a word disappeared from the American vocabulary. That word is segregation.*
>
> —Douglas Massey and Nancy Denton, American Apartheid *(1993)*

In the waning days of the summer of 1957, the nation's attention was riveted on an unfolding drama in Little Rock, Arkansas. There, Governor Orval Faubus, who earlier had cultivated a reputation as a racial moderate, had declared in flat contradiction of a federal court order that nine black students—the first black students to be admitted to a white school in Little Rock—would not be permitted to enroll in Central High School. "Blood will run in the streets," Faubus warned, if the youngsters tried to enter the school, and the first intrepid black student was driven off, the vengeful crowd shouting "Get her! Lynch her! . . . Get a rope and drag her over to this tree."

Although the impasse was broken when, after three weeks of violence, President Eisenhower finally ordered army paratroopers to escort the black youngsters into Central High, the military presence didn't mean peace. When harassment of the nine students continued unabated, the federal trial judge, fearful of yet more "chaos, bedlam and turmoil," shifted course, agreeing to postpone integration for two years, until 1960; meanwhile, the nine black students who had survived a year at Central High would be reassigned to the all-black high school (Irons 1988, 111).

It was this order, appealed by the NAACP, that the Supreme Court took up in special session in September 1958. This was four weeks before the Court Term was scheduled to begin, and the timing of the oral argument was meant to dramatize the significance of the case: only three times before in the Court's history had the justices convened during a recess (Irons and Guitton 1993, 249–263). While this was not the first occasion on which a Dixie official had vowed to perpetuate the regime of school segregation struck down in *Brown v. Board of Education* (1954), it represented the most direct and frontal defiance of the federal judiciary, and so the Court felt compelled to respond swiftly. Barely 24 hours after oral arguments, the justices ordered that integration in Little Rock proceed without delay; two weeks later, it issued a more detailed decree in *Cooper v. Aaron* (1958).

The opinion in the Little Rock case is remarkable neither for its rhetorical flourishes nor for its constitutional boldness. Unlike the Segregation Cases, there is no heartstrings-tugging plea to end segregation in order not to inflict damage upon the "hearts and minds" of the young, no tacit overruling of a sixty-year-old precedent. Instead, what makes *Cooper* memorable is the declaration of judicial will that is so palpably on display, the jurists' insistence on their right to the last word in matters of constitutional law. This is less *Brown* revisited than *Marbury v. Madison* (1803) *redux*.

Often in its history, the Supreme Court has been called upon to act as "teacher in a vital national seminar" (Rostow 1952); so too here. Each of the justices individually signed the opinion in *Cooper v. Aaron,* and that remarkable gesture—Earl Warren as John Hancock in this declaration of judicial independence—was a tangible manifestation of the justices' determination to prevail. The Segregation Cases, the Court insisted, embodied the law of the land to which government officials and ordinary citizens alike owed allegiance.

Fast Forward

Shift time and geography some 30 years to DeKalb County, Georgia; then, a few years later, shift once more to Kansas City, Missouri (*Freeman v. Pitts* 1992; *Missouri v. Jenkins* 1995). These are the most recent school desegregation cases to be heard by the Supreme Court, and their contrast with *Cooper v. Aaron* could not be plainer. The justices, so pointedly unanimous about the right course of action in Little Rock, have become badly split and publicly querulous, disinclined even to conceal their disdain for their colleagues' opposing views. The issues to be decided have much less to do with great principles—simple justice (Kluger 1976)—than with the details of political and judicial management. Whatever the Supreme Court may subsequently say about desegregation, these opinions confirm what has been apparent for years: that an era during which the Court embraced an integrationist vision of racial fairness has ended. The persistence of segregation, it seems, no longer troubles the sleep of the justices.

In DeKalb County, a leafy Atlanta suburb, school officials sought an end to pupil busing mandated by the trial court which, decades after the original litigants had graduated from high school, was still issuing supplementary orders. These officials insisted that they had done their job. The public schools were "unitary" according to the standards laid down by the Court. The fact that some schools in the county remained mostly black while others were mainly white was not government's fault, but rather a matter of housing prices and individual preferences—factors entirely outside public officials' control. It was time, they believed—long past time, really—to be freed from court oversight.

In Kansas City, a quarrel over money had broken out between the city and the state over who should pay for enticements to integration. Missouri objected to having to underwrite the costs of magnet schools, specially designed institutions which offered everything from Olympic size swimming pools to the latest in electronic gadgetry in order to lure white suburbanites to the almost entirely black urban school system.

In the DeKalb County litigation, the school board prevailed; and the state got its way in Missouri. The array of opinions in these two cases reveals desegregation to be in full retreat. The integrationist-minded justices who once ruled the Court became fixated on the minutiae of school board behavior in DeKalb County and the precise terms of the legal complaint in Kansas City. It was the opponents who displayed passion and summoned principle to defend individual liberty and assail judicial paternalism. As a matter of rhetoric, these moments belong to Clarence Thomas, who has gentrified Orval Faubus' angry sentiments, rendering them the stuff of constitutional law.

How could the death of the integrationist ideal have happened so swiftly?

Just Schools

"No single issue has more moral force than *Brown*," wrote J. Harvie Wilkinson, III a generation ago in *From Brown to Bakke*. "Few struggles have been morally more significant than the one for racial integation of American life. Yet school integration may be the most political item on the Court's agenda" (Wilkinson 1979, 151). From a matter of high principle in *Brown*, desegregation rapidly descended into the swamp of defiance (as in Little Rock), evasion, avoidance, and delay. The Court, frustrated by the success of these tactics, sought a clear standard against which to measure compliance with its orders. It settled upon a numerical standard which took racial balance as its starting point.

In *Green v. County School Board* (1968), freedom of choice, the justification the rural Virginia district preferred for having accomplished only token integration, was simply a euphemism for evading *Brown*. It made obvious sense to order that the district's two elementary schools reflect the racial composition of the school district—that there be "a system without a 'white' school and a 'Negro' school, but just schools." However, when in the *Swann* (1971) case this same "just schools" standard was applied in formulaic fashion to urban, residentially segregated Charlotte, North Carolina, thousands of students had to be bused to school over substantial distances.

Until *Swann*, desegregation occupied the unchallenged moral high ground in national discourse. *Brown* enjoyed near-iconic status; while justices might disagree among themselves about the constitutional status of civil rights demonstrations, to dissent in a school case was a sacrilege. But *Swann* changed all that. The ruling evoked a national chorus of complaint, whipped up by chief chorister Richard Nixon. It didn't matter that pupils had been bused to school since Henry Ford's time—that, as the NAACP pithily and accurately pointed out, "It's Not the Distance, It's the Niggers" (Mills 1973, 322) which best explained the anti-busing sentiment. The Supreme Court's decision to discuss the issue entirely in terms of numbers— racial balance substituting for historically-rooted understandings of racial justice, on the one hand and educationally rooted understandings of equal opportunity on the other—proved to be a fatal misrepresentation of the problem.

Just one year after *Swann,* and nearly twenty years after *Brown,* the first dissents were registered in a Supreme Court desegregation case (*Wright v. City Council of Emporia* 1972), when Nixon's appointees voted as a bloc to loosen judicial control. A year later, in the Denver case, the justices, again divided made numbers rather than principle the heart of their first ruling on segregation in the North (*Keyes v. Denver School District* 1973).

An incautious Supreme Court, willing to confront the full measure of school segregation, might have advanced "a sweeping and interconnected view of American racial history. It might have seen school segregation as a product of prejudice in jobs, housing, politics, public facilities, the military, with discrimination and segregation in each part of American life reverberating through the whole" (Wilkinson 1979, 140; see generally, Myrdal 1972). With much less strain on their constitutional role as interpreters of the law, the justices could have decided that fixing a single national standard for school segregation was both legally and morally right (Hochschild 1984).

In 1954, when the opinion in the Segregation Cases was announced, North and South seemed to occupy different moral universes, and merging those universes required a second Reconstruction (Orfield 1969; Rodgers and Bullock 1976). The Supreme Court refused even to hear a desegregation case from the North throughout the 1960s, as if waiting for the apparently intractable legal and political issues posed by those lawsuits to be tamed in lower court opinions.

By the 1970s, however, it could plausibly be said that the racial situation in Denver was not so different from Charlotte, either in fact or law. On both sides of Mason's and Dixon's line, the constitutional injustice stemmed from government-sanctioned—indeed, government-promoted—segregation in housing, which combined with school boards' use of racially distinct neighborhoods to define attendance zones, resulting in segregated public schools. While Northern officials piously contended that such segregation was *de facto*—that it just happened—since government officials drew these attendance zones, the government was always a player, never an innocent party. As Justice Douglas bluntly pointed out in *Keyes,* the Denver case, "the State is barred from creating by one device or another ghettoes that determine the school one is compelled to attend" (*Keyes v. Denver School District* 1973, 205).

A few years earlier, in the Charlotte case, the justices had come close to adopting such a nationwide standard, but when it became clear that such an opinion would not command unanimous assent the majority, still bewitched by unanimity, backed off. Never again would there be a majority on the high court for such a ruling.

To cobble together a solid majority in the Denver case, Justice Brennan, the avatar of racial liberalism, wrote an opinion that combined the by-now familiar fixation on numbers with a hyper-legalist analysis. Before a federal court could order desegregation in the North, Brennan announced, there had to be proof of intentional past wrongdoing on the part of local school officials which substantially affected the racial composition of the schools. Even as the segregation-promoting character of housing policy was ignored in this equation, burdens of pleading and burdens of proof became the order of the day. The result was Dickensian litigation, daunting to all but the most experienced and best-financed litigants. The outcomes of such litigation varied from place to place in the North—what to one judge was illicit official behavior seemed entirely innocent to another—and this inconsistency made for more popular unhappiness with the courts. Why us, the citizens of San Francisco asked, and not them, referring to San Jose, and the question was really unanswerable (Kirp 1982; Kirp and Jensen 1984).

Brown had deliberately been written in language fit for the Sunday newspaper supplements. In *Keyes,* by contrast, the lack of a persuasive rationale anchored in a morally-driven conceptualization of official wrong-doing made the decision seem a crude imposition of judicial will, not necessarily the right thing to do.

The triumph of artlessly executed hyper-legalism over simple justice became complete in *Milliken v. Bradley* (1975). In that case, the justices overturned, by a 5-4 vote, an order requiring desegregation, not just for the city of Detroit but for the surrounding suburbs as well. This opinion ignored mountains of evidence concerning the complicity of state and suburban officials in walling off Detroit from the surrounding suburbs, evidence on which the trial judge based his decree. *Milliken* sent an unmistakable message—urban apartheid would not be overcome through judicial decree.

The Detroit decision effectively spelled the end of judicial activism in public school desegregation. The constitutional war was over. DeKalb County, Georgia and Kansas City, Missouri were merely mopping-up operations.

Back to the Future

Racial justice acquired meaning outside as well as inside the courtroom during these years. What had seemed so simple in Little Rock in 1957—that nine intrepid black adolescents should not be turned away from a public high school because of their race—had become more complicated by the 1970s. In both the South and the North, residential segregation had increased, making school desegregation logistically harder to accomplish. Nor was it so clear that, in terms of educational outcomes, busing was worth the political and social price (St. John 1975). New black voices were being heard, many of them unsympathetic to the desegregation project. Some black leaders had come to reject integration in favor of black-run schools (Levin 1970; Fantini, Gittell and Magat 1970), even as others grew impatient while waiting, seemingly forever, for the promise of *Brown* to be realized in their communities (Bell 1978). Anyplace where desegregation landed on the agenda, it became *the* issue, demanding massive amounts of time, energy and money. During the past generation, issues having more to do with pedagogy and educational philosophy, less to do with racial justice—the back-to-basics movement; the push for educational excellence; the demand, through vouchers or charter schools, for greater choice of school—have seized the spotlight.

The Supreme Court cannot be faulted for failing to make good on its promise, implicit in Little Rock and spelled out a decade later in *Green,* that state-inflicted segregation would be eliminated "root and branch." To accomplish this would have required the active support of other branches of government and ultimately the citizenry (Hochschild 1995; Kirp 1984; Kirp, Dwyer, and Rosenthal 1996). But the Court can fairly be criticized for announcing a universal obligation to desegregate America's schools, then through its busing decrees imposing the burden selectively; as well as for failing to risk greatly to preserve its integrationist ideal of racial justice, instead bowing (in *Keyes, Milliken* and the later cases) to the pragmatics of politics in a way the justices had rejected in *Cooper v. Aaron.* If the achievement of a unitary society was really beyond the capacity of justices, the past generation's desegregation decisions have nonetheless undercut the moral authority of constitutional law.

The 40 year-old story of Little Rock has come full circle—like parent, like child. Even as the children of Linda Brown, the named plaintiff in the Segregation Cases, went to segregated schools in Topeka, it's unlikely that the offspring of those nine remarkable teenagers in Little Rock attended integrated public schools. There is a difference between then and now, though: Now hardly any voices are raised in protest.

References

Bell, Derrick. 1978. "Waiting on the Promise of *Brown.*" *Law and Contemporary Problems* 39:341.

Brown v. Board of Education. 1954:347 U.S. 483.

Cooper v. Aaron. 1958. 358 U.S. 1.

Fantini, Mario, Marilyn Gittell, and Richard Magat. 1970. *Community Control and the Urban School.* New York: Praeger.

Freeman v. Pitts. 1992. 503 U.S. 467.

Green v. County School Board. 1968. 391 U.S. 430.

Hochschild, Jennifer. 1984. *The New American Dilemma: Liberal Democracy and School Desegregation.* New Haven: Yale University Press.

_____. 1995. *Facing Up to the American Dream: Race, Class, and the Soul of the Nation.* Princeton: Princeton University Press.

Irons, Peter. 1988. *The Courage of Their Convictions.* New York: Free Press.

_____, and Stephanie Guitton, eds. 1993. *May It Please the Court.* New York: New Press.

Missouri v. Jenkins. 1995, 515 U.S. 70.

Keyes v. Denver School District. 1973. 413 U.S. 189.

Kirp, David. 1977. "School Desegregation and the Limits of Legalism." *Public Interest* 47:101.

_____. 1982. *Just Schools: The Idea of Racial Equality in American Education.* Berkeley and Los Angeles: University of California Press.

_____, John Dwyer, and Larry Rosenthal. 1996. *Our Town: Race, Housing, and the Soul of Suburbia.* New Brunswick, NJ: Rutgers University Press.

_____, and Donald Jensen, eds. 1984. *School Days, Rule Days.* London and Philadelphia: Falmer Press.

Kluger, Richard. 1976. *Simple Justice.* New York: Knopf.

Levin, Henry, ed. 1970. *Community Control of Schools.* Washington DC: Brookings Institution.

Marbury v. Madison. 1803. 5 U.S. 137.

Massey, Robert, and Nancy Denton. 1993. *American Apartheid.* Cambridge, MA: Harvard University Press.

Milliken v. Bradley. 1975. 418 U.S. 717.

Mills, Nicholas, ed. 1973. *The Great School Bus Controversy.* New York: Teachers College Press.

Myrdal, Gunnar, ed. 1972. *An American Dilemma: The Negro Problem and Modern Democracy.* New York: Pantheon.

Orfield, Gary. 1969. *The Reconstruction of Southern Education.* New York: John Wiley.

_____. 1996. *Dismantling Desegregation: The Quiet Reversal of Brown v. Board of Education.* New York: New Press.

Peltason, Jack. 1961. *Fifty-Eight Lonely Men.* Urbana IL: University of Illinois Press.

Rodgers, Harvey Jr., and Charles S. Bullock, III. 1976. *Coercion to Compliance.* Lexington MA: D.C. Heath.

Rosenberg, Gerald. 1991. *The Hollow Hope: Can Courts Bring about Social Change?* Chicago: University of Chicago Press.

Rostow, Eugene. 1952. "The Democratic Character of Judicial Review." *Harvard Law Review* 66:208.

St. John, Nancy. 1975. *School Desegregation: Outcomes for Children.* New York: Wiley.

Swann v. Charlotte-Mecklenberg Board of Education. 1971. 302 U.S. 1.

Symposium. 1976. "Is School Desegregation Still a Good Idea?" *School Review* 84:309.

Wilkinson, J. Harvie, III. 1979. *From Brown to Bakke: The Supreme Court and School Integration: 1954–1978.* New York: Oxford University Press.

Wright v. City Council of Emporia. 1972. 407 U.S. 451.

Additional Resources

Suggested Readings

Branch, Taylor. *Parting the Waters: America in the King Years 1954–63.* New York: Simon & Schuster, 1988. A monumental account of the civil rights struggle from the Eisenhower years, through the rise of King, to the presidential contest of 1960. Comprehensive history of the Montgomery bus boycott, lunch counter sit-ins, Freedom Rides, James Meredith's integration of the University of Mississippi, and the murder of Medgar Evers.

Burns, Stuart. *Daybreak of Freedom: The Montgomery Bus Boycott.* Chapel Hill: University of North Carolina Press, 1997. A collection of original source documents of the year-long protest of racial segregation in Montgomery, Alabama. The book contains information on key figures such as King and his inner circle and others who were involved, including interviews with bus drivers, maids, and cooks.

Curry, Constance. *Silver Rights.* New York: Harcourt Brace, 1995. Compelling story of an African American family in Mississippi and their struggle to desegregate the all-white schools in the 1960s.

King, Martin Luther, Jr. *Stride toward Freedom: The Montgomery Story.* New York: Harper, 1958. King's personal account of the Montgomery bus boycott. It also contains an exploration of his philosophy of nonviolence.

Kluger, Richard. *Simple Justice.* New York: Knopf, 1975. A comprehensive and detailed history of the NAACP court battles for school desegregation leading up to and culminating in the *Brown* decision of 1954.

Martin, Waldo. *The Brown Decision: A Brief History with Documents.* Boston: Bedford Books, 1998. A study of race, law, and social change. Martin illustrates the history of legal battles to democratize public education in the United States. Invaluable to students at all levels. It contains copies of original *Brown* documents along with the popular press reaction to the 1954 decision.

Morris, Aldon. *The Origins of the Civil Rights Movement: Black Communities Organizing for Change.* New York: Free Press, 1984. A major work on the civil rights struggles of the 1950s and 1960s. With emphasis on local community groups along with national and regional organizations, the book is a first-rate account of the movement.

Robinson, JoAnn. *The Montgomery Bus Boycott and the Women Who Started It.* Edited by David Garrow. Knoxville: University of Tennessee Press, 1987. A participant-observation study of the historic boycott in 1955–56.

Williams, Randall. *Johnnie, The Life of Johnnie Rebecca Carr.* Montgomery, Alabama: Black Belt Press, 1996. An interesting account of the Montgomery bus boycott as seen through the life of a friend of Rosa Parks. Written for children.

Web Sites

http://brownvboard.org/brwnqurt/03-1/03-1a.htm

In conjunction with the 45th anniversary of the *Brown* decision, the September 1999 issue of *The Brown Quarterly* is featured on this Web site. The site contains separate sections on the lawyers, current National Parks Service efforts to preserve school sites, and many oral histories of those who were part of early school desegregation.

www.midsouth.rr.com/civilrights/

The National Civil Rights Museum is located in Memphis, Tennessee, on the site of the Lorraine Motel, where Dr. King was assassinated in 1968. The museum Web site highlights school desegregation in Little Rock, Arkansas, and Oxford, Mississippi. It also features a section on the Montgomery Bus Boycott and Rosa Parks. The "Interactive Tours" section offers an overview of civil rights related history dating back to the Abolitionists.

www.huarchivesnet.howard.edu

This Web site, at the Moorland-Spingarn Research Center at Howard University, offers an electronic journal, HUArchivesNet, dealing with African American history. It also holds an oral history collection of the civil rights movement.

www.shsw.wisc.edu

This civil rights collection at the State Historical Society of Wisconsin contains an oral history collection of the integration of Central High School in Little Rock, Arkansas. It also houses the archives of the Congress for Racial Equality (CORE). In the archives section is the "Social Action Collection."

www.seattletimes.com/mlk/movement/PT/phototour.html

This photo tour of the civil rights movement includes coverage of the events of Montgomery and Little Rock along with a section devoted to Martin Luther King's life. The Web site centers primarily around civil rights issues and Seattle, Washington.

http://www.cr.nps.gov/nr/travel/civilrights/

This site presents all the historical places of the civil rights movement that can be explored by clicking on "Main Map," and from the "List of Sites."

Chapter 4

Student Activism and the Emergence of a Mass Movement, 1960–1965

During the early 1960s, the struggle against racism and discrimination developed new strategies and revitalized old ones. The involvement of college students brought enthusiasm and optimism to the movement—younger, more impatient activists who escalated the civil rights struggle and broadened its base. Creating a spiral of activity, they were involved throughout the Southern states, and their tactics spread in several directions, encompassing sit-ins, freedom rides, jail-ins, boycotts, voter registration drives, and marches. This was the beginning of a new phase of the movement. With the encouragement of Ella Baker, students formed their own, separate organization, the Student Nonviolent Coordinating Committee (SNCC), which, along with the NAACP, SCLC, and CORE, dominated the civil rights movement. Beyond this, in local communities groups of civil rights workers joined together during these years to desegregate century-old segregated institutions.

By this time, civil rights activities had become a media staple and the issue acquired national significance. National newspaper coverage along with the increasingly sophisticated use of television news reporting brought the movement into most American households, and the appalling segregated conditions throughout the South presented the media with images that dramatized the movement. Violence and tragedy stemming from the Southern reaction to 1960s civil rights activities became a national concern. With federal laws and Supreme Court decisions beginning to disassemble segregation, the civil rights movement saw the government as an ally, but segregated conditions remained in the South, and massive resistance to change developed.

The period from 1960 to 1965, from the sit-ins in Greensboro, North Carolina, and Nashville, Tennessee, to the now-famous Selma-to-Montgomery march, was well documented by the media. The front-page coverage of confrontation made civil rights more of a national issue; a sense of national crisis, far beyond the Jim Crow communities of the South, was demonstrated by movement leaders and communicated by the media. Martin Luther King's "Letter from Birmingham City Jail" (Reading 4.4), which reiterates that the goal of America is freedom, conveys the moral sentiment of the movement. While in jail without paper, King wrote the letter in the margins of an old copy of the *New York Times;* it was to become the most widely reprinted document of the civil rights movement. The confrontations between the young students and blacks on one hand and opposition Southern whites backed by the local politicians and police on the other framed a clear picture of injustice, but new federal legislation needed the support of legislators outside the South.

Sit-Ins

*Student Activism
and the
Emergence of
a Mass
Movement,
1960–1965*

"I'm sorry, we don't serve you here." This response from the waitress at the F. W. Woolworth's lunch counter in Greensboro, North Carolina, to the four black college freshmen from North Carolina A & T who ordered coffee and doughnuts affirmed the lingering Southern way of selective segregation. The black customers showed the waitress their Woolworth's receipts from shopping at other counters in the store. But, in 1960, North Carolina lunch counters remained segregated. Although the four students, Ezell Blair Jr., Franklin McCain, Joseph McNeil, and David Richmond, were members of NAACP Youth Councils, their action was not sponsored by any organization. The news of the sit-in spread throughout the 10 black colleges in the Greensboro area. Within a few days, students from those colleges and the local black churches had organized sit-ins at other segregated lunch counters, and the action spread to cities, primarily, across the South. Chain stores—like Woolworth's—that practiced selective segregation and discrimination were also subject to pickets in New York City and other Northern cities.

The Reverend James Lawson of Nashville, who had been planning sit-ins in that city, was contacted by one of the sit-in leaders from North Carolina. A pacifist who was imprisoned for refusing to serve in the military during the Korean War, Lawson was interested in the nonviolent approach to social change. He ran a series of workshops in nonviolence for students who wanted to challenge segregation. Lawson's teachings were extremely influential with the students, who learned nonviolence and discipline, both cornerstones to effective social change in this period of the civil rights movement. The Nashville Student Movement that arose from those workshops made plans to challenge department store lunch counters in Nashville. The students from the historically black colleges in the Nashville area were motivated by reports of the Greensboro sit-ins. These student sit-ins demonstrated the dissatisfaction of young blacks with the culture of segregation in the South.

Two months after the sit-ins, on Easter weekend, the student leaders were invited to a meeting of the Southern Christian Leadership Conference (SCLC) to coordinate future civil rights action. Executive director of SCLC, Ella Baker, gave the opening address, "More than a Hamburger." "Political Mama," by Joanne Grant (Reading 4.1), examines that weekend when the Student Nonviolent Coordinating Committee (SNCC) was born. The leaders of SCLC wanted the students to follow them as the youth arm of the organization. The students, however, wanted to be more independent. They, instead, followed the advice of Baker to create an independent organization. In her speech, Baker argued that the lunch counter sit-ins were about larger issues of civil and human rights, issues "bigger than a hamburger." She gave the students a strong sense of purpose encouraging them to be democratic and independent. Although SNCC challenged the existing movement leadership, the NAACP and local organizations supported the students with money, legal aid, and advice.

Sitting down to have a cup of coffee or occupying any seat in a movie theater may be taken for granted today, but in 1960 lunch counter segregation epitomized the humiliation of blacks. Demonstrators carried signs that read, "We do not picket just because we want to eat. We can eat at home or walking down the street. We picket to protest the lack of dignity and respect shown us as human beings." The sit-ins sparked a parallel movement against segregation in interstate transportation, the Freedom Rides, where interracial students traveled on interstate buses (Wexler, 1993:114).

Student protests were having an effect in breaking down segregation. Civil rights activities attracted the attention of the presidential campaigns of John Kennedy and Richard Nixon. Both candidates needed the Southern vote and were careful when dealing with civil rights issues, so the movement played a key role in the election. When Martin Luther King was placed in a Georgia jail, people from the Kennedy campaign influenced a Georgia judge from behind the scenes to release him. Taylor Branch (1988:374) points out how the news of King's release spread throughout the black community:

> Far removed from these twin storms of political attention, beneath the notice of campaign professionals, the Kennedy campaign's **"blue bomb"** was spreading through the Negro culture by means of the most effective private communications medium since the Underground Railroad—the church. Nearly two million copies were being shipped by bus, train, and airplane— duplicated and bundled, picked up and unbundled, praised from ten thousand pulpits and handed out.

Kennedy went on to win the closest election in American history with the help of the black vote.

In spring 1961, student activism took form in Jackson, Mississippi, when black students from Tougaloo College held a sit-in at the segregated public library. A few days later sympathetic white students joined them in a protest march. This example of local activism demonstrates the indigenous character of the civil rights struggle. Taylor Branch (1988:485) describes the building of a social movement:

> From the Montgomery bus boycott to the confrontations of the sit-ins, then on to the Rock Hill jail-in and now to the mass assault on the Mississippi prisons, there was a "movement" in both senses of the word—a moving spiritual experience, and a steady expansion of scope. The theater was spreading through the entire South. One isolated battle had given way to many scattered ones, and now in the Mississippi jails they were moving from similar experiences to a common experience.

Freedom Rides

Late in 1960, the U.S. Supreme Court, in *Boynton v. Virginia,* extended its prohibition against segregation on buses and trains to terminals. Early in 1961 the Congress of Racial Equality (CORE) planned to have black and white "freedom riders" ride through the South and challenge interstate transportation segregation. James Farmer, the national director of CORE, modeled the Freedom Rides after the little-publicized 1947 "Journey of Reconciliation," when integrated CORE volunteers defied segregation in the upper Southern states. Since federal law was on their side, the 1961 CORE plan was to get arrested, stay in jail **("jail-no-bail"),** attract national publicity, and then get the Justice Department to enforce the law.

282

*Student Activism
and the
Emergence of
a Mass
Movement,
1960–1965*

Howell Raines's "Freedom Riders" (Reading 4.2) illustrates James Farmer's strategy for CORE to force the South to comply with federal interstate transportation law. In that reading, fellow rider John Lewis describes his experiences of being beaten and put in jail in Birmingham and Montgomery. The attorney general of Alabama obtained an injunction saying that it was unlawful for interracial groups to travel in that state. Both Alabama and Mississippi, defying federal law, imposed old state segregation statutes, so that traveling through those states carried the risk of violence and death. The riders' fear was heightened when a Freedom Riders' bus was firebombed outside Anniston, Alabama, and the rides almost ended after a mob attacked a bus arriving in Birmingham. However, a group of students mostly from the Nashville sit-ins, in the face of increasing threats of violence, pressed on to Jackson, Mississippi, where over 300 were arrested. Finally, in late September 1961, the Interstate Commerce Commission (ICC) issued regulations banning all segregated seating in interstate vehicles and terminals.

Mass Demonstrations, Albany, Georgia (1961–62)

The southwestern Georgia town of Albany was a segregationist stronghold. SNCC, under direction of field secretary Charles Sherrod, came to help the black community organize against segregation and formed the Albany Movement, an umbrella organization that coordinated all the civil rights groups in the community. The Albany Movement involved mass demonstrations whose participants for the first time included untrained protesters and even mothers and children. The fervor of freedom songs was important to the demonstrators in Albany, as they were to the entire movement, providing unity and popular appeal. Martin Luther King, who initially was not involved in the desegregation effort in Albany, was eventually invited to speak there. The presence of King and SCLC offended members of SNCC who had begun to view King's strategies as too slow and conciliatory. Media attention centered on King and the tactics of Albany's police chief, Laurie Prichett. Prichett planned to defeat the "jail-no-bail" strategy of the Albany Movement. Having read King's *Stride toward Freedom,* he tried to restrain the police from being violent even while they arrested the civil rights demonstrators. Prichett was successful. In July, King and SCLC's Ralph Abernathy were jailed. For the federal government, however, King in jail meant bad publicity, and bail for his release was paid anonymously. Later that month, a federal judge issued a restraining order to end the nine-month civil rights demonstration, but one week later, an appeals judge set aside the injunction.

When the opportunity arose, the federal government did not enforce the ICC desegregation ruling. Tensions between SNCC and King began to surface. Dubbing King "de Lawd," SNCC activists viewed him as an uninvited guest. The initial squabbling between SNCC, SCLC, and local civil rights organizations came to the attention of the city commissioners who played on the division and made a deal with local black organizations to desegregate the train and bus terminals if the demonstrations were stopped. King left Albany in August, and the Albany Movement continued to mobilize an entire community without him. Adam Fairclough, in "Confrontation: Albany and Birmingham" (Reading 4.3), depicts the failure of Albany and the success of Birmingham's **"Project C"** confrontation.

Mass Demonstrations, Birmingham, Alabama (1963)

Pat Watters, a white Southern reporter who was drawn into the movement after hearing the freedom riders singing on a passing bus, wrote (1993:233):

> "There wasn't any real strategy in Albany," Andy Young recalled in 1970. "I remember being around and not knowing what to do . . . We didn't know then how to mobilize people in masses. We learned in Albany. We put together the team of SCLC staff people there that later won the victories. They hadn't even known each other before . . . There's always tension between the analytical and the religious in these circumstances. But they came together in Birmingham."

Hardened by defeat, King decided to explode the political equivalent of a bomb under the federal government. At the invitation of the Reverend Fred Shuttlesworth, he went to Birmingham, Alabama (Fairclough, 1990:71). Fairclough points out that in 1963, Birmingham exemplified all that was extreme, vicious, and violent in Southern racism. The segregated city was rife with political conflict, and two city governments—one headed by Eugene "Bull" Connor and the other by a newly elected mayor—made the city vulnerable. Despite public opinion urging black leaders to hold off in their actions and demands, the protests as planned in Project C started.

The civil rights demonstrations, including economic boycotts, affected businesses. The federal government thought the protests were ill timed, and there was pressure on SCLC to call off demonstrations and get out of town. SCLC, however, decided to stay on and push for its demands that Birmingham desegregate. Black school children volunteered and generated the movement's creative tension to push the white power structure into negotiations on racial discrimination (Eskew, 1997:337). This strategy was employed because adults, who were connected to the system, risked their jobs and housing by participating in the protests. Hundreds of children were arrested, and on a Friday when one thousand children lined up to march, Connor brought out dogs and fire hoses.

Live coverage of police dogs and fire hoses turned on black children shocked the nation. These photos provided a lasting image of brutality in Birmingham, and the *New York Times* headlines of May 13 read "U.S. Sends Troops into Alabama after Riots Sweep Birmingham; Kennedy Alerts State's Guard." The American public was witness to the serious gap between equality and discrimination, and Birmingham business leaders, who disapproved of the confrontational police tactics, agreed to desegregate lunch counters and to hire black workers. This outraged the white community. At a night rally, one thousand white-robed Ku Klux Klansmen denounced the businessmen's agreement, and the hotel where King stayed was bombed, leading to a riot. Soon Kennedy sent in federal troops. The agreement was eventually implemented, but more bombings would occur in Birmingham. Most tragically, in September 1963, Klansmen bombed the Sixteenth Street Baptist Church, killing four little black girls and wounding many more people. In the weeks preceding the blast, Governor George Wallace encouraged massive white resistance against desegregation and the same month made his stand at the schoolhouse door to prevent the integration of the University of Alabama.

284

*Student Activism
and the
Emergence of
a Mass
Movement,
1960–1965*

Birmingham became a symbol of victory and success for the national civil rights movement. The vicious tactics of Bull Connor against demonstrators, especially children, provoked national outrage. Indeed, this contributed to the passage of the Civil Rights Act of 1964. The wheels of change, beginning with the New Deal and continuing through the *Brown* decision, found triumph in the act. Birmingham desegregated, and the movement achieved its goals of gaining access to public accommodations and equal employment opportunities. Later, with the implementation of the Voting Rights Act of 1965, Birmingham's black population was registered. In essence, the demonstrations brought Birmingham to the nation's attention and forced a resolution of racial issues (Eskew, 1977:338). During the Birmingham demonstrations, King was arrested and placed in solitary confinement. It was during this time that he composed the famous "Letter from Birmingham City Jail." Considered by some the moral highpoint of the movement, the letter from prison marked a turning point in his life as a leader. He rebounded from failure in Albany to emerge as the national leader of the civil rights movement.

Mass March on Washington

King's leadership, symbolic or real, was further established with the mass March on Washington. Against the wishes of the Kennedy administration, black leaders A. Philip Randolph and Bayard Rustin planned a "March on Washington for Jobs and Freedom." On August 28, 1963, the day after the death of W. E. B. Du Bois, over 200,000 demonstrated in front of the Lincoln Memorial. Keith Miller and Emily Lewis, in "Touchstones, Authorities and Marion Anderson: The Making of 'I Have a Dream,'" (Reading 4.5), trace the construction of King's historic speech, comparing the "Dream" speech to "The Negro and the Constitution," one that he gave in 1944 as a 15-year-old boy. In that early speech, King gave tribute to Marion Anderson and her 1939 Easter Sunday performance in front of the Lincoln Memorial where the NAACP head, Walter White, arranged for her to perform after Anderson had been prevented from singing at Constitution Hall. The similarities between the speeches are striking. King's "I Have A Dream" speech, with its emotional, moral tone, was visionary in that he spoke about freedom for all Americans. It projected hope and optimism. Though the effects of the historic March are difficult to measure, the event projected civil rights into American mainstream politics. King had the ability to arouse the human spirit and burden the consciences of white liberals. Clearly, he was becoming a national figure.

One of the March organizers, Bayard Rustin, saw the 1964 presidential election as a key point in the political future of civil rights. Rustin's platform for the future, "From Protest to Politics: The Future of the Civil Rights Movement" (Reading 4.6), urged blacks to engage in coalition politics within the Democratic Party. For him, political coalitions were inescapable.

One year later the most comprehensive civil rights legislation to date was passed by Congress. The Civil Rights Act of 1964 banned discrimination in public accommodations and provided for equal employment opportunity by declaring discrimination based on race, color, religion, sex, or national origin an unlawful practice. In terms of voting, it banned the use of literacy tests as a requirement for voting, unless written tests were given to everyone. In effect, the act abolished legal segregation and guaranteed a more favorable climate for civil rights legislation in the future.

Voter Registration and Freedom Summer

In the early 1960s SNCC began a voter registration project in Mississippi. Led by Robert Moses, young SNCC workers worked with the rural black community toward getting voters registered. This "direct action" method used by SNCC challenged the older, more established NAACP legal method of fighting segregation. The NAACP field secretary, Medgar Evers, tried to get SNCC, NAACP, CORE, and SCLC to work together. In an effort to focus on politics, especially registration of voters, an umbrella organization was formed, the Council of Federated Organizations (COFO).

Following the assassination of Evers in June 1963, plans were made to bring hundreds of college students to Mississippi to register black voters for a real election, the 1964 presidential election. Bloom (1987:172–3) writes:

> The movement of the early sixties passed largely into the hands of the newly mobilized students. Virtually all of these were middle-class. They did not necessarily come from the middle class; few did. But that they or their parents could provide the money necessary to put them through college was an important marker; and once through college, most were bound for a middle-class existence. Yet, they were faced with indignities that were incongruous with the status they expected in life. There was, moreover, in that, with the rigid structure of segregation and second-class citizenship, there were not sufficient opportunities to accommodate the expansion of this stratum. Unless these youth broke through the system, perhaps most, of them would be forever frustrated.

The student project run by SNCC, known as Freedom Summer, was to register blacks systematically in order to form the Freedom Democratic Party that would challenge the white-only Mississippi Democratic Party. The SNCC strategy was to bring whites to Mississippi for summer voter registration. Student volunteers were recruited from black colleges in the South as well as from Ivy League colleges in the Northeast and large universities in the Midwest. During the first week of the project, tragedy struck. Three civil rights workers, two white and one black, disappeared. Their bodies were eventually found buried on a farm near Philadelphia, Mississippi. A local policeman and Klansmen had shot them. The bodies were discovered in early August, three weeks before the Democratic Party National Convention to be held in Atlantic City, New Jersey. Again, national press coverage highlighted the dramatic images of racial injustice in the South with its ugly violent overtones, this time in Mississippi. The sense of fear and gloom did not prevent Freedom Summer from forging ahead.

After registering nearly 60,000 blacks, COFO set up a new political party, the Mississippi Freedom Democratic Party (MFDP). Its goal was to challenge the state Democratic Party's delegation with regard to the seating of the regular Mississippi delegates at the Democratic Convention. Capturing the attention of the country was the powerful testimony of a black sharecropper, Fannie Lou Hamer. She spoke passionately about racial injustice in Mississippi, posing the profoundly troubling question, Is this America? in front of a national television

286

*Student Activism
and the
Emergence of
a Mass
Movement,
1960–1965*

audience. Despite her emotional and riveting appeal, President Johnson opposed the MFDP challenge, but he offered a compromise of two at-large seats to the MFDP instead of the number requested. The compromise contained a provision that in 1968 the National Democratic Party would refuse to seat any state delegation that practiced discrimination. Although some black leaders such as King and Roy Wilkins favored the compromise as a symbolic victory, the MFDP rejected it. Jaded but not defeated, the group returned to Mississippi.

Freedom Summer was important because it led to the creation of the MFDP. The civil rights movement reached a new level of success in voter registration. But the political maneuverings of the Democrats in Atlantic City alienated many in SNCC, some of whom moved in a radical direction that would become identified with black power. Many other Freedom Summer volunteers became activists for free speech, the women's movement, and demonstrated against the Vietnam War. In 1968, the MFDP was seated at the Democratic National Convention in Chicago with Fannie Lou Hamer as a delegate.

Selma and the Voting Rights Act of 1965

The civil rights movement achieved international recognition when Martin Luther King was awarded the Nobel Peace Prize in Oslo, Norway, in 1964. Shortly after that, King spoke to blacks in Selma, Alabama, about using their right to vote to send representatives to the statehouse who would uphold equal justice for all, replacing those who stood in the doorways of universities to keep people out. In 1963 George Wallace personified Southern resistance. His schoolhouse stand to prevent blacks from enrolling and his slogan "Segregation now, segregation tomorrow, and segregation forever" appealed to the Southern white uneasiness with civil rights. The Wallace appeal was especially dangerous to the movement because it sent a message to violent groups, such as the Ku Klux Klan, that they had the support of Alabama's state government. The media captured the contrast between Nobel Peace prizewinner King and the sharp resistant tone of Wallace.

More than half of Dallas County, Alabama, where Selma is located, was black but less than one percent of the black citizens were registered to vote. For over a year, SNCC had worked unsuccessfully to register black voters. Selma's Sheriff James Clark had a history of resisting integration efforts by intimidation and harassment tactics. In 1963 he allowed whites to attack blacks trying to integrate lunch counters. Then he arrested the demonstrators for trespassing. In January 1965, SCLC began a campaign of daily marches to the courthouse. When one of the demonstrators, Amelia Boynton, chose not to move from the courthouse although ordered to do so by Sheriff Clark, he grabbed her by the coat and shoved her. The next morning newspapers around the country carried photographs of Clark's strong-arm tactics. Later that week, one hundred of Selma's black, middle-class teachers marched in protest of Boynton's treatment and arrest. Risking their jobs, the courageous Selma teachers' march inspired reluctant blacks to join the demonstrations and encouraged others to join the effort to register to vote. The following Monday, hundreds of demonstrators, including King, were arrested. The media covered the events, and President Johnson called a nationally televised press conference proclaiming that all Americans have the right to vote.

Police brutality in the nearby town of Marion became front-page news. State troopers and local police along with other angry whites attacked blacks leaving a church after a rally. Dozens were beaten and two blacks were killed.

Frustrated in their attempts to register voters, SCLC leader James Bevel proposed a march to Montgomery, the state capital, to make their case directly to Wallace. The 50-mile march along Route 80 to Montgomery was to take place on Sunday, March 7, now known as Bloody Sunday. Governor George Wallace signed an order to prevent the march and Alabama state troopers attacked the peaceful marchers at the Edmund Pettus Bridge. Networks interrupted their regular programming to broadcast vivid, live footage to millions of Americans. So shocking was the sight of troopers beating civilians that the national public became enraged. Later that week another attempt at a march, this time led by King, was turned around by King to avoid another violent conflict. Pressure continued to mount when a sympathetic white Unitarian minister, James Reeb, was beaten to death.

Federal Judge Frank Johnson ruled that SCLC had a legal and constitutional right to march from Selma to Montgomery. In response Governor Wallace announced that the state of Alabama could not protect the marchers or guarantee their safety. Asserting his support, President Johnson federalized the Alabama National Guard and sent FBI agents, federal troops, and federal marshals to protect the marchers. Finally, the march began on Sunday, March 21. National television recorded the drama. For the next five days the Selma-to-Montgomery march was front-page news in the United States and the world. (The photograph on the cover of this book is of the marchers along Route 80 walking to Montgomery.) The media captured the incredible symbolism of the end of the march: civil rights marchers carrying American flags arriving at the state capital with its Confederate flag flying overhead.

The night the march ended, Viola Liuzzo, a white housewife from Michigan, attempted to drive black marchers back to Selma. The Ku Klux Klan shot her dead. Once again, the nation was shocked and more insistent that Congress pass the Voting Rights Act.

After passing the Civil Rights Act of 1964, President Lyndon Johnson continued to support civil rights by calling for the passage of new federal legislation to secure the voting rights of blacks. In the wake of the brutal events of Selma in 1965 Johnson pleaded with the nation for voting rights for blacks and an end to racism. Seen and heard by approximately 70 million Americans, Johnson's speech (Reading 4.7) adopted the civil rights slogan, "We shall overcome." Soon afterwards The Voting Rights Act of 1965 was passed. The act, which closed loopholes in the 1964 measure, abolished all remaining deterrents to exercising the right to vote. Further, it authorized federal supervision of voter registration where necessary. By taking registration out of the hands of local segregationists and putting it in the hands of federal officials, Johnson was able to ensure that blacks would be able to register to vote. This was a major victory for the movement. Racial justice was now a national priority, supported by the majority of Americans both black and white and backed by the federal government. Johnson called the act "one of the most monumental laws in the entire history of American freedom" when he signed it into law in August 1965.

Southern Reaction to the Mass Movement

*Student Activism
and the
Emergence of
a Mass
Movement,
1960–1965*

When a Trailways bus carrying the Freedom Riders arrived in Birmingham on Mother's Day in 1961, local thugs beat some riders. There was no local police protection. Birmingham's police commissioner, "Bull" Connor, told the local Ku Klux Klan that he would allow them about 15 minutes to attack the riders, and Alabama governor John Patterson advised the Freedom Riders to leave the state as quickly as possible. This incident was typical of the reaction to civil rights activities, where incidents of violence along with clever local political and legal maneuvering worked hand in hand to maintain segregation. Governor George Wallace continued this tradition of Southern racism by promoting resistance to change. Between 1963 and 1966, 12 people died in his state in civil rights slayings. Wallace went on to run for president in 1968 advocating, "states' rights," a code phrase for segregation.

In 1962, when James Meredith tried to integrate the University of Mississippi at Oxford, riots and opposition protests broke out. Southern resistance was quelled by the use of federal troops, a practice that became a common formula for civil rights activities in the South. The resistance to desegregation was widespread and often included local political and police authorities. The Ku Klux Klan was on the rise and White Citizens Councils planned resistance to desegregation.

Opposition to the movement was not limited to politics and people in the South. Douglas Blackmon, in "Silent Partner: How the South's Fight to Uphold Segregation Was Funded Up North" (Reading 4.8), demonstrates the financial path used by a New York millionaire, Wickliffe Preston Draper, to contribute large sums of money to the Mississippi State Sovereignty Commission, an agency created to fight the civil rights movement. The 1964 Republican presidential candidate, Senator Barry Goldwater of Arizona, claimed to be in favor of civil rights but in the Senate he voted against the Civil Rights Act. Although he did not hold public office at the time, Ronald Reagan was opposed to both the Civil Rights Act of 1964 and the Voting Rights Act of 1965.

Conclusion

Student activism of the early sixties energized and propelled the civil rights movement. Coalitions of civil rights organizations worked toward the common goal of desegregation whether the objective was voter registration or equal access to public facilities. Indeed, there was conflict between SNCC and the other, older rights organizations. Despite the SNCC belief that, "if we leave it to the adults, nothing will happen," the black community supported the students. SNCC worked to pressure mainstream Democratic Party politics in Mississippi, establishing a political party. SNCC volunteers labored in Selma to register blacks to vote before SCLC and other groups became involved. The march from Selma to Montgomery became a symbol of a successful civil rights campaign. It reflected the triumphs of the decade, especially the right to vote and access to public facilities. The coalition, which carried the movement through those years of change (1960–65), did not, however, last.

Often lost in the dramatic details of events and activities captured by the media is the long perspective or a more comprehensive analysis of movement. Constitutional giants like Thurgood Marshall (Reading 2.5) and Charles Hamilton

Houston (Reading 2.4), who established the NAACP legal program, created the legal means for change. A. Philip Randolph (Reading 1.5), the acknowledged "dean" of the movement, convinced Franklin Roosevelt to create the Fair Employment Practice Commission in 1941. The critical role of women in the black Baptist church (Reading 2.2) is sometimes lost in the media preoccupation with black "leaders." Finally, with the focus of study on key civil rights sites there is a tendency to overlook the struggle of hundreds of local civil rights groups contributing out of the limelight to the same goal of equality. The resulting broad-based support to ensure constitutional rights made the civil rights movement successful in the early years of the sixties.

Key Terms, Figures, and Concepts

The Albany Movement
Marian Anderson
direct action
freedom riders
McCartheyism

Mississippi Freedom Democratic Party (MFDP)
Mississippi State Sovereignty Commission
The Pioneer Fund
sit-in
Voting Rights Act of 1965

Important Questions to Consider

1. Was integration sufficient to deal with the problems of segregation faced by blacks? What other social issues were parts of the struggle for civil rights?

2. How was the strategy to integrate interstate bus transportation different from prior integration strategy?

3. What were the factors that enabled Martin Luther King and Project C to be successful in Birmingham in 1963? How and why did riots take place?

4. Explore the issue of nonviolence in Albany, Georgia, and Birmingham, Alabama.

5. What roles did white supporters play during the sit-ins, freedom rides, and voter registration drives?

Political Mama

Joanne Grant, a former member of the Student Nonviolent Coordinating Committee (SNCC), was a close associate of Ella Baker. She began her career in civil rights as assistant to W. E. B. Du Bois. She is author of Ella Baker: Freedom Bound *and producer of* Fundi: The Story of Ella Baker.

The chief emphasis I tried to make was their right to make their own decision. . . . The only reason that I became relevant . . . was because I had lived through certain experiences and had had certain opportunities to gather information and organizational experience. . . . I have always felt that if there is any time in our existence that you have a right to make mistakes it should be when you're young, cause you have some time to live down some of the mistakes, or to offset them. I felt that what they [the students] were doing was certainly . . . creative [and] much more productive than anything that had happened in my life, and it shouldn't be stifled. . . . I must have sensed also that it was useless to try to put the brakes on, because it was unleashed enthusiasm . . . an overflow of a dam that had been penned up for years, and it had to run its course.

JJust as Rosa Parks decided one day that she was not going to move to the back of the bus, the four North Carolina students who sat down at a whites-only Woolworth's lunch counter on February 1, 1960, also decided not to move. Thus began the new challenge to the system of legally supported racial segregation that had been in existence for decades. To Ella Baker it was a dream come true. Here was the beginning of the civil rights revolution which she had looked forward to since the days of the 1930s when she had ventured from neighborhood to neighborhood listening to speeches that carried the promise of change.

Within days the sit-ins spread across the South—where segregation was not simply custom, but the law—through North Carolina, to Maryland, Tennessee, Virginia, Alabama, Georgia, Kentucky, and South Carolina. Hundreds of students were arrested. They were taunted with racial epithets and often attacked by mobs of angry whites.

This upsurge was what Ella Baker had been waiting for. She received a call from an excited SCLC board member, Fred L. Shuttlesworth, who said that she must inform Martin of the amazing new development. Immediately grasping the momentousness of the event, she dutifully informed King and promptly set about the task of organizing this potential force into a cohesive one. She began to plan for a gathering of representatives from the protest areas, convincing the SCLC to put up $800 to cover the expenses of the meeting. She persuaded King to sign a call to "chart new goals and achieve a more unified sense of direction for training and action in Nonviolent Resistance." To supplement the sit-in meeting that was scheduled for Easter weekend, April 15 to 17, in Raleigh, North Carolina, SCLC also planned nonviolence training for young people at three locations in the spring: Nashville, Mobile, and Shreveport.

Baker rushed out a follow-up letter to protesting students. Citing the courageous, dedicated, and thoughtful leadership manifested by the hundreds of Negro students who presented new challenges for the future, she urged that the "great potential for social change" called for a determination of the question, Where do we go from here?

In preparation for the April meeting Baker went to Raleigh and reached an agreement with Shaw University on meeting rooms, meals, and accommodations. Since Shaw could only house about forty people, Baker contacted nearby St. Augustine College, the YMCA, and local residents whom she had met as a student there and during her travels for the NAACP. Baker arranged to stay with a Shaw alumna who had been in the class behind her, Effie Yeargan, a distant cousin of Max Yergin, a radical theorist whom Baker had met during her Shaw days and whom she had encountered again during her early days in Harlem. Yeargan was one of the founders of the Raleigh Citizens Association, which was organized to host the students, cosponsor the gathering, and provide whatever subsidiary housing was necessary.

Having taken care of the logistics, Baker then went on to deal with policy. She began to press the issue of the independence of the students, which was to be the most important question at the meeting. In a memo to King and Abernathy, she eased into her agenda by remarking that on a trip to Raleigh-Durham she had had a chance meeting with Glenn Smiley of the **Fellowship of Reconciliation [FOR]** and Douglas Moore, a young Durham minister. She pointed out that they "agreed that the meeting should be youth centered and that the adults attending would serve in an advisory capacity, and should mutually agree to 'speak only when asked to do so.' " This was to become the central issue at the meeting, yet Baker's concerns were broader: She wanted an organization to develop.

She wrote Anne Braden, the codirector of the Southern Conference Educational Fund (SCEF), expressing the hope that "out of this meeting will come some workable machinery for maintaining affective [*sic*] communication between youth leaders in areas of recent and future protest activities, and a larger degree of coordinated strategy." She added that she hoped that "several work-teams of young persons can be financed for work in the South this summer. The need for developing more experienced young workers in the field of civil rights is obvious, I am sure. This may be only a dream of mine, but I think it can be made real."

Determined to make the meeting a success, Baker set about the task of identifying the leaders of the various demonstrations. She scanned newspaper accounts, contacted people with whom she had worked, and wrote to heads of student bodies. She dispatched Reverend Moore on a tour of North Carolina and Virginia to urge demonstrators to send a representative. Lawson and CORE also contacted activists. In the end over two hundred delegates attended the Raleigh meeting, as well as observers from such organizations as FOR, CORE, the **American Friends Service Committee**, the National Student Association, and the YWCA. Nineteen schools and colleges from the North were represented. Baker said that while the conference

292

*Student
Activism
and the Emergence
of a Mass
Movement,
1960–1965*

was too large to be a leadership training workshop, it became "a mountaintop experience of enthusiasm."

Though the meeting was an exciting and productive one, there were problems. At the start a conflict arose over who would preside at the opening session. Baker suggested James Lawson, FOR's Southern regional secretary, who had recently been expelled from Vanderbilt University for his sit-in activities. Lawson was a leading advocate of nonviolence and had been training Nashville students in nonviolent techniques. King and Abernathy wanted Baker to open the conference, but she argued for Lawson, pointing out that he was closer in age to the students and that she was not "an advocate of nonviolence in the true sense." Baker prevailed. Her next contretemps was with the press, which she insisted be excluded from some sessions. She had, as she put it, "quite a run-in" with the reporters, but on this issue, too, she prevailed.

Soon thereafter, the major conflict came into play. This was the controversy that Baker had anticipated and had tried to prepare King for in her March memo. At issue was the question of the students' independence: Should the students set up a separate organization or become affiliated with an existing one? The leading contenders for the role of adult sponsor were SCLC and CORE. On Saturday morning Baker was summoned to a caucus. Present were King; his second in command, Ralph Abernathy; Wyatt Tee Walker, soon to become Baker's successor as director of the SCLC; and Lawrence Reddick, the SCLC historian.

The adult leaders did not seem to know where the conference was heading, so they asked Baker, who seemed to have more influence with the delegates than they did. She said that it was too soon to predict the outcome, but that it was more important to establish a temporary continuations committee "to permit the students to find their own sense of direction."

It soon became clear what the real purpose of the caucus was: to find out from her what the students might do—or more precisely, to figure out a way to coerce the students into becoming the youth arm of the SCLC. When the meeting participants began to divide up the delegations that each one would lobby, Baker dug in her heels, stating that she would have no part in dragooning delegations. Walker proposed in his calm, ministerial way that he could take care of Virginia. "Martin said he could talk to the Atlanta group and that he thought that Ralph [Abernathy] should take care of Alabama."

So Baker walked out of the caucus. She was furious at the temper of the discussion and outraged by the ministers' plans to manipulate the students. The sit-ins were, to her, the beginning of a new approach in the fight for equality. She did not want to see it coopted, corrupted, or changed. She felt that the students had something new to offer and to make the student movement a youth arm of an adult organization was a mistake. The adults had no understanding of the young people's vision. The young people were daring. They had something new to contribute. Up to now there had been no rebellion to match what had taken place after the first sit-in. She did not want this outpouring to be stifled.

Baker's departure signaled the beginning of a new phase for the civil rights movement. It was no longer to be controlled by a stodgy ministerial or bureaucratic presence. It was to be led by a new force.

The plenary session that followed was volatile. It became so tense that they resorted to, in Baker's words, "the old soothing syrup" of "We Shall Overcome" to cool things down. Angry as she was over the plan to manipulate the students, she did nothing to prevent the maneuvering to secure votes in favor of affiliation—although she did speak out in the sessions for the young people's right to make their own decisions.

It could be claimed that SCLC had some grounds for seeking to adopt the young people. After all, it was SCLC money that had made the conference possible. It was the method of co-optation that aggravated Baker: She did not believe in arm-twisting. She did believe in the students, and in their promise.

It is doubtful that King exerted pressure on the students to affiliate with SCLC, but Ella Baker's stance was clear: Hope lay with the students. For her there was no illusion about what the ministers of SCLC could accomplish toward her goal of the development of a mass organization.

Charles McDew, an Orangeburg, South Carolina, student who was later to become SNCC chairman, said that Baker lobbied the students individually and advocated—at a closed meeting the students held without observers or other adults—the creation of an independent organization. At the meeting's end the students had established the Temporary Student Nonviolent Coordinating Committee, made plans for continuations committee meetings, and adopted a statement of purpose, drafted by Lawson, that incorporated the principle of nonviolence, which "nurtures the atmosphere in which reconciliation and justice become actual possibilities."

> We affirm the philosophical or religious ideal of nonviolence as the foundation of our purpose, the presupposition of our faith, and the manner of our action. Nonviolence as it grows from Judaic-Christian traditions seeks a social order of justice permeated by love. Integration of human endeavor represents the crucial first step towards such a society.
>
> Through nonviolence, courage displaces fear; love transforms hate. Acceptance dissipates prejudice; hope ends despair. Peace dominates war; faith reconciles doubt. Mutual regard cancels enmity. Justice for all overthrows injustice. The redemptive community supersedes systems of gross social immorality.
>
> Love is the central motif of nonviolence. Love is the force by which God binds man to Himself and man to man. Such love goes to the extreme; it remains loving and forgiving even in the midst of hostility. It matches the capacity of evil to inflict suffering with an even more enduring capacity to absorb evil, all the while persisting in love.
>
> By appealing to conscience and standing on the moral nature of human existence, nonviolence nurtures the atmosphere in which reconciliation and justice become actual possibilities.

At the mass meeting on Saturday night King delivered the main address and Baker spoke on the significance of the conference, sounding the theme with which she became identified. The lunch counter sit-ins were about larger issues, she said; they were "bigger than a hamburger."

At the first meeting of the continuations committee in May 1960, Marion Barry, a Fisk University student who had participated in Lawson's nonviolent training sessions and in the Nashville sit-ins, was elected chair. By then the protest movement had spread across the South. There were hundreds of arrests, and violent confrontations had occurred in several cities. One of the reasons for the rapid spread of the demonstrations was the press attention they received, though Baker also felt that word of mouth was the strongest impetus: "A sister to a brother,

294

*Student
Activism
and the Emergence
of a Mass
Movement,
1960–1965*

members of the same fraternity, girlfriend to boyfriend, or simply calling up contracts, friends asking, 'What is happening on your campus?' " More importantly, the actions "were getting results."

Baker felt strongly that the liberation movements in Africa and other parts of the world spurred on the U.S. civil rights movement. One of the most significant influences was the Sharpeville massacre on March 21, 1960. South African police fired into a crowd of eight thousand blacks who were staging a peaceful march; 69 people were killed and 180 were wounded. Here at home the failure to implement the 1954 *Brown* decision and the ineffectiveness of the Civil Rights Act of 1957 led to rising disappointment and "the developing climate of alienation of the young from the Establishment." She also pointed to the "additional impact on black youngsters of the rising independence of black people in Africa and other parts of the world."

Baker had arranged for office space for the coordinating committee in a spare room at SCLC headquarters at 208 Auburn Avenue, and she got Jane Stembridge, a Union Theological Seminary student, to become the administrator. (They soon had to move out of the SCLC space, but Baker cajoled the landlord into renting them a tiny office across the street at a reduced rent.) Throughout this formative period SCLC lent its support to the fledgling organization. King and Baker attended all the meetings, and SCLC gave encouragement as well as some financial aid.

During these early days some of Atlanta's "liberal" community criticized Baker for failing to keep the students sufficiently in check. Baker, however, felt that the students didn't need adult supervision, that "they had the right to make mistakes when they were young." Besides, she was exhilarated by the movement. To her it was "more productive than anything that had happened in [her] life." She felt strongly that it "shouldn't be stifled" and sensed, as others did not, that "it was useless to put the brakes on, because it was enthusiasm unleashed—an overflow of a dam that had been penned up for years and it had to run its course." Those who wanted to impose rules on the students wouldn't get anywhere because they simply could not communicate with them.

Nashville sit-in leader John Lewis noted that although Baker was much older than the students, "in terms of ideas and philosophy and commitment she was one of the youngest persons in the movement." SNCC worker Judy Richardson extended this judgment in an interview in 1993: "What was nice about Miss Baker is you never felt that she had a personal agenda that she was trying to put on. It was always about what is good for the organization, for black people, for whatever the larger issue was. [With] other adults you never really knew what else was hidden . . . what else they were trying to get through that they weren't talking about."

In May, after the founding meeting of the Temporary Student Nonviolent Coordinating Committee, Baker organized a meeting in the chapel of Morris Brown College. Kenneth Kaunda, a leader of what was then known as Northern Rhodesia (Zambia), spoke, primarily to the students but also to some adults who had participated in the student movement. Then Baker addressed a workshop at **Highlander Folk School** on "The Place of the White Southerner in the Current Struggle," speaking on "What Can Be Done That Hasn't Been Done?" This meeting was one of the few at which Baker appeared in "movement attire," abandoning her neat business suit for trousers and a sleeveless blouse.

In the midst of helping the students set up the coordinating group, she was organizing the second State-wide Institute on Non-Violent Resistance to Segregation and preparing for her departure from SCLC on August 1, 1960. And as if this was not enough to occupy her, she was also soliciting clothing for the people of Fayette and Haywood counties in Tennessee who were being severely harassed for attempting to register to vote. Many had been evicted from plantations and were living in a tent city.

At the end of July Baker wrote to her many contacts in the South informing them of her impending departure from SCLC, saying: "My successor, the Reverend Wyatt Tee Walker, is a young man of vision, and I am confident that with him the program of the Conference will expand to meet the challenges that we face in the months and years ahead." She credited the demonstrating students for the inclusion of civil rights planks in both the Democratic and Republican party platforms. Baker had promoted the idea that the coordinating committee should send a delegation to each of the party conventions and had helped draft their testimony. She pointed out, however, that "planks and promises are only good when they are followed by action. That is why we must increase our determination to get all of our families, friends, and neighbors registered."

Then, as she so often did, she quoted from the Bible: "Now is our salvation nearer than when we first believed. Therefore, we must cast off the works of darkness and put on the armour of light." She continued: "The 'works of darkness' are ignorance, doubt and fear; but armed with truth and knowledge, faith and courage, we can and must follow the light of freedom to complete and certain victory." At the end she offered a small prayer: "May God grant you good health and increased courage to continue the fight for human justice and freedom for all mankind." There were also personal touches in the letter: she wrote that she cherished the fellowship shared and the cooperation received and spoke of her need for rest and a cataract operation, gave her New York address, and invited the addressees to visit her if in New York in August or September. After that, she assured them, she expected to be back in the Southern struggle.

By this time, Robert Moses, who was to become one of the movement's most respected leaders, had arrived in Atlanta as an SCLC volunteer. A math teacher at Horace Mann High School in New York, he had been a volunteer in the Friends of SCLC office there, the brainchild of Rustin and Levison. Baker had not been apprised of Moses's impending arrival and no one had prepared work for him to do. Consequently, after a talk with Baker he began working in the SNCC office, where he became friends with Stembridge—perhaps in part because of their common bond as philosophy students. Moses credited Ella Baker and Jane Stembridge with getting him out of SCLC and into SNCC. "They knew I was disgruntled and gave me a way out," Moses said.

Baker soon sent Moses off on a tour of Mississippi, Louisiana, and Alabama to convince demonstrators in protest areas to send delegates to the founding conference of SNCC, which was to be held at Atlanta University on October 14–15, 1960. Baker had returned to Atlanta from a trip to New York, where she had attended Jackie's [Jacqueline Brockington, Ella Baker's niece] wedding, to help the students prepare. There were few reporters present (myself among them), but the conference was a joyous occasion. When the delegates from Mississippi came in, they were greeted with a standing ovation. Mississippi was the toughest state, and the students from other areas, already battle-scarred, were paying tribute to the courage of the participants on the newest front.

The conference adopted the statement of purpose that had come out of the Raleigh meeting, dropped "temporary" from the name of the organization, formal-

296

*Student
Activism
and the Emergence
of a Mass
Movement,
1960–1965*

ized its relationship to the protest areas (meaning the places where sit-ins had taken place), and voted to publish the *Student Voice* monthly. SNCC (pronounced "Snick") was to be made up of one representative from each of sixteen states plus the District of Columbia. In addition, there was to be a staff made up of field secretaries and an expanded office staff. The constitution proclaimed: "SNCC shall serve as a channel of coordination and communication for the student movement. By direction of its Executive Committee through its staff it shall have authority to initiate programs in areas where none presently exists, and to work closely with local protest groups in the intensification of the movement." In the formulation of the constitution it was decided to omit the phrase "in the South" from this paragraph, though SNCC remained a Southern-based movement. The constitution provided for voting members from other organizations, one representative each from the National Student Association, the National Student Christian Movement, and the National College and Youth Branch of the NAACP. There were to be observers from the American Friends Service Committee, American Civil Liberties Union, CORE, FOR, NAACP, SCLC, SCEF, National Student YWCA, the Southern Regional Council, and "any other group to be selected by the Student Nonviolent Coordinating Committee."

Drawn by the excitement the movement engendered, many of these observers soon became SNCC staffers. Almost anyone who had contact with the rebelling students wanted to join in some way. Some promptly signed on for the duration at the going salary, $10.99 a week. Others went back North and joined support groups.

In the fluid days of the early 1960s, SNCC's structure was altered often. SNCC meetings were round-the-clock discussions of the organization's shape and function. Baker would sit in silence for much of the time, more often than not wearing a cotton face mask to protect her against the cigarette smoke. Like her mother, she suffered from respiratory troubles.

In these marathon meetings Baker used her old technique of asking questions. "I was not too sure that I had the answer," she recalled later. But often, her questions directed the discussions. Her technique was much like that of Nelson Mandela, who had learned it from his mentor, a tribal chieftain. Mandela wrote in his autobiography, *Long Walk to Freedom,* "I have always endeavored to listen to what each and every person in a discussion had to say before venturing my own opinion. Oftentimes, my own opinion will simply represent a consensus of what I heard in the discussion." Mandela always remembered the chieftain's axiom that a leader is like a shepherd: "He stays behind the flock, letting the most nimble go out ahead, whereupon the others follow, not realizing that all along they are being directed from behind." This was, indeed, Baker's way.

Baker was a listener. Her practice was to hear everyone out and to accept ideas from even the youngest in the group—"if it was a good idea." She taught the young people in SNCC that everyone had something to give, thus helping them learn to respect each other. SNCC chair Charles McDew recalled that she would pick out a kernel that was a good idea. "Somebody may have spoken for 8 hours, and 7 hours and 53 minutes was utter bullshit, but 7 minutes was good. She taught us to glean out the 7 minutes."

This was a different way of working. Many adults tried telling the students how to behave, citing greater experience and knowledge, but this, Baker said, could not work for several reasons. In the first place, the young people were confident that there was something new about their movement, that it was innovative and successful to a far greater extent, achieving results more rapidly than earlier attempts had done. Then, too, Baker felt that the students were exhilarated by the speed with which their movement had grown. In a sense, they were leading the adults. She was convinced that despite King's growing prominence as a spokesman, SNCC was providing the cutting edge.

Baker's prescience was confirmed early in 1961 by two significant events: SNCC's move into the rural areas of Mississippi and the advent of the Freedom Rides.

At the urging of Baker, Bob Moses had made a second swing through Mississippi in 1961. There, at Baker's suggestion, he met with veteran activist Amzie Moore, whom Baker had known for several years. Inspired by Moore and C. S. Bryant in McComb, Moses laid out a plan for voter registration.

Taking two field secretaries with him, he set up headquarters in McComb, one of the poorest parts of the state. The group began working on voter registration. Their efforts soon drew national attention because of the violent reactions they encountered.

In the meantime CORE had started the Freedom Rides. Integrated groups of students, ministers, and priests boarded interstate buses to ride from Washington, D.C., to New Orleans with an intent to seek service in terminals along the route. In Alabama they were met by violent mobs. In Anniston, their bus was burned. In Birmingham, a white mob gathered and they were beaten as they disembarked; there were no police in sight. In Montgomery, law enforcement officers stood by idly, looking on as the riders were brutally beaten.

Attorney General Robert Kennedy called for a "cooling-off period," pressuring the students to stop the rides and focus on voter registration for the duration of a round of negotiations with bus company officials and local government representatives. So serious was the effort that draft deferments were offered to SNCC workers in exchange for concentrating on the vote. Largely through the attorney general's efforts, the Taconic and Field foundations and the Stern Family Fund provided money to the Southern Regional Council, which set up a tax-exempt arm, the Voter Education Project (VEP). Headed by Wiley Branton, a lawyer from Greenwood, Mississippi, VEP made grants to voter registration efforts, distributing over half a million dollars. SNCC received only $24,000 in 1962 and 1963.

The voter registration work led to the first major controversy in SNCC. The disagreement was over whether the organization should devote itself exclusively to direct action or to voter registration. This was the most serious of the organization's conflicts because it nearly caused a split—averted only by Baker's intervention. She was not about to watch her baby, her pride and joy, be destroyed by a doctrinal dispute. During a heated discussion at a meeting at the Highlander Center, Baker abandoned her custom of sitting on the sidelines and took an active part. She pointed out that direct action was a necessary adjunct to voter registration because the resistance to Negro voting attempts would be so strong that it would lead to protest demonstrations. They could do both, she said, and this essentially resolved the issue. SNCC proceeded to set up two sections, with Diane Nash, a Fisk student and a devoted adherent of Gandhian nonviolence, heading up direct action and Charles Jones, a young minister from Charlotte, North Carolina, as director of voter registration. As Baker observed later, however, "it became obvious there was no irreconcilable difference between the two tactics." Soon Jones and Nash would themselves decide that there was no need for the two posts.

298

*Student
Activism
and the Emergence
of a Mass
Movement,
1960–1965*

By now SNCC felt the need for a strong executive secretary. The field secretaries voiced a need for someone to take charge, to give direction and hold the organization together. It was clear, however, that they did not want anyone to tell them what to do, to boss them around or cramp their style. Because they were confident that she had no interest in becoming a "Supreme Leader," they asked Baker to take the job. She declined, saying that she believed the post should be held by a younger person. Diane Nash and the direct action group urged James Forman to accept. He agreed, though somewhat reluctantly; he had come South to get into the action and did not look forward to an administrative job. Forman was from Chicago, but he had spent some years and many summers on his grandmother's farm in Mississippi. He was teaching in Chicago when the movement called him first to Fayette County, Tennessee, and then, in August 1961, to Monroe, North Carolina, where the national spotlight was turned on Robert F. Williams, a proponent of desegregation and of armed self-defense. Williams had been charged with kidnapping a white couple. He maintained that he was concerned about their safety and had offered them shelter when they drove into the black part of town during a period of high tension.

Baker, too, had been drawn to the Monroe confrontation. Here was a standoff between a black militant and the white power structure. The situation would appeal to any person who thought that the individual had a right to stand up and fight. Baker, however, did not go during the height of the crisis, when Monroe was swarming with representatives of the news media. As usual, she held back, waiting until she felt she could do useful work, after the headline-makers had departed. "Usually you need people [later]," she said, "and not too many people go when the point of high focus has passed."

She did visit in August 1962, to be of comfort to a woman whose only son had drowned. The kidnapping trial had been postponed, but Baker made the overnight trip because, as she wrote to Anne Braden, "there are some other developments which bear looking into." But her primary reason for going was because she felt the woman "ought to have somebody to be concerned. That was all."

Forman arrived at SNCC at a crucial time. He was able to reconcile opposing forces by applying his gruff assessment that whatever was happening in local areas (known as "the field") was more important than whatever squabbles were taking place in the home office. He was able to maintain a sense of balance; in this he was in tune with Baker's drive to keep the organization focused.

If Baker was the mother of SNCC, Forman was the dad. Both were transplanted Northerners with Southern roots. Forman, though not close to Baker in age, was older than the other SNCC members, and both were forceful personalities. While Forman says of her in his book, *The Making of Black Revolutionaries:* "without her there would be no story of the Student Nonviolent Coordinating Committee," there was a subtle undercurrent of friction between them.

Yet in an interview in 1968 Baker praised Forman as "the guy who made [SNCC] into an organization . . . a fighting force." She said that he "had a sensitivity about people that almost amounted to his playing a father role." The students "felt he was young enough for them to relate to, and yet, at the same time to combine that sense of comradeship with a father image."

Forman wielded enormous influence and did much to shape SNCC as it grew and changed. From the moment he stepped into the tiny SNCC office at 197½ Auburn Avenue until the day SNCC withered away, Forman was a formidable presence. While Baker and Forman agreed on many fundamental issues, their relationship was an ambivalent one. They agreed on the need for SNCC to be an organization with a structure; they disagreed on how to achieve this. Some of their differences stemmed from their ways of working. Baker, the elder stateswoman, would sit quietly in meetings without a word—sometimes for hours—breaking her silence with a meaningful question or pronouncement. Forman, on the other hand, would take charge immediately, making his proposals at the outset. Forman's proposals were often too grandiose for Baker's taste—like the 1965 purchase of a building for SNCC headquarters and a printing press. Baker was skeptical, too, of the ties to the Black Panthers that Forman and Stokely Carmichael pushed.

They did agree on the basic thrust of SNCC, the emphasis on developing the grass roots—although Forman did not have quite the same degree of confidence in the abilities of local leadership as Baker. But that may be too rash a judgment: perhaps Forman was just a man in a hurry. Certainly, he was less patient than Baker, who had been in the struggle so long. Baker, for her part, tried to adjust her goals to the timetable that Forman lived by. She respected his intensity, his revolutionary fervor, and his genius for organization; she simply wished that he would slow down.

They both felt that given SNCC's impetus it might be possible to build a revolutionary movement. Forman had a concept of building local organizational "cells" that would expand in concentric circles into a revolutionary force. Baker expressed somewhat the same idea to John Britton in 1968. Almost as an aside she referred to the Communist Party and "its cell groupings," commenting, "I don't think we had any more effective demonstration of organizing people for whatever purpose. . . . But the idea of getting small groups of people together, understanding what they wanted them to understand, and getting them organized for that—this is a good pattern."

Baker agreed with Forman on the need to push the federal government for more action on civil rights, yet she probably would not have gone as far as he did. She backed SNCC's sit-in at the U.S. Department of Justice in protest of its inaction, and she was amused and somewhat admiring of Forman's rebuff to the powers on high. (When told that the White House was calling, Forman invariably would say, "Tell them I'm not in.")

Many conflicts arose in SNCC. Baker calmly sat through the long and heated debates, only intervening at crucial moments to help bring about a resolution. One such issue was the extent of participation in SNCC by Northerners. It was obvious to many Southern students, even as early as the April meeting in Raleigh, that Northern students were more politically sophisticated, more skilled verbally. To the Southern students they seemed to be "taking over," so from the beginning it was decided that SNCC should be a Southern-based, Southern-run organization. Yet, the problem of Northern participation kept coming up, reaching its peak in 1964, when the question of recruiting hundreds of volunteers from around the country for Mississippi Summer was under consideration.

One other debate was almost a constant: organizational structure. As always, Baker felt that an organization should have regular procedures, a clear idea of who was responsible for what and to whom: in other words, a chain of command. On this point she and Forman were united. By September 1961, Forman was executive secretary, succeeding Ed King. Convinced that King was not up to the job, Baker had persuaded him to return to college. (There was clearly a pragmatic side to

300

*Student
Activism
and the Emergence
of a Mass
Movement,
1960–1965*

Baker's nature, but it was tempered by her concern for the individual's well-being, as in this case: Push him out, but do it gently. Baker arranged for scholarship funds for King and maintained a correspondence with him over the next few years, cheering him on and forwarding money when it was needed. She had a genuine interest in helping him achieve his potential. By helping King further his studies, she helped him to grow.)

SNCC changed its structure often, partly in response to the growth of the movement, partly in response to changes in the movement's goals and direction. Between 1960 and 1965, SNCC's staff grew from sixteen to well over two hundred and its budget went from nearly nothing to over a million dollars. Such growth necessitated a change in structure to prevent chaos. By 1963, for instance, SNCC operated a fleet of about a hundred cars. Named the Sojourner Truth Motor Fleet, it had to be supervised; someone had to know where each car was, how long its lease would run, what its state of repair was. In sum, myriad details had to be handled. And this was only one of many items that cried out for a line of command.

In addition, since SNCC was based on local movements, it had to adapt quickly to changing conditions in each area. A wide range of issues had to be dealt with. Even as the fight for equal access to public accommodations (kneel-ins at churches, wade-ins at swimming pools, sleep-ins in hotel lobbies) was in motion, SNCC was already sponsoring a Christmas boycott of Atlanta stores and a struggle for black employment in Nashville and elsewhere. While there was some discernible progression from one phase of the movement to another, in actuality many forms of struggle were in progress simultaneously.

As the movement evolved, Baker's influence as a mentor was evident. Her professed aversion to the teaching profession did not prevent her from becoming a teacher—not in a formal sense, but there was no way that she could avoid this calling since she was intent on developing new leaders from among the local populace wherever she might find herself. Throughout her career she had seen that there were local people who were unhappy with their lot but did not know how to make changes. They had to be taught.

The designation "fundi" seemed to characterize her. *Fundi,* which I used as the film title for the documentary about her, is a Swahili word which denotes the person in a community who passes on the wisdom of the elders, the crafts, the knowledge. This is not done in an institutional way, a way which Baker would have rejected, but as an oral tradition, handed down from one generation to the next.

As SNCC developed, and the emphasis changed from civil rights to economic issues, there was always a need for education—workshops, study groups, training institutes. Many were set in motion by Baker, who felt strongly that a movement could not be based simply on oratory and action, but must be grounded in knowledge. When she worked for the NAACP, she had insisted on training, both for staff members and for local organizers, and she never let up on her drive to instill in organizers the need for facts to back up their rhetoric. She also recognized that the community needed educating, and this was the hard part. She helped to develop literature that could give the local community an understanding of the issues. Even middle-class, educated voters needed to be taught how their lives were linked with those who were less advantaged.

Baker had a profound influence on SNCC in this regard, but her impact in other areas was no less significant, as the minutes of SNCC staff meetings clearly show. For example, from the minutes of the June 9–11, 1961, meeting in Louisville,

Kentucky: "After discussion on [the Mississippi Project] by Miss Ella Baker, it was decided that the financial and personnel problems were too great for immediate summer commencement of this program. It was moved to table this matter until the July meeting."

But an even more powerful indication are the recollections of Charles McDew, the second chairman of SNCC: "I never told this to a soul. . . . Ella made me chairman. The meeting had been very long and you could tell there was this fight [for the chairmanship] going on between the forces in Atlanta and the forces in Nashville and the forces from Virginia, and Miss Baker said, 'Would you want to be chairman?' I said, no-o-o, not for love or money, and she said, 'Don't you understand [that] you're the only one here who doesn't want to be chairman?' She asked me if they were to elect me, would I be willing to be chairman, and I said, 'Well, I'll think about it.' The next day she asked if I had thought about it. She said, 'If you're interested in seeing that you all get something done, then you should be chairman. You owe it to yourself and the rest of us to be chairman.' We were clearly at an impasse because of all that maneuvering, and Miss Baker said, 'You are the only one here without a constituency. I mean if you want to help us, then you should accept being chairman.' I believe that she talked to other people, but I hadn't talked to a soul except Miss Baker, and, hell, I was convinced. I know Miss Baker made me chairman of SNCC, period." McDew served for the next two years.

McDew recalled that, as chair, he broke the tie in the vote on whether to continue with direct action or concentrate on voter registration. "That was one of the times she lobbied me. She said, 'If you go to Mississippi and see Mr. Steptoe, Mr. Turnbow, or Amzie [local leaders], you will see that you can't do voter registration without direct action.'"

Meanwhile, Harry Belafonte, an early supporter of the students, had invited sit-in leaders to meet with him in Washington in late June 1961 to discuss voter registration. Out of the meeting rose a vision of a student movement of 100,000 to 200,000, and a consensus was reached that "the voter registration project should be given top priority by SNCC while other direct action projects such as sit-ins, etc. be simultaneously steped [sic] up." In October a temporary executive committee was appointed at an SNCC staff meeting, consisting of Baker, Belafonte, McDew, Connie Curry, and two members each from the voter registration and direct action staffs. It was mandated to "work deliberately to expand and democratize the organization of SNCC, to seek the development of a functioning communications system which will clarify the nature of the movement to the country, and to provide students with stimulus and strategic information." This committee was given broad powers to define the functions of SNCC officers and staff, but it functioned only for a month. At the next staff meeting, in November, a pared-down executive committee was created. Forman had begun to establish order.

Baker's travel schedule for the summer of 1961 seemed as heavy as in her NAACP days. She went to Jackson, Mississippi, to work with Bob Moses for 5 days, then to Berkeley to attend a SLATE conference. At the beginning of August she went to Columbus, Ohio, to attend the NSA's fifth Southern Students Human Relations Seminar. From there she made a stop in Cincinnati to visit Fred Shuttlesworth's wife, Ruby, who was a great friend and had been ill. She also spent time in Raleigh, North Carolina, and Jackson, Tennessee, helping to organize voter registration campaigns.

302

*Student
Activism
and the Emergence
of a Mass
Movement,
1960–1965*

In the midst of this she was asked to become the guardian of Brenda Travis, a McComb high school student who was being held in a reform school after she had participated in voter registration demonstrations. Baker took over as her temporary guardian and arranged for her to go to summer camp in Michigan, to which she took Brenda, and boarding school in North Carolina.

In 1961, Charles Sherrod and Charles Jones went to Albany, Georgia, to do voter registration; they spent some weeks talking with the local people in preparation for the drive. Then, on November 1, 1961, the first of the Albany sit-ins took place. Nine students sat in at the bus terminal, and on December 10 a group from the Atlanta SNCC office took a "freedom ride" on the train to the Albany railroad station and were arrested. This touched off mammoth demonstrations, which increased over the next few months. The Albany Movement was formed soon after, with William G. Anderson as president and Slater King as vice president. By the time that Baker went to Albany in mid-December more than seven hundred people had been arrested. In typical fashion Baker, away from the television cameras and news reporters, was busily noting down the needs of those about to demonstrate and go to jail. The questions she was asking ranged from "Do you have a toothbrush?" to "Have you informed your parents where you are?" to "Have you thought through the question of **jail-no-bail?**"

These were for her the essentials, what in those days was called the "nitty-gritty," the guts of the issue, the core of the problem. This was what she dealt with.

4.2   **Howell Raines**

Freedom Riders

Howell Raines is author of My Soul Is Rested: Movement Days in the Deep South Remembered. *He is a news correspondent in the Washington, D.C., office of the* New York Times. *Raines interviews James Farmer, Hank Thomas, and John Lewis in the following excerpt.*

> *Yes, we are the Freedom Riders
> And we ride a long Greyhound;
> White or black, we know no difference,
> Lord, for we are Glory bound . . .*
>
>   —Southern collegiate folk song of the sixties

James Farmer

He had left CORE to become national program director of the NAACP, and he watched from the sidelines as the sit-inners practiced the direct-action techniques he had tested twenty years earlier. But he would not miss the next great wave of confrontation to sweep the South. Rejoining CORE as national director early in 1961, he started it.

I was impressed by the fact that most of the activity thus far had been of local people working on their local problems—Greensborans sitting-in in Greensboro and Atlantans sitting-in in Atlanta—and the pressure of the opposition against having outsiders come was very, very great. If any outsider came in . . . , "Get that outside agitator." . . . I thought that this was going to limit the growth of the Movement. . . . We somehow had to cut across state lines and establish the position that we were entitled to act any place in the country, no matter where we hung our hat and called home, because it was our country.

We also felt that one of the weaknesses of the student sit-in movement of the South had been that as soon as arrested, the kids bailed out. . . . This was not quite Gandhian and not the best tactic. A better tactic would be to remain in jail and to make the maintenance of segregation so expensive for the state and the city that they would hopefully come to the conclusion that they could no longer afford it. Fill up the jails, as Gandhi did in India, fill them to bursting if we had to. In other words, stay in without bail.

So those were the two things: cutting across state lines, putting the movement on wheels, so to speak, and remaining in jail, not only for its publicity value but for the financial pressure it would put upon the segregators. We decided that a good approach here would be to move away from restaurant lunch counters. That had been the Southern student sit-in movement, and anything we would do on that would be anticlimactic now. We would have to move into another area and so we decided to move into the transportation, interstate transportation. . . .

It would be necessary, he decided, to violate custom and local law to focus attention on the federal laws barring discrimination in interstate transportation. He knew that in 1946 the Supreme Court had ruled against segregated seating on interstate buses, and in 1960, against segregated terminal facilities. The rulings were uniformly ignored throughout the South.

So we, following the Gandhian technique, wrote to Washington. We wrote to the Justice Department, to the FBI, and to the President, and wrote to Greyhound Bus Company and Trailways Bus Company and told them that on May first or May fourth—whatever the date was,* I forget now—we were going to have a Freedom Ride. Blacks and whites were going to leave Washington, D.C., on Greyhound and Trailways, deliberately violating the segregated seating requirements and at each rest stop would violate the segregated use of facilities. And we would be nonviolent, absolutely nonviolent, throughout the campaign, and we would accept the consequences of our actions. This was a deliberate act of civil disobedience. . . .**

Did Justice try to head you off?

No, we got no reply. We got no reply from Justice. Bobby Kennedy, no reply. We got no reply from the FBI. We got no reply from the White House, from President Kennedy. We got no reply from Greyhound or Trailways. *We got no replies.* [Laughs]

He recruited an interracial group of thirteen and brought them to Washington for a week's training.

---

*May 4.
**Before beginning the Salt March, Gandhi sent a letter of warning to British authorities, although he did not outline the specifics of his strategy.

304

*Student
Activism
and the Emergence
of a Mass
Movement,
1960–1965*

We had some of the group of thirteen sit at a simulated counter asking for coffee. Somebody else refused them service, and then we'd have others come in as white hoodlums to beat 'em up and knock them off the counter and club 'em around and kick 'em in the ribs and stomp 'em, and they were quite realistic, I must say. I thought they bent over backwards to be realistic. I was aching all over. [Laughs] And then we'd go into a discussion as to how the roles were played, whether there was something that the Freedom Riders did that they shouldn't have done, said that they shouldn't have said, something that they didn't say or do that they should have, and so on. Then we'd reverse roles and play it over and over again and have lengthy discussions of it.

I felt, by the way, that by the time that group left Washington, they were prepared for anything, even death, and this was a possibility, and we knew it, when we got to the Deep South.

Through Virginia we had no problem. In fact they had heard we were coming, Greyhound and Trailways, and they had taken down the For Colored and For Whites signs, and we rode right through. Yep. The same was true in North Carolina. Signs had come down just the previous day, blacks told us. And so the letters in advance did something.

In South Carolina it was a different story. . . . John Lewis started into a white waiting room in some town in South Carolina* . . . and there were several young white hoodlums, leather jackets, ducktail haircuts, standing there smoking, and they blocked the door and said, "Nigger, you can't come in here." He said, "I have every right to enter this waiting room according to the Supreme Court of the United States in the Boynton case."**

They said, "Shit on that." He tried to walk past, and they clubbed him, beat him, and knocked him down. One of the white Freedom Riders . . . Albert Bigelow,*** who had been a Navy captain during World War II, big, tall, strapping fellow, very impressive, from Connecticut—then stepped right between the hoodlums and John Lewis. Lewis had been absorbing more of the punishment. They then clubbed Bigelow and finally knocked him down, and that took some knocking because he was a pretty strapping fellow, and he didn't hit back at all. [They] knocked him down, and at this point police arrived and intervened. They didn't make any arrests. Intervened.

Well, we went through the rest of South Carolina without incident and then to Atlanta, Georgia, and there we met with Dr. King. We called him and told him we were coming, and he had dinner with us and wished us well. Went to Albany first and then Atlanta. And when we were in Atlanta—my father by the way, was in Freedman's Hospital here in Washington with cancer, and I got word just about two hours before the buses left Atlanta that my father had died, and I had to go back and bury him. My mother insisted until her death five years later that my father willed his death at that time, willed the timing of it because he had my schedule. I had talked with him here in Washington during our training session, when he was in the hospital before I left, and told him what we were going to do, and he said, "Well, that's an interesting idea and I hope you survive it." He

---

*Rock Hill.
**The 1960 Supreme Court case outlawing segregated facilities at bus terminals.
***Despite his military background, a Quaker pacifist. He was best known for sailing the yacht *Golden Rule* into an atomic testing area in the Pacific as a protest against nuclear warfare.

said, "I think the most dangerous part of it will be through Bama," as he put it, "and Mississippi. There, somebody will probably take a potshot at you, and I just hope they miss." And my mother says that every morning he would take out my itinerary and look at it and say, "Well, now, let's see where Junior is today." And he was relaxed about it until I got to Atlanta, and he says, "Oh, tomorrow he goes through Bama."

He died, and she says that he willed the timing of it to bring me back. It's apocryphal I'm sure. At any rate I had to return then to bury him and informed the Freedom Riders that I would rejoin them as soon as I had gotten this family obligation out of the way. I must confess that while I felt guilty at leaving, there was also a sense of relief at missing this leg of the trip, because all of us were scared. There was one reporter who was one of the Freedom Riders at this stage, and that was Simeon Booker of Johnson publications, *Jet* and *Ebony*. Simeon had come to me just before I got the telegram telling me of my father's death, or the phone call, and he said, "Jim, you know, I've decided that you are the only Freedom Rider I can outrun. So what I'm going to do is to stick with you on this trip, and I figure it's the fellow bringing up the rear who's gonna get caught." [Laughs]

Hank Thomas

The Freedom Ride didn't really get rough until we got down in the Deep South. Needless to say, Anniston, Alabama, I'm never gonna forget that, when I was on the bus that they threw some kind of incendiary device on.

He was on the first of two buses to cross into "Bama." When it pulled into the depot at Anniston, a Klan hotbed about sixty miles from Birmingham, the bus was surrounded by white men brandishing iron bars. Anniston police held them back long enough for the bus to reach the highway again, but about six miles outside town the pursuing mob caught up.

I got real scared then. You know, I was thinking—I'm looking out the window there, and people are out there yelling and screaming. They just about broke every window out of the bus.... I really thought that that was going to be the end of me.

How did the bus get stopped?

They shot the tires out, and the bus driver was forced to stop.... He got off, and man, he took off like a rabbit, and might well have. I couldn't very well blame him there. And we were trapped on the bus. They tried to board. Well, we did have two FBI men aboard the bus. All they were there to do were to observe and gather facts, but the crowd apparently recognized them as FBI men, and they did not try to hurt them.

It wasn't until the thing was shot on the bus and the bus caught afire that everything got out of control, and ... when the bus was burning, I figured ... [pauses] ... panic did get ahold of me. Needless to say, I couldn't survive that burning bus. There was a possibility I could have survived the mob, but I was just so afraid of the mob that I was gonna stay on that bus. I mean, I just got that much afraid. And when we got off the bus ... first they closed the doors and wouldn't let us off. But then I'm pretty sure they realized, that somebody said,

306

*Student
Activism
and the Emergence
of a Mass
Movement,
1960–1965*

"Hey, the bus is gonna explode," because it had just gassed up, and so they started scattering then, and I guess that's the way we got off the bus.* Otherwise, we probably all would have been succumbed by the smoke, and not being able to get off, probably would have been burned alive or burned on there anyway. That's the only time I was really, really afraid. I got whacked over the head with a rock or I think some kind of a stick as I was coming off the bus.

What happened in Anniston after the bus was attacked?

We were taken to the hospital. The bus started exploding, and a lot of people were cut by flying glass. We were taken to the hospital, most of us, for smoke inhalation.

By whom?

I don't remember. I think I was half out of it, half dazed, as a result of the smoke, and, gosh, I can still smell that stuff down in me now. You got to the point where you started having the dry heaves. Took us to the hospital, and it was incredible. The people at the hospital would not do anything for us. They would not. And I was saying, "You're *doctors,* you're medical personnel." They wouldn't. Governor Patterson got on statewide radio and said, "Any rioters in this state will not receive police protection." And then the crowd started forming outside the hospital, and the hospital told us to leave. And we said, "No, we're not going out there," and there we were. A caravan from Birmingham, about a fifteen-car caravan led by the Reverend Fred Shuttlesworth, came up from Birmingham to get us out.

Without police escort, I take it?

Without police escort, but every one of those cars had a shotgun in it. And Fred Shuttlesworth had got on the radio and said—you know Fred, he's very dramatic—"I'm going to get my people." [Laughs] He said, "I'm a nonviolent man, but I'm going to get my people." And apparently a hell of a lot of people believed in him. Man, they came there and they were a welcome sight. And each one of 'em got out with their guns and everything and the state police were there, but I think they all realized that this was not a time to say anything because, I'm pretty sure, there would have been a lot of people killed.

The black drivers were openly carrying guns?

Oh, yeah. They had rifles and shotguns. And that's how we got back to Birmingham. . . . I think I was flown to New Orleans for medical treatment, because

---

*John Patterson, then governor of Alabama, maintains that he and his public safety director, Floyd Mann, were indirectly responsible for the Freedom Riders' getting off the burning bus: "Floyd recommended that we send a state plainclothes investigator to Atlanta to catch the bus and ride with the Freedom Riders, and we did. Now this has never been reported that I know of in any paper. . . . We sent a man named E. L. Cowling. . . . He went over to Atlanta and caught the bus, and he was on the bus when they came to Anniston. . . . So Cowling walked up to the door of the bus and drew his pistol and backed the crowd away from the bus and told them that if anybody touched anybody he'd kill them. And he got the Freedom Riders off the burning bus. That's true."

still they were afraid to let any of us go to the hospitals in Birmingham, and by that time—it was what, two days later—I was fairly all right. I had gotten most of the smoke out of my system.

No one received any attention in the hospital in Anniston?

No, no. Oh, we did have one girl, Genevieve Hughes, a white girl, who had a busted lip. I remember a nurse applying something to that, but other than that, nothing. Now that I look back on it, man, we had some vicious people down there, wouldn't even so much as *treat* you. But that's the way it was. But strangely enough, even those bad things then don't stick in my mind that much. Not that I'm full of love and goodwill for everybody in my heart, but I chalk it off to part of the things that I'm going to be able to sit on my front porch in my rocking chair and tell my young'uns about, my grandchildren about.

Postscript: That same day, Mother's Day, May 14, 1961, the second bus escaped the mob in Anniston and made it to Birmingham. At the Trailways station there, white men armed with baseball bats and chains beat the Freedom Riders at will for about fifteen minutes before the first police arrived. In 1975 a former Birmingham Klansman, who was a paid informant of the FBI at the time, told the Senate Select Committee on Intelligence that members of the Birmingham police force had promised the Klansmen that no policemen would show up to interfere with the beatings for at least fifteen minutes. In 1976 a Birmingham detective who refused to be interviewed on tape told me that account was correct—as far as it went. The detective said that word was passed in the police department that Public Safety Commissioner Eugene "Bull" Connor had watched from the window of his office in City Hall as the crowd of Klansmen, some brandishing weapons, gathered to await the Freedom Riders. Asked later about the absence of his policemen, Connor said most of them were visiting their mothers.

John Lewis

He had left the Freedom Ride in South Carolina to keep an appointment for a job interview. Returning to Nashville on May 14, he learned of the attacks in Anniston and Birmingham and that CORE, heeding Attorney General Robert Kennedy's request for a "cooling-off" period, had canceled the ride altogether. He and a group of sit-in veterans believed that if the Freedom Ride did not continue, segregationists would conclude that they could, indeed, defeat the Movement with violence and intimidation. Using money left over from the sit-in treasury and ignoring the advice of Nashville's SCLC affiliate, they bought tickets for Birmingham and announced that the Freedom Ride was on again.

At the Birmingham city limit, a policeman halted their bus and informed the driver that he was taking charge of the vehicle. When the bus pulled into the station, the "Birmingham police department put up newspapers all around the bus windows so you couldn't see out, and no one could see in." Shielded from inspection, they waited until "Bull" Connor arrived on the scene and ordered them taken into "protective custody." Thus began one of the most bizarre episodes of the Movement.

308

*Student
Activism
and the Emergence
of a Mass
Movement,
1960–1965*

So they took us all to the jail, the Birmingham city jail. Now this was on a Wednesday. We went to jail and stayed in jail Wednesday night. We didn't eat anything. We went on a hunger strike.

What sort of treatment did you get from the police?

They were very, very nice. They didn't rough us up or anything like that, just very nice, as I recall. They put us in jail, segregated us . . . and that Thursday we stayed in jail all day. That Thursday night around midnight, "Bull" Connor and two reporters . . . and maybe one or two detectives came up to the jail, and "Bull" Connor said they were going to take us back to Nashville, back to the college campus where we belonged. We said, "Well, we don't want to go back. We have a right to be on this Freedom Ride. We have a right to travel. We plan to go to Montgomery, and from Montgomery we're going to Jackson and to New Orleans." And he insisted. And people just sort a went limp, so they had people literally to pick us up and place us into these cars. . . .

Anyway, they drove us on the highway, and "Bull" Connor was really funny. I was in the car that he was in and this young lady, Katherine Burke. He was really funny, he was really joking with us, saying that he was gonna take us back to Nashville, and we told him we would invite him to the campus, and he could have breakfast with us and that type of thing. He said he would like that. It was that type of conversation that we had going with "Bull" Connor.

We got to the Tennessee-Alabama line. . . . They dropped us off, saying . . . "You can take the bus back to Nashville." They literally left us there. We didn't know anybody, didn't know any place to go. This is true.

Did it cross your mind that you might be being set up?

Oh, yeah, oh, yeah. We just didn't know what had happened, and it was still dark. It was early morning-like.

The Birmingham police, including the police commissioner, had physically loaded you up in a car and carried you to the state line, a matter of 150 miles.

That's right. That's right. And *left*, us, just left us. What we did, we started walking down a road, and we saw a railroad track, and we crossed this railroad track and went to an old house. There was an elderly couple there, must have been in their late sixties, early seventies. We knocked on the door, and they let us in, and they was just really frightened. They'd heard about the Freedom Riders.

This was a black couple?

Black couple. They were just really, really frightened. They didn't know what to do. They didn't really want to let us in, but they did, and we called Nashville and told 'em what had happened. Called Diane Nash on the telephone. She was in the local student movement office there in Nashville, and she wanted to know whether we wanted to continue the ride or whether we wanted a car to pick us up to bring us back to Nashville. We told her to send a car to take us back to Birmingham. We wanted to continue the ride.

In the meantime, we hadn't had anything to eat, and we were very hungry. 'Cause this is now Friday morning, and we hadn't had anything to eat since, I guess, early Wednesday. This man, this elderly man, got in his pickup truck and went around during the early morning to two or three stores and bought something like bologna and bread and cornflakes. Anyway, we had a little meal there, and apparently some of the white people in the community came by, and he told 'em some of his relatives were visiting from Nashville. We waited around till the car from Nashville got there, and this was really something else. It was seven of us and the driver now, eight of us, got in that car on our way back to Birmingham, and we heard a reporter on the radio saying the students had been taken to the state line and apparently they were . . . back in Nashville on their college campuses. . . .

So we drove back to Birmingham, and Rev. Shuttlesworth and several other ministers from the Alabama Christian Movement for Human Rights met us there, and we went directly back to the Greyhound bus station. And we tried to get on the bus around, I recall, three o'clock, on the Greyhound bus from Birmingham to Montgomery, and apparently Greyhound canceled the bus taking off. We were going to try to get on one at five-something, and this bus driver said something that I'll never forget. He said, "I only have one life to give and I'm not going to give it to CORE or the NAACP."

He and his group, along with about twenty fresh volunteers from Nashville, spent the night on the wooden benches of the bus station. Departing from their previous practice, the police repelled a white mob which gathered during the night. Finally a reporter who was covering the story brought a message: "Apparently you all are going to get a chance to go. Attorney General Kennedy has been in contact with Greyhound."

The same bus driver came out to the bus about eight-thirty on Saturday morning, and we got on a bus from Birmingham to Montgomery. And apparently the arrangement was that every so many miles there would be a state patrol car and there would be a plane. We did see—I don't know whether it was the arrangement or not—we did see a small plane flying up above the bus for so many miles and we did have the patrol car. . . .*

It was a nice ride between Birmingham and Montgomery. A few miles outside of Montgomery you just didn't see anything. You didn't see the plane, didn't see the state patrol car. It seemed like everything sort of disappeared, and the moment that we arrived in that station, it was the strangest feeling to me. It was something strange, that you knew something. It was really weird. It was an eerie feeling. There was a funny peace there, a quietness. You didn't see anything happening. Apparently, when you really look back, the mob there must have been so planned and was so out of sight . . . it just sorta appeared, just appeared

You didn't see any sign of it as you went into the bus station?

None. Just didn't see anything. When we drove up, we didn't see anything. . . . We got most of the young ladies in a cab. So they got in a cab and the black cab driver didn't want to drive, because at that time there was two white students,

---

*In fact, an airplane and sixteen highway patrol cars accompanied the bus, despite Governor Patterson's public statement that "we are not going to escort those agitators. We stand firm on that position."

310

*Student
Activism
and the Emergence
of a Mass
Movement,
1960–1965*

young ladies from Peabody or Scarritt, and in Alabama there was a law that you couldn't have an integrated cab. So the two young ladies got out, and at that very time, this mob started all over the place. So everybody, all the young ladies, got away, and the two young white girls were running down the street trying to get away. That's when John Siegenthaler got hit.** And at that time, the rest of us, mostly fellas, just literally standing there because we couldn't run—no place to go really.***

This was out in the lot?

Just out in the lot. And if you've been at the bus station, there's a rail there. . . . Down below is the entrance to the courthouse, the Post Office building. So when the mob kept coming, several of the people, several of the fellas jumped over and were able to get in the basement of the Post Office, and the postmaster there opened it and made it possible for people to come in and escape the mob. And I said—I remember saying that we shouldn't run, we should just stand there, 'cause the mob was beating people. And the last thing that I recall, I was hit with a crate, a wooden crate what you have soda in, and was left lying in the street. And I remember the Attorney General of Alabama, MacDonald Gallion, serving this injunction that Judge Walter B. Jones had issued saying that it was unlawful for interracial groups to travel. While I was lying there on the ground, he brought this injunction.

4.3　　　　　　　　　　　　　　　　　　　　　　　　　　　　**Adam Fairclough**

Confrontation: Albany and Birmingham

Adam Fairclough holds the chair of modern American history at the University of Leeds. He is author of Race and Democracy: The Civil Rights Struggle in Louisiana, 1915–1972, To Redeem the Soul of America: The Southern Christian Leadership Conference and Martin Luther King, Jr., *and* Martin Luther King, Jr.

On December 14, 1961, King received a telegram from Dr. William G. Anderson, a black osteopath, urging him to "come and join the Albany Movement."

**Robert Kennedy's administrative assistant, sent to Alabama as an observer.
***Freedom Rider William Harbour: "There was nobody there. I didn't see anybody standin' around the bus station. I saw some taxicabs there. That was about it. So the bus driver opened the bus door up and just walked away from the bus. I guess in less than fifteen minutes, we had a mob of people, five or six hundred people with ax handles, chains and everything else. . . . Soon as we walked off the bus, John Lewis said to me, 'Bill, it doesn't look right. . . .'

"Everything happened so quick. There was a standstill for the first two or three minutes. . . . They were closin' in on us, and we were standin' still tryin' to decide what should we do in order to protect the whites we had with us. But then you had a middle-aged white female hollerin', 'Git them niggers, git them niggers . . . ,' and that urged the crowd on. From then on, they was constantly movin' in. I don't think she ever hit anybody or threw anything whatsoever. Just the idea she started, just kept pushin' and pushin' and pushin'. . . . It started just like that."

King arrived in the southwest Georgia town having promised to make a speech. But he stayed to lead a march, was arrested and jailed, and found himself embroiled in a remarkable protest movement.

The Albany Movement owed its existence to Cordell Reagon and Charles Sherrod, two young SNCC workers who hoped to instigate the kind of audacious tactics pioneered by the sit-ins and the Freedom Rides. At first, only students and young people took them seriously, but their flamboyant behavior soon made older blacks sit up and take notice. The pair engineered a series of dramatic incidents at the bus and train stations to show that the city was still enforcing segregation, despite the new federal edict on interstate travel. The ensuing arrests angered the black community, and hundreds protested by marching to city hall under the banner of the Albany Movement, a coalition of black organizations that Dr. Anderson had agreed to head. The city council was determined, however, to maintain segregation. The police arrested nearly five hundred marchers and insisted on a cash bond of $100 from each person—money that many could not pay. Black leaders felt they were in over their heads, and some were losing their nerve. They hoped that King would be able to retrieve the situation.

Looking around the crowded pews of Shiloh Baptist Church on December 15, King could see an impressive cross section of Albany's black community: old men in creased blue overalls, professionals in white shirts and ties, maids and housewives, students and schoolchildren. He could sense the "movement spirit," that magic ingredient that inspired ordinary people to do extraordinary things. It was almost palpable in the emotional atmosphere of the packed church and, above all, in the extemporized verses and simple, powerful melodies of the "freedom songs," which had titles like "Ain't Gonna Let Nobody Turn Me 'Round" and "I Woke Up This Morning with My Mind Set on Freedom." King also heard a stirring rendition of "We Shall Overcome." SNCC workers had learned this union song, which had started life as a hymn, in 1960. Sung slowly with improvised counterpoints and swelling harmonies, it soon became the anthem of the civil rights movement. The Albany Movement reminded King of the inspiring early days of the Montgomery bus boycott: here was a ready made movement—enthusiastic, apparently united, and eager to bestow its leadership on him.

King seized the moment. "Don't stop now," he urged his audience at the end of a riveting speech. "Keep moving. Walk together children, don't you get weary. There's a great camp meeting in the sky." The following day, accompanied by Dr. Anderson and Ralph Abernathy, his friend and colleague from SCLC, King headed a slow, quiet procession toward city hall. All 257 marchers were arrested for "parading without a permit." King vowed to spend Christmas in jail, and the staff of SCLC embarked on a frantic campaign to drum up national support and publicity.

To King's dismay, however, the campaign of direct action rapidly fell apart, and all his subsequent attempts to achieve a clear-cut victory proved unavailing. In August 1962, after two more spells in jail, he left Albany as segregated as he had found it. Whites had failed to yield any ground whatever. What went wrong? Among the many factors that conspired to frustrate the Albany Movement, two stand out: disunity, and the guile of chief of police Laurie G. Pritchett.

The emotional response that greeted King's arrival disguised a welter of factionalism among the blacks who composed the leadership of the movement. The lines of division and suspicion ran this way and that, strangling the prospects for unity. Part of the problem lay in organizational rivalry. When it learned of SNCC's

312

*Student
Activism
and the Emergence
of a Mass
Movement,
1960–1965*

presence in Albany, the NAACP instructed its local officials to cold-shoulder SNCC's efforts to form a united front. This narrow sectarianism typified the NAACP's attitude to other civil rights groups. But SNCC's dealings with King betrayed similar pettiness. Struggling to establish its own identity, SNCC acquiesced in Dr. Anderson's invitation to King but resisted the notion of surrendering the leadership to him. Some of the locals who headed the Albany Movement also developed misgivings about King's role; they especially resented the assertive manner of Wyatt T. Walker, whom King had recruited as SCLC's executive director. Oblivious to these tensions, King had to deal with the fact that Dr. Anderson, in jail with him, showed signs of succumbing to mental stress.

The upshot was a debacle that verged on farce. Egged on by Ella Baker, who had left SCLC in 1960 belittling King as a "prophetic leader who turns out to have heavy feet of clay," the SNCC workers prevailed upon Marion Page, Anderson's deputy, to show King the door. On December 17 Page told reporters that the Albany Movement needed no "outside help"; the next day he agreed to call off the demonstrations in return for the release of the imprisoned marchers. King emerged from jail, alongside Anderson, to find that Page had settled for the flimsiest of concessions. Local whites gloated as he left Albany; newspaper reports of his departure read like obituaries.

Characteristically, King swallowed his humiliation and refused to engage in recriminations. Returning for his trial on July 10, 1962, he reentered the campaign, determined to salvage something from the fiasco of December. For the next month his presence invigorated the protests: blacks marched in the streets, prayed on the steps of city hall, boycotted the downtown stores, and conducted sit-ins at white-only restaurants. And when SNCC workers mocked him as "De Lawd," berated him for his caution, and chastised him for being "bourgeois," King reciprocated with endless patience. He and the others in SCLC were older men, he explained; they had families and mortgages and were bound to be more conservative. "We would like to think that you are the creative antagonists who make this sort of situation, and that we . . . come in and help you work in them." SNCC tolerated King's intervention because local blacks adored him, and his presence secured much-needed publicity. As one SNCC worker conceded, King could "cause more hell to be raised by being in jail one night than anyone else could if they bombed city hall."

At every point, however, King's tactics backfired, and the enthusiasm of the black population began to flag. When King chose to spend forty-five days in jail rather than pay a $178 fine, the mayor of Albany surreptitiously paid the money, forcing the astonished prisoner to walk away free. Inevitably, some blacks muttered about King turning "chicken." As he struggled to regain the initiative, the campaign stalled once again when the city authorities obtained an injunction against further marches from federal judge Robert Elliott. Over the strenuous objections of SNCC, King insisted on obeying the court order. The chief judge of the federal appeals court, Elbert Tuttle, soon voided Elliott's injunction, but an outbreak of rock- and bottle-throwing by some blacks persuaded King to further delay the resumption of demonstrations. The protests finally got underway again, and King spent two weeks in jail after another arrest. But the campaign's momentum had been irretrievably lost. When he left jail after receiving a suspended sentence, he also left Albany.

Whites could thank Laurie G. Pritchett, chief of police, for King's discomfiture. The fat, drawling Pritchett looked like the archetypal southern cop, but his calm, canny handling of the demonstrations defied the stereotype. As an efficient police chief who discouraged brutality, Pritchett understood the political dimensions of the challenge posed by black protests. The danger to segregation, he realized, lay not so much in the pressure of demonstrations but rather in the possibility of direct federal intervention in southern affairs. And he perceived—more keenly than King at this stage—that nothing would encourage federal intervention more surely than a violent response to nonviolent protest. Pritchett's strategic approach was to read King's account of the Montgomery bus boycott, *Stride Toward Freedom,* which have him valuable insight into the thinking of his adversary, and to consult other police chiefs who had succeeded in containing black protests. The plan was clear: a policy of arresting demonstrators, applied firmly but without violence, would obviate federal intervention and suffocate nonviolent protests. During the first half of 1962, anticipating King's return, Pritchett drilled his men: "At each roll call they were lectured and shown films on how to conduct themselves."

As King and SCLC licked their wounds, they pondered the lessons of the campaign. On the one hand, the movement in Albany represented a significant escalation of the civil rights struggle. For the first time, an entire black community had been mobilized for a broad attack on segregation, and large numbers of ordinary people—not only students—had gone to jail. On the other hand, Albany painfully illustrated the limitations of nonviolent direct action. In India the British had been a tiny minority. In every southern state, blacks were clearly outnumbered; in Albany they constituted only a third of the population. Moreover, because most blacks depended upon white employers, relatively few, five percent at most, were prepared to risk jail. Talk of a "nonviolent army" that would "fill up the jails" had been exposed as wishful thinking. King's army had been pitifully small, and Pritchett ensured a plenitude of jail space. By countering civil rights demonstrations with the repressive machinery of the law, the white authorities turned the contest into a war of attrition that blacks could not win.

In such an unequal contest, only strong intervention by the federal government could tip the scales in favor of the weaker protagonist. In May 1962 King called upon President Kennedy to issue a "Second Emancipation Proclamation," urging him to throw the full weight of his office behind the struggle for black civil rights. Kennedy did not seriously entertain the idea, and he avoided entanglement in the Albany situation. Instead, Robert Kennedy, as Attorney General, sought to dissuade King from pressing the demonstrations; while critical of the city's refusal to negotiate, Kennedy tacitly endorsed its restrained, low-key handling of the protests. The administration's "neutrality" infuriated the normally equable King. Arguing with Kennedy over the phone, he complained that the government had no comprehension of what blacks in Albany were up against. "This can't go on," he insisted. "I'm tired. We're sick of it."

Reflecting upon the government's inaction, King arrived at an uncomfortable conclusion: shallow political considerations, not reason or morality, guided the administration's actions. If a crisis threatened political embarrassment, if violence and disorder got out of hand, then the government would indeed intervene. If, however, southern racists quietly stifled black protests, then it acquiesced in the status quo. This seemed to be the lesson of the Freedom Rides. In Alabama, where the white authorities had summoned up the Klan to brutally assault the protesters, Kennedy acted in a most forceful manner, but when the Mississippi authorities

314

*Student
Activism
and the Emergence
of a Mass
Movement,
1960–1965*

simply jailed the Freedom Riders, ensuring that no mobs gathered, the government did nothing. Evidently, the absence of overt violence in Albany made it a minor local difficulty that could safely be ignored. The crisis at "Ole Miss" in October 1962 underscored the point. When the entry of James Meredith, an African American, into the University of Mississippi prompted rioting by white segregationists— violence that left two people dead—Kennedy sent in troops.

Hardened by defeat, King decided to explode the political equivalent of a bomb under the federal government. He would launch demonstrations in Birmingham, Alabama.

The sheer audacity of King's decision was astonishing. Birmingham now prides itself as a model of racial harmony; it even boasts a museum that honors the civil rights movement. In 1963, however, Birmingham exemplified all that was extreme, vicious, and violent in southern racism. Founded by aggressive capitalists after the Civil War, Birmingham was a coal and steel center that possessed none of the genteel ways and paternalistic traditions of older cities like New Orleans or even Montgomery. In the 1930s Birmingham experienced bitter industrial conflict and saw the emergence of a militant labor movement. But the city disproved the notion that racism and capitalism were antithetical: rigid segregation characterized industry as well as public life, and the white union branches provided a steady stream of recruits for the Ku Klux Klan. Indeed, Birmingham boasted some of the most dangerous Klan groups in the South.

Above all, Birmingham meant Theophilus G. "Bull" Connor, who bore the ironic title Commissioner of Public Safety, a post that included supervision of the police and fire departments. First elected in 1937, Connor became friendly with the city's industrialists but also retained his popularity with white workers. Connor was a fervent racist and his publicity-conscious and high-handed actions to defend segregation outraged northern liberals but delighted Birmingham's white voters. In 1938 he insulted First Lady Eleanor Roosevelt. Ten years later he arrested a U.S. senator. By the late 1950s he had become a law unto himself, and his methods had become increasingly thuggish. He used his control of the police force to tap telephones, spy on meetings, and frame opponents. With the protection and cooperation of the police, the Klan bombed black churches, brutally assaulted the Freedom Riders, and castrated a black man for the sheer hell of it. Birmingham became so notorious for racial violence that a group of whites framed a new city charter that abolished Connor's job of public safety commissioner. When voters approved the change, Connor decided to run for mayor.

The Reverend Fred L. Shuttlesworth emerged as Connor's most forceful and determined black opponent. Impulsive, excitable, and egocentric, Shuttlesworth almost single-handedly kept black protest alive in Birmingham after the suppression of the NAACP in 1956. Intent on integrating the most segregated city in the South, he was blasted out of bed by dynamite, beaten up by white mobs, and repeatedly arrested by Connor's police. The diminutive clergyman displayed a bravado that amused blacks and caused them to shake their heads in admiration and amazement. The organization he built up over the years, the Alabama Christian Movement for Human Rights, was the strongest of the local groups that made up SCLC. With several hundred devoted followers and a handful of ministers he could count on, Shuttlesworth provided SCLC with a solid base upon which to build its campaign.

King started with several advantages. In Albany he had stumbled into a protest not of his making and not under his control; the white authorities had been able to keep him off-balance. In Birmingham he would not be plagued by divided and confused authority, and he would begin with the element of surprise. Whereas in Albany the whites had put up a solid front of resistance, in Birmingham they were split between the hardliners, who backed Connor for mayor, and the moderates, who preferred the more conciliatory Albert Boutwell. King also had a team behind him. Wyatt Walker, the clergyman hired in 1960 to breathe life into SCLC, provided the drive, discipline, and administrative talent that the more easygoing and reflective King sometimes lacked. With Shuttlesworth's advice, Walker drafted a detailed campaign plan that identified targets, specified tactics, and dealt with the minutiae of recruiting demonstrators.

A small group of organizers assisted Walker. Andrew Young, thirty-one years old, came from New Orleans; his ordination in the mainly white Congregational church made him something of a rarity among black ministers, but it gave SCLC important contacts with the white clergy. Young had the organizational know-how to function as Walker's number two, and he also possessed the social and diplomatic skills to negotiate with southern whites. James Bevel, who was in his early twenties, had none of Young's social polish but possessed far more experience at the grass roots of the civil rights movement; as a veteran of the sit-ins and the Freedom Rides, he had spent two years in Mississippi. Although he was a rabble-rousing orator, Bevel regarded himself as an expert on Gandhian tactics. He had picked up many of his ideas from James Lawson, a Methodist minister and articulate intellectual who had been expelled from Vanderbilt University for his role in the Nashville sit-in movement. In Birmingham Lawson developed a program for training demonstrators in nonviolence. Dorothy Cotton, who normally worked in SCLC's citizenship education program, worked alongside Lawson and also performed more general duties. Two other staff members answered directly to King. Ralph D. Abernathy, King's best friend, served him as companion and troubleshooter. Bernard Lee, a young man, acted as King's secretary, bodyguard, and general factotum. No rigid lines separated these roles. SCLC had no armchair generals or deskbound bureaucrats: everyone pitched in.

King had two broad objectives in Birmingham. The first was to force white leaders to begin the process of desegregation. He regarded the precise scope of any agreement as unimportant; any concessions, however small, would constitute a victory. In order to achieve a victory, therefore, King focused on the desegregation of Birmingham's downtown department stores, a relatively narrow goal. Fred Shuttlesworth was unhappy with such a limited objective, but King did not want to risk the failure of an overambitious assault against segregation across the board. As Walker recalled, "We knew that as Birmingham went, so went the South. And we felt that if we could crack that city, then we could crack any city." Learning from Albany, however, King realized that it would be useless to demand concessions from the city government, which could not afford to lose face in the eyes of the largely white electorate. SCLC therefore ensured that its primary demand, the desegregation of department store eating facilities, could be satisfied with or without the agreement of white politicians. The pressure of demonstrations, underpinned by a black boycott of the city's downtown shopping district, would force the city's businessmen to the negotiating table.

A negotiated settlement, however, also depended on SCLC's second goal, federal intervention. In order to bring about federal action King had to tread a very fine line. Without the restraining influence of national publicity, which carried the

316

*Student
Activism
and the Emergence
of a Mass
Movement,
1960–1965*

possibility of federal interference, the white authorities would feel free to suppress the demonstrations with whatever force they deemed necessary. King was counting on the news media to inhibit Bull Connor from employing his customary brutality. But King also had to discredit Connor in the eyes of the nation, thus embarrassing the government into assuming responsibility for ending the crisis. He had to make Connor show his true colors, but without provoking bloodshed.

The resolution of this paradox lay in King's use of symbolism. Although he sought a confrontation between demonstrators and police, he envisaged a tightly controlled one that strove for dramatic effect rather than physical conflict. One journalist likened the campaign to a carefully staged morality play, and this was precisely the effect King intended. The campaign had to maintain a sense of momentum and drama: the demonstrations needed to build up to a powerful climax. Walker tried to anticipate every contingency so that SCLC could retain the initiative.

But everything about the Birmingham project was risky. King would be charged with extreme provocation, especially as white moderates were attempting to drive Connor from office. Nor could King count on black unity. Many middle-class blacks were appalled by the prospect of King, an outsider, mounting demonstrations with Shuttlesworth, whom they considered an irresponsible firebrand, at the very time that Connor was becoming discredited and the political situation balanced on a knife-edge. Lest they tip the balance to Connor in the imminent mayoral election, SCLC prepared for the campaign in secret, which severely limited the opportunity to mobilize black support in advance. Blacks in this tough steeltown, moreover, would look upon nonviolence with puzzlement and cynicism; many possessed guns and routinely carried knives. The possibility of a bloodbath, which would discredit not only Connor but King as well, could not be discounted. As he faced the supreme challenge of his career, King somberly warned his colleagues that some of them might not leave Birmingham alive.

At first little went according to plan. Although Boutwell won more votes than Connor in the mayoral election, King had to further delay the campaign because a runoff was necessary for Boutwell to achieve the required overall majority. When the protests finally began on April 3, 1963, few people volunteered for jail, and many blacks, including leading ministers and businessmen, openly criticized the campaign. King had anticipated black opposition, but its depth took him by surprise. Many resented having been kept in the dark and felt that King should allow Boutwell a honeymoon period. King had to spend a week rallying black support—although he was careful not to admit that SCLC's refusal to permit another delay stemmed from its eagerness to confront Connor, who through legal strategems was clinging to his post as Commissioner of Public Safety.

Connor declined to play the role that SCLC's script assigned him, however. The Birmingham police exhibited uncharacteristic restraint and were content simply to arrest all demonstrators for "parading without a permit." Even so, and despite King's exhortations, few people joined the marches. The mass meetings were enthusiastic enough, but fear of arrest and loss of employment deterred most blacks from walking down the aisle to the front of the church when King's aides appealed for volunteers. With the campaign apparently coming undone, the prospect of either negotiations or federal intervention seemed remote.

The campaign soon reached a crisis point: King needed to lead a march and go to jail in order to revive media interest and stimulate black support. There were also reasons, though, why King should stay out of jail. The city authorities had obtained a blanket injunction against the demonstrations, and King had never hith-erto disobeyed a court order. Moreover, SCLC had exhausted its bail fund, and at a tense strategy meeting many argued that only King could raise enough money to get the incarcerated demonstrators released. Ralph Abernathy lamely argued that he could not accompany King to jail because he had to preach the Easter Sunday service at his Atlanta church. Daddy King implored his son not to march. King withdrew to a side room in order to pray. When he rejoined the anxious group, he was wearing denim jeans and a rough work shirt—his prison clothes. Colleagues later cited the decision as evidence of the religious inspiration that guided King; the day of his arrest, Good Friday, invested it with additional symbolism. Yet King's "faith act" was never really in doubt. He had long ago resolved to break any in-junction issued by the Alabama courts, knowing that an appeal to the federal courts would entail years of litigation.

King dreaded solitary confinement. Separated from Abernathy after his arrest on April 12, "those were the longest, most frustrating and bewildering hours I have lived," he remembered. "You will never know the meaning of utter dark-ness until you have lain in such a dungeon, knowing that sunlight is streaming overhead and still seeing only darkness below." A gregarious man, he hated being alone. He ached to see his new daughter, born a few days earlier. He worried about the bail money. And he experienced straightforward fear. In New York **Stanley Levison** speculated that Connor was trying to "break" King. Walker, too, feared for his safety and advised an anxious Mrs. King to make direct contact with the president. Coretta King's messages eventually reached Robert Kennedy, who returned her calls. Connor was "very difficult to deal with," the attorney general explained. Nevertheless, he assured her of the ad-ministration's concern. The following day, President Kennedy added his own reassurances. "We sent the FBI into Birmingham last night," he divulged. "We've checked on your husband, and he's all right."

A few minutes later, King's jailers allowed him to take a telephone call from Coretta. The news of Kennedy's conversation with his wife surprised and pleased him. It gave the campaign a "new dimension," he believed. Guessing correctly that Connor had the line tapped, he told Coretta to immediately inform "the Reverend" (Wyatt Walker) of Kennedy's intercession. The administration's concern for King's safety did not imply active intervention. Well aware that King was trying to force his hand, Kennedy had no intention of being drawn in against his will; indeed, he disclaimed any legal authority for involvement. Nevertheless, the government found the situation in Birmingham disturbing. "The Negro population has no confidence at all in the local police," one official advised Robert Kennedy. "And there is no doubt but that a good number of Negroes carry weapons."

King also received the welcome news that singer Harry Belafonte, a staunch supporter, had managed to raise $50,000 in bail money. But an additional worry now nagged at King. White moderates, whose support he desperately wanted, were displaying little sympathy for the protests. They criticized the timing and the tactics of the campaign, and some questioned King's motives. Over the years King had become hardened to criticism, but attacks from southern churchmen saddened, irritated, and finally angered him. Reading the local newspaper in his cell, he came across an open letter signed by eight of Alabama's most respected white clergymen. Denouncing the demonstrations for inciting hatred and violence, their statement

318

*Student
Activism
and the Emergence
of a Mass
Movement,
1960–1965*

praised the conduct of the police, called for negotiations between "local leaders," and urged blacks to shun King's campaign.

Depressed, and then furious, King penned a rebuttal, filling up the margins of the newspaper with his spiky handwriting. In what amounted to twenty impassioned pages he castigated the eight clergymen for their superficial analysis, rebuked self-styled white moderates for their "shallow understanding," and charged the white church with hypocrisy and lack of moral commitment.

At the core of "Letter from Birmingham City Jail" [Reading 4.4] was the most systematic exegesis of civil disobedience that King ever gave. He called upon such diverse authorities as Socrates, the Old Testament prophets, Thomas Aquinas, and Martin Buber to testify in his defense. He likened himself to Saint Paul, another "outsider," and Jesus, another "extremist." He frankly avowed that his demonstrations sought to create "tension" and "crisis," but insisted, with a bow to Niebuhr, that only pressure could induce privileged groups to act justly. Besides, he pointed out, "We merely bring to the surface the tension that is already alive." He denied the charge of provocation, arguing that blacks were not to be blamed if whites responded to their peaceful protests with violence. And he bluntly warned of a "frightening racial nightmare" if blacks surrendered to bitterness and hatred because whites refused to negotiate with responsible leaders like himself.

King also employed pathos, describing the pain he felt seeing the impact of discrimination upon his own children.

> You suddenly find your tongue twisted and your speech stammering as you seek to explain to your six-year-old daughter why she can't go to the public amusement park that has just been advertised on television, and see the tears welling up in her eyes when she is told that Funtown is closed to colored children, and see ominous clouds of inferiority beginning to form in her little mental sky, and see her beginning to distort her personality by developing an unconscious bitterness toward white people. . . . [Y]ou have to concoct an answer to a five-year-old son who is asking: "Daddy, why do white people treat colored people so mean?"

King's polemic had no influence on the campaign. But when "Letter from Birmingham City Jail" was published it soon became the most widely-read, widely-reprinted and oft-quoted document of the civil rights movement. It was the most powerful and influential piece of writing that King ever produced.

When King left jail after nine days, he stood trial for violating the state court injunction. Judge William Jenkins recognized that King behind bars was an embarrassment to the city: instead of jailing him for civil contempt until he apologized to the court, he found him guilty of criminal contempt only. The latter carried but a short sentence, and King would remain free during the lengthy appeals process. This moral victory, however, did not help King. The white authorities were still handling the demonstrations gingerly. Although the old city government was exploiting legal technicalities to cling to power, the courts would soon confirm Boutwell's election and Connor would be out of office. Without Connor, the chances of engineering a dramatic confrontation with the police would fade. The press were already losing interest in the demonstrations, whose ranks were dwindling. Walker began delaying the start of the daily marches so that large crowds of black bystanders gathered: their presence conveyed an illusion of mass support. But the illusion would soon wear thin unless SCLC recruited more demonstrators.

James Bevel suggested a way of doing just that. He proposed going into the city's black schools to enlist children in their thousands. The magnitude of such a step worried King: at what age should SCLC permit children to join the demonstrations, and should they allow children to take part if the parents objected? By the end of April children as young as nine were going to jail, but only with their parents' permission. Recruiting them en masse was a different proposition. It would not only incur the opposition of many parents but also in all likelihood be perceived by the outside world as cowardly manipulation. Nevertheless, King tacitly encouraged Bevel to organize a mammoth demonstration composed of schoolchildren. On May 2, which Bevel dubbed "D-Day," thousands of black children deserted their classrooms and converged on the Sixteenth Street Baptist Church, the gathering point for demonstrators. Leaving the church in groups of fifty, they walked into the arms of waiting policemen to be hauled away in paddy wagons. About six hundred went to jail that day, and by May 7 well over two thousand were in custody.

The "children's crusade" finally made Connor snap. Angered by the crowds of black spectators that were becoming bigger and bolder each day, he told the police to utilize German shepherds to keep them in check. He then ordered the fire department to disperse the throngs with their high-pressure hoses. The press had a field day; the scenes were broadcast across America and around the world. Overnight, the black community united behind the protests: so many people came to the mass meetings that it took four churches to accommodate them all. King could hardly contain his joy. "This is the most inspiring movement that has ever taken place in the United States of America," he told a packed church on May 5. "There are those who write history, there are those who make history, there are those who experience history. . . . You are certainly making history and you are experiencing history. And you will make it possible for the historians of the future to write a marvellous chapter. Never in the history of this nation have so many people been arrested for the cause of freedom and human dignity."

Sickened and embarrassed by the spectacle and fearful of a racial explosion, President Kennedy asked his brother to bring the two sides together. On May 3 Robert Kennedy's most talented mediator, Burke Marshall, arrived in Birmingham with instructions to halt the descent into chaos. A week later, after tense and exhausting negotiations, and the application of direct pressure by the president and attorney general, a committee of white businessmen accepted some of the movement's demands. The principal concession appeared slight: department stores agreed to desegregate their eating facilities and hire black sales assistants. But King had achieved his goal and also played his last card. Untrained in nonviolence, the black crowds were becoming unruly, and he could not contain the violent elements much longer. Claiming victory, he ended the demonstrations. But as the protests stopped in Birmingham, African Americans poured into the streets all over the South. King had unleashed the biggest wave of black militancy since Reconstruction.

Letter from Birmingham City Jail

Martin Luther King is the most celebrated civil rights leader of the twentieth century. As a young minister in Montgomery, Alabama, he became the spokesman for the legendary bus boycott in 1955 and later head of SCLC. He wrote Stride toward Freedom: The Montgomery Story, *his personal account of that struggle. In 1964 King was awarded the Nobel Peace Prize. He was assassinated in 1968.*

My dear Fellow Clergymen,

While confined here in the Birmingham city jail, I came across your recent statement calling our present activities "unwise and untimely." Seldom, if ever, do I pause to answer criticism of my work and ideas. If I sought to answer all of the criticisms that cross my desk, my secretaries would be engaged in little else in the course of the day, and I would have no time for constructive work. But since I feel that you are men of genuine good will and your criticisms are sincerely set forth, I would like to answer your statement in what I hope will be patient and reasonable terms.

I think I should give the reason for my being in Birmingham, since you have been influenced by the argument of "outsiders coming in." I have the honor of serving as president of the Southern Christian Leadership Conference, an organization operating in every southern state with headquarters in Atlanta, Georgia. We have some eighty-five affiliate organizations all across the South—one being the Alabama Christian Movement for Human Rights. Whenever necessary and possible we share staff, educational and financial resources with our affiliates. Several months ago our local affiliate here in Birmingham invited us to be on call to engage in a nonviolent direct-action program if such were deemed necessary. We readily consented and when the hour came we lived up to our promises. So I am here, along with several members of my staff, because we were invited here. I am here because I have basic organizational ties here.

Beyond this, I am in Birmingham because injustice is here. Just as the eighth century prophets left their little villages and carried their "thus saith the Lord" far beyond the boundaries of their hometowns; and just as the Apostle Paul left his little village of Tarsus and carried the gospel of Jesus Christ to practically every hamlet and city of the Graeco-Roman world, I too am compelled to carry the gospel of freedom beyond my particular hometown. Like Paul, I must constantly respond to the Macedonian call for aid.

Moreover, I am cognizant of the interrelatedness of all communities and states. I cannot sit idly by in Atlanta and not be concerned about what happens in Birmingham. Injustice anywhere is a threat to justice everywhere. We are caught in an inescapable network of mutuality, tied in a single garment of destiny. Whatever affects one directly affects all indirectly. Never again can we afford to live with the narrow, provincial "outside agitator" idea. Anyone who lives in the United States can never be considered an outsider anywhere in this country.

You deplore the demonstrations that are presently taking place in Birmingham. But I am sorry that your statement did not express a similar concern for the conditions that brought the demonstrations into being. I am sure that each of you would want to go beyond the superficial social analyst who looks merely at effects, and does not grapple with underlying causes. I would not hesitate to say that it is unfortunate that so-called demonstrations are taking place in Birmingham at this time, but I would say in more emphatic terms that it is even more unfortunate that the white power structure of this city left the Negro community with no other alternative.

In any nonviolent campaign there are four basic steps: (1) collection of the facts to determine whether injustices are alive, (2) negotiation, (3) self-purification, and (4) direct action. We have gone through all of these steps in Birmingham. There can be no gainsaying of the fact that racial injustice engulfs this community.

Birmingham is probably the most thoroughly segregated city in the United States. Its ugly record of police brutality is known in every section of this country. Its injust treatment of Negroes in the courts is a notorious reality. There have been more unsolved bombings of Negro homes and churches in Birmingham than any city in this nation. These are the hard, brutal and unbelievable facts. On the basis of these conditions Negro leaders sought to negotiate with the city fathers. But the political leaders consistently refused to engage in good faith negotiation.

Then came the opportunity last September to talk with some of the leaders of the economic community. In these negotiating sessions certain promises were made by the merchants—such as the promise to remove the humiliating racial signs from the stores. On the basis of these promises Rev. Shuttlesworth and the leaders of the Alabama Christian Movement for Human Rights agreed to call a moratorium on any type of demonstrations. As the weeks and months unfolded we realized that we were the victims of a broken promise. The signs remained. Like so many experiences of the past we were confronted with blasted hopes, and the dark shadow of a deep disappointment settled upon us. So we had no alternative except that of preparing for direct action, whereby we would present our very bodies as a means of laying our case before the conscience of the local and national community. We were not unmindful of the difficulties involved. So we decided to go through a process of self-purification. We started having workshops on nonviolence and repeatedly asked ourselves the questions, "Are you able to accept blows without retaliating?" "Are you able to endure the ordeals of jail?" We decided to set our direct-action program around the Easter season, realizing that with the exception of Christmas, this was the largest shopping period of the year. Knowing that a strong economic withdrawal program would be the by-product of direct action, we felt that this was the best time to bring pressure on the merchants for the needed changes. Then it occurred to us that the March election was ahead and so we speedily decided to postpone action until after election day. When we discovered that Mr. Connor was in the run-off, we decided again to postpone action so that the demonstrations could not be used to cloud the issues. At this time we agreed to begin our nonviolent witness the day after the run-off.

This reveals that we did not move irresponsibly into direct action. We too wanted to see Mr. Connor defeated; so we went through postponement after postponement to aid in this community need. After this we felt that direct action could be delayed no longer.

You may well ask, "Why direct action? Why sit-ins, marches, etc.? Isn't negotiation a better path?" You are exactly right in your call for negotiation. Indeed, this is the purpose of direct action. Nonviolent direct action seeks to create such

322

*Student
Activism
and the Emergence
of a Mass
Movement,
1960–1965*

a crisis and establish such creative tension that a community that has constantly refused to negotiate is forced to confront the issue. It seeks so to dramatize the issue that it can no longer be ignored. I just referred to the creation of tension as a part of the work of the nonviolent resister. This may sound rather shocking. But I must confess that I am not afraid of the word tension. I have earnestly worked and preached against violent tension, but there is a type of constructive nonviolent tension that is necessary for growth. Just as Socrates felt that it was necessary to create a tension in the mind so that individuals could rise from the bondage of myths and half-truths to the unfettered realm of creative analysis and objective appraisal, we must see the need of having nonviolent gadflies to create the kind of tension in society that will help men to rise from the dark depths of prejudice and racism to the majestic heights of understanding and brotherhood. So the purpose of the direct action is to create a situation so crisis-packed that it will inevitably open the door to negotiation. We, therefore, concur with you in your call for negotiation. Too long has our beloved Southland been bogged down in the tragic attempt to live in monologue rather than dialogue.

One of the basic points in your statement is that our acts are untimely. Some have asked, "Why didn't you give the new administration time to act?" The only answer that I can give to this inquiry is that the new administration must be prodded about as much as the outgoing one before it acts. We will be sadly mistaken if we feel that the election of Mr. Boutwell will bring the millennium to Birmingham. While Mr. Boutwell is much more articulate and gentle than Mr. Connor, they are both segregationists, dedicated to the task of maintaining the status quo. The hope I see in Mr. Boutwell is that he will be reasonable enough to see the futility of massive resistance to desegregation. But he will not see this without pressure from the devotees of civil rights. My friends, I must say to you that we have not made a single gain in civil rights without determined legal and nonviolent pressure. History is the long and tragic story of the fact that privileged groups seldom give up their privileges voluntarily. Individuals may see the moral light and voluntarily give up their unjust posture; but as Reinhold Niebuhr has reminded us, groups are more immoral than individuals.

We know through painful experience that freedom is never voluntarily given by the oppressor; it must be demanded by the oppressed. Frankly, I have never yet engaged in a direct action movement that was "well-timed," according to the timetable of those who have not suffered unduly from the disease of segregation. For years now I have heard the word "Wait!" It rings in the ear of every Negro with a piercing familiarity. This "Wait" has almost always meant "Never." It has been a tranquilizing thalidomide, relieving the emotional stress for a moment, only to give birth to an ill-formed infant of frustration. We must come to see with the distinguished jurist of yesterday that "justice too long delayed is justice denied." We have waited for more than 340 years for our constitutional and God-given rights. The nations of Asia and Africa are moving with jetlike speed toward the goal of political independence, and we still creep at horse and buggy pace toward the gaining of a cup of coffee at a lunch counter. I guess it is easy for those who have never felt the stinging darts of segregation to say, "Wait." But when you have seen vicious mobs lynch your mothers and fathers at will and drown your sisters and brothers at whim; when you have seen hate-filled policemen curse, kick, brutalize and even kill your black brothers and sisters with impunity; when you see the vast majority of your twenty million Negro brothers smothering in an airtight cage of poverty in the midst of an affluent society; when you suddenly find your tongue twisted and your speech stammering as you seek to explain to your six-year-old daughter why she can't go to the public amusement park that has just been advertised on television, and see tears welling up in her little eyes when she is told that Funtown is closed to colored children, and see the depressing clouds of inferiority begin to form in her little mental sky, and see her begin to distort her little personality by unconsciously developing a bitterness toward white people; when you have to concoct an answer for a five-year-old son asking in agonizing pathos: "Daddy, why do white people treat colored people so mean?"; when you take a cross-country drive and find it necessary to sleep night after night in the uncomfortable corners of your automobile because no motel will accept you; when you are humiliated day in and day out by nagging signs reading "white" and "colored"; when your first name becomes "nigger" and your middle name becomes "boy" (however old you are) and your last name becomes "John," and when your wife and mother are never given the respected title "Mrs."; when you are harried by day and haunted by night by the fact that you are a Negro, living constantly at tiptoe stance never quite knowing what to expect next, and plagued with inner fears and outer resentments; when you are forever fighting a degenerating sense of "nobodiness"; then you will understand why we find it difficult to wait. There comes a time when the cup of endurance runs over, and men are no longer willing to be plunged into an abyss of injustice where they experience the blackness of corroding despair. I hope, sirs, you can understand our legitimate and unavoidable impatience.

You express a great deal of anxiety over our willingness to break laws. This is certainly a legitimate concern. Since we so diligently urge people to obey the Supreme Court's decision of 1954 outlawing segregation in the public schools, it is rather strange and paradoxical to find us consciously breaking laws. One may well ask, "How can you advocate breaking some laws and obeying others?" The answer is found in the fact that there are two types of laws: there are *just* and there are *unjust* laws. I would agree with Saint Augustine that "An unjust law is no law at all."

Now what is the difference between the two? How does one determine when a law is just or unjust? A just law is a man-made code that squares with the moral law or the law of God. An unjust law is a code that is out of harmony with the moral law. To put it in the terms of Saint Thomas Aquinas, an unjust law is a human law that is not rooted in eternal and natural law. Any law that uplifts human personality is just. Any law that degrades human personality is unjust. All segregation statutes are unjust because segregation distorts the soul and damages the personality. It gives the segregator a false sense of superiority, and the segregated a false sense of inferiority. To use the words of Martin Buber, the great Jewish philosopher, segregation substitutes an "I-it" relationship for the "I-thou" relationship, and ends up relegating persons to the status of things. So segregation is not only politically, economically and sociologically unsound, but it is morally wrong and sinful. Paul Tillich has said that sin is separation. Isn't segregation an existential expression of man's tragic separation, an expression of his awful estrangement, his terrible sinfulness? So I can urge men to disobey segregation ordinances because they are morally wrong.

Let us turn to a more concrete example of just and unjust laws. An unjust law is a code that a majority inflicts on a minority that is not binding on itself.

324

*Student
Activism
and the Emergence
of a Mass
Movement,
1960–1965*

This is difference made legal. On the other hand a just law is a code that a majority compels a minority to follow that it is willing to follow itself. This is sameness made legal.

Let me give another explanation. An unjust law is a code inflicted upon a minority which that minority had no part in enacting or creating because they did not have the unhampered right to vote. Who can say that the legislature of Alabama which set up the segregation laws was democratically elected? Throughout the state of Alabama all types of conniving methods are used to prevent Negroes from becoming registered voters and there are some counties without a single Negro registered to vote despite the fact that the Negro constitutes a majority of the population. Can any law set up in such a state be considered democratically structured?

These are just a few examples of unjust and just laws. There are some instances when a law is just on its face and unjust in its application. For instance, I was arrested Friday on a charge of parading without a permit. Now there is nothing wrong with an ordinance which requires a permit for a parade, but when the ordinance is used to preserve segregation and to deny citizens the First Amendment privilege of peaceful assembly and peaceful protest, then it becomes unjust.

I hope you can see the distinction I am trying to point out. In no sense do I advocate evading or defying the law as the rabid segregationist would do. This would lead to anarchy. One who breaks an unjust law must do it *openly, lovingly* (not hatefully as the white mothers did in New Orleans when they were seen on television screaming, "nigger, nigger, nigger"), and with a willingness to accept the penalty. I submit that an individual who breaks a law that conscience tells him is unjust, and willingly accepts the penalty by staying in jail to arouse the conscience of the community over its injustice, is in reality expressing the very highest respect for law.

Of course, there is nothing new about this kind of civil disobedience. It was seen sublimely in the refusal of Shadrach, Meshach and Abednego to obey the laws of Nebuchadnezzar because a higher moral law was involved. It was practiced superbly by the early Christians who were willing to face hungry lions and the excruciating pain of chopping blocks, before submitting to certain unjust laws of the Roman Empire. To a degree academic freedom is a reality today because Socrates practiced civil disobedience.

We can never forget that everything Hitler did in Germany was "legal" and everything the Hungarian freedom fighters did in Hungary was "illegal." It was "illegal" to aid and comfort a Jew in Hitler's Germany. But I am sure that if I had lived in Germany during that time I would have aided and comforted my Jewish brothers even though it was illegal. If I lived in a Communist country today where certain principles dear to the Christian faith are suppressed, I believe I would openly advocate disobeying these anti-religious laws. I must make two honest confessions to you, my Christian and Jewish brothers. First, I must confess that over the last few years I have been gravely disappointed with the white moderate. I have almost reached the regrettable conclusion that the Negro's great stumbling block in the stride toward freedom is not the White Citizen's Counciler or the Ku Klux Klanner, but the white moderate who is more devoted to "order" than to justice; who prefers a negative peace which is the absence of tension to a positive peace which is the presence of justice; who constantly says, "I agree with you in the goal you seek, but I can't agree with your methods of direct action"; who paternalistically feels that he can set the timetable for another man's freedom; who lives by the myth of time and who constantly advised the Negro to wait until a "more convenient season." Shallow understanding from people of good will is more frustrating than absolute misunderstanding from people of ill will. Lukewarm acceptance is much more bewildering than outright rejection.

I had hoped that the white moderate would understand that law and order exist for the purpose of establishing justice, and that when they fail to do this they become dangerously structured dams that block the flow of social progress. I had hoped that the white moderate would understand that the present tension of the South is merely a necessary phase of the transition from an obnoxious negative peace, where the Negro passively accepted his unjust plight, to a substance-filled positive peace, where all men will respect the dignity and worth of human personality. Actually, we who engage in nonviolent direct action are not the creators of tension. We merely bring to the surface the hidden tension that is already alive. We bring it out in the open where it can be seen and dealt with. Like a boil that can never be cured as long as it is covered up but must be opened with all its pus-flowing ugliness to the natural medicines of air and light, injustice must likewise be exposed, with all of the tension its exposing creates, to the light of human conscience and the air of national opinion before it can be cured.

In your statement you asserted that our actions, even though peaceful, must be condemned because they precipitate violence. But can this assertion be logically made? Isn't this like condemning the robbed man because his possession of money precipitated the evil act of robbery? Isn't this like condemning Socrates because his unswerving commitment to truth and his philosophical delvings precipitated the misguided popular mind to make him drink the hemlock? Isn't this like condemning Jesus because His unique God-consciousness and never-ceasing devotion to His will precipitated the evil act of crucifixion? We must come to see, as federal courts have consistently affirmed, that it is immoral to urge an individual to withdraw his efforts to gain his basic constitutional rights because the quest precipitates violence. Society must protect the robbed and punish the robber.

I had also hoped that the white moderate would reject the myth of time. I received a letter this morning from a white brother in Texas which said: "All Christians know that the colored people will receive equal rights eventually, but it is possible that you are in too great of a religious hurry. It has taken Christianity almost two thousand years to accomplish what it has. The teachings of Christ take time to come to earth." All that is said here grows out of a tragic misconception of time. It is the strangely irrational notion that there is something in the very flow of time that will inevitably cure all ills. Actually time is neutral. It can be used either destructively or constructively. I am coming to feel that the people of ill will have used time much more effectively than the people of good will. We will have to repent in this generation not merely for the vitriolic words and actions of the bad people, but for the appalling silence of the good people. We must come to see that human progress never rolls in on wheels of inevitability. It comes through the tireless efforts and persistent work of men willing to be co-workers with God, and without this hard work time itself becomes an ally of the forces of social stagnation. We must use time creatively, and forever realize that the time is always ripe to do right. Now is the time to make real the promise of democracy, and transform our pending national elegy into a creative psalm of broth-

326

*Student
Activism
and the Emergence
of a Mass
Movement,
1960–1965*

erhood. Now is the time to lift our national policy from the quicksand of racial injustice to the solid rock of human dignity.

You spoke of our activity in Birmingham as extreme. At first I was rather disappointed that fellow clergymen would see my nonviolent efforts as those of the extremist. I started thinking about the fact that I stand in the middle of two opposing forces in the Negro community. One is a force of complacency made up of Negroes who, as a result of long years of oppression, have been so completely drained of self-respect and a sense of "somebodiness" that they have adjusted to segregation, and, of a few Negroes in the middle class who, because of a degree of academic and economic security, and because at points they profit by segregation, have unconsciously become insensitive to the problems of the masses. The other force is one of bitterness and hatred, and comes perilously close to advocating violence. It is expressed in the various black nationalist groups that are springing up over the nation, the largest and best known being Elijah Muhammad's Muslim movement. This movement is nourished by the contemporary frustration over the continued existence of racial discrimination. It is made up of people who have lost faith in America, who have absolutely repudiated Christianity, and who have concluded that the white man is an incurable "devil." I have tried to stand between these two forces, saying that we need not follow the "do-nothingism" of the complacent or the hatred and despair of the black nationalist. There is the more excellent way of love and nonviolent protest. I'm grateful to God that, through the Negro church, the dimension of nonviolence entered our struggle. If this philosophy had not emerged, I am convinced that by now many streets of the South would be flowing with floods of blood. And I am further convinced that if our white brothers dismiss us as "rabble-rousers" and "outside agitators" those of us who are working through the channels of nonviolent direct action and refuse to support our nonviolent efforts, millions of Negroes, out of frustration and despair, will seek solace and security in black nationalist ideologies, a development that will lead inevitably to a frightening racial nightmare.

Oppressed people cannot remain oppressed forever. The urge for freedom will eventually come. This is what happened to the American Negro. Something within has reminded him of his birthright of freedom; something without has reminded him that he can gain it. Consciously and unconsciously, he has been swept in by what the Germans call the **Zeitgeist**, and with his black brothers of Africa, and his brown and yellow brothers of Asia, South America and the Caribbean, he is moving with a sense of cosmic urgency toward the promised land of racial justice. Recognizing this vital urge that has engulfed the Negro community, one should readily understand public demonstrations. The Negro has many pent-up resentments and latent frustrations. He has to get them out. So let him march sometime; let him have his prayer pilgrimages to the city hall; understand why he must have sit-ins and freedom rides. If his repressed emotions do not come out in these nonviolent ways, they will come out in ominous expressions of violence. This is not a threat; it is a fact of history. So I have not said to my people "get rid of your discontent." But I have tried to say that this normal and healthy discontent can be channelized through the creative outlet of nonviolent direct action. Now this approach is being dismissed as extremist. I must admit that I was initially disappointed in being so categorized.

But as I continued to think about the matter I gradually gained a bit of satisfaction from being considered an extremist. Was not Jesus an extremist in love—"Love your enemies, bless them that curse you, pray for them that despite-fully use you." Was not Amos an extremist for justice—"Let justice roll down like waters and righteousness like a mighty stream." Was not Paul an extremist for the gospel of Jesus Christ—"I bear in my body the marks of the Lord Jesus." Was not Martin Luther an extremist—"Here I stand; I can do none other so help me God." Was not John Bunyan an extremist—"I will stay in jail to the end of my days before I make a butchery of my conscience." Was not Abraham Lincoln an extrem-ist— "This nation cannot survive half slave and half free." Was not Thomas Jef-ferson an extremist—"We hold these truths to be self-evident, that all men are created equal." So the question is not whether we will be extremist but what kind of extremist will we be. Will we be extremists for hate or will we be extremists for love? Will we be extremists for the preservation of injustice—or will we be extremists for the cause of justice? In that dramatic scene on Calvary's hill, three men were crucified. We must not forget that all three were crucified for the same crime—the crime of extremism. Two were extremists for immorality, and thusly fell below their environment. The other, Jesus Christ, was an extremist for love, truth and goodness, and thereby rose above his environment. So, after all, maybe the South, the nation and the world are in dire need of creative extremists.

I had hoped that the white moderate would see this. Maybe I was too opti-mistic. Maybe I expected too much. I guess I should have realized that few members of a race that has oppressed another race can understand or appreciate the deep groans and passionate yearnings of those that have been oppressed and still fewer have the vision to see that injustice must be rooted out by strong, persistent and determined action. I am thankful, however, that some of our white brothers have grasped the meaning of this social revolution and committed themselves to it. They are still all too small in quantity, but they are big in quality. Some like Ralph McGill, Lillian Smith, Harry Golden and James Dabbs have written about our strug-gle in eloquent, prophetic and understanding terms. Others have marched with us down nameless streets of the South. They have languished in filthy roach-infested jails, suffering the abuse and brutality of angry policemen who see them as "dirty nigger-lovers." They, unlike so many of their moderate brothers and sisters, have recognized the urgency of the moment and sensed the need for powerful "action" antidotes to combat the disease of segregation.

Let me rush on to mention my other disappointment. I have been so greatly disappointed with the white church and its leadership. Of course, there are some notable exceptions. I am not unmindful of the fact that each of you has taken some significant stands on this issue. I commend you, Rev. Stallings, for your Christian stance on this past Sunday, in welcoming Negroes to your worship service on a non-segregated basis. I commend the Catholic leaders of this state for inte-grating Springhill College several years ago.

But despite these notable exceptions I must honestly reiterate that I have been disappointed with the church. I do not say that as one of the negative critics who can always find something wrong with the church. I say it as a minister of the gospel, who loves the church; who was nurtured in its bosom; who has been sustained by its spiritual blessings and who will remain true to it as long as the cord of life shall lengthen.

I had the strange feeling when I was suddenly catapulted into the leadership of the bus protest in Montgomery several years ago that we would have the support of the white church. I felt that the white ministers, priests and rabbis of the South

328

*Student
Activism
and the Emergence
of a Mass
Movement,
1960–1965*

would be some of our strongest allies. Instead, some have been outright opponents, refusing to understand the freedom movement and misrepresenting its leaders: all too many others have been more cautious than courageous and have remained silent behind the anesthetizing security of the stained-glass windows.

In spite of my shattered dreams of the past, I came to Birmingham with the hope that the white religious leadership of this community would see the justice of our cause, and with deep moral concern, serve as the channel through which our just grievances would get to the power structure. I had hoped that each of you would understand. But again I have been disappointed. I have heard numerous religious leaders of the South call upon their worshippers to comply with a deseg-regation decision because it is the *law,* but I have longed to hear white ministers say, "Follow this decree because integration is morally *right* and the Negro is your brother." In the midst of blatant injustices inflicted upon the Negro, I have watched white churches stand on the sideline and merely mouth pious irrelevancies and sanctimonious trivialities. In the midst of a mighty struggle to rid our nation of racial and economic injustice, I have heard so many ministers say, "Those are social issues with which the gospel has no real concern," and I have watched so many churches commit themselves to a completely otherworldly religion which made a strange distinction between body and soul, the sacred and the secular.

So here we are moving toward the exit of the twentieth century with a re-ligious community largely adjusted to the status quo, standing as a taillight behind other community agencies rather than a headlight leading men to higher levels of justice.

I have traveled the length and breadth of Alabama, Mississippi and all the other southern states. On sweltering summer days and crisp autumn mornings I have looked at her beautiful churches with their lofty spires pointing heavenward. I have beheld the impressive outlay of her massive religious education buildings. Over and over again I have found myself asking: "What kind of people worship here? Who is their God? Where were their voices when the lips of Governor Barnett dripped with words of interposition and nullification? Where were they when Governor Wallace gave the clarion call for defiance and hatred? Where were their voices of support when tired, bruised and weary Negro men and women decided to rise from the dark dungeons of complacency to the bright hills of creative protest?"

Yes, these questions are still in my mind. In deep disappointment, I have wept over the laxity of the church. But be assured that my tears have been tears of love. There can be no deep disappointment where there is not deep love. Yes, I love the church; I love her sacred walls. How could I do otherwise? I am in the rather unique position of being the son, the grandson and the great-grandson of preachers. Yes, I see the church as the body of Christ. But, oh! How we have blemished and scarred that body through social neglect and fear of being nonconformists.

There was a time when the church was very powerful. It was during that period when the early Christians rejoiced when they were deemed worthy to suffer for what they believed. In those days the church was not merely a thermometer that recorded the ideas and principles of popular opinion; it was a thermostat that transformed the mores of society. Wherever the early Christians entered a town the power structure got disturbed and immediately sought to convict them for being "disturbers of the peace" and "outside agitators." But they went on with the conviction that they were "a colony of heaven," and had to obey God rather than man. They were small in number but big in commitment. They were too God-intoxicated to be "astronomically intimidated." They brought an end to such ancient evils as infanticide and gladiatorial contest.

Things are different now. The contemporary church is often a weak, ineffectual voice with an uncertain sound. It is so often the arch-supporter of the status quo. Far from being disturbed by the presence of the church, the power structure of the average community is consoled by the church's silent and often vocal sanction of things as they are.

But the judgment of God is upon the church as never before. If the church of today does not recapture the sacrificial spirit of the early church, it will lose its authentic ring, forfeit the loyalty of millions, and be dismissed as an irrelevant social club with no meaning for the twentieth century. I am meeting young people every day whose disappointment with the church has risen to outright disgust.

Maybe again, I have been too optimistic. Is organized religion too inextricably bound to the status quo to save our nation and the world? Maybe I must turn my faith to the inner spiritual church, the church within the church, as the true *ecclesia* and the hope of the world. But again I am thankful to God that some noble souls from the ranks of organized religion have broken loose from the paralyzing chains of conformity and joined us as active partners in the struggle for freedom. They have left their secure congregations and walked the streets of Albany, Georgia, with us. They have gone through the highways of the South on tortuous rides for freedom. Yes, they have gone to jail with us. Some have been kicked out of their churches, and lost support of their bishops and fellow ministers. But they have gone with the faith that right defeated is stronger than evil triumphant. These men have been the leaven in the lump of the race. Their witness has been the spiritual salt that has preserved the true meaning of the gospel in these troubled times. They have carved a tunnel of hope through the dark mountain of disappointment.

I hope the church as a whole will meet the challenge of this decisive hour. But even if the church does not come to the aid of justice, I have no despair about the future. I have no fear about the outcome of our struggle in Birmingham, even if our motives are presently misunderstood. We will reach the goal of freedom in Birmingham and all over the nation, because the goal of America is freedom. Abused and scorned though we may be, our destiny is tied up with the destiny of America. Before the Pilgrims landed at Plymouth we were here. Before the pen of Jefferson etched across the pages of history the majestic words of the Declaration of Independence, we were here. For more than two centuries our foreparents labored in this country without wages; they made cotton king; and they built the homes of their masters in the midst of brutal injustice and shameful humiliation—and yet out of a bottomless vitality they continued to thrive and develop. If the inexpressible cruelties of slavery could not stop us, the opposition we now face will surely fail. We will win our freedom because the sacred heritage of our nation and the eternal will of God are embodied in our echoing demands.

I must close now. But before closing I am impelled to mention one other point in your statement that troubled me profoundly. You warmly commended the Birmingham police force for keeping "order" and "preventing violence." I don't believe you would have so warmly commended the police force if you had seen its angry violent dogs literally biting six unarmed, nonviolent Negroes. I don't believe you would so quickly commend the policemen if you would observe their ugly and inhuman treatment of Negroes here in the city jail; if you would watch them

330

*Student
Activism
and the Emergence
of a Mass
Movement,
1960–1965*

push and curse old Negro women and young Negro girls; if you would see them slap and kick old Negro men and young boys; if you will observe them, as they did on two occasions, refuse to give us food because we wanted to sing our grace together. I'm sorry that I can't join you in your praise for the police department.

It is true that they have been rather disciplined in their public handling of the demonstrators. In this sense they have been rather publicly "nonviolent." But for what purpose? To preserve the evil system of segregation. Over the last few years I have consistently preached that nonviolence demands that the means we use must be as pure as the ends we seek. So I have tried to make it clear that it is wrong to use immoral means to attain moral ends. But now I must affirm that it is just as wrong, or even more so, to use moral means to preserve immoral ends. Maybe Mr. Connor and his policemen have been rather publicly nonviolent, as Chief Pritchett was in Albany, Georgia, but they have used the moral means of nonviolence to maintain the immoral end of flagrant racial injustice. T. S. Eliot has said that there is no greater treason than to do the right deed for the wrong reason.

I wish you had commended the Negro sit-inners and demonstrators of Birmingham for their sublime courage, their willingness to suffer and their amazing discipline in the midst of the most inhuman provocation. One day the South will recognize its real heroes. They will be the James Merediths, courageously and with a majestic sense of purpose facing jeering and hostile mobs and the agonizing loneliness that characterizes the life of the pioneer. They will be old, oppressed, battered Negro women, symbolized in a seventy-two-year-old woman of Montgomery, Alabama, who rose up with a sense of dignity and with her people decided not to ride the segregated buses, and responded to one who inquired about her tiredness with ungrammatical profundity: "My feet is tired, but my soul is rested." They will be the young high school and college students, young ministers of the gospel and a host of their elders courageously and nonviolently sitting-in at lunch counters and willingly going to jail for conscience's sake. One day the South will know that when these disinherited children of God sat down at lunch counters they were in reality standing up for the best in the American dream and the most sacred values in our Judeo-Christian heritage, and thusly, carrying our whole nation back to those great wells of democracy which were dug deep by the Founding Fathers in the formulation of the Constitution and the Declaration of Independence.

Never before have I written a letter this long (or should I say a book?). I'm afraid that it is much too long to take your precious time. I can assure you that it would have been much shorter if I had been writing from a comfortable desk, but what else is there to do when you are alone for days in the dull monotony of a narrow jail cell other than write long letters, think strange thoughts, and pray long prayers?

If I have said anything in this letter that is an overstatement of the truth and is indicative of an unreasonable impatience, I beg you to forgive me. If I have said anything in this letter that is an understatement of the truth and is indicative of my having a patience that makes me patient with anything less than brotherhood, I beg God to forgive me.

I hope this letter finds you strong in the faith. I also hope that circumstances will soon make it possible for me to meet each of you, not as an integrationist or a civil rights leader, but as a fellow clergyman and a Christian brother. Let us all hope that the dark clouds of racial prejudice will soon pass away and the deep fog of misunderstanding will be lifted from our fear-drenched communities and in some not too distant tomorrow the radiant stars of love and brotherhood will shine over our great nation with all of their scintillating beauty.

331

4.5 The Making of 'I Have a Dream'

Yours for the cause of Peace and Brotherhood, Martin Luther King Jr.

4.5   Keith D. Miller and Emily M. Lewis

Touchstones, Authorities, and Marian Anderson: The Making of 'I Have a Dream'

Keith Miller is assistant professor of English at Arizona State University. He is author of Voice of Deliverance: The Language of Martin Luther King Jr. and Its Sources. *Emily Lewis is a former graduate student at Arizona State University.*

On Easter Sunday 1939, when Marian Anderson sang 'America' ('My country 'tis of thee/Sweet land of liberty') from the steps of the Lincoln Memorial, the event served as both a culmination and a beginning—the culmination of a long effort to identify Abraham Lincoln as a symbol of racial equality and the beginning of a method of formalized protest that would climax when Martin Luther King Jr. delivered 'I Have a Dream' on those same steps twenty-four years later.

After the **Daughters of the American Revolution** had prevented Anderson from singing at Constitution Hall because of her race, First Lady Eleanor Roosevelt resigned from the DAR, and NAACP chief Walter White arranged for Anderson to perform at the Lincoln Memorial before 75 000 people. Harold Ickes, Secretary of Interior, introduced Anderson by commenting on the appropriateness of the setting: 'In this great auditorium under the sky all of us are free. When God gave us this wonderful outdoors and the sun, the moon and the stars, He made no distinction of race, or creed, or color.'

As Scott Sandage explains, by scheduling the concert as a response to the controversy, 'black organizers transformed a recital of sacred music at a national shrine into a political rally.' Sandage argues that, by reinterpreting the Lincoln Memorial, the NAACP and Anderson helped revise the memory of Abraham Lincoln from that of the National Saviour to that of the Great Emancipator.

Such an effort was necessary because northern white leaders had sought to define Lincoln as an icon unrelated to slavery and emancipation. When designers planned the Lincoln Memorial and commissioned a sculptor to chisel the giant statue housed inside, they envisioned their work not as a tribute to the liberator of slaves but instead 'as a symbol of national consensus, linking North and South on holy, national ground.' At the dedication in 1922 the chief planner of the Lincoln Memorial, former president William Howard Taft, gave a lengthy speech that en-

332

*Student
Activism
and the Emergence
of a Mass
Movement,
1960–1965*

tirely ignored the subject of slavery. In another address at the dedication, President Warren Harding insisted that Lincoln 'would have been the last man in the republic to resort to arms to effect . . . abolition. Emancipation was a means to the great end—maintained union. . . .'

On other occasions as well, white officials exalted Lincoln by extracting him from the divisiveness of slavery and emancipation. In 1916 President Woodrow Wilson accepted as a national site the farm where Lincoln was born. Credentialing himself, Wilson stated, 'I have read many biographies of Lincoln.' He hailed Lincoln as 'a man of singular, delightful, vital genius' and a 'natural ruler of men' with a 'great heart that seemed to comprehend all mankind.' Nowhere in his **panegyric** did Wilson mention slavery or emancipation. Nowhere did he even allude to the Civil War. Rather he portrayed Lincoln as a god-like figure involved in human affairs yet somehow elevated above them.

African-Americans, however, interpreted national symbols differently than did presidents. In his famous 1852 **jeremiad** 'What to the Slave Is the Fourth of July?', Frederick Douglass attacked slavery in part by contrasting the promises of the Declaration of Independence to the horrors of bondage. When Henry Highland Garnet denounced slavery, he invoked George Washington, Thomas Jefferson, Moses, and the Christian religion as his authorities.

After slavery ended, African-American orators continue to make arguments similar to those offered by Douglass and Garnet. These later speakers contrasted the values enunciated in the Declaration of Independence, the newly amended Constitution, and the Bible to the ugly racism institutionalized in American life. Following Douglass and Garnet, these black leaders urged whites to end prejudice and hypocrisy by living up to the noble ideals of democracy and brotherhood that whites claimed to embrace. Adding Lincoln to the gallery of sanctified religious and patriotic figures whom they invoked, these orators interpreted the Emancipation Proclamation as another touchstone of democracy and freedom.

Early in this century George William Cook compared Christ's preaching to the Declaration of Independence. James Curtis and M. C. B. Mason compared Lincoln to Christ and called for equal rights. In his speech 'Abraham Lincoln and Fifty Years of Freedom', Abraham Walters praised 'the immortal Emancipator', demanded racial equality and claimed, 'Mr. Lincoln was the first to suggest to his party the enfranchisement of the Negro.' Ernest Lyon celebrated the fiftieth anniversary of the Emancipation Proclamation by evoking Lincoln and the Constitution and by describing African-American triumphs against great odds. Lyon concluded his speech optimistically: ' . . . since Right is Right and God is God, Right must ultimately prevail.' In yet another oration honouring the fiftieth anniversary of the Emancipation Proclamation, William Lewis asserted that Lincoln 'walked with God'; Lewis identified Jefferson, Lincoln and Christianity by claiming that Lincoln, in effect, declared, '"The Negro is a man' " and " 'my [Lincoln's] ancient faith tells me that all men are created equal.' "

During inaugural week of 1909, Francis Grimke entered his pulpit in Washington, DC, cited Lincoln, and issued a jeremiad to whites who failed to live by their expressed values: 'The secession of the Southern States in 1860 was a small matter compared with the secession of the Union itself from the great principles enunciated in the Declaration of Independence, in the Golden Rule, in the Ten Commandments, in the Sermon on the Mount.' After invoking these touchstones, Grimke protested the pattern of segregation unfolding across the

South. He bemoaned the loss of the vote, rejoiced that blacks were generally 'dissatisfied' and advocated the need to struggle against 'this great evil of race prejudice.' He ended optimistically, affirming 'The right is bound, sooner or later, to triumph' and explaining 'A better day is coming; but we have got to help to bring it about.'

At the consecration of the Lincoln Memorial in 1922 Robert Russa Moton, who replaced Booker T. Washington as president of Tuskegee Institute, was the only speaker to violate the careful process of crafting Lincoln's image as a national healer who stood above the issue of race. Unlike Taft and Harding, Moton dared to tie Lincoln to **manumission**. He hailed Lincoln as 'the great emancipator', who implemented part of Jefferson's promise that 'all men are created equal'; further, he challenged Americans to make their nation 'an example for all the world of equal justice and equal opportunity for all.' Although Moton had his say, white officials apparently won this particular battle over the memory of Lincoln. Blacks were allowed to witness the dedication of the Lincoln Memorial only from a segregated area where they sat behind white spectators—an arrangement that obviously conflicted with Moton's call for 'equal justice.'

Despite their setback in contesting the image of Lincoln at the 1922 dedication, blacks continued to call for equality by appealing to sanctified touchstones and authorities. African-Americans acted on a rhetorical assumption that Kenneth Burke articulates: 'if the excommunicated would avoid the corner of negativism, he must recruit a group who steal the insignia of the orthodox.' Burke explains, 'The stealing back and forth of symbols is the approved method whereby the Outs avoid "being driven into a corner"'. By fusing their demands to hallowed emblems, blacks claimed that the American civil religion necessitated racial equality. In this argument, rejecting equal rights meant rejecting all things dear and holy.

But in order to appeal successfully to the emblem of Lincoln, African-Americans first had to win the rhetorical war over what Lincoln symbolized. They did not enjoy the luxury of explaining how Lincoln intertwined his roles as National Saviour and Great Emancipator—a task that Frederick Douglass undertook in 1876 when dedicating a monument to Lincoln. No, they needed simply to define Lincoln as the emancipator—period. Then he could serve as a rhetorically useful authority and a link to connect Christianity and Jefferson's words—'all men are created equal'—to their own situation.

Although white Americans' memory of Lincoln appears to have gradually evolved from National Unifier (in 1922) to Emancipator (in 1938), Anderson's 1939 performance at the Lincoln Memorial proved decisive in garnering massive, positive publicity that permanently associated the image of Lincoln with the theme of racial equality. She and the NAACP thereby won a decisive battle in the rhetorical contest to seize and command the symbol of Lincoln, culminating the combined rhetorical efforts of Curtis, Mason, Lyon, Walters, Lewis, Grimke and Moton. Forever would Lincoln's name be coupled with what Kenneth Burke would call the 'god-terms' of 'freedom' and 'equality.'

Not only did Anderson's performance end the struggle over what Lincoln represented, it also inaugurated a stylized form of dissent in a specific location. Sandage explains:

A standardized civil rights protest ritual evolved from the elements in Marian Anderson's concert, such as using mass rallies instead of pickets, performing patriotic and spiritual music, choosing a religious format, inviting prominent

334

*Student
Activism
and the Emergence
of a Mass
Movement,
1960–1965*

platform guests, self-policing the crowds to project an orderly image, alluding to Lincoln in publicity and oratory, and insisting on using the memorial rather than another site.

Although this formalized ritual was new, it simply constituted a refined form of the same argument that Douglass, Garnet and other black orators had used before, namely criticizing whites for preaching equality and justice while practising segregation and injustice. In this refined political ceremony, not only did blacks again protest exploitation and argue from authority, they claimed the same specific authorities—Moses, Christ, Jefferson and Lincoln—that Douglass, Garnet and other African-American speakers had cited singly or in combination. And they argued from the same benchmarks—the Bible, the Declaration of Independence and the Emancipation Proclamation. Through her singing Anderson added 'America' ('My country 'tis of thee/Sweet land of liberty') to the list of touchstones.

Two years after the Anderson concert, A. Philip Randolph started a March on Washington Movement, threatening President Franklin Roosevelt with a huge demonstration that would conclude at the Lincoln Memorial. Fearful of Randolph's march, Roosevelt supplied an executive order outlawing segregation in the defence industry. In 1943 Randolph organized a small band that gathered at the memorial on Lincoln's birthday and sang the spiritual 'Go Down, Moses.' Other protests followed at the site.

Of course African-Americans continued to dissent in places other than the Lincoln Memorial. In 1944 a fifteen-year-old boy from Atlanta won a local oratorical contest (and qualified for a state contest) by disputing racism. His name was Martin Luther King, Jr. Whether King wrote this address, 'The Negro and the Constitution', or borrowed it from an unacknowledged and as-yet-undiscovered source, he identified himself with it and delivered it with enough conviction to win a contest.

In this speech the teenage King followed familiar practices. His chief themes were identical with those of Francis Grimke. Both Grimke and King lambasted racial inequity, advocated the right to vote, applauded the black struggle for freedom, and concluded with a note of high optimism. Like Mason and Lyon, King discussed the beginning of American slavery in 1620. Like Lyon, King claimed that emancipation left blacks in a rather pitiful, undeveloped state. Again like Lyon—albeit much more briefly—King announced that African-Americans had nonetheless important contributions.

In 'The Negro and the Constitution' the young King also appealed to hallowed emblems in order to contrast America's gaudy promises to its disturbing practices. Like Grimke, King recalled the Golden Rule. Like Curtis and Mason, King identified Christ and Lincoln. Like Lewis and Moton, King incorporated Jefferson's assertion from the Declaration of Independence: 'all men are created . . . equal'. Like Lyon, Walters and Lewis, King alluded to the number of years that had passed since the Emancipation Proclamation. And just as Grimke merged his voice with lyrics from the 'Battle Hymn of the Republic', King merged his own voice with lyrics from 'Lift Every Voice and Sing', sometimes known as the Negro National Anthem.

In the same oration the youthful King analysed the importance of Anderson's 1939 concert:

Marian Anderson was barred from singing in Constitution Hall, ironically enough by the professional daughters of the very men who founded this nation for liberty and equality. But this tale had a different ending. The nation rose in protest, and gave a stunning rebuke to the Daughters of the American Revolution and a tremendous ovation to the artist, Marian Anderson, who sang in Washington on Easter Sunday and fittingly, before the Lincoln Memorial.

After remarking the distinguished members of the audience and the size of crowd, King explained,

> [Anderson] sang as never before with tears in her eyes. When the words of "America" and "Nobody Knows de Trouble I Seen" rang out over that great gathering, there was a hush on the sea of uplifted faces, black and white, and a new baptism of liberty, equality, and fraternity.

Here the adolescent King associated the American Revolution, Constitution Hall, Washington, DC, and the Lincoln Memorial—where Anderson 'fittingly' sang—with the 'god-terms' of 'liberty' and 'equality.' Like the organizers who staged Anderson's concert on Easter, King skilfully fused sacred and patriotic messages, mentioning the timing of the concert on Easter Sunday and claiming that it initiated a 'new baptism of liberty.' The baptism occurred when Anderson sang 'America' and a spiritual and thereby identified patriotism and African-American culture.

Wanting his tribute to Anderson to be more than a panegyric, the teenage King transformed it into a values appeal in his protest against segregation: 'Yet [Miss Anderson] cannot be served in the public restaurants of her home city, even after it has declared her to be its best citizen.'

In 1955, eleven years later, the Montgomery bus boycott catapulted King onto the national stage. In 1957, King and NAACP chief Roy Wilkins planned a Prayer Pilgrimage to the Lincoln Memorial on the third anniversary of the Supreme Court decision in *Brown v. the Board of Education*. On the steps of the memorial, gospel soloist Mahalia Jackson sang 'America.' Wearing his pulpit robe at that same spot, King delivered 'Give Us the Ballot', the major speech of the Prayer Pilgrimage. He urged the nation to obey the desegregation order of the Supreme Court and repeatedly implored Congress for the right to vote. He closed by referring to Moses and by quoting ten lines from 'Lift Every Voice and Sing'—the same hymn he had excerpted thirteen years earlier in 'The Negro and the Constitution'.

In the nineteen years between 'The Negro and the Constitution', and 'I Have a Dream', King remembered Marian Anderson. To understand his references to her in 1963, we need to return to her 1939 performance at the Lincoln Memorial. There she helped construct her musical persona by singing 'America', an Italian aria, Schubert's 'Ave Maria', and several spirituals. By selecting 'America', she bolstered her credentials as a patriot; by choosing 'Ave Maria', she became a worthy purveyor of the finest classical music; by picking beautiful and religiously orthodox spirituals, she argued for the importance of the people who produced them. By creating her musical persona out of such disparate materials, Anderson presented herself as a loyal, black American soaked in the finest European culture.

The mature King constructed his rhetorical persona in an analogous fashion. Seeking legitimacy, he carefully fixed himself within the coordinates of Christian, Euro-American moral and intellectual traditions. In an autobiographical essay, 'Pilgrimage to Nonviolence', he maintained that his ideas sprang from reading prestigious Euro-American philosophers and theologians even though he repeatedly copied the words of fellow preachers and friends to explain what he claimed to

336

*Student
Activism
and the Emergence
of a Mass
Movement,
1960–1965*

have learned from Marx and other renowned thinkers. He dotted—and sometimes saturated—his discourse with quotations from and references to Shakespeare, Jefferson, Lincoln, Thoreau, Emerson, the American Revolution, the Civil War, emancipation, *Brown v. Board of Education,* Moses, Christ and other biblical figures—each of whom served as an authority or touchstone that helped clarify a current situation. He garnered many of these quotations and references from books of sermons by preachers whose names he rarely mentioned.

Balancing his use of Euro-American icons and history lessons, King frequently incorporated into his addresses the lyrics of spirituals, gospel songs and hymns, using them to cap several of his most important orations. Like Lyon, he highlighted his African-American identity by occasionally spotlighting outstanding black achievers who had overcome extremely formidable obstacles.

One of the achievers King chronicled was Anderson. In 'The American Dream', a sermon delivered in February 1963, he applauded her: 'From poverty-stricken conditions . . . Marian Anderson rose up to be the world's greatest contralto, so that Toscanini had to cry out: "A voice like this comes only once in a century." And Sibelius of Finland said: "My roof is too low for such a voice." '

At the end of the homily he referred to Lincoln, 'who had the vision to see that this nation could not survive half slave and half free', and quoted Jefferson—'all men are created equal'.

In 'Dives and Lazarus,' a sermon delivered in March 1963, King spoke more about Anderson. Borrowing from white preacher/scholar George Buttrick and from British preacher Leslie Weatherhead, King expounded the theme of interrelatedness, explaining the need to recognize one's dependence on others. He introduced his analysis of Anderson by talking about 'that great experience I had in reading the autobiography of Marian Anderson'. Published in 1956, Anderson's autobiography is one of only a handful of books that King ever claimed to have read after the start of the Montgomery bus boycott.

After noting Anderson's autobiography, King cited Anderson as someone with a keen sense of obligation to her extraordinary mother. He devoted 342 words to detailing the enormous sacrifices that Mrs Anderson made to further Marian Anderson's education and Mrs Anderson's unlimited joy when she heard her daughter sing 'Ave Maria' and a spiritual at Carnegie Hall. Then he related Marian Anderson's gratitude to her mother. He recalled that someone had asked Marian Anderson about 'the happiest moment' in her life, inquiring,

> Was it the moment that Toscanini said that you possess the "voice that comes only once in a century"? Miss Anderson said "No." Was it the moment that you sang before Sibelius of Finland and he said, "My roof is too low for your voice"? Miss Anderson said "No". . . . What was it then? . . . "The happiest moment in my life was when I could say, 'Mother, you may stop working now.' "

Here King established Anderson's musical status by indicating that she sang Schubert's classic 'Ave Maria' in Carnegie Hall, easily the most famous auditorium in the nation. He reinforced and upgraded that status by noting the acclaim lavished upon her by the greatest living conductor of European classical music (Toscanini) and by the greatest living composer of European classical music (Sibelius). No one could dismiss such authorities.

King further explained that Anderson served as a stellar ambassador of the African-American community, one who brought spirituals to an arena where they could be savoured by the best-trained and most discriminating of musical ears. As if this were not enough, King ventured, Anderson maintained perspective on her rare fame. She was happiest when earning enough money to rescue her hard-working mother from a life of endless toil. King urged his listeners to emulate her recognition of interdependence.

King concluded by turning the whole theme of interrelatedness—including his exegesis of the parable of Dives and Lazarus and his long Anderson illustration—into an argument against white supremacy, a doctrine that denied interdependence. He thereby transmuted his Anderson illustration into a values appeal against racism, just as he had done in 'The Negro and the Constitution'.

One hundred years after the Emancipation Proclamation, a few months after delivering 'Dives and Lazarus', King joined A. Philip Randolph, Roy Wilkins and other civil rights advocates in orchestrating a massive March on Washington. A galaxy of religious figures—including a Roman Catholic archbishop, the president of the American Jewish Congress, and a leader of the National Council of Churches—joined 200 000 others at the Lincoln Memorial. There they sang 'Go Down, Moses', the spiritual that Randolph's small group had brought to the same spot twenty years earlier.

From the steps of the memorial, various speakers offered highly predictable values appeals in demanding strong civil rights legislation. Randolph invoked Jesus Christ. Wilkins quoted the New Testament. Moderate Whitney Young claimed that civil rights were 'constitutionally guaranteed'. Youthful militant John Lewis called for agitation 'until the Revolution of 1776 is completed.' Joan Baez sang the spiritual 'Oh Freedom'. Jewish leader Joachim Prinz cited the Pledge of Allegiance and urged action on behalf of 'the image, the dream, the idea, and the aspiration of America itself'. Walter Reuther, President of the United Auto Workers, lamented the 'moral gap between American democracy's noble promises and its ugly practices in the field of civil rights.' He added, 'There is too much high octane hypocrisy in America.'

Nearing the end of the proceedings, Randolph introduced Marian Anderson, who calmed the huge crowd with a spiritual, and Mahalia Jackson, who revived everyone with an up-tempo spiritual bewailing the slaves' mistreatment and implying that justice would come.

After Prinz's remarks, King's turn came. A few days earlier, he had told a friend that he wanted to give 'a sort of Gettysburg Address'. That intention was obvious when, in his second sentence, King echoed the opening of Lincoln's famous oration and alluded to the enormous statue of Lincoln gazing at his back; 'Five score years ago, a great American, in whose symbolic shadow we stand today, signed the Emancipation Proclamation.'

In its structure and themes, King's 'I Have a Dream' closely resembles Francis Grimke's jeremiad of 1909. Like Grimke, King protested the loss of the vote and measured white racism against the Declaration of Independence and the Bible. Grimke rejoiced that blacks were 'dissatisfied'; King asserted that blacks 'can never be satisfied' with injustice. And, like Grimke (and Lyon), King ended with a strikingly hopeful vision based on the promises of the American civil religion.

Further, as Dave Barboza observes, the form and themes of 'I Have a Dream' strongly resemble those of King's 'The Negro and the Constitution.' The major purpose of each speech is to protest racial injustice. One theme common to the orations is the need to recognize interdependence. In 'The Negro and the Consti-

338

*Student
Activism
and the Emergence
of a Mass
Movement,
1960–1965*

tution' King argued that slaves established 'the empire of King cotton' that made possible the unique 'status of life and hospitality' enjoyed by southern whites. In addition he maintained that white Americans' health hinged on racial justice. Because diseases spread from blacks to whites, he argued, a 'healthy nation' was impossible as long as blacks were 'harboring germs of disease which recognize no color lines.' In 'I Have a Dream', he contended that African-Americans needed to recognize interdependence: 'many of our white brothers . . . have come to realize that their destiny is tied up with our destiny and they have come to realize that their freedom is inextricably bound to our freedom. We cannot walk alone.'

Many of the same, ritualized values appeals animate 'The Negro and the Constitution' and 'I Have a Dream'. Following a pattern established (or confirmed) by Grimke, King in both orations marshalled ritualized appeals to protest an American nightmare; then he paradoxically offered hope based on the same civil religion. In 'The Negro and the Constitution' King ventured that, despite the Civil War and emancipation, 'Black America still wears chains'. In 'I Have a Dream' he used the same metaphor to describe the same nightmare: 'One hundred years [after emancipation] . . . the Negro is still sadly crippled by the manacles of segregation.' In 'The Negro and the Constitution' he objected that Marian Anderson could not 'spend the night in any good hotel in America'. In 'I Have a Dream' he decried blacks' inability to 'gain lodging in . . . the hotels of the cities'.

In both 'The Negro and the Constitution' and 'I Have a Dream', he piled one racist scandal on top of another, organized each pile in parallel sentences beginning with 'We cannot', and included a biblical scale to weigh each injustice—in the first, a reference to Jesus; in the second, an excerpt from the prophet Amos. Compare:

'The Negro and the Constitution'

We cannot have an enlightened democracy with one great group living in ignorance.
We cannot have a healthy nation with one tenth of the people . . . harboring germs of disease which recognize no color lines . . .
We cannot have a nation orderly and sound with one group so ground down . . . that it is almost forced into . . . crime.
We cannot be truly Christian people so long as we flaunt [sic] the central teachings of Jesus: brotherly love and the Golden Rule.
We cannot come to full prosperity with one great group so ill-delayed that it cannot buy goods.

'I Have a Dream'

We can never be satisfied as long as the Negro is the victim of the unspeakable horrors of police brutality. . . .
We cannot be satisfied as long as the Negro's basic mobility is from a smaller ghetto to a larger one.
We cannot be satisfied as long as our children are stripped of their selfhood . . . by signs saying 'For Whites Only.'
We cannot be satisfied as long as a Negro in Mississippi cannot vote. . . .
No, we . . . will not be satisfied until justice rolls down like waters and righteousness like a mighty stream.

By the time King reached this 'We cannot' litany in 'The Negro and the Constitution', he had already alluded to Lincoln, the Emancipation Proclamation, and constitutional amendments outlawing discrimination; he had already quoted Jefferson's 'all men are created equal'; and—in the section on Anderson—he had already cited Constitution Hall, the American Revolution, Easter Sunday, the Lincoln Memorial, 'America' and a spiritual.

By the time he reached the 'We cannot' litany of 'I Have a Dream', he had already echoed the Gettysburg Address; turned a Shakespearean phrase inside out; alluded to a teaching of Jesus; and noted the Emancipation Proclamation, the Constitution, and the Declaration of Independence, which he had quoted.

Extending a metaphor for seven sentences, King used familiar benchmarks to contend that the 'architects of our republic' had offered a 'check' that promised freedom. 'America', he complained, 'has given the Negro people a bad check', which kited due to 'insufficient funds'. Yet the promise of Jefferson's Declaration is sacred and will surely be redeemed: 'We refuse to believe that there are insufficient funds in the great vaults of opportunity of this nation. And so we've come to cash this check.' This appeal to sterling promises—whose realization is currently thwarted but eventually certain—underlies the entire speech, just as it did Grimke's oration and 'The Negro and the Constitution'.

Like Grimke's speech, 'The Negro and the Constitution' ended with great optimism as King blended sacred and secular appeals: 'My heart throbs anew in the hope that inspired by the example of Lincoln, imbued with the spirit of Christ, [Americans] will cast down the last barrier to perfect freedom.' Continuing 'I Have a Dream', King quoted again from the Declaration—'all men are created equal'—and included an extended, visionary metaphor from Isaiah that reappeared in the New Testament and in Handel's 'Messiah' ('every valley shall be. . . ') .

King ended 'I Have a Dream' by borrowing, adjusting, and adding to the conclusion of a speech that black pastor Archibald Carey gave at the 1952 Republican Convention. Carey had argued against segregation by citing emancipation and appealing to Jesus, Paul, the Hebrew Bible and the Declaration. Carey began his conclusion by quoting 'America':

We, Negro Americans, sing with all loyal Americans:

My country 'tis of thee, Sweet land of liberty. Of thee I sing—Land where my fathers died, Land of the Pilgrim's pride. From every mountainside Let freedom ring!

That's exactly what we mean—from every mountainside, let freedom ring. Not only from the Green Mountains and White Mountains of Vermont and New Hampshire; not only from the Catskills of New York; but from the Ozarks in Arkansas, from the Stone Mountain in Georgia, from the Blue Ridge Mountains of Virginia—let it ring not only for the minorities of the United States, but for . . . the disinherited of all the earth—may the Republican Party, under God, from every mountainside, LET FREEDOM RING!

Compare Carey's words to those in 'I Have a Dream':

This will be the day when all of God's children will be able to sing with new meaning:

My country 'tis of thee, sweet land of liberty. Of thee I sing—Land where my fathers died, Land of the Pilgrims' pride. From every mountainside Let freedom ring!

340

*Student
Activism
and the Emergence
of a Mass
Movement,
1960–1965*

So let freedom ring from the prodigious hilltops of New Hampshire. Let freedom ring from the mighty mountains of New York. Let freedom ring from the heightening Alleghenies of Pennsylvania. . . . Let freedom ring from Stone Mountain of Georgia. Let freedom ring from Lookout Mountain of Tennessee. Let freedom ring from every hill and molehill in Mississippi. From every mountainside, let freedom ring!

Unlike Carey, King reached the climax of the peroration when he stated emphatically, 'Let freedom ring from every hill and molehill in Mississippi. . . .' Inasmuch as Mississippi is a low-lying state, this imagery revived the earlier metaphor of geographical transformation that King had quoted from Isaiah—'every valley shall be exalted'. Thus he brilliantly merged Biblical eschatology and the 'god-term' of freedom that, by now, was firmly identified with Jefferson and Lincoln.

King further improved Carey's conclusion by quoting a spiritual. King envisioned a day when whites would overcome the contradictions between American promise and American practice, and everyone would 'join hands and sing in the words of the old Negro spiritual, "Free at last! Free at last! Thank God, Almighty. We're free at last." ' Through the word 'free', he again fused the slaves' desires with Isaiah's dramatic prophecy and the goals of Jefferson and Lincoln.

By singing 'America' and a spiritual at her 1939 concert, Anderson had similarly merged the slaves' desires with the goals of Jefferson, Lincoln and Christianity—an identification that essentially repeated the values appeals of Grimke and others. In 'The Negro and the Constitution', King remarked this identification by observing that, by singing 'America' and a spiritual, Anderson had precipitated a 'new baptism of liberty'. In 'I Have a Dream', he offered a strikingly parallel appeal.

James Cone, David Garrow, Lewis Baldwin and Keith D. Miller contend that King's religion, politics, ideas and eloquence stem from his immersion in the black church, not, as a generation of scholars has argued, from his graduate training in Euro-American philosophy and theology. Alexandra Alvarez, Robert Harrison and Linda Harrison, and Miller argue that 'I Have a Dream' reflects King's exposure to his father's folk preaching.

Clearly 'I Have a Dream' sprang not only from African-American folk sermons, but also from the black oratorical (and sometimes homiletic) tradition of Douglass, Garnet, Lyon and Grimke. At her 1939 concert Anderson refined their values appeals into what became a political ritual at the Lincoln Memorial. In a speech he gave at the age of fifteen, long before he enrolled in graduate school, King offered decidedly comparable appeals throughout and analysed Anderson's concert as an example of such appeals. In 'I Have a Dream', he re-enacted the political ritual that Anderson had begun and that he had interpreted when he was fifteen.

'I Have a Dream' did not succeed despite its 'historical self-consciousness' as one critic has claimed. Instead, 'I Have a Dream' triumphed because through it King perfected the values appeals that his black predecessors (and he himself) had standardized, stylized, formalized and ritualized.

'I Have a Dream' is an acutely paradoxical oration. It is scintillating. It is incandescent. It is nonpareil. But it is also brilliantly and profoundly conventional.

From Protest to Politics: The Future of the Civil Rights Movement

Bayard Rustin played a leading role in organizing the 1963 March on Washington. He was an eminent figure in the civil rights movement without ever becoming a genuine leader.

The decade spanned by the 1954 Supreme Court decision on school desegregation and the Civil Rights Act of 1964 will undoubtedly be recorded as the period in which the legal foundations of racism in America were destroyed. To be sure, pockets of resistance remain; but it would be hard to quarrel with the assertion that the elaborate legal structure of segregation and discrimination, particularly in relation to public accommodations, has virtually collapsed. On the other hand, without making light of the human sacrifices involved in the direct-action tactics (sit-ins, freedom rides, and the rest) that were so instrumental to this achievement, we must recognize that in desegregating public accommodations, we affected institutions which are relatively peripheral both to the American socio-economic order and to the fundamental conditions of life of the Negro people. In a highly industrialized, 20th-century civilization, we hit Jim Crow precisely where it was most anachronistic, dispensable, and vulnerable—in hotels, lunch counters, terminals, libraries, swimming pools, and the like. For in these forms, Jim Crow does impede the flow of commerce in the broadest sense: it is a nuisance in a society on the move (and on the make). Not surprisingly, therefore, it was the most mobility-conscious and relatively liberated groups in the Negro community—lower-middle-class college students—who launched the attack that brought down this imposing but hollow structure.

The term "classical" appears especially apt for this phase of the civil rights movement. But in the few years that have passed since the first flush of sit-ins, several developments have taken place that have complicated matters enormously. One is the shifting focus of the movement in the South, symbolized by Birmingham; another is the spread of the revolution to the North; and the third, common to the other two, is the expansion of the movement's base in the Negro community. To attempt to disentangle these three strands is to do violence to reality. David Danzig's perceptive [1964] article, "The Meaning of Negro Strategy," correctly saw in the Birmingham events the victory of the concept of collective struggle over individual achievement as the road to Negro freedom. And Birmingham remains the unmatched symbol of grass-roots protest involving all strata of the black community. It was also in this most industrialized of Southern cities that the single-issue demands of the movement's classical stage gave way to the "package deal." No longer were Negroes satisfied with integrating lunch counters. They now sought advances in employment, housing, school integration, police protection, and so forth.

Thus, the movement in the South began to attack areas of discrimination which were not so remote from the Northern experience as were Jim Crow lunch counters. At the same time, the interrelationship of these apparently distinct areas became increasingly evident. What is the value of winning access to public accom-

342

*Student
Activism
and the Emergence
of a Mass
Movement,
1960–1965*

modations for those who lack money to use them? The minute the movement faced this question, it was compelled to expand its vision beyond race relations to economic relations, including the role of education in modern society. And what also became clear is that all these interrelated problems, by their very nature, are not soluble by private, voluntary efforts but require government action—or politics. Already Southern demonstrators had recognized that the most effective way to strike at the police brutality they suffered from was by getting rid of the local sheriff—and that meant political action, which in turn meant, and still means, political action within the Democratic party where the only meaningful primary contests in the South are fought.

And so, in Mississippi, thanks largely to the leadership of Bob Moses, a turn toward political action has been taken. More than voter registration is involved there. A conscious bid for *political power* is being made, and in the course of that effort a tactical shift is being effected: direct-action techniques are being subordinated to a strategy calling for the building of community institutions or power bases. Clearly, the implications of this shift reach far beyond Mississippi. What began as a protest movement is being challenged to translate itself into a political movement. Is this the right course? And if it is, can the transformation be accomplished? . . .

The civil rights movement is evolving from a protest movement into a full-fledged *social movement*—an evolution calling its very name into question. It is now concerned not merely with removing the barriers to full *opportunity* but with achieving the fact of *equality*. From sit-ins and freedom rides we have gone into rent strikes, boycotts, community organization, and political action. As a consequence of this natural evolution, the Negro today finds himself stymied by obstacles of far greater magnitude than the legal barriers he was attacking before: automation, urban decay, *de facto* school segregation. These are problems which, while conditioned by Jim Crow, do not vanish upon its demise. They are more deeply rooted in our socio-economic order; they are the result of the total society's failure to meet not only the Negro's needs, but human needs generally.

Moderates and Militants

These propositions have won increasing recognition and acceptance, but with a curious twist. They have formed the common premise of two apparently contradictory lines of thought which simultaneously nourish and antagonize each other. On the one hand, there is the reasoning of the *New York Times* moderate who says that the problems are so enormous and complicated that Negro militancy is a futile irritation, and that the need is for "intelligent moderation." Thus, during the first New York school boycott, the *Times* editorialized that Negro demands, while abstractly just, would necessitate massive reforms, the funds for which could not realistically be anticipated, therefore the just demands were also foolish demands and would only antagonize white people. Moderates of this stripe are often correct in perceiving the difficulty or impossibility of racial progress in the context of present social and economic policies. But they accept the context as fixed. They ignore (or perhaps see all too well) the potentialities inherent in linking Negro demands to broader pressures for radical revision of existing policies. They apparently see nothing strange in the fact that in the last twenty-five years we have spent nearly a trillion dollars fighting or preparing for wars, yet throw up their hands before the need for overhauling our schools, clearing the slums, and really abolishing poverty. My quarrel with these moderates is that they do not even envision radical changes; their admonitions of moderation are, for all practical purposes, admonitions to the Negro to adjust to the status quo, and are therefore immoral.

The more effectively the moderates argue their case, the more they convince Negroes that American society will not or cannot be reorganized for full racial equality. **Michael Harrington** has said that a successful war on poverty might well require the expenditure of a $100 billion. Where, the Negro wonders, are the forces now in motion to compel such a commitment? If the voices of the moderates were raised in an insistence upon a reallocation of national resources at levels that could not be confused with tokenism (that is, if the moderates stopped being moderates), Negroes would have greater grounds for hope. Meanwhile, the Negro movement cannot escape a sense of isolation.

It is precisely this sense of isolation that gives rise to the second line of thought I want to examine—the tendency within the civil rights movement which, despite its militancy, pursues what I call a "no-win" policy. Sharing with many moderates a recognition of the magnitude of the obstacles to freedom, spokesmen for this tendency survey the American scene and find no forces prepared to move toward radical solutions. From this they conclude that the only viable strategy is shock; above all, the hypocrisy of white liberals must be exposed. These spokesmen are often described as the radicals of the movement, but they are really its moralists. They seek to change white hearts—by traumatizing them. Frequently abetted by white self-flagellants, they may gleefully applaud (though not really agreeing with) Malcolm X because, while they admit he has no program, they think he can frighten white people into doing the right thing. To believe this, of course, you must be convinced, even if unconsciously, that at the core of the white man's heart lies a buried affection for Negroes—a proposition one may be permitted to doubt. But in any case, hearts are not relevant to the issue; neither racial affinities nor racial hostilities are rooted there. It is institutions—social, political, and economic institutions—which are the ultimate molders of collective sentiments. Let these institutions be reconstructed *today*, and let the ineluctable gradualism of history govern the formation of a new psychology.

My quarrel with the "no-win" tendency in the civil rights movement (and the reason I have so designated it) parallels my quarrel with the moderates outside the movement. As the latter lack the vision or will for fundamental change, the former lack a realistic strategy for achieving it. For such a strategy they substitute militancy. But militancy is a matter of posture and volume and not of effect.

A Revolutionary Struggle

I believe that the Negro's struggle for equality in America is essentially revolutionary. While most Negroes—in their hearts—unquestionably seek only to enjoy the fruits of American society as it now exists, their quest cannot *objectively* be satisfied within the framework of existing political and economic relations. The young Negro who would demonstrate his way into the labor market may be motivated by a thoroughly bourgeois ambition and thoroughly "capitalist" considerations, but he will end up having to favor a great expansion of the public sector of the economy. At any rate, that is the position the movement will be forced to take as it looks

344

*Student
Activism
and the Emergence
of a Mass
Movement,
1960–1965*

at the number of jobs being generated by the private economy, and if it is to remain true to the masses of Negroes.

The revolutionary character of the Negro's struggle is manifest in the fact that this struggle may have done more to democratize life for whites than for Negroes. Clearly, it was the sit-in movement of young Southern Negroes which, as it galvanized white students, banished the ugliest features of McCarthyism from the American campus and resurrected political debate. It was not until Negroes assaulted *de facto* school segregation in the urban centers that the issue of quality education for *all* children stirred into motion. Finally, it seems reasonably clear that the civil rights movement, directly and through the resurgence of social conscience it kindled, did more to initiate the war on poverty than any other single force.

It will be—it has been—argued that these by-products of the Negro struggle are not revolutionary. But the term revolutionary, as I am using it, does not connote violence; it refers to the qualitative transformation of fundamental institutions, more or less rapidly, to the point where the social and economic structure which they comprised can no longer be said to be the same. The Negro struggle has hardly run its course; and it will not stop moving until it has been utterly defeated or won substantial equality. But I fail to see how the movement can be victorious in the absence of radical programs for full employment, abolition of slums, the reconstruction of our educational system, new definitions of work and leisure. Adding up the cost of such programs, we can only conclude that we are talking about a refashioning of our political economy. It has been estimated, for example, that the price of replacing New York City's slums with public housing would be $17 billion. Again, a multi-billion dollar federal public-works program, dwarfing the currently proposed $2 billion program, is required to reabsorb unskilled and semi-skilled workers into the labor market—and this must be done if Negro workers in these categories are to be employed. "Preferential treatment" cannot help them.

Political Power

I am not trying here to delineate a total program, only to suggest the scope of economic reforms which are most immediately related to the plight of the Negro community. One could speculate on their political implications—whether for example, they do not indicate the obsolescence of state government and the superiority of regional structures as viable units of planning. Such speculations aside, it is clear that Negro needs cannot be satisfied unless we go beyond what has so far been placed on the agenda. How are these radical objectives to be achieved? The answer is simple, deceptively so: *through political power.*

There is a strong moralistic strain in the civil rights movement which would remind us that power corrupts, forgetting that the absence of power also corrupts. But this is not the view I want to debate here, for it is waning. Our problem is posed by those who accept the need for political power but do not understand the nature of the object and therefore lack sound strategies for achieving it; they tend to confuse political institutions with lunch counters.

A handful of Negroes, acting alone, could integrate a lunch counter by strategically locating their bodies so as *directly* to interrupt the operation of the proprietor's will; their numbers were relatively unimportant. In politics, however, such a confrontation is difficult because the interests involved are merely *represented.* In the execution of a political decision a direct confrontation may ensue (as when federal marshals escorted James Meredith into the University of Mississippi—to turn from an example of non-violent coercion to one of force backed up with the threat of violence). But in arriving at a political decision, numbers and organizations are crucial, especially for the economically disenfranchised. (Needless to say, I am assuming that the forms of political democracy exist in America, however imperfectly, that they are valued, and that elitist or putschist conceptions of exercising power are beyond the pale of discussion for the civil rights movement.)

Neither that movement nor the country's twenty million black people can win political power alone. We need allies. The future of the Negro struggle depends on whether the contradictions of this society can be resolved by a coalition of progressive forces which becomes the *effective* political majority in the United States. I speak of the coalition which staged the March on Washington, passed the Civil Rights Act, and laid the basis for the Johnson landslide—Negroes, trade unionists, liberals, and religious groups.

A Coalition Strategy

There are those who argue that a coalition strategy would force the Negro to surrender his political independence to white liberals, that he would be neutralized, deprived of his cutting edge, absorbed into the Establishment. Some who take this position urged last year that votes be withheld from the Johnson-Humphrey ticket as a demonstration of the Negro's political power. Curiously enough, these people who sought to demonstrate power through the non-exercise of it, also point to the Negro "swing vote" in crucial urban areas as the source of the Negro's independent political power. But here they are closer to being right: the urban Negro vote will grow in importance in the coming years. If there is anything positive in the spread of the ghetto, it is the potential political power base thus created, and to realize this potential is one of the most challenging and urgent tasks before the civil rights movement. If the movement can wrest leadership of the ghetto vote from the machines, it will have acquired an organized constituency such as other major groups in our society now have.

But we must also remember that the effectiveness of a swing vote depends solely on "other" votes. It derives its power from them. In that sense, it can never be "independent," but must opt for one candidate or the other, even if by default. Thus coalitions are inescapable, however tentative they may be. And this is the case in all but those few situations in which Negroes running on an independent ticket might conceivably win. "Independence," in other words, is not a value in itself. The issue is which coalition to join and how to make it responsive to your program. Necessarily there will be compromise. But the difference between expediency and morality in politics is the difference between selling out a principle and making smaller concessions to win larger ones. The leader who shrinks from this task reveals not his purity but his lack of political sense.

The task of molding a political movement out of the March on Washington coalition is not simple, but no alternatives have been advanced. We need to choose our allies on the basis of common political objectives. It has become fashionable in some no-win Negro circles to decry the white liberal as the main enemy (his hypocrisy is what sustains racism); by virtue of this reverse recitation of the reactionary's litany (liberalism leads to socialism, which leads to Communism) the Negro is left in majestic isolation, except for a tiny band of fervent white initiates.

346

*Student
Activism
and the Emergence
of a Mass
Movement,
1960–1965*

But the objective fact is that [Senators James] *Eastland* and [Barry] *Goldwater* are the main enemies—they and the opponents of civil rights, of the war on poverty, of medicare, of social security, of federal aid to education, of unions, and so forth. The labor movement, despite its obvious faults, has been the largest single organized force in this country pushing for progressive social legislation. And where the Negro-labor-liberal axis is weak, as in the farm belt, it was the religious groups that were most influential in rallying support for the Civil Rights Bill.

The durability of the coalition was interestingly tested during the election. I do not believe that the Johnson landslide proved the "white backlash" to be a myth. It proved, rather that economic interests are more fundamental than prejudice: the backlashers decided that loss of social security was, after all, too high a price to pay for a slap at the Negro. This lesson was a valuable first step in re-educating such people, and it must be kept alive, for the civil rights movement will be advanced only to the degree that social and economic welfare gets to be inextricably entangled with civil rights.

The 1964 Elections

The 1964 elections marked a turning point in American politics. The Democratic landslide was not merely the result of a negative reaction to Goldwaterism; it was also the expression of a majority liberal consensus. The near unanimity with which Negro voters joined in that expression was, I am convinced, a vindication of the July 25th statement by Negro leaders calling for a strategic turn toward political action and a temporary curtailment of mass demonstrations. Despite the controversy surrounding the statement, the instinctive response if met with in the community is suggested by the fact that demonstrations were down 75 per cent as compared with the same period in 1963. But should so high a percentage of Negro voters have gone to Johnson, or should they have held back to narrow his margin of victory and thus give greater visibility to our swing vote? How has our loyalty changed things? Certainly the Negro vote had higher visibility in 1960, when a switch of only 7 per cent from the Republican column of 1956 elected President Kennedy. But the slimness of Kennedy's victory—of his "mandate"—dictated a go-slow approach on civil rights, at least until the Birmingham upheaval.

Although Johnson's popular majority was so large that he could have won without such overwhelming Negro support, that support was important from several angles. Beyond adding to Johnson's total national margin, it was specifically responsible for his victories in Virginia, Florida, Tennessee, and Arkansas. Goldwater took only those states where fewer than 45 per cent of eligible Negroes were registered. That Johnson would have won those states had Negro voting rights been enforced is a lesson not likely to be lost on a man who would have been happy with a unanimous electoral college. In any case, the 1.6 million Southern Negroes who voted have had a shattering impact on the Southern political party structure, as illustrated in the changed composition of the Southern congressional delegation. The "backlash" gave the Republicans five House seats in Alabama, one in Georgia, and one in Mississippi. But on the Democratic side, seven segregationists were defeated while all nine Southerners who voted for the Civil Rights Act were re-elected. It may be premature to predict a Southern Democratic party of Negroes and white moderates and a Republican party of refugee racists and economic conservatives, but there certainly is a strong tendency toward such a realignment; and an additional 3.6 million Negroes of voting age in the eleven Southern states are still to be heard from. Even the *tendency* toward disintegration of the Democratic party's racist wing defines a new context for Presidential and liberal strategy in the congressional battles ahead. Thus the Negro vote (North as well as South), while not *decisive* in the Presidential race, was enormously effective. It was a dramatic element of a historic mandate which contains vast possibilities and dangers that will fundamentally affect the future course of the civil rights movement.

The liberal congressional sweep raises hope for an assault on the seniority system, **Rule Twenty-two,** and other citadels of Dixiecrat-Republican power. The overwhelming of this conservative coalition should also mean progress on much bottlenecked legislation of profound interest to the movement. . . . Moreover, the irrelevance of the South to Johnson's victory gives the President more freedom to act than his predecessors had and more leverage to the movement to pressure for executive action in Mississippi and other racist strongholds.

Reshaping the Democratic Party

None of this *guarantees* vigorous executive or legislative action, for the other side of the Johnson landslide is that it has a Gaullist quality. Goldwater's capture of the Republican party forced into the Democratic camp many disparate elements which do not belong there. Big Business being the major example. Johnson, who wants to be President "of all people," may try to keep his new coalition together by sticking close to the political center. But if he decides to do this, it is unlikely that even his political genius will be able to hold together a coalition so inherently unstable and rife with contradictions. It must come apart. Should it do so while Johnson is pursuing a centrist course, then the mandate will have been wastefully dissipated. However, if the mandate is seized upon to set fundamental changes in motion, then the basis can be laid for a new mandate, a new coalition including hitherto inert and dispossessed strata of the population.

Here is where the cutting edge of the civil rights movement can be applied. We must see to it that the reorganization of the "consensus party" proceeds along lines which will make it an effective vehicle for social reconstruction, a role it cannot play so long as it furnishes Southern racism with its national political power. (One of Barry Goldwater's few attractive ideas was that the Dixiecrats belong with him in the same party.) And nowhere has the civil rights movement's political cutting edge been more magnificently demonstrated than at Atlantic City, where the Mississippi Freedom Democratic party [FDP] not only secured recognition as a bona fide component of the national party but in the process routed the representatives of the most rabid racists—the white Mississippi and Alabama delegations. While I still believe that the FDP made a tactical error in spurning the compromise, there is no question that they launched a political revolution whose logic is the displacement of Dixiecrat power. They launched that revolution within a major political institution and as part of a coalitional effort.

The role of the civil rights movement in the reorganization of American political life is programmatic as well as strategic. We are challenged now to broaden our social vision, to develop functional programs with concrete objectives. We need to propose alternatives to technological unemployment, urban decay, and the rest. We need to be calling for public works and training, for national economic planning, for federal aid to education, for attractive public housing—all this on a suf-

348

*Student
Activism
and the Emergence
of a Mass
Movement,
1960–1965*

ficiently massive scale to make a difference. We need to protest the notion that our integration into American life, so long delayed, must now proceed in an atmosphere of competitive scarcity instead of in the security of abundance which technology makes possible. We cannot claim to have answers to all the complex problems of modern society. That is too much to ask of a movement still battling barbarism in Mississippi. But we can agitate the right questions by probing at the contradictions which still stand in the way of the "Great Society." The questions having been asked, motion must begin in the larger society, for there is a limit to what Negroes can do alone.

4.7   **Lyndon B. Johnson**

The Voting Rights Act Should Be Passed

Lyndon B. Johnson was a Texas senator who became president of the United States in 1963 after the assassination of John Kennedy. He supported and signed into effect the Civil Rights Act of 1964 and the Voting Rights Act of 1965.

I speak tonight for the dignity of man and the destiny of democracy. I urge every member of both parties, Americans of all religions and of all colors, from every section of this country, to join me in that cause.

At times history and fate meet at a single time in a single place to shape a turning point in man's unending search for freedom. So it was at Lexington and Concord. So it was a century ago at Appomattox. So it was last week in Selma, Alabama.

There, long-suffering men and women peacefully protested the denial of their rights as Americans. Many were brutally assaulted. One good man, a man of God, was killed.

There is no cause for pride in what has happened in Selma. There is no cause for self-satisfaction in the long denial of equal rights of millions of Americans.

But there is cause for hope and for faith in our democracy in what is happening here tonight.

For the cries of pain and the hymns and protests of oppressed people have summoned into convocation all the majesty of this great government of the greatest nation on earth.

Our mission is at once the oldest and the most basic of this country: to right wrong, to do justice, to serve man.

In our time we have come to live with the moments of great crisis. Our lives have been marked with debate about great issues, issues of war and peace, issues of prosperity and depression. But rarely in any time does an issue lay bare the secret heart of America itself. Rarely are we met with a challenge, not to our growth or abundance, or our welfare or our security, but rather to the values and the purposes and the meaning of our beloved nation.

The issue of equal rights for American Negroes is such an issue. And should we defeat every enemy, and should we double our wealth and conquer the stars and still be unequal to this issue, then we will have failed as a people and as a nation.

For with a country as with a person, "What is a man profited, if he shall gain the whole world, and lose his own soul?"

There is no Negro problem. There is no Southern problem. There is no Northern problem. There is only an American problem. And we are met here tonight as Americans, not as Democrats or Republicans, we are met here as Americans to solve that problem.

America's Promise

This was the first nation in the history of the world to be founded with a purpose. The great phrases of that purpose still sound in every American heart, North and South: "All men are created equal"—"government by consent of the governed"—"give me liberty or give me death." Those are not just clever words. Those are not just empty theories. In their name Americans have fought and died for two centuries, and tonight around the world they stand there as guardians of our liberty, risking their lives.

Those words are a promise to every citizen that he shall share in the dignity of man. This dignity cannot be found in a man's possessions. It cannot be found in his power or in his position. It really rests on his right to be treated as a man equal in opportunity to all others. It says that he shall share in freedom, he shall choose his leaders, educate his children, provide for his family according to his ability and his merits as a human being.

To apply any other test—to deny a man his hopes because of his color or race, or his religion, or the place of his birth—is not only to do injustice, it is to deny America and to dishonor the dead who gave their lives for American freedom.

Our fathers believed that if this noble view of the rights of man was to flourish, it must be rooted in democracy. The most basic right of all was the right to choose your own leaders. The history of this country in large measure is the history of expansion of that right to all of our people.

The Right to Vote

Many of the issues of civil rights are very complex and most difficult. But about this there can and should be no argument. Every American citizen must have an equal right to vote. There is no reason which can excuse the denial of that right. There is no duty which weighs more heavily on us than the duty we have to ensure that right.

Yet the harsh fact is that in many places in this country men and women are kept from voting simply because they are Negroes.

Every device of which human ingenuity is capable has been used to deny this right. The Negro citizen may go to register only to be told that the day is wrong, or the hour is late, or the official in charge is absent. And if he persists and if he manages to present himself to the registrar, he may be disqualified because he did not spell out his middle name or because he abbreviated a word on the application. And if he manages to fill out an application he is given a test. The

350

*Student
Activism
and the Emergence
of a Mass
Movement,
1960–1965*

registrar is the sole judge of whether he passes this test. He may be asked to recite the entire constitution, or explain the most complex provisions of state laws. And even a college degree cannot be used to prove that he can read and write.

For the fact is that the only way to pass these barriers is to show a white skin.

Experience has clearly shown that the existing process of law cannot overcome systematic and ingenious discrimination. No law that we now have on the books—and I have helped to put three of them there—can ensure the right to vote when local officials are determined to deny it.

In such a case our duty must be clear to all of us. The Constitution says that no person shall be kept from voting because of his race or his color. We have all sworn an oath before God to support and to defend that Constitution. We must now act in obedience to that oath.

A New Law

Wednesday I will send to Congress a law designed to eliminate illegal barriers to the right to vote.

The broad principle of that bill will be in the hands of the Democratic and Republican leaders tomorrow. After they have reviewed it, it will come here formally as a bill. I am grateful for this opportunity to come here tonight at the invitation of the leadership to reason with my friends, to give them my views and to visit with my former colleagues.

I have had prepared a more comprehensive analysis of the legislation which I have intended to transmit to the clerks tomorrow, but which I will submit to the clerks tonight; but I want to really discuss with you now briefly the main proposals of this legislation.

This bill will strike down restrictions to voting in all elections—Federal, State, and local—which have been used to deny Negroes the right to vote.

This bill will establish a simple, uniform standard which cannot be used however ingenious the effort to flout our Constitution.

It will provide for citizens to be registered by officials of the United States government, if the state officials refuse to register them.

It will eliminate tedious, unnecessary lawsuits which delay the right to vote.

Finally, this legislation will ensure that properly registered individuals are not prohibited from voting.

I will welcome the suggestions from all of the members of Congress. I have no doubt that I will get some on ways and means to strengthen this law and to make it effective. But experience has plainly shown that this is the only path to carry out the command of the Constitution.

To those who seek to avoid action by their national government in their own communities, who want to and who seek to maintain purely local control over elections, the answer is simple.

Open your polling places to all your people.

Allow men and women to register and vote whatever the color of their skin.

Extend the rights of citizenship to every citizen of this land.

There is no constitutional issue here. The command of the Constitution is plain.

There is no moral issue. It is wrong to deny any of your fellow Americans the right to vote in this country.

There is no issue of states rights or national rights. There is only the struggle for human rights.

I have not the slightest doubt what will be your answer.

But the last time a President sent a civil rights bill to the Congress it contained a provision to protect voting rights in Federal elections. That civil rights bill was passed after eight long months of debate. And when that bill came to my desk from the Congress for my signature, the heart of the voting provision had been eliminated.

This time, on this issue, there must be no delay, or no hesitation or no compromise with our purpose.

We cannot, we must not refuse to protect the right of every American to vote in every election that he may desire to participate in. And we ought not, we must not wait another eight months before we get a bill. We have already waited a hundred years and more and the time for waiting is gone.

So I ask you to join me in working long hours, nights, and weekends if necessary, to pass this bill. And I don't make that request lightly. Far from the window where I sit with the problems in our country, I recognize that from outside this chamber is the outraged conscience of a nation, the grave concern of many nations and the harsh judgment of history on our acts.

But even if we pass this bill, the battle will not be over. What happened in Selma is part of a far larger movement which reaches into every section and state of America. It is the effort of American Negroes to secure for themselves the full blessings of American life.

Our Cause

Their cause must be our cause too. Because it is not just Negroes, but really it is all of us, who must overcome the crippling legacy of bigotry and injustice. And we shall overcome.

As a man whose roots go deeply into Southern soil I know how agonizing racial feelings are. I know how difficult it is to reshape the attitudes and the structure of our society.

But a century has passed, more than a hundred years, since the Negro was freed. And he is not fully free tonight.

It was more than a hundred years ago that Abraham Lincoln, the great President of the Northern party, signed the Emancipation Proclamation, but emancipation is a proclamation and not a fact.

A century has passed, more than a hundred years since equality was promised. And yet the Negro is not equal.

A century has passed since the day of promise. And the promise is unkept.

The time of justice has now come. I tell you that I believe sincerely that no force can hold it back. It is right in the eyes of man and God that is should come. And when it does, I think that day will brighten the lives of every American. . . .

The real hero of this struggle is the American Negro. His actions and protests, his courage to risk safety and even to risk his life, have awakened the conscience of this nation. His demonstrations have been designed to call attention to injustice, designed to provoke change, designed to stir reform. He has called upon us to make good the promise of America. And who among us can say that we would have made the same progress were it not for his persistent bravery, and his faith in American democracy.

Silent Partner: How the South's Fight To Uphold Segregation Was Funded Up North

New York Millionaire Secretly Sent Cash to Mississippi Via Morgan Guaranty

'Wall Street Gang' Pitches In

Douglas A. Blackmon, author of "Silent Partner: How the South's Fight to Uphold Segregation was Funded Up North," is a staff reporter for the Wall Street Journal.

JACKSON, Miss.—On the afternoon of Sept. 12, 1963, a vice president of Morgan Guaranty Trust Co. sent a telegram to the Mississippi State Sovereignty Commission, the agency created by local politicians to fight the civil-rights movement and preserve racial segregation.

A Morgan client, the telegram said, was "setting aside as an anonymous gift" stock valued at $100,000. There was one condition: "Donor would like the fact and amount of the gift to be kept confidential."

The matter was referred directly to Mississippi Gov. Ross Barnett, who agreed to the terms and, that same day, sent Morgan instructions on where to send the cash.

Once the money arrived in Mississippi, it was funneled to an account in Washington, D.C., where segregationists were launching a fierce campaign to defeat landmark civil-rights legislation abolishing segregation in most public facilities. And in the ensuing months, the mystery contributor would follow up with additional, substantial gifts to help the cause.

For nearly four decades, the role of that donor remained concealed in the files of the now-defunct Sovereignty Commission. But last year, a federal judge ordered the unsealing of more than 130,000 commission files. The documents triggered a painful examination of some of the South's most heinous racial crimes. Little explored, though, was the trove of ledgers, invoices and correspondence recording the commission's finances.

Those records show large transfers of money by Morgan on behalf of a client who turns out be a wealthy and reclusive New Yorker named Wickliffe Preston Draper. Mr. Draper used his private banker to transfer nearly $215,000 in stock and cash to the Sovereignty Commission for use in its fight against the Civil Rights Act. The entire budget for the effort amounted to about $300,000. Adjusted for inflation, Mr. Draper's contributions would be worth more than $1.1 million today.

The Sovereignty Commission files do more than simply document one man's role. They show that some of the most virulent resistance to civil-rights progress in the 1960s was supported and funded from the North, not just the South. The files also highlight the ethical issues that confront an institution like Morgan Guaranty, the private-banking unit of J. P. Morgan & Co., when it is drawn, even unwittingly, into a client's support for repugnant causes.

Since the 1930s, Mr. Draper had been a client of Guaranty Trust, which became Morgan Guaranty when it merged with J. P. Morgan in 1959. It isn't clear whether he used Guaranty to help with funding some of his earlier race-related efforts, such as a program in the 1930s to encourage white military pilots to have more children, or research in the 1950s to prove the superiority of whites and the dangers of mixed-race marriages.

When Mr. Draper died in 1972, Morgan was an executor of his estate, overseeing distributions totaling about $5 million to two race-oriented foundations. The primary beneficiary was the Pioneer Fund, an organization Mr. Draper helped found and which became known in recent years for funding research cited in "**The Bell Curve**," a book arguing that blacks are genetically inclined to be less intelligent than whites or Asians. In his will, Mr. Draper instructed that after his death, the Pioneer Fund use Morgan for financial advice; the fund did so for two decades.

Morgan today says that "racism is deplorable" and that the bank doesn't "support institutions that further racist causes." Moreover, the bank notes that it has been a consistent donor to African-American causes, giving more than $3.3 million of its own money to civil-rights-related groups since the late 1960s.

Morgan insists that the Sovereignty Commission transactions it processed for Mr. Draper were routine procedures carried out on behalf of a client, over which the bank had no influence or control.

"A thousand times a day, somebody sends money to an organization that 30 years later looks really terrible," says Morgan spokesman Joe Evangelista. "We can't tell our customers how to spend their money."

Mr. Evangelista says the role Morgan played was no different from the way Wall Street banks today facilitate gifts to organizations that could be equally controversial. He cites donations made to Planned Parenthood (often criticized for its pro-choice stance), or to the Boy Scouts of America (which prohibits gays from becoming troop leaders). Morgan's policy, he says, is to pass no judgment on any client's activities, except in the "rare situation" when "the wishes of a client . . . conflict with the principles that we stand for as a firm." In those cases, the firm may close a client's account, Mr. Evangelista says.

Since the Sovereignty Commission was a legal, state-created entity, says Hildy J. Simmons, a managing director at Morgan Guaranty, the bank had no choice but to follow its client's wishes. It would be no different today. "As long as the receiving party is legal, we have no discretion," says Ms. Simmons.

Morgan did close the asset-management account it maintained for the Pioneer Fund after the furor erupted over "The Bell Curve" in 1994, according to people familiar with the situation. The bank won't give details on why it did so.

That option is something banks should consider, says Thomas Donaldson, a business-ethics professor at the Wharton School of the University of Pennsylvania in Philadelphia. "Good bankers should have the words 'Know thy client' tattooed somewhere on their chests," Mr. Donaldson says. "When the activities of the client or customer reach the point where they offend vital, deeply held values of the institution, you have to say no."

But many banks aren't comfortable with that posture, and with good reason, says George J. Benston, a banking professor at the Goizueta Business School at

354

*Student
Activism
and the Emergence
of a Mass
Movement,
1960–1965*

Emory University in Atlanta. "One would like any institution to operate with its customers neutrally. You don't want some bank officer making a judgment on whether a customer's donations are moral."

Brahmin Roots

Wickliffe Draper was, in many ways, a typical Yankee aristocrat. He was born in Hopedale, Mass., in 1891. His father was a top executive in the textile-machinery giant Draper Corp. His mother was from a blue-blood Kentucky family. An uncle was a Massachusetts governor. His younger sister married a nephew of President William Howard Taft.

Mr. Draper reveled in adventure. At Harvard College, from which he graduated in 1913, he excelled in shooting. A volunteer in both world wars, he used the title "colonel" for most of his life. In 1924, he inherited about half of his father's estate, which was valued at the then-enormous sum of nearly $11 million. In 1938, he reported to his Harvard classmates that his diversions over the 25 years since college included "shooting jaguar in Matto Grosso and deer in Sonora, elephant in Uganda and chamois in Steiermark, ibex in Baltistan and antelope in Mongolia; . . . pigsticking in India."

By the late 1930s, for reasons that still aren't clear, Mr. Draper had also developed a fascination with racial genetics. In 1937, he helped found the Pioneer Fund. The foundation was devoted to supporting eugenics, a school of thinking which held that races can be genetically "improved" through mating practices, such as encouraging intelligent people to marry, or sterilizing handicapped individuals. Many eugenicists of the day, including some Pioneer founders, believed that whites were superior to blacks in intellect and other attributes, says Barry Mehler, a historian at Minnesota's Ferris State University, who has studied the fund extensively.

The charter of the Pioneer Fund said the organization would support research and programs aimed at "race betterment." Scholarship programs would give special consideration to "children who are deemed to be descended predominantly from white persons who settled in the original 13 states." (In 1985, Pioneer amended its charter, saying it supports programs aimed at "human race betterment," and also deleting the reference to "white persons.")

Today, officials of the fund deny that it seeks to prove the inferiority of any race and maintain that it funds only legitimate genetic research, regardless of its findings. The organization says its past and present leaders were not biased for or against any race.

One of the first major projects of the Pioneer Fund under Dr. Draper was a program to encourage officers of the all-white U.S. Army Air Corps, predecessor of the Air Force, to have more children. Mr. Draper and other directors of the foundation believed that the Pioneer Fund should encourage a higher birth rate among the best of the white race. So the fund offered to establish annuities to pay for the education of any child born in 1940 to a pilot who had already fathered at least three children.

Among the original Pioneer Fund directors who endorsed the plan was John Marshall Harlan II, a prominent New York attorney who would be appointed to the U.S. Supreme Court in 1957. President Franklin D. Roosevelt's secretary of war, Harry H. Woodring, personally approved the plan, according to Justice Harlan's papers, now stored at Princeton University.

Memos to Mr. Harlan make clear that the plans were fulfilled. "During the calendar year 1940 there were 12 children born to officers in the Army Air Corps . . . eligible to receive scholarships," wrote a psychologist hired to oversee the program. Mr. Draper made arrangements, according to records kept by Mr. Harlan, for an annuity to be established for each of the children at Guaranty Trust, the predecessor to Morgan Guaranty.

After World War II, the never-married Mr. Draper became increasingly reclusive. He stopped submitting updates to his Harvard class and lived alone in Manhattan, in a spacious East 57th Street penthouse duplex, surrounded by hunting weapons and mounted animal heads. For several years, he paid young researchers to visit his apartment and teach him genetic theory.

"For $10 an hour, I tutored Draper . . . every time I was in New York," says Bruce Wallace, a retired Virginia Polytechnic University professor who adds that he disagreed with Mr. Draper's views. "His contention was that the geneticists had all the figures but they were afraid to add them all up. . . . He was quite set on the idea that there was superiority and inferiority. I don't think he would have placed blacks among the superior."

The theories embraced by Mr. Draper fell out of favor after the war, and as the horrors of the Nazi regime became apparent, many of his old allies distanced themselves from their previous work. But through the 1950s, Mr. Draper continued to push for research to demonstrate white superiority; he also espoused sending American blacks, on a voluntary basis, to live in Africa, says the Pioneer Fund.

In 1957, the state of Mississippi created the Sovereignty Commission. Operating on an appropriation of about $100,000 a year, the commission penetrated most of the major civil-rights organizations in Mississippi, even planting clerical workers in the offices of activist attorneys. It informed police about planned marches or boycotts and encouraged police harassment of African-Americans who cooperated with civil rights groups. Its agents obstructed voter registration by blacks and harassed African-Americans seeking to attend white schools. On occasion, the commission also took steps to discourage violence by Ku Klux Klan and other extremist groups.

Precisely how Mr. Draper became connected to the commission isn't clear. But the relationship appears to have blossomed shortly after a national address by President John F. Kennedy in June 1963. The president proposed wide-reaching legislation to outlaw segregation in public facilities. Mississippi leaders scrambled to mount a vigorous fight.

They turned to John C. Satterfield, a brilliant litigator from Yazoo City, Miss., and the immediate past president of the American Bar Association. By the end of the 1960s, Time magazine would label him "the most prominent segregationist lawyer in the country."

Within days of President Kennedy's speech, Mr. Satterfield headed to Washington to meet with top politicians and business groups. The response was encouraging. "We in the South now have new and important allies who never before seemed seriously concerned," wrote Erle Johnston Jr., director of the Sovereignty Commission. "It was a thrill to me to see how the gentlemen at these meetings looked to Mississippi for leadership."

The result was a new national lobbying organization, called the Coordinating Committee for Fundamental American Freedoms. The Sovereignty Commission

356

*Student
Activism
and the Emergence
of a Mass
Movement,
1960–1965*

provided money to rent a Washington office and hire staff, and largely controlled the group from Mississippi.

On July 22, 1963, Mr. Satterfield received the first private contribution to the cause, a $10,000 Morgan Guaranty cashier's check drawn from Mr. Draper's accounts. It was deposited into a special account in the Mississippi state treasury and logged into Sovereignty Commission records with a simple notation: "Morgan Guaranty Trust Co."

Over the next year, Mississippi leaders repeatedly claimed that the campaign was being financed by broad grass-roots support in Mississippi and across the U.S. In truth, contributions from Mississippi citizens never topped $30,000. A surviving partner of Mr. Satterfield's law firm says the attorney obliquely referred to the source of the big money simply as "the Wall Street gang."

On Sept. 12, Mississippi Gov. Barnett received the telegram in which Morgan Vice President Arthur W. Rossiter Jr. said $100,000 in stock had been earmarked for the Mississippi commission. After the shares were sold, the gift totaled $98,612. It was entered into Sovereignty Commission records as "Donation from Morgan Guaranty Trust Company." Four months later, another telegram arrived from Mr. Rossiter, this time signaling the impending arrival of an additional $105,000 from Mr. Draper.

The money was derived from Mr. Draper's shares of Reynolds Tobacco, General Motors, Standard Oil of New Jersey and Addressograph-Multigraph. Morgan sold the stock at Mr. Draper's direction, collected commissions on the sales, and moved the proceeds into what it calls a temporary Sovereignty Commission account at Morgan Guaranty. The Sovereignty Commission eventually forwarded the funds to Washington.

Throughout, Mr. Rossiter insisted that the source of the money never be disclosed. "This represents an anonymous gift to your Commission and the donor has specifically requested that the fact and the amount of the gift be kept strictly confidential," he wrote in one letter.

Mr. Draper's money buoyed a sweeping attack on the civil-rights bill. The Sovereignty Commission's Washington arm coordinated opposition efforts among less-organized groups, pushed trade associations to fight the bill and lobbied Congress. It sent ghost-written editorials to newspapers around the country and bought ads in 500 daily and weekly papers. By April 1964, the group had distributed 1.4 million pamphlets and mailings, Sovereignty Commission records indicate.

The opposition effort was swathed in the issues of protecting states' rights and reining in an overreaching federal government. The advertisements said the bill would create an "omnipotent president" and a "dictatorial attorney general."

But commission records make clear that the effort co-financed by Mr. Draper was grounded on bitterly racist notions. Citing several white-supremacist tracts, an internal memorandum by Mr. Satterfield said Americans had to be shown that the conditions of blacks in the U.S. were the result of "heredity . . . not discrimination." At the heart of the matter, the memo said, were "the intelligence, criminality and immorality of the Negro."

The Sovereignty Commission campaign triggered thousands of letters. Despite that, Congress approved the Civil Rights Act of 1964, and President Lyndon B. Johnson signed it into law.

Frustrated by the defeat, Mr. Satterfield pressed Mississippi's new governor, Paul Johnson, to help start a new national organization, designed to demonstrate that the plight of blacks in the South was the result not of "mistreatment and discrimination" but the "completely different nature of Negro citizens and white citizens," he wrote the governor.

"Certain groups in the east who prefer anonymity" were ready to back the effort with $200,000, Mr. Satterfield wrote, if the state would match the contribution. As a gesture of seriousness, an unnamed northern benefactor had sent $50,000.

The donor was, again, Mr. Draper. His gift arrived via Morgan on June 2, 1964. Gov. Johnson endorsed the plan, and the Legislature quickly appropriated $200,000.

But the segregationists suffered another setback, this time at the hands of their most rabid elements. Klan members abducted civil-rights workers Michael Schwerner, Andrew Goodman and James Chaney in the town of Philadelphia, Miss. The three were beaten, shot to death and buried in an earthen dam. Six weeks later, the workers' 1963 Ford station wagon was found burned along an isolated road, still bearing Mississippi licence tag H 25503, a number logged into Sovereignty Commission files by an informant a few weeks earlier.

The national outcry brought an end to the new alliance between Mississippi officials and Mr. Draper. Gov. Johnson's office was flooded with telegrams, many simply repeating the words "justice, justice, justice." Increasingly isolated, Mississippi leaders took at least symbolic steps to halt violence. The state's own $200,000 appropriation was quietly returned to the Mississippi treasury.

Later, the $50,000 from Mr. Draper was returned to his attorney in New York, Harry F. Weyher, who deposited it into the escrow account of his firm, records show. Mr. Weyher, who has been president of the Pioneer Fund for more than 40 years, says he doesn't recall the flow of funds, though he did remember meeting with Mr. Satterfield in the 1960s.

Mr. Draper maintained his interest in the fight to preserve segregation in the South. In the late 1960s and 1970s, he sent dozens of checks to private academies that had opened up to accommodate white families fleeing newly integrated public schools, estate records show.

After Mr. Draper died in 1972, Morgan continued to manage his holdings while the will was being sorted out. Five years later, his assets were distributed according to Mr. Draper's wishes.

He gave about $1 million to family members, and also bequeathed $3.3 million to the Pioneer Fund and $1.7 million to the Puritan Foundation. (The Pioneer Fund isn't related to the mutual fund of the same name.) The Puritan Foundation listed as its address the law firm of Mr. Satterfield, the Mississippi lawyer. In 1978, the fund was merged into another nonprofit called the Council School Foundation, according to Rutgers University Prof. William Tucker, who is researching Mr. Draper's activities. That Mississippi group was created to support private schools that catered to white students.

A State's Stigma

Citing bank policy, executives at Morgan won't discuss whether the bankers who worked with Mr. Draper knew of his racial leanings or the true nature of the Sovereignty Commission.

358

*Student
Activism
and the Emergence
of a Mass
Movement,
1960–1965*

Still, Morgan was dealing with prominent Mississippi segregationists at a time when the national media were focused on the state, and when some on Wall Street and in New York's political community were concerned about maintaining business ties there. Mr. Barnett, the governor of Mississippi, had been pictured on the front page of the New York Times in 1962 during a bloody standoff with federal troops forcing the integration of the University of Mississippi.

The Mississippi state treasurer at the time, William F. Winter, said that Wall Street firms charged higher interest rates on the state's bonds, due to the stigma of having ties to Mississippi. In 1965, one such issue was canceled due to a lack of bids on Wall Street.

Morgan says none of that is relevant. The bank likely had clients supporting the civil-rights movement as well, executives say. And, adds Mr. Evangelista, "doing business with a particular client doesn't mean that we endorse that client's beliefs or actions." It would be "offensive" for a bank to police how its clients conduct their affairs.

"That's a privilege of being rich in America," says Ms. Simmons at Morgan. "You can spend your money the way you want to."

Additional Resources

Suggested Readings

Branch, Taylor. *Parting the Waters: America in the King Years 1954–63.* New York: Simon & Schuster, 1988. A monumental account of the civil rights struggle from the Eisenhower years through the rise of King to the presidential contest of 1960. Comprehensive history of the Montgomery bus boycott, lunch counter sit-ins, freedom rides, James Meredith's integration of the University of Mississippi, and the murder of Medgar Evers.

Branch, Taylor. *Pillar of Fire: America in the King years 1963–65.* New York: Simon & Schuster, 1998. Second volume in his *America in the King Years* trilogy, it captures the intensity of this historical period. Places the movement in the larger perspective of the 1960s within the context of the Vietnam War, Lyndon Johnson's Great Society program, civil rights workers, and Malcolm X.

Dittmer, John. *Local People: The Struggle for Civil Rights in Mississippi.* Urbana and Chicago: University of Illinois Press, 1995. An analytical history of lesser-known civil rights activists in the struggle for racial justice in Mississippi.

Eskew, Glenn T. *But for Birmingham: The Local and National Movements in the Civil Rights Struggle.* Chapel Hill: University of North Carolina Press, 1997. A detailed and comprehensive exploration of the civil rights struggle in Birmingham, Alabama. An excellent analysis of the intersection of local and national organizations.

Grant, Joanne. *Ella Baker: Freedom Bound.* New York: John Wiley, 1998. A biography of the little-known civil rights activist who influenced many radicals of the civil rights era.

Kasher, Steven. *The Civil Rights Movement: A Photographic History, 1954–68.* New York: Abbeville Press, 1996. History in the making from the camera's eye. The book combines research, writing, and carefully selected, striking photographs of the movement presented in chronological form.

McAdam, Doug. *Freedom Summer.* New York: Oxford University Press, 1988. An in-depth study of the young student civil rights volunteers who went to Mississippi in 1964. The book discusses what happened to the volunteers after the Summer Project ended.

Moody, Anne. *Coming of Age in Mississippi.* New York: Laurel, 1968. An autobiography of growing up poor and black in the rural South and becoming a civil rights worker. The book illustrates the development of a woman dedicated to social change.

Watters, Pat. *Down to Now: Reflections on the Southern Civil Rights Movement.* Athens, Georgia: The University of Georgia Press, 1993. A detailed writing of some of the events of the civil rights movement, especially the sit-ins, freedom rides, the Albany Campaign and Birmingham. The book was written mostly from the author's own recollections, tapes, and notes.

Wexler, Sanford. *The Civil Rights Movement: An Eyewitness History.* New York: Facts on File, 1993. Contains hundreds of firsthand accounts and documents of civil rights events assembled in chronological order. Traces the origins of the movement to the nineteenth-century rise of the Ku Klux Klan and the denial of basic rights to blacks.

Young, Andrew. *An Easy Burden: The Civil Rights Movement and the Transformation of America.* New York: Harper Collins, 1996. Written by a former director of the Southern Christian Leadership Conference (SCLC), this is a personal account of the movement from the point of view of King's aide.

Web Sites

www.tulane.edu/~so-inst

This Web site of the Southern Institute for Education and Research contains information on the history of civil rights in Louisiana. There is a special section devoted to the *Plessey* decision.

www.pilotonline.com/millenium/stories9/mc/9rig.html

The "decade of change," the 1960s, is the topic of this Web site. Articles analyzing the 1960s, ranging from popular culture to the Vietnam War to the civil rights movement, are available.

http://pioneer.netserv.chula.ac.th/~crabtree/civilrights.htm

This Web site offers a look into the state of Alabama and civil rights movement activities there. It contains brief biographies of Martin Luther King as well as George Corley Wallace.

http://www-dept.usm.edu/~mcrohb/transcripts.html

Established by the Mississippi Department of Archives and History, this excellent Web site contains full transcripts of oral history interviews with civil rights workers and white Southern opponents. Included are transcripts of a Mississippi State Trooper, Fannie Lou Hamer, and several lesser-known activists.

http://bcri.bham.al.us

This is the Web site of the Birmingham Civil Rights Institute, which depicts civil rights events that took place in Birmingham and other cities. It is a descriptive guide through the museum holdings including its extensive archives collection.

www.albanycivilrights.org

The Albany Civil Rights Museum at Mt. Zion, Georgia, has a long-term goal of developing a virtual museum. The focus of the site is on the grass-roots history of the Albany Movement and the SNCC Freedom Singers who started there.

Chapter 5

The Militant Years, 1966–1968

By the mid-1960s legislative gains driven by the civil rights movement changed the political and social environment and offered protection and new opportunities for blacks. Civil rights victories, however, came at an incredibly high human cost. Many lives—black and white—were lost at the hands of white Southerners who could not tolerate change in their caste system. Southern authorities often sanctioned the violence.

This was a period when change threatened mainstream America too. The civil rights movement, with its apparent success on one hand and frustration on the other, mirrored the conflict and confusion of the larger culture. Student rebellions, nascent feminism, and the antiwar movement all challenged the establishment. These issues—sexuality, a controversial war, and antiestablishment views—along with the civil rights movement came to characterize the decade of the sixties.

The expectations created by the civil rights movement met with frustration in the mid-1960s. The violent Southern reaction to the voter registration drive during Freedom Summer undermined SNCC's commitment to integration. Murders, beatings, and general harassment of rights advocates contributed to an increasing impatience and anger among the blacks in the organization. Furthermore, problems within the organization, such as with issues of race and sex, became apparent. Racial tensions erupted between black and white SNCC workers. Volunteer white women had to deal with the constant advances of black male SNCC staffers, which aroused the jealousy of black women; white women often sought to ease their guilt by permitting blacks to exploit them sexually and financially. These internal problems were compounded by what psychiatrist Robert Coles called "battle fatigue" resulting from "long periods of unremitting dangers and disappointments" (Matusow, 1969:144). Quarrels over leadership and strategy continued during the 1964–65 winter, when John L. Lewis, chairman of SNCC, demanded that blacks lead their own movement. In "From Civil Rights to Black Power: The Case of SNCC, 1960–1966" (Reading 5.1), Allen Matusow demonstrates how a new urgency, symbolized in the slogan Black Power, evolved within SNCC. Although it grew out of the experiences and disillusionment of the civil rights workers in the South, it was also fueled by the ghetto uprisings in Northern cities (Bloom, 1987:208).

By the end of the summer of 1965 a spirit akin to black nationalism was rising within the organization (Matusow, 1981). SNCC was now attracted to the language of the Muslim hero of the urban ghetto, Malcolm X. Clayborne Carson, writing *In Struggle, SNCC and the Black Awakening of the 1960s*, saw an interesting turn in the movement (Carson, 1981:192):

> Southern blacks took pride in their own efforts to initiate and direct the course of their local movements even while accepting outside assistance.

After 1964 this racial pride grew stronger as they began to exercise newly won civil rights and became more confident of their leadership abilities. SNCC workers recognized the growth in black consciousness, but had only begun to articulate the significance of the emerging sense of racial potency and pride.

Urban Riots

Unlike the volunteers in SNCC, the ghetto masses never had to disabuse themselves of the colorblind assumptions of the civil rights movement (Matusow, 1969:147). While SNCC's frustrations took the form of militant rhetoric, ghetto rage took the form of riot.

Just days after the Voting Rights Act of 1965 was signed into law by President Lyndon Johnson, a violent uprising took place in the Watts ghetto in southwest Los Angeles. The looting and burning shocked the nation. National Guardsmen were sent in to restore order. In the end, 34 people were killed and thousands were jailed. Martin Luther King flew to Los Angeles and "was completely undone" by the conditions in Watts. This made King more conscious than ever that the economic problems of poor blacks constituted the movement's most difficult challenge.

Typically, incidents of police brutality precipitated violence in many Northern cities. During the next three years riots took place in cities like Newark and Detroit. The national media focus on the civil rights movement that proved to be its strong ally now began to highlight a new side to the race issue. The phrase "the long, hot summer" replaced the popular image of the civil rights movement. Urban riots were not a planned part of the civil rights movement, however, riots, not new in U.S. history, now replaced voter registration as the subject matter of the race issue. The association of nonviolence with the civil rights movement gave way to fiery, militant rhetoric and urban violence.

In "Ghetto Revolts, Black Power, and the Limits of the Civil Rights Coalition" (Reading 5.2), Jack Bloom points out how conditions of poverty, police brutality, and class despair formed the social base of a new trend toward black militancy that grew up independently of King and the Southern movement. A sense of despair and futility among urban blacks fueled an attitude critical of Martin Luther King and attracted many of them to the ideas of Malcolm X. The element of protest of the ghetto revolts had a similar impact on black self-esteem as the civil rights demonstrations: black pride grew.

Malcolm X

The class concerns of disadvantaged blacks were particularly important outside the South. In "Meeting Malcolm" (Reading 5.3), Michael Eric Dyson highlights Malcolm X's role in the civil rights movement. The Muslim appeal was directed toward the socially dispossessed, the morally compromised, and the economically desperate members of the black community, groups of people who were hitherto unaffected by the civil rights movement. Black nationalist ideas such as racial self-help and black unity found a waiting audience among them. Malcolm's appeal to the disconnected was strong. He was a former prisoner who had led a life of crime. Converted to the Muslim religion during his prison sentence, 1946–1952, he became a charismatic figure with exceptional oratorical skills whose appeal was not limited to Northern, urban blacks.

One of Malcolm X's early speeches (April 1964) "The Ballot or the Bullet" (Reading 5.4), included the line, "I don't see any American dream. I see an American nightmare." Perhaps as a challenge to King's ideal of an integrated dream, Malcolm X introduced the idea of culturally separate black and white communities. The speech was critical of U.S. politics and especially of the Democratic Party. Elements of black nationalism were present and growing in such organizations as CORE and SNCC.

SNCC, which was influenced by Malcolm X and impressed with him, invited him to Selma, Alabama, in February 1965. Speaking to a Southern audience, Malcolm X encouraged the state of Alabama to support King and SNCC because their demands were reasonable. He had been highly critical of Martin Luther King in the past, and this speech demonstrated a softening in his position. Later that month Malcolm X was assassinated while speaking in Harlem. Historian Eric Foner (1998:283) points out:

> When he was assassinated in 1965 by members of the Nation of Islam—the nationalist religious group in which he had risen to prominence and had then abandoned—Malcolm X left neither a consistent ideology nor a coherent organization. But in death, his powerful language and call for blacks to rely on their own resources struck a chord among younger civil rights activists. More than any other individual, Malcolm X was the intellectual father of "Black Power," a slogan that first came to national attention in 1966 when SNCC leader Stokely Carmichael and other young blacks employed it during a civil rights march in Mississippi.

James Meredith's March against Fear, 1966

In the summer of 1966, James Meredith set out to march from Memphis, Tennessee, to Jackson, Mississippi, to demonstrate the importance of voting to achieve social change. Meredith, who integrated the University of Mississippi at Oxford in 1962, was shot on the second day of the march just after he passed the Mississippi state line. Many civil rights organizations stepped in to continue the march from the point where Meredith was shot. King wanted the march to lead to another civil rights act, one that would include a provision for federal protection of civil rights workers. His strategy, however, came in conflict with a manifesto drafted by Stokely Carmichael, the newly elected chairman of SNCC, who, in contrast to King's philosophy and discipline of nonviolence, emphasized the need for power. Carmichael wanted to condemn the Johnson administration for its lax enforcement of existing civil rights acts. This was not the first time King was opposed by SNCC. The Albany, Georgia, campaign of 1962 (see Reading 4.3) was one of the first public disagreements between the young SNCC workers and King's SCLC. Now, the coalition of civil rights groups assembled to finish the march was forced to deal with Carmichael's criticism of nonviolence. Put off by his insults and provocation, both the Urban League and the NAACP refused to sign his manifesto and dropped out of the march. King did sign and forged ahead clinging to his philosophy of nonviolence while watching the movement turn in a more militant direction.

Henry Hampton and Steve Fayer's "The Meredith March, 1966, 'Hit Them Now'" (Reading 5.5) is an interview account of how the slogan Black Power came to provide an electrifying phrase for the movement's lexicon. Black Power became a rallying cry heard far beyond Greenwood, Mississippi, where Stokely Carmichael introduced it to marchers and local blacks in the Delta. Black Power touched a nerve in America (Hampton & Fayer, 1990). The media reported the concept as a new and dangerous development in the civil rights struggle. The slogan helped to undermine what was once a national consensus for civil rights legislation and inspired fear in a country living through its fourth year of urban unrest.

The rift within the movement became evident to the entire nation as the media dramatized the differences between Martin Luther King's philosophy of nonviolence and Stokely Carmichael's militant rhetoric challenging the nonviolent approach to change. The term Black Power became a symbolic departure from King's popular slogan Freedom Now. King feared the phrase Black Power would alienate the white majority he counted on for positive public opinion and legislative support. SNCC moved away from its early emphasis on nonviolence and community organizing to a philosophy of Black Power. This coincided with a vote to exclude all whites from positions of leadership within SNCC.

Stokely Carmichael's "Toward Black Liberation" (Reading 5.6) developed a definition of Black Power that reached beyond traditional black dependence on the "good-will of white liberals." Black Power rhetoric was simultaneously inspirational and inflammatory; it inspired impatient civil rights activists and younger blacks but threatened mainstream blacks and whites who could not separate militancy from violence.

The effectiveness of nonviolence was frequently debated and criticized within the black community and within the movement as continued violence from white Southerners threatened the movement. Howard Zinn, in "The Limits of Nonviolence" (Reading 5.7), argued that nonviolent protest in some parts of the South did not work. Examining the Albany campaign of 1962, Zinn warned that if the federal government did not intervene between the local police and blacks in areas in the deep South, a violent revolt could occur. In this selection, written in 1964, Zinn arrived at a similar conclusion to the Black Power advocates. Two years later, Stokely Carmichael wrote "Toward Black Liberation" (Reading 5.6).

John L. Lewis noted as far back as 1964, "There's been a radical change in our people since 1960; the way they dress, the music they listen to, their natural hairdos—all of them want to go to Africa . . . I think people are searching for a sense of identity, and they're finding it" (Carson 1981:101). Clearly, there was a developing racial consciousness.

For SNCC members, always impatient with the slow pace of change, Black Power became an instant rallying cry. It articulated a mood rather than a program, but the slogan expressed a tendency that had been present for a long time and had been gaining strength in the black community. Black Power divided the movement and fueled white backlash. James Meredith's was the last great march of the Southern civil rights movement. It served as a historical marker for the end of the civil rights coalition and the beginning of black pride. SNCC symbolized this change of direction.

The drift toward militancy marked a deviation from the tradition of organizing, which was, historically, the strength of SNCC programs that had led to real structural change. Charles Payne, in "Mrs. Hamer Is No Longer Relevant" (Reading 5.8), cites SNCC's increasingly dogmatic style emanating from the shift toward middle-class volunteers. Countering SNCC's tradition of local organizing, the post-1966 volunteers were attracted by the new fiery rhetoric. This move away from moral anchors in the communities—the local people with whom SNCC traditionally shared close ties—drew criticism from Ella Baker and other founding members. When Fannie Lou Hamer opposed the idea of expulsion of whites, some claimed that she was "no longer relevant" and dismissed her position.

Black Panther Party

The Lowndes County Freedom Association, a political party established by SNCC, used a black panther as its symbol, in part to contrast it with the white rooster of the Alabama Democratic Party and the elephant of the Republican Party. The black cat represented an image that would become a symbol of a controversial and misunderstood philosophy.

Growing antagonism between the black community and the white police department in Oakland, California, led Huey Newton and Bobby Seale to found a new political party, the Black Panthers for Self-Defense. The Black Panthers patrolled Oakland streets to protect black residents against police brutality. The group came to national attention when they marched onto the floor of the California state legislature carrying weapons. Newton structured the party after the Black Muslims, "minus the religion." Its Ten Point Program introduced the idea of economic self-determination into the civil rights struggle. Bobby Seale set the tone and voiced the wider concerns of the group. He argued forcefully against the Vietnam War. This antiwar position represented another direction, albeit a troublesome one, in the movement. Martin Luther King opened himself to criticism on April 4, 1967, when he gave a speech at Riverside Church in New York City critical of the U.S. involvement in the Vietnam War.

Although their rhetoric was militant and confrontational, the Panthers made intelligent demands for economic reform. Garnering support in the ghetto with urban social and political programs and a Power to the People slogan, membership in the Black Panther Party began to peak in the late 1960s. The media began to highlight radical blacks instead of those who believed in nonviolence. Protests against the Vietnam War, demonstrations all over the country, the Black Panthers' closed fist salute, are reminiscent even today of the troubled days of the late 1960s.

King began to lose patience with the media's preoccupation with militant rhetoric. CBS reporter Daniel Schorr described a conversation he had with King before his assassination on April 4, 1968:

> Well it's because of what you people in television are doing. I don't know if you are aware of it, but you keep driving people like me, who are non-violent, into saying more and more militant things, and if we don't say things militantly enough for you, we don't get on the evening news. And

who does? Stokely Carmichael and H. Rap Brown. By doing this you are, first of all, selecting the more militant black leaders to be civil rights leaders, because everybody sees your television programs. And secondly, you're putting a premium on violence. (Hampton & Fayer, 1990:457)

Conclusion

For many activists and historians, the civil rights movement ended after the Selma March in 1965. Some suggest that the movement ended with the assassination of King. Yet others argue that the struggle for civil rights is not over because the goal of full equality has not been achieved. The triumphs of the Civil Rights Act of 1964 and the Voting Rights Act of 1965 brought many movement efforts in the South to a close. Nevertheless, it is a mistake to view the movement as abruptly ending in 1965. On a local level, many Southern blacks elected African Americans to office who helped their communities achieve a greater political democracy and economic opportunity than would have been possible in the old Southern caste system. The Civil Rights Act of 1968 (The Fair Housing Act) focused on eradicating discrimination in housing and on protecting the right of blacks to vote. Existing civil rights legislation was expanded to prohibit sexual discrimination in education (Title IX).

Without question, the civil rights movement put fundamental reforms in place. De jure segregation as a system was dismantled through the legal battles of the NAACP and the grassroots protests of the movement. Jim Crow laws were soundly defeated as unconstitutional. Voter registration drives contributed thousands of blacks to the rolls. In the face of massive opposition, new political parties were formed and existing ones were challenged for their racist practices. Carson (1981:301) notes:

> Black people who never participated in the collective struggles of the 1960s have also benefited from them. Indeed, blacks who chose not to participate in black struggles and who are primarily concerned with pursuing personal goals rather than assuming social responsibilities are the ones most likely to gain the rewards of American society. As Willie Ricks commented, "Black folks walking around in suits and ties, having jobs, that's an outgrowth of SNCC."

Many whites who participated in the civil rights movement, especially those who took part in Freedom Summer, became involved in other protest and reform efforts of the sixties. For example, a Freedom Summer volunteer, Mario Savio, led the free speech movement at the University of California at Berkeley. Many women became involved in the women's movement. Other volunteers became involved with the movement against the Vietnam War. In later years, the Save the Earth or ecological movement attracted former civil rights activists. Many progressive and left-leaning students emerged from civil rights activities. Historian Eric Foner (1998:299–300) elaborates:

> It is hardly surprising that the civil rights revolution, soon followed by the rise of the New Left and the second wave of feminism, inspired many other Americans to articulate their grievances and claim their own rights. By the late sixties, movements for Chicano rights, and others dotted the political

landscape. Many borrowed the confrontational tactics of the black movement and the New Left, adopting language of "power" and "liberation" and their derisive stance toward traditional organizations and legal approaches.

Using protests and marches in attacking injustice hardly began in the sixties, but the events of that decade, especially the civil rights movement, made them more salient and important in American culture. Because of the civil rights movement and the actions it fostered—sit-ins, boycotts, marches, freedom rides, voter registration drives, and school integration—the United States became a more open, tolerant country. The movement may not claim complete victory, but socially, politically, and structurally America was a changed society at the end of the 1960s.

Key Figures, Terms, and Concepts

Atlanta Project
Black nationalism
Chicago Eight
civil rights coalition
Deacons for Defense
Franz Fanon's *Wretched of the Earth*

Alex Haley
Korean War
Nation of Islam
Alvin Poussaint
rust belt cities
Third World

Important Questions to Consider

1. Malcolm X is credited with evolving the idea of Black Power that came to be associated with SNCC. What were his ideas about black nationalism? To what extent did these ideas influence the actions of SNCC?

2. Evaluate the phrase, "the media giveth and the media taketh away" in terms of the civil rights movement before and after 1965.

3. What is meant by the loss of the organizing tradition in the civil rights movement? How did this long-standing tradition yield to a concern with presenting a militant image to the press?

4. The idea of Black Power became instantly popular during 1966. Define Black Power using the ideas of Malcolm X, Stokely Carmichael, and Bobby Seale.

5. Evaluate the basic division within the civil rights movement. Explain the differences in the social base of the advocates of nonviolence in comparison to the advocates of Black Power.

From Civil Rights to Black Power: The Case of SNCC, 1960–1966

Allen J. Matusow is coeditor with Barton J. Bernstein of Twentieth Century America: Recent Interpretations.

T he transformation of black protest in the 1960's from civil rights to black power has seemed in retrospect an inevitable development. When the inherent limitations of the civil rights movement finally became apparent and when the expectations that the movement created met frustration, some kind of militant reaction in the black community seemed certain. However predictable this development may have been, it tells little about the concrete events that led to the abandonment of the civil rights program and to the adoption of a doctrine that is in many ways its opposite. For black power was not plucked whole from impersonal historical forces; nor was its content the only possible expression of rising black militancy. Rather, black power both as a slogan and a doctrine was in large measure the creation of a small group of civil rights workers who in the early 1960's manned the barricades of black protest in the Deep South. The group was called the Student Nonviolent Coordinating Committee (SNCC). Through its spokesman, Stokely Carmichael, SNCC first proclaimed black power and then became its foremost theoretician. Others would offer glosses on black power that differed from SNCC's concept, but because SNCC had contributed so much to the civil rights movement, no other group could speak with so much authority or command a comparable audience. Although SNCC borrowed freely from many sources to fashion black power into a doctrine, the elements of that doctrine were in the main the results of SNCC's own history. An examination of that history reveals not only the roots of black power but also the sad fate of the whole civil rights movement.

Founded in 1960, SNCC was an outgrowth of the historic sit-in movement, which began in Greensboro, North Carolina, on February 1 of that year. Four freshmen from a local Negro college attempted to desegregate the lunch counter at a Woolworth's five and ten store. The example of these four sent shock waves through the black colleges of the South and created overnight a base for a campaign of massive civil disobedience. The new generation of black students seemed suddenly unwilling to wait any longer for emancipation at the hands of the federal courts and in the next months supplied most of the recruits for the nonviolent army of 50,000 that rose spontaneously and integrated public facilities in 140 Southern cities. For the students on the picket lines, the prophet of the sit-in movement was Dr. Martin Luther King, the leader of the successful Montgomery bus boycott of 1955–56. The students found in King's nonviolent philosophy a ready-made ethic, a tactic, and a conviction of righteousness strong enough to sustain them on a sometimes hazardous mission. It was King's organization, the Southern Christian Leadership Conference (SCLC), that first suggested the need for some central direction of the sit-in movement. At the invitation of SCLC's executive secretary, some 300 activist students from throughout the South met in Raleigh, North Carolina, in April 1960, to discuss their problems. The students agreed to form a coordinating body, which became SNCC, and in May 1960, hired a secretary and opened an office in Atlanta. In October the organization decided to become a permanent one, and 235 delegates approved a founding statement inspired by King's philosophy:

> We affirm the philosophical or religious ideal of nonviolence as the foundation of our purpose, the presupposition of our belief, and the manner of our action. . . . Through nonviolence, courage displaces fear. Love transcends hate. Acceptance dissipates prejudice; hope ends despair. Faith reconciles doubt. Peace dominates war. Mutual regards cancel enmity. Justice for all overwhelms injustice. The redemptive community supersedes immoral social systems.

In truth, the Christian rhetoric of SNCC's founding statement was not appropriate. The author of the statement was James Lawson, a young minister who never actually belonged to SNCC. Most of the students who rallied to the sit-ins in 1960 accepted King's teachings more out of convenience than conviction and respected his courage more than his philosophy. For while King believed that Christian love was an end in itself and that Negro nonviolence would redeem American society, the students preferred to participate in America rather than to transform it. Sociologists who examined the attitudes of protesters in the black colleges found not alienation from American middle-class values but a desire to share fully in middle-class life. In a perceptive piece written for *Dissent,* Michael Walzer supported these findings from his own first-hand impressions of the sit-ins. Walzer concluded that the students were materialistic as well as moral, were "willing to take risks in the name of both prosperity and virtue," and had as their goal "assimilation into American society." As for nonviolence, Walzer wrote, "I was told often that 'when one side has all the guns, then the other side is non-violent.'"

In the beginning, the philosophical inconsistencies of the sit-ins did not trouble SNCC, for it stood at the forefront of a movement whose ultimate triumph seemed not far distant. But within months, as mysteriously as it began, the sit-in movement vanished. By the spring of 1961 the black campuses had lapsed into their customary quiescence, their contribution to the civil rights movement at an end. As for SNCC, since October 1960, the student representatives from each Southern state had been meeting monthly to squander their energies trying to coordinate a movement that was first too amorphous and then suddenly moribund. SNCC's attempts in early 1961 to raise up new hosts of students proved ineffectual, and lacking followers, the organization seemed without a future. Then in May 1961, the Freedom Rides restored a sense of urgency to the civil rights movement and gave SNCC a second life.

On May 14, 1961, members of the Congress of Racial Equality (CORE) began the Freedom Rides to test a Supreme Court decision outlawing segregation in transportation terminals. On May 20, after one of CORE's integrated buses was bombed near Anniston, Alabama, and another was mobbed in Birmingham, CORE decided to call off its rides. But amid sensational publicity, students from Nashville and Atlanta, many associated with SNCC, rushed to Birmingham to continue the journey to New Orleans. After mobs assaulted this second wave of riders, the Federal Government stepped in to protect them, and they were permitted to go as far as Jackson, where local authorities put them in jail for defying segregation ordinances.

Throughout the summer of 1961 some 300 citizens from all over America took Freedom Rides that brought them to the jails of Jackson. For SNCC the Freedom Rides provided a temporary outlet for activism and, more important, inspired radical changes in the structure and purpose of the organization.

Perhaps the most important result of the Freedom Rides for SNCC was to focus its attention on the Deep South. Most of the sit-ins had occurred in the cities and larger towns of the Upper South, and the victories there had come with relative ease. Now the magnitude of the task confronting the civil rights movement became clearer. As some in SNCC had already perceived, sit-ins to desegregate public places offered no meaningful benefits to poverty-stricken tenant farmers in, say, Mississippi. In order to mobilize the black communities in the Deep South to fight for their rights, sporadic student demonstrations would be less useful than sustained efforts by full time field workers. In the summer of 1961, as SNCC was beginning to grope toward the concept of community action, the Federal Government stepped in with an attractive suggestion.

Embarrassed by the Freedom Rides, Attorney General Robert F. Kennedy moved to direct the civil rights movement into paths that, in his view, were more constructive. Kennedy suggested that the civil rights organizations jointly sponsor a campaign to register Southern black voters. Such a drive, its proponents argued, would be difficult for even extreme segregationists to oppose and eventually might liberalize the Southern delegation in Congress. When the Justice Department seemed to offer federal protection for registration workers and when white liberals outside the Administration procured foundation money to finance anticipated costs, the civil rights groups agreed to undertake the project. Within SNCC, advocates of direct action fought acceptance of the project, but the issue was compromised and a threatened split was averted. SNCC's decision to mobilize black communities behind efforts to secure political rights decisively changed the character of the organization. It thereafter ceased to be an extracurricular activity of student leaders and became instead the vocation of dedicated young men and women who temporarily abandoned their careers to become full time paid workers (or "field secretaries") in the movement. Moreover, as SNCC workers drifted away from the black campuses and began living among Deep South blacks, they cast aside the middle-class goals that had motivated the sit-ins of 1960 and put on the overalls of the poor. Begun as middle-class protest, SNCC was developing revolutionary potential.

In Mississippi the major civil rights groups (NAACP, SCLC, CORE, and SNCC) ostensibly joined together to form the Council of Federated Organizations (COFO) to register black voters. But in reality, except for one Mississippi congressional district where CORE had a project of its own, COFO was manned almost entirely by SNCC people. The director of COFO was SNCC's now legendary Robert Moses, a product of Harlem with a Masters degree in philosophy from Harvard, whose courage and humanity made him the most respected figure in the organization. Moses had entered Pike County, Mississippi, alone in 1961, stayed on in spite of a beating and a jail term, and in the spring of 1962 became COFO's director in charge of voting projects in Vicksburg, Cleveland, Greenwood, and a few other Mississippi towns. Although SNCC also had registration projects in Arkansas, Alabama, and Georgia, it concentrated on Mississippi, where the obstacles were greatest.

Throughout 1962 and into 1963 SNCC workers endured assaults, offered brave challenges to local power structures, and exhorted local blacks to shake off fear and stand up for freedom. But SNCC scored no breakthroughs to sustain morale, and while its goals remained outwardly unchanged, its mood was turning bitter. To SNCC the hostility of local racists was not nearly so infuriating as the apparent betrayal that it suffered at the hands of the Justice Department. SNCC believed that in 1961 the Kennedy Administration had guaranteed protection to registration workers, but in Mississippi in 1962 and 1963, SNCC's only contact with federal authority consisted of the FBI agents who stood by taking notes while local policemen beat up SNCC members. SNCC and its supporters insisted that existing law empowered the Federal Government to intervene, but the Justice Department contended that it was in fact powerless. SNCC doubted the sincerity of the Government's arguments and became convinced that the Kennedys had broken a solemn promise for political reasons. Thus by 1963 SNCC was already becoming estranged from established authority and suspicious of liberal politicians.

SNCC's growing sense of alienation cut it off even from other civil rights organizations and most importantly from Dr. King, who by 1963 had become a fallen idol for SNCC workers. They believed that King was too willing to compromise, wielded too much power, and too successfully monopolized the funds of the movement. Doubts about King had arisen as early as the Freedom Rides, when students turned to him for advice and leadership and received what they considered only vague sympathy. In fact, after CORE called off the first ride, King privately supported Robert Kennedy's plea for a "cooling-off" period. But much to SNCC's annoyance, when militant voices prevailed and the rides continued, the press gave King all the credit. In Albany, Georgia, in December 1961, after SNCC aroused the black population to pack the local jails for freedom, King came to town, got arrested, monopolized the headlines, and almost stole the leadership of the Albany campaign from SNCC. In SNCC's view, dependence on King's charisma actually weakened the civil rights movement, for it discouraged development of leadership at the grass-roots level. Why, SNCC asked, did King use his huge share of civil rights money to maintain a large staff in Atlanta, and why did he never account for the funds that he so skillfully collected? As King lost influence on SNCC, dissenting attitudes about nonviolence, implicit since 1960, came to be frankly articulated. When Robert Penn Warren asked Robert Moses what he thought of King's philosophy, Moses replied,

> We don't agree with it, in a sense. The majority of the students are not sympathetic to the idea that they have to love the white people that they are struggling against. . . . For most of the members, it is tactical, it's a question of being able to have a method of attack rather than to be always on the defensive.

During the March on Washington in August 1963, the nation almost caught a glimpse of SNCC's growing anger. John Lewis, the chairman of SNCC and one of the scheduled speakers, threatened to disrupt the harmony of that happy occasion by saying what he really thought. Only with difficulty did moderates persuade Lewis to delete the harshest passages of his address. So the nation did not know that SNCC scorned Kennedy's civil rights bill as "too little and too late." Lewis had intended to ask the 250,000 people gathered at the Lincoln Memorial,

> What is there in this bill to insure the equality of a maid who earns $5 a week in the home of a family whose income is $100,000 a year? . . . This nation is still a place of cheap political leaders who build their careers on immoral com-

promises and ally themselves with open forms of political, economic, and social exploitation. . . . The party of Kennedy is also the party of Eastland. The party of Javits is also the party of Goldwater. Where is *our* party? . . . We cannot depend on any political party, for the Democrats and the Republicans have betrayed the basic principles of the Declaration of Independence.

In those remarks that he never delivered, Lewis used both the language of Christian protest and images alive with the rage of SNCC field workers. "In the struggle we must seek more than mere civil rights; we must work for the community of love, peace, and true brotherhood." And,

the time will come when we will not confine our marching to Washington. We will march through the South, through the heart of Dixie, the way Sherman did. We shall pursue our "scorched earth" policy and burn Jim Crow to the ground—nonviolently. We shall fragment the South into a thousand pieces and put them back together in the image of democracy.

The crucial milestone of SNCC's road to radicalism was the Freedom Summer of 1964. Freedom Summer grew out of a remarkable mock election sponsored by SNCC in the autumn of 1963. Because the mass of Mississippi's black population could not legally participate in choosing the state's governor that year, Robert Moses conceived a freedom election to protest mass disfranchisement and to educate Mississippi's blacks to the mechanics of the political process. COFO organized a new party called the Mississippi Freedom Democrats, printed its own ballots, and in October conducted its own poll. Overwhelming the regular party candidates, Aaron Henry, head of the state NAACP and Freedom Democratic nominee for governor, received 70,000 votes, a tremendous protest against the denial of equal political rights. One reason for the success of the project was the presence in the state of 100 Yale and Stanford students, who worked for two weeks with SNCC on the election. SNCC was sufficiently impressed by the student contribution to consider inviting hundreds more to spend an entire summer in Mississippi. Sponsors of this plan hoped not only for workers but for publicity that might at last focus national attention on Mississippi. By the winter of 1963–64, however, rising militancy in SNCC had begun to take on the overtones of black nationalism, and some of the membership resisted the summer project on the grounds that most of the volunteers would be white.

Present from the beginning, by mid-1964 whites made up one-fifth of SNCC's approximately 150 full time field secretaries. Though whites had suffered their fair share of beatings, some blacks in SNCC were expressing doubts about the role of white men in a movement for black freedom. At a staff meeting at Greenville, Mississippi, in November 1963, a debate on the proposed Freedom Summer brought the issue of white-black relations into the open. In his book *SNCC: The New Abolitionists*, Howard Zinn, who attended this meeting, summarizes the views of the militants:

Four or five of the Negro staff members now urged that the role of whites be limited. For whites to talk to Mississippi Negroes about voter registration, they said, only reinforced the Southern Negro's tendency to believe that whites were superior. Whites tended to take over leadership roles in the movement, thus preventing Southern Negroes from being trained to lead. Why didn't whites just work in the white Southern community? One man noted that in Africa the new nations were training black Africans to take over all important government positions. Another told of meeting a Black Muslim in Atlanta who warned him that whites were taking over the movement. "I had the feeling inside. I felt what he said was true."

But Fannie Lou Hamer disagreed. Mrs. Hamer had been a time-keeper on a cotton plantation and was one of the local Mississippi blacks whom SNCC discovered and elevated to leadership. Speaking for the majority of the meeting, she said, "If we're trying to break down this barrier of segregation, we can't segregate ourselves." Thus in February 1964, SNCC sent an invitation to Northern college students to spend their summer vacation in Mississippi.

In retrospect, the summer of 1964 was a turning point in the civil rights movement. When the summer began, SNCC was still operating within the framework of liberal America, still committed to integration and equal political rights for all citizens. But by the end of the summer of 1964, the fraying cords that bound SNCC to liberal goals and values finally snapped. In a sense, much of later black power thought was merely a postscript to SNCC's ill-fated summer project.

In June 1964, more than 700 selected students, judged by a staff psychiatrist at MIT to be "an extraordinarily healthy bunch of kids," came to Oxford, Ohio, for two week-long orientation sessions conducted by veteran SNCC workers. The atmosphere in Oxford, tense from the outset, became on June 22 pervaded with gloom. Robert Moses quietly told the volunteers that three workers had gone into Neshoba county in Mississippi the day before and had not been heard from since. One was Michael Schwerner, a CORE staff member; the second was James Chaney, a black SNCC worker from Mississippi; and the third was Andrew Goodman, a student volunteer who had finished his orientation in Ohio a few days before. (In August the bodies of these three were discovered in their shallow graves near Philadelphia, Mississippi.)

The volunteers in Ohio had to face not only their own fear but also unanticipated hostility from the SNCC workers whom they had come to assist. Tensions between black workers and white volunteers seethed under the surface for some days and then finally erupted. One night SNCC showed a film of a grotesque voting registrar turning away black applicants. When the student audience laughed at the scene, six SNCC people walked out, enraged at what they considered an insensitive response. There followed an exchange between the workers and the volunteers, in which the students complained that the staff was distant, uncommunicative, and "looked down on us for not having been through what they had." A SNCC worker replied,

> If you get mad at us for walking out, just wait until they break your head in, and see if you don't have something to get mad about. Ask Jimmy Travis over there what he thinks about the project. What does he think about Mississippi? He has six slugs in him, man, and the last one went right through the back of his neck when he was driving a car outside Greenwood. Ask Jesse here—he has been beaten so that we wouldn't recognize him time and time and time and time again. If you don't get scared, pack up and get the hell out of here because we don't need any favors of people who don't know what they are doing here in the first place.

The bitter words seemed to have a **cathartic** effect, and the meeting culminated in emotional singing. Said one volunteer a bit too optimistically, "The crisis is past, I think."

From one perspective the story of the two months that followed is one of the human spirit triumphant. Though three more people were killed, eighty others were beaten, thirty-five churches were burned, and thirty other buildings bombed, few turned back; black and white together, the civil rights workers in Mississippi worked for racial justice. The student volunteers taught in Freedom Schools, where 3,000 children were given their first glimpse of a world beyond Mississippi. They organized the disfranchised to march on county courthouses to face unyielding registrars. Most importantly, they walked the roads of Mississippi for the Freedom Democratic Party (FDP). Denying the legitimacy of the segregated Democratic party, COFO opened the FDP to members of all races and declared the party's loyalty to Lyndon Johnson. The goal of the FDP in the summer of 1964 was to send a delegation to the Democratic convention in Atlantic City to challenge the credentials of the regular Democrats and cast the state's vote for the party's nominees. To mount this challenge against the racist Democrats of Mississippi, COFO enrolled 60,000 members in the FDP and then organized precinct, county, and state conventions to choose 68 integrated delegates to go north. The FDP, in which tens of thousands of black Mississippi citizens invested tremendous hopes, was a true grass-roots political movement and the greatest achievement of Freedom Summer.

Although the FDP brought to Atlantic City little more than a sense of moral outrage, it nevertheless managed to transform its challenge of the Mississippi regulars into a major threat to the peace of the national party. Mrs. Hamer helped make this feat possible by her electrifying (and televised) testimony before the **credentials committee** on how Mississippi policemen had beaten her up for trying to register to vote. As Northern liberals began rallying to the FDP, the managers of the convention sought a compromise that would satisfy the liberals and at the same time keep the bulk of the Southern delegations in the convention. President Johnson favored a proposal to seat all the Mississippi regulars who pledged their loyalty to the party, to deny any voting rights to the FDP delegates, but to permit them to sit on the floor of the convention. In addition, he proposed that at future conventions no state delegations chosen by racially discriminatory procedures would be accredited. But because this compromise denied the FDP's claims of legitimacy, the FDP and many liberals declared it unacceptable and threatened to take their case to the floor of the convention, a prospect that greatly displeased the President. Johnson then sent Senator Hubert Humphrey to Atlantic City to act as his agent in settling the controversy. Unsubstantiated rumors had it that if Humphrey's mission failed, the President would deny the Senator the party's vice-presidential nomination. In close touch with both the White House and the **credentials committee**, Humphrey proposed altering the original compromise by permitting two FDP delegates to sit in the convention as delegates at large with full voting rights. This was as far as Johnson would go, and at the time it seemed far enough. Though the Mississippi white regulars walked out, no Southern delegations followed them, and, at the same time, most liberals felt that the Administration had made a genuine concession. Black leaders, including Dr. King, pleaded with the FDP to accept Humphrey's compromise. But the FDP denied that the compromise was in any sense a victory. Angered at Humphrey's insistence that he alone choose the two at-large delegates, the FDP announced that it had not come to Atlantic City "begging for crumbs." Mrs. Hamer, by now a minor national celebrity, said of Humphrey's efforts, "It's a token of rights on the back row that we get in Mississippi. We didn't come all this way for that mess again."

To the general public the FDP appeared to be a band of moral zealots hostile to reasonable compromise and ungrateful for the real concession that the party had offered. The true story was more complicated. Aware that total victory was impossible, the FDP had in fact been quite willing to accept any proposal that recognized its legitimacy. At the beginning of the controversy Oregon's Congresswoman Edith Green offered a compromise that the FDP found entirely acceptable. Mrs. Green proposed that the convention seat every member of both delegations who signed a pledge of loyalty and that Mississippi's vote be divided between the two groups according to the number of seated delegates in each. Since only eleven members of the credentials committee (10 percent of the total) had to sign a minority report to dislodge the Green compromise from committee, the FDP seemed assured that its case would reach the convention floor, where many believed that the Green compromise would prevail over Johnson's original proposal. FDP's hopes for a minority report rested chiefly on Joseph Rauh, a member of the credentials committee, leader of the Democratic party in the District of Columbia, veteran of innumerable liberal crusades, and, happily, adviser and legal counsel of the FDP. But Rauh was also a friend of Hubert Humphrey and an attorney for Humphrey's strong supporter, Walter Reuther. After Humphrey came on the scene with his compromise, Rauh backed away from the minority report.

In his semi-official history of the Mississippi Summer Project, *The Summer That Didn't End,* Len Holt presents the FDP and SNCC interpretation of what happened. Presumably pressured by his powerful friends, Rauh broke a promise to the FDP and would not support the Green compromise. One by one the FDP's other allies on the committee backed away—some to protect jobs, others to keep alive hopes for federal judgeships, and one because he feared the loss of a local antipoverty program. In the end the FDP failed to collect the needed signatures, and there was no minority report. The angry rhetoric that the FDP delegates let loose in Atlantic City was in reality inspired less by Humphrey's compromise than by what the FDP regarded as its betrayal at the hands of the white liberals on the credentials committee. By the end of the Democratic convention SNCC was convinced that membership in the Democratic coalition held little hope for Southern blacks and that, lacking power, they would always be sold out by the liberals. In Atlantic City the phrase "white power structure" took on concrete meaning. Freedom Summer, which began with SNCC fighting for entrance into the American political system, ended with the radical conviction that that system was beyond redemption.

In the end the Freedom Summer Project of 1964 not only destroyed SNCC's faith in the American political system; it also undermined its commitment to integration. Within the project racial tensions between white and black workers were never successfully resolved. Though many white volunteers established warm relationships with the local black families that housed them, healthy communication between students and veteran SNCC workers proved difficult at best. Staff members resented the officious manner of better-educated volunteers and feared that the white students were taking over the movement. "Several times," one volunteer wrote, "I've had to completely re-do press statements or letters written by one of them." Said a SNCC worker, "Look at those fly-by-night freedom fighters bossing everybody around." SNCC people found it hard to respect the efforts of volunteers who they knew would retreat at the end of the summer to their safe middle-class world. One sensitive white female volunteer wrote that SNCC workers "were automatically suspicious of us, the white volunteers; throughout the summer they put us to the test, and few, if any, could pass. . . . It humbled, if not humiliated, one to realize that *finally they will never accept me."* By the end of the summer a spirit akin to black nationalism was rising inside the SNCC organization.

The overall failure of Freedom Summer administered a blow to SNCC's morale from which the organization almost did not recover. In November 1964, Robert Coles, a psychiatrist who had worked closely with SNCC, wrote about the tendency of veteran workers to develop battle fatigue. Even heroic temperaments, he said, could not escape the depression that inevitably results from long periods of unremitting dangers and disappointments. But by the fall of 1964 battle fatigue was no longer just the problem of individual SNCC members; it was pervading the entire organization. One patient told Coles,

> I'm tired, but so is the whole movement. We're busy worrying about our position or our finances, so we don't do anything. . . . We're becoming lifeless, just like all revolutions when they lose their first momentum and become more interested in preserving what they've won than going on to new challenges. . . . Only with us we haven't won that much, and we're either holding to the little we have as an organization, or we get bitter, and want to create a new revolution. . . . You know, one like the Muslims want which is the opposite of what we say we're for. It's as if we completely reverse ourselves because we can't get what we want.

Uncertain of their purpose, SNCC workers in the winter of 1964–65 grew introspective. Months were consumed in discussing the future of whites in the movement and the proper structure of the organization. Fresh from a trip to Africa where he met the black nationalist Malcolm X, John Lewis, Chairman of SNCC, spoke for the majority in early 1965 when he demanded that blacks lead their own movement. At the same time, quarrels over organization almost tore SNCC apart. Some workers became "high on freedom" and advocated a romantic anarchism that rejected bureaucratic structure and leadership. Robert Moses, for instance, believed that SNCC workers should "go where the spirit say go, and do what the spirit say do." Moses was so disturbed by his own prestige in the movement, that he changed his name, drifted into Alabama, and thereafter was only vaguely connected with SNCC. Meanwhile SNCC's field work tended to fall into neglect.

In the summer of 1965 SNCC brought 300 white volunteers into Mississippi for its second and last summer project. The result was a shambles. Racial tensions caused some projects to break up and prevented serious work in others. Problems only dimly perceived a year before assumed stark clarity, and SNCC's resentment of the volunteers became overt and unambiguous. At staff meetings blacks would silence white students with such remarks as "How long have you been here?" and "How do you know what it's like being black?" and "If you don't like the way we do it, get the hell out of the state." Not all the blame for the final breakdown of race relations in SNCC, however, belonged to the black staff. The questionable motivation of some of the white students led Alvin Poussaint, a black psychiatrist close to SNCC, to add a new neurosis to medical terminology—the white African Queen or Tarzan complex. The victim of this neurosis harbored repressed delusions of himself as an "intelligent, brave, and handsome white man or woman, leading the poor down-trodden and oppressed black men to freedom and salvation."

But the most serious obstacle to healthy race relations inside SNCC was sex, and in this dimension, as really in all others, the villain was neither black worker nor white student, but rather the sad and twisted history of race relations in America. The white girl who came South to help SNCC found herself, according to Dr. Poussaint, "at the center of an emotionally shattering crossfire of racial tensions that have been nurtured for centuries." In the summer of 1965 a veteran black civil rights worker in SCLC tried to warn white girls of the perils that awaited them in their dealings with black men in the movement:

> What you have here is a man who had no possible way of being a man in the society in which he lives, save one. And that's the problem. The only way or place a Negro man has been able to express his manhood is sexually and so you find a tremendous sexual aggressiveness. And I say quite frankly, don't get carried away by it and don't get afraid of it either. I mean, don't think it's because you're so beautiful and so ravishing that this man is so enamoured of you. It's not that at all. He's just trying to find his manhood and he goes especially to the places that have robbed him of it. . . . And so, in a sense, what passes itself as desire is probably a combination of hostility and resentment—because he resents what the society has done to him and he wants to take it out on somebody who symbolizes the establishment of society.

At the end of the summer a white girl spoke of her experiences:

> Well, I think that the white female should be very well prepared before she comes down here to be bombarded. And she also has to be well prepared to tell them to go to hell and be prepared to have them not give up. . . . I've never met such forward men as I have in Mississippi.

The problem was complicated by the jealousy of black girls toward their white rivals, and by neurotic whites who sought to ease their guilt by permitting blacks to exploit them sexually and financially. On leaving their projects to go home, a few white girls told Poussaint, "I hate Negroes." By the end of the summer of 1965 no one could any longer doubt that the blacks reciprocated the feeling.

The year 1965 was a lost one for SNCC. For the first time since its founding, it was no longer on the frontier of protest, no longer the keeper of the nation's conscience, no longer the driving force of a moral revolution. The civil rights acts of 1964 and 1965 brought the civil rights movement, for which SNCC had suffered so much, to a triumphant conclusion, but SNCC had lost interest in integrated public accommodations and equal political rights. SNCC seemed to be losing its sense of mission and after years of providing heroes for the black protest movement, it now needed a hero of its own. Significantly it chose Malcolm X, the black nationalist who had been assassinated by Muslim rivals in February 1965. Only a few years before, SNCC and Malcolm X had seemed to occupy opposite poles of black protest. Thus while SNCC's John Lewis was toning down his speech at the March on Washington, Malcolm X was saying,

> Who ever heard of angry revolutionists all harmonizing "We Shall Overcome . . . Suum Day . . ." while tripping and swaying along arm-in-arm with the very people they were supposed to be angrily revolting against? Who ever heard of angry revolutionists swinging their bare feet together with their oppressors in lily-pad park pools, with gospels and guitars and "I Have a Dream" speeches?

While policemen were clubbing SNCC workers in Mississippi, Malcolm X was saying, "If someone puts a hand on you, send him to the cemetery." While SNCC was pondering the meaning of Atlantic City, Malcolm X was saying, "We *need* a Mau Mau. If they don't want to deal with the Mississippi Freedom Democratic Party, then we'll give them something else to deal with." While black nationalists were still a minority in SNCC, Malcolm X was calling for black control of black politicians in black communities, black ownership of ghetto businesses, and black unity "to lift the level of our community, to make our society beautiful so that we will be satisfied in our own social circles and won't be running around here trying to knock our way into a social circle where we're not wanted." This was the language that had made Malcolm X the hero of the urban ghetto, and it was the language appropriate in 1965 to SNCC's militant mood. In a certain sense Malcolm X was the link that connected SNCC with the black radicalism that was arising in the North.

Unlike SNCC, the ghetto masses never had to disabuse themselves of the colorblind assumptions of the civil rights movement. Trapped permanently in their neighborhoods, the poor blacks of the North have always been painfully conscious of their racial separateness. As Essien-Udom, a historian of black nationalism, has written, blackness "is the stuff of their lives and an omnipresent, harsh reality. For this reason the Negro masses are instinctively 'race men.'" But the civil rights movement nevertheless had its consequences in the ghetto. The spectacle of Southern blacks defying their white tormentors apparently inspired among Northern blacks race pride and resurgent outrage at the gap between American ideals and black realities. Thus the civil rights movement had the ironic effect of feeding the nationalist tendency in the ghetto to turn inward, to separate, and to identify the white men outside as the enemy. SNCC's frustrations exploded intellectually in the formulation of black power doctrines, but ghetto rage took the form of riot.

The riot of August 1965, in Watts (the sprawling ghetto of Los Angeles) dwarfed the violent outbursts of the previous year and awakened America to the race crisis in her big cities. A social trauma of the first order, the Watts riot resulted in 35 deaths, 600 burned and looted buildings, and 4,000 persons arrested. Above all it revealed the dangerous racial hatred that had been accumulating unnoticed in the nation's black ghettos. The official autopsy of Watts denied by implication that it was a revolt against white oppression. The McCone Commission (after its chairman, John McCone), appointed by California's Governor Pat Brown to investigate the riot, estimated that only 10,000 Watts residents, or 2 percent of the population in the riot area, had actually been on the streets during the uprising. This minor fraction, the Commission contended, was not protesting specific grievances, which admittedly existed in abundance, but was engaged in an "insensate rage of destruction" that was "formless, quite senseless." Critics of the McCone report have ably challenged these findings. (For example, Robert Fogelson points out that "to claim that only 10,000 Negroes rioted when about 4,000 were arrested is to presume that the police apprehended fully 40 percent of the rioters.") In reality, a rather large minority of the riot-age population in Watts was on the streets during the riot, and one of the Commission's own staff reports revealed, the riot had significant support inside the ghetto, especially in the worst slum areas.

On the crucial question of the riot's causes, observers on the scene agreed that the rioters were animated by a common anger against whites. Robert Blauner, a staff member for the McCone Commission and its severest critic, has written,

> Most of the actions of the rioters appear to have been informed by the desire to clear out an alien presence, white men, rather than to kill them. . . . It was primarily an attack on property, particularly white-owned businesses. . . . The spirit of the Watts rioters appears similar to that of anti-colonial crowds demonstrating against foreign masters.

Said Bayard Rustin, a moderate black intellectual who was in Watts during the riot, "The whole point of the outburst in Watts was that it marked the first major rebellion of Negroes against their masochism and was carried on with the express purpose of asserting that they would no longer quietly submit to the deprivation of slum life." Thus in 1965, for different reasons, both the ghetto masses and the members of SNCC were seized by militant anti-white feelings, and it was this congruence of mood that would shortly permit SNCC to appeal to a nation-wide black audience.

After a year on the periphery of the black protest movement, SNCC in 1966 moved again to the forefront. In May 1966, at a time when the organization was apparently disintegrating, 135 staff members (25 of them white) met in Nashville to thrash out their future. Early in the emotional conference, by a vote of 60 to 22, John Lewis, the gentle advocate of nonviolence, retained the chairmanship of SNCC by defeating the challenge of the militant Stokely Carmichael. But as the conference went on, the arguments of the militants began to prevail. When the staff voted to boycott the coming White House conference on civil rights, Lewis announced that he would attend anyway, and the question of the chairmanship was then reopened. This time SNCC workers chose Carmichael as their new leader by a vote of 60 to 12. The conference next issued a statement calling, among other things, for "black Americans to begin building independent political, economic, and cultural institutions that they will control and use as instruments of social change in this country."

A few weeks later the full meaning of Carmichael's election became clear to the whole nation. The occasion was the famous Meredith march through Mississippi in June of 1966. James Meredith, the man who integrated the University of Mississippi in 1962 with the help of the United States Army, embarked on a 200-mile walk from Memphis to Jackson to show the black people of Mississippi that they could walk to the voting booths without fear. On June 6, 28 miles out of Memphis, a white man felled Meredith with buckshot. Erroneously believing that Meredith had been killed, civil rights leaders immediately flew to Mississippi to continue his walk against fear. So it was that arm in arm, Martin Luther King of SCLC, Floyd McKissick of CORE, and Stokely Carmichael of SNCC marched down U.S. Highway 51.

Early efforts of the three leaders to maintain surface unity rapidly broke dawn. Significantly, the first issue that divided them was the role of white people in the Meredith march. King's workers publicly thanked Northern whites for joining the procession. McKissick also thanked the Northerners but announced that black men must now lead the civil rights movement. And Carmichael mused aloud that maybe the whites should go home. As the column moved onto the back roads and Southern white hostility increased, the leadership of the march failed to agree on how to respond to violence. In Philadelphia, Mississippi, Dr. King conducted a memorial service for Goodman, Chaney, and Schwerner and told a crowd of 300 jeering whites that the murderers of the three men were no doubt "somewhere around me at this moment." Declaring that "I am not afraid of any man," King then delivered a Christian sermon. But after the service was over and local whites got rough, the marchers returned punch for punch.

The real spokesman for the march, it soon developed, was not King but Stokely Carmichael. In one town, after spending a few hours in jail, Carmichael told a crowd "I ain't going to jail no more. I ain't going to jail no more," and he announced "Every courthouse in Mississippi ought to be burned down to get rid of the dirt." Carmichael then issued the cry that would make him famous. Five times be shouted "Black Power!" and, the *New York Times* reported, "each time the younger members of the audience shouted back, 'Black Power.'" Informed of this new slogan, Dr. King expressed disapproval, and SCLC workers exhorted crowds to call not for black power but for "freedom now." Nevertheless, by the end of the Meredith march, black power had become a force to reckon with.

At its inception in June, 1966, black power was not a systematic doctrine but a cry of rage. In an article in the *New York Times Magazine,* Dr. Poussaint tried to explain the psychological origin of the anger expressed in the new slogan:

> I remember treating Negro workers after they had been beaten viciously by white toughs or policemen while conducting civil rights demonstrations. I would frequently comment, "You must feel pretty angry getting beaten up like that by those bigots." Often I received a reply such as: "No, I don't hate those white men, I love them because they must really be suffering with all that hatred in their souls. Dr. King says the only way we can win our freedom is through love. Anger and hatred has never solved anything."
>
> I used to sit there and wonder, "Now, what do they really do with their rage?"

Poussaint reported that after a while these workers vented their mounting rage against each other.

> While they were talking about being nonviolent and "loving" the sheriff that just hit them over the head, they rampaged around the project houses beating up each other. I frequently had to calm Negro civil rights workers with large doses of tranquilizers for what I can describe clinically only as acute attacks of rage.

In time the civil rights workers began to direct their anger against white racists, the Federal Government, and finally white people in the movement. Said Poussaint:

> This rage was at a fever pitch for many months, before it became crystallized in the "Black Power" slogan. The workers who shouted it the loudest were those with the oldest battle scars from the terror, demoralization, and castration which they experienced through continual direct confrontation with Southern white racists. Furthermore, some of the most bellicose chanters of the slogan had been, just a few years before, examples of nonviolent, loving passive resistance in their struggle against white supremacy. These workers appeared to be seeking a sense of inner psychological emancipation from racists through self-assertion and release of aggressive angry feelings.

In the months following the Meredith march, SNCC found itself at the center of a bitter national controversy and spokesman for an enlarged constituency. The anger implicit in the slogan "black power" assured SNCC a following in the ghettos of the North and ended its regional confinement. Through its leader, Stokely Carmichael, SNCC labored through 1966 and into 1967 to give intellectual substance to the black power slogan, seeking especially to frame an analysis that would be relevant to black Americans of all sections. Although his speeches were often inflammatory, Carmichael in his writing attempted serious, even restrained, argument suitable for an educated audience. But the elements of black power were not, in truth, derived from rational reflection but from wretched experience—from the beatings, jailhouses, and abortive crusades that SNCC veterans had endured for six years. SNCC had tried nonviolence and found it psychologically destructive. (The "days of the free head-whipping are over," Carmichael and his collaborator Charles Hamilton wrote. "Black people should and must fight back.") SNCC, for example, had believed in integration and tried it within its own organization, but black and white together had not worked. (Integration, said Carmichael, "is a subterfuge for the maintenance of white supremacy" and "reinforces, among both black and white, the idea that 'white' is automatically better and 'black' is by definition inferior.") SNCC had allied with white liberals in the Democratic party and had come away convinced that it had been betrayed. (In dealing with blacks, Carmichael said, white liberals "perpetuate a paternalistic, colonial relationship.") SNCC had struggled for equal political rights but concluded finally that political inequality was less oppressive than economic exploitation. In 1966 SNCC felt it was necessary to go beyond the assertion of these hard conclusions and to attempt to impose on them systematic form. So it was that after years of activism divorced from ideology, SNCC began to reduce its field work and concentrate on fashioning an intellectual rationale for its new militancy. At a time when the black protest movement was floundering and its future direction was uncertain, SNCC stepped forward to contribute the doctrines of black power, which were really the culmination of its career. No history of SNCC would be complete, therefore, without some consideration of those doctrines.

According to Stokely Carmichael, the black masses suffer from two different but reinforcing forms of oppression: class exploitation and white racism. To illustrate this point, he relies on an analogy apparently inspired by Franz Fanon's *Wretched of the Earth,* a book with considerable influence in black power circles. The black communities of contemporary America, Carmichael says, share many of the characteristics of African colonies under European rule. Thus as Africa once enriched its imperialist masters by exporting valuable raw materials to Europe, so now do the American ghettos "export" their labor for the profit of American capitalists. In both Africa and America, white men own local businesses and use them to drain away any wealth somehow possessed by the subject population. As in Africa, there exists in the ghetto a white power structure that is no abstraction, but is a visible and concrete presence—the white landlords, for instance, who collect rent and ignore needed repairs, the city agencies and school systems that systematically neglect black people, the policemen who abuse black citizens and collect payoffs from white racketeers. By far the most insidious method devised by the white imperialists for perpetuating class exploitation has been the use of race as a badge of inferiority. Colonial masters, says Carmichael, "purposely, maliciously, and with reckless abandon relegated the black man to a subordinated, inferior status in society. . . . White America's School of Slavery and Segregation, like the School of Colonialism, has taught the subject to hate himself and deny his humanity." As the colonies of Africa have done, black Americans must undergo "political modernization," liberate their communities, and achieve self-determination. And like Africa, the ghetto must win the struggle by its own effort.

For Carmichael, liberation begins with eradication of the effects of white racism. To overcome the shame of race bred in them by white men, blacks must develop a cultural identity, rediscover the rich African civilization from which they originally came, and learn from their history that they are a "vibrant, valiant people." Freed of their damaging self-image, they can begin to challenge the capitalist values that have enslaved them as a class. The white middle class, says Carmichael, has fostered esteem for "material aggrandizement," is "without a viable conscience as regards humanity," and constitutes "the backbone of institutional racism in this country." Black men, however, will develop values emphasizing "the dignity of man, not . . . the sanctity of property," "free people," not "free enterprise." "The society we seek to build among black people, then, is not a capitalist one. It is a society in which the spirit of community and humanistic love prevail." To complete the process of liberation, black men will have to purge the ghetto of exploiting institutions and develop structures that conform to their new values.

The reconstruction of the black community, Carmichael contends, should be in the hands of black people in order to "convey the revolutionary idea . . . that black people are able to do things themselves." Among other acts of liberation that they can perform, ghetto blacks should conduct rent strikes against slum landlords and boycotts against the ghetto merchant who refuses to " 'invest' say forty to fifty percent of his net profit in the indigenous community." Governmental structures that have violated the humanity of blacks will have to be either eliminated from the ghetto or made responsive to their black constituency. The school system must be taken from professionals, most of whom have demonstrated "insensitivity to the needs and problems of the black child" and given to black parents, who will control personnel and curriculum. The indifference of the existing political parties to black people necessitates formation of separate (parallel) black organizations, both in the 110 Southern counties with black majorities and in the ghettos of the North. According to Carmichael, it is simply naive to think that poor and powerless blacks have anything in common with the other components of the Democratic coalition. White liberals inevitably fall under the "overpowering influence" of their racist environment, and their demands for civil rights are "doing for blacks." Labor unions accept the existing order and, in the case of the AFL, even discriminate against black workers. Black political parties, Carmichael believes, will alone be devoted to real change and will in fact make possible emancipation from dominant American values and power centers.

Carmichael professes to believe that black power is not really a departure from American practice. "Traditionally," he writes, "for each new ethnic group, the route to social and political integration into America's pluralistic society has been through the organization of their own institutions with which to represent their communal needs within the larger society." Once in possession of power, blacks then could reenter the old coalitions for specific goals. But "let any ghetto group contemplating coalition be so tightly organized, so strong, that . . . it is an 'undigestible body' which cannot be absorbed or swallowed up." Given Carmichael's scheme for a radical reconstruction of American society, it is not surprising that the only group that he someday hopes to make his ally is the poor whites.

As several critics have pointed out, Carmichael's version of black power is hardly more than a collection of fragments, often lacking in clarity, consistency, and conviction. Thus, for example, Carmichael talks about the need for parallel institutions but offers only one example—black political organizations. He claims that these organizations can regenerate the entire political system but typically neglects to explain concretely how this regeneration is to be achieved. He calls for radical rejection of American values and institutions but at the same time portrays the black community as merely another ethnic group turning temporarily inward to prepare for later integration into American society. According to Carmichael, ghetto blacks are an exploited proletariat kept in bondage to enrich America's capitalist class; yet black workers seem more like a *lumpenproletariat* threatened with loss of economic function and forced to the margin of the American economy. Carmichael fails to reveal the mechanisms by which big business keeps the black man exploited, and indeed it seems doubtful that big business especially profits from the depressed condition of such a large group of potential consumers. But the real criticism of black power is not that as a body of thought it lacks coherence and sustained argument. Its greatest weakness is its failure to propose adequate solutions.

Carmichael began his argument by maintaining that black men suffer from two separate but related forms of discrimination—racial and economic. When Carmichael proposes ways for black men to undo the effects of racism, he makes good sense. Certainly black men should uncover their cultural roots and take pride in what has been of worth in their heritage. Certainly liberal paternalism is now anachronistic and black men should lead their own organizations. Nonviolence probably *was* psychologically damaging to many who practiced it, and integration into a hostile white society is not only an unrealistic goal but demeaning to a self-respecting people. Furthermore, some middle-class values, as Carmichael maintains, are less than ennobling, and elements of the black man's life style do have intrinsic merit. But it is doubtful whether black self-respect can ever be achieved without a solution of the second problem confronting ghetto blacks, and it is here that Carmichael's version of black power is most deficient.

Concerned primarily with humanizing social and governmental structures inside the ghetto, Carmichael has little to say about ending poverty in black America. Although more responsive policemen and schoolteachers and less dishonest slum lords and merchants will no doubt be a great step forward, these aspects of ghetto life are of less consequence than unemployment or poverty wages. Within the ghetto the resources for economic reconstruction are simply not available and since Carmichael rejects coalitions outside the ghetto, he is barred from offering a realistic economic strategy. It is this weakness that led the black intellectual and long-time civil rights leader Bayard Rustin to oppose black power. Pointing to the futility of separatist politics in a society in which the black man is a minority, Rustin calls for "a liberal-labor-civil rights coalition which would work to make the Democratic party truly responsive to the aspirations of the poor, and which would develop support for programs (specifically those outlined in A. Philip Randolph's $100 billion Freedom Budget) aimed at the reconstruction of American society in the interest of greater social justice." Rustin's goals are considerably less apocalyptic than Carmichael's, but they are far more realistic. Carmichael's radical ruminations about a socialist alliance of poor whites and poor blacks seem fantasies irrelevant to American social realities. Although Carmichael's vision holds out hope for some distant time, it offers no meaningful proposals for the present.

The true significance of black power lies not in the doctrines into which it evolved but in the historical circumstances that gave it birth. The real message of black power is that after years of struggle to make America an open and just society, an important group of civil rights workers, instructed by the brute facts of its own history, gave up the fight. Black power was a cry of rage directed against white bigots who overcame righteous men by force, a cry of bitterness against white liberals who had only a stunted comprehension of the plight of the black poor, and a cry of frustration against gains that seemed meager when compared to needs. It is possible, however, that even rage can perform a useful function, and if the black power slogan brings about a constructive catharsis and helps rouse the black masses from apathy, then the intellectual shortcomings of black power doctrines may seem of little consequence, and what began as a cry of despair may yet play a creative role in the black protest movement. Therefore, whether the history of SNCC in this decade will be considered triumph or tragedy depends on events yet to occur.

5.2

Jack M. Bloom

Ghetto Revolts, Black Power, and the Limits of the Civil Rights Coalition

Jack M. Bloom, author of Class, Race, and the Civil Rights Movement, *is a professor of sociology at Indiana University/Northwest. He was a movement activist in the 1970s.*

With the passage of the Voting Rights Act in 1965, the civil rights movement finished its program of legal gains. This legislation, and the process by which it was achieved, broke the central thrust of black subjection in the South. By this time the focus of activity was already moving to the North. There, where blacks were legally free and equal, they were consigned to live apart in black "ghettos," many in poverty, almost all substantially worse off than whites, with inferior education and medical care.

These ghettos, where huge numbers gave blacks a sense of strength and power, became the breeding grounds for anger and militance. By 1964 they became the site of a long series of explosive upheavals—the ghetto riots—that eloquently made the case that the black movement had not ended with the civil rights movement, that more was needed to redress black grievances. The riots served notice that racial subjection had ceased to be merely a Southern problem—it was alive and well throughout the nation, even if in a different form.

The actions of the ghetto blacks forced everyone to take notice: the federal government, white liberals, and civil rights leaders all had to respond. The government created a poverty program to ease some of the distress and to get blacks off the streets. When it became clear that this response was inadequate, that some substantive redistribution of wealth and power would be necessary, the former allies of the battle against southern intransigence—the Northern middle class, the Democratic party, and the federal government—refused to take the path asked of them. More concessions were ruled out.

The youth of the second wave and SNCC were affected by these outbursts. Though they had little connection to them, they understood and sympathized with the frustration and anger that motivated riots. The urban revolt confirmed their own sense of the failures of white society and of the strength of blacks. These youth gave general expression to this sense in their call for black power—a call that echoed through the black ghettos, as the rioters and their defenders adopted it as their own.

King felt the need to respond to the discontent illustrated by the riots and to try to fashion a program consistent with his principles and his strategy that could meet the needs made evident by the rioters. He could not do so with the old civil rights coalition, but his attempt to fashion a new coalition, based on more radical principles, failed.

The civil rights movement had won its victories because blacks had been able to assemble a coalition that altered the balance of power within the nation. That coalition had brought about structural change within the South; but that same coalition put limits on the extent of change it was willing to support. It had cohered around a specific program: abolishing the state-sanctioned forms of discrimination in the South, particularly those having to do with segregation and the right to vote. Completing this program had required an intensive struggle and the defeat of the ruling elite of the region.

All of these developments had added up to the modernization of the South—bringing its politics into alignment with its new economic structure, and with the rest of the country. Support could be won for this program from the federal government, the Northern Democratic party, some businesses, and the middle classes. This support was forthcoming, despite the intensive struggle for power that it entailed, because the social class being displaced from power was anachronistic to modern society, and because second-class citizenship for blacks came to be viewed both as morally unacceptable and as a political liability to the nation. For the Southern middle class and businessmen, the turmoil created when black insistence met white resistance made the status quo a social and economic liability, as well. That was especially so because what blacks were asking for in the civil rights movement was unthreatening to modern capitalism and therefore acceptable even if at times unpalatable. The ghetto revolts, however, raised the specter of class upheaval and seemed to demand the redistribution of wealth and power, and this demand was unacceptable to those who had been the allies of the black movement. Blacks' allies were unwilling to undermine their own power and privileges. Class considerations had shaped the position of blacks originally; a changed class structure had enable blacks to get the leverage to alter their position. But so long as they operated within that structure, there were limits to what they could achieve. They did not escape its confines.

Race and Class Outside the South

The class concerns of disadvantaged blacks were of particular importance outside the South. There, in the ghettos to which Southern blacks had made their way, they encountered circumstances different from those that they had fled. There was still segregation. Many restaurants refused to serve blacks. There were sometimes volatile flareups over the use of parks. If a black person dared to move into a white neighborhood or to use a "white" beach, riots might break out, as they had in the past. But these indignities were not state-sanctioned; they did not have the systematic use of police power behind them; they were not ubiquitous. There was no class whose well-being depended upon the total subordination of blacks, as was the case in the South. In many ways, blacks were free from the overt oppression they had left. They were able to use public facilities, such as restrooms, water fountains, buses, and trains, without discrimination. They could try on clothes, purchase automobiles, go to movies. They could vote and, since the thirties, participate in unions. In that sense, their flight to the North was a success.

But Northern blacks frequently stated that they preferred the South, because there they at least "knew where they stood." This expression meant that while the ideology in the North was one of equality, the reality was quite different. Whites did not openly treat blacks with contempt, as they did in the South: they did not flaunt their hostility. Jobs were not openly denied to blacks because they were black; jobs were simply not offered. Houses and apartments that were available over the telephone had been quickly sold or rented when people with black skin appeared.

Housing was an important component to black suffering in the urban ghettos of the North. Blacks were kept in segregated housing areas by a combination of interests. They were limited to certain areas by "racial steering," in which realtors refused to show blacks housing in areas reserved for whites; by "restrictive covenants" in which contracts were written (and enforced by the courts, until 1948) that forbade the owner to sell to a black person; and by the physical attacks of whites who, when a black family moved into a previously all-white neighborhood, would stop at little to drive them out.

In the fifties, even as court decisions favored blacks in the South, and as the movement there grew, the federal government continued and deepened its involvement in segregated housing. It did so through two programs. The Federal Housing Authority's insured housing loan program refused to underwrite loans to racially mixed areas. In 1959, the United States Commission on Civil Rights estimated that minorities had gotten less than 2 percent of the $120 billion in housing underwritten by the FHA since World War II, and all of that was in segregated housing. The FHA had very early recommended the use of restrictive covenants and continued to underwrite housing that used them for eighteen months after the Supreme Court decision that outlawed them. The massive federally financed highway construction program, carried out in the fifties and sixties, as blacks were arriving in the Northern cities, also reinforced residential segregation. Though it was not established for racial purposes, the program enabled whites to flee these cities and to abandon large parts of them to the blacks.

The result of these policies was the creation of black ghettos—areas of the city where blacks were forced to live and from which most could not escape, even if they had the funds to enable them to buy or rent in more expensive areas of the city or in the suburbs. Renters and landlords were able to obtain substantially higher rents and purchase prices than would be justified by fair market value for apartments and houses when blacks' choices were limited in this way. For the same dollar, they simply got less than whites, and though they earned less, they had to pay more. In these ghettos, blacks were crammed in. Poorer blacks were forced to double up because of the inadequate space at overly high prices. Huey Newton, founder of the Black Panther party, recalled the house he had lived in as a child in Oakland, California: "The floor was either dirt or cement, I cannot remember exactly; it did not seem to be the kind of floor that 'regular' people had in their homes." In this house,

> I slept in the kitchen. That memory returns often. Whenever I think of people crowded into a small living space, I always see a child sleeping in the kitchen and feeling upset about it; everybody knows that the kitchen is not supposed to be a bedroom. That is all we had, however. I still burn with the sense of unfairness I felt every night as I crawled into the cot near the icebox.

Absentee landlords often compounded these problems by failing to maintain their properties adequately. As a result, slums were created or worsened. Government exacerbated this tendency also, by building public housing in black areas and by providing high-rise housing that packed thousands or even tens of thousands of people into small areas. When "urban renewal" was applied to the impoverished black areas, it forced blacks to move and to crowd into the remaining slums, thereby worsening them, or to expand the boundaries of the ghetto.

The California state legislature tried to come to grips with this issue by passing a law that did away with restrictive covenants and discrimination in housing and rental properties. This law was seen as appropriate to a part of the country that had supported federal action directed toward the South's discriminatory policies. However, in 1964, a referendum was placed on the state ballot to repeal the law, and it passed by a two-to-one vote, thereby administering a stinging rebuff to blacks. Apparently, Northern white support for civil rights was limited to the South. Richard Townsend, a resident of Watts, the black community of Los Angeles, described how the residents of that community reacted to the vote:

> The attitude of the people in Watts was "I didn't really want to move there, but it's just the idea of you didn't want me anyway; it was like a bar you put there, that we didn't want to cross it, but you put it there, so that's pretty mean, it indicates how you feel about me. So, for that reason, I feel a certain way about you."

The extra charges on ghetto residents were not limited to housing. Trapped in the ghetto by poverty and by a lack of good public transportation, they were also forced to pay more than the white middle class for goods and services. They often had inferior merchandise to choose from, and they paid more for it. Because they were short on cash, they frequently bought on credit, for which they were charged exorbitant terms. Thus, they were enveloped in a web of exploitation.

With the neighborhood school system, segregated housing meant segregated schools, and segregated schools generally meant inferior education. In part, that was because white school districts had more money to spend. But it was also a result of more deliberate policies. Within city districts, less experienced teachers were assigned to black schools, as was inferior equipment. In Boston in 1963, CORE reported that 27 percent less was spent per pupil in black than in white schools, while in Chicago in 1962 it was found that appropriations per pupil were 21 percent less in all-black schools than in those for white. According to Charles Silberman:

> A distinguished Chicago minister who lives in an integrated area was horrified to discover that when the Negro registration in his child's school began to

climb, the school was shifted in mid-year from one District Superintendent to another, who had an all-Negro district. After this transfer had been made, the school lost its speech therapist, remedial reading teacher and other special services. The following year, shortages of textbooks began to show up and then the school began getting an inordinate number of permanent substitutes.

The problem was not only inferior facilities and staff. It was also the attitude of the teachers and administrators, mostly white, who denigrated the children. Anthropologist Gerry Rosenfield told of his experience at a black school in Harlem: "One teacher's class preceded ours down the stairway at dismissal time each day. Without fail, every afternoon, she turned to the children, halted them and shouted: 'Shut those thick lips! Can't you behave like human beings?' " Dick Gregory recalled his childhood in school bitterly:

> The teacher thought I was stupid. Couldn't speak, couldn't read, couldn't do arithmetic. Just stupid. Teachers were never interested in finding out that you couldn't concentrate because you were so hungry, because you hadn't had any breakfast. All you could think about was noontime, would it ever come? . . . The teacher thought I was a troublemaker. All she saw from the front of the room was a little black boy who squirmed in this idiots' seat and made noises and poked the kids around him. I guess she couldn't see a kid who made noises because he wanted someone to know he was there.

Perhaps worst of all, the economic opportunities to which many blacks had flocked were terribly elusive. They found themselves consigned to the worst jobs, when they could find work at all. Skilled jobs, white-collar and professional jobs, were largely closed off to them. Even in manufacturing they were channeled into the dirtiest, most unsafe, and lowest-paying work. In service industries, they were kept away from the public. In restaurants, they were dishwashers and busboys but not waiters or waitresses or managers. In hotels, they were not allowed to tend bar or serve in the front. Education did not provide an out, as it did for whites. Studies showed that blacks with a college degree earned no more than whites who had not gone beyond the eighth grade.

All of these circumstances were worsened by the fact that the postwar boom came to an end very early for blacks. In 1967, economist Arthur Ross called 1953 "the last year in which Negroes enjoyed relatively good times. . . ." The recession of the fifties hit blacks hard. During 1954, the black unemployment rate jumped from 4.1 percent to 8.9 percent, which was double the unemployment rate of whites, a ratio that has not improved since. And blacks stayed unemployed considerably longer than whites. In 1958 they accounted for 25 percent of the long-term unemployed, and in 1962, 29 percent, even though they were only 11 percent of the labor force. This number was made worse by the fact that a great number of blacks simply dropped out of the labor force, presumably because of discouragement. The number of these would-be workers increased from 270,000 in 1954 to 405,000 in 1964. Those most affected by this trend were the youth. The participation of black teenagers in the labor market fell from 56.1 percent in 1950 to 37.7 percent in 1964, a much more precipitous decline than that among white teenagers.

In their earnings, blacks were losing ground to whites in the fifties and early sixties, and that was true in every region. The losses were not only relative; real wages were falling, as well. Blacks in the city suffered a very high level of poverty:

in Los Angeles during the first half of the sixties, the poverty rate among blacks hovered between 30 and 31 percent. That blacks left the South to go to other regions, where they were better paid, kept the overall statistic from appearing worse. Poverty created a great deal of personal strain. Huey Newton recalled of his childhood:

> My father's constant preoccupation with bills was the most profound and persistent memory of my childhood. We were always in debt, always trying to catch up. . . . For me, no words . . . were as profane as "the bills." It killed me a little each time they were mentioned, because I could see the never-ending struggle and agony my father went through trying to cope with them.

As a result of these conditions, a high proportion of blacks were on the welfare rolls. Welfare came with a price: the dignity of those receiving it. Welfare workers were free to inspect the homes of the recipients at any time, and at times they did so at night to see if there was a male breadwinner present. As a result, men were driven from their families to make them eligible for **Aid to Families with Dependent Children.** Families could be broken up in other ways, as well. Malcolm X and his siblings were taken from their mother and put in foster homes, partly through efforts of the welfare department. A welfare mother described to Robert Coles the demeaning and destructive impact of her lack of power over her life and those of her children. She told him she was

> tired of everything they try to do to help us. They send us those welfare checks, and with them comes that lady who peeks around every corner here, and gives me those long lectures on how I should do everything—like her, of course. Then they take my kids to the Head Start thing, and first thing I hear is the boys' fingernails is dirty, and they don't use the right words, and the words they do use, no one can make them out. They try to take them to those museums and places, and tell them how sorry life is here at home and in the neighborhood, and how they is no good, and something has to be done to make them better—like the rich ones, I guess. But the worst is they just make you feel no good at all. They tell you they want to help you, but if you ask me they want to make you into them, and leave you without a cent of yourself left to hang on to.

Blacks in the cities of the North were everywhere faced with white authority: in the schools, in the welfare department, and especially with the police. Police were mostly white; they sometimes aggressively patrolled high-crime areas, namely, the black ghettos; they stopped people indiscriminately, simply because they were black. In the sixties the police were frequently referred to as an occupying army; they were felt to demean, to harm and attack residents but not to protect them.

The most humiliating conditions in the South did not exist in the North or were relatively easily done away with. A condition of class despair and anger remained, a condition that was substantially worsened by less overt, but still serious, racial discrimination. The anger especially emerged in response to the apparent hypocrisy of a society that proclaimed the equality of all but then denied it to blacks. Jimmie Sherman, who grew up in the Watts area of Los Angeles, recalled:

> As a child I used to dream of being . . . a general, a lawyer, a man who flew those big shiny planes. . . . I even wanted to be President. But sadly enough,

dreams withered with time, and age brought me closer to reality—a reality I wanted no part of. I began to notice many things around me—things I did not like, but could do nothing about. I noticed my mother going out to the white folks' houses, scrubbing their floors and serving their food every day. I realized that my father, the man I idolized and imitated, had been cleaning sewers all of his life and getting nowhere. I even heard a white man call him "boy" a couple of times. That really made me mad. It made him mad, too. But what could he do but take it? I noticed the old shacky house we lived in—the cold splintered floors, the torn curtains, the broken chairs we sat in, the pie pans and jelly jars we ate and drank from. I noticed the roaches crawling on the walls, across the floors, and breeding all over the house, and the junk and the trash that piled up and scattered in the yard. And for the first time, *I realized that I was in poverty.* Then I discovered that we weren't the only family in that bag. My friends were in bad shape, too. Their parents were also servants, and they were living on beans and grits and hand me downs, just as we were. And *I discovered that being black had something to do with it.* (emphasis added)

For Sherman, racial subjection meant poverty—without the ideological justification of black inferiority. He was free to dream as a child, but it soon became clear that the dreams of gold were destined to turn into dross—because of his race.

Malcolm X and Northern Lower-Class Blacks

These conditions formed the social base of a new trend toward black militancy that grew up independently of King and the Southern movement. "This sense of despair and futility led us into rebellious attitudes," wrote Huey Newton. Blacks in the North, freed from the heavy hand of Southern police repression, were heartened by the victories won by their brethren and angered by the violence they saw visited upon Southern blacks for no legitimate reason. This anger augmented the hostility they felt toward their own police and other authority figures. They were less accepting than Southern blacks of nonviolence and of exhortations to love their oppressors.

They were thus open to an approach critical of King. One key source of the critique was the Nation of Islam, more popularly known as the Black Muslims, an organization that militantly raised the banner of black nationalism. They, and in particular their spokesman, Malcolm X, rejected the civil rights goal of integration, saw whites simply as an enemy, and pointedly refused to endorse the program of nonviolent resistance. Black solidarity was their program.

Toward the end of the 1950s, the Black Muslims had begun to develop a reputation in the North. In 1957, Minister Malcolm X had led a crowd of some two thousand to a police station in Harlem to demand that a prisoner who had been injured by the police be examined and treated, if necessary. The crowd had its way, whereupon Malcolm sent them home. Word of this incident spread, and with it the reputation of Malcolm and the Muslims. Benjamin Goodman, who became one of Malcolm's followers, described its impact on him:

Here was a man who could walk boldly into the jaws of the lion, walk proud and tall into the territory of the enemy, the station house of the twenty-eighth precinct, and force the enemy to capitulate. Here was a man who could help restore the heritage, the pride of race and pride of self, that had been carefully stripped from us over the four hundred years of our enslavement here in white America.

Louis Lomax's television documentary "The Hate That Hate Produced" brought a great deal of publicity to the Black Muslim organization when it was broadcast in 1959, and with publicity came rapid growth. Increased numbers meant, in turn, a greater hearing especially for Malcolm X, who abrasively attacked the established civil rights leadership: "We do not want leaders who are handpicked for us by the white men. We don't want any more Uncle Toms. We don't want any more leaders who are puppets or parrots for the white man."

Malcolm, and the Black Muslims generally, called for black separatism. They stressed that blacks should be an independent nation:

> Can you not see that our former "leaders" have been fighting for the wrong thing . . . the wrong kind of freedom? Mr. Muhammed says we must have some land where we can work hard for ourselves, make ourselves equal, and live in dignity. Then and only then we won't have to beg the white man for the crumbs that fall occasionally from his table. No one respects or appreciates a beggar.

Malcolm was criticized for that demand by whites and by more moderate blacks. The idea that the American government could or would yield some of its territory was utopian, they suggested. And it was ridiculous to believe that all or even most blacks would transplant themselves to this new nation. What these critics often missed was that many blacks were stirred not by the demand for land per se but by the connotations expressed by it of militancy and impatience. Many blacks in the 1920s supported Marcus Garvey, who had called upon American blacks to return to Africa, even though they had no thought of really doing so. Malcolm's expression of anger and impatience and the Muslim rejection of integration as a goal had a similar effect:

> When someone sticks a knife into my back nine inches and then pulls it out six inches they haven't done me any favor. They should not have stabbed me in the first place. . . . During slavery they inflicted the most extreme form of brutality against us to break our spirit, to break our will . . . after they did all of this to us for three hundred ten years, then they come up with some so-called Emancipation Proclamation. . . . And today the white man actually runs around here thinking he is doing the black people a favor.

Malcolm rejected nonviolence, and he countered King directly on this issue. It didn't work, he said, because whites were fundamentally immoral:

> Don't change the white man's mind. You can't change his mind, and that whole thing about appealing to the moral conscience of America—America's conscience is bankrupt. She lost all conscience. They don't know what morals are.

To encourage nonviolence on the part of blacks was to mislead disastrously and dangerously. Malcolm X would make this point, using lurid imagery.

> Just as the slavemaster of that day used Tom, the house Negro, to keep the field Negroes in check, the same old slavemaster today has Negroes who are nothing but moderate Uncle Toms, twentieth century Uncle Toms, to keep you and me in check, to keep us under control, keep us passive and peaceful

and nonviolent. That's Tom making you nonviolent. It's like when you go to the dentist, and the man's going to take your tooth. You're going to fight him when he starts pulling. So he squirts some stuff in your jaw called novocaine, to make you think they're not doing anything to you. So you sit there and because you've got all of that novocaine in your jaw, you suffer—peacefully. Blood running all down your jaw, and you don't know what's happening. Because someone has taught you to suffer—peacefully.

Instead, he counseled,

be peaceful, be courteous, obey the law, respect everyone; but if someone puts his hand on you, send him to the cemetery. That's a good religion. In fact, that's that old-time religion. . . . Preserve your life, it's the best thing you've got. And if you've got to give it up, let it be even-steven.

Malcolm insisted that the civil rights movement's white allies—those to whom King looked for support in the struggle against the segregationists: the federal government, the Northern Democratic party, and the white middle class—could not be trusted:

Roosevelt promised, Truman promised, Eisenhower promised. Negroes are still knocking on the door begging for civil rights. Do you mean to tell me that in a powerful country like this, a so-called Christian country, that a handful of men from the South can prevent the North, the West, the Central States and the East from giving Negroes the rights the Constitution says they already have? No! I don't believe that and neither do you. *No white man really wants the black man to have his rights, or he'd have them!* The United States does everything else it wants to do. (emphasis in original)

The Black Muslims were rooted in and speaking directly to Northern, urban, lower-class blacks. Malcolm himself was one of many who were recruited out of the prisons, and others came from the streets. The bulk were laborers or unemployed. They were less directly concerned with the issue of segregation that confronted blacks in the South except and so far as they identified with their kinsmen. But the treatment blacks received in the South, and their own concerns, angered these ghetto blacks. It was their anger that Malcolm X both articulated and encouraged.

Malcolm was well aware of who his constituency was, and he was pleased about it and comfortable with it. Alex Haley, with whom Malcolm worked closely in producing his autobiography, recalled:

Where I witnessed the Malcolm X who was happiest and most at ease among members of our own race was when sometimes I chanced to accompany him on what he liked to call "my little daily rounds" around the streets of Harlem, among the Negroes that he said the "so-called black leaders" spoke of "as black masses statistics." On these tours, Malcolm X generally avoided the arterial 125th Street in Harlem; he plied the side streets, especially in those areas which were thickest with what he described as "the black man down in the gutter where I came from," the poverty-ridden with a high incidence of dope addicts and winos. Malcolm X here indeed was a hero. Striding along the sidewalks, he bathed all whom he met in the boyish grin, and his conversation with any who came up was quiet and pleasant. . . .

Malcolm encouraged his followers to think of themselves as different from what he viewed as King's middle- and upper-class supporters, and he pointedly charged that King's approach was not relevant to his people:

> When you have two different people, one sitting on a hot stove, one sitting on the warm stove, the one sitting on the warm stove thinks progress is being made. He's more patient, But the one who is sitting on the hot stove, you can't let him up fast enough. You have the so-called Negro in this country, the upper-class Negro or the so-called high-class Negro or, as Franklin Frazier calls them, the "black bourgeoisie." They aren't suffering the extreme pain that the masses of the black people are. And it is the masses of the black people today, I think you'll find, who are the most impatient, the most angry, because they're the ones who are suffering the most.

These lower-class blacks did indeed suffer from different problems and saw solutions different from those favored by the constituency mobilized by King.

Malcolm X and the Black Movement Outside the South

Despite this trend, the civil rights movement outside the South began with middle-class demands. There was, for example, some substantial emphasis on desegregating housing. As with the right to use public accommodations in the South, that was largely for the benefit of those who could afford to move to more expensive areas but were prohibited from doing so by racial discrimination. Over time, increasing concern was given to issues of greater importance to lower-class blacks. CORE and other organizations held demonstrations around the needs of those displaced by urban renewal; they raised demands for black jobs—on retail establishments, on banks and other businesses, on the construction trades. Civil rights activists made an issue of school segregation in the North.

Increasingly, the issue of police brutality was brought into relief by the highly publicized attacks on blacks in the South. Outside the South, police mistreatment of blacks was an issue of common concern. A study of blacks in Los Angeles, after the outbreak of racial unrest in the Watts area, showed that large percentages of blacks had seen or had themselves been subject to police mistreatment. (Almost one-quarter asked said that they had personally been treated with lack of respect by the police, and almost 40 percent had seen it happen to others. One-fifth had been unnecessarily rousted and frisked, and two-fifths had seen it happen; almost the same numbers applied to people who were stopped while driving and whose cars were searched; 5.1 percent had had their homes searched, and 15.2 percent had seen it; 7.8 percent had experienced unnecessary force in being arrested, and 36.9 percent had seen it; 3.9 percent had been beaten while in police custody, and over 20 percent had witnessed such conduct.) The Black Muslims, led by Malcolm X, hammered at this issue and set themselves apart from the civil rights movement by their ridicule of nonviolence as a response to such mistreatment.

Organizations such as CORE became concerned over their class composition, and as they did so, they also began to question the utility of an interracial movement. They demanded black leadership on principle, but in actuality the proposal reflected the perception that the needs, concerns, and and interests of whites diverged from those of blacks, especially when the blacks represented were of a different class from the middle- and upper-class whites who supported or were active in the movement.

The demonstrations in Birmingham had an electrifying effect upon blacks in the North, just as they did in the South. Demonstrations proliferated as the movement mushroomed. Ministers, unions, student organizations, and others provided financial and political backing for the black movement. One hundred thousand marched in San Francisco, and King joined with Walter Reuther in the summer of 1963, after Birmingham, to lead a march of 125,000 on a Freedom Walk in Detroit. Data from a national *Newsweek* poll taken in that summer showed widespread backing for and involvement in the black movement: 80 percent thought that demonstrations worked; 46 percent felt a personal obligation to get involved; 48 percent were prepared to demonstrate even if it meant going to jail.

As the tempo of black struggle grew in 1963, Malcolm increasingly spoke to concerns. King's confrontation in Birmingham helped to provide Malcolm with an audience that was far more receptive to his ideas. But the Birmingham movement and its aftermath slowed recruitment into the Black Muslims, to whom many had previously turned because of their militancy. The Muslims spoke in militant terms, but they remained inactive. Those blacks who wished to participate in the struggle for black equality, and who previously might have been attracted to the Muslims, began to look elsewhere. The civil rights movement now provided a place for them to put their energy. Malcolm himself wanted to play a role in the racial conflicts of the sixties, and ultimately that goal lay behind his rupture with Muhammed. Malcolm explained the impact this tendency was having:

> Privately, I was convinced that our nation of Islam could be an even greater force in the American black man's overall struggle—if we engaged in more *action*. It could be heard increasingly in the Negro communities: "Those Muslims *talk* tough, but they never *do* anything, unless somebody bothers Muslims."
> I moved around among outsiders more than most other Muslim officials. I felt the very real potentiality that, considering the mercurial moods of the black masses, this labeling of Muslims as "talk only" could see us, powerful as we were, one day suddenly separated from the Negro's front-line struggle. (emphasis in original)

Malcolm did not wish to be separated from that struggle. So, while the Black Muslims continued to refrain from black activity, Malcolm's pronouncements became increasingly harsh and political. His departure from the organization was only months away.

As this conflict developed, Malcolm was able to stay at the center of black and white consciousness by articulating the growing black mood of anger. He persistently hammered away at the viciousness of the whites and at the apparent limitations put on the actions of blacks by their leaders.

You don't have to criticize Reverend Martin Luther King, Jr. His actions criticize him. Any Negro who teaches other Negroes to turn the other cheek is disarming the Negro. . . . And men like King—their job is to go among Negroes and teach Negroes "Don't fight back." He doesn't tell them "don't fight each other." "Don't fight the white man" is what he's saying in essence, because the followers of Martin Luther King, Jr. will cut each other from head to foot, but they will not do anything to defend themselves against the attacks of the white man. . . . *White* people follow King. *White* people pay King. *White* people subsidize King. *White* people support King. But the masses of black people don't support Martin Luther King, Jr. (emphasis in original)

"They controlled you," he said of the civil rights leaders, "but they have never incited you or excited you. . . . They contained you."

The anger articulated by Malcolm X reflected the wounds that had been rubbed raw in the Northern black population. They had seen the brutality of Southern police and of those who flagrantly and successfully violated the law. They themselves had gained little from the civil rights movement, and their material concerns had not been addressed at all. The angry mood deepened in both the South and the North when a bomb exploded in a church in Birmingham about a month after the March on Washington, in the fall of 1963. Four young black girls were killed, and Malcolm's angry words rang out:

As long as the white man sent you to Korea, you bled. He sent you to Germany, you bled. He sent you to the South Pacific to fight the Japanese, you bled. You bleed for people, but when it comes to seeing your own churches being bombed and little black girls murdered, you haven't got any blood. You bleed when the white man says bleed, you bite when the white man says bite; and you bark when the white man says bark. I hate to say this about us, but it's true. How are you going to be nonviolent in Mississippi, as violent as you were in Korea?

Malcolm counseled militancy as necessary for blacks to achieve their goals:

When I was in Africa, I noticed some of the Africans got their freedom faster than others. . . . I noticed that in the areas where independence had been gotten, someone got angry. And in areas where independence had not been achieved yet, no one was angry.

He stressed to his followers the culpability of Northern whites in black oppression, and he contended that it was not only Southern blacks who suffered:

What has Mississippi got to do with Harlem? It isn't actually Mississippi; it's America. America is Mississippi. . . . There's no such thing as the South—it's America. If one room in your house is dirty, you've got a dirty house. . . . Don't say that that room is dirty but the rest of my house is clean. You're over the whole house. . . . And the mistake that you and I make is letting these Northern crackers shift the weight to the Southern crackers. . . . This country is a country whose governmental system is run by committees. . . . Out of 46 committees that govern the foreign and domestic direction of this country, 23 are in the hands of Southern racists . . . because in the areas from which they come, the black man is deprived of his right to vote. . . . So, what happens in Mississippi and the South has a direct bearing on what happens to you and me here in Harlem.

Malcolm felt that blacks had to have control over their lives:

> We're against a segregated school system.... But this does not mean that a school is segregated because it's all black. A segregated school means a school that is controlled by people who have no real interest in it whatsoever.... They never refer to the white section as a segregated community. It's the all-Negro section that's a segregated community. Why? The white man controls his own school, his own bank, his own economy, his own politics, his own everything, his own community—but he also controls yours. When you're under someone else's control you're segregated.

Control was necessary in order to enable blacks to attain the benefits to which they were entitled:

> Just because you're in this country doesn't make you an American. No you've got to go farther than that before you can become an American. You've got to enjoy the fruits of Americanism.

Ghetto Rebellions

Malcolm's biting words expressed and focused a mood of anger that festered while the organized civil rights movement grew. The extent of his influence cannot be measured; that it was substantial cannot be doubted. As the movement in the North grew, it produced a variety of manifestations: school boycotts protesting not only segregation but also the unequal allocation of resources; demonstrations at construction sites, as blacks demanded a share of the well-paying jobs in the industry; "shop-ins," where demonstrators filled grocery carts with goods and then walked off and left them in order to pressure the stores to hire blacks; sit-ins in hotels for the same purpose; and a threat to block the entrances to the New York World's Fair during the summer of 1964. Over and over, the charge of police brutality reverberated as the demonstrators encountered the police. This experience provided a common point of reference to the travails of the civil rights workers in the South.

It was the charge of police brutality after a white police lieutenant shot a fifteen-year-old boy that precipitated the Harlem riot in the summer of 1964. This upheaval was the first of the ghetto rebellions in the Northern cities. It may have been coincidence that this riot, and almost all of those that followed that year, took place within weeks of the Democratic convention, either before, during, or after. But it was the summer of the Schwerner-Chaney-Goodman murders, and information about the terrible harassment to which civil rights workers were subject had been well aired in the North. Fannie Lou Hamer testified on television to the Democratic Credentials Committee concerning the brutal beatings she suffered that summer for her activity; it was after her testimony that Malcolm reminded blacks of the similarity between Mississippi and the rest of the nation.

Shooting incidents such as the one in Harlem were not uncommon, but the response was. Before the Harlem riot was over, riots had spread to Brooklyn and Bedford-Stuyvesant. And immediately thereafter, new riots broke out in Rochester, New York; then Jersey City, New Jersey. During the Democratic convention, there was more rioting in Patterson and Elizabeth, New Jersey, and somewhat later in Philadelphia.

These riots were not minor disturbances. In Rochester, for example, 4 people died, hundreds were injured, and 976 were arrested. Property damage was estimated at near three million dollars, and the Governor of New York mobilized 1,500 National Guardsmen. Thus was inaugurated a new period in the black movement. Malcolm X warned after the summer bout of 1964 that "more and worse riots will erupt. The black man has seen the white man's underbelly of guilty fear." He was right about there being more to come. The riots took place for the most part outside the South, in the new urban ghettos. They illustrated a depth of alienation and disaffection from the American mainstream previously unimagined by white society.

The summer of 1964 was only the first wave in what was to become a sea of riotous upheaval. The next summer saw an uprising in Watts, the black ghetto of Los Angeles, that dwarfed those of the previous year. The riot proceeded for six days. When it was over, 35 people had been killed, 28 of them black; 900 were injured, and over 3,500 had been arrested. The police had been unable to cope with the dimensions of the uprising, and over 12,000 National Guardsmen were called in; entire city blocks were burned to the ground; buses and ambulances were stoned; snipers fired at police and fireman, and even at airplanes. David Sears and John McConahay noted that the number of law enforcement agents employed was "equal to the 17,000 troops necessary to conquer Cuba in the Spanish-American War."

Watts was the largest, but by no means the only, such riot that year. There were others in Chicago and San Diego. In 1966, over two dozen cities were struck by riots. The summer of 1967 saw many more such upheavals, including one in Detroit that substantially exceeded the scale even of the Watts rebellion: 43 dead, over 1,000 injured, 7,000 arrested, and fifty million dollars of property destruction. More followed through the rest of the sixties, with a big wave in 1968, after the murder of Martin Luther King.

The riots had an immense political impact: they shifted both the geographical and the political focus of the black movement. They went beyond the matter of civil rights to raise a wide variety of political, economic, and social issues. They forced the government to respond with new programs, the civil rights leaders to reshape their strategies and even their goals; they intensified the political struggles within the black movement, and they confronted white society with the dilemma of how to respond. Finally, their impact on blacks themselves was profound.

Riots or Revolt?

These riots proceeded for several years, during which there was heated debate over who had participated in them, what they were about, and why they occurred. Because they were first and primarily a Northern urban phenomenon, they were a shock to Northern liberals, who had supported and been moved by the black struggle in the South, and who felt that conditions in the North were superior. They upset the big-city political machines and bosses, who had provided an important share of the support for the civil rights movement in the South, and the riots forced these officials to reconsider their relations with the black community resident in their localities.

Politicians often tried to deflect the political impact of the upheavals by terming them mere riots rather than expressions of protest. They contended that the riots were irrational, senseless acts and that the rioters were either an urban underclass—the dregs of society—or newly arrived from the South, and hence really protesting, irrationally, Southern conditions when they were safely in the North. In any case, they charged that the rioters represented a tiny part of the black population and were in no sense representative. They thus implied that the riots did not represent a general feeling of black discontent with conditions in the Northern cities.

There were several critiques of this view, but it was most sharply attacked by Sears and McConahay, T. M. Tomlinson, and Nathan Caplan. These scholars held that the riots were the work of what Sears, McConahay, and Tomlinson called "the new urban black" and what Caplan called the "new ghetto man." The rioters, they held, were socialized in the North and were responding specifically to Northern grievances, using Northern-engendered responses. Moreover, they argued that these "new urban blacks" were relatively well educated and of a higher class status than blacks in general. Tomlinson referred to the rioters as the "cream of Negro youth in particular and urban Negro citizens in general." The political implication of this contention ran directly counter to the politicians' characterization of the riots and rioters. The riots were seen as a response to real grievances and thus as a legitimate form of political expression. (This thesis was, in its turn, attacked by Abraham Miller, Louis H. Bolce, and Mark R. Halligan. They charged that Sears and McConahay had seriously miscalculated their data by confusing dependent and independent variables. They argued that Caplan, who summarized a whole series of studies, erred by collapsing categories, and that he thereby confused civil rights protestors with rioters, a distinction that Miller et al. felt had to be retained. They contended that the rioters were part of the unstable underclass and not necessarily raised in the North.)

The evidence indicates something different from these analyses. The rioters included a large part of the eligible population in the areas of the city in which rioting took place—generally from 10 to 20 percent. They were representative of the broader populace, a large percentage of which was quite sympathetic to the rioters and their actions. There was participation of the underclass in these outbursts, but in general the participants lived in the riot areas and were not the hard-core unemployed. Their income was basically the same as nonrioters', and their employment status does not appear to have diverged sharply from the nonrioters', although the lower-status occupations were overrepresented.

A survey in Newark found the very poor to be less supportive of violence than those who were better off, and the study in Watts found that the most active churchgoers were most likely to have been participants, indicating the stable character of the rioters (although the next most likely were those who went to church least). Rioters tended to believe in the work ethic about the same as nonrioters; and they had a crime rate prior to the riots similar to that of nonrioters, but they tended to have committed *fewer* serious crimes prior to that riot.

Robert B. Hill and Robert M. Fogelson, who looked at those actually arrested in the riots, concluded that "the occupational distributions of the arrestees and the residents are quite similar" and that "if age is . . . held constant, the rioters were about as likely to be unskilled and unemployed as the potential rioters." It appears, then, reasonable to conclude that the rioters were fairly representative of the black, urban population. While that means they were not necessarily an underclass, they were without question on overwhelmingly lower-class population.

The participants in these upheavals did not lash out blindly. They were selective: public facilities, such as libraries, went untouched; so did black-owned stores and those that were felt to treat ghetto residents fairly. In one study of the residents of one of the areas of conflagration in Detroit, most thought that the riot was not a product of impulsive behavior. Fifty-seven percent thought that "most of the people who started the trouble in Detroit had been thinking about it for a long time."

These lower-class black riots were the product of the first generation of blacks raised in the North. Robert Fogelson, using a sample of those arrested, demonstrated that in a large number of riots in different cities over several years, on the first day of rioting young men raised in the urban ghettos outside the South constituted the largest share of the arrestees. Moreover, he noted that in later years, blacks socialized in the North came increasingly to be represented among those arrested. He concluded:

> Apparently the upcoming generation of urban blacks, the young and single blacks born in the Northern ghettos, joined in the riots first; and it was particularly active in the rioting and burning. The current generation of urban blacks, the mature and married blacks born in the rural South, joined in thereafter; and it was particularly active in the rioting and looting. What is more, the upcoming (and presumably more militant) generation has increased its participation over time much more rapidly than the older generation. Hence the fairly typical young adults born and raised in the Northern ghettos who reached maturity in the 1950's and 1960's were not just the main source of rioters. They were also the rioters who joined in at the beginning, who engaged in the most serious forms of violence and who in all likelihood, will predominate in future riots.

The riots were carried out to a significant extent by people who were raised in the conditions of the Northern urban ghettos and who had their own distinctive response to those conditions. Even the Southern blacks who participated in the riots evidently were not simply expressing resentment over Southern conditions and circumstances; they were also responding to distinctly Northern conditions. They were aware of, concerned about, and affected by the Southern drama, and the successes of the civil rights movement had provided them with a sense of power. But they had their own problems, and it was to these they were responding.

Angus Campbell and Howard Schuman, in a study of blacks in fifteen cities that experienced riots in 1968, found significant grievances directed toward any number of features of ghetto life. When people were asked a series of questions concerning their experiences with the police, over 50 percent stated that the police did not come quickly enough when called; almost 40 percent felt they were disrespectful and insulting; 36 percent felt they searched people in their neighborhood without good reason; 35 percent felt they roughed people up unnecessarily. These findings were corroborated in the Los Angeles study of blacks after the Watts upheaval. Said one man:

> If they stop a white man, they don' bother him, but a Negro they hope to find dope or pills [or] stolen merchandise. They hope to "get lucky" on a Negro and get him to do or say the wrong thing, or call in on you. On a Sunday afternoon, you can't even go out for a decent ride. . . . The police is always hiding out trying to sneak up on people. You are tense and nervous looking

for them at all times. Even the children are afraid. They start running when they see the police because they have heard how the policemen beat their fathers and brothers. They have seen how they stop them for nothing.

Findings were similar with respect to feelings about merchants. People felt that the merchants overcharged them, served them inferior merchandise, and treated them with a lack of respect. In the Los Angeles study, people felt aggrieved about their treatment by public agencies, public officials, the white-dominated media, and their own representatives. Racial discrimination was felt to be still pervasive:

I've run into more prejudice here than I did in the South. The kids in the South can go to school anywhere now, but here we are zoned so that we are still segregated *de facto*. When a white kid gets out of school, he can qualify for a job in aircraft with his high school training, but not our kids. Here at Centinela High they give them woodburning and mess like that and they get bad grades because they aren't interested. They don't fail them anymore, they just pass them along and when they get sixteen, they kick them out.

Thus, real grievances existed, based on distinctly Northern conditions. But grievances alone were not sufficient to bring about upheaval. The young men and women who grew up in the urban ghettos of the North and West were much freer than those who had come before them of the debilitating effects of racial self-hatred. They had been socialized to believe they were equal to whites. They were much less inclined to self-derogation than their Southern counterparts or those older than they in the cities. They exhibited racial pride. This new generation of urban blacks was politically sophisticated and well informed. It felt capable of affecting policy.

These blacks were, at the same time, quite militant; they had grown up learning not, as had many Southern blacks, to contain their anger but rather to express it effectively. Huey Newton recalled:

In our working and lower class community we valued the person who successfully bucked authority. Group prestige and acceptance were won through defiance and physical strength. . . . Fighting has always been a big part of my life, as it is in the lives of most poor people. . . . We were really trying to affirm our masculinity and dignity, and using force in reaction to the social pressures exerted against us. For a proud and dignified people fighting was one way to resist dehumanization.

Joe R. Feagin and Harlan Hahn argued that prior to and during the course of the riots, there was growing support among blacks for the use of violence. Many others were prepared to justify the use of violence, even if they themselves would not use it. Increasingly, support grew for use of these means, so that James Geschwender contended that the distinction between protest and riots was disappearing.

The riots took place in a climate of increasing protest. Northern blacks had been watching the civil rights movement and the treatment blacks received in the South. They were infuriated by it. Cries of "Selma!" were heard in the Watts riot, which took place only months after the demonstrations in Alabama, indicating how extensive was the impact of the events there. Douglas Glasgow, who studied a group of the black underclass who had participated in the riot, reported that the group had watched the civil rights struggles on television. They had observed the white violence and blacks' accepting it by turning the other cheek. "The men resolved that they would never passively accept this treatment from the 'man.' Whereas earlier they had turned much of the anger in on themselves . . . their rage and resentment now arose to a new high and was externalized."

Many Northern blacks were disillusioned with the federal government, and a large number of those who rioted had also participated in civil rights demonstrations. They and others had little faith in the procedures that existed for handling grievances. In Watts, 40 percent were found to have lost faith in conventional approaches. Again and again, researchers found that blacks viewed the riots as an expression of protest and as a way of forcing changes. James Geschwender noted that, as a result of these riots, negotiations proceeded in several cases between the authorities and black leaders, sometimes including black youth. The riots emerged as a form of protest, a way to win black gains, under conditions where most participants felt that there was no other way to win them. Said one:

> It was an attempted emergence from passivity. Too long now we Negroes have had things done *to* and *for* us, but seldom *by* us. This was our initial try. . . . I feel that it was something that the white folks had been inviting. They set the stage and wrote most of the script leading to this drama. (emphasis in original)

That was why many called the riots revolts, or even insurrections, indicating that they had a political character and were not merely outbursts of looters and hoodlums.

Ghetto Revolts and the Break with White America

The protest character of these ghetto revolts was further illustrated by the way in which the black community viewed them. King toured the riot area in Watts during the last day of the riot. There a young man proudly told him: "We won!" Looking at the mayhem and destruction, King asked how he could say that. "Because we made them pay attention to us," was the response. His was not an isolated sentiment. In a survey of Watts, 58 percent of the area residents and 57 percent of the arrestees thought that the effect of the riot would be favorable, while only 18 percent and 27 percent respectively anticipated unfavorable results. Thirty-eight percent of the residents and 54 percent of the arrestees thought that the Watts riot "helped the Negro's cause"; 84 percent and 80 percent respectively thought that it made whites "more aware of Negro problems"; 51 percent and 49 percent thought that it made "whites more sympathetic to Negro problems." One respondent commented: "Things will be better. We will have new buildings and the whites now realize that the Negro isn't going to be pushed around like before."

Real gains were won as a result of the riots. The funds generally allocated to the poverty program were increased during the riot period and those cities that experienced riots got the largest share of antipoverty money. One study showed that the amount of antipoverty money allocated to Los Angeles dramatically increased after the Watts uprising. James Button argued that his statistical analysis of the allocation of these funds demonstrated that "the black riots had a greater direct positive impact than any other independent variable upon total Office of Economic Opportunity expenditure increases in the latter 1960's." Jobs were also provided for the unemployed.

King contended that the gains produced by the riots were small and that those who argued they were significant

> always end up with stumbling words when asked what concrete gains have been won as a result. At best, the riots have produced a little anti-poverty money allotted by frightened government officials, and a few water-sprinklers to cool the children of the ghettos. It is something like improving the food in the prison while the people remain securely incarcerated behind bars.

A great deal had to do with perception. An important part of the riots was their impact on black self esteem, which was similar to that of the civil rights demonstrations: black pride grew. This effect was evidenced in many ways. Sears and McConahay found that black pride increased over time in Watts, as people had the opportunity to discuss and assimilate the impact of the upheaval. Campbell and Schuman found that racial pride was widespread in the cities they surveyed.

During the riot period, this changing attitude had its reflection in a number of developments. The term *Negro* fell into disrepute; those wanting to emphasize racial pride called themselves "blacks," the linguistic counterpart to "whites." The use of hair straighteners was greatly diminished, and the process of males' "conking" their hair—soaking it in lye to take out the curl—came virtually to an end. Young blacks wore "naturals"—they let their hair grow out in a way that no white hair could. "Black is beautiful" became a widespread slogan that emphasized the new attitude. In the colleges and universities, black students fought for and frequently won the establishment of black studies programs.

Nationalism grew, particularly among the young. Campbell and Schuman reported that from about 10 to 20 percent of those aged sixteen to nineteen agreed with a variety of statements that could be described as nationalist, or as separatist, and among these Malcolm X was particularly well regarded. Nationalist and separatist organizations grew and proliferated in the latter years of the sixties and even social relations became severely curtailed.

This growing nationalist sentiment was only partially a product of a sense of black strength. In part also, it emerged from a growing sense, mirrored in the young black activists in the South, that whites would not support them in their efforts to restructure American society so as to improve substantially their life chances. The rebuff administered by Californians in 1964 to middle-class blacks who wanted to expand their housing selection was one such indication. There were many others.

Campbell and Schuman found that whites and blacks had very different assessments about the riots. Close to 50 percent of whites felt that riots were wholly or partially for the purpose of looting; over 60 percent attributed the causes of the riots to radicals, looters, and Communists; almost 85 percent thought they had been planned in advance; nearly 50 percent felt that the best way to prevent future riots was to increase police control. Perhaps most dramatic, given the black perception that the ghetto rebellions would improve their circumstances and the way whites viewed them, was that about 65 percent of the whites felt that the riots hurt the black cause, most because they felt that those upheavals increased antiblack sentiments. Sixty-eight percent of whites interviewed in Los Angeles after Watts felt that blacks were pushing too fast, and 56 percent thought blacks were "asking for special treatment from whites to which they were not entitled." William Brink and Louis Harris, in a poll done for *Newsweek* magazine in 1966, found that the whites' assessment of racial matters was entirely different from the blacks': 85 percent felt that demonstrations hurt the black cause, and certainly that riots did so. Seventy percent thought blacks were moving too fast. As in California, most whites (58 percent) did not want blacks moving into their neighborhood, "and this figure rises to 76 per cent among whites living in the areas where Negroes would like to move." For this reason a national open-house bill was defeated in the election year of 1966.

These sentiments were reflected in government action. While at first monies were poured into rioting ghettos, by the summer of 1967 the then-secretary of the Department of Housing and Urban Development stated: "We were very careful *not* to allow a riot city to receive a lot of new money, as we didn't want to appear to respond to violence" (emphasis in original). Instead, both federal and local governments began emphasizing repression. President Johnson mobilized the army in 1967, not to protect integration, as President Eisenhower had done in Little Rock a decade earlier, but to suppress the Detroit uprising; and the National Guard was mobilized for the same purpose twenty-nine times that summer. City after city stockpiled armaments; new legislation was passed to prevent riots and to suppress crime.

There was thus ample reason for blacks to feel that their needs were not being met, and perhaps would not be met. Though they gained antipoverty money and jobs, these did not begin to deal with the problems they faced. The very fact of the rioting itself, in which invariably more blacks were hurt than whites, and in which black neighborhoods were seriously damaged, often losing most or all of their stores, indicated a sense of despair and alienation. That was particularly so among lower-class blacks. The Brink and Harris survey found that while Southern blacks, especially those of the middle class, had made some substantial progress, "the Negroes who have shared the least in the rewards of progress are those living in the big-city slums and ghettos, mainly in the North." While 70 percent of the black population said that they had seen progress, only 29 percent of lower-class blacks did. "In the case of jobs, only 24 percent of them feel they are better off now, compared with 54 percent of Negroes overall." Economist Vivian Henderson corroborated this sense when he testified before the National Advisory Commission on Civil Disorders:

> No one can deny that all Negroes have benefited from civil rights laws and desegregation in public life in one way or another. The fact is, however, that the masses of Negroes have not experienced tangible benefits in any significant way. This is so in education and housing. It is critically so in the area of jobs and economic security. Expectations of Negro masses for equal job opportunity programs have fallen short of fulfillment. Negroes have made gains.... But... the masses of Negroes have been virtually untouched by these gains.

The commission itself summed up in its conclusion what many blacks felt: "Our nation is moving toward two societies, one black and one white—separate and unequal."

It was not, however, merely a matter of color. Blacks outside the South met a rebuff because whites, who were willing to support changes in the South to accommodate blacks there, were unwilling to do so when demands for change were brought in their own backyards. That was one important element of the situation. But the needs of blacks in the North and the demands raised by them for jobs, housing, health, welfare—for a slice of the American pie—went far beyond what blacks in the South had demanded. Blacks in the North and West were seeking a restructuring not just of the South but of American society generally, and as such they ran up against the interests that had supported the civil rights movement. They began to lose those allies, and it was largely out of this process of isolation that the demand for black power emerged and became the dominant tendency among these new urban blacks.

Ghetto Revolts and Black Power

The anger that emanated from the black ghettos of the North was particularly important because the social weight of these black concentrations was so great. By the mid-sixties, one-half of the black population lived in the North, almost all crowded into the big cities. The disturbances blacks created in those metropolises were magnified because the extensive destruction and the widespread challenge to authority took place in the nation's cultural, financial, manufacturing, and political centers. Turmoil in Little Rock or Montgomery was significant; in Chicago or New York or Los Angeles it was far more so. And the riots had a national impact, as they began to eclipse the civil rights struggle and to exert a great pull on the civil rights activists themselves. Cleveland Sellers recalled:

> We were all very conscious of the fact that the axis of the struggle appeared to be shifting away from the rural South to the cities in the North. The totally unexpected rebellions in Harlem, Watts, Chicago and Philadelphia made a big impact on our thinking.

SNCC and CORE had already begun to turn away from both the goals and the strategy of the civil rights movement. After the MFDP [Mississippi Freedom Democratic Party] experience, many SNCC activists began to look more carefully at Malcolm X, and they began to explore ties with him. They drew the conclusion that the effort to attain civil rights was insufficient. One SNCC activist wrote that she understood this point only after winning the Voting Rights Act:

> We found that it was a shallow victory. After the earlier sit-ins, the civil rights movement had had to stop and ask: "What have we gained by winning the right to a cup of coffee downtown?" In the same way, we who had worked for voting rights now had to ask ourselves what we had gained. In both cases the answer was the same: Negroes were in fact not basically better off with this new right than they had been before; they were still poor and without the power to direct their own lives.

In part because of their own experiences, in part because the ghetto revolts demanded a new black agenda, SNCC and CORE activists began to propose major structural changes in America. In the manifesto *Black Power*, SNCC leader Stokeley Carmichael and Charles V. Hamilton explained black power. Elsewhere, Hamilton argued that the ghetto riots were

> acts which deny the very legitimacy of the system itself. The entire value structure which supports property rights over human rights, which *sanctions* the intolerable conditions in which the black people have been *forced* to live is questioned.

This statement, and many others like it, indicated clearly that the effort to resolve issues of *racial* concern had led many black activists to challenge the *class* structure. Now they were going beyond the anachronistic form of class domination that had characterized the South to attack the structure of modern American capitalism.

In the spring of 1966, after the Selma campaign and the Watts riot, a bitter faction fight in SNCC resulted in the election of radical Stokeley Carmichael as chairman of the organization. As a result, those who were leaning toward nationalism took over the leadership of the most militant civil rights organization. That summer, during a civil rights march in Mississippi that was jointly sponsored by SNCC, CORE, and the SCLC, Carmichael seized the opportunity to make known and to popularize his position. There, in front of the media, he raised the cry of "black power" as the new slogan for the black movement. The cry grew out of the experiences and disillusionment of the civil rights workers in the South, but it was fueled by the ghetto uprisings. Had it expressed only the sentiments of frustrated civil rights activists in the South, its impact would have been minimal. But it clearly tapped into the developing consciousness of masses of urban ghetto blacks. With the help of the media, the cry spread across the country, and Carmichael became a major national black spokesman.

Black riots had helped to give rise to the slogan; they also helped to provide it with meaning. While talking with King, Carmichael endowed the slogan with a relatively innocuous meaning: "Martin, you know as well as I do that practically every other ethnic group in America has done just this. The Jews, the Irish and the Italians did it, why can't we?" But circumstances gave the slogan a much angrier tone. The expression "black power" was articulated in the midst of the fourth long, hot summer of angry black activity. The summer of 1966, and those that followed with their massive explosions of human anger in the black ghettos, endowed the phrase "black power" with the connotations of militance and nationalism, of black anger and hostility to whites. Above all, it seemed to signify the willingness of blacks to seek this course alone, unencumbered by whites, who did not share the same oppressive conditions to which blacks were subject and who, many blacks felt, did not and could not share the deep sense of urgency to transform their lives and their conditions.

In adopting the slogan "black power," Carmichael and others were consciously rejecting the limits set by the civil rights coalition. It was a mistake, said Carmichael and Hamilton, to assume that "a politically and economically secure group can collaborate with a politically and economically insecure group." Such alliances were held to be unviable because the coalition partners had widely differing goals. While blacks needed fundamental social transformation, the others didn't: "At bottom, those groups accept the American system and want only—if at all—to make peripheral, marginal reforms in it. Such reforms are inadequate to rid the society of racism." Thus, given the "power-oriented nature of American politics," the partners in the civil rights coalition "are unpredictable allies when a conflict of interest arises."

King responded to the ideological offensive represented by black power by arguing that the slogan was self-defeating because it did not provide a strategy capable of success. "No one has ever heard the Jews publicly chant a slogan of Jewish power, but they have power. Through group identity, determination and creative endeavor, they have gained it. The same thing is true of the Irish and

Italians." He objected to the slogan of "black power" because, he maintained, it isolated blacks.

"Black power" did isolate the black movement, and whites certainly did turn away from it in the later sixties and early seventies. But in truth it should be plain that black power was also a *response* to the isolation of the black movement that was already taking place. As blacks perceived the need to go beyond the simple struggle for civil rights and to extend their demands to dig deeper into the foundation of American society, they saw themselves increasingly isolated as whites deserted them.

Black power, and indeed the riots themselves, were as much an expression as a cause of the disintegration of the civil rights coalition, and of the isolation of blacks that was attendant upon it. That alliance had made the movement victorious in its effort to end legal segregation and discrimination against blacks in the South. It was possible because the dominant section of the nation had an interest in ending segregation, owing to the political and economic difficulties it caused. But neither the federal government nor any of the other allies of blacks had any interest in carrying out the far-reaching social and economic changes that would be necessary to deal with the full range of black needs. There was no pressure from the middle classes to do so. On the contrary, many actually opposed black demands when they were directed at social issues that went beyond simple racial discrimination. Even in this realm, they often did not view issues such as housing and school desegregation with sympathy. Whereas in the South turmoil created by blacks again and again had brought the business and middle classes to seek to conciliate the demand for change, the disorder of the ghetto riots had no such effect; if anything, attitudes hardened in response to these outbursts. The result was for many blacks to turn inward, but the turn inward was a response to the turn away from the black movement by whites.

Ghetto Revolts and Martin Luther King: Search for a New Coalition

King and his supporters could not escape the turmoil outside the South that had such a great impact on the black movement and on civil rights activists, organizations, and leaders. They too were moved by it and felt compelled to respond to it by altering their agenda. If King and his strategy of nonviolent direct action were to retain their leadership, he had now to turn to the ghettos, where, Bayard Rustin stated, "Roy [Wilkins, then head of the NAACP], Martin and I haven't done a thing about it. We've done plenty to get votes in the South and seats in lunch rooms, but we've had no progress for these youngsters." So, King proposed a project in Chicago, to begin in 1966.

In making this move, King was, in one sense, gambling. The problems he was facing—poverty and slumlords; black exclusion from jobs; housing that was segregated because whites refused to sell or rent to, or live near, blacks—were very different from and much more difficult to resolve than the legal discrimination he had fought with such success in the South. Moreover, as Northern blacks and those in SNCC had already found, King's allies in the Southern campaigns—the Northern Democratic party and liberal white opinion—now turned out to be his adversaries. In Chicago, King was not dealing with an outlawed section of the country that had kept blacks in their place and prevented modernization. Mayor Daley's political machine was the bedrock of the national Democratic party. But that party saw little that needed change in Chicago or elsewhere outside of the South. When King entered this territory, he did so without the backing of the potent civil rights coalition. In this circumstance, he was risking failure. But in another sense it was no gamble at all; if he didn't undertake this campaign, he would be abandoning the field.

King was able to develop impressive support. He got some from the AFL-CIO unions; the United Auto Workers sent in organizers to set up a rent strike. He had a meeting with the powerful leaders of the black gangs in Chicago and persuaded them to give nonviolence a try. He was able to hold some large demonstrations. However, he succeeded in winning little.

In the midst of this campaign, from the rural backlands of Mississippi, intruded the drama that recast the movement. When James Meredith had enrolled at the University of Mississippi in 1962, he had precipitated a white riot, which forced President Kennedy to federalize the Mississippi National Guard. Now, in the summer of 1966, Meredith had begun a "March against Fear" in that state to prove that blacks could go anywhere they wished. He had not gone far when he was shot and seriously wounded. King and other civil rights leaders immediately flew down to Mississippi to visit Meredith and to continue his march.

There were deep differences between the groups represented, ranging from the newly installed heads of SNCC and CORE, Stokeley Carmichael and Floyd McKissick, to the far more conservative Roy Wilkins of the NAACP and Whitney Young of the Urban League. Wilkins and Young balked over demands for a march manifesto that charged the federal government with failure to carry out a real civil rights program. King accepted the manifesto but had to battle over two other issues: whether whites should be allowed on the march and whether it would be nonviolent. King prevailed on the first issue, and ostensibly on the second, as well. But a group from Louisiana, the Deacons for Self-Defense, escorted the march, and they were quietly armed. It was on this march that Carmichael had raised the cry of black power.

All of that made the Chicago campaign more crucial for King. If he could succeed there, his nonviolent approach would be proved against the advocates of black power. But he did not succeed in Chicago: in the summer of 1966 a riot broke out in that city, followed shortly by another riot in Cleveland. King, without the support of the civil rights coalition, was able to secure little in the way of real concessions from the Daley machine, and eventually he packed up and returned to Atlanta. By the time the summer was over, the black movement had a new face: it was more radical, more militant, more nationalist.

King thus faced a new situation. He perceived that the civil rights coalition had run its course, and in his last book, *Where Do We Go from Here: Chaos or Community?* he wrote that:

> It evokes happy memories, to recall that our victories in the past decade were won with a broad coalition of organizations representing a wide variety of interests. But we deceive ourselves if we envision the same combination backing structural changes in the society. It did not come together for such a program and will not reassemble for it.

This perception did not lead King to abandon the pursuit of coalition politics. Rather, he attempted to counter the isolating trend of black power. "In a multiracial society," he affirmed, "no group can make it alone." So, he sought to create a new coalition. Who would the new allies be? He was groping toward a solution that put more emphasis on class politics. "There are, in fact, more poor white Americans than there are Negro," he pointed out. And these whites were indeed, in his view, potential allies:

> Racism is a tenacious evil, but it is not immutable. Millions of underprivileged whites are in the process of considering the contradiction between segregation and economic progress. White supremacy can feed their egos but not their stomachs. They will not go hungry or forego the affluent society to remain racially ascendant.

It was to these people, as well as to the well-intentioned middle-class whites, that King hoped to turn in what had to be a much more radical confrontation with American society than he had heretofore attempted. One example of his thinking is found in his address before the tenth-anniversary convention of the SCLC in 1967:

> We must honestly face the fact that the Movement must address itself to the question of restructuring the whole of American society. There are 40 million poor people here. And one day we must ask the question, "Why are there 40 million poor people in America?" And when you begin to ask that question, you are raising questions about the economic system, about a broader distribution of wealth. When you ask that question, you begin to question the capitalistic economy. And to ask questions about the whole society. We are called upon to help the discouraged beggars in life's market place. But one day we must come to see that an edifice which produces beggars needs restructuring. It means that questions must be raised. You see, my friends, when you deal with this, you begin to ask the question, "Who owns the oil?" You begin to ask the question, "Who owns the iron ore?" You begin to ask the question, "Why is it that people have to pay water bills in a world that is two-thirds water?" These are questions that must be asked.

King denied the inevitable charge that he was a Marxist. Nonetheless, he went on to contend that:

> When I say question the whole society, it means ultimately coming to see that the problem of racism, the problem of economic exploitation, and the problem of war are all tied together.... A nation that will keep people in slavery for 244 years will "thingify" them, make them things. Therefore they will exploit them, and poor people generally economically. And a nation that will exploit economically will have to have foreign investments . . . and will have to use its military might to protect them. All of these problems are tied together. What I am saying today is that we must go from this convention and say, "America, you must be born again!"

It was in this spirit, and in hope of creating a new coalition that could successfully tackle the economic issues that had been raised by the black movement, that King began preparation for the Poor People's March on Washington, which he envisioned as a confrontation. He also turned to union organizing. That was the new strategy he had to offer. If successful, he felt that it would restore nonviolent direct action as the centerpiece of social change and enable blacks to break out of the isolation that was being imposed upon them as they refused to cease their struggles. A class program that posed issues in terms of economic equality might, he hoped, create a new spirit of unity. King and the SCLC embarked upon a serious campaign that involved them in strikes and union organizing in Atlanta; Memphis; Detroit; Birmingham; St. Petersburg, Florida; and Charleston, Georgetown, and Florence, South Carolina. His murder in Memphis took place when he was involved in such activity. That was part of his alternative to what he considered the blind alley of black power.

The new alliance, however, never emerged. King's death cut short his efforts to create it, so we can never know what might have happened. But there is no indication that in those prosperous times any substantial section of whites would have heeded his call. If black power was a blind alley, King does not appear to have had an approach that at that time was more likely to be successful. The Black Panther party attempted to create such a coalition, within the framework of black power, in 1968 and 1969. While it was able to gain some white support from the anti-Vietnam War movement, it was not sufficiently powerful to have any major impact on the structure of American society. The black movement appeared to have gone about as far as it was capable of going at that time, given the political alignments.

5.3   Michael Eric Dyson

Meeting Malcolm

Michael Eric Dyson is author of Making Malcolm: The Myth and Meaning of Malcolm X, Reflecting Black: African-American Cultural Criticism, *and* Between God and Gansta Rap: Bearing Witness to Black Culture. *He is the Ida B. Wells-Barnett University Professor of religious studies at DePaul University in Chicago.*

> *First, I don't profess to be anybody's leader. I'm one of 22 million Afro-Americans, all of whom have suffered the same things. And I probably cry out a little louder against the suffering than most others and therefore, perhaps, I'm better known. I don't profess to have a political, economic, or social solution to a problem as complicated as the one which our people face in the States, but I am one of those who is willing to try any means necessary to bring an end to the injustices that our people suffer.*
>
> —Malcolm X, in *By Any Means Necessary: Speeches, Interviews, and a Letter, by Malcolm X*

Malcolm X, one of the most complex and enigmatic African-American leaders ever, was born Malcolm Little on May 19, 1925, in Omaha, Nebraska. Since his death in 1965, Malcolm's life has increasingly acquired mythic stature. Along with Martin Luther King, Jr., Malcolm is a member of the pantheon of twentieth-century black saints. Unlike that of King, however, Malcolm's heroic rise was both aided and complicated by his championing of black nationalism and his advocacy of black self-defense against white racist violence.

Malcolm's ideas of black nationalism were shaped virtually from the womb by the example of his parents, Earl and Louise Little, both members of Marcus Garvey's Universal Negro Improvement Association (UNIA). As president of the Omaha branch of the UNIA, Earl Little, who was also an itinerant Baptist preacher, vigorously proclaimed the Garveyite doctrine of racial self-help and black unity, often with Malcolm at his side. Louise Little served as reporter of the Omaha UNIA. A native of Grenada, Louise was a deeply spiritual woman who presided over her brood of eight children even as she endured the abuse of her husband, and together they heaped domestic violence on their children.

According to Malcolm, his family was driven from Omaha by the Ku Klux Klan while he was still an infant, forcing them to seek safer habitation in Lansing, the capital city of Michigan eighty miles northwest of Detroit. Their respite was only temporary, however; the Little family house was burned down by a white hate group, the Black Legionnaires, during Malcolm's early childhood in 1929. This experience of racial violence, which Malcolm termed his "earliest vivid memory," deeply influenced his unsparing denunciation of white racism during his public career as a black nationalist leader.

When Malcolm was only six, his father died after being crushed under a streetcar. It is unclear whether Earl died at the hands of the Black Legionnaires, as Malcolm reports in his autobiography, or whether his death was accidental, as recent scholarship has suggested. In either case, his loss bore fateful consequences for the Little family because Louise Little was faced with raising eight children alone during the Great Depression. She eventually suffered a mental breakdown, and her children were dispersed to different foster homes.

Malcolm's life after his family's breakup went from bleak to desperate, as he was shuttled between several foster homes. Malcolm stole food to survive and began developing hustling habits that he later perfected in Boston, where he went to live with his half-sister Ella after dropping out of school in Lansing after completing the eighth grade. Before leaving school, Malcolm had become eighth-grade class president at Mason Junior High School. But a devastating rebuff from a teacher—who discouraged Malcolm in his desire to become an attorney by claiming that it was an unrealistic goal for "niggers"—finally sealed Malcolm's early fate as an academic failure.

It was in Boston that Malcolm encountered for the first time the black bourgeoisie, with its social pretensions and exaggerated rituals of cultural self-affirmation, leading him to conclude later that the black middle class was largely ineffective in achieving authentic black liberation. It was also in Boston's Roxbury and New York's Harlem that Malcolm was introduced to the street life of the northern urban poor and working class, gaining crucial insight about the cultural styles, social sufferings, and personal aspirations of everyday black people. Malcolm's hustling repertoire ranged from drug dealing and numbers running to burglary, the last activity landing him in a penitentiary for a six- to ten-year sentence. Malcolm's prison period—lasting from 1946 to 1952—marked the first of several extraordinary transformations he underwent as he searched for the truth about himself and his relation to black consciousness, black freedom and unity, and black religion.

While in prison, Malcolm read widely and argued passionately about a broad scope of subjects, from biblical theology to Western philosophy, voraciously absorbing the work of authors as diverse as Louis S. B. Leakey and Friedrich Nietzsche. Malcolm read so much during this period that his eyesight became strained, and he began wearing his trademark glasses. It was during his prison stay that Malcolm experienced his first religious conversion, slowly evolving from a slick street hustler and con artist to a sophisticated, self-taught devotee of Elijah Muhammad and the Nation of Islam, the black nationalist religious group that Muhammad headed. Malcolm was drawn to the Nation of Islam because of the character of its black nationalist practices and beliefs: its peculiar gift for rehabilitating black male prisoners; its strong emphasis on black pride, history, culture, and unity; and its unblinking assertion that white men were devils, a belief that led Muhammad and his followers to advocate black separation from white society.

Within a year of his release from prison on parole in 1952, Malcolm became a minister with the Nation of Islam, journeying to its Chicago headquarters to meet face to face with the man whose theological doctrines of white evil and black racial superiority had given Malcolm new life. Through a herculean work ethic and spartan self-discipline—key features of the black puritanism that characterized the Nation's moral orientation—Malcolm worked his way in short order from assistant minister of Detroit's Temple Number One to national spokesman for Elijah Muhammad and the Nation of Islam. In his role as the mouthpiece for the Nation of Islam, Malcolm brought unprecedented visibility to a religious group that many critics had either ignored or dismissed as fundamentalist fringe fanatics. Under Malcolm's leadership, the Nation grew from several hundred to a hundred thousand members by the early 1960s. The Nation under Malcolm also produced forty temples throughout the United States and purchased thirty radio stations.

During the late 1950s and early 1960s, enormous changes were rapidly occurring within American society in regard to race. The momentous *Brown v. Board of Education* Supreme Court decision, delivered in 1954, struck down the "separate-but-equal" law that had enforced racially segregated public education since 1896. And in 1955, the historic bus boycott in Montgomery, Alabama—sparked by seamstress Rosa Parks's refusal to surrender her seat to a white passenger, as legally mandated by a segregated public-transportation system—brought its leader, Martin Luther King, Jr., to national prominence. King's fusion of black Christian civic piety and traditions of American public morality and radical democracy unleashed an irresistible force on American politics that fundamentally altered the social conditions of millions of blacks, especially the black middle classes in the South.

The civil rights movement, though, barely affected the circumstances of poor southern rural blacks. Neither did it greatly enhance the plight of poor northern urban blacks, whose economic status and social standing were severely handicapped by forces of deindustrialization: the rise of automated technology that displaced human wage earners, the severe decline in manufacturing and in retail and wholesale trade, and escalating patterns of black unemployment. These social and economic trends, coupled with the growing spiritual despair that beginning in the early 1950s gripped Rust Belt cities like New York, Chicago, Philadelphia, Detroit, Cleveland, Indianapolis, and Baltimore, did not initially occupy the social agenda of the southern-based civil rights movement.

Malcolm's ministry, however, as was true of the Nation of Islam in general, was directed toward the socially dispossessed, the morally compromised, and the economically desperate members of the black proletariat and ghetto poor who were unaided by the civil rights movement. The Nation of Islam recruited many of its members among the prison populations largely forgotten by traditional Christianity (black and white). The Nation also proselytized among the hustlers, drug dealers, pimps, prostitutes, and thieves whose lives, the Nation contended, were ethically impoverished by white racist neglect of their most fundamental needs: the need for self-respect, the need for social dignity, the need to understand their royal black history, and the need to worship and serve a black God. All of these were provided in the black nationalist worldview of the Nation of Islam.

Malcolm's public ministry of proselytizing for the Nation of Islam depended heavily on drawing contrasts between what he and other Nation members viewed as the corruption of black culture by white Christianity (best symbolized in Martin Luther King, Jr., and segments of the civil rights movement) and the redemptive messages of racial salvation proffered by Elijah Muhammad. Malcolm relentlessly preached the virtues of black self-determination and self-defense even as he denounced the brainwashing of black people by Christian preachers like King who espoused passive strategies of resistance in the face of white racist violence.

Where King advocated redemptive suffering for blacks through their own bloodshed, Malcolm promulgated "reciprocal bleeding" for blacks and whites. As King preached the virtues of Christian love, Malcolm articulated black anger with unmitigated passion. While King urged nonviolent civil disobedience, Malcolm promoted the liberation of blacks by whatever means were necessary, including (though not exclusively, as some have argued) the possibility of armed self-defense. While King dreamed, Malcolm saw nightmares.

It was Malcolm's unique ability to narrate the prospects of black resistance at the edge of racial apocalypse that made him both exciting and threatening. Malcolm spoke out loud what many blacks secretly felt about racist white people and practices, but were afraid to acknowledge publicly. Malcolm boldly specified in lucid rhetoric the hurts, agonies, and frustrations of black people chafing from an enforced racial silence about the considerable cultural costs of white racism.

Unfortunately, as was the case with most of his black nationalist compatriots and civil rights advocates, Malcolm cast black liberation in terms of masculine self-realization. Malcolm's zealous trumpeting of the social costs of black male cultural emasculation went hand in hand with his often aggressive, occasionally vicious, put-downs of black women. These slights of black women reflected the demonology of the Nation of Islam, which not only viewed racism as an ill from outside its group, but argued that women were a lethal source of deception and seduction from within. Hence, Nation of Islam women were virtually desexualized through "modest" dress, kept under the close supervision of men, and relegated to the background while their men took center stage. Such beliefs reinforced the already inferior position of black women in black culture.

These views, ironically, placed Malcolm and the Nation of Islam squarely within misogynist traditions of white and black Christianity. It is this aspect, especially, of Malcolm's public ministry that has been adopted by contemporary black urban youth, including rappers and filmmakers. Although Malcolm would near the end of his life renounce his sometimes vitriolic denunciations of black women, his contemporary followers have not often followed suit.

But as the civil rights movement expanded its influence, Malcolm and the Nation came under increasing criticism for its deeply apolitical stance. Officially, the Nation of Islam was forbidden by Elijah Muhammad to become involved in acts of civil disobedience or social protest, ironically containing the forces of anger and rage that Malcolm's fiery rhetoric helped unleash. This ideological constraint stifled Malcolm's natural inclination to action, and increasingly caused him great discomfort as he sought to explain publicly the glaring disparity between the Nation's aggressive rhetoric and its refusal to become politically engaged.

Malcolm's growing dissatisfaction with the Nation's apolitical posture only deepened his suspicions about its leadership role in aiding blacks to achieve real liberation. Malcolm also became increasingly aware of the internal corruption of the Nation—unprincipled financial practices among top officials who reaped personal benefit at the expense of the rank and file, and extramarital affairs involving leader Elijah Muhammad. Moreover, there is evidence that Malcolm had privately forsaken his belief in the whites-are-devils doctrine years before his widely discussed public rejection of the doctrine after his 1964 split from the Nation of Islam, his embrace of orthodox Islamic belief, and his religious pilgrimage to Mecca.

The official cause of Malcolm's departure from the Nation of Islam was Elijah Muhammad's public reprimand of Malcolm for his famous comments that President John F. Kennedy's assassination merely represented the "chickens coming home to roost." Malcolm was saying that the violence the United States had committed in other parts of the world was returning to haunt this nation. Muhammad quickly forbade Malcolm from publicly speaking, initially for ninety days, motivated as much by jealousy of Malcolm's enormous popularity among blacks outside the Nation of Islam as by his desire to punish Malcolm for a comment that would bring the Nation undesired negative attention from an already racially paranoid government.

In March 1964, Malcolm left the Nation of Islam after it became apparent that he could not mend his relationship with his estranged mentor. He formed two organizations, one religious (Muslim Mosque) and the other political (Organization of Afro-American Unity, or OAAU). The OAAU was modeled after the Organization of African Unity and reflected Malcolm's belief that broad social engagement provided blacks their best chance for ending racism. Before establishing the OAAU, however, Malcolm fulfilled a longstanding dream of making a hajj to Mecca. While there, Malcolm wrote a series of letters to his followers detailing his stunning change of heart about race relations, declaring that his humane treatment by white Muslims and his perception of the universality of Islamic religious truth had forced him to reject his former narrow beliefs about whites. Malcolm's change of heart, though, did not blind him to the persistence of American racism and the need to oppose its broad variety of expressions with aggressive social resistance.

After his departure from the Nation of Islam, Malcolm traveled extensively, including trips to the Middle East and Africa. His travels broadened his political perspective considerably, a fact reflected in his new appreciation of socialist movements (though he didn't embrace socialism) and a new international note in his public discourse as he emphasized the link between African-American liberation and movements for freedom throughout the world, especially in African nations. Malcolm didn't live long enough to fulfill the promise of his new directions. On February 21, 1965, three months shy of his fortieth birthday, Malcolm X was gunned down by Nation of Islam loyalists as he prepared to speak to a meeting of the OAAU. Fortunately, Malcolm had recently completed his autobiography with the help of Alex Haley. That work, *The Autobiography of Malcolm X,* stands as a classic of black letters and American autobiography.

Malcolm lived only fifty weeks after his break with the Nation of Islam, initiating his last and perhaps most meaningful transformation of all: from revolutionary black nationalist to human rights advocate. Although Malcolm never gave up on black unity or self-determination—and neither did he surrender his acerbic wit on behalf of the voiceless millions of poor blacks who could never speak their pain before the world—he did expand his field of vision to include poor, dispossessed people of color from around the world, people whose plight resulted from class inequality and economic oppression as much as from racial domination. Had he lived, we can only hope that vexing contemporary problems from gender oppression to homophobia might have exercised his considerable skills of social rage and incisive, passionate oratory in giving voice to fears and resentments that most people can speak only in private.

During the last year of his life, Malcolm's social criticism and political engagement reflected a will to spontaneity, his analysis an improvisatory and fluid affair that drew from his rapidly evolving quest for the best means available for real black liberation—but a black liberation connected to the realization of human rights for all suffering peoples. In the end, Malcolm's moral pragmatism and experimental social criticism linked him more nearly to the heart of African-American culture and American radical practices than it might have otherwise appeared during his controversial career. Malcolm's complexity resists neat categories of analysis and rigid conclusions about his meaning.

It is this Malcolm—the Malcolm who spoke with uncompromising ardor about the poor, black, and dispossessed, and who named racism when and where he found it—who appealed to me as a young black male coming to maturity during the 1970s in the ghetto of Detroit. I took pleasure in his early moniker Detroit Red, feeling that our common geography joined us in a project to reclaim the dignity of black identity from the chaotic dissemblances and self-deceptions instigated by racist oppression.

But the riots of 1967—with their flames of frustration burning bitterly in my neighborhood, a testament to the unreconciled grievances that fueled racial resentments—had already confirmed Malcolm's warnings about the desperate state of urban black America. And the death of Martin Luther King, Jr., one year later ruptured the veins of nonviolent response to black suffering, evoking seizures of social unrest in the nerve centers of hundreds of black communities across the nation. King's death and Malcolm's life forced me to grapple with the best remedy for resisting racism.

As a result, I turned more frequently to a means of communication and combat that King and Malcolm had favored and that had been nurtured in me by my experience in the black church: rhetorical resistance. In African-American cultures, acts of rhetorical resistance are often more than mere words. They encompass a complex set of symbolic expressions and oral interactions with the "real" world. These expressions and interactions are usually supported by substantive black cultural traditions—from religious worship to social protest—that fuse speech and performance. Much of the ingenuity and inventiveness of black rhetorical resistance was evident in the church-based civil rights movement and in black nationalist struggles for self-determination in the 1960s.

One form of rhetorical resistance that has been prominently featured throughout black cultural history is the black sermon, the jewel in the crown of black sacred rhetoric. Here, a minister, or another authorized figure, thrives in the delivery of priestly wisdom and prophetic warning through words of encouragement and comfort, of chastening and challenge. Martin and Malcolm, of course, were widely acknowledged masters of black sacred rhetoric—as well as brilliant political rhetoricians whose deft weaving of spiritual uplift and secular complaint forged a powerful basis for black action in a bruising white world. The excellent examples of Martin and Malcolm—along with the more immediate impact of my pastor, Frederick G. Sampson—brought me to believe that words can have world-making and life-altering consequences.

In the years following Malcolm's and Martin's deaths, I participated in all manner of black public oral performance—from church plays and speeches to poetry recitations and oratorical contests—that whetted my appetite for the word. At eleven, I wrote a speech for the local Optimist Club that won me a first-place trophy and a photograph and headline in the *Detroit News* that read "Boy's Plea Against Racism Wins Award." Martin's and Malcolm's spirit hovered intimately around my performance. Their presence in word also inspired my decision to become an ordained Baptist minister, and sustained me as I became, in quick succession, a teen-age father, a welfare recipient, a wheel-brake-and-drum-factory laborer, and a pastor in the South.

As I have matured, journeying from factory worker to professor, it is the Malcolm who valued truth over habit who has appealed most to me, his ability to be self-critical and to change his direction an unfailing sign of integrity and courage. But these two Malcolms need not be in ultimate, fatal conflict, need not be fractured by the choice between seeking an empowering racial identity and linking ourselves to the truth no matter what it looks like, regardless of color, class, gender, sex, or age. They are both legitimate quests, and Malcolm's career and memory are enabling agents for both pursuits. His complexity is our gift.

5.4   Malcolm X

The Ballot or the Bullet

Malcolm X was a Black Muslim minister who, in contrast to the philosophy of nonviolent civil disobedience, advocated liberation of blacks by any means necessary. Appealing to a segment of Northern urban poor and working-class blacks with critical rhetoric, Malcolm became a leader emphasizing self-determination for blacks. His ideas had a profound influence on many black students involved in the civil rights movement. He was assassinated in 1965.

Mr. Moderator, Brother Lomax, brothers and sisters, friends and enemies: I just can't believe everyone in here is a friend and I don't want to leave anybody out. The question tonight, as I understand it, is "The Negro Revolt, and Where Do We Go From Here?" or "What Next?" In my little humble way of understanding it, it points toward either the ballot or the bullet.

Before we try and explain what is meant by the ballot or the bullet, I would like to clarify something concerning myself. I'm still a Muslim, my religion is still Islam. That's my personal belief. Just as Adam Clayton Powell is a Christian minister who heads the Abyssinian Baptist Church in New York, but at the same time takes part in the political struggles to try and bring about rights to the black people in this country; and Dr. Martin Luther King is a Christian minister down in Atlanta,

Georgia, who heads another organization fighting for the civil rights of black people in this country; and Rev. Galamison, I guess you've heard of him, is another Christian minister in New York who has been deeply involved in the school boycotts to eliminate segregated education; well, I myself am a minister, not a Christian minister, but a Muslim minister; and I believe in action on all fronts by whatever means necessary.

Although I'm still a Muslim, I'm not here tonight to discuss my religion. I'm not here to try and change your religion. I'm not here to argue or discuss anything that we differ about, because it's time for us to submerge our differences and realize that it is best for us to first see that we have the same problem, a common problem—a problem that will make you catch hell whether you're a Baptist, or a Methodist, or a Muslim, or a nationalist. Whether you're educated or illiterate, whether you live on the boulevard or in the alley, you're going to catch hell just like I am. We're all in the same boat and we all are going to catch the same hell from the same man. He just happens to be a white man. All of us have suffered here, in this country, political oppression at the hands of the white man, economic exploitation at the hands of the white man, and social degradation at the hands of the white man.

Now in speaking like this, it doesn't mean that we're antiwhite, but it does mean we're anti-exploitation, we're anti-degradation, we're anti-oppression. And if the white man doesn't want us to be anti-him, let him stop oppressing and exploiting and degrading us. Whether we are Christians or Muslims or nationalists or agnostics or atheists, we must first learn to forget our differences. If we have differences, let us differ in the closet; when we come out in front, let us not have anything to argue about until we get finished arguing with the man. If the late President Kennedy could get together with Khrushchev and exchange some wheat, we certainly have more in common with each other than Kennedy and Khrushchev had with each other.

If we don't do something real soon, I think you'll have to agree that we're going to be forced either to use the ballot or the bullet. It's one or the other in 1964. It isn't that time is running out—time has run out. 1964 threatens to be the most explosive year America has ever witnessed. The most explosive year. Why? It's also a political year: It's the year when all of the white politicians will be back in the so-called Negro community jiving you and me for some votes. The year when all of the white political crooks will be right back in your and my community with their false promises, building up our hopes for a letdown, with their trickery and their treachery, with their false promises which they don't intend to keep. As they nourish these dissatisfactions, it can only lead to one thing, an explosion; and now we have the type of black man on the scene in America today—I'm sorry, Brother Lomax—who just doesn't intend to turn the other cheek any longer.

Don't let anybody tell you anything about the odds are against you. If they draft you, they send you to Korea and make you face 800 million Chinese. If you can be brave over there, you can be brave right here. These odds aren't as great as those odds. And if you fight here, you will at least know what you're fighting for.

I'm not a politician, not even a student of politics; in fact, I'm not a student of much of anything. I'm not a Democrat, I'm not a Republican, and I don't even consider myself an American. If you and I were Americans, there'd be no problem. Those Honkies that just got off the boat, they're already Americans; Polacks are already Americans; the Italian refugees are already Americans. Everything that came out of Europe, every blue-eyed thing, is already an American. And as long as you and I have been over here, we aren't Americans yet.

Well, I am one who doesn't believe in deluding myself. I'm not going to sit at your table and watch you eat, with nothing on my plate, and call myself a diner. Sitting at the table doesn't make you a diner, unless you eat some of what's on that plate. Being here in America doesn't make you an American. Being born here in America doesn't make you an American. Why, if birth made you American, you wouldn't need any legislation, you wouldn't need any amendments to the Constitution, you wouldn't be faced with civil-rights filibustering in Washington, D.C., right now. They don't have to pass civil-rights legislation to make a Polack an American.

'No, I'm not an American. I'm one of the 22 million black people who are the victims of Americanism. One of the 22 million black people who are the victims of democracy, nothing but disguised hypocrisy. So, I'm not standing here speaking to you as an American, or a patriot, or a flag-saluter, or a flag-waver—no, not I. I'm speaking as a victim of this American system. And I see America through the eyes of the victim. I don't see any American dream; I see an American nightmare.

These 22 million victims are waking up. Their eyes are coming open. They're beginning to see what they used to only look at. They're becoming politically mature. They are realizing that there are new political trends from coast to coast. As they see these new political trends, it's possible for them to see that every time there's an election the races are so close that they have to have a recount. They had to recount in Massachusetts to see who was going to be governor, it was so close. It was the same way in Rhode Island, in Minnesota, and in many other parts of the country. And the same with Kennedy and Nixon when they ran for president. It was so close they had to count all over again. Well, what does this mean? It means that when white people are evenly divided, and black people have a bloc of votes of their own, it is left up to them to determine who's going to sit in the White House and who's going to be in the dog house.

It was the black man's vote that put the present administration in Washington, D.C. Your vote, your dumb vote, your ignorant vote, your wasted vote put in an administration in Washington, D.C., that has seen fit to pass every kind of legislation imaginable, saving you until last, then filibustering on top of that. And your and my leaders have the audacity to run around clapping their hands and talk about how much progress we're making. And what a good president we have. If he wasn't good in Texas, he sure can't be good in Washington, D.C. Because Texas is a lynch state. It is in the same breath as Mississippi, no different; only they lynch you in Texas with a Texas accent and lynch you in Mississippi with a Mississippi accent. And these Negro leaders have the audacity to go and have some coffee in the White House with a Texan, a Southern cracker—that's all he is—and then come out and tell you and me that he's going to be better for us because, since he's from the South, he knows how to deal with the Southerners. What kind of logic is that? Let Eastland be president, he's from the South too. He should be better able to deal with them than Johnson.

In this present administration they have in the House of Representatives 257 Democrats to only 177 Republicans. They control two-thirds of the House vote. Why can't they pass something that will help you and me? In the Senate, there are 67 senators who are of the Democratic Party. Only 33 of them are Republicans. Why, the Democrats have got the government sewed up, and you're the one who sewed it up for them. And what have they given you for it? Four years in office, and just now getting around to some civil-rights legislation. Just now, after everything else is gone, out of the way, they're going to sit down now and play with you all summer long—the same old giant con game that they call filibuster. All those are in cahoots together. Don't you ever think they're not in cahoots together, for the man that is heading the civil-rights filibuster is a man from Georgia named Richard Russell. When Johnson became president, the first man he asked for when he got back to Washington, D.C., was "Dicky"—that's how tight they are. That's his boy, that's his pal, that's his buddy. But they're playing that old con game. One of them makes believe he's for you, and he's got it fixed where the other one is so tight against you, he never has to keep his promise.

So it's time in 1964 to wake up. And when you see them coming up with that kind of conspiracy, let them know your eyes are open. And let them know you got something else that's wide open too. It's got to be the ballot or the bullet. The ballot or the bullet. If you're afraid to use an expression like that, you should get on out of the country, you should get back in the cotton patch, you should get back in the alley. They get all the Negro vote, and after they get it, the Negro gets nothing in return. All they did when they got to Washington was give a few big Negroes big jobs. Those big Negroes didn't need big jobs, they already had jobs. That's camouflage, that's trickery, that's treachery, window-dressing. I'm not trying to knock out the Democrats for the Republicans, we'll get to them in a minute. But it is true—you put the Democrats first and the Democrats put you last.

Look at it the way it is. What alibis do they use, since they control Congress and the Senate? What alibi do they use when you and I ask, "Well, when are you going to keep your promise?" They blame the Dixiecrats. What is a Dixiecrat? A Democrat. A Dixiecrat is nothing but a Democrat in disguise. The titular head of the Democrats is also the head of the Dixiecrats, because the Dixiecrats are a part of the Democratic Party. The Democrats have never kicked the Dixiecrats out of the party. The Dixiecrats bolted themselves once, but the Democrats didn't put them out. Imagine, these lowdown Southern segregationists put the Northern Democrats down. But the Northern Democrats have never put the Dixiecrats down. No, look at that thing the way it is. They have got a con game going on, a political con game, and you and I are in the middle. It's time for you and me to wake up and start looking at it like it is, and trying to understand it like it is; and then we can deal with it like it is.

The Dixiecrats in Washington, D.C., control the key committees that run the government. The only reason the Dixiecrats control these committees is because they have seniority. The only reason they have seniority is because they come from states where Negroes can't vote. This is not even a government that's based on democracy. It is not a government that is made up of representatives of the people. Half of the people in the South can't even vote. Eastland is not even supposed to be in Washington. Half of the senators and congressmen who occupy these key positions in Washington, D.C., are there illegally, are there unconstitutionally.

I was in Washington, D.C., a week ago Thursday, when they were debating whether or not they should let the bill come onto the floor. And in the back of the room where the Senate meets, there's a huge map of the United States, and on that map it shows the location of Negroes throughout the country. And it shows that the Southern section of the country, the states that are most heavily concentrated with Negroes, are the ones that have senators and congressmen standing up filibustering and doing all other kinds of trickery to keep the Negro from being able to vote. This is pitiful. But it's not pitiful for us any longer; it's actually pitiful for the white man, because soon now, as the Negro awakens a little more and sees the vise that he's in, sees the bag that he's in, sees the real game that he's in, then the Negro's going to develop a new tactic.

These senators and congressmen actually violate the constitutional amendments that guarantee the people of that particular state or county the right to vote. And the Constitution itself has within it the machinery to expel any representative from a state where the voting rights of the people are violated. You don't even need new legislation. Any person in Congress right now, who is there from a state or a district where the voting rights of the people are violated, that particular person should be expelled from Congress. And when you expel him, you've removed one of the obstacles in the path of any real meaningful legislation in this country. In fact, when you expel them, you don't need new legislation, because they will be replaced by black representatives from counties and districts where the black man is in the majority, not in the minority.

If the black man in these Southern states had his full voting rights, the key Dixiecrats in Washington, D.C., which means the key Democrats in Washington, D.C., would lose their seats. The Democratic party itself would lose its power. It would cease to be powerful as a party. When you see the amount of power that would be lost by the Democratic Party if it were to lose the Dixiecrat wing, or branch, or element, you can see where it's against the interests of the Democrats to give voting rights to Negroes in states where the Democrats have been in complete power and authority ever since the Civil War. You just can't belong to that party without analyzing it.

I say again, I'm not anti-Democrat, I'm not anti-Republican, I'm not anti-anything. I'm just questioning their sincerity, and some of the strategy that they've been using on our people by promising them promises that they don't intend to keep. When you keep the Democrats in power, you're keeping the Dixiecrats in power. I doubt that my good Brother Lomax will deny that. A vote for a Democrat is a vote for a Dixiecrat. That's why, in 1964, it's time now for you and me to become more politically mature and realize what the ballot is for; what we're supposed to get when we cast a ballot; and that if we don't cast a ballot, it's going to end up in a situation where we're going to have to cast a bullet. It's either a ballot or a bullet.

In the North, they do it a different way. They have a system that's known as gerrymandering, whatever that means. It means when Negroes become too heavily concentrated in a certain area, and begin to gain too much political power, the white man comes along and changes the district lines. You may say, "Why do you keep saying white man?" Because it's the white man who does it. I haven't ever seen any Negro changing any lines. They don't let him get near the line. It's the white man who does this. And usually, it's the white man who grins at you the most, and pats you on the back, and is supposed to be your friend. He may be friendly, but he's not your friend.

So, what I'm trying to impress upon you, in essence, is this: You and I in America are faced not with a segregationist conspiracy, we're faced with a government conspiracy. Everyone who's filibustering is a senator—that's the government. Everyone who's finagling in Washington, D.C., is a congressman—that's the government. You don't have anybody putting blocks in your path but people who are a part of the government. The same government that you go abroad to fight for and die for is the government that is in a conspiracy to deprive you of your voting rights, deprive you of your economic opportunities, deprive you of decent housing, deprive you of decent education. You don't need to go to the employer alone, it is the government itself, the government of America, that is responsible for the oppression and exploitation and degradation of black people in this country. And you should drop it in their lap. This government has failed the Negro. This so-called democracy has failed the Negro. And all these white liberals have definitely failed the Negro.

So, where do we go from here? First, we need some friends. We need some new allies. The entire civil-rights struggle needs a new interpretation, a broader interpretation. We need to look at this civil-rights thing from another angle—from the inside as well as from the outside. To those of us whose philosophy is black nationalism, the only way you can get involved in the civil-rights struggle is give it a new interpretation. That old interpretation excluded us. It kept us out. So, we're giving a new interpretation to the civil-rights struggle, an interpretation that will enable us to come into it, take part in it. And these handkerchief-heads who have been dillydallying and pussyfooting and compromising—we don't intend to let them pussyfoot and dillydally and compromise any longer.

How can you thank a man for giving you what's already yours? How then can you thank him for giving you only part of what's already yours? You haven't even made progress, if what's being given to you, you should have had already. That's not progress. And I love my Brother Lomax, the way he pointed out we're right back where we were in 1954. We're not even as far up as we were in 1954. We're behind where we were in 1954. There's more segregation now than there was in 1954. There's more racial animosity, more racial hatred, more racial violence today in 1964, than there was in 1954. Where is the progress?

And now you're facing a situation where the young Negro's coming up. They don't want to hear that "turn-the-other-cheek" stuff, no. In Jacksonville, those were teenagers, they were throwing Molotov cocktails. Negroes have never done that before. But it shows you there's a new deal coming in. There's new thinking coming in. There's new strategy coming in. It'll be Molotov cocktails this month, hand grenades next month, and something else next month. It'll be ballots, or it'll be bullets. It'll be liberty, or it will be death. The only difference about this kind of death—it'll be reciprocal. You know what is meant by "reciprocal"? That's one of Brother Lomax's words, I stole it from him. I don't usually deal with those big words because I don't usually deal with big people. I deal with small people. I find you can get a whole lot of small people and whip hell out of a whole lot of big people. They haven't got anything to lose, and they've got everything to gain. And they'll let you know in a minute: "It takes two to tango; when I go, you go."

The black nationalists, those whose philosophy is black nationalism, in bringing about this new interpretation of the entire meaning of civil rights, look upon it as meaning, as Brother Lomax has pointed out, equality of opportunity. Well, we're justified in seeking civil rights, if it means equality of opportunity, because all we're doing there is trying to collect for our investment. Our mothers and fathers invested sweat and blood. Three hundred and ten years we worked in this country without a dime in return—I mean without a dime in return. You let the white man walk around here talking about how rich this country is, but you never stop to think how it got rich so quick. It got rich because you made it rich.

You take the people who are in this audience right now. They're poor, we're all poor as individuals. Our weekly salary individually amounts to hardly anything. But if you take the salary of everyone in here collectively it'll fill up a whole lot of baskets. It's a lot of wealth. If you can collect the wages of just these people right here for a year, you'll be rich—richer than rich. When you look at it like that, think how rich Uncle Sam had to become, not with this handful, but millions of black people. Your and my mother and father, who didn't work an eight-hour shift, but worked from "can't see" in the morning until "can't see" at night, and worked for nothing, making the white man rich, making Uncle Sam rich.

This is our investment. This is our contribution—our blood. Not only did we give of our free labor, we gave of our blood. Every time he had a call to arms, we were the first ones in uniform. We died on every battlefield the white man had. We have made a greater sacrifice than anybody who's standing up in America today. We have made a greater contribution and have collected less. Civil rights, for those of us whose philosophy is black nationalism, means: "Give it to us now. Don't wait for next year. Give it to us yesterday, and that's not fast enough."

I might stop right here to point out one thing. Whenever you're going after something that belongs to you, anyone who's depriving you of the right to have it is a criminal. Understand that. Whenever you are going after something that is yours, you are within your legal rights to lay claim to it. And anyone who puts forth any effort to deprive you of that which is yours, is breaking the law, is a criminal. And this was pointed out by the Supreme Court decision. It outlawed segregation. Which means segregation is against the law. Which means a segregationist is breaking the law. A segregationist is a criminal. You can't label him as anything other than that. And when you demonstrate against segregation, the law is on your side. The Supreme Court is on your side.

Now, who is it that opposes you in carrying out the law? The police department itself. With police dogs and clubs. Whenever you demonstrate against segregation, whether it is segregated education, segregated housing, or anything else, the law is on your side, and anyone who stands in the way is not the law any longer. They are breaking the law, they are not representatives of the law. Any time you demonstrate against segregation and a man has the audacity to put a police dog on you, kill that dog, kill him, I'm telling you, kill that dog. I say it, if they put me in jail tomorrow, kill—that—dog. Then you'll put a stop to it. Now, if these white people in here don't want to see that kind of action, get down and tell the mayor to tell the police department to pull the dogs in. That's all you have to do. If you don't do it, someone else will.

If you don't take this kind of stand, your little children will grow up and look at you and think "shame." If you don't take an uncompromising stand—I don't mean go out and get violent; but at the same time you should never be nonviolent unless you run into some nonviolence. I'm nonviolent with those who are nonviolent with me. But when you drop that violence on me, then you've made me go insane, and I'm not responsible for what I do. And that's the way every Negro should get. Any time you know you're within the law, within your legal rights, within your moral rights, in accord with justice, then die for what you believe in. But don't die alone. Let your dying be reciprocal. This is what is meant by equality. What's good for the goose is good for the gander.

When we begin to get in this area, we need new friends, we need new allies. We need to expand the civil-rights struggle to a higher level—to the level of human rights. Whenever you are in a civil-rights struggle, whether you know it or not, you are confining yourself to the jurisdiction of Uncle Sam. No one from the outside world can speak out in your behalf as long as your struggle is a civil-rights struggle. Civil rights comes within the domestic affairs of this country. All of our African brothers and our Asian brothers and our Latin-American brothers cannot open their mouths and interfere in the domestic affairs of the United States. And as long as it's civil rights, this comes under the jurisdiction of Uncle Sam.

But the United Nations has what's known as the charter of human rights, it has a committee that deals in human rights. You may wonder why all of the atrocities that have been committed in Africa and in Hungary and in Asia and in Latin America are brought before the UN, and the Negro problem is never brought before the UN. This is part of the conspiracy. This old, tricky, blue-eyed liberal who is supposed to be your and my friend, supposed to be in our corner, supposed to be subsidizing our struggle, and supposed to be acting in the capacity of an adviser, never tells you anything about human rights. They keep you wrapped up in civil rights. And you spend so much time barking up the civil-rights tree, you don't even know there's a human-rights tree on the same floor.

When you expand the civil-rights struggle to the level of human rights, you can then take the case of the black man in this country before the nations in the UN. You can take it before the General Assembly. You can take Uncle Sam before a world court. But the only level you can do it on is the level of human rights. Civil rights keeps you under his restrictions, under his jurisdiction. Civil rights keeps you in his pocket. Civil rights means you're asking Uncle Sam to treat you right. Human rights are something you were born with. Human rights are your God-given rights. Human rights are the rights that are recognized by all nations of this earth. And any time any one violates your human rights, you can take them to the world court. Uncle Sam's hands are dripping with blood, dripping with the blood of the black man in this country. He's the earth's number-one hypocrite. He has the audacity—yes, he has—imagine him posing as the leader of the free world. The free world!—and you over here singing "We Shall Overcome." Expand the civil-rights struggle to the level of human rights, take it into the United Nations, where our African brothers can throw their weight on our side, where our Asian brothers can throw their weight on our side, where our Latin-American brothers can throw their weight on our side, and where 800 million Chinamen are sitting there waiting to throw their weight on our side.

Let the world know how bloody his hands are. Let the world know the hypocrisy that's practiced over here. Let it be the ballot or the bullet. Let him know that it must be the ballot or the bullet.

When you take your case to Washington, D.C., you're taking it to the criminal who's responsible; it's like running from the wolf to the fox. They're all in cahoots together. They all work political chicanery and make you look like a chump before the eyes of the world. Here you are walking around in America, getting ready to be drafted and sent abroad, like a tin soldier, and when you get over there, people ask you what are you fighting for, and you have to stick your tongue in your cheek. No, take Uncle Sam to court, take him before the world.

By ballot I only mean freedom. Don't you know—I disagree with Lomax on this issue—that the ballot is more important than the dollar? Can I prove it? Yes. Look in the UN. There are poor nations in the UN; yet those poor nations can get together with their voting power and keep the rich nations from making a move. They have one nation—one vote, everyone has an equal vote. And when those brothers from Asia, and Africa and the darker parts of this earth get together, their voting power is sufficient to hold Sam in check. Or Russia in check. Or some other section of the earth in check. So, the ballot is most important.

Right now, in this country, if you and I, 22 million African-Americans—that's what we are—Africans who are in America. You're nothing but Africans. Nothing but Africans. In fact, you'd get farther calling yourself African instead of Negro. Africans don't catch hell. You're the only one catching hell. They don't have to pass civil-rights bills for Africans. An African can go anywhere he wants right now. All you've got to do is tie your head up. That's right, go anywhere you want. Just stop being a Negro. Change your name to Hoogagagooba. That'll show you how silly the white man is. You're dealing with a silly man. A friend of mine who's very dark put a turban on his head and went into a restaurant in Atlanta before they called themselves desegregated. He went into a white restaurant, he sat down, they served him, and he said, "What would happen if a Negro came in here?" And there he's sitting, black as night, but because he had his head wrapped up the waitress looked back at him and says, "Why, there wouldn't no nigger dare come in here."

So, you're dealing with a man whose bias and prejudice are making him lose his mind, his intelligence, every day. He's frightened. He looks around and sees what's taking place on this earth, and he sees that the pendulum of time is swinging in your direction. The dark people are waking up. They're losing their fear of the white man. No place where he's fighting right now is he winning. Everywhere he's fighting, he's fighting someone your and my complexion. And they're beating him. He can't win any more. He's won his last battle. He failed to win the Korean War. He couldn't win it. He had to sign a truce. That's a loss. Any time Uncle Sam, with all his machinery for warfare, is held to a draw by some rice-eaters, he's lost the battle. He had to sign a truce. America's not supposed to sign a truce. She's supposed to be bad. But she's not bad any more. She's bad as long as she can use her hydrogen bomb, but she can't use hers for fear Russia might use hers. Russia can't use hers, for fear that Sam might use his. So, both of them are weaponless. They can't use the weapon because each's weapon nullifies the other's. So the only place where action can take place is on the ground. And the white man can't win another war fighting on the ground. Those days are over. The black man knows it, the brown man knows it, the red man knows it, and the yellow man knows it. So they engage him in guerrilla warfare. That's not his style. You've got to have heart to be a guerrilla warrior, and he hasn't got any heart. I'm telling you now.

I just want to give you a little briefing on guerrilla warfare because, before you know it, before you know it—It takes heart to be a guerrilla warrior because you're on your own. In conventional warfare you have tanks and a whole lot of other people with you to back you up, planes over your head and all that kind of stuff. But a guerrilla is on his own. All you have is a rifle, some sneakers and a bowl of rice, and that's all you need—and a lot of heart. The Japanese on some of those islands in the Pacific, when the American soldiers landed, one Japanese sometimes could hold the whole army off. He'd just wait until the sun went down, and when the sun went down they were all equal. He would take his little blade and slip from bush to bush, and from American to American. The white soldiers couldn't cope with that. Whenever you see a white soldier that fought in the Pacific, he has the shakes, he has a nervous condition, because they scared him to death.

The same thing happened to the French up in French Indochina. People who just a few years previously were rice farmers got together and ran the heavily-mechanized French army out of Indochina. You don't need it—modern warfare today won't work. This is the day of the guerrilla. They did the same thing in Algeria. Algerians, who were nothing but Bedouins, took a rifle and sneaked off to the hills, and de Gaulle and all of his highfalutin' war machinery couldn't defeat those guerrillas. Nowhere on this earth does the white man win in a guerrilla warfare. It's not his speed. Just as guerrilla warfare is prevailing in Asia and in parts of Africa and in parts of Latin America, you've got to be mighty naive, or you've got to play the black man cheap, if you don't think some day he's going to wake up and find that it's got to be the ballot or the bullet.

I would like to say, in closing, a few things concerning the Muslim Mosque, Inc., which we established recently in New York City. It's true we're Muslims and our religion is Islam, but we don't mix our religion with our politics and our economics and our social and civil activities—not any more. We keep our religion in our mosque. After our religious services are over, then as Muslims we become involved in political action, economic action and social and civic action. We become involved with anybody, anywhere, any time and in any manner that's designed to eliminate the evils, the political, economic and social evils that are afflicting the people of our community.

The political philosophy of black nationalism means that the black man should control the politics and the politicians in his own community; no more. The black man in the black community has to be re-educated into the science of politics so he will know what politics is supposed to bring him in return. Don't be throwing out any ballots. A ballot is like a bullet. You don't throw your ballots until you see a target, and if that target is not within your reach, keep your ballot in your pocket. The political philosophy of black nationalism is being taught in the Christian church. It's being taught in the NAACP. It's being taught in CORE meetings. It's being taught in SNCC (Student Nonviolent Coordinating Committee) meetings. It's being taught in Muslim meetings. It's being taught where nothing but atheists and agnostics come together. It's being taught everywhere. Black people are fed up with the dillydallying, pussyfooting, compromising approach that we've been using toward getting our freedom. We want freedom now, but we're not going to get it saying "We Shall Overcome." We've got to fight until we overcome.

The economic philosophy of black nationalism is pure and simple. It only means that we should control the economy of our community. Why should white people be running all the stores in our community? Why should white people be running the banks of our community? Why should the economy of our community be in the hands of the white man? Why? If a black man can't move his store into a white community, you tell me why a white man should move his store into a black community. The philosophy of black nationalism involves a re-education program in the black community in regards to economics. Our people have to be made to see that any time you take your dollar out of your community and spend it in a community where you don't live, the community where you live will get poorer and poorer, and the community where you spend your money will get richer and richer. Then you wonder why where you live is always a ghetto or a slum area. And where you and I are concerned, not only do we lose it when we spend it out of the community, but the white man has got all our stores in the community tied up; so that though we spend it in the community, at sundown the man who runs the store takes it over across town somewhere. He's got us in a vise.

So the economic philosophy of black nationalism means in every church, in every civic organization, in every fraternal order, it's time now for our people to become conscious of the importance of controlling the economy of our community. If we own the stores, if we operate the businesses, if we try and establish some industry in our own community, then we're developing to the position where we are creating employment for our own kind. Once you gain control of the economy of your own community, then you don't have to picket and boycott and beg some cracker downtown for a job in his business.

The social philosophy of black nationalism only means that we have to get together and remove the evils, the vices, alcoholism, drug addiction, and other evils that are destroying the moral fiber of our community. We ourselves have to lift the level of our community, the standard of our community to a higher level, make our own society beautiful so that we will be satisfied in our own social circles and won't be running around here trying to knock our way into a social circle where we're not wanted.

So I say, in spreading a gospel such as black nationalism, it is not designed to make the black man re-evaluate the white man—you know him already—but to make the black man re-evaluate himself. Don't change the white man's mind—you can't change his mind, and that whole thing about appealing to the moral conscience of America—America's conscience is bankrupt. She lost all conscience a long time ago. Uncle Sam has no conscience. They don't know what morals are. They don't try and eliminate an evil because it's evil, or because it's illegal, or because it's immoral; they eliminate it only when it threatens their existence. So you're wasting your time appealing to the moral conscience of a bankrupt man like Uncle Sam. If he had a conscience, he'd straighten this thing out with no more pressure being put upon him. So it is not necessary to change the white man's mind. We have to change our own mind. You can't change his mind about us. We've got to change our own minds about each other. We have to see each other with new eyes. We have to see each other as brothers and sisters. We have to come together with warmth so we can develop unity and harmony that's necessary to get this problem solved ourselves. How can we do this? How can we avoid jealousy? How can we avoid the suspicion and the divisions that exist in the community? I'll tell you how.

I have watched how Billy Graham comes into a city, spreading what he calls the gospel of Christ, which is only white nationalism. That's what he is. Billy Graham is a white nationalist; I'm a black nationalist. But since it's the natural tendency for leaders to be jealous and look upon a powerful figure like Graham with suspicion and envy, how is it possible for him to come into a city and get all the cooperation of the church leaders? Don't think because they're church leaders that they don't have weaknesses that make them envious and jealous—no, everybody's got it. It's not an accident that when they want to choose a cardinal [as Pope] over there in Rome, they get in a closet so you can't hear them cussing and fighting and carrying on.

Billy Graham comes in preaching the gospel of Christ, he evangelizes the gospel, he stirs everybody up, but he never tries to start a church. If he came in trying to start a church, all the churches would be against him. So, he just comes in talking about Christ and tells everybody who gets Christ to go to any church where Christ is; and in this way the church cooperates with him. So we're going to take a page from his book.

Our gospel is black nationalism. We're not trying to threaten the existence of any organization, but we're spreading the gospel of black nationalism. Anywhere there's a church that is also preaching and practicing the gospel of black nationalism, join that church. If the NAACP is preaching and practicing the gospel of black nationalism, join the NAACP. If CORE is spreading and practicing the gospel of black nationalism, join CORE. Join any organization that has a gospel that's for the uplift of the black man. And when you get into it and see them pussyfooting or compromising, pull out of it because that's not black nationalism. We'll find another one.

And in this manner, the organizations will increase in number and in quantity and in quality, and by August, it is then our intention to have a black nationalist convention which will consist of delegates from all over the country who are interested in the political, economic and social philosophy of black nationalism. After these delegates convene, we will hold a seminar, we will hold discussions, we will listen to everyone. We want to hear new ideas and new solutions and new answers. And at that time, if we see fit then to form a black nationalist party, we'll form a black nationalist party. If it's necessary to form a black nationalist army, we'll form a black nationalist army. It'll be the ballot or the bullet. It'll be liberty or it'll be death.

It's time for you and me to stop sitting in this country, letting some cracker senators, Northern crackers and Southern crackers, sit there in Washington, D.C., and come to a conclusion in their mind that you and I are supposed to have civil rights. There's no white man going to tell me anything about my rights. Brothers and sisters, always remember, if it doesn't take senators and congressmen and presidential proclamations to give freedom to the white man, it is not necessary for legislation or proclamation or Supreme Court decisions to give freedom to the black man. You let that white man know, if this is a country of freedom, let it be a country of freedom; and if it's not a country of freedom, change it.

We will work with anybody, anywhere, at any time, who is genuinely interested in tackling the problem head-on, nonviolently as long as the enemy is nonviolent, but violent when the enemy gets violent. We'll work with you on the voter-registration drive, we'll work with you on rent strikes, we'll work with you on school boycotts—I don't believe in any kind of integration; I'm not even worried about it because I know you're not going to get it anyway; you're not going to get it because you're afraid to die; you've got to be ready to die if you try and force yourself on the white man, because he'll get just as violent as those crackers in Mississippi, right here in Cleveland. But we will still work with you on the school boycotts because we're against a segregated school system. A segregated school system produces children who, when they graduate, graduate with crippled minds. But this does not mean that a school is segregated because it's all black. A segregated school means a school that is controlled by people who have no real interest in it whatsoever.

Let me explain what I mean. A segregated district or community is a community in which people live, but outsiders control the politics and the economy of that community. They never refer to the white section as a segregated community. It's the all-Negro section that's a segregated community. Why? The white man controls his own school, his own bank, his own economy, his own politics, his own everything, his own community—but he also controls yours. When you're under someone else's control, you're segregated. They'll always give you the lowest or the worst that there is to offer, but it doesn't mean you're segregated just because you have your own. You've got to control your own. Just like the white man has control of his, you need to control yours.

You know the best way to get rid of segregation? The white man is more afraid of separation than he is of integration. Segregation means that he puts you away from him, but not far enough for you to be out of his jurisdiction; separation means you're gone. And the white man will integrate faster than he'll let you separate. So we will work with you against the segregated school system because it's criminal, because it is absolutely destructive, in every way imaginable, to the minds of the children who have to be exposed to that type of crippling education.

Last but not least, I must say this concerning the great controversy over rifles and shotguns. The only thing that I've ever said is that in areas where the government has proven itself either unwilling or unable to defend the lives and the property of Negroes, it's time for Negroes to defend themselves. Article number two of the constitutional amendments provides you and me the right to own a rifle or a shotgun. It is constitutionally legal to own a shotgun or a rifle. This doesn't mean you're going to get a rifle and form battalions and go out looking for white folks, although you'd be within your rights—I mean, you'd be justified; but that would be illegal and we don't do anything illegal. If the white man doesn't want the black man buying rifles and shotguns, then let the government do its job. That's all. And don't let the white man come to you and ask you what you think about what Malcolm says—why, you old Uncle Tom. He would never ask you if he thought you were going to say, "Amen!" No, he is making a Tom out of you.

So, this doesn't mean forming rifle clubs and going out looking for people, but it is time, in 1964, if you are a man, to let that man know. If he's not going to do his job in running the government and providing you and me with the protection that our taxes are supposed to be for, since he spends all those billions for his defense budget, he certainly can't begrudge you and me spending $12 or $15 for a single-shot, or double-action. I hope you understand. Don't go out shooting people, but any time, brothers and sisters, and especially the men in this audience— some of you wearing Congressional Medals of Honor, with shoulders this wide, chests this big, muscles that big—any time you and I sit around and read where they bomb a church and murder in cold blood, not some grownups, but four little girls while they were praying to the same god the white man taught them to pray to, and you and I see the government go down and can't find who did it.

Why, this man—he can find Eichmann hiding down in Argentina somewhere. Let two or three American soldiers, who are minding somebody else's business way over in South Vietnam, get killed, and he'll send battleships, sticking his nose in their business. He wanted to send troops down to Cuba and make them have what he calls free elections—this old cracker who doesn't have free elections in his own country. No, if you never see me another time in your life, if I die in the morning, I'll die saying one thing: the ballot or the bullet, the ballot or the bullet.

If a Negro in 1964 has to sit around and wait for some cracker senator to filibuster when it comes to the rights of black people, why, you and I should hang our heads in shame. You talk about a march on Washington in 1963, you haven't seen anything. There's some more going down in '64. And this time they're not going like they went last year. They're not going singing. "We Shall Overcome." They're not going with white friends. They're not going with placards already painted for them. They're not going with round-trip tickets. They're going with one-way tickets.

And if they don't want that nonnonviolent army going down there, tell them to bring the filibuster to a halt. The black nationalists aren't going to wait. Lyndon B. Johnson is the head of the Democratic Party. If he's for civil rights, let him go into the Senate next week and declare himself. Let him go in there right now and declare himself. Let him go in there and denounce the Southern branch of his party. Let him go in there right now and take a moral stand—right now, not later. Tell him, don't wait until election time. If he waits too long, brothers and sisters, he will be responsible for letting a condition develop in this country which will create a climate that will bring seeds up out of the ground with vegetation on the end of them looking like something these people never dreamed of. In 1964, it's the ballot or the bullet. Thank you.

5.5   Henry Hampton and Steve Fayer

The Meredith March, 1966: "Hit Them Now"

Henry Hampton is coauthor of Voices of Freedom: An Oral History of the Civil Rights Movement from the 1950s through the 1980s. *He was a documentary filmmaker who produced the* Eyes on the Prize *series. Hampton died in 1989.*
Steve Fayer, a series writer for Eyes on the Prize, *is coauthor of* Voices of Freedom.

JJames Meredith wore a pith helmet against the Mississippi sun and carried an ivory-headed African cane as he walked down U.S. 51 on June 6, 1966. Just the day before, the thirty-two-year-old civil rights veteran had set out on a 220-mile "March Against Fear" from Memphis, Tennessee, to Jackson, Mississippi. His announced purpose: to encourage blacks in his home state to register and vote. Four years earlier, when Meredith had integrated the Oxford campus of Ole Miss, he had strong support from the major civil rights organizations and the federal government. Then, his was a cause the movement was ready to embrace. Now, at the beginning of his 1966 march, Meredith, a man few could get close to or understand, was ignored by almost all of his former allies. "A black **Don Quixote**," *Newsweek* called him.

Crossing the state line into Mississippi with only four supporters in his entourage, Meredith seemed to be making an eccentric and empty gesture, marching in a personal crusade at a time when the nation had grown tired of marches. Then, on the second day, a white unemployed hardware clerk from Memphis, forty-year-old Aubrey James Norvell, trampled out a hiding place in a thicket of oak and honeysuckle at the roadside and waited. "I just want James Meredith," Norvell called when the marchers appeared. And then he fired his sixteen-gauge automatic shotgun. Two of three blasts found their mark and sent Meredith sprawling.

An Associated Press photographer snapped Meredith writhing in a pool of blood. In a matter of hours, Meredith's lonely walk became, in the words of one reporter, "the biggest parade since Selma." The first wire service bulletins on the shooting mistakenly indicated that Meredith had been killed. Later, he was reported in satisfactory condition at a Memphis hospital after emergency surgery.

Martin Luther King, Jr., rushed from Atlanta to be at Meredith's bedside. Joining him were Stokely Carmichael, just elected chairman of SNCC, Floyd McKissick of CORE, and the older moderates—the NAACP's Roy Wilkins and Whitney Young of the National Urban League. SNCC program secretary Cleveland Sellers traveled to Memphis with Carmichael.

Cleveland Sellers

In Memphis we met with Martin King and Floyd McKissick from CORE and some of the other leaders who had come in from around the country. In looking at the march we recognized that Meredith was planning to march through what was essentially the second congressional district in Mississippi. That was the area that we had all worked in the summer of '64 and through 1965. So we felt comfortable that we knew many of the people that could be intricately involved in giving the march some perspective and focus. At that point we seized upon the opportunity to go forward and encourage that the march would continue.

On the first day, Floyd McKissick and Martin King and Stokely and myself and a few other people went out to continue to march. We thought that the theme of the march, March Against Fear, was very important. And we thought that not following through on that would send a negative message to the black community and a very positive message to the white Citizens' Council and Ku Klux Klan types. We also thought that it was an opportunity to begin to raise the question of blacks controlling their own destiny. We were in areas that was almost seventy percent black, and we felt like we could begin to talk about registering to vote, and we talked about empowerment and we talked about using the model of Lowndes County and adapting it to Mississippi. We also believed that it was time for the black community to take the responsibility for assuring that it had a successful march. We had seen Selma and we had seen Albany, Georgia, and we had seen Birmingham, where we had an entourage of press and leaders and once the objective was reached, they would leave behind a vacuum and a lot of frustration. If there was going to be a march, we wanted [local] people to share in the leadership development, share in making decisions on what the march objectives were. We wanted them to share in providing the resources and in the actual marching. We felt the Meredith March could be a showcase, a focal point where we could begin to talk about doing programs differently from the way they had been done across the South prior to that time.

We returned to the Lorraine Motel in Memphis, and at that point we met up with Roy Wilkins and Whitney Young, representing the NAACP and the Urban League. SNCC had some concerns about how the march would unfold. We raised several issues. One was the inclusion of the Deacons for Defense [an armed, black self-defense group from Bogalusa, Louisiana]. We wanted them to be involved in the march. Two, we did not want a national call to be made. We wanted to keep the march indigenous to Mississippi, indigenous to the South primarily. The question of a March Against Fear impacted directly on people in Mississippi, and we felt like in order to make that statement they had to be involved. They had to make the step out and say that I am not frightened by vigilantes and Ku Klux Klans and people who are going to try to oppress me and take advantage of me. What happened then is that those more moderate civil rights leaders, Roy Wilkins and Whitney Young, were reluctant about the inclusion of the Deacons for Defense. They wanted to have a national call and they wanted to bring in people so that they could generate the resources external to Mississippi to carry off the march. We discussed that issue, we were able to lobby Floyd McKissick to our position, and then it came to a vote, and the final decision had to be made by Martin King. Martin King did side with us in the effort to put the march together, and that infuriated Roy Wilkins and Whitney Young. They went through the whole litany of calling us rabble-rousers and saying we didn't understand the dynamics of the civil rights movement and all that, and they slammed their briefcases shut and stomped out of the meeting, going back to New York.

King agreed to participate, but only after getting assurance that the march would not exclude whites and would be nonviolent. SNCC was successful, however, in arguing for the inclusion of the Deacons for Defense and Justice.

Cleveland Sellers

The Deacons for Defense was a group whose responsibility was to defend their communities or themselves against attack. It was never a group of retaliation. We involved them to protect the marchers. They were in fact armed and their responsibility was to make sure that the march was safe. If they could eliminate an aggressive action or eliminate sharpshooters or people taking advantage of the march, then that's what they would do. We tried to learn from them. They would tell us certain things we needed to know along the way. They would go into the wooded areas. They would check cars out. They would keep their eyes on all of these things, but the spirit was around self-defense. This is something emerging inside of the movement. What we're beginning to see is a shift away from just talking about nonviolence, and in order for you to shift away you see other philosophies and other tactics creeping in. Now we're talking about empowerment. We're talking about black empowerment. Not only registering to vote—we'd already secured the 1965 Voting Rights Act—but how to vote and how to get the kind of power so that you wouldn't have to worry about being a registered voter and the person who you have elected is the one who comes to your house and beats you up and drags you off to jail. We were beginning to raise those kinds of questions and to try to find solutions to the problems that people faced in their communities.

Floyd McKissick had recently succeeded James Farmer as national director of CORE, having previously served as one of its attorneys. In 1951, McKissick had been the first black to receive a law degree from the University of North Carolina. He had known James Meredith for many years.

Floyd McKissick

When we got on the Meredith March, the Deacons for Defense and Justice came to protect the marchers from attacks when the law enforcement officers would not respond. They were armed. And the question was: Are we going to tell the Deacons to go home? And someone said, "They basically grew out of CORE organization and community organizations in Mississippi. You tell them to go home." I said, "No, I refuse to tell them to go home. I think they have a right to be on the march. I think we should tell them, as we tell everybody else, that we believe in nonviolence, but I'll not tell these people to go home, because they have a right to be here and protect themselves and other people." In other words, I don't believe in a standard for white and a standard for black. I think that violence and nonviolence is equally distributed among all races.

> Andrew Young had been opposed to the march on the grounds that King was overextended. Also, unlike Selma, this was not an SCLC-sponsored event, and the role of whites and the role of nonviolence were hotly debated.

Andrew Young

The SCLC was aggressively nonviolent. But Martin made distinctions between defensive violence and retaliatory violence. He was far more understanding of defensive violence. Martin's attitude was you can never fault a man for protecting his home and his wife. We saw the Deacons as defending their home and their wives and children. Now Martin said he would never himself resort to violence even in self-defense, but he would not demand that of others. That was a religious commitment into which one had to grow.

The role of white people on the march began to be discussed. There was a decision on the part of some of the blacks in SNCC that we don't just want to get people free, we want to develop indigenous black leadership. And one of the ways to force the development of indigenous black leadership is to get rid of all this paternalism. Now, they and we were paternalists ourselves in many ways, because we were outsiders just as whites were. That's the reason SCLC never went along with that. We felt yes, we have to develop local leadership, but you don't want to blame the frustrations of local leadership development on whites alone. We were also partially responsible for usurping some of the leadership.

Kwame Ture (Stokely Carmichael)

The disagreement over whites was not on having whites. The disagreement was on having white leadership on the march. The question of white leadership in SNCC was one which had already raised conflict since 1963 in the March on Washington. SNCC was very clear here. White liberals could work with SNCC but they could not tell SNCC what to do or what to say. We were very strong about this because of the inferiority imposed upon our people through exploitation that makes it appear as if we are not capable of leading ourselves.

Cleveland Sellers

The three groups—SNCC, CORE, and the SCLC—began to pool our legal resources and contact the people for setting up mass meetings and rallies along the highway. We began to get people involved. The idea of Martin Luther King marching against fear in Mississippi was an idea whose time had come, and many people responded from throughout the state. So we were successful in generating the interest and the crowds that we would not have generated if we had gone the other way and made the calls for a number of people to come in from the North. But we did not want the march to be overtaken by a lot of whites from outside of the community, as had happened in some of the other communities. We thought that it became important, if we are talking about self-determination and pride and effort against fear, for black folk to make that statement.

Kwame Ture (Stokely Carmichael)

We decided to use the march for an education purpose. Number one, we wanted to push strongly our struggle against the war in Vietnam. It's one of the areas where we started to hit them with it seriously. And of course we wanted to throw out "Black Power" [as a slogan] for the mass of the people. So we prepared the terrain.

Brother Willie Ricks was sent ahead as the advance scout, and as we grew bigger sometimes he would have twenty or forty people under his direction. His task was to spread them out to plantations, speak to the sharecroppers. Tell them the march was coming through and to give little Black Power speeches to get the reaction. About three nights before Greenwood, about two o'clock in the morning, Ricks came back and he was giving a report. Cleve Sellers was sitting next to me, and Ricks was saying, "We ought to drop it now. The people are ready for it. I said it the other day and they dropped their hoes." And I said to Cleve, "You know, you sent the wrong man out, because we need a clear analysis here and this man is given to exaggerations and talking all sorts of nonsense in hyperbolic terms." Ricks said, "I'm telling you the truth." So as Ricks was telling us about how great the people were, we were moving into Greenwood. Now, I myself had been in Greenwood. I had worked in the [SNCC] project there. I had spent time in the jail in Greenwood so many times the police knew me. The police chief knew me. Everyone in town knew me. So we decided we couldn't go wrong in Greenwood, SNCC's strongest base in the Delta. This is where we will launch Black Power. Unfortunately for the police, we went to set up some tents there and the police had decided to arrest me. So when I got arrested, Ricks was on the side there. He said, "Let them arrest you. We'll get you out of jail, and you come out and make the speech tonight." And he disappears. Anyway, I went to jail but I was bought out, and when I was released it was at night. The speeches were going on, and I was in line. Ricks came back and said, "We have everything prepared. We're ready for Black Power. We've spoke about it all day."

> Although no national call had been issued, David Dawley, a student at the University of Michigan, joined the Meredith March along with a number of other whites.

David Dawley

That afternoon in Greenwood, I was in a crowd that was listening to speakers from a porch. Willie Ricks from SNCC was introduced, and Ricks was angry and he was lashing out at whites like a cracking whip. And as he talked, there was a chill, there was a feeling of a rising storm. Willie Ricks asked people what they wanted, and they answered, "Freedom Now." Willie Ricks exhorted the crowd to demand not "Freedom Now" but "Black Power." He kept talking at the crowd, and when he asked what they wanted, they answered "Freedom Now," but more answered "Black Power," until eventually "Black Power" began to dominate until finally everyone together was thundering, "Black Power, Black Power." And that was chilling. That was frightening. Suddenly the happy feeling of the march was threatened. Suddenly I felt threatened. It seemed like a division between black and white. It seemed like a hit on well-intentioned northern whites like me, that the message from Willie Ricks was "Go home, white boy, we don't need you."

Around the tents [later that day] after listening to Willie Ricks, the atmosphere was clearly different. There was a surface of more anger and more hostility. There was a release of more hostility toward whites. Suddenly, I was a "honky," not "David." When there was small groups of two or three younger black men who might be talking to each other, where a couple of days earlier we might stand around and listen, now they told us to "move out of the way, honky." Others wanted us to know that there was no danger and that we were welcome. But clearly now there was a division.

> In a speech he gave the evening of June 16, in Greenwood, Stokely Carmichael issued the call for Black Power in a more public forum than the porches that Willie Ricks had used earlier.

Kwame Ture (Stokely Carmichael)

Luckily for us, that night King had to go to do a taped television thing, I think for "Meet the Press," in Memphis. So he was not there. He had other people there, but they were not a threat to us. It meant the whole night belonged to us and we were in Greenwood, in SNCC territory. So Ricks had everybody primed. He said, "Just get to your speech. We're going against 'Freedom Now,' we're going for 'Black Power.' Don't hit too much on 'Freedom Now' but hit the need for the power." So we built up on the need for power and just when I got there, before I got it, Ricks was there, saying, "Hit them now. Hit them now." And I kept saying, "Give me time. Give me time." When we finally got there and we dropped it—Black Power— of course they had been primed and they responded immediately. But I, myself, to be honest, didn't expect that enthusiastic response. And the enthusiastic response not only shocked me but gave me more energy to carry it on further. By the time we got down that night, SCLC was running around everywhere. We knew it was finished. We had made our victory. They could not bring Freedom Now back. It was over. From now on, it was Black Power. We continued with the slogan. King was immediately rushed back. It was too late. We had a meeting the following morning where King tried his best to ask me not to use the term Black Power. But I told him that really I could not do that. That this was an organizational decision, not mine. And like him, I represent an organization and I must represent that organization or I resign from the position which I hold, and I was not prepared to do that, so we would have to use the term.

We expected the press to be completely against us, to use all sorts of terms, but that was not our problem. King was on the march. And since King was on the march, they could not attack the march without attacking King. And King could not leave the march. So their hands would be tied. King obviously could not attack us. If you will look everywhere, King has never attacked Black Power. He said he wouldn't use the term, because of the connotation it conjures up.

Floyd McKissick

I liked the expression Black Power, and it was not the first time it had been used. It wasn't the first time that Stokely had used it. I had used the expression, and many other people had used it. [Writers W.E.B.] Du Bois and Richard Wright certainly had used the expression of black people getting their power. I think it scared people because they did not understand. They could not subtract violence from power. They could only see power as having a violent instrument accompanying it. In the last analysis, it was a question of how Black Power would be defined. And it was never really defined. We talked in CORE about constructive militancy as Black Power. As we marched, we would give the African cry for freedom. Many people were disturbed because, they said, this is becoming too non-American. We're going back to our roots too much and SNCC was talking about nationalism at that time. These were some of the fuzzy parts of the march, which some of the other national organizations objected to.

> After Greenwood, the media would not let go of the Black Power idea, and neither would Stokely Carmichael. Night after night, he and the SNCC organizers called for Black Power, while King's followers countered with Freedom Now.
>
> Arlie Schardt, a correspondent for *Time* magazine, had been covering the civil rights movement since early 1962.

Arlie Schardt

Greenwood was a kind of milestone because it was there, although Stokely Carmichael had been talking about Black Power from the very beginning of the march, that it was really dramatized. Stokely gave a very, very fiery address that evening, in which he basically told the group that they couldn't count on support or cooperation or help from the white man, and that blacks had to do it on their own, that blacks were being sent off to fight and die in Vietnam and yet they couldn't even vote. They had no rights at all in the communities where they lived, and they were going to have to gather their own courage and not worry about outside help. He began leading the crowd in a chant for Black Power, which of course many people began interpreting as a call for black separatism.

I wasn't startled by it because I had heard Stokely talking for several days by this time, along the same line. There were talks as we walked along the highway. He made brief little talks, even to the chief of police in Greenwood. We went around during the day and he made calls where there were officials that he knew well and told them that it was a new day and that Negroes—at that time the word *black* was just beginning to be used—were tired of waiting and that they were going to gain their rights on their own. But it was a change, even though I knew him well and we had had many a meal together and walked on marches together. His attitude toward me as a white reporter and toward other white reporters he knew just as well was different. There was a definite barrier between us, and he wanted us to call him "sir" from then on; he wanted a little more formality, at least publicly, in our relationship, which had been very casual in the past because there had been a tremendous amount of dialogue and long interviews and everything. It was "Keep your distance, this is a new day now, and I mean it at all levels." I'm paraphrasing Stokely, but there was a definite change there, no question about it.

The media coverage of the march was interesting because there was a tendency, I thought, to overplay it. There were a couple of reasons for that. One is that there were a lot of reporters who were new to this beat who were coming in from a lot of papers around the country as the march began to pick up momentum and as this Black Power theme began to get some publicity. The second reason was that the theme was never really clearly articulated. Or at least what it meant was never clearly defined. And so it was open to very broad interpretations. There were some whites, for their own reasons, who wanted to take this as a signal of real black hostility and enmity, and there were others who simply didn't know how to read what was being said. Therefore it was left open to the idea that this was a dramatic change in the civil rights movement in which blacks were telling the whites, "Get out and forget it. We're on our own," and that it was antiwhite. But there was a lot of confusion because there was no unanimity about this. Most of the black leaders were still arguing strongly for integration as the only approach to take to achieve justice throughout the country.

Andrew Young

Martin saw Stokely as a young man with tremendous potential and ability. Black Power itself was something Martin disagreed with tactically. In fact, what he said all the time was "Jews have power, but if you ever accuse them of power, they deny it. Catholics have power, but they always deny it. In a pluralistic society, to have real power you have to deny it. And if you go around claiming power, the whole society turns on you and crushes you." It was not black power that he was against, it was the slogan Black Power, because he said, "If you really have power you don't need a slogan."

David Dawley

We left the march a couple of days later. Basically we had come for a few days. We had to return to finals. We were not unhappy to leave the march. When we came, we had felt wanted. We felt needed. When we left, we didn't feel wanted. So we went back to Michigan to fight another war. We were activists. We were interested in changing the United States. So we listened to what SNCC was saying, and there was a sense that this was a time when blacks had the right to define the movement and that blacks would lead the strategy. And the strategy coming out of Black Power from SNCC was that blacks should organize with blacks and whites should organize with whites. I accepted that strategy. My friends accepted that strategy. So we moved on to work with whites on issues that we felt we should work with. In the next year that was not civil rights, that was Vietnam.

> Some concerned Americans began to wonder if the call to Black Power was a call for a race war. Vice President Hubert Humphrey, long a civil rights supporter, called Black Power "reverse racism." Roy Wilkins called the new slogan "the father of hate and the mother of violence." Many blacks, however, welcomed the idea. *Ebony* editor Lerone Bennett, Jr., wrote that Black Power "was

in the air" before Carmichael made his speech. "It was in the heads and hearts of long-suffering men who had paid an enormous price for minuscule gains."

On June 24, James Meredith rejoined the march in the town of Canton. There had been violence all along the route in Mississippi—near Hernando, when Meredith was shot; in Philadelphia, where King and the marchers were attacked by whites with hoes and ax handles; and in Canton on June 23, when state and local police had attacked with tear gas and clubs—but the protest had not lost sight of Meredith's goal. By the time he led the march into Jackson, three weeks after he first set out, four thousand new black voters had been registered in Mississippi, a state where only 7 percent of eligible black voters had been allowed on the rolls.

The march also provided an electrifying phrase for the movement's lexicon. "Black Power" became a rallying cry heard by blacks far beyond Greenwood, Mississippi. It also inspired fear in a country living through its fourth year of urban unrest. Black Power touched a nerve, in a very nervous white America.

5.6   Stokely Carmichael (Kwame Ture)

Toward Black Liberation

Stokely Carmichael (Kwame Ture) was the former chairman of SNCC. Active in voter registration throughout the South, Carmichael is credited with developing the concept of black power. He wrote Black Power: The Politics of Liberation in America *with Charles Hamilton, a political scientist. He died in 1998.*

Traditionally, for each new ethnic group, the route to social and political integration into America's pluralistic society has been through the organization of their own institutions with which to represent their communal needs within the larger society. This is simply stating what the advocates of black power are saying. The strident outcry, *particularly* from the liberal community, that has been evoked by this proposal can only be understood by examining the historic relationship between Negro and White power in this country.

Negroes are defined by two forces, their blackness and their powerlessness. There have been traditionally two communities in America. The White community, which controlled and defined the forms that all institutions within the society would take, and the Negro community which has been excluded from participation in the power decisions that shaped the society, and has traditionally been dependent upon, and subservient to the White community.

This has not been accidental. The history of every institution of this society indicates that a major concern in the ordering and structuring of the society has been the maintaining of the Negro community in its condition of dependence and oppression. This has not been on the level of individual acts of discrimination between individual whites against individual Negroes, but as total acts by the White community against the Negro community. This fact cannot be too strongly emphasized—that racist assumptions of white superiority have been so deeply ingrained in the structure of the society that it infuses its entire functioning, and is so much a part of the national subconscious that it is taken for granted and is frequently not even recognized.

Let me give an example of the difference between individual racism and institutionalized racism, and the society's response to both. When unidentified white terrorists bomb a Negro Church and kill five children, that is an act of individual racism, widely deplored by most segments of the society. But when in that same city, Birmingham, Alabama, not five but 500 Negro babies die each year because of a lack of proper food, shelter and medical facilities, and thousands more are destroyed and maimed physically, emotionally and intellectually because of conditions of poverty and deprivation in the ghetto, that is a function of institutionalized racism. But the society either pretends it doesn't know of this situation, or is incapable of doing anything meaningful about it. And this resistance to doing anything meaningful about conditions in that ghetto comes from the fact that the ghetto is itself a product of a combination of forces and special interests in the white community, and the groups that have access to the resources and power to change that situation benefit, politically and economically, from the existence of that ghetto.

It is more than a figure of speech to say that the Negro community in America is the victim of white imperialism and colonial exploitation. This is in practical economic and political terms true. There are over 20 million black people comprising ten percent of this nation. They for the most part live in well-defined areas of the country—in the shanty-towns and rural black belt areas of the South, and increasingly in the slums of northern and western industrial cities. If one goes into any Negro community, whether it be in Jackson, Miss., Cambridge, Md. or Harlem, N.Y., one will find that the same combination of political, economic, and social forces are at work. The people in the Negro community do not control the resources of that community, its political decisions, its law enforcement, its housing standards; and even the physical ownership of the land, houses, and stores *lie outside that community.* . . .

In recent years the answer to these questions which has been given by most articulate groups of Negroes and their white allies, the "liberals" of all stripes, has been in terms of something called "integration." According to the advocates of integration, social justice will be accomplished by "integrating the Negro into the mainstream institutions of the society from which he has been traditionally excluded." It is very significant that each time I have heard this formulation it has been in terms of "the Negro," the individual Negro, rather than in terms of the community.

This concept of integration had to be based on the assumption that there was nothing of value in the Negro community and that little of value could be created among Negroes, so the thing to do was to siphon off the "acceptable" Negroes into the surrounding middle-class white community. Thus the goal of the movement for integration was simply to loosen up the restrictions barring the entry of Negroes into the white community. Goals around which the struggle took place, such as public accommodation, open housing, job opportunity on the executive level (which is easier to deal with than the problem of semi-skilled and blue collar jobs which involve more far-reaching economic adjustments), are quite simply middle-class goals, articulated by a tiny group of Negroes who had middle-class aspirations. It is true that the student demonstrations in the South during the early sixties, out of which SNCC came, had a similar orientation. But while it is hardly a concern of a black sharecropper, dishwasher, or welfare recipient whether a certain fifteen-dollar-a-day motel offers accommodations to Negroes, the overt symbols of white superiority and the imposed limitations on the Negro community had to be destroyed. Now, black people must look beyond these goals, to the issues of collective power.

Such a limited class orientation was reflected not only in the program and goals of the civil rights movement, but in its tactics and organization. It is very significant that the two oldest and most "respectable" civil rights organizations have constitutions which *specifically* prohibit partisan political activity. CORE once did, but changed that clause when it changed its orientation toward black power. But this is perfectly understandable in terms of the strategy and goals of the older organizations. The civil rights movement saw its role as a kind of liaison between the powerful white community and the dependent Negro one. The dependent status of the black community apparently was unimportant since—if the movement were successful—it was going to blend into the white community anyway. We made no pretense of organizing and developing institutions of community power in the Negro community, but appealed to the conscience of white institutions of power. The posture of the civil rights movement was that of the dependent, the suppliant. The theory was that without attempting to create any organized base of political strength itself, the civil rights movement could, by forming coalitions with various "liberal" pressure organizations in the white community—liberal reform clubs, labor unions, church groups, progressive civic groups—and at times one or other of the major political parties—influence national legislation and national social patterns.

I think we all have seen the limitations of this approach. We have repeatedly seen that political alliances based on appeals to conscience and decency are chancy things, simply because institutions and political organizations have no consciences outside their own special interests. The political and social rights of Negroes have been and always will be negotiable and expendable the moment they conflict with the interests of our "allies." If we do not learn from history, we are doomed to repeat it, and that is precisely the lesson of the Reconstruction. Black people were allowed to register, vote and participate in politics because it was to the advantage of powerful white allies to promote this. But this was the result of white decision, and it was ended by other white men's decision before any political base powerful enough to challenge that decision could be established in the southern Negro community. (Thus at this point in the struggle Negroes have no assurance—save a kind of idiot optimism and faith in a society whose history is one of racism—that if it were to become necessary, even the painfully limited gains thrown to the civil rights movement by the Congress will not be revoked as soon as a shift in political sentiments should occur.)

The major limitation of this approach was that it tended to maintain the traditional dependence of Negroes, and of the movement. We depended upon the good-will and support of various groups within the white community whose interests were not always compatible with ours. To the extent that we depended on the financial support of other groups, we were vulnerable to their influence and domination.

* * * *

Now we've got to talk about this thing called the serious coalition. You know what that's all about? That says that black folks and their white liberal friends can get together and overcome. We have to examine our white liberal friends. And I'm going to call names this time around. We've got to examine our white liberal friends who come to Mississippi and march with us, and can afford to march because our mothers, who are their maids, are taking care of their house and their children; we got to examine them [applause]. Yeah; I'm going to speak the truth tonight. I'm going to tell you what a white liberal is. You talking about a white college kid joining hands with a black man in the ghetto, that college kid is fighting for the right to wear a beard and smoke pot, and we fighting for our lives [cheers and applause]. We fighting for our lives [continued applause].

That missionary comes to the ghetto one summer, and the next summer he's in Europe, and he's our ally. That missionary has a black mammy, and he stole our black mammy from us. Because while she was home taking care of them, she couldn't take care of us. That's not our ally [applause]. Now I met some of those white liberals on the march, and I asked one man, I said, look here brother. I said, you make what, about twenty-five thousand dollars a year? He mumbled. I said, well dig. Look here. Here are four black Mississippians. They make three dollars a day picking cotton. See they have to march; you can afford to march. I say, here's what we do. Take your twenty-five thousand dollars a year divide it up evenly. Let all five of you make five thousand dollars a year. He was for everybody working hard by the sweat of their brow [laughter and shouts]. That's a white liberal, ladies and gentlemen. That's a white liberal. You can't form a coalition with people who are economically secure. College students are economically secure; they've already got their wealth; we fighting to get ours. And for us to get it is going to mean tearing down their system, and they are not willing to work for their own destruction. Get that into your own minds now [applause]. Get that into your own minds now [continued applause]. . . .

When I talk about Black Power, it is presumptuous for any white man to talk about it, because I'm talking to black people [applause]. And I've got news for our liberal friend Bobby Kennedy. I got news for that white man. When he talks about his Irish Catholic power that made him to the position where he is that he now uses black votes in New York City to run for the presidency in 1972, he ought to not say a word about Black Power. Now the Kennedys built a system of purely Irish Catholic power with Irish Nationalism interwoven into it. Did you know that? And that's how come they run, rule, own Boston lock stock and barrel including all the black people inside it. That's Irish power. And that man going to get up and tell you-all; well he shouldn't talk about Black Power. He ran and won in New York City on Black Power; his brother became president because Black Power made him president [shouts and applause]. Black Power made his brother president [continued applause]. And he's got the white nerve to talk about Black Power [continued applause].

The Limits of Nonviolence

Howard Zinn is a professor emeritus of political science at Boston University, an activist, and author of SNCC: The New Abolitionists *and* A People's History of the United States.

When I went to Albany, Georgia, during the first wave of demonstrations and mass arrests in December of 1961, I had been in Atlanta for five years and thought I had learned some important things about the South, as observer and minor participant in the civil rights struggle. I had written an optimistic article for *Harper's Magazine* about the possibility of changing the *behavior* (not immediately his *thinking*) of the white southerner without violence, by playing upon his self-interest, whether through economic pressure or other means which would forcefully confront him with hard choices. And in Atlanta, I saw such changes come about, through the pressure of lawsuits, sit-ins, boycotts, and sometimes by just the threat of such actions. Nonviolence was not only hugely appealing as a concept. It worked.

And then I took a good look at Albany, and came back troubled. Eight months later, when the second crisis broke out in Albany, in the summer of 1962, I drove down again from Atlanta. The picture was the same. Again, mass demonstrations and mass arrests. Again, the federal government stood by impotent while the chief of police took control of the constitutional rights of citizens.

My optimism was shaken but still alive. To those people around me who said that Albany was a huge defeat, I replied that you could not measure victories and defeats only by tangible results in the desegregation of specific facilities, that a tremendous change had taken place in the thinking of Albany's Negroes, that expectations had been raised which could not be stilled until the city was transformed.

Today, over a year later, after studying events in Birmingham and Gadsden and Danville and Americus, after interviewing staff workers of the Student Nonviolent Coordinating Committee just out of jail in Greenwood, Mississippi, watching state troopers in action in Selma, Alabama, and talking at length to voter registration workers in Greenville, Mississippi, I am rethinking some of my old views. Albany, it seems to me, was the first dramatic evidence of a phenomenon which now has been seen often enough to be believed: that there is a part of the South impermeable by the ordinary activities of nonviolent direct action, a monolithic South completely controlled by politicians, police, dogs, and prod sticks, And for this South, special tactics are required.

One portion of the South has already been removed from the old Confederacy. This part of the South, represented by places like Richmond, Memphis, Nashville, Louisville, and Atlanta, is still fundamentally segregationist—as is the rest of the nation, North and South—but the first cracks have appeared in a formerly solid social structure. In these places, there is fluidity and promise, room for maneuver and pressure and accommodation; there is an economic elite sophisticated enough to know how badly it can be hurt by outright resistance, and political leaders shrewd enough to take cognizance of a growing Negro electorate. There will be much conflict yet in Atlanta and in Memphis. But the tactics of nonviolent direct action can force ever greater gains there.

Where Slavery Still Lingers

Then there is the South of Albany and Americus, Georgia; of Gadsden and Selma, Alabama; of Danville, Virginia; of Plaquemine, Louisiana; of Greenwood and Hattiesburg and Yazoo City, Mississippi—and a hundred other towns of the Black Belt. Here, where the smell of slavery still lingers, politicians are implacable, plantation owners relentless, policemen unchecked by the slightest fear of judgment. In these towns of the Black Belt, a solid stone wall separates black from white, and reason from fanaticism; nonviolent demonstrations smash themselves to bits against this wall, leaving pain, frustration, bewilderment, even though the basic resolve to win remains alive, and some kind of ingenuous optimism is left untouched by defeat after defeat.

I still believe that the Albany Movement, set back again and again by police power, has done a magnificent service to the Negroes of Albany—and ultimately, to the whites who live in that morally cramped town. I still believe that the three hundred Negroes who waited on line near the county courthouse in Selma, Alabama from morning to evening in the shadow of clubs and guns to register to vote, without even entering the doors of that courthouse, accomplished something. But I no longer hold that a simple repetition of such nonviolent demonstrative action— which effectively broke through barriers in the other part of the South—will bring victory. I am now convinced that the stone wall which blocks expectant Negroes in every town and village of the hard-core South, a wall stained with the blood of children, as well as others, and with an infinite capacity to absorb the blood of more victims—will have to be crumbled by hammer blows.

Federal Government Must Act

This can be done, it seems to me, in one of two ways. The first is a Negro revolt, armed and unswerving, in Mississippi, Alabama and southwest Georgia, which would result in a terrible waste of human life. That may be hard to avoid unless the second alternative comes to pass: the forceful intervention of the national government, to smash, with speed and efficiency, every attempt by local policemen or politicians to deprive Negroes (or others) of the rights supposedly guaranteed by the Constitution.

Unaware of the distinction between the two Souths, not called upon for such action in places like Atlanta and Nashville, and uncommitted emotionally and ideologically to racial equality as a first-level value, the national government has played the role of a hesitant, timorous observer. It will have to move into bold action, or face trouble such as we have not seen yet in the civil rights crisis. This is my thesis here, and the story of Albany, Georgia may help illustrate it.

Federal law was violated again and again in Albany, yet the federal government did not act. In effect, over a thousand Negroes spent time in prison, and thousands more suffered and sacrificed, in ways that cannot be expressed adequately on paper, as a mass substitute for federal action.

Judicial decisions in this century have made it clear that the Fourteenth Amendment, besides barring officials from dispensing unequal treatment on the basis of race, also prohibits them from interfering with the First Amendment rights of free speech, petition, and assembly. Yet in Albany over one thousand Negroes were locked up in some of the most miserable jails in the country for peacefully attempting to petition the local government for a redress of grievances. *And the Justice Department did nothing.*

Section 242 of the U.S. Criminal Code, which comes from the Civil Rights Act of 1866 and the Enforcement Act of 1870, creates a legal basis for prosecution of: "Whoever, under color of any law . . . wilfully subjects . . . any inhabitant of any State . . . to the deprivation of any rights, privileges, or immunities secured or protected by the Constitution and laws of the United States. . . . " Three times in succession, in November and December 1961, the police of the city of Albany, by arresting Negroes and whites in connection with their use of the terminal facilities in that city, violated a right which has been made clear beyond a shadow of a doubt. Yet the federal government took no action.

Today, the wheels of the nonviolent movement are churning slowly, in frustration, through the mud of national indifference which surrounds the stone wall of police power in the city of Albany. As if to give a final blow to the Albany Movement, the Department of Justice is now prosecuting nine of its leaders and members, who face jail sentences up to ten years, in connection with the picketing of a white grocer who had served on a federal jury. One of the defendants is Dr. W. G. Anderson, former head of the Albany Movement. Another is Slater King, now heading the Movement. *It is the bitterest of ironies that Slater King, who pleaded in vain for federal action while he himself was jailed, while his wife was beaten by a deputy sheriff, while his brother was beaten, is now being vigorously prosecuted by the U.S. Department of Justice on a charge which can send him to jail for five years.*

The simple and harsh fact, made clear in Albany, and reinforced by events in Americus, Georgia, in Selma and Gadsden, Alabama, in Danville, Virginia, in every town in Mississippi, is that the Federal Government abdicated its responsibility in the Black Belt. The Negro citizens of that area were left to the local police. The United States Constitution was left in the hands of Neanderthal creatures who cannot read it, and whose only response to it has been to grunt and swing their clubs.

Federal Presence Must Be Felt

The responsibility is that of the president of the United States, and no one else. It is his job to enforce the law. And the law is clear. Previously the civil rights movement joined in thrusting the responsibility on Congress when the president himself, without any new legislation, had the constitutional power to enforce the 14th Amendment in the Black Belt.

The immediate necessity is for a *permanent* federal presence in the Deep South. I am not talking of occupation by troops, except as an ultimate weapon. I am suggesting the creation of a special force of federal agents, stationed throughout the Deep South, and authorized to make immediate on-the-spot arrests of any local official who violates federal law. The action would be preventive, before a crisis has developed, and would snuff out incipient fires before they got going, by swift, efficient action. Such a force would have taken Colonel Al Lingo into custody as he was preparing to use his electric prod sticks on the Freedom Walkers crossing the border into Alabama. Such a force would have taken Governor [George] Wallace to the nearest federal prison the very first time he blocked the entrance of a Negro student into the University of

Alabama, and would have arrested Sheriff Jim Clark as he moved to drag those two SNCC youngsters off the steps of the federal building in Selma.

Many liberals are affronted by such a suggestion; they worry about civil war. My contention is that the white southerner submits—as do most people—to a clear show of authority; note how Governors Wallace and [Ross] Barnett gave in at the last moment rather than go to jail. Once southern police officials realize that the club is in the other hand, that *they* will be behind bars, that *they* will have to go through all the legal folderal of getting bond and filing appeal, etc. which thousands of Negroes have had to endure these past few years—things will be different. The national government needs to drive a wedge, as it began to do in the First Reconstruction, between the officialdom and the ordinary white citizen of the South, who is not a rabid brute but a vacillating conformist.

Burke Marshall, head of the Civil Rights Division of the Department of Justice, has been much disturbed by this suggestion of "a national police force or some other such extreme alternative." If a national police force is extreme, then the United States is already "extremist," because the Federal Bureau of Investigation is just that. It is stationed throughout the country and has the power to arrest anyone who violates federal law. Thus, it arrests those who violate the federal statutes dealing with bank robberies, interstate auto thefts and interstate kidnapping. But it does *not* arrest those who violate the civil rights laws. I am suggesting an organization of special agents, who will arrest violators of civil rights laws the way the F.B.I. arrests bank robbers.

The continued dependence on nonviolence by the civil rights movement is now at stake. Nonviolent direct action can work in social situations where there are enough apertures through which economic and political and moral pressure can be applied. But it is ineffective in a totally closed society, in those Black Belt towns of the Deep South where Negroes are jailed and beaten and the power structure of the community stands intact.

The late President Kennedy's political style was one of working from crisis to crisis rather than undertaking fundamental solutions—like a man who settles one debt by contracting another. This can go on and on, until the day of reckoning. And that day may come, in the civil rights crisis, this summer just before the election.

There is a strong probability that this July and August [1964] will constitute another "summer of discontent." The expectations among Negroes in the Black Belt have risen to the point where they cannot be quieted. CORE (Congress of Racial Equality), SCLC (Southern Christian Leadership Conference) and the intrepid youngsters of the Student Nonviolent Coordinating Committee, are determined to move forward.

With the probability high of intensified activity in the Black Belt this summer, the President will have to decide what to do. He can stand by and watch Negro protests smashed by the local police, with mass jailings, beatings, and cruelties of various kinds. Or he can take the kind of firm action suggested above, which would simply establish clearly what the Civil War was fought for a hundred years ago, the supremacy of the U.S. Constitution over the entire nation. If he does not act, the Negro community may be pressed by desperation to move beyond the nonviolence which it has maintained so far with amazing self-discipline.

Thus, in a crucial sense, the future of nonviolence as a means for social change rests in the hands of the President of the United States. And the civil rights movement faces the problem of how to convince him of this, both by words and by action. For, if nonviolent direct action seems to batter itself to death against the police power of the Deep South, perhaps its most effective use is against the national government. The idea is to persuade the executive branch to use its far greater resources of nonviolent pressure to break down the walls of totalitarian rule in the Black Belt.

The latest victim of this terrible age of violence—which crushed the life from four Negro girls in a church basement in Birmingham, and in this century has taken the lives of over fifty million persons in war—is President John F. Kennedy, killed by an assassin's bullet. To President Johnson will fall the unfinished job of ending the violence and fear of violence which has been part of the everyday life of the Negro in the Deep South.

Charles Payne

Mrs. Hamer Is No Longer Relevant

The Loss of the Organizing Tradition

Charles Payne, author of I've Got the Light of Freedom, The Organizing Tradition and the Mississippi Freedom Struggle, *is professor of African American studies, sociology, and urban affairs at Northwestern University and is the Charles Deering McCormick Professor of Teaching Excellence.*

Even the hatred of squalor
Makes the brow grow stern.
Even anger against injustice
Makes the voice grow harsh. Alas, we
Who wished to lay the foundations of kindness
Could not ourselves be kind.

—Bertolt Brecht

So my rationalization for it is that the kids tried the established methods and they tried at the expense of their lives, which is much different from the accommodating role of trying that had previously been used. . . . So they began to look for other answers.

—Ella Baker

On many college campuses today, Black student organizations do not use traditional titles for their officers. Instead of presidents and treasurers they have "facilitators" or "coordinators." On some campuses, there is not a single member of the organization with any idea why Black students forming organizations in the late 1960s didn't use the more common terms. The language chosen by the students of the sixties reflects the fact that they were still in touch, in greatly varying degrees, with an entire philosophy about social change that cautioned against hierarchy and centralized leadership. Contemporary students are almost entirely unaware of that heritage.

To take another example, columnist Clarence Page opens a recent Public Broadcasting documentary on Black conservatives by claiming that for most of this century civil rights leaders have focused on outside help rather than the Black community's own resources; now, he says, in the 1990s some conservative Black leaders are focusing on Black self-help. I suspect few viewers, including few Black viewers, will question his premise: that the civil rights movement was something that had little to do with the Black community's own sacrifices and resources. The ideological right has successfully appropriated the movement's history and reinscribed it to support the conservative line, and even contemporary Black activists are often sufficiently alienated from their own history as to not recognize its theft.

In the late sixties and early seventies, the themes of the community-organizing tradition—the developmental perspective, an emphasis on building relationships, respect for collective leadership, for bottom-up change, the expansive sense of how democracy ought to operate in everyday life, the emphasis on building for the long haul, the antibureaucratic ethos, the preference for addressing local issues—were reflected, in varying combinations, in some anti-poverty campaigns, in various forms of nationalist organizing, in struggles on college campuses. In some cases, Deep South organizers carried the organizing philosophy with them as they moved on to other struggles. One can certainly find contemporary examples of activists self-consciously working within the organizing tradition (and far more of activists using that tradition's rhetoric). It is still fair to say that the organizing tradition as a political and intellectual legacy of Black activists has been effectively lost, pushed away from the table by more top-down models.

In the sixties, organizing represented just one culture of activism among the several that made up the movement. It never had much visibility to those outside the movement. Outsiders saw the sit-ins, the Freedom Rides, Freedom Summer, Atlantic City, but not deeper traditions that lay underneath them. Nonetheless, at a critical juncture in our history, some of the country's most innovative and influential activists were working within and redefining an organizing tradition, and through them, the concerns of that tradition were part of the larger dialogue in the Black community about direction and means. That is seldom the case now.

In part certainly, organizing lost ground because to people hungry for change it often looked like such a tortuously slow road that people began experimenting with other activist styles. The radical-nationalist thrusts that came to dominate much Black activism after the mid-sixties represent not one but several distinguishable activist cultures, some of them diametrically opposed to the assumptions of the organizing tradition. Some—I stress the *some* here—of those operating under the new political banners had no problem with hierarchy so long as they could be at the top of it, no problem with cults of personality so long as they got to pick the personalities, little conception of individual growth as a political issue, more interest in the dramatic gesture than in building at the base, and little concern with building interpersonal relationships that reflected their larger values. The basic metaphor of solidarity became "nation," not "family." The last may be especially important. The larger movement—not just SNCC and not just the civil rights movement—underwent a loss of community similar to what happened at the local level in Greenwood. While their analysis was in fact growing sharper in many ways, movement activists increasingly lost the ability to relate to one another in human terms. Even had there been no other changes, that alone would probably have been enough to prevent much organizing. In the movement's sense of "organize," in the transformative sense, it is probably safe to say that you cannot organize people you do not respect. You can lead them, you can inspire them, you can make speeches at them, but you cannot organize them. Some of the more self-consciously radical thrusts, notwithstanding rhetoric to the contrary, were simply contemptuous of the individual.

Near the end of 1964, Bob Moses wrote that SNCC was like a boat in the water that had to be repaired to stay afloat but had to stay afloat in order to be repaired. Too many issues needed to be addressed simultaneously. Between the fall of 1964 and the spring of 1966, SNCC was trying to resolve a staggering number of questions, many of them products of the organization's disillusionment with American society. What did "integration" mean, and was the country worth integrating into? How would it be possible to accommodate both the need of individual members for freedom of conscience and action and the need of the organization for discipline? What was the proper role of whites in the context of increasing race consciousness among Blacks? How is it possible to provide leadership without being manipulative? Is it possible to be both moral and politically effective? How could the organization speak to economic inequalities, rural and urban? If neither the federal government nor liberals could be trusted, where were the movement's allies? Could allies or models be found in the Third World? How should the organization respond to the anger in the urban ghettoes and the periodic violent uprisings it generated? What are the limits on what local leadership can accomplish? Should existing social structures be reformed or new ones created? What was to be the role of women in the movement? What should be the movement's position on Vietnam?

Even had there been fewer questions, discussion about them was increasingly taking place in an atmosphere of mutual distrust and recriminations, a deteriorating social climate that would ultimately lead to SNCC members threatening one another with weapons, to members calling the police to settle disputes among themselves, to the members of one faction "firing" all the members of another faction and being "fired" by them in turn. We are still far from fully understanding the causes of these changes, but an important part of the explanation may be that the transition from the Beloved Community to Black Power was accompanied by a jettisoning of some of the moral and social anchors that had helped regulate relationships among activists when SNCC was in its community-organizing phase.

Even allowing for some nostalgic exaggeration on the part of early SNCC members, there is not much doubt that most members at that time really did find the movement an oasis of personal trust, an extended family more sustaining than some real families. Joyce Ladner remembers Medgar Evers introducing her to a CORE worker who had come into the state to lay groundwork for the Freedom Rides. "We didn't ask questions. You didn't ask questions back then. We just accepted him as he was." Bob Moses compared SNCC's ability to release from its members levels of personal energy that they themselves never knew they had to nuclear fusion. The sense of trust and community was an important part of that, and its erosion was an important part of the organization's growing ineffectiveness. Instead of making individuals feel larger and stronger, it made them weaker. "They began to sort of eat on each other," Ella Baker put it.

Jim Forman and Bob Moses always represented somewhat opposite tendencies in SNCC. Forman, while aware of the need for field workers to have considerable autonomy, thought the organization needed to be run like a real organization if it was going to be effective. Moses, while aware of the need for some minimal level of organizational discipline was much more afraid of the possibility of too much organization suffocating the spirit. These differences did not prevent them from working together. In the wake of the 1964 Summer Project, they jointly developed a plan to expand SNCC's range of operation and to take advantage of the momentum created by the Summer Project. Called the Black Belt Project, the intention was to establish new projects in counties with large Black populations, from Virginia to Texas, this time using Black volunteers to minimize racial conflict as well as the chances of undermining the confidence of local participants. Preliminary inquiries suggested that both Black college students and local Black communities were going to be receptive to the idea. The plan was introduced for approval at a staff meeting that fall but never fully discussed. As soon as it was introduced, some members began questioning the motives of its authors and arguing that there should have been more staff input in its development, reacting as if it were a final decision rather than a proposal. Discussion got side-tracked into a consideration of the basic issue of decision-making. Some members objected to the plan, apparently without revealing their real motives for doing so. Some took the plan to be a power-play on the part of those who had done the preliminary planning. Apparently, in that climate, neither Forman nor Moses felt comfortable pushing the plan. The plan was tabled. Forman later wrote that the kind of confusion that characterized discussion of the Black Belt plan would have been "unimaginable" one or two years earlier. SNCC had then been a smaller, more tightly knit group, "moving on the assumption of great unity of purpose and good intentions as well as a willingness to compromise."

The inability to implement the Black Belt Project was a sign of things to come. Time and again, the substance of ideas could not be discussed because of a climate of suspicion and emotional strain, so that the organization was unable to implement any new projects or even effectively maintain old ones. The climate would become progressively more debilitating. Mary King noted:

> Until late 1965 it was possible to disagree in SNCC and yet not feel reviled, because the underlying bonds were strong. Personal hostility was now [in 1965] being expressed. This did not feel like SNCC to me. It was foreign—dissonant.

Mrs. Hamer commented on the changes at least once. In late 1966 at a dinner at which SNCC workers were honoring her, Mrs. Hamer "turned upon her old friends, as much in sadness as in anger, for growing 'cold' and unloving."

One of the factors contributing to the new and unhealthy climate was the expansion of the staff. At the end of the Summer Project, about eighty volunteers elected to stay on, a decision approved with some misgiving by the staff. The Mississippi staff almost doubled in size. At the same rime, the increased national visibility of SNCC following the Summer Project attracted new members to SNCC projects across the South and outside of it. In late 1963, the organization only had about one hundred fifty full-time staff. By the summer of 1965, it had swollen to more than two hundred staff and two hundred fifty full-time volunteers. According to SNCC's Cleveland Sellers:

This growth, coupled with the changing nature of struggle, was responsible for the emergence of several opposing factions. Although SNCC had always contained individuals who strongly disagreed with each other on various minor issues, it had never really had to contend with large factions divided by basic political differences. I spent much of the spring and summer of 1965 attending long, involved staff meetings where the various factions haggled and argued over everything from the "true nature of freedom" to the cost of insurance.

It is misleading to suggest that early SNCC members disagreed only over "minor" matters, but disagreements in the early years seldom led to the rigid, politicized factions, each quick to suspect the worst of the other factions, that developed after 1964. If the expansion had not occurred so rapidly, or if it had come when the organization had a stable direction programmatically, or if SNCC had been a more hierarchical organization, or if the people coming in had come from social backgrounds more like those of the veterans, the effects might not have been so damaging. At the same time it was trying to reassess its entire program, respond to the morale problems caused by disillusionment with liberal America and by the lingering resentments from the debate over whether there should have even been a Summer Project, SNCC was adding a group of largely upper-middle-class white northerners to what had been predominantly a southern Black movement.

SNCC's membership had always come from diverse backgrounds. Mary King notes that the early members included rural Blacks, northern middle-class Blacks, upper-class southern Blacks, New England Quakers, Jews, white ethnics, members of the Left, and southern whites. "Our heterogeneity—a strength while we were small . . .—was strained to the breaking point when we expanded quickly. It resulted in irreconcilable schisms."

Organizational size was always an important consideration to Ella Baker. She generally preferred smaller organizations. She was much impressed by cell structures like that of the Communist party: "I don't think we had any more effective demonstration of organizing people for whatever purpose." She envisioned small groups of people working together but also retaining contact in some form with other such groups, so that coordinated action would be possible whenever large numbers really were necessary. I know of no place where she fully explains her thinking, but, given her values, it is almost certain that she would have been put off by the undemocratic tendencies of larger organizations as well as by their usual failure to provide the kind of environment that encouraged individual growth. I suspect that she also favored smaller organizations precisely because they were less likely to factionalize or develop climates of distrust.

The changing social base of its membership, as well as the rapid expansion in the number of members, contributed to the increasingly negative social climate. That climate, then, contributed to its inability to execute its program, which in turn aggravated internal relations even further. After 1964 there are more reports of staff members acting irresponsibly or just not working at all. In Greenwood, Mary Boothe remembers the post-1964 period as a time when there were staff meetings all the time but very little follow-up. There were similar problems across the state. Referring to the fall of 1964, Clayborne Carson writes:

Some of those involved in the Summer Project abandoned their responsibilities, citing fatigue and a desire to allow local black residents to assume greater control over civil rights activities in their communities. Freedom schools and community centers in Mississippi were closed, owing to the absence of dependable personnel. "People were wandering in and out of the organization," Marion Barry recalled. "Some worked, some didn't work." There was a noticeable increase in marijuana usage, which contributed to the discipline problems.

In the years between 1964 and 1966, Jack Newfield notes, "drinking, auto accidents, petty thievery, pot smoking, personality clashes, inefficiency and anti-white outbursts all increased." According to Forman, even some of those "who had come to SNCC as disciplined, dedicated workers became dysfunctional and disgusted within a year or two." After the winter of 1965, Cleveland Sellers remembers, "Although most of us were under twenty-five, we seemed to have aged. Our faces were haggard, our nerves overwrought. Arguments over trifles dominated all our meetings." He recalls relationships deteriorating to a point where two factions had a stand-off involving "pool cues, baseball bats, knives and a couple of pistols." The issue at stake was whether people at a conference could be admitted to breakfast without a meal ticket.

When Cleveland Sellers was elected program secretary in 1965 he was determined to set the house back in order, and he quickly sent letters to all staffers asking them to explain what they were doing. The move generated substantial resentment among some old members, who thought SNCC should still operate like an extended family, and some newer members, who thought it smacked of authoritarianism. The various initiatives by Sellers and others were insufficient to halt the decline. By 1966, SNCC projects in Mississippi had weakened to the point where both the NAACP and SCLC were considering expanding their activities to take advantage of the vacuum.

Factions contributed to programmatic ineffectiveness. Sellers describes two of the important factions as the Floaters and the Hardliners, putting himself in the latter group. His admittedly biased description portrays Floaters as equally divided between Blacks and whites, generally well-educated and committed to integrationist ideals. They were resistant to organizational discipline, upholding the right of the individual to follow the dictates of individual conscience, an important principle in early SNCC. "Go where the spirit say go," they used to say, "Do what the spirit say do." In the early years, the small size of the organization and the fact that the membership was so highly self-selected probably ensured that personal freedom wouldn't too often become personal license. In later years. according to Miss Baker, "the right of people to participate in the decisions that affect their lives . . . began to be translated into the idea that each person working had a right to decide what ought to be done. So you began to do your own thing."

Hardliners tended to be Blacks, with less formal education than Floaters, were more likely to be field organizers, and were less concerned with personal freedom than with organizational effectiveness, which they saw as requiring a greater degree of centralization and accountability. In retrospect, Mary King thought that while the problems were difficult ones, they could have been resolved had the discussion not taken place in an atmosphere of suspicion and paranoia.

Program ineffectiveness was probably also a function of the reluctance of some new members to work with local leaders in the old way. On the one hand,

Ivanhoe Donaldson, who had driven truckloads of food to Leflore during the winter of 1962–63, had moved to Columbus and, cooperating with local leaders, had set up what appeared to be a very promising community development corporation. On the other hand, Carson attributes the modest success of the attempt to organize in Vine City ghetto in Atlanta to the failure of the leadership "to acquire the support of strong, indigenous adult leaders who had traditionally provided entree for SNCC field secretaries." Many of those in the leadership of the project were relatively recent members of SNCC. Where the veterans were almost always respectful of local leadership, sometimes to the point of romanticizing it, some of the new members had no respect for local leaders at all, seeing them as clear examples of political backwardness. At a 1966 meeting where the expulsion of whites had been proposed, Mrs. Hamer fought the idea. A few separatists discounted her position since she was "no longer relevant" and not at their level of development.

Attitudes like that may have been part of the reason organizers began leaving rural areas. At the same time, ghetto uprisings and the passage of the civil rights bill caused more concern with taking the movement to the cities. Traditionally, the great majority of staff members had been stationed in the rural South. By October of 1966, only a third of the staff remained in such areas, the rest being placed in urban centers in the South or outside of it. According to Carson, most of those who joined in 1966 were urban Blacks drawn to the militant image of SNCC rather than to the kind of organizing it had done in rural areas, and "few wanted to engage in the difficult work of gaining the trust and support of southern black people who were older than themselves and less aware of the new currents of black nationalist thought." More harshly, Forman claims that too many of the newcomers were simply middle-class Black elitists, unwilling to work with poor people.

Drifting away from the close ties they had once shared with local people meant that the movement was drifting away from one of its moral anchors. In earlier years, Bob Moses had noted that being rooted in the lives of local people kept the movement from going off on tangents. Similarly, Martha Prescod Norman pointed out that the decision to work with people like Mrs. Hamer and Amzie Moore implied a decision to conduct oneself in a manner acceptable within their moral code. Some of the contentious and dogmatic behavior that came to characterize the movement in the middle sixties would never have been tolerated by local people. For many of the local people with whom SNCC had worked, nothing excused a lack of personal courtesy, and abstract ideas about political direction were less important than relationships with concrete individuals.

The loss of faith in nonviolence meant the loss of another moral anchor. Nonviolence is frequently talked about in tactical terms, in terms of its impact on the outside world, but the internal effects of the nonviolent, Christian tradition may have been equally important. Although not a proponent of nonviolence herself, Ella Baker noted with approval that in SNCC's early days the kids "were so keen about the concept of nonviolence that they were trying to exercise a degree of consciousness and care about not being violent in their judgment of others." So long as significant numbers of members were making an effort to live their daily lives according to the dictates of stringent moral codes, there was something to balance whatever forces might have generated interpersonal bitterness. As organizers generally lost faith in American values, rejected the nonviolent, Christian tradition, and drifted away from their close contacts with the rural poor, they failed to create or find any functionally equivalent system for regulating their day-to-day behavior with one another. Without some such system, activists could become as much a danger to one another as to the social order.

The increasingly dogmatic style represents an especially important break with SNCC's heritage. It is quite different from the attitude with which the first organizers entered Mississippi. SNCC members had often prided themselves on their non-ideological character, on the way in which they developed ideas out of action. By the mid-sixties, ideas were taking on a primacy of their own, which meant a tendency to be unable to learn further from experience.

As a counter-example, consider Charlie Cobb's experience with the Julian Bond campaign. During the spring of 1965 Bond, at the urging of Ivanhoe Donaldson, ran for a seat in the Georgia House. By this time, probably a majority of SNCC members had deep doubts about participating in the political system. Some of those who did not participate in Bond's campaign called those who did sell-outs, symbolized by the exchange of overalls for coats and ties among campaign workers. Charles Cobb decided to participate despite his own misgivings: "I will confess that I was also worried about the corrupting influence of politics in general. I felt, and I still feel, the threat . . . American 'politics' has on people who 'play the game'—you know, like touch . . . and be tainted." At the time, according to Cobb, most of the staff thought that city people were hardest to organize; they were "too apathetic." "We don't know yet what can tap and sustain the energies of the people locked up in the city ghettoes." Bond ran a campaign very much in the SNCC tradition. His workers went door to door, asking people what their problems were and what they wanted from a state representative (which often required explaining what a state representative was, since these people had never really had one before). On the basis of their responses, Bond fashioned a platform that stressed economic issues. He won the primary and the election by comfortable margins. Cobb learned a good deal from the effort. In the final analysis, he wrote, urban organizing is the same as rural: "What people need—all over!—is something they can grab hold of, or build, that is their own." He found that his own fears "about controlling people or manipulating them blurred in the give and take dialogue (which implies give and take of decision-making and ideas) with the community." After the campaign he was fascinated by the idea of communities "moving in and out of traditional American political forms. It implies a creation of instability of these political forms, created by people whose needs are not being and probably will not be met by the forms anyway. I think it is to our advantage to have oppressive government unstable."

Cobb's stance was open-ended. He took part in the campaign despite misgivings; he was willing to experiment with a tactic he thought dubious. The experiment then changed his thinking to something more complex than an either-or choice about whether to participate in the system. Much of what was dynamic in SNCC is reflected in Cobb's attitude, and that dynamism would be lost in a more dogmatic climate.

The more doctrinaire climate also meant a tendency to see one another in increasingly stereotypical, one-dimensional terms. Ella Baker and Septima Clark understood clearly that the matron in the fur coat or the self-important preacher were hardly models of progressive thought, but they still assumed that such people could be worked with and could make a contribution. This ability to see people in their full complexity was increasingly lost in the more dogmatic phase of the movement, and as had been the case with southern racists, labels came increasingly to substitute for an awareness of the contradictions and complexities of individuals.

Once, in the context of an argument within SNCC over who had the right to participate in the movement, Miss Baker, with uncharacteristic rhetorical flourish, said, "We need to penetrate the mystery of life and perfect the mastery of life and the latter requires understanding that human beings are human beings." Making allowances for the ordinary human imperfections and contradictions of one's comrade became increasingly unlikely as the movement became increasingly dogmatic.

SNCC's increasing radicalism meant increasingly problematic relations with former allies. In the wake of the Atlantic City convention, they found relations with northern liberals and funding sources strained. In November 1964, the NAACP, still very angry over Atlantic City, left the COFO coalition, citing SNCC dominance. COFO disbanded altogether a year later. After Atlantic City, SNCC also found itself red-baited more frequently, a problem exacerbated even more in early 1966, when SNCC spoke out officially against the Vietnam War, the first major civil rights group to do so (although King as an individual had earlier made known his opposition). Most SNCC members seem to have opposed the war from the very beginning but the organization refrained from taking a stand until Sammy Younge, an Alabama SNCC worker and a navy veteran, was killed for trying to use a white restroom. Their statement on Vietnam argued that "the murder of Samuel Younge in Tuskegee, Alabama, is no different from the murder of people in Vietnam." In 1966, the liberal establishment was still largely behind the war. Even a year later, when Martin Luther King, against the advice of his staff, spoke out very aggressively against the war, he was sharply criticized by much of the liberal community. For SNCC, liberal reaction to its position on the war was more evidence of liberal hypocrisy. All apart from the war issue, SNCC's increasing emphasis on economic issues meant that it was going to have more trouble with liberals. "We are raising fundamental questions," Bob Moses said, "about how the poor sharecropper can achieve the Good Life, questions liberalism is incapable of answering." By 1967, most members thought of themselves as anti-capitalist, anti-imperialist members of the Third World.

Reconciling the more global concerns with the daily problems of the sharecropper and the ghetto dweller did not prove easy. The deepening radicalism led to Stokely Carmichael's election as chairman. In 1965, when few SNCC projects were going well, he had led an effort in Lowndes County, Alabama, that resulted in the creation of what was becoming a very powerful Black political party. His work there was very much in the community-organizing tradition, basic door-to-door organizing to create vehicles to empower the powerless. His success increased his prestige within the organization. His election in May 1966 reflected that, and it was also a repudiation of the tradition of Christian nonviolence symbolized by John Lewis, who had been chair since 1963. The shift from the religious Alabaman to the brasher, more eloquent New Yorker also symbolized a shift in the organization's self-presentation. Carmichael was seen as more militant on racial issues than Lewis, although his nationalism never precluded effective working relations with whites, a distinction largely lost on the press.

Traditionally, SNCC chairmen had not become media figures, but that changed under Carmichael, primarily because of the Black Power controversy. In early June, less than a month after the election, James Meredith began his March Against Fear, intending to walk from Memphis to Jackson to prove that it could be done. He was shot from ambush on the second day. A coalition of civil rights groups quickly formed to continue the march. Almost as quickly, the NAACP and Urban League, deliberately baited by Carmichael, pulled out. He refused to give them a reassuring statement about continued commitment to nonviolence. CORE, increasingly nationalistic itself, SNCC, and SCLC continued the march into the Delta, stopping in towns along the way to stimulate voter registration, getting a good response from local residents. In Greenwood, where Carmichael was well known from the time he had spent there in 1963 and 1964, he was arrested in a dispute over whether the marchers could use school grounds to pitch their tents. Bailed out (by Father Machesky), he showed up at that evening's rally boiling mad. When he spoke, he announced that this was his twenty-seventh arrest, and he intended for it to be his last. It was time for some changes. For years, Black people had been shouting "Freedom Now!" and had little to show for it. Cops were still doing anything they pleased. It was time to start shouting "Black Power!"

SNCC members had been discussing the idea of Black Power, and one, Willie Ricks, had used it in speeches. Carmichael himself seems to have been surprised by how positively the slogan was received by the crowd. The phrase catapulted him into the national spotlight. For some months, few reporters could see anything in it but anti-white sentiment. Nationalism, separatism, racism, and Black Power were frequently discussed as if they meant the same thing. The press was not helped by the fact that Carmichael was consistently, and probably deliberately, ambiguous in his subsequent explanations of the idea. More conservative civil rights organizations immediately criticized the slogan. Martin Luther King, who had been on the march, refused to join the condemnations, private misgivings notwithstanding. He was himself going through a period of frustration with SCLC's programs and a period of philosophical transition. He also had long-standing relationships with some SNCC members. He stressed the more pragmatic elements of the slogan and noted that there was nothing wrong with racial pride. He also noted that some policymakers were trying to exploit the controversy over the phrase to justify resistance to change.

SNCC had long been disdainful of SCLC for acting as if building a movement and making speeches were the same things. With Carmichael's increased national visibility, SNCC increasingly found itself acting the same way. Although he had planned to spend the year rebuilding southern projects and trying to replicate his success in Lowndes County, he found himself flying all over the nation making speeches and stirring controversies, while organizing projects continued to drift. His speech-making gave SNCC a central role in the national reexamination of racial and economic issues and generated badly needed funds, but it generated internal resentment as well. Other members suddenly found themselves being regarded by the public as Stokely's followers, which came as news to them. While no one denied that Carmichael had paid his dues in the field, so had dozens of other organizers, and they were not getting the kind of public adulation Carmichael was getting. Some members began calling him Stokely Starmichael. It did not help that some of his statements were intemperate and unauthorized, as if policy were now being made at the podium. Carmichael acknowledged the validity of many of the criticisms and for a while followed the restrictions placed on his public speaking by other staff members. When he left the chairmanship in the spring of 1967, he again announced his desire to return to the field as an organizer, but in fact he continued to play the role of militant nationalist spokesman. Having stepped on the stage, he seemed unable to step back off. The pattern of substituting rhetoric at the top for program at the bottom continued after he stepped down. "Rather than encouraging local leaders to develop their own ideas," Clayborne Carson contends, "SNCC was becoming merely one of many organizations seeking to speak on behalf of black communities."

Other organizations were having similar problems. As early as 1963, Septima Clark, then with SCLC complained:

> Many states are losing their citizenship schools because there is no one to do follow-up work. I have done as much as I could. In fact, I'm the only paid staff worker doing field visitation. I think that the staff of the SCLC working with me in the Citizenship Education Program feels that the work is not dramatic enough to warrant their time. Direct action is so glamorous and packed with emotion that most young people prefer demonstration over genuine education. It seems to me as if Citizenship Education is all mine except when it comes time to pick up the checks.

Similarly, grassroots organizing, slowly developing local leadership, must have seemed undramatic in the atmosphere of 1966–67, even to such a successful and experienced organizer as Carmichael.

For Ella Baker, the increased reliance on the press and the need of leaders for public recognition was a common element in the degeneration of social movements, a part of the pattern by which initially progressive American movements have traditionally been rendered ineffective. She contended that the labor movement had succumbed to what she called the American weakness of receiving some recognition from the powers-that-be and then taking on some of the characteristics and values of their former enemies. Similarly, in the NAACP of the forties and fifties, she thought that the thirst for recognition was one of the factors leading to accommodationist politics at a time when many of the members were ready for a more militant program. Too many leaders thought that as long as *they* were getting some attention from the press, as long as *they* could call important whites on the phone, the Race was making progress. In the 1960s, she thought that some Black Power spokespersons became so enamored of the coverage they were receiving from the press as to begin performing for the press.

> I think they got caught up in their own rhetoric. Even this business of the press, I think, has its explanation. To me, it is a part of our system which says that success is registered in terms of, if not money, then how much prestige and how much recognition you have. . . . So these youngsters with their own need for recognition began to respond to the press.

The substance of the Black Power idea didn't trouble her; the lack of organizing did. She noted that she had seen Carmichael explain Black Power in ways that should have made sense to any person willing to look at the facts.

> But this began to be taken up, you see, by youngsters who had not gone through any experiences or any steps of thinking and it did become a slogan, much more of a slogan, and the rhetoric was far in advance of the organization for achieving that which you say you're out to achieve.

> [What was needed was] a greater degree of real concentration on organizing people. I keep bringing this up. I'm sorry but it's part of me. I just don't see anything to be substituted for having people understand their position and understand their potential power and how to use it. This can only be done, as I

see it, through the long route, almost, of actually organizing people in small groups and parlaying those into larger groups.

The national and international reaction to the Black Power controversy probably obscured the need for real organizing. Perhaps nothing in SNCC's history, not even the Summer Project, had given the organization so much visibility. Quite apart from the way in which some leaders may have been affected by the need for recognition, the fact that the organization itself was getting so much attention, however hostile, probably contributed to a sense that they were getting things done, they were shaking the world.

The high-flying rhetoric of Carmichael and others was a far cry from SNCC's early style in Mississippi. Bob Moses, for example, although he hadn't thought the problem out fully at the time, responded to the enormity of the problems in Mississippi by understating everything:

> I remember that all during that time period my talk, my speech and everything was very, sort of sparse. I didn't know any other way to talk there. You were always afraid of getting people thinking that something was going to happen that wasn't going to happen. . . . You needed people who were going to accept what was going to happen and were somehow going to steel themselves to be part of what you knew was going to happen as opposed to promising people something that you knew wasn't going to happen. . . . Your tools are really the people, those are your tools. So the question is how do you attract the tools that you need from among those people? Well, it isn't by getting people who are going to respond to the big speech.

The issue of white participation in SNCC came to a head during Carmichael's tenure as chair. SNCC's small size in its early years was probably particularly important in maintaining the sense of interracial fraternity. Most of the whites were from the North, but it may also have been significant that some of the most active and visible whites were southerners—Bob Zellner from Alabama (who grew up in the same church as George Wallace), Casey Hayden from Texas, Jane Stembridge from Virginia, Connie Curry from North Carolina, Sam Shirah from Alabama. They frequently seemed more at ease interacting with Blacks than did their northern white counterparts, at least partly because southern whites and southern Blacks shared so much culturally. MacArthur Cotton, a Black SNCC member, appreciated the fact that white southerners came to the movement by a particularly hard road: "I found a closeness with southern whites. That probably had a lot to do with commitment. You step out of one of these towns in Alabama or Mississippi, talking about you going to be a freedom fighter, you committed."

Racial tensions were also minimized by the fact that there just weren't that many whites in the organization before 1964, and leadership was generally in Black hands. In 1961, Zellner was the only white member on a staff of sixteen, and it would be a year before another white, Bill Hansen, joined him. Of the forty-one field staff in Mississippi in late 1963, there were six whites. In the Leflore County area during the same period, I know of only two whites who were there for any length of time. After 1964, the proportion of whites in the overall organization went up to about twenty percent, although it didn't maintain that level very long.

Historically, the involvement of outsiders in movements of the oppressed has been unstable. In one article on the subject, Gary Marx and Michael Useem look at three cases of outsider involvement in minority movements—whites in the nineteenth-century abolitionist movement, upper-caste Hindus in the movement for **untouchable** rights in India, and whites in the modern American civil rights movement. Outsider involvement became problematic in all three cases, and for similar reasons in each case.

First, despite broad agreement on the need for change, outsiders and minorities were likely to disagree ideologically, frequently because minority-group members favored more radical strategies. Second, the privileged backgrounds of outsiders in the broader world were often replicated or thought to be replicated inside the movement. They often, for example, had skills that tended to make them gravitate toward administrative roles. Third, outsiders often brought some of the prejudices of the outside world with them, even if in diluted forms. Many white abolitionists were quite sure they knew what was best for Blacks. Ex-slaves like Frederick Douglass had to fight for the right to speak for themselves. Finally, while outsiders often played important roles in the early phases of movements, the passage of time often made their roles more problematic, no matter whether the movement was successful or not. As participation made minorities more self-confident, they wanted to depend less on others. Sources of conflict that are present from the beginning become more and more nettlesome with increased interaction between the two groups. The failure to reach goals may lead to a desire for internal restructuring of the movement or to scapegoating. In the end, even Gandhi's participation in India's Untouchable movement became problematic.

What happened in the civil rights movement is not historically unusual. By 1964, some SNCC members worried that the presence of whites in large numbers could interfere with the development of the self-confidence of the local people; that no matter how individually liberal whites might be, in appearing to rely upon them the movement added to the stereotype that Blacks were dependent on whites for everything; that some white members were trying to act out personal philosophies that were not always consistent with the movement's needs or were just acting our personal problems; that some white members had trouble accepting leadership from Blacks, partly because they thought of themselves as messiahs. Perhaps every veteran had a version of the story in which a Black organizer pleaded and pleaded with some old farmer to go register without success. Then some white organizer comes along, and the farmer goes right away because anything a white person says must be right. On the other hand, some young local Black people working with SNCC could not stop using white SNCC members as punching bags against whom they could release pent-up racial frustrations.

There was broad agreement within the organization, including among many white members, that some of these were valid problems, but different people took different lessons from that. Many, probably a majority, thought that it was time that white organizers started working in white communities. Others thought that whites had to go altogether. Among those taking the hardest line were the members of the Atlanta Project, an attempt to demonstrate that urban areas could be successfully organized. Half of the members were from the North, many were veterans, but only a few had been with SNCC in its earliest years. Most had not been as exposed to the nonviolent, Christian period of the movement and were not as likely to have long-standing personal relations with individual whites. Black members who had gone through that earlier period even as they adopted nationalist ideology were more likely to envision a continuing role for at least those individual whites with whom they had shared jail cells, cigarette butts, and beatings.

Members of the Atlanta Project were among those within the organization engaging in a new form of race-baiting. While members of the press kept the organization on the defensive by constantly raising the specter of Black racism, members of the Atlanta Project kept other Black SNCC members on the defensive by constantly questioning their loyalty to the race. The Atlanta separatists also acquired a general reputation for being difficult to work with. "They ignored memos, refused to return phone calls and rarely attended general staff meetings," according to Cleveland Sellers. Some of the lack of cooperation may be attributable to the fact that some members were jealous of Carmichael or to the fact that from their perspective, the persons running the organization, even though largely nationalist, had not achieved the level of consciousness they had reached.

Members of the Atlanta Project forced a "final" resolution of the racial question at a staff meeting in upstate New York in December 1966. To the chagrin of many present, they refused to allow any other business to be discussed until that issue was disposed of. Debate went on for several frustrating and emotional days. Carmichael argued for the whites-organizing-whites idea rather than exclusion. In the end, the vote was for exclusion of whites, with nineteen voting for the motion, eighteen against, and twenty-four official abstentions. (Perhaps another twenty-odd members were not present for the vote, held at two in the morning.)

The December vote did not lay the race question to rest. In May of 1967, Bob and Dottie Zellner presented the central committee with a proposal under which they would organize a poor white community in New Orleans. They had already acquired their own funding, but they wanted to operate the project as SNCC members without any special restrictions because of their race. Zellner had been in SNCC almost since its inception and held a special status. Sellers, one of the leaders of the nationalist thrust, said Zellner "commanded the unqualified respect of everyone in the organization. He was a damned good man. No one questioned his courage or his commitment." During the uneasy debate over the proposal, Forman, also an architect of SNCC's nationalist position, called Zellner his best friend. The decision not to accept the Zellners' proposal was painfully made by the committee, most of whose members, with the exception of Forman, had not been in the organization as long as Zellner. Someone wanted to deliver the decision by mail rather than look the Zellner in the face. Forman condemned that proposal for cowardice. What comes through from all accounts of the meeting is the ambivalence of SNCC's officers, committed though they were to the nationalist path. In the name of ideological principle, they were doing something that just did not sit right in the gut. Like nearly all of the whites expelled from the organization, the Zellners refused to talk with an eager national press.

The Zellners stayed in the organization longer than did many members of the Atlanta Project. A few months after the December meeting at which they had pushed the expulsion of whites, Atlanta Project staff were themselves fired from SNCC after they had responded to a disagreement over use of a staff car by sending Jim Forman a threatening letter. There was talk among the Project members of settling their expulsion with force, but that was averted. They had, though, made a contribution to the growing pattern of dogmatism within SNCC that would outlast their actual presence. "In their uncompromising effort to impose their ideas on other SNCC workers, they further undermined the trust, mutual respect, and interdependence without which SNCC could not survive," according to Carson. Still, it is not clear that they were any more dogmatic than any of the other factions.

The expulsion of whites from SNCC and from some other movement organizations is taken to be a watershed in our social history, but emphasizing racial antagonisms in this way can be misleading. American intellectuals have often stressed the interracial to the exclusion of the intraracial. For the same reason that the deaths of Black activists never had the public impact of the deaths of white activists, social commentary on the movement in the middle of the decade sometimes focused on how Blacks and whites were interacting almost to the exclusion of looking at how Blacks were interacting with one another. Thus, we don't fully appreciate one of the central ironies of the period, that while elaborating an ideology that gave a new primacy to racial unity, Black activists increasingly lost the capacity to work effectively with one another. Once that happened, the status of whites in the movement was more or less beside the point. The expulsion of whites has to be understood as one expression of a more pervasive deterioration in social relationships. Charlie Cobb refers to it as a period of tribalism, a time when activists began making invidious distinctions among themselves based on educational background, region of origin, philosophy of organization, placement on the field or office staff, length of movement service.

One important dividing line was that between northern and southern Blacks. Tensions had been present from the beginning. At SNCC's founding conference in 1960, Miss Baker had been at some pains to keep southern students and northern ones apart, precisely because the northern students were better schooled and exposed to a broader range of social philosophies. Miss Baker thought it important that the basically southern character of the early struggle not be suddenly overwhelmed by all these ideas the southern students weren't yet prepared to discuss.

Even among Black students, each group came to Raleigh conference with its own reputation. The North Carolina kids had been the most activist and had the prestige that went with that. The Atlanta kids were seen as swell-heads, and they did have a pretty high opinion of themselves. They quickly learned that in this context, they lost points because they hadn't engaged in much direct action, and no one at the conference was especially impressed with the ringing proclamations they had issued. The Nashville group was the most steeped in the study of nonviolence and civil disobedience, probably the only group to have a regular pattern of workshops, and like the North Carolina kids, they already had a great deal of practical experience. The Howard group was thought to be more articulate than any of the others in a formal sense and better prepared to argue their positions. Miss Baker noted that kids from the southern tradition were strong on the flowery oratory but less good at reasoned dialogue. The Howard group was also seen as more aggressive than the other students, often inappropriately aggressive, a reputation that would follow them and other northern students so long as the movement in the South lasted.

Joyce Ladner, who appreciated the students, white and Black, who came from the North and once thought they might be the South's salvation, still felt a deeper sense of communion with students who shared her southern background.

I strongly agreed with the southerners, Black southerners in the movement much more than I did with northerners because they understood more. I used to feel that there were occasions when northerners didn't fully understand and they could go back to their own homes. So I had a special affinity with people like MacArthur Cotton, Sam Block, Willie Peacock, James Peacock, Hollis and Curtis. They were people like me. I always felt we had much more of a stake in what happened in the South, in Mississippi.

Hollis Watkins expressed the differences more sharply. He referred to northern students as "the children of those who ran" from the South. He found northern Black students less dependable, more given to rash behavior. They were great philosophers, he said; they could rap for days, but they might or might not be around when something serious had to be done. Those who had not been politically active in the North were actually less trouble than those who came down with some prior experience. If they already had any kind of civil rights experience, you couldn't tell them anything. They already had all the answers. Willie Peacock noted that "we [Southerners] had spiritual values; most of them did not.... They tried to rationalize everything. Because of our different realities, we clashed on many issues." Other southern-born organizers expressed similar feelings. Northerners had too little respect for the local people and their customs. Above all, perhaps, they were simply seen as arrogant and pushy, too prone to seeing themselves as saviors.

Similarly, James Forman has been sharply critical of certain attitudes that he attributed to middle-class northerners, whatever their color. He attributes much of the disorder of the post-1964 period to their increasing influence within the organization, and the egotism and elitism they brought with them. He also sees them as the source of a kind of **bourgeois liberalism** that made them so concerned with retaining a kind of moral purity they were unwilling to exercise the power they might have exercised.

As with race, these antagonisms were at least partly a struggle over ownership of the movement. According to Mary King, the involvement of the white and powerful tended to make local field staff, those who had risked the most to build the movement, feel excluded. That is no doubt true, but it does not apply only to the involvement of whites. When the Summer Project was still under debate, local staff objected to the idea of large numbers of white students coming down, but many were also uncomfortable with the idea of large numbers of Black students coming down, and the Greenwood staff objected to SNCC's national office coming to Greenwood. Although they differed in intensity, there were objections to outsiders, period, and the objections were almost certainly related to the fact that the outsiders, white or Black, were perceived as taking the movement away from the people who had built it at the local level. As had been expected, national attention focused on the outsiders. There are any number of stories from the Summer Project in which a reporter is in a room with several veterans of the Mississippi movement and Susie Sophomore from Swarthmore, who has been in Mississippi all week. The reporter, of course, wants to talk with Susie. Similarly, as some SNCC members became nationally known spokespersons, they tended not to be the southern-born members of the field staff, but northern Blacks. The southern-born staff was pushed aside inside their own movement, and their resentment showed at times in quite visible disdain for johnny-come-latelys, some of whom had never organized anything and never put their bodies on the line. Fighting back, newcomers sometimes treated whatever SNCC had done prior to their coming as irrelevant and old-fashioned anyway. It was the kind of escalating spiral that could go on endlessly with the real issues never being discussed.

At their most destructive, the various manifestations of tribalism encouraged subgroups of activists to try to establish some higher legitimacy by playing games of moral superiority—Blacker Than Thou, More Dedicated Than Thou, More Revolutionary Than Anybody. In the absence of successful program, it allowed one to maintain a self-identity as being on the side of the angels. Of course, it also helped make organizational life, or even rational discussion, virtually impossible.

The social and political atmosphere of the late sixties was inimical in so many ways to the organizing tradition that it is impossible to be precise about just which of many factors were most important. The social climate that developed in much of the movement community after 1965 was certainly a very important problem. The social climate of the Mississippi movement in the early sixties was developmental in several different respects. In the latter period, it was much more judgmental, more divisive, more negative, sometimes characterized by a dogmatism that militated against thinking freely and experimenting widely. In the name of radicalism, people started destroying their friends. Political work became increasingly media-mediated, increasingly focused on charismatic personalities. The patient path of actual organizing seemed much less attractive. At their worst, the new militant spokespersons were just the modern version of the old southern preacher, Reverend Chickenwing transformed into Brother Abdullah. Rushing off into brave new forms of struggle, activists frequently left behind some of the forms of thinking and doing, some of the relationships that had sustained and anchored activists in Mississippi and elsewhere.

Black Power was and is an unsettling idea. While there is much truth in characterizing it a radical slogan that, at least within SNCC, seldom developed a comparably radical program, the idea of Black Power was a central element in a national debate that changed, probably permanently, the way Americans think about race. For substantial numbers of Black activists and intellectuals, it legitimated their right to think without constant reference to what pleased whites. It added legitimacy to the idea that Blacks have as much right to defend themselves as anyone else, that the legal rights of Blacks cannot be dependent on how loving and nonviolent they are, that Blacks need not beg and plead for what white Americans take for granted. It helped make it possible for an important minority of Black Americans to identify with non-white people the world over and with their own African backgrounds and to begin looking for reasons to take pride in a history that had too often been treated as stigma and degradation. It was a part of several social currents that encouraged Black and white intellectuals to think about social problems in terms that were more institutional and less personal. If it developed in ways that represented a turning away from the styles of many older, rural Blacks, it also captured and gave expression to a growing mood of frustration and urgency among younger Blacks.

The benefits were not without costs. Although few in number, SNCC and CORE organizers had great impact on the shape of political discourse among Blacks nationally. In the best of worlds, as those who had been a part of the organizing tradition began moving to other political styles, some thought would have been given to preserving and passing on whatever had been learned from years of struggle in Deep South communities. In fact, real-world urgencies and the emotional climate of the time left little time for calm reflection. The idealism and high hopes of the early years had been thrown back in their faces. Joyce Ladner said:

> I think a lot of the acting out that people have gone through, the turning on
> each other, came about in part because of the big, idealistic bubble having been

burst in so many places. . . . If this that I believed and in which I've invested so much psychic energy all these years doesn't work, then what am I to believe?

In turning on one another, they were turning away from the local people of the South and the sense of community that local people had done so much to create within the movement. If the movement's formally radical phase achieved less than it might have, the erosion of community is at least partly responsible for that.

However unwittingly, however compelling the reasons, the activist tradition in the Black community lost touch with the kinds of questions raised by the organizing experience in Mississippi, a loss that has certainly contributed to the impoverishment of political discussion in that community for the last two decades.

Additional Resources

Suggested Readings

Carmichael, Stokely, and Charles V. Hamilton. *Black Power: The Politics of Liberation in America.* New York: Vintage, 1967. Presents a political framework and ideology of black power. An outline of 1960s political action for blacks that would include development of new political structures along with a critique of coalition politics.

Carson, Clayborne. *In Struggle: SNCC and the Black Awakening of the 1960s.* Cambridge: Harvard University Press, 1981. A major contribution to the understanding of the black protest movement of the 1960s. It is a balanced treatment of student involvement in civil rights protest beginning with the sit-ins up to the decline of black radicalism.

Cleaver, Eldridge. *Soul on Ice.* New York: Dell, 1968. Autobiography written by a leader of the Black Panther Party when he was in California's Folsom State Prison. Contains commentary on the many forces in his life including religion and Malcolm X, James Baldwin, the Vietnam War, and popular music.

Dyson, Michael Eric. *Making Malcolm: The Myth and Meaning of Malcolm X.* New York: Oxford University Press, 1995. A lucid analysis of Malcolm X examining his role in contemporary society with essays on hip-hop culture, black films, and the lives of poor black men.

Hampton, Henry, and Steve Fayer. *Voices of Freedom: An Oral History of the Civil Rights Movement from the 1950s through the 1980s.* New York: Bantam Books, 1990. An interesting presentation of interviews of civil rights movement activists. It is the companion to the video series *Eyes on the Prize.*

King, Mary. *Freedom Song: A Personal Story of the 1960s Civil Rights Movement.* New York: Quill Books, 1987. A chronicle of SNCC's development from a nonviolent reform group to a black power revolutionary group. Critical of SNCC's treatment of women.

Malcolm X with Alex Haley. *The Autobiography of Malcolm X.* New York: Grove Press, 1965. A personal history and Black Nationalist views in the words of Malcolm X. A classic account of the Muslim who had a profound effect on many black Americans.

Marable, Manning. *Black Leadership: Four Great American Leaders and the Struggle for Civil Rights.* New York: Columbia University Books, 1998. A look at four black leaders including former Chicago mayor Harold Washington and Louis Farrakhan.

"Report of the National Advisory Commission on Civil Disorders." New York: E. P. Dutton, 1968. Commissioned by President Lyndon Johnson to study the causes of urban civil disorder, the Kerner Commission warned that the nation was moving toward two separate societies, one black and one white—separate and unequal.

Seale, Bobby. *Seize the Time: The Story of the Black Panther Party and Huey P. Newton.* New York: Random House, 1968. Written by one of the founders of the Black Panther Party, it is part autobiography and part history with an explanation of the Party's philosophy.

Zinn, Howard. *SNCC: The New Abolitionists.* Boston: Beacon Press, 1965. A study of SNCC and its direct action nonviolent campaign of the 1960s. SNCC achieved its greatest success in voter registration drives in Mississippi.

Web Sites

www.olemiss.edu/depts/english/ms-writers/dir/meredith_james

This is the Mississippi Writers Page Web site. It has a section devoted to the life and work of James Meredith. Documenting the integration of the University of Mississippi in 1962 and the "March against Fear," the site offers first-hand accounts of these pivotal moments.

www.bcpl.net/~dbroida/mxlinks.html

This host Web site offers links to information on Malcolm X including his speeches as well as exerpts from *The Autobiography of Malcolm X.* Additionally there are links to Martin Luther King's documents including his "Vietnam" speech.

www.brothermalcolm.net/mxcontext.html

This is a research site devoted to information on Malcolm X. It contains a chronology of his life, an extensive bibliography site, information on his family life, a webliography, and a study guide. There is a link to the Malcolm X collection at Emory University.

www.afroam.org/history/Panthers/panther-lead.html

This Web site offers information on the Black Panther Party. There are biographies of Bobby Seale, Huey Newton, Angela Davis, and Eldridge Cleaver. The site also offers links to other black history resources.

www-dept.usm.edu/~mcrohb/

This Web site is from the Center for Oral History and Cultural Heritage at the University of Southern Mississippi. It features a civil rights movement oral history bibliography. There are interviews of people in Mississippi who reflect upon the civil rights activities in that state between 1954 and 1972.

Chapter 6

Integration or Segregation?

T he issues that drove the African American struggle for freedom persist even today. Although integration has been achieved in many areas of society, segregation still exists. In the contemporary context, the question of racial equality has taken on the added dimension of class. The focus on poverty was a significant change in the direction of the civil rights movement. Similarly, raising the question of class in assessing the effects of the movement promotes a critical understanding of the movement. Why did middle-class blacks benefit more from civil rights policies? How do we account for the growing black urban and rural underclass? How far did the movement go? How are problems of race prejudice and discrimination addressed today? These issues dominate postmovement civil rights. The race and class issues impact employment, residential segregation or resegregation, affirmative action, and perceptions of equality.

Urban violence and the militant rhetoric of Black Power aroused white America. Following the Detroit riots in 1967, President Johnson appointed an advisory committee headed by Illinois governor Otto Kerner to look into the causes of the riots. In March 1968 the Kerner Commission issued its findings in *The Report of the National Advisory Commission on Civil Disorders,* which portrayed a divided America: two societies, black and white, separate and unequal. The report demonstrated the urgency and seriousness of the problems of race and poverty. Not since Gunnar Myrdal's *American Dilemma,* published in 1944, had such a comprehensive analysis of race linked black-white relations to prejudice among whites. Myrdal had shown that the core American value of egalitarianism was a dilemma for whites because they deviated from these values in their treatment of blacks. In similar fashion, in 1968 *The Kerner Report* urged the nation to generate "new will" and tear down racial barriers, citing conditions of poverty as significant factors in problems of urban violence.

The Paradox of Success

The legislative "road-from-*Brown*" included the important Civil Rights Act of 1964 and Voting Rights Act of 1965. Based on these laws, changes in American society stemming from the civil rights movement slowly became institutionalized. Movement success resulted in increased voter registration of blacks in the South. Viewed as evidence that American democracy worked against great odds, this change led to increased voter participation and the election of black officials in traditionally segregated states. Supreme Court decisions in the decades of the 1950s and 1960s unanimously favored the dismantling of old line segregationist practices and policy. Public schools and universities were desegregated, lunch counters were integrated, Jim Crow was eliminated in public transportation, and segregated public accommodations were forced to change. These visible legal and political changes were easily measured as civil rights victories.

On the other hand, in examining American culture—the beliefs, values, and norms that sociologists consider to understand a way of life—desegregation and integration of the post–civil rights movement proved to be paradoxical. Legislative gains were challenged by a reaction from mainstream America and the post-movement years of the 1970s and 1980s never embodied the culture of integration and equality visualized by the civil rights leaders. Orlando Patterson in *The Ordeal of Integration* (1997:17) asserts:

> The paradox is this: for the great majority of Afro-Americans, these are genuinely the best of times, but for a minority they would seem to be, relatively, among the worst, at least since the ending of formal Jim Crow laws. . . . On the other hand, there is no denying the fact that in absolute terms, Afro-Americans are better off now than at any other time in their history. The civil rights movement effectively abolished the culture of post-juridical slavery, which, reinforced by racism and legalized segregation, had denied Afro-American people the basic rights of citizenship in the land of their birth.

The paradox manifests at two levels: First, those who benefited most from the movement were middle-class blacks. The crumbling of the legal walls of segregation permitted them to enjoy benefits of freedom and justice, as they should have all along. At the same time, poor and low-income blacks remained poor. Social scientists noted poverty of the urban underclass amid the progress of the civil rights movement, and the term underclass became synonymous with poor blacks living in segregated areas of cities.

On another level, paradox is still a part of black middle-class status. Although blatant racism has faded, subtle forms of prejudice and racism are a constant reminder to all blacks that race still matters. Expressing the contradictions of racial progress, journalist Ellis Cose writes in *The Rage of a Privileged Class* (1993:1):

> Despite its very evident prosperity, much of America's black middle class is in excruciating pain. And that distress—although most of the country does not see it—illuminates a serious American problem: the problem of the broken covenant, of the pact ensuring that if you work hard, get a good education, and play by the rules, you will be allowed to advance and achieve to the limits of your ability.

The paradox of material success juxtaposed with lingering racial insults and disguised beliefs of inferiority confounds our assessment of the civil rights movement. Laws changed and opportunities arose. To what extent have attitudes changed?

White Backlash

Following the death of Martin Luther King and the failure of the Poor People's Campaign to convince legislators of the urgency of addressing the issue of poverty, civil rights goals became lost in America's national agenda, and by the late 1960s white backlash to change was evident in many areas, including presidential politics. The cryptic racism of President Richard Nixon was barely disguised by his law and order campaign in the 1968 national election. That theme appealed to white fears of urban riots and became the white backlash code of the times.

Nixon's successor, President Gerald Ford, was criticized by Democrats as "the most veto-prone Republican president in the twentieth century." Ford not only continued with Nixon's policies of strong opposition to school busing and school integration, but his relentless opposition to open housing and school desegregation was criticized by the U.S. Civil Rights Commission for accelerating the trend toward resegregation. Beginning in 1980, the Reagan-Bush administrations made countless appointments of conservative, anti–civil rights judges.

As integration spread in different parts of the country, the currents of backlash followed. Neoconservatives and their popular pundits consolidated their attack on the welfare system and targeted blacks in the process. Raymond Franklin's "From Civil Rights to Civic Disgrace" (Reading 6.1) contrasts the many important issues central to the civil rights struggle of the 1950s and 1960s with the backlash that began with the fear of Black Power and continues today. White backlash, especially during the Reagan-Bush years, took many forms, both overt and covert. An ex-Klansman, David Duke, ran for the U.S. Senate in 1990. He received over 40 percent of Louisiana voter support. Explaining Duke's attraction, one supporter stated, "Blacks are taking everything. They're taking everything from us, and the white race is going down the tubes. It's about time someone spoke up for the white people." Was Duke an isolated phenomenon or a national phenomenon? His appeal—a white backlash appeal—was not limited to racists but encompassed a vast group of white, middle-class voters who felt that they were being ignored.

Franklin views the attempts to explain black subordination in terms of the race-versus-class debate. Clearly, white backlash is race based, but it cannot be understood outside the context of the economics of dominant-subordinate relations. For Franklin, it is the race-class tension that drives black-white relations.

Affirmative Action

In the 1990 North Carolina race for the U.S. Senate, the conservative Republican Jesse Helms used a television ad to win his reelection campaign against a black Democrat, Harvey Gantt. The "White Hands" ad depicted a pair of white hands crumbling a job rejection letter while a background voice stated, "You needed that job. And you were the best qualified. But they had to give it to a minority because of racial quota. Is that really fair?" This telling example of exaggerating and exploiting affirmative action reflects the reaction of a sizable white minority to this controversial policy.

Affirmative action became the most widely discussed and controversial policy coming out of civil rights legislation. Affirmative action refers to public policy designed to increase educational and employment opportunities for blacks and other minority groups that have been historically excluded. It is aimed at countering institutional discrimination, that is, a denial of equality and opportunity to individuals or groups resulting from the normal operations of a society. Originally intended to protect blacks, affirmative action now protects other groups, including Asian Americans, Hispanics, Native Americans, and women.

Years after the civil rights struggle and legislation protecting blacks from different forms of discrimination, race remains a determining factor in many areas of life.

The idea of affirmative action surfaced in 1961, when newly elected president John F. Kennedy signed an executive order establishing the President's Commission on Equal Employment Opportunity. The order provided that federal contractors take "affirmative action to ensure that applicants are employed, and employees are treated during their employment, without regard to their race, creed, color, or national origin." Further, the order urged contractors to promote information about employment among racial groups, especially among blacks who had been previously excluded from employment.

The Johnson administration began to redefine affirmative action. In a speech given at Howard University in 1965, "To Fulfill These Rights," President Johnson extended affirmative action policy by reiterating that special procedures were needed beyond what was written in the careful language of the Civil Rights Act of 1964. Johnson stated, "You do not take a person who, for years, has been hobbled by chains and liberate him, bring him to the starting line of a race and then say, 'You are free to compete with all others' and still justly believe you have been completely fair." Johnson stipulated that "equity as a result" and "not just legal equity" had to be provided for those groups who have experienced a historical pattern of exclusion from competing on fair terms.

When the Nixon administration took over office from the Johnson administration in 1969, the policy of affirmative action was uncertain. Nicolaus Mills in *Debating Affirmative Action* (1994:9) points out:

> Nixon had made his opposition to the liberalism of Johnson's Great Society programs part of his campaign, and his administration was in a position to halt, if not reverse, the new version of affirmative action that the Johnson Labor Department had brought about. . . . The Nixon administration chose, however, not to alter the course affirmative action had begun to take in the Johnson years. It sought instead to make sure that the urban unrest of the late 1960s, exacerbated in no small measure by joblessness among young blacks, did not become one of its problems. The change from a Johnson Labor Department headed by liberal Willard Wirtz, to one headed by George Shultz, the former dean of the University of Chicago Business School—who years later would become secretary of state under Ronald Reagan—gave new momentum to affirmative action.

In Order No. 4, 1970, the Labor Department redefined affirmative action as "a set of specific and result-oriented procedures." The old notion of discriminatory intent was left far behind one year later when the Supreme Court ruled in the case of *Griggs v. Duke Power Company* (1971) that affirmative action functions as a remedy for adverse-effect discrimination. This means that discrimination can result even though there is no intent to discriminate on the part of an institution. In *Griggs v. Duke Power Company,* the Court unanimously supported the concept of disparate impact (sometimes called adverse-effect discrimination). Blacks seeking employment at Duke Power claimed their rights were violated because they needed a high school diploma or a passing score on a standardized test. The Court agreed, stating that Duke Power's requirements could not be shown to have "a manifest relationship to the employment in question," but they could be shown to act as "built-in headwinds" against minorities, and that was enough to make them illegal (Mills, 1994:12).

In 1978 the Supreme Court, in a 5-4 decision in *Regents of the University of California v. Bakke,* prohibited reserving a specific number of places for minorities in college admissions. The Court ordered the medical school of the University of California at Davis to admit Allan Bakke, a white engineer who had originally been denied admission. The justices ruled that the school had violated Bakke's constitutional rights by establishing a fixed quota system for minority students. The Court, however, added that it was constitutional for universities to adopt flexible admission programs that use race as one factor in making decisions (Schaefer, 1995).

In the case of *United Steelworkers of America v. Weber* (1979) the Court ruled by a vote of 5-2 that the labor union did not have to admit a white lab technician, Brian Weber, to a training program in Louisiana. The justices held that it was constitutional for the union to run a program for training skilled technicians that, to promote affirmative action, admitted one African American for every white.

In "Persuasion and Distrust: The Affirmative Action Debate" (Reading 6.2), Randall Kennedy defends the affirmative action program. He looks into the role of covert motivations in reaction to affirmative action. Are opponents of affirmative action enemies of equality? Is this opposition a mere continuation of the campaign against blacks? Kennedy concludes that the policy of affirmative action should be retained because it is useful in overcoming entrenched racial hierarchy:

George Lipsitz provides another perspective in the affirmative action debate. He writes in *The Possessive Investment in Whiteness* (1998:222):

> The stigma that is supposed to haunt those helped by affirmative action evidently does not apply to white people, for example, to the 20 percent of Harvard undergraduates who received preferential treatment because their parents were alumni, consequently increasing by three times their likelihood of admission compared to applicants not connected to the college through family ties. At Harvard, alumni children are twice as likely to be admitted as a Latino or black student. The class of 1992 at that institution included two hundred marginally qualified applicants who gained admission because their parents attended Harvard, a greater number than the combined total of black, Chicano, Native American, and Puerto Rican members of the class. Apparently advantages only carry a stigma when people of color receive them.

In other words, the stigma of preferential treatment does not apply to whites; a policy that benefits whites escapes criticism and backlash.

The stigma that Lipsitz describes eludes Stephen Carter, whose "Racial Preferences? So What?" (Reading 6.3) is an example of the inherent contradictions of the affirmative action issue. Carter's admission to Harvard Law School illustrates the frustrations of blacks and affirmative action. He asserts that a large segment of blacks must be willing to meet the affirmative action question head-on. To the question, Did you get into school because of a special program? Carter's reply is, Yes, I got into law school because of racial preferences. So What?

In stark contrast to the Supreme Court of the 1950s, the decades of the 1980s and 1990s saw the Court divided on practically all civil rights cases. The unified Court of the *Brown* era was clear in its efforts to end school desegregation. Moreover, it proved to be an important ally in reaching many of the goals of the civil rights movement. This major shift in the role of the Court from supporting civil rights issues to slowing down and sometimes confusing the public with its complex determinations was exacerbated during the Reagan years. Earlier civil rights Court decisions were aimed at a segregated school system or public accommodation. On the defense now were people with whom white America could identify. Whether it was the future medical doctor Allan Bakke or a factory worker like Brian Weber, white Americans began to see affirmative action as civil rights gone too far. The notion of preferential treatment for minorities was seen as a form of discrimination against whites. In their minds and sometimes in the eyes of the Court it became reverse discrimination.

President Reagan appointed a corporate lawyer, William Bradford Reynolds, to be head of the Civil Rights Division of the Justice Department. To run the Equal Employment Opportunity Commission, Reagan chose Clarence Thomas, a conservative who as an African American described himself as "unalterably opposed to programs that force or even cajole people to hire a certain percentage of minorities." By making sure that his key civil rights appointees had a hard-line opposition to affirmative action policy, Reagan continued his history of legislative opposition to civil rights. With a skillful appeal to white racial resentments in covert ways, Reagan's presidential campaign started in the town of Philadelphia, Mississippi, the site of the murder of three civil rights workers in 1964 by local whites. It was here that Reagan announced, "I believe in states' rights." Lost in the conservative shift was the reality of continued discrimination and the very slow progress toward integration in occupations with a tradition of segregation.

Clearly, civil rights groups were not as politically influential as they had been in prior decades. Nevertheless, they pushed Congress for a new civil rights bill in an attempt to combat the split decisions of the Court in the 1970s and 1980s. The Bush administration was at first hostile to the Kennedy-Hawkins proposal that aimed at assisting minorities and women to prove workplace discrimination, and finally President Bush vetoed the bill after declaring that he supported the idea of civil rights. The proposed Civil Rights Act of 1990 passed by large majorities in the House and the Senate but fell one vote short of an override to Bush's veto. Public perception in the early 1990s showed that among whites there was widespread belief that civil rights leaders were more interested in special preferences than equal opportunity.

Another attempt at civil rights legislation proved to be successful. Initially calling it the "quota bill," President Bush signed the Civil Rights Act of 1991, which would help minorities with workplace discrimination. Nicolaus Mills (1994:25) summarizes:

> The Supreme Court's cluster of 1989 civil rights decisions was no longer the law. The new Civil Rights Act shifted the burden of proof in disparate-impact cases back to the employment practice that resulted in disparate impact to demonstrate that the practice was both "job related" and "consistent with business necessity." The Act also provided remedies for intentional discrimi-

nation and unlawful harassment in the workplace, allowing women and minorities who were victims of intentional discrimination to collect up to $300,000 in compensatory damages.

Affirmative action proponents argue that the policy is about equal opportunity; it functions as a remedy for discrimination and as a corrective for disadvantage. Additionally, they cite the benefits to the nation as a whole. For example, the absence of black police officers in many cities exacerbates the tension between the police and black communities.

Opponents see affirmative action programs as the cause of another social problem. Resentment and reverse discrimination lead to a new concept of the "victim." The furor over Bakke promoted the image of the white male as the new perceived victim. Critics add that those who defend affirmative action are voicing "politically correct" views. They also contend that the goals of diversity are antithetical to the original vision of civil rights.

Residential Segregation

Douglas Massey and Nancy Denton (1993:2–3) are concerned that the word "segregation" has virtually disappeared from the American vocabulary:

> The effect of segregation on black well-being is structural, not individual. Residential segregation lies beyond the ability of any individual to change; it constrains black life chances irrespective of personal traits, individual motivations, or private achievements. For the past twenty years this fundamental fact has been swept under the rug by policymakers, scholars, and theorists of the urban underclass. Segregation is the missing link in prior attempts to understand the plight of the urban poor. As long as blacks continue to be segregated in American cities, the United States cannot be called a race-blind society.

In "The Perpetuation of the Underclass" (Reading 6.4), Massey and Denton apply the argument that poverty among blacks results from deliberate segregation. For them, the central issue is not whether African Americans prefer to live near whites or whether integration is a desirable social goal, but how the restrictions on individual liberty implied by severe segregation undermine the social and economic well being of individuals. The perpetuation of an urban underclass is ensured by keeping it in poverty, segregated, and politically marginalized.

Sociologist William Julius Wilson argues in *When Work Disappears: The World of the New Urban Poor* that, essentially, for many cities residential segregation has become economic segregation. The disappearance of work and the consequences of that disappearance for both social and cultural life are the central problems of the inner-city ghetto (1996: xix). Work has disappeared from black neighborhoods into the global economy. His analysis, however, includes the role of class as evidenced by his early book, *The Declining Significance of Race*. In essence, he describes a new social formation in which the urban poor— overwhelmingly black—are without hope of jobs because there are no jobs. Wilson contends that simply eliminating racial barriers is not enough. He proposes programs, recalling the ideas of the New Deal and Martin Luther King, to address the problem of poverty.

In contrast to poor and socially segregated communities, Lise Funderburg describes the integrated middle-class community of Montclair, New Jersey, in "Integration Anxiety" (Reading 6.5). What sets Montclair apart from the proto-typical suburb is the enduring mix of race and class. Recently, researchers for the Department of Housing and Urban Development (HUD) cited the willingness of residents to identify their community as diverse. The long tradition of inte-grated life in Montclair, however, has its share of problems of prejudice, which is manifested in concerns with **racial tipping,** social patterns among public school children, and teachers' low expectations of poor black children. In ad-dition, there are intraracial class divisions. Socioeconomic status concerns make maintaining a truly integrated community even more challenging. Massey and Denton (Reading 6.4) note that places like Montclair are forced to adapt to a racially segregated world and undertake heroic efforts to keep themselves islands of integration in the broader sea of segregation (Funderburg, 1999).

Contemporary Discrimination

Although the legal barriers of segregation fell, new, invisible fences that reflected more subtle forms of discrimination were being built. The apparent decline of overt discrimination was accompanied by new and covert forms of racism. That race continues to shape American life today is Michael Eric Dyson's theme in "In a Color-Blind Society, We Can Only See Black and White" (Reading 6.6). Making the point that the most vitriolic forms of racism have been forced un-derground by the success of the civil rights movement, Dyson shows how race is much more complex today than during the era of segregation. Prejudice and discrimination persist, but they are harder to prove and far more difficult to analyze than the undisguised examples of racial hatred before the movement, the church burnings, cross burnings, and lynchings.

Dyson describes a recent example of the Supreme Court ruling against black voters. Congressional districts drawn in response to the 1965 Voting Rights Act to give minorities more just electoral representation, were ruled unconsti-tutional by the Supreme Court in 1996. Arguing for the ideal of a color-blind society, the Court, in a 5-4 decision, invalidated the districts because race played a predominant role in their formation. Law professor Patricia Williams says, "The rules may be color-blind, but people are not." The disagreement about race issues reflected in the highest court mirrors the confusion about race and civil rights in American life today. Dyson believes that racial disparities in edu-cation, income, and employment need to be addressed before promoting the idea of a color-blind society.

Another example of 1990s backlash and subtle discrimination is discussed in "Turning Back the Clock on Voting Rights" (Reading 6.7) written by investi-gative reporter Ron Nixon, who exposes the double standard of voter-fraud in-vestigation in Alabama. Directed at successful black politicians, voter-fraud investigation virtually bypassed white politicians. Voting rights activists fear that abusive prosecution will intimidate black voters in the state.

The covert nature of antiblack discrimination, the subtle and invisible forms, are described in a study by Joe R. Feagin in "The Continuing Significance of Race" (Reading 6.8). Drawing on 37 in-depth interviews of middle-class blacks, Feagin describes how blacks have developed the strategies of verbal confrontation and withdrawal in response to subtle discrimination. He shows how racism plays out in ways that whites cannot see.

Robert Staples, in "The Illusion of Racial Equality" (Reading 6.9), points out that the media creates a distorted image of equality when the success of icons of popular culture—black athletes and entertainers—is offered as evidence of racial equality. Staples sees this as a gross overgeneralization, an illusion that is promoted as reality. Behind this picture is the "quiet anger" of the black middle class, who are forced to accommodate new and subtle forms of prejudice and discrimination.

Future Matters Concerning Race

Writer and social critic Stanley Crouch presents Martin Luther King's idea that people should be judged by the content of their character and not by the color of their skin. He uses this as a starting point to argue that the contemporary discussion of civil rights issues is flawed in that some blacks further a separatist rather than integrationist vision. In "Blues-Collar Clarity" (Reading 6.10), Crouch argues that the current battle with "white middle-class standards" is a distortion of the civil rights movement. The best of the Afro American tradition—Frederick Douglass, Albert Murray, and Harriet Tubman—are symbols of great American achievement. Crouch believes that the current discussion of race focuses too much on the decay that has taken place in lower-class black communities.

Strongly critical of the idea that there were two Americas—one black, one white—that ignores the regional, religious, and ethnic complexities of American culture, Crouch sees such analyses as an oversimplification. For him, the traditional civil rights goal of complete integration should be the focus of African Americans.

The final selection offers the student a sensitive reflection from the point of view of an American black. What is the role of race for American blacks? Randall Kennedy, in "My Race Problem—and Ours" (Reading 6.11), explores the question. We do not make decisions in a vacuum. They occur within a social and economic structure. Kennedy writes, "The difficulties that disproportionately affect black Americans are not 'black problems' whose solutions are the special responsibility of black people. They are our problems, and their solution or amelioration is the responsibility of us all, irrespective of race." With this statement Kennedy rejects the idea that skin color creates an "obligation" to members of a particular race, asking, rather, whether higher ideals should link all individuals in society. Looking toward the future, how much will race matter?

Key Figures, Terms, and Concepts

affirmative action
Bob Jones University v. United States
disparate impact
David Duke
Griggs v. Duke Power Company

institutional discrimination
Daniel Patrick Moynihan
Thomas Sowell
urban underclass
"chocolate city–vanilla suburb"

1. Explain what is meant by affirmative action. Should affirmative action be a core strategy in public policy?

2. Does institutional discrimination seem less objectionable than overt discrimination? Explain with examples from the readings.

3. What is meant by the urban underclass? Explain the relationship between policies that lead to segregation and the perpetuation of the underclass. What public policy can address both race and poverty?

4. Account for the dramatic shift of federal support for civil rights from the Johnson administration to a rolling back of legislative gains by the Reagan-Bush administrations.

5. Compare and contrast modern, subtle forms of prejudice and discrimination with those that characterize the culture of segregation. Why do you think such behavior still exists?

From Civil Rights to Civic Disgrace

Raymond Franklin, professor of economics at Queens College of the City University of New York, is director of the Michael Harrington Center for Democratic Values and Social Change. He is author of Shadows of Race and Class *and* American Capitalism: Two Visions.

T he hopeful changes many expected from the civil rights movement in the sixties proved unwarranted. By the mid-seventies, many liberals and conservatives had come to believe that the civil rights movement had outlived its usefulness. Throughout the first half of the eighties we witnessed a resurgence of racially motivated incidents throughout the country that appeared to signify a hardening of white resistance and a serious interruption in the economic progress and social integration of blacks. These developments constitute the "disgrace" that informs the title of this chapter.

In the course of the civil rights movement's relative success in the legal and political sphere, followed by its relative disappointment in the economic and social one, a number of derivative issues emerged that became integral to the black population's struggles for a fundamental change in status. These issues include the legacy of slavery, IQism, the juxtapositioning of a growing black middle class and the rise of a black underclass, black male-female relations and family patterns; they became a subtext in a broad debate about relationships of race and class in American society. This chapter establishes the changing context in which these issues emerged.

The interpretive emphasis is focused through the stereoscopic lenses of race and class. Rather than accepting one or the other, or reducing one into the other, I argue that black-white conflict can best be understood by the specific interplay between race and class as they unfold in history, are constructed in theory, and, not least, are employed to make meaning out of everyday experiences. This requires looking simultaneously at race differences between populations and class divisions within the separate racial communities. Because of the failure of scholars, politicians, activists, and ordinary citizens to understand the complex pattern and structure in which race and class interact between and within communities, the oscillating shadows that both cast are not understood and identified.

America's New International Role

When World War II ended, the leaders of our political institutions inherited a cluster of embarrassments. We fought and won a war against fascism, in opposition to the idea of a master race and notions of racial superiority. We inherited the role of international police and leaders of the Western world against a backdrop of rising Third World nationalism, especially on the continent of Africa. We soon became engaged in a cold war with the Soviet Union and consequently found ourselves competing for the allegiances of these newly formed nations. Both liberal anticommunists and conservatives agreed that racial segregation and overt discrimination had to end, if for no other reason than the fact that such practices interfered with our struggle against international communism. Walter Reuther, addressing the fiftieth anniversary meeting of the NAACP, warned that segregation "can be American democracy's Achilles heel in Asia and Africa where the great millions of the human family live." Acting secretary of state Dean Acheson wrote:

> The existence of discrimination against minority groups in the United States is a handicap in our relations with other countries. The Department of State . . . has good reason to hope for a continued effectiveness of public and private efforts to do away with these discriminations.

Similar utterances were made by prominent black leaders up to and beyond the 1954 *Brown v. Board of Education of Topeka* decision. U.S. officialdom was ready, even if the American people were not, for legal changes, if properly pressured.

As the patriotic outpouring of "brotherly" love among all races, creeds, and colors dwindled soon after World War II, the postwar "normalcy" patterns established themselves. American people immersed themselves in their work, getting ahead, accumulating consumer goods, and enlarging their families. On a few major university campuses, a minority of radical and liberal students struggled against the quota system in professional schools that required photographs and other such information that would clearly identify one's religion, ethnicity, or race. And while the NAACP was working arduously and continuously at undermining the legal foundations of segregation, it was still possible up to the early 1950s to find nationally used high school and college textbooks writing mythological histories about happy slaves, the implications of which were extended to embrace the willingness of contemporary blacks to accommodate to their subordinate position.

Stereotypical history and its depictions are always difficult to destroy, especially if the subordinate group has pariah status. Nevertheless, the landmark Supreme Court decision in May 1954, *Brown v. Board of Education,* triggered a chain of actions and reactions that permanently shifted black-white relations and uprooted typical images established in white minds since the earliest days of our history. The unanimous declaration, overturning *Plessy v. Ferguson* (1896), that segregation was inherently unequal and damaging moved key aspects of the struggle from the de jure to the de facto level.

The Civil Rights Struggle

The most significant single event to follow the *Brown v. Board of Education* decision was the Montgomery bus boycott, which began in 1955 when Mrs. Rosa Parks refused to surrender her bus seat to a white man upon command by the bus driver. The boycott, which lasted one year, injected a new sense of collective power and pride into the black community and brought moral and financial support from northern middle-class whites and union leaders; it also represented a new combination of class forces and conflict in the southern context. Many older black middle-class leaders, whose strategies for change mainly involved appeals to and deals with members of the "responsible" white elite, linked themselves to a new stratum of young clergy who were educated and had matured in the post-World War II period. These younger religious leaders had assimilated more fully the spirited struggles for nationhood by Third World nations. To this must be added the new black urban working class that also emerged from World War II. Last, the rise of a sizable southern business class should not go unnoticed. Unlike the rural white planters whose manifest racism could ignore the mood of the rest of the country when they intimidated isolated black farmers, the urban businessmen, with regional and national competitors, worried daily about downtown sales affected by the boycott.

The Montgomery experience had a ripple effect and led to desegregation struggles in a number of southern cities. Perhaps of greater importance, the boycott validated the mandate for demonstrations to integrate not only buses, but lunch counters, restaurants, libraries, churches, theaters, amusement parks, beaches, and, more generally, "any public business licensed by the state." While these varied tactics were for the most part aimed at breaking down the walls of de facto segregation, which now was officially illegal, their use required considerable courage and involved a radical departure from the slower legal testing procedures and standard pressure group politics. The tactics were seen as a threat to the social order. They were perceived by many whites as a "territorial" invasion that violated the property owner's sense of prerogatives and freedom to choose, which to blacks meant white freedom to exclude. Insofar as the state has an obligation to maintain order and protect private property, the demonstrators, as a sign of their own commitment, were ready to accept violence against themselves in order to raise the moral conscience of the nation. The white majority at this time, it should be recalled, had little immediate sympathy with black causes and social journeys. But insofar as the national government had an obligation to enforce the law of the land, which included, of course, the Supreme Court decision, black struggles were legitimate. Thus, the march of events from 1954 to the march on Washington in 1963 put the national government in an ambiguous position. With TV cameras reporting violence against blacks around the world on the one hand, and the legal legitimacy of black goals on the other, federal troops reluctantly and hesitatingly were used to protect black protesters. In the course of these events, local white southern extremists (White Citizens Councils) grew in alarming strength, driving white urban moderates into a state of limbo. A race war was in the making. Polarization within the southern white community was matched by the emergence of the Student Nonviolent Coordinating Committee (SNCC) in mid-1960, a group soon perceived as a more militant alternative to Martin Luther King, Jr.'s Southern Christian Leadership Conference. Civil rights concerns previously viewed as leading edge demands of the black middle class gradually turned into social justice and black power demands under the youthful SNCC leadership. The struggle to desegregate Birmingham in the spring of 1963, followed by the march on Washington in August of the same year, marked a turning point.

The Birmingham battle called into operation every segment of the black population, including the working class, the lower class, and young children. Demonstrators filled the jails; downtown business came to a standstill; Sheriff Eugene ("Bull") Connor, a symbol of southern racism, responded with "dogs, firehoses, and clubs" to some SNCC stone throwers. He also turned the hoses and dogs on perfectly peaceful demonstrators. The events of Birmingham "caused a national revulsion," leading to the capitulation of Birmingham's business community. Following the march on Washington that drew two hundred thousand persons from all parts of the country—black and white, young and old, rich and poor, union and nonunion—John F. Kennedy's proposed civil rights bill was approved by Congress.

The summer of 1964 marked the Mississippi Summer Project. Large numbers of northern white college students, fired up with a sense of idealism, descended on Mississippi in a voter registration drive. Whites learned personally about red-necks and life-threatening terror just by exercising what was viewed as a normal right "back home." A significant number of blacks experienced a sense that whites were taking over. It was said of whites that they were "running offices, freedom schools, and campaigns by virtue of their superior education and the sole fact of their being white, and that they thereby prevented blacks from controlling their own movement." Compounding this loaded situation, some white women "became sexually involved with black men," an issue that had explosive political and racial dimensions in Mississippi. In the course of the personal becoming political, a black feminist affirmation emerged—an issue to which we shall return at a later juncture.

Between 1963 and 1966, the crescendo of demands for civil and voting rights rose to unprecedented levels and spilled over into western and northern urban centers. These non-southern voices were less focused on civil and voting rights and more on jobs, urban renewal, welfare, schooling, health care, job training, slum conditions, and, not least, desegregation in housing. The outcome was not only the passing of the Civil Rights Act (1964) and Voting Rights Act (1965), but also President Lyndon Baines Johnson's announcement of his War on Poverty. Some of these programs focused on race-specific problems and issues and became a source of white backlash in subsequent years. These included Johnson's executive order on affirmative action, preferential treatment intent, federal funding of local control and participation to fight city hall, and compensatory education.

Simultaneous with the War on Poverty there emerged, beginning in 1966, the black power movement. The minority voice of Malcolm X, which had persisted unflinchingly alongside King's broader-based civil rights movement between 1954 and 1963, now received national attention. De facto desegregation proved more difficult to eliminate than de jure. In some situations, class differences between black and white school districts frequently appeared too substantial, given the pace of events, to sustain integration goals and interracial alliances. But in many other communities, rhetorical euphemisms developed to obstruct integration. Whites used class—even in the absence of serious class differences—when they meant race. And when class differences were clearly absent, "cultural differences" often became the excuse to prevent integration. Finally, even when desegregation occurred—with or without class differences between the races—it often led to resegregation within schools. Thus, alleged class and cultural differences between the races prevented the momentum of the civil rights movement from achieving genuine integration of the established black middle and working classes with their white counterparts.

In any event, the frustrations and expectations of the black middle class were an important factor in the emergence of the black power ideology among SNCC organizers. Distinguished by their youth and nonministerial origins, SNCC leaders such as Stokely Carmichael and John Lewis represented a new breed of southern-based, college-educated blacks. They constituted yet another wave of leadership as SNCC began to compete with the Southern Christian Leadership Conference.

Black Power: 1966–72

Under the general rubric of black power, four themes developed between 1966 and 1972. Although some of these themes are not novel, they were articulated with new energy and defined by the history-making civil rights movement that preceded it. Black community development, black capitalism, cultural nationalism, and revolutionary nationalism all embraced a common ideology: the need for black identity based on some combination of race and culture, the need for black self-determination, and the need to overcome white economic and cultural domination. Whatever the emphasis, black power advocates always opted for independent forms of action. In the economic sphere, independent action meant controlling resources to develop some fraction of a racially based economy. Politically, race advocates argued for their own ideology and legislative agenda. For the cultural domain, they focused on the "positives" of black history and experience, returning, if necessary, to the glories of the black population's preslave roots. In principle, although not always in fact, black power advocates eschewed alliances with whites and glossed over status and interest differences within the black community.

A brief comment about each specific theme will serve to illuminate the differences among them. Black community development was discussed in terms of community control. The main innovative dimension revolved around the creation of ghetto-based resource and financial planning agencies in the form of community development corporations. The goals of these corporations were, first, to implement the creation of ghetto-based enterprises to absorb some portion of unemployed and underemployed blacks; second, to improve the competitive performance and quality of existing ghetto enterprises owned by black capitalists; and third, to acquire sufficient political power and autonomy to affect the flow of resources out of the ghetto, as well as to extract resource transfers from "foreign" exploiters.

These activities were racially unifying to the extent that they relate to the unemployed black masses, to some black businesspersons, to black professionals and technicians who sought to employ their human capital know-how in service to the black community, and to the black politicians and ideologues who saw the need to develop effective electoral constituencies and the perpetuation of black power ideas in general.

Black capitalism, our second black power theme, had a more limited vision, although it was often advertised as more realistic since it had the endorsement of the white establishment. Black capitalism as an instrument of black salvation has a long history of failure in a variety of guises. These range from grand visions of black retail chain stores, manufacturing plants, development banks and enterprise zones to the modest policies of the Small Business Administration for what are essentially family entrepreneurial undertakings in and on the margins of ghettos. Black capitalism is consistent with conservative self-help schemes and the urging of black workers to internalize self-discipline and the work ethic.

Cultural nationalism, the third black power theme, involved a number of general scenarios: nativism, a focus on the portion of the black experience derived from Africa; a liberation struggle from the bonds of white supremacy and from the internalized self-denigration associated with enslavement; and, not least, overcoming the black "identity crisis" associated with the destruction of the black cultural and historical heritage by emphasizing, publicizing, and developing black contributions to civilization and American society. An inspired cultural nationalism requires the development of a black intelligentsia on a scale much larger than that envisioned years earlier by W. E. B. Du Bois.

Revolutionary nationalism, the last of the black power themes, is distinguished by its utopian economic program and its focus on direct action tactics and super-militant rhetoric. Whereas cultural nationalists tended to say little that was specific in the area of altering the economy, the revolutionary nationalists, in the spirit of Marxism-Leninism, projected the need for black ownership of "banks and industries and stores"; control of "local, state and national governments, courts and police forces"; [and] a consequential role in the administration of "schools, and universities, churches, public places, foundations, etc." Since revolutionary nationalists aimed at altering the class structure, their implicit logic required class alliances with white workers; their actual organizing style emphasized race.

The Backlash

The density of the supermilitant spirit—which was part real and part a media creation—had to have a short life. It burned too fast to evolve and endure. It provoked a profound backlash among all strata of white American society, and provoked a limited backlash among some segments of the black community as well. The story of this backlash constitutes the next phase of the black struggles for full and equal status. This phase began "officially" in 1972 with Daniel Patrick Moynihan's "benign neglect" statement:

> The time may have come when the issue of race could benefit from a period of benign neglect. The subject has been too much talked about. The forum has been too much taken over by hysterics, paranoids, and boodlers. . . . We may need a period [in which] extremists are [denied] opportunities for martyrdom, heroics, histrionics or whatever.

Burned and hurt by the liberal and black community's rejection of his black family plan in 1968 with its reference to the pathological status of the black family whose initial dependent and matrifocal characteristics were allegedly determined by enslavement, Moynihan had drifted into the Nixon administrative fold. Under the banner of "law and order," conservatives aimed their political guns at putting down white university student disruptions and black street protests. Even before Moynihan's call for "benign neglect," the white backlash was under way in a variety of forms.

In reaction to the perceived failure of the War on Poverty, Arthur Jensen, education professor at the University of California, kicked up a storm in his 1969 article on differences in IQ between blacks and whites. After "proving" through a vast array of statistics that roughly 80 percent of an individual's intelligence is inherited, Jensen concluded that compensatory education for blacks had failed because of their inferior biological endowment. Blacks are not educable in the same way as whites, and, therefore, investment in their intellectual development is a waste of resources.

As university-based black power advocates pushed for the creation of black studies departments and curriculum changes to reflect the history and nature of the black experience, white ethnic students quickly responded with "me too." If a black studies program is to be created, why not an Irish or Italian or a Greek or a Jewish studies program? Do not we white ethnics likewise have legacies and problems that need appreciation and understanding? This issue became most acute as black and Jewish interests acted out their respective scenarios. Because black power rhetoric was identified with Third World peoples, it often became anti-Israel and anti-Semitic. As a result, the traditional black-Jewish alliance on campuses to end discrimination and bigotry dissolved. Thus, what started as a black academic demand to create a curriculum that would compensate for the cultural genocide experienced by blacks fed into a white backlash. Ethnic demands produced instead interethnic rivalry and balkanization on many large university campuses.

Gradually, the culturally diverse ethnic programs, often underfinanced, became a form of cultural window-dressing within the larger and typical liberal arts curriculum. Traditional departments began introducing a range of ethnic courses that further reduced the need for minority students to find identity by becoming an ethnic studies major. Perhaps, as Jesse M. Vazquez suggests, "outside forces will revitalize the reasons that gave birth to black studies programs." I am more doubtful about such possibilities.

Probably the most critical backlash was stimulated by school busing of blacks into white neighborhoods to achieve the mandatory goals of integration. Busing was viewed as an invasion by blacks into white turf, which included not only "their" schools, but also "their" communities, "their" parks, and "their" shopping areas. "Their" constituted an invisible territorial sovereignty assumed in each white neighborhood when blacks moved into it. The whites most affected by these alleged black invasions were the more affluent blue-collar workers and lower-middle-class white-collar ones. It was the stratum immediately above the black community, not the upper-middle-class professionals residing in the much richer suburbs, that felt most threatened by busing orders from the courts.

As the struggle for integration spread, the currents of the blacklash reduced themselves to a more general rejection of the twelve or so major central cities throughout the nation in which poor blacks had become concentrated. This was noted by the liberal urban sociologist Herbert Gans:

> Most voters—and the politicians that represent them—are not inclined to give the cities the funds and powers to deal with poverty, or segregation. This disinclination is by no means as arbitrary as it may seem, for the plight of the urban poor, the anger of the rebellious, and the bankruptcy of the municipal treasury have not yet hurt or even seriously inconvenienced the vast majority of Americans. . . . Many Americans . . . are opposed to significant governmental activity on behalf of the poor and black. . . . Not only do they consider taxes an imposition on their ability to spend their earnings, but they view governmental expenditures as economic waste. . . . In effect, then, the cities and the poor and the blacks are politically outnumbered. This state of affairs suggests the . . . most important reasons for the national failure to act: the structure of American democracy and majority rule.

Between 1972 and the election of Ronald Reagan in 1980, civil rights groups activated their concern for affirmative action. A new stratum of black college students had risen who were seeking entry into professional schools and middle positions in the bureaucracies that ran public and private enterprises. This effort emerged in a larger economic context marked by "stagflation"—slow growth, creeping unemployment, and inflation. Real income in this period for large numbers of blue- and white-collar workers had become stagnant and even declined. Maintaining family living standards often took two full-time income earners. The acuteness of this new condition of stagflation was accompanied, moreover, by a diminishing faith in the federal government to correct the situation with policies that would increase output and employment and stabilize prices. In fact, the government was increasingly perceived as part of the problem rather than as part of the solution.

In this context, neoconservative scholars and pundits consolidated their attack on the welfare society and reaffirmed the virtues of the self-propelled market system. Welfare policies, once celebrated for their success, increasingly became viewed as the black nemesis that maintained black dependency on state subsidies. As real income declined for the lower middle classes, the tax burden could readily be blamed on the cost of the welfare system that sustained blacks who were unwilling to work.

As more middle-class blacks in the seventies found jobs and acquired middle-income status, especially among two-income families, they moved to the periphery of the central city or into marginally integrated suburbs; paradoxically, some returned to settle in the South they have traditionally fled. In any event, they abandoned, like many whites before them, the older urban neighborhoods and, in doing so, they contributed to the increased concentration and isolation of the black poor and underclass that continued to reside in the inner cities throughout the nation.

These various currents of change in the seventies proved conceptually unsettling for black intellectuals and leaders. The demise of the black power and separatist upsurge precipitated a confusing debate about whether race or class now composed the foundation of racism and the black malaise. The submerged civil rights leaders, having succeeded in the sixties in changing the legal structure, re-emerged with a focus on affirmative action. Both the former black power advocates and civil rights leaders moved in the direction of integrationist goals. Both groups tended to avoid entering into a public debate about the continued destruction of the black family and the growing black underclass, a matter that was finally corrected with a vengeance in the mid-eighties by William Julius Wilson's book *The Truly Disadvantaged.*

Imamu Amiri Baraka's disillusionment with Kenneth Gibson's mayoralty in Newark led to the most celebrated black separatist conversion of the mid-seventies, and it illustrates well the pervasive intellectual confusion of that time. Baraka, formerly LeRoi Jones—established playwright, poet, publicist, and political strategist—announced in 1974 his conversion to Marxism-Leninism and advocated that all workers, black and white, join hands to struggle against capitalism.

In the same year, a number of black intellectuals, many of whom were strong nationalists, were driven to debate the relationship between race and class at the Sixth Pan-African Congress in Tanzania. The African-based socialists, to the dismay of many American blacks, equated the degradation of their position to class rather than race. Race advocates, on the other hand, were "suspicious, even disdainful, of alliances with whites." The class analysis was seen as "a way out, a way to take off their African clothes, change back to their names, refry their hair, pick up white friends again." Less disdainful arguments returned to a position articulated by Malcolm X years earlier: blacks must organize separately and then integrate from a position of strength. One participant shunned all ideologically motivated positions and insisted that pragmatism should determine the extent of black-white collaboration. Finally, it was pointed out that black unity was an illusion because of class differences within the black community: "Regardless of chit'lins, fried chicken and soul, dancing-doin-it and rhythm, there are basic conflictual differences among blacks and those are class differences." This last observation received increasingly more attention as the decade of the seventies came to a close.

With more individual blacks acquiring the benefits of college education—one of the major fruits of the whole black upsurge from 1954 to 1970—it was natural for civil rights leaders to reflect the interests of this group and shift their attention to affirmative action. While the evidence suggests, contrary to some neoconservative claims, that affirmative action efforts to recruit and upgrade blacks to middle-level jobs were successful, the affirmative action ideology was not without its contradictions. First, it was increasingly viewed as reverse discrimination. A few highly publicized cases proved to middle-class whites that affirmative action was unfair; it violated rules of merit by putting less qualified blacks into positions that otherwise would have gone to whites. When seniority and some promotional rules in white-dominated unions were challenged by black affirmative action advocates, fears of affirmative action acquired a wider base; they entered the spontaneous rhetoric of the white middle-class backlash. Second, affirmative action that was initially race specific became generalized. When women, Hispanics, and Asian-Americans became defined as minorities and eligible for affirmative action regardless of their respective income and status differences, the concept of a minority representing more than 50 percent of the population lost some of its logical meaning. Third, the singular focus of affirmative action, an interest namely of middle-class blacks, ignored the truly disadvantaged blacks who possessed neither education nor skills to compete effectively. Finally, it has almost become fashionable among some contemporary black conservative scholars to argue that affirmative action is demoralizing to blacks themselves. It accents black inferiority on the assumption that promotion or entrance into a good college would not have occurred in the absence of preferential treatment. It lowers self-esteem and induces the acceptance of lower standards. It indirectly "encourages blacks to exploit their own victimization. Like inferiority, victimization is what justifies preference, so that to receive the benefits of preferential treatment one must . . . become invested in the view of one's self as a victim." And not least, it creates an illusion among blacks that "they [whites] owe us this" and that living blacks should be paid "for the historic suffering of the race."

The first book to give serious theoretical and empirical attention to the rise of the black middle class in the post-civil rights period was William J. Wilson's *Declining Significance of Race,* published in 1978. Although vituperatively received by many black intellectuals, it stimulated a vigorous debate about class and race and the growing integration of the black middle class in the work sphere of American society.

Wilson argues that the rise in demand for white-collar workers in the private and public sectors, combined with the success of the civil rights movement in removing the barriers for black entry into white-collar jobs, spawned a new, black middle class. The top third of the black population has now achieved integration in the economic sphere. Blacks, especially young college-educated ones, have acquired equal chances in the labor market to exchange their skills, goods, or services on the same basis as whites. Race has ceased to function as an important screening mechanism in the allocation of educated blacks. Income differences, therefore, between whites and blacks in the middle white-collar areas of employment have almost disappeared. Thus, it is class, not race, that increasingly determines the economic fate of blacks. By implication, the race category per se loses its theoretical relevance.

The situation that defines the bottom third of the black population is somewhat different. While historic racism may account for the lack of skills and education of poor blacks, their concentration in our central cities and their current isolation and impoverishment are due to the impersonal forces of technological change, capital flight, and demographic movement out of the inner cities on the part of both whites and better-off blacks. Insofar as these poor blacks are at a disadvantage, they compare to poor whites who likewise have been bypassed by technology and job upgrading in the postindustrial era. More neutral class policies, rather than race-specific ones, are the order of the day.

Unjustifiably in my judgment, many of Wilson's black critics viewed his interpretation as completely dissolving race considerations in his explanation of the current nature of black subordination. In contrast to black reactions, white liberals and conservatives saw virtue in the direction of Wilson's analysis. It legitimized the liberal and conservative political inclinations to yield further to their working- and middle-class white constituencies who were "tired" of hearing about the special needs of black people. Allegedly color-blind policies enabled white politicians to avoid allusion to race-specific programs; perhaps it even enabled them to justify avoiding policies for the poor in toto.

By the time the 1980s rolled around, the incremental retreats from the early civil rights days to the election of Ronald Reagan had accumulated into a well-formulated backlash, a revision, if you will, of the meaning and impact of the black struggles in the post-World War II period. The individual who most clearly summarized the delegitimization of the whole black struggle was Thomas Sowell, a prominent black conservative economist and intellectual. Writing thirty years after the historic *Brown v. Board of Education of Topeka* decision in 1954 and twenty years after the Civil Rights Act of 1964, Sowell's book *Civil Rights: Rhetoric or Reality?* raised the following questions:

> How much of the promise has [the] judicial and legislative events [brought into being by the civil rights movement] been fulfilled? How much has it been perverted? How well has the social vision behind the civil rights movement been understood—or even questioned?

Sowell's answers to these and related questions have become the litany of America's neoconservative doctrine and, perhaps, the inner speech of many liberals silently drifting to the right.

The civil rights movement in Sowell's eyes ultimately failed. What began as a movement specific to blacks soon became a universal vision that failed to serve black interests. Contrary to his intention, Thomas Sowell proves the extent to which America is a racist society—the extent to which white America is capable of putting the lid on the black American quest for social justice.

Sowell's arguments and "observations" delegitimize the process by which the civil rights movement specific to blacks was transformed into a civil rights vision allegedly applicable to all oppressed people. In the absence of any knowledge of Sowell's race, background, and intentions, readers of his *Civil Rights: Rhetoric or Reality?* often assume that he is a white scholar venting his disgust with blacks. While blatantly untrue, Sowell's arguments can be interpreted to feed such a view. From his perspective, the civil rights movement has spawned a race relations industry with leaders who do more harm than good, whose interests are to perpetuate themselves, and who use and are used by the mass media to sensationalize issues that have a dubious reality and may even do damage to black causes.

The civil rights vision has linked black economic success to black politics. This is unfortunate, since little evidence exists to show that political activity and economic success are related. "It would perhaps be easier to find an inverse correlation," writes Sowell, "between political activity and economic success than a direct correlation. Groups that have the skills for other things seldom concentrate in politics." Sowell repeatedly cites the economic success of Asian-Americans who allegedly "made it" like many immigrant groups of the past, that is, through hard work and no politics.

Sowell charges the civil rights vision with being simpleminded. It reduces the explanation of black-white statistical differences to only two alternatives: (a) innate inferiority, which, of course, the civil rights vision rejects, or (b) discriminatory practices by our social institutions, which it accepts. In putting all its emphasis on the latter assumption, the civil rights vision becomes simplistic and unable to stand up to scientific scrutiny, especially when one seeks to explain the relative progress of other ethnic groups. By "scientific scrutiny," Sowell means comparing income and occupational differences among groups after consideration of other "causal" factors such as age, region, time of entry into the United States, migration patterns, cultural habits, and wasted energies devoted to pursuits other than hard work. His conclusion is always in the direction of reducing racist and discriminatory factors in accounting for black failure to "make it" relative to other "equally" discriminated against racial and ethnic minorities who have "made it."

Perhaps Sowell wails most strongly against affirmative action. He argues that once the civil rights movement was transformed to defend the aged, the disabled, women, Native Americans, Hispanics, and so on, 70 percent of the population became minority groups, an absurdity that makes affirmative action useless. Instead of viewing the broadening base of affirmative action as the leading edge in an effort to change our national priorities about which, where, and how people work—as an effort, even if momentarily not successful, to establish deep changes in the ground rules guiding our goals to achieve social justice—Sowell sees it as solely inducing a white backlash, as discouraging employers from hiring blacks or other minority groups, and, finally, as nurturing black inferiority because affirmative action suggests that blacks are unable to make it by the merit standards that judge the majority. He makes a similar interpretation about busing: busing for school integration is an axiomatic disaster, since it not only leads to a white backlash but also speaks to the idea that it is impossible for all black schools to be of a high quality.

In sum, by pushing confrontation with the white power structure too far, by making overt efforts to acquire economic progress through affirmative action that benefits middle- but not lower-class blacks, by seeking to use the government to correct today's statistical discrepancies that are a result of past wrongs and not of present institutional practices, blacks could lose everything. The black civil rights vision in action is pushing the majority of white society into a corner from which it may lash out with an antiblack reaction that could bring down the promise of freedom for all.

What should blacks do? Blacks should, according to Sowell, accept the system as it stands and do what all other past and present immigrant groups have done. This general prescription involves the following specific recommendations: (a) Let businesspeople apply their own criteria for organizing the efficient use of workers within their enterprises; too much interference with their prerogatives will increase their hiring and promotion costs and lead to a decrease in demand for black employees. (b) Blacks should throw themselves into the competitive jungle like everyone else, even if it means accepting menial, low-paid work; by learning work discipline and being forced to shape up in a real world, blacks will do better in the long run than by accepting government handouts. And finally, (c) instead of black power and civil rights ideologies, blacks should adopt the work ethic, become work addicts, and seek self-sufficiency through establishing small businesses. Besides, suggests Sowell, these propositions are more consonant with the real basis upon which black progress has always rested: hard work in the context of rapid economic growth. Black opportunities are more a function of the pushes and pulls of impersonal market forces and less a result of black political and social posturing about racism. If posturing is necessary, black leaders should emphasize positive black achievements and the success of the black middle class.

Sowell's overall assessment of the evolution of the civil rights movement from the early fifties to the present is, in my view, an articulation of white America's drift to the right based on the judgment that blacks have pushed whites beyond their limits of toleration; it constitutes the rationalization of rising neoconservative forces. It is as if Sowell were hired to articulate what "responsible" white conservatives would not say for fear of being accused of overt racist sentiments. This judgment has been poignantly made by Derrick Bell, a black Harvard University legal scholar. In discussing the way white policymakers are currently seeking to abandon the enforcement of civil rights laws and the blaming of black poverty either on blacks themselves or on the social policies upon which they rely, it is always a good practice to obtain some black experts for achieving "deceptive authenticity." Thomas Sowell, in the view of Derrick Bell, is one such black expert:

> [Thomas Sowell], knowingly or not, dispense[s] a product that fills the present national need for outrageous anti-black comment. Many whites welcome it. . . . Spout[ing] . . . white-racist rhetoric . . . obtains a spurious legitimacy because it emanates from a black mouth.

Whether or not Sowell has acted as mouthpiece for the racist undertones of the conservative drift over the past fifteen years or so is not relevant for the immediate purposes at hand. I personally believe that the "mouthpiece" castigation is unwarranted. He no doubt would dismiss the accusation as an ad hominem attack. Nevertheless, our racist heritage includes the way whites use color and then stand back to observe how blacks devour each other, as if whites were not a part of the fray or the problem it represents. Be that as it may, Sowell has performed a service, insofar as one might wish to view it as such, by articulating in a coherent form the way many white backlashers and conservatives view black struggles.

One last comment is required about Sowell's civil rights revisionist interpretation. Sowell's overall perspective has an unintended contradiction that undermines some of his glib comparisons between blacks and other ethnic groups. . . . Sowell argues that "blacks have a history in the United States that is quite different from that of other American ethnic group. The massive fact of slavery looms over more than half of that history."

This fact of slavery, he continues, was followed by Jim Crow laws and virulent, biologically defined racism relegating blacks to membership in an inferior subspecies of the human race. As a result, Sowell reminds us, "blacks are black for life. They do not have the option simply to change their names and life-styles and blend into the general population."

An origin and history as profoundly unique as Sowell claims militates against facile comparisons between African-Americans and other ethnic groups. Not only may black history and its legacy be unique, but white racial sentiments toward blacks may be uniquely different from the white majority's chauvinistic attitude toward other ethnic minorities. All chauvinism is not equal in character and intensity.

As the current wave of ethnic affirmations is paraded under the rhetorical banner of multiculturalism, the unfinished economic and social agenda stimulated by the civil rights movement is being aborted, if not completely abandoned. It is ironic that the declining economic position of at least 30 to 40 percent of the black population throughout the 1980s should coalesce alongside rising antiblack sentiments. As one supporter of the known ex-Klansman, David Duke (who received 40 percent of the vote in his campaign for the state senate in Louisiana), stated: "Blacks are just taking everything. They're taking everything from us, and the white race is going down the tubes. It's about time someone spoke up for the white people." Extreme overt sentiments, of course, are not the norm, however close they may be to the private thoughts of others. They are, in my judgment, part of a white backlash continuum: witness the fact that President Bush vetoed the 1990 civil rights bill, which focused on enhancing certainty in employment for minorities. The veto, according to informed opinion, was related to the social and political climate that enabled President Bush to "alienate black leaders, but [placate] the much larger number of whites" with references to the bill's reliance on quotas.

Conclusion

Assessing the critical events that marked the civil rights struggle and its metamorphosis into a civic disgrace evokes endemic issues that perennially emerge in the conflictual history and experiences of black-white relations. Black affirmations and white reactions to them reveal the changing faces of our latent and manifest racist impulses. The issues, as the struggles from the fifties to the nineties illustrate, range from the meaning of the slave experience to possibilities for a new era of black-white relations beyond the derogatory dependency status allegedly established by the welfare state.

In attempts to explain black subordination and understand black-white conflict, there is a long-standing debate between those who view the enduring black malaise as rooted and defined in terms of race from which socioeconomic status is derived, and those who see it as primarily anchored in the black population's class position from which cultural characteristics are derived. The shorthand mode in this debate is simply race versus class. How to allocate the respective roles of these two opposing organizing principles, repeatedly employed to explain racism and the relative subordination of blacks, involves looking at the vacillating shadows cast by the interaction of race and class. These interactions have changed as one explores the entrapment of the black population from its African roots to North American enslavement, from enslavement to the development of a rigid agricultural tenancy system, from rural impoverishment to ghettoization. Consequential portions of the black community have been periodically locked into social and economic enclaves that nurtured subordination and racism in a variety of vulgar and subtle forms, including self-denigration and dependency. In the course of historical shifts in circumstances, we have witnessed the use of race or class categories to explain the subordination of blacks. Whites use myopic race perceptions to produce class differences, or employ class differences to rationalize racial exclusionary practices. Blacks, for defensive and offensive reasons, vacillate between racially oriented themes that transcend class and class themes that subordinate race.

Illustrations abound. The origin of slavery is seen as an outgrowth of the class exigencies of the southern plantation owners; it is also understood as arising out of a deeply rooted racialist mind-set that constitutes a part of Western cultural tradition predating black enslavement. In a parallel manner, the evolution and manifestation of black cultural habits are viewed as tied to a history that transcends the slave experience, thereby directing our focus to the black population's African roots; or they are seen as more reflective of the white domination of blacks in the American context.

Dimensions of this debate never seem to die. Moynihan raised the ghost of the slave legacy to account for the state of the black family's deterioration and dependency; black power advocates asserted that it was the racial-cultural legacy, despite enslavement, that sustained the black family's survival.

Comparing black-white differences in income and occupational achievements, especially as they relate to schooling and scholastic performance, social scientists periodically turn to the notion of inherited mental capacities. Hereditary explanations have a long, checkered, and seamy history in which there is little cause for pride. Nevertheless, biologically driven arguments appear to be a cat with many lives, reemerging with different and more subtle stripes. Why and when this approach gets injected into the social equation of black-white differences illustrates, frequently with a vengeance, how class conflicts can be transformed into racist social instruments by professional academicians and scientists to affect the allocation of resources to blacks.

In the political and civil rights struggles of the 1960s there emerged an implicit debate between Martin Luther King, Jr., and Malcolm X that centered on class versus race. King, in orienting blacks, often reminded his followers that they were mainly working people, and they therefore shared common interests with unions and all other working people. Class ought to transcend race. Malcolm X, in contrast, advocated organizing around race. Whites in all classes, and especially those in the working class, despised blacks. Progress in dealing with issues that confront us required that we first organize as blacks. In the tradition of black power advocates, this meant emphasizing the need for black identity based on some combination of race and culture shared by all blacks—regardless of the specific class, status, education, and income differences within the black community. It is precisely here that William J. Wilson's analysis intercedes with the argument that class has replaced race in "determining life-chances in the modern industrial period." Middle-class blacks now have the same goals as middle-class whites and poor blacks now have shared interests with poor whites. Discrimination based on race, in one interpretation of Wilson's argument, ceases to become a vital determinant; race affirmations and explanations lose their appeal.

Whatever doubts Wilson's well-argued thesis cast on the continuing influence of race, a virulent strain of social racism in everyday life appeared to rise and spread throughout the eighties. It was noted by the very same black middle class that Wilson identified as having acquired equal economic life chances. This social racism outside the work sphere is unlikely to proceed without affecting the status of the blacks who are "making it" economically. Beyond the underclass and the style of life it conjures (a major source of social racism), there are "everyday" occurrences in black life that are transmitted through the mass media and defined in racially degrading terms. Teenage pregnancy, for example, is rarely described as simply a problem of young poor women. Black teenagers are generally identified, along with a possible motive for pregnancy, for example, the acquisition of income from the welfare system in order to avoid work. Is this alleged adaptation explicable by race or class? In the popular mind there is often little doubt.

The swelling undertones of hostile racial sentiments and the need for racial pride perhaps constitute the basis of Jesse Jackson's political rise in the current period. His political mobilization of blacks sometimes involved the employment of class and race themes in a single voice. On the one hand, in his speeches made in 1984 and 1988, Jackson called for the need to "leave the racial battle ground and come to the economic common ground." Class commonality is what will unite blacks and whites. On the other hand, Jackson's idiom, cadence, and incantation are that of a black preacher talking to his people. For the most part, Jackson's message is geared to the racial and cultural experiences of blacks.

Jackson's rise to the status of a power broker in the Democratic party is viewed by many white Democrats as an embarrassment; that feeling is a self-evident, if veiled, reflection of racist sentiments. The Democrats need to turn out the black vote in larger numbers and, of course, also need the more volatile white middle-class vote. To the extent that the party is too race specific, it will lose the white vote. To the extent that it avoids race issues or substitutes a race orientation for a broad or vague class one, it will fail to enlarge the black vote. This dilemma is part of the unsolved race-class tension that drives black-white relations.

Underlying my major themes—the economics of dominant-subordinate relations and their aggregation to produce a race-class nexus that affects many aspects of American life—is a historic foundation that necessarily requires a statement about the legacy of slavery. Since the mid-seventies, unfortunately, the discussion of the unique slave roots shaping the trajectory of black-white relations has diminished. A correction of this lapse is in order.

6.2   **Randall Kennedy**

Persuasion and Distrust: The Affirmative Action Debate

Randall Kennedy was a law clerk for former Supreme Court justice Thurgood Marshall. He is author of Race, Crime, and the Law. *Currently he is professor of law at Harvard University Law School.*

The controversy over affirmative action constitutes the most salient current battlefront in the ongoing conflict over the status of blacks in American life. No domestic struggle has been more protracted or more riddled with ironic complication. One frequently noted irony is that the affirmative action controversy has contributed significantly to splintering the coalition principally responsible for the civil rights revolution. That coalition was comprised of a broad array of groups—liberal Democrats, moderate Republicans, the national organizations of the black and Jewish communities, organized labor, and others—that succeeded in invalidating de jure segregation and passing far-reaching legislation in support of the rights of blacks, including the Civil Rights Act of 1964 and the Voting Rights Act of 1965.

For over a decade this coalition has been riven by bitter disagreement over the means by which American society should attempt to overcome its racist past. Opponents of affirmative action maintain that commitment to a nonracist social environment requires strict color-blindness in decision-making as both a strategy and a goal. In their view, "one gets beyond racism by getting beyond it now: by a complete, resolute, and credible commitment *never* to tolerate in one's own life—or in the life or practices of one's government—the differential treatment of other human beings by race." Proponents of affirmative action insist that only *malign* racial distinctions should be prohibited; they favor *benign* distinctions that favor blacks. Their view is that "[i]n order to get beyond racism, we must first take race into account" and that "in order to treat some persons equally, we must treat them differently."

Part I of this Commentary considers aspects of two principal objections to affirmative action; that it harms rather than helps blacks in American society, and that it violates the Constitution. My discussion does not attempt to analyze this large and complicated subject comprehensively but rather seeks to focus upon certain vexing areas of the public debate. I conclude that affirmative action should generally be retained as a tool of public policy because, on balance, it is useful in overcoming entrenched racial hierarchy.

Part II explores an issue widely ignored by academic commentators: whether covert motivations play a role in the political, judicial, and intellectual reaction against affirmative action. I defend the utility of the question and suggest an answer to it. I argue that division within the civil rights coalition is not the *only* conflict permeating the affirmative action controversy. Also involved is a much older conflict involving sectors of our society that have never authentically repudiated the "old style religion" of white supremacy. The most important of these sectors is the Reagan administration. I contend that a tenacious and covert resistance to further erosion of racial hierarchy explains much of the Reagan administration's racial policy, especially its attacks on affirmative action.

I focus on both overt and covert discourse, because the affirmative action debate cannot be understood without acknowledging simultaneously the force of the openly stated arguments for and against preferential treatment and the submerged intuitions that disguise themselves with these arguments. To disregard either of these features of the debate is to ignore an essential aspect of the controversy. To appreciate both is to recognize the frustrating complexity of our racial situation.

I. The Efficacy and Lawfulness of Affirmative Action

The Case for Affirmative Action

Affirmative action has strikingly benefited blacks as a group and the nation as a whole. It has enabled blacks to attain occupational and educational advancement in numbers and at a pace that would otherwise have been impossible. These breakthroughs engender self-perpetuating benefits: the accumulation of valuable experience, the expansion of a professional class able to pass its material advantages and elevated aspirations to subsequent generations, the eradication of debilitating stereotypes, and the inclusion of black participants in the making of consequential decisions affecting black interests. Without affirmative action, continued access for black applicants to college and professional education would be drastically narrowed. To insist, for example, upon the total exclusion of racial factors in admission decisions, especially at elite institutions, would mean classes of college, professional, and graduate students that are virtually devoid of African-American representation.

Furthermore, the benefits of affirmative action redound not only to blacks but to the nation as a whole. For example, the virtual absence of black police even in overwhelmingly black areas helped spark the ghetto rebellions of the 1960s. The integration of police forces through strong affirmative action measures has often led to better relations between minority communities and the police, a result that improves public safety for all. Positive externalities have accompanied affirmative action programs in other contexts as well, most importantly by teaching whites that blacks, too, are capable of handling responsibility, dispensing knowledge, and applying valued skills.

The Claim That Affirmative Action Harms Blacks

In the face of arguments in favor of affirmative action, opponents of the policy frequently reply that it actually harms its ostensible beneficiaries. Various interrelated claims undergird the argument that affirmative action is detrimental to blacks. The most weighty claim is that preferential treatment exacerbates racial resentments, entrenches racial divisiveness, and thereby undermines the consensus necessary for effective reform. The problem with this view is that intense white resentment has accompanied every effort to undo racial subordination no matter how careful the attempt to anticipate and mollify the reaction. The Supreme Court, for example, tried mightily to preempt white resistance to school desegregation by directing that it be implemented with "all deliberate speed." This attempt, however, to defuse white resistance may well have caused the opposite effect and, in any event, doomed from the outset the constitutional rights of a generation of black schoolchildren. Given the apparent inevitability of white resistance and the uncertain efficacy of containment, proponents of racial justice should be wary of allowing fear of white backlash to limit the range of reforms pursued. This admonition is particularly appropriate with respect to affirmative action insofar as it creates vital opportunities the value of which likely outweigh their cost in social friction. A second part of the argument that affirmative action hurts blacks is the claim that it stigmatizes them by implying that they simply cannot compete on an equal basis with whites. Moreover, the pall cast by preferential treatment is feared to be pervasive, hovering over blacks who have attained positions without the aid of affirmative action as well as over those who have been accorded preferential treatment. I do not doubt that affirmative action causes some stigmatizing effect. It is unrealistic to think, however, that affirmative action causes most white disparagement of the abilities of blacks. Such disparagement, buttressed for decades by the rigid exclusion of blacks from educational and employment opportunities, is precisely what engendered the explosive crisis to which affirmative action is a response. Although it is widely assumed that "qualified" blacks are now in great demand, with virtually unlimited possibilities for recognition, blacks continue to encounter prejudice that ignores or minimizes their talent. In the end, the uncertain extent to which affirmative action diminishes the accomplishments of blacks must be balanced against the stigmatization that occurs when blacks are virtually absent from important institutions in the society. The presence of blacks across the broad spectrum of institutional settings upsets conventional stereotypes about the place of blacks and acculturates the public to the idea that blacks can and must participate in all areas of our national life. This positive result of affirmative action outweighs any stigma that the policy causes.

A third part of the argument against affirmative action is the claim that it saps the internal morale of blacks. It renders them vulnerable to a dispiriting anxiety that they have not truly earned whatever positions or honors they have attained. Moreover, it causes some blacks to lower their own expectations of themselves. Having grown accustomed to the extra boost provided by preferential treatment, some blacks simply do not try as hard as they otherwise would. There is considerable power to this claim; unaided accomplishment does give rise to a special pride felt by both the individual achiever and her community. But the suggestion that affirmative action plays a major role in undermining the internal morale of the black community is erroneous.

Although I am unaware of any systematic evidence on the self-image of beneficiaries of affirmative action, my own strong impression is that black beneficiaries do not see their attainments as tainted or undeserved—and for good reason. First, they correctly view affirmative action as rather modest compensation for the long period of racial subordination suffered by blacks as a group. Thus they do not feel that they have been merely *given* a preference; rather, they see affirmative discrimination as a form of social justice. Second, and more importantly, many black beneficiaries of affirmative action view claims of meritocracy with skepticism. They recognize that in many instances the objection that affirmative action represents a deviation from meritocratic standards is little more than disappointed nostalgia for a golden age that never really existed. Overt exclusion of blacks from public and private institutions of education and employment was one massive affront to meritocratic pretensions. Moreover, a long-standing and pervasive feature of our society is the importance of a wide range of nonobjective, nonmeritocratic factors influencing the distribution of opportunity. The significance of personal associations and informal networks is what gives durability and resonance to the adage: It's not *what* you know, it's *who* you know. As Professor Wasserstrom wryly observes, "Would anyone claim that Henry Ford II [was] head of the Ford Motor Company because he [was] the most qualified person for the job?"

Finally, and most importantly, many beneficiaries of affirmative action recognize the thoroughly political—which is to say contestable—nature of "merit"; they realize that it is a malleable concept, determined not by immanent, preexisting standards but rather by the perceived needs of society. Inasmuch as the elevation of blacks addresses pressing social needs, they rightly insist that considering a black's race as part of the bundle of traits that constitute "merit" is entirely appropriate.

A final and related objection to affirmative action is that it frequently aids those blacks who need it least and who can least plausibly claim to suffer the vestiges of past discrimination—the offspring of black middle-class parents seeking preferential treatment in admission to elite universities and black entrepreneurs seeking guaranteed set-asides for minority contractors on projects supported by the federal government. This objection, too, is unpersuasive. First, it ignores the large extent to which affirmative action has pried open opportunities for blue-collar black workers. Second, it assumes that affirmative action should be provided only to the most deprived strata of the black community or to those who can best document their victimization. In many circumstances, however, affirmative action has developed from the premise that special aid should be given to strategically important sectors of the black community—for example, those with the threshold ability to integrate the professions. Third, although affirmative action has primarily benefited the black middle class, that is no reason to condemn preferential treatment. All that fact indicates is the necessity for additional social intervention to address unmet needs in those sectors of the black community left untouched by affirmative action. One thing that proponents of affirmative action have neglected to emphasize strongly enough is that affirmative discrimination is but part—indeed a rather small part—of the needed response to the appalling crisis besetting black communities. What is so remarkable—and ominous—about the affirmative action debate is that so modest a reform calls forth such powerful resistance.

Does Affirmative Action Violate the Constitution?

The constitutional argument against affirmative action proceeds as follows: *All* governmental distinctions based on race are presumed to be illegal and can only escape that presumption by meeting the exacting requirements of "strict scrutiny." Because the typical affirmative action program cannot meet these requirements, most such programs are unconstitutional. Behind this theory lies a conviction that has attained its most passionate and oft-quoted articulation in Alexander Bickel's statement:

> The lesson of the great decisions of the Supreme Court and the lesson of contemporary history have been the same for at least a generation: discrimination on the basis of race is illegal, immoral, unconstitutional, inherently wrong, and destructive of democratic society. Now this is to be unlearned and we are told that this is not a matter of fundamental principle but only a matter of whose ox is gored.

Among the attractions of this theory are its symmetry and simplicity. It commands that the government be color blind in its treatment of persons, that it accord benefits and burdens to black and white individuals according to precisely the *same* criteria—no matter whose ox is gored. According to its proponents, this theory dispenses with manipulable sociological investigations and provides a clear *rule* that compels consistent judicial application.

In response, I would first note that the color-blind theory of the Constitution is precisely that—a "theory," one of any number of competing theories that seek to interpret the Fourteenth Amendment's Delphic proscription of state action that denies any person "the equal protection of the laws." Implicitly recognizing that neither a theory of original intent nor a theory of textual construction provides suitable guidance, Professor Bickel suggests that a proper resolution of the affirmative action dispute can be derived from "the great decisions of the

Supreme Court." Certainly what Bickel had in mind were *Brown v. Board of Education* and its immediate progeny, the cases that established the foundation of our postsegregation Constitution. To opponents of affirmative action, the lesson of these cases is that, except in the narrowest, most exigent circumstances, race can play no legitimate role in government decision-making.

This view, however, is too abstract and ahistorical. In the forties, fifties, and early sixties, against the backdrop of laws that used racial distinctions to exclude blacks from opportunities available to white citizens, it seemed that racial subjugation could be overcome by mandating the application of race-blind law. In retrospect, however, it appears that the concept of race-blindness was simply a proxy for the fundamental demand that racial subjugation be eradicated. This demand, which matured over time in the face of myriad sorts of opposition, focused upon the *condition* of racial subjugation; its target was not only procedures that overtly excluded blacks on the basis of race, but also the self-perpetuating dynamics of subordination that had survived the demise of American apartheid. The opponents of affirmative action have stripped the historical context from the demand for race-blind law. They have fashioned this demand into a new totem and insist on deference to it no matter what its effects upon the very group the Fourteenth Amendment was created to protect. *Brown* and its progeny do not stand for the abstract principle that governmental distinctions based on race are unconstitutional. Rather, those great cases, forged by the gritty particularities of the struggle against white racism, stand for the proposition that the Constitution prohibits any arrangements imposing racial subjugation—whether such arrangements are ostensibly race neutral or even ostensibly race blind.

This interpretation, which articulates a principle of antisubjugation rather than antidiscrimination, typically encounters two closely related objections. The first objection is the claim that the constitutional injury done to a white whose chances for obtaining some scarce opportunity are diminished because of race-based allocation schemes is legally indistinguishable from that suffered by a black victim of racial exclusion. Second, others argue that affirmative discrimination based on racial distinctions cannot be satisfactorily differentiated from racial subjugation absent controversial sociological judgments that are inappropriate to the judicial role.

As to the first objection, the injury suffered by white "victims" of affirmative action does not properly give rise to a constitutional claim, because the damage does not derive from a scheme animated by racial prejudice. Whites with certain credentials may be excluded from particular opportunities they would receive if they were black. But this diminished opportunity is simply an incidental consequence of addressing a compelling societal need: undoing the subjugation of African Americans. Whites who would be admitted to professional schools in the absence of affirmative action policies are not excluded merely because of prejudice, as were countless numbers of blacks until fairly recently. Rather, whites are excluded "because of a rational calculation about the socially most beneficial use of limited resources for [professional] education."

As to the second objection, I concede that distinctions between affirmative and malign discrimination cannot be made in the absence of controversial sociological judgments. I reject the proposition, however, that drawing these distinctions is inappropriate to the judicial role. Such a proposition rests upon the assumption that there exists a judicial method wholly independent of sociological judgment. That assumption is false; to some extent, whether explicitly or implicitly, *every* judicial decision rests upon certain premises regarding the irreducibly controversial nature of social reality. The question, therefore, is not whether a court will make sociological judgments, but the content of the sociological judgments it must inevitably make.

Prior to *Brown,* the Supreme Court's validation of segregation statutes rested upon the premise that they did not unequally burden the black. A perceived difficulty in invalidating segregation statutes was that, as written, such laws were race neutral; they excluded white children from black schools just as they excluded black children from white schools. The Court finally recognized in *Brown* that racial subjugation constituted the social meaning of segregation laws. To determine that social meaning, the Court had to look past form into substance and judge the legitimacy of segregation laws given their intended and actual effects. Just as the "neutrality" of the segregation laws obfuscated racial subjugation, so, too, many the formal neutrality of race-blind policies also obfuscate the perpetuation of racial subjugation. That issue can only be explored by an inquiry into the context of the race-blind policy at issue, an inquiry that necessarily entails judicial sociology.

II. The Question of Racism

The Need for Motive Analysis

Much has been written about the issues discussed in Part I of this Comment. However, there remains a disturbing lacuna in the scholarly debate. Whether racism is partly responsible for the growing opposition to affirmative action is a question that is virtually absent from many of the leading articles on the subject. These articles typically portray the conflict over affirmative action as occurring in the context of an overriding commitment to racial fairness and equality shared by *all* the important participants in the debate. For example, a recent article by Professors Richard Fallon and Paul Weiler depicts the conflict in terms of "contending models of racial justice"—a depiction suggesting that, despite its bitterness, the affirmative action debate is at least bounded by common abhorrence of explicit racial hierarchy. This portrait, however, of conflict-within-consensus is all too genial. It conjures up the absurd image of Benjamin Hooks and William Bradford Reynolds embracing one another as ideological brethren, differing on the discrete issue of affirmative action but united on the fundamentals of racial fairness. It obscures the emotions that color the affirmative action debate and underestimates the alienation that separates antagonists. It ignores those who believe that much of the campaign against affirmative action is merely the latest in a long series of white reactions against efforts to elevate the status of blacks in American society. These observers perceive critics of affirmative action not merely as *opponents* but as *enemies.* They perceive ostensibly nonracist objections to affirmative action as rationalizations of white supremacy. They fear that the campaign against affirmative action is simply the opening wedge of a broader effort to recapture territory "lost" in the Civil Rights Revolution of the 1960s. And it is precisely this apprehension that explains the bitterness and desperation with which they wage the affirmative action struggle— emotions that are simply inexplicable in terms of the picture of race relations portrayed by conventional analyses.

The conventional portrait also implicitly excludes from consideration those whose opposition to affirmative action stems from racism. It concedes the presence of prejudice "out there" in the workaday world of ordinary citizens. But it assumes that "in here"—in the realm of scholarly discourse and the creation of public policy—prejudice plays no role. In other words, conventional scholarship leaves largely unexamined the possibility that the campaigns against affirmative action now being waged by political, judicial, and intellectual elites reflect racially selective indifference, antipathy born of prejudice, or strategies that seek to capitalize on widespread racial resentments.

Why have scholars consistently avoided scrutinizing the motives of policy-makers and fellow commentators? The explanations offered for the absence of such inquiry resemble those advanced to explain the futility or inappropriateness of inquiry into legislative motive. One objection centers on the evidentiary difficulties involved in ascertaining someone's motives. If the devil himself knoweth not the mind of man, how can mortal commentators know the motivation of officials and fellow analysts? A second objection is that the cost of the inquiry, including the inevitable possibility of error, outweighs any gains. A third objection is that, whatever the propriety of motive review in adjudication, it is an improper mode of analysis within intellectual discourse because it strongly tends toward ad hominem attacks on honesty that are impossible to disprove. Moreover, scrutiny of motive is a mode of analysis easily susceptible of reductionism: by focusing on the proponent of an idea and his suspected aims, one tends to reduce the idea itself to the status of a mere instrument. A fourth objection is that motive-centered inquiries are irrelevant: after all, a policy stemming from bad motives can nevertheless turn out to be a positive contribution to the public good, fully justifiable on the basis of sound reasons unrelated to covert and evil motives.

These objections serve a useful cautionary function. They fail, however, to show that motive analysis is misplaced in intellectual discussion and policy analysis. First, awkward problems in assembling evidence regarding the suspected objectives of a scholar or public official need not justify a wholesale rejection of the inquiry. Such problems merely indicate that a motive-centered analysis is difficult—not that it is improper or unfruitful. Second, although motive analysis does entail the possibility that a person or institution may be wrongly accused of harboring racist sentiments, forgoing such inquiry also imposes a high cost: loss of information regarding the nature of our society. Conclusions as to motive are admittedly uncertain, but so are the conclusions that result from many of the most important inquiries we are forced to make in our intellectual as well as personal and political lives. Furthermore, while charging someone with either consciously or unconsciously falsifying his motives is undeniably an insult, it is equally undeniable that the search for truth often causes pain—and that the deliberate hiding of motive constitutes an affront to all of those to whom the lie is addressed.

Third, the danger that concern with motive will overshadow attentiveness to ideas is simply another of the many dangers of excess that adhere to *any* methodology. The proper reaction is not wholesale rejection, but rather a disciplined use of the methodology that is informed by the limits of any one particular line of inquiry. Finally, to suggest that a policy is completely distinct from the motive from which it arises simply distorts reality. The animating motive is an integral aspect of the context in which a policy emerges, and there is no such thing as a policy without a context. A policy is "not a crystal, transparent and unchanged, it is the skin of a living thought and may vary greatly in color and content according to the circumstances and the time in which it is used." In other words, no unchanging essence exists within any policy, including a policy rejecting affirmative action. Such a policy could have a wide variety of meanings, depending upon, among other things, the motive behind the policy. Rejecting affirmative action for nonracist reasons is simply not the same policy as rejecting affirmative action for reasons infected with racism. The two policies share obvious traits: they both reject preferential treatment. But they also differ fundamentally—the former may constitute an error, the latter is certainly an insult.

Motivation, then, always matters in determining the meaning of a policy, although it is not all that matters. But attentiveness to motive should be an important aspect of ongoing analysis of the affirmative action controversy for other reasons as well. The simple but basic desire to document accurately the history of our era is justification enough for inquiring into the motives animating political action. That inquiry is essential to answering the most difficult of the questions that beset historians—the question of *why* particular actions are taken, given decisions made. Furthermore, baleful consequences attend dependence upon false records of social reality. After all, blindness to contemporary social realities helped spawn the monstrous lie, propagated by the Supreme Court in *Plessy v. Ferguson,* that the segregation of African Americans had nothing to do with racial oppression. Bitter experience should remind us, then, that in matters touching race relations there is an especially pressing need to keep the record straight.

The Importance of Motive Inquiry:
The Case of the Reagan Administration

A good way to begin setting the record straight is by assessing the motives of those in high public office. Suspicion characterizes the disposition with which I begin that assessment. My suspicion stems from the recognition that racism in America is an enormously powerful ideological institution, considerably older than the political institutions of our republic, and has often influenced the actions of the executive branch and indeed all levels of government. My preexisting distrust is heightened, however, by the particular background of the Reagan administration and, more specifically, by the political biography of Ronald Reagan himself.

As President, Ronald Reagan declared himself "heart and soul in favor of the things that have been done in the name of civil rights and desegregation." This commitment, he maintained, accounted for his opposition to affirmative discrimination. What justifies skepticism toward the President's account is his long history of suspect views on racial issues. His active opposition to racial distinctions *benefiting* African Americans is not matched by analogous opposition to racial distinctions *harming* African Americans. Indeed, a strikingly consistent feature of President Reagan's long political career has been his resistance to practically every major political effort to eradicate racism or to contain its effects. During the height of the civil rights revolution, he opposed the Civil Rights Act of 1964, the Voting Rights Act of 1965, and the Open Housing Act of 1968, legislation that his own assistant attorney general rightly described as "designed to make equal opportunity a reality."

Of course, although opposition to this landmark legislation is itself tremendously revealing, limits exist to the inferences that one can properly draw from positions adopted over twenty years ago. But President Reagan provided additional reasons for distrusting his explanation of his racial policies. Repeatedly his administration showed callous disregard for the particular interests of blacks and resisted measures designed to erode racial hierarchy. These actions included the administration's opposition (1) to the amendments that strengthened and extended the Voting Rights Act, (2) to anything more than the most cramped reading of the Civil Rights Act of 1964, (3) to creating a national holiday honoring Dr. Martin Luther King, Jr., (4) to maintaining the integrity of agencies involved in federal enforcement of civil rights, and (5) to imposing sanctions on South Africa for its policy of apartheid.

Perhaps the most instructive episode was the position the Reagan Administration took in the now infamous *Bob Jones University* case on the issue of tax exemption for private schools that discriminate against blacks. The platform of the Republican party in 1980 promised that its leaders would "halt the unconstitutional regulatory vendetta launched . . . against independent schools." President Reagan fulfilled that pledge by reversing the policy of the Internal Revenue Service (IRS) denying exempt status to discriminatory private schools. The administration stated that it had acted out of a desire to end the IRS's usurpation of powers beyond those authorized by Congress. Subsequent revelations called the honesty of this explanation into doubt. That apparent dishonesty—coupled with the administration's overwhelming defeat in the Supreme Court—turned the tax exemption imbroglio into one of the administration's most politically embarrassing moments. For present purposes, however, the significance of the episode lies in the stark illustration it provides of the underlying impulse behind the Reagan administration's racial policy—an impulse to protect the prerogatives of whites at the least hint of encroachment by claims of racial justice.

There are, of course, alternative explanations to the one advanced above. One could disaggregate the record of Ronald Reagan and his administration and rationalize each position on a case-by-case basis, by reference to concerns having nothing to do with racist sentiments or strategies. Concerns about freedom of association might have prompted Reagan's opposition to the Civil Rights Act of 1964. Concerns about federalism might account for his opposition to the Voting Rights Act of 1965. Concerns about the proper allocation of responsibility between the executive and legislative branches might explain the administration's stance in the tax exemption controversy. And authentic regard for the philosophical premises of individualism might theoretically explain the administration's opposition to affirmative action.

The problem with this mode of defense is that it ignores the strong *systematic* tilt of the administration's actions. It disregards as well the political milieu in which debate over affirmative action and other racial policies has been waged over the past decade—a period during which there has been a discernible attenuation of public commitment to racial justice and, even more troubling, a startling reemergence of overt racial animosity. The Reagan administration's policies reflect, reinforce, and capitalize on widespread feelings that blacks have received an undeserved amount of the nation's attention. Unburdened by the inhibitions imposed by public office, ordinary white citizens have expressed quite openly the feelings that color their analysis of the affirmative action issue. The Reagan administration expertly tapped these feelings for political gain by dint of arguments for race-blindness that were, in fact, exquisitely attuned to the racial sensitivities of the dominant white majority. Those who have ignored racism as an important element of the affirmative action controversy should consider SPONGE (The Society for the Prevention of

Niggers Getting Everything), an organization of disaffected whites in the Canarsie section of Brooklyn, New York, whose arresting title is more revealing of at least part of the opposition to affirmative action than many commentators seem willing to acknowledge.

III. Conclusion

In the end, perhaps the most striking feature of the affirmative action debate is the extent to which it highlights the crisis of trust besetting American race relations. Proponents of affirmative action view their opponents with suspicion for good reason. They know that not all of their opponents are racist; they also know that many of them are. Such suspicions corrode reasoned discourse. Contending claims to truth and justice are often reduced by opposing camps to disguised grasps for power and privilege. It would be a mistake, however, to suppose that the antidote to such corrosion is willful blindness to pretext. The only thing that will enable affirmative action—or any similarly controversial policy—to be debated in an atmosphere free of suspicion is for the surrounding social context to be decisively transformed. The essential element of this transformation is the creation of a sentiment of community strong enough to enable each group to entrust its fate to the good faith and decency of the other—the sort of feeling that in the 1960s impelled groups of black and white mothers to exchange their children during civil rights marches. Only the presence of such sentiment can enable the force of persuasion to supplant the force of distrust.

At this point, *even if* a demonstration of policy and fact decisively pointed toward eliminating affirmative action, many of its proponents might well refuse to recognize such a showing and continue to support preferential treatment. Their reaction would stem in large measure from their fears regarding the ulterior motives of their opponents. This is another reason why, as a practical matter, motive is so important. As long as suspect motivation justifiably remains a point of apprehension, inquiry into "the merits" of affirmative action will play a peripheral, instrumental role in the resolution of the controversy.

6.3

Stephen L. Carter

Racial Preferences? So What?

Stephen Carter is the William Nelson Cromwell professor of law at Yale University Law School. He was a law clerk for Supreme Court justice Thurgood Marshall. He is author of The Culture of Disbelief *and* Reflections of an Affirmative Action Baby.

Those of us who have graduated from professional school over the past fifteen to twenty years and are not white travel a career path that is frequently bumpy with suspicions that we did not earn the right to be where we are. We bristle when others raise what might be called the affirmative action question—"Did you get into a school because of a special program?" That prickly sensitivity reveals a rarely mentioned cost of racial preferences. The cost I have in mind is to the psyches of the beneficiaries themselves, who simultaneously want racial preferences to be preserved and to force the world to pretend that no one benefits from them. And therein hangs a tale.

For law students at the leading law schools, the autumn brings the recruiting season, the idyllic weeks when law firms from around the country compete to lavish lunches and dinners and other attentions upon them, all with the professed goal of obtaining the students' services—perhaps for the summer, perhaps for a longer term. This year, however, the nation's largest firm, Baker & McKenzie, has been banned from interviewing students at the University of Chicago Law School, and is on probation—that is, enjoined to be on its best behavior—at some others.

The immediate source of Baker & McKenzie's problems was a racially charged interview that a partner in the firm conducted last fall with a black third-year Chicago law student. The interviewer evidently suggested that other lawyers might call her "nigger" or "black bitch," and wanted to know how she felt about that. Perhaps surprised that she played golf, he observed that "there aren't too many golf courses in the ghetto." He also made a comment suggesting that students admitted under a racially conscious affirmative action program were less qualified than students admitted in any other way.

The law school reacted swiftly, and the firm was banned from campus. Because I am black myself, and teach in a law school, I suppose the easiest thing for me to do would be to clamor in solidarity for suspension or worse.

Yet I find myself strangely reluctant to applaud the school's action. Instead, I am disturbed rather than excited by the vision of law schools' circling the wagons to defend their minority students against insensitive remarks. The Chicago action is part of a trend on campuses across the nation to punish those who utter remarks deemed disparaging to racial and ethnic groups. At the many schools that are considering forbidding such remarks, the comments are referred to as "harassment" (which in many cases they certainly are)—evidently in an effort to show that it is conduct, not speech, for which punishment is proposed.

It strikes me as paradoxical that universities, traditionally bastions of free thought, should suddenly be taking the lead in punishing speech because they find it offensive. But it is not my intention to defend the interviewer, most of whose reported questions and comments were inexplicable and inexcusable. I am troubled, however, by my suspicion that there would still have been outrage—not as much, but some—had the interviewer asked only the affirmative action question.

I suspect this because in my own student days, something over a decade ago, when an interviewer from a major law firm in Washington addressed this very question to a Yale student who was not white, the student voices—including my own—howled in protest. But with the passing years, I have come to wonder whether our anger might not have been misplaced.

To be sure, the question was boorish. And because the interviewer had a grade record and résumé right in front of him, it was probably irrelevant as well. But lots of interviewers ask questions that meet the tests of boorishness and irrelevance.

At Yale a decade ago, we called the question racist. I have heard it said that the Baker & McKenzie interviewer's question on affirmative action was racist. I also understand that at least one university is considering a proposal that would deem it harassment per se for a (white?) student to question the qualifications of nonwhite classmates. But we can't change either the truths or the myths about racial preferences by punishing those who speak them.

This clamor for protection from the affirmative action question is the best evidence of the terrible psychological pressure that racial preferences put on their beneficiaries. Indeed, it sometimes seems as though the programs are not supposed to have any beneficiaries—or at least, that no one is permitted to suggest that they have any.

And that's ridiculous. If one supports racial preferences in professional school admissions, one must be prepared to treat them like any other preference in admissions. One must believe that they make a difference, that is, that some students would not be admitted if the preferences did not exist. This is not a racist observation. It is not normative in any sense. It is simply a fact. A good deal of emotional underbrush might be cleared away were the fact simply conceded, and made the beginning, not the end, of any discussion of preferences.

For once it is conceded that the programs have beneficiaries, it follows that some of us who are professionals and are not white must be among them, and supporters of preferences must stop pretending otherwise. Rather, some large segment of us must be willing to meet the affirmative action question head-on, to say, "Yes, I got into law school because of racial preferences. So what?"—and, having said it, must be ready with a list of what we have accomplished with the opportunities that the preferences provided.

Now, this is a costly concession, because it carries all the baggage of the battle over the relationship between preferences and merit. I take no position on that dispute here, but I do think that the bristling when the question is raised suggests a deep-seated fear that the dichotomy might be real. In any case, it is not racism or harassment to point out that racial preferences make a difference. And if admitting that preferences make a difference leaves a funny aftertaste in the mouths of proponents, they might be more comfortable fighting against preferences rather than for them.

For my part, the matter is simple: I got into law school because I'm black. And I can prove it.

As a senior at Stanford, I applied to about a half dozen law schools. Yale, where I would ultimately enroll, came through fairly early with an acceptance. So did all but one of the others. The last school, Harvard, dawdled and dawdled. Finally, toward the end of the admission season, I received a letter of rejection.

Then, within days, two different Harvard officials and a professor contacted me by telephone to apologize. They were quite frank in their explanation for the "error." I was told by one official that the school had initially rejected me because "we assumed from your record that you were white." (The words have always stuck in my mind, a tantalizing reminder of what is expected of me.) Suddenly coy, he went on to say that the school had obtained "additional information that should have been counted in your favor"—that is, Harvard had discovered the color of my skin. And if I had already made a deposit to confirm my decision to go elsewhere, well, that, I was told, would "not be allowed" to stand in my way should I enroll at Harvard.

Naturally, I was insulted by this miracle. Stephen Carter, the white male, was not good enough for the Harvard Law School; Stephen Carter, the black male, not only was good enough, but rated agonized telephone calls urging him to attend. And Stephen Carter, color unknown, must have been white: How else would he have achieved what he did in college? Except that my college achievements were obviously not sufficiently spectacular to merit acceptance had I been white. In other words, my academic record was too good for a black Stanford undergraduate but not good enough for a white Harvard Law student. Because I turned out to be black, however, Harvard was quite happy to scrape me from what it apparently considered the bottom of the barrel.

My objective is not to single out Harvard for special criticism; on the contrary, I make no claim that a white student with my record would have been admitted to any of the leading law schools. The insult that I felt came from the pain of being reminded so forcefully that I was good enough for a top law school only because I happened to be black.

Naturally, I should not have been insulted at all; that is what racial preferences are for—racial preference. But I was insulted and went off to Yale instead, even though I have now and had then absolutely no reason to imagine that Yale's judgment was based on different criteria than Harvard's. Because Yale is far more selective, the chances are very good that I was admitted at Yale for essentially the same reason that I was admitted at Harvard—the color of my skin made up for evident deficiencies in my academic record.

So I am unable to fool myself: Without that leg up, the thumb on the scale, the extra points due to skin color—choose your own metaphor—I would not be where I am today. And I, too, must be able to say, "So what?" and go on from there.

Whatever the pain it might cause, the affirmative action question, whether at Yale more than a decade ago or at Chicago last year, should come as no surprise. And if those of us who have benefited from racial preferences are not prepared to treat the question in a serious manner, to admit to the advantage that we have been given, then we are not after all the beneficiaries of affirmative action: We are its victims.

6.4   **Douglas S. Massey and Nancy A. Denton**

The Perpetuation of the Underclass

Douglas Massey is coauthor of American Apartheid: Segregation and the Making of the Underclass. *He is chair and professor of sociology at the University of Pennsylvania.*
Nancy Denton is coauthor of American Apartheid: Segregation and the Making of the Underclass. *She is associate professor of sociology at the State University of New York, Albany.*

One notable difference appears between the immigrant and Negro populations. In the case of the former, there is the possibility of escape, with improvement in economic status in the second generation.

—1931 report to President Herbert Hoover
by the Committee on Negro Housing

If the black ghetto was deliberately constructed by whites through a series of private decisions and institutional practices, if racial discrimination persists at remarkably high levels in U.S. housing markets, if intensive residential segregation continues to be imposed on blacks by virtue of their skin color, and if segregation concentrates poverty to build a self-perpetuating spiral of decay into black neighborhoods, then a variety of deleterious consequences automatically follow for individual African Americans. A racially segregated society cannot be a race-blind society: as long as U.S. cities remain segregated—indeed, hypersegregated—the United States cannot claim to have equalized opportunities for blacks and whites. In a segregated world, the deck is stacked against black socioeconomic progress, political empowerment, and full participation in the mainstream of American life.

In considering how individuals fare in the world, social scientists make a fundamental distinction between individual, family, and structural characteristics. To a great extent, of course, a person's success depends on individual traits such as motivation, intelligence, and especially, education. Other things equal, those who are more highly motivated, smarter, and better educated will be rewarded more highly in the labor market and will achieve greater socioeconomic success.

Other things generally are not equal, however, because individual traits such as motivation and education are strongly affected by family background. Parents who are themselves educated, motivated, and economically successful tend to pass these traits on to their children. Children who enter the middle and upper classes through the accident of birth are more likely than other, equally intelligent children from other classes to acquire the schooling, motivation, and cultural knowledge required for socioeconomic success in contemporary society. Other aspects of family background, moreover, such as wealth and social connections, open the doors of opportunity irrespective of education or motivation.

Yet even when one adjusts for family background, other things are still not equal, because the structural organization of society also plays a profound role in shaping the life chances of individuals. Structural variables are elements of social and economic organization that lie beyond individual control, that are built into the way society is organized. Structural characteristics affect the fate of large numbers of people and families who share common locations in the social order.

Among the most important structural variables are those that are geographically defined. Where one lives—especially, where one grows up—exerts a profound effect on one's life chances. Identical individuals with similar family backgrounds and personal characteristics will lead very different lives and achieve different rates of socioeconomic success depending on where they reside. Because racial segregation confines blacks to a circumscribed and disadvantaged niche in the urban spatial order, it has profound consequences for individual and family well-being.

Social and Spatial Mobility

In a market society such as the United States, opportunities, resources, and benefits are not distributed evenly across the urban landscape. Rather, certain residential areas have more prestige, greater affluence, higher home values, better services, and safer streets than others. Marketing consultants have grown rich by taking advantage of this "clustering of America" to target specific groups of consumers for wealthy corporate clients. The geographic differentiation of American cities by socioeconomic status does more than conveniently rank neighborhoods for the benefit of demographers, however; it also creates a crucial connection between social and spatial mobility.

As people get ahead, they not only move up the economic ladder, they move up the residential ladder as well. As early as the 1920s, sociologists at the University of Chicago noted this close connection between social and spatial mobility, a link that has been verified many times since. As socioeconomic status improves, families relocate to take advantage of opportunities and resources that are available in greater abundance elsewhere. By drawing on benefits acquired through residential mobility, aspiring parents not only consolidate their own class position but enhance their and their children's prospects for additional social mobility.

In a very real way, therefore, barriers to spatial mobility are barriers to social mobility, and where one lives determines a variety of salient factors that affect individual well-being: the quality of schooling, the value of housing, exposure to crime, the quality of public services, and the character of children's peers. As a result, residential integration has been a crucial component in the broader process of socioeconomic advancement among immigrants and their children. By moving to successively better neighborhoods, other racial and ethnic groups have gradually become integrated into American society. Although rates of spatial assimilation have varied, levels of segregation have fallen for each immigrant group as socioeconomic status and generations in the United States have increased.

The residential integration of most ethnic groups has been achieved as a by-product of broader processes of socioeconomic attainment, not because group members sought to live among native whites per se. The desire for integration is only one of a larger set of motivations, and not necessarily the most important. Some minorities may even be antagonistic to the idea of integration, but for spatial assimilation to occur, they need only be willing to put up with integration in order to gain access to socioeconomic resources that are more abundant in areas in which white families predominate.

To the extent that white prejudice and discrimination restrict the residential mobility of blacks and confine them to areas with poor schools, low home values, inferior services, high crime, and low educational aspirations, segregation undermines their social and economic well-being. The persistence of racial segregation makes it difficult for aspiring black families to escape the concentrated poverty of the ghetto and puts them at a distinct disadvantage in the larger competition for education, jobs, wealth, and power. The central issue is not whether African Americans "prefer" to live near white people or whether integration is a desirable social goal, but how the restrictions on individual liberty implied by severe segregation undermine the social and economic well-being of individuals.

Extensive research demonstrates that blacks face strong barriers to spatial assimilation within American society. Compared with other minority groups, they are markedly less able to convert their socioeconomic attainments into residential contact with whites, and because of this fact they are unable to gain access to crucial resources and benefits that are distributed through housing markets. Dollar for dollar, blacks are able to buy fewer neighborhood amenities with their income than other groups.

Among all groups in the United States, only Puerto Ricans share blacks' relative inability to assimilate spatially; but this disadvantage stems from the fact that many are of African origin. Although white Puerto Ricans achieve rates of spatial assimilation that are comparable with those found among other ethnic groups, those of African or racially mixed origins experience markedly lower abilities to convert socioeconomic attainments into contact with whites. Once race is controlled, the "paradox of Puerto Rican segregation" disappears.

Table 6.1

Characteristics of neighborhoods inhabited by blacks and whites at different income levels in Philadelphia, 1980

Level of Household Income

	Poor ($8,000)		Middle ($20,000)		Affluent ($32,000)	
	Whites	Blacks	Whites	Blacks	Whites	Blacks
Percentage of births to unwed mothers	40.7	37.6	10.3	25.8	1.9	16.7
Median value of homes (in thousands of 1980 dollars)	$19.4	$27.1	$38.0	$29.5	$56.6	$31.9
Percentage of students scoring below 15th percentile on SAT in local high school	39.3	35.5	16.5	26.6	5.7	19.2

Source: Douglas S. Massey, Gretchen A. Condran, and Nancy A. Denton, "The Effect of Residential Segregation on Black Social and Economic Well-Being," *Social Forces* 66 (1987):46–47, 50.
Note: Household income is in 1979 dollars.

Given the close connection between social and spatial mobility, the persistence of racial barriers implies the systematic exclusion of blacks from benefits and resources that are distributed through housing markets. We illustrate the severity of this black disadvantage with data specially compiled for the city of Philadelphia in 1980 (see Table 6.1). The data allow us to consider the socioeconomic character of neighborhoods that poor, middle-income, and affluent blacks and whites can be expected to inhabit, holding education and occupational status constant.

In Philadelphia, poor blacks and poor whites both experience very bleak neighborhood environments; both groups live in areas where about 40% of the births are to unwed mothers, where median home values are under $30,000, and where nearly 40% of high school students score under the 15th percentile on a standardized achievement test. Families in such an environment would be unlikely to build wealth through home equity, and children growing up in such an environment would be exposed to a peer environment where unwed parenthood was common and where educational performance and aspirations were low.

As income rises, however, whites are able to escape this disadvantaged setting by relocating to a more advantaged setting. With a middle-class income ($20,000 1979 dollars), whites no longer reside in a neighborhood where unwed parenthood predominates (only 10% of births are to single mothers) and housing values are well above $30,000. At the same time, school performance is markedly better: only 17% of students in the local high school score below the 15th percentile.

Once whites achieve affluence, moreover, negative residential conditions are left far behind. Affluent whites in Philadelphia (those with a 1979 income of $32,000) live in neighborhoods where only 2% of the births are to unwed mothers, where the median home value is $57,000, and where a mere 6% of high school students score below the 15th percentile on achievement tests. Upwardly mobile whites, in essence, capitalize on their higher incomes to buy their way into improved residential circumstances.

Blacks, in contrast, remain mired in disadvantage no matter what income they achieve. Middle-income blacks live in an area where more than a quarter of the births are to unwed mothers, where housing values languish below $30,000, and where 27% of all students in the local high school score below the 15th percentile. Even with affluence, blacks achieve neighborhood environments that compare unfavorably with those attained by whites. With an income of $32,000, a black family can expect to live in a neighborhood where 17% of all births are to unwed mothers, home values are barely over $30,000, and where a fifth of high school students score below the 15th percentile.

For blacks, in other words, high incomes do not buy entrée to residential circumstances that can serve as springboards for future socioeconomic mobility; in particular, blacks are unable to achieve a school environment conducive to later academic success. In Philadelphia, children from an affluent black family are likely to attend a public school where the percentage of low-achieving students is three times greater than the percentage in schools attended by affluent white children. Small wonder, then, that controlling for income in no way erases the large racial gap in SAT scores. Because of segregation, the same income buys black and white families educational environments that are of vastly different quality.

Given these limitations on the ability of black families to gain access to neighborhood resources, it is hardly surprising that government surveys reveal blacks to be less satisfied with their residential circumstances than socioeconomically equivalent whites. This negative evaluation reflects an accurate appraisal of their circumstances rather than different values or ideals on the part of blacks. Both races want the same things in homes and neighborhoods; blacks are just less able to achieve them. Compared with whites, blacks are less likely to be homeowners, and the homes they do own are of poorer quality, in poorer neighborhoods, and of lower value. Moreover, given the close connection between home equity and family wealth, the net worth of blacks is a small fraction of that of whites, even though their incomes have converged over the years. Finally, blacks tend to occupy older, more crowded dwellings that are structurally inadequate compared to those inhabited by whites; and because these racial differentials stem from segregation rather income, adjusting for socioeconomic status does not erase them.

The Politics of Segregation

Socioeconomic achievement is not only a matter of individual aspirations and effort, however; it is also a matter of collective action in the political arena. Generations of immigrants have entered American cities and struggled to acquire political power as a means to enhance individual mobility. Ultimately most were incorporated into the pluralist political structure of American cities. In return for support at the polls, ethnic groups were awarded a share of public services, city contracts, and municipal jobs in rough proportion to their share of the electorate. The receipt of these public resources, in turn, helped groups consolidate their class position and gave their members a secure economic base from which to advance further.

The process of political incorporation that followed each immigrant wave grew out of shared political interests that were, to a large extent, geographically determined. Although neighborhoods may have been labeled "Polish," "Italian," or "Jewish," neighborhoods in which one ethnic group constituted a majority were rare, and most immigrants of European origin never lived in them. As a result, levels of ethnic segregation never reached the heights typical of black-white segregation today.

This geographic diversification of ethnicity created a situation in which ethnic groups necessarily shared common political interests. In distributing public works, municipal services, and patronage jobs to ethnic groups in return for their political support, resources were also allocated to specific neighborhoods, which typically contained a diverse array of ethnicities. Given the degree of ethnic mixing within neighborhoods, political patronage provided to one group yielded substantial benefits for others as well. Building a new subway stop in an "Italian" neighborhood, for example, also provided benefits to Jews, Poles, and Lithuanians who shared the area; and allocating municipal jobs to Poles not only benefited merchants in "Polish" communities but generated extra business for nearby shopkeepers who were Hungarian, Italian, or Czech.

At the same time, threats to curtail municipal services encouraged the formation of broad, interethnic coalitions built around common neighborhood interests. A plan to close a firehouse in a "Jewish" neighborhood, for example, brought protests not only from Jews but from Scandinavians, Italians, and Slovaks who shared the neighborhood and relied on its facilities. These other ethnics, moreover, were invariably connected to friends and relatives in other neighborhoods or to co-ethnic politicians from other districts who could assist them in applying political pressure to forestall the closure. In this way, residential integration structurally supported the formation of interethnic coalitions, providing a firm base for the emergence of pluralist political machines.

Residential integration also made it possible for ethnic groups to compete for political leadership throughout the city, no matter what their size. Because no single group dominated numerically in most neighborhoods, politicians from a variety of backgrounds found the door open to make a bid for elective office. Moreover, representatives elected from ethnically diverse neighborhoods had to pay attention to all voters irrespective of ethnic affiliation. The geographic distribution of political power across ethnically heterogeneous districts spread political influence widely among groups and ensured that all were given a political voice.

The residential segregation of blacks, in contrast, provided no basis for pluralist politics because it precluded the emergence of common neighborhood interests; the geographic isolation of blacks instead forced nearly all issues to cleave along racial lines. When a library, firehouse, police station, or school was built in a black neighborhood, other ethnic groups derived few, if any, benefits; and when important services were threatened with reduction or removal, blacks could find few coalition partners with whom to protest the cuts. Since no one except blacks lived in the ghetto, no other ethnic group had a self-interest in seeing them provided with public services or political patronage.

On the contrary, resources allocated to black neighborhoods detracted from the benefits going to white ethnic groups; and because patronage was the glue that held white political coalitions together, resources allocated to the ghetto automatically undermined the stability of the pluralist machine. As long as whites controlled city politics, their political interests lay in providing as few resources as possible to African Americans and as many as possible to white ethnic groups. Although blacks occasionally formed alliances with white reformers, the latter acted more from moral conviction than from self-interest. Because altruism is notoriously unreliable as a basis for political cooperation, interracial coalitions were unstable and of limited effectiveness in representing black interests.

The historical confinement of blacks to the ghetto thus meant that blacks shared few political interests with whites. As a result, their incorporation into local political structures differed fundamentally from the pluralist model followed by other groups. The geographic and political isolation of blacks meant that they had virtually no power when their numbers were small; only when their numbers increased enough to dominate one or more wards did they acquire any influence at all. But rather than entering the pluralist coalition as an equal partner, the black community was incorporated in a very different way: as a machine within a machine.

The existence of solid black electoral districts, while undermining interracial coalition-building, did create the potential for bloc voting along racial lines. In a close citywide election, the delivery of a large number of black votes could be extremely useful to white politicians, and inevitably black political bosses arose to control and deliver this vote in return for political favors. Unlike whites, who exercised power through politicians of diverse ethnicities, blacks were typically represented by one boss, always black, who developed a symbiotic and dependent relationship with the larger white power structure.

In return for black political support, white politicians granted black bosses such as Oscar DePriest or William Dawson of Chicago and Charles Anderson of Harlem a share of jobs and patronage that they could, in turn, distribute within the ghetto. Although these bosses wielded considerable power and status within the black community, they occupied a very tenuous position in the larger white polity. On issues that threatened the white machine or its constituents, the black bosses could easily be outvoted. Thus patronage, services, and jobs were allocated to the ghetto only as long as black bosses controlled racial agitation and didn't threaten the color line, and the resources they received typically compared unfavorably to those provided to white politicians and their neighborhoods.

As with black business owners and professionals, the pragmatic adaptation of black politicians to the realities of segregation gave them a vested interest in the ghetto and its perpetuation. During the 1950s, for example, William Dawson joined with white ethnic politicians to oppose the construction of public housing projects in white neighborhoods, not because of an ideological objection to public housing per se, but because integration would antagonize his white political sponsors and take voters outside of wards that he controlled.

The status quo of a powerful white machine and a separate but dependent black machine was built on shifting sand, however. It remained viable only as long as cities dominated state politics, patronage was plentiful, and blacks comprised a minority of the population. During the 1950s and 1960s, white suburbanization and black in-migration systematically undermined these foundations, and white machine politicians became progressively less able to accommodate black demands while simultaneously maintaining the color line. Given the declining political clout of cities, the erosion of their tax base, and the rising proportion of blacks in cities, municipal politics became a racially charged zero-sum game that pitted politically disenfranchised blacks against a faltering coalition of ethnic whites.

In cities where blacks came to achieve an absolute majority—such as Baltimore, Newark, Gary, Detroit, Cleveland, and Washington, D.C.—the white political machine was destroyed as blacks assumed power and ended white patronage. In cities where the share of blacks peaked at around 40%—as in Chicago and Philadelphia—blacks were able to acquire power only by pulling liberal whites and disaffected Hispanics into a tenuous coalition, but given prevailing patterns of segregation these alliances were not politically stable. Chicago, for example, quickly reverted to white control in a way that succinctly illustrates the vulnerability of black politicians under conditions of racial segregation.

By the beginning of the 1980s, black in-migration to Chicago had stopped, white out-migration had leveled off, and the movement of Hispanics into the city was accelerating. As the share of blacks stalled at just above 40%, it became clear that they would not soon, if ever, comprise a majority of Chicago's population. Latinos had become the swing voters and whoever pulled them into a coalition would rule the city. Mexican Americans and Puerto Ricans, however, had traditionally been ignored by the city's white machine politicians, and in frustration they joined with blacks in 1983 to elect the city's first black mayor, Harold Washington.

But under black leadership the fruits of political power did not come fast enough to satisfy rising Latino expectations. Given the high degree of residential segregation between blacks and Hispanics, resources provided to black constituents had few spillover benefits for Mexican Americans or Puerto Ricans, and when Mayor Washington died early in his second term, they bolted from the black politicians to form a new coalition with the chastened and now politically receptive ethnic whites. Together Latinos and European whites constituted a working majority of voters who elected a new white mayor, Richard M. Daley, son of the city's last white political boss. Given their relative integration, moreover, white Europeans and Latinos found a stable basis for coalition politics based on geographically structured self-interest.

Chicago's Latinos now appear to be following the pluralist political model of earlier European immigrant groups; and because they are the only major group in the city whose numbers are growing, their political power and influence can only be expected to increase. As long as the working coalition between Latinos and European whites holds, blacks will be unable to win citywide power. The political isolation of blacks continues because of the structural limitations imposed on them by racial segregation, which guarantees that they have will few interests in common with other groups.

Even in cities where blacks have assumed political leadership by virtue of becoming a majority, the structural constraints of segregation still remain decisive. Indeed, the political isolation experienced by blacks in places such as Newark and Detroit is probably more severe than that experienced earlier in the century, when ghetto votes were at least useful to white politicians in citywide elections. Once blacks gained control of the central city and whites completed their withdrawal to the surrounding suburbs, virtually all structural supports for interracial cooperation ended.

In the suburbs surrounding places such as Newark and Detroit, white politicians are administratively and politically insulated from black voters in central cities, and they have no direct political interest in their welfare. Indeed, money that flows into black central cities generally means increased taxes and lower net incomes for suburban whites. Because suburbanites now form a majority of most state populations—and a majority of the national electorate—the "chocolate city–

vanilla suburb" pattern of contemporary racial segregation gives white politicians a strong interest in limiting the flow of public resources to black-controlled cities.

In an era of fiscal austerity and declining urban resources, therefore, the political isolation of blacks makes them extremely vulnerable to cutbacks in governmental services and public investments. If cuts must be made to balance strained city budgets, it makes political sense for white politicians to concentrate the cuts in black neighborhoods, where the political damage will be minimal; and if state budgets must be trimmed, it is in white legislators' interests to cut subventions to black-controlled central cities, which now represent a minority of most states' voters. The spatial and political isolation of blacks interacts with declining public resources to create a powerful dynamic for disinvestment in the black community.

The destructiveness of this dynamic has been forcefully illustrated by Rodrick and Deborah Wallace, who trace the direct and indirect results of a political decision in New York City to reduce the number of fire companies in black and Puerto Rican neighborhoods during the early 1970s. Faced with a shortage of funds during the city's financial crisis, the Fire Department eliminated thirty-five fire companies between 1969 and 1976, twenty-seven of which were in poor minority areas located in the Bronx, Manhattan, and Brooklyn, areas where the risk of fire was, in fact, quite high. Confronted with the unpleasant task of cutting services, white politicians confined the reductions to segregated ghetto and barrio wards where the political damage could be contained. The geographic and political isolation of blacks and Puerto Ricans meant that their representatives were unable to prevent the cuts.

As soon as the closings were implemented, the number of residential fires increased dramatically. An epidemic of building fires occurred within black and Puerto Rican neighborhoods. As housing was systematically destroyed, social networks were fractured and institutions collapsed; churches, block associations, youth programs, and political clubs vanished. The destruction of housing, networks, and social institutions, in turn, caused a massive flight of destitute families out of core minority areas. Some affected areas lost 80% of their residents between 1970 and 1980, putting a severe strain on housing in adjacent neighborhoods, which had been stable until then. As families doubled up in response to the influx of fire refugees, overcrowding increased, which led to additional fires and the diffusion of the chaos into adjacent areas. Black ghettos and Puerto Rican barrios were hollowed out from their cores.

The overcrowded housing, collapsed institutions, and ruptured support networks overwhelmed municipal disease prevention efforts and swamped medical care facilities. Within affected neighborhoods, infant mortality rates rose, as did the incidence of cirrhosis, gonorrhea, tuberculosis, and drug use. The destruction of the social fabric of black and Puerto Rican neighborhoods led to an increase in the number of unsupervised young males, which contributed to a sharp increase in crime, followed by an increase in the rate of violent deaths among young men. By 1990, this chain reaction of social and economic collapse had turned vast areas of the Bronx, Harlem, and Brooklyn into "urban deserts" bereft of normal community life.

Despite the havoc that followed in the wake of New York's fire service reductions, the cuts were never rescinded. The only people affected were minority members who were politically marginalized by segregation and thereby prevented, structurally, from finding allies to oppose the service reductions. Although residential segregation paradoxically made it easier for blacks and Puerto Ricans to elect city councillors by creating homogeneous districts, it left those that were elected relatively weak, dependent, and unable to protect the interests of their constituents.

As a result of their residential segregation and resultant political isolation, therefore, black politicians in New York and elsewhere have been forced into a strategy of angrily demanding that whites give them more public resources. Given their geographic isolation, however, these appeals cannot be made on the basis of whites' self-interest, but must rely on appeals to altruism, guilt, or fear. Because altruism, guilt, and fear do not provide a good foundation for concerted political action, the downward spiral of black neighborhoods continues and black hostility and bitterness grow while white fears are progressively reinforced. Segregation creates a political impasse that deepens the chasm of race in American society.

Under the best of circumstances, segregation undermines the ability of blacks to advance their interests because it provides ethnic whites with no immediate self-interest in their welfare. The circumstances of U.S. race relations, however, can hardly be described as "best," for not only do whites have little self-interest in promoting black welfare, but a significant share must be assumed to be racially prejudiced and supportive of policies injurious to blacks. To the extent that racism exists, of course, the geographic and political isolation of the ghetto makes it easier for racists to act on their prejudices. In a segregated society, blacks become easy targets for racist actions and policies.

The Isolation of the Ghetto

The high degree of residential segregation imposed on blacks ensures their social and economic isolation from the rest of American society. As we have seen, in 1980 ten large U.S. cities had black isolation indices in excess of 80 (Atlanta, Baltimore, Chicago, Cleveland, Detroit, Gary, Newark, Philadelphia, St. Louis, and Washington, D.C.), meaning that the average black person in these cities lived in a neighborhood that was at least 80% black. Averages in excess of 80% occur when a few blacks live in integrated areas, and the vast majority reside in areas that are 100% black.

Such high levels of racial isolation cannot be sustained without creating a profound alienation from American society and its institutions. Unless ghetto residents work outside of their neighborhoods, they are unlikely to come into contact with anyone else who is not also black, and if they live in an area of concentrated poverty, they are unlikely to interact with anyone who is not also *poor* and black. The structural constraints on social interaction imposed by segregation loom large when one considers that 36% of black men in central cities are either out of the labor force, unemployed, or underemployed, a figure that rises to 54% among black men aged 18 to 29.

The role that segregation plays in undermining blacks' connection to the rest of society has been demonstrated by William Yancey and his colleagues at Temple University. They undertook a representative survey of people in the Philadelphia urban area and asked them to describe the race and ethnicity of their friends and neighbors. Not surprisingly, blacks were far more concentrated residentially than any other group, even controlling for social and economic background. They were also very unlikely to report friendships with anyone else but blacks, and this remarkable racial homogeneity in their friendship networks was explained entirely by their residential concentration; it had nothing to do with group size, birthplace, socioeconomic status, or organizational membership. Unlike other groups, blacks were prevented from forming friendships outside their group because they were so residentially segregated: spatial isolation leads to social isolation.

The intense isolation imposed by segregation has been confirmed by an ethnographic study of blacks living in Chicago's poorest neighborhoods. Drawing on detailed, in-depth interviews gathered in William Julius Wilson's Urban Family Life Survey, Sophie Pedder found that one theme consistently emerged in the narratives: poor blacks had extremely narrow geographic horizons. Many of her informants, who lived on Chicago's South Side, had never been into the Loop (the city's center), and a large number had never left the immediate confines of their neighborhood. A significant percentage only left the neighborhood after reaching adulthood. According to Pedder, this racial isolation "is at once both real, in that movement outside the neighborhood is limited, and psychological, in that residents feel cut off from the rest of the city."

Thus residents of hypersegregated neighborhoods necessarily live within a very circumscribed and limited social world. They rarely travel outside of the black enclave, and most have few friends outside of the ghetto. This lack of connection to the rest of society carries profound costs, because personal contacts and friendship networks are among the most important means by which people get jobs. Relatively few job seekers attain employment by responding to ads or canvassing employers; most people find jobs through friends, relatives, or neighbors, and frequently they learn of jobs through acquaintances they know only casually.

The social isolation imposed on blacks by virtue of their systematic residential segregation thus guarantees their economic isolation as well. Because blacks have weak links to white society, they are not connected to the jobs that white society provides. They are put at a clear disadvantage in the competition for employment, and especially for increasingly scarce jobs that pay well but require little formal skill or education. This economic isolation, moreover, is cumulative and self-perpetuating: because blacks have few connections outside the ghetto, they are less likely to be employed in the mainstream economy, and this fact, in turn, reduces the number and range of their connections to other people and institutions, which further undermines their employment chances. Given the levels of residential segregation typically found in large American cities, therefore, the inevitable result is a dependent black community within which work experience is lacking and linkages to legitimate employment are weak.

The Language of Segregation

The depth of isolation in the ghetto is also evident in black speech patterns, which have evolved steadily away from Standard American English. Because of their intense social isolation, many ghetto residents have come to speak a language that is increasingly remote from that spoken by American whites. Black street speech, or more formally, Black English Vernacular, has its roots in the West Indian creole and Scots-Irish dialects of the eighteenth century. As linguists have shown, it is by no means a "degenerate," or "illogical" version of Standard American English; rather, it constitutes a complex, rich, and expressive language in its own right, with a consistent grammar, pronunciation, and lexicon all its own. It evolved independently from Standard American English because blacks were historically separated from whites by caste, class, and region; but among the most powerful influences on black speech has been the residential segregation that blacks have experienced since early in the century.

For several decades, the linguist William Labov and his colleagues have systematically taped, transcribed, and analyzed black and white speech patterns in American cities. In city after city they have found that whites "constitute a single speech community, defined by a single set of norms and a single, extraordinarily uniform structural base. Linguistic features pass freely across ethnic lines within the white community. But not across racial lines: black(s) . . . have nothing to do with these sound changes in process." Divergent black and white speech patterns provide stark evidence of the structural limits to interracial communication that come with high levels of residential segregation.

Whereas white speech has become more regionally specialized over time, with linguistic patterns varying increasingly between metropolitan areas, Labov and his colleagues found precisely the opposite pattern for Black English: it has become progressively more uniform across urban areas. Over the past two decades, the Black English Vernaculars of Boston, Chicago, Detroit, New York, and Philadelphia have become increasingly similar in their grammatical structure and lexicon, reflecting urban blacks' common social and economic isolation within urban America. Although black speech has become more uniform internally, however, as a dialect it has drifted farther and farther away from the form and structure of Standard American English. According to Labov's measurements, blacks and whites in the United States increasingly speak different tongues, with different grammatical rules, divergent pronunciations, and separate vocabularies.

Labov has concluded that this separate linguistic evolution stems from the high degree of segregation imposed on blacks in U.S. urban areas, which confines them to isolated and self-contained linguistic communities. In a series of critical tests, he and Wendell Harris demonstrated that the less contact blacks have with whites, the greater their reliance on Black English Vernacular and the less their ability to speak Standard American English. Blacks who live within the ghetto, in particular, display speech patterns that are quite remote from the dialect spoken by most white Americans. Because of segregation, the languages spoken by blacks and whites are moving toward mutual unintelligibility.

The recognition of Black English Vernacular's progressive evolution away from Standard American English in no way implies that it is inferior as a language; nor does the fact that whites may have a difficult time understanding Black English mean that it is flawed as a medium of human communication. The linguistic drift of black English does, however, symbolize the breakdown of communication between the races, and suggests at least two additional barriers to black socioeconomic advancement.

U.S. schools rely almost exclusively on the standard dialect for instruction and exposition. Thus when children grow up speaking Black English Vernacular rather than Standard American English, their educational progress is seriously hampered. When ghetto children enter schools where texts and instructional materials all are written in Standard English, and where teachers speak primarily in this dialect, they experience a culture shock akin to that felt by immigrant children from non-English-speaking countries. Because the language they are being taught to read and write is not the same as the one they speak, their confidence and self-esteem are threatened, thereby undermining the entire learning process. Unless special efforts are made to compensate for the wide discrepancy between the language of the classroom and the spoken language of everyday life, formal education is likely to be a frustrating and alienating experience for ghetto children.

Acquiring fluency in Standard English is difficult for black children whose entire social world is bounded by the ghetto and whose families have no familiarity with the mainstream dialect. Children learn language through frequent interaction with other speakers. Although they will be able to understand Standard English from exposure to television, radio, and other media, children growing up in the ghetto will not be able to speak it unless they have had the opportunity to use it actively to manipulate their social environment. The passive consumption of mass media does not provide this sort of active learning experience. Without systematic reinforcement in other social contexts, ghetto dwellers are unlikely to learn to speak a style of English familiar to most whites.

The educational barriers facing ghetto children are exacerbated by teachers and school administrators who view Black English as "wrong," "bad," or "inferior," thereby stigmatizing black children and further undermining their motivation to learn. In many school settings, Black English is pejoratively stereotyped and taken to indicate a lack of intelligence, an absence of motivation, or the presence of a learning disability. These perceptions lead to a lowering of expectations and to the systematic tracking of ghetto children into remedial courses, thereby making low achievement a self-fulfilling prophecy. Thus black educational progress is hampered not only because segregation concentrates poverty within ghetto schools but also because segregation confines blacks to an isolated linguistic community. Segregation ensures that black children will speak a nonstandard dialect of English that is not taught, spoken, or appreciated in the American school system.

The difficulties caused by a reliance on Black English do not stop at the classroom door. Facility with Standard English is required for many jobs in the larger economy, especially those that carry good prospects for socioeconomic advancement and income growth. To the extent that an exclusive reliance on Black English undermines employability, therefore, it constitutes a second barrier to socioeconomic achievement.

The ability to speak, write, and communicate effectively in Standard English is essential for employment in most white-collar jobs. The ability to speak Standard English, at least, is also widely demanded by employers for clerical or service positions that bring jobholders into frequent contact with the general public, most of whom are white. Employers make frequent use of language as a screening device for blue-collar jobs, even those that involve little or no interaction with the public. They assume that people who speak Black English carry a street culture that devalues behaviors and attitudes consistent with being a "good worker," such as regularity, punctuality, dependability, and respect for authority.

The inability to communicate in Standard American English, therefore, presents serious obstacles to socioeconomic advancement. Black Americans who aspire to socioeconomic success generally must acquire a facility in Standard English as a precondition of advancement, even if they retain a fluency in black speech. Successful blacks who have grown up in the ghetto literally become bilingual, learning to switch back and forth between black and white dialects depending on the social context.

This "code switching" involves not only a change of words but a shift between contrasting cultures and identities. Although some people acquire the ability to make this shift without difficulty, it causes real social and psychological problems for others. For someone raised in the segregated environment of the ghetto, adopting white linguistic conventions can seem like a betrayal of black culture, a phony attempt to deny the reality of one's "blackness." As a result, black people who regularly speak Standard American English often encounter strong disapproval from other blacks. Many well-educated blacks recall with some bitterness the ridicule and ostracism they suffered as children for the sin of "talking white."

The Culture of Segregation

This struggle between "black" and "white" speech patterns is symptomatic of a larger conflict between "black" and "white" cultural identities that arises from residential segregation. In response to the harsh and isolated conditions of ghetto life, a segment of the urban black population has evolved a set of behaviors, attitudes, and values that are increasingly at variance with those held in the wider society. Although these adaptations represent rational accommodations to social and economic conditions within the ghetto, they are not widely accepted or understood outside of it, and in fact are negatively evaluated by most of American society.

Middle-class American culture generally idealizes the values of self-reliance, hard work, sobriety, and sacrifice, and adherence to these principles is widely believed to bring monetary reward and economic advancement in society. Among men, adherence to these values means that employment and financial security should precede marriage, and among women they imply that childbearing should occur only after adequate means to support the raising of children have been secured, either through marriage or through employment. In the ideal world, everyone is hardworking, self-sufficient, and not a burden to fellow citizens.

In most white neighborhoods the vast majority of working age men are employed. Because jobs are available and poverty is relatively uncommon, most residents can reasonably expect to conform to ideal values most of the time. Men generally do find jobs before marrying and women have reason to believe that men will help support the children they father. Although these ideals may be violated with some frequency, there is enough conformity in most white neighborhoods for them to retain their force as guides for behavior; there are still enough people who exemplify the values to serve as role models for others. Those failures that do occur are taken to reflect individual flaws, and most whites derive a sense of self-esteem and prestige by conforming to the broader ideals of American society.

Ghetto blacks, however, face very different neighborhood conditions created by residential segregation. A large share live in a geographically isolated and racially homogeneous neighborhood where poverty is endemic, joblessness is rife, schools are poor, and even high school graduates are unlikely to speak Standard English with any facility. Employment opportunities are limited, and given the social isolation enforced by segregation, black men are not well connected to employers in the larger economy. As a result, young men coming of age in ghetto areas are relatively unlikely to find jobs capable of supporting a wife and children, and black women, facing a dearth of potential husbands and an absence of educational institutions capable of preparing them for gainful employment, cannot realistically hope to conform to societal ideals of marriage and childbearing.

The conditions of the ghetto, in short, make it exceedingly difficult to live up to broader societal values with respect to work, marriage, and family formation, and poor blacks are thus denied the opportunity to build self-esteem and to acquire prestige through channels valued in the wider society. As a result, an alternative status system has evolved within America's ghettos that is defined *in opposition to* the basic ideals and values of American society. It is a culture that explains and legitimizes the social and economic shortcomings of ghetto blacks, which are built into their lives by segregation rather than by personal failings. This culture of segregation attaches value and meaning to a way of life that the broader society would label as deviant and unworthy.

The effects of segregation on black cultural identity were first noted by the psychologist Kenneth Clark in *Dark Ghetto:* "Because the larger society has clearly rejected [the black ghetto dweller], he rejects . . . the values, the aspirations, and techniques of that society. His conscious or unconscious argument is that he cannot hope to win meaningful self-esteem through the avenues ordinarily available to more privileged individuals, [which] have been blocked for him through inadequate education, through job discrimination, and through a system of social and political power which is not responsive to his needs." As a psychological defense mechanism, therefore, ghetto dwellers evolve a cultural identity defined in opposition to the larger ideals of white society.

The anthropologists John Ogbu and Signithia Fordham, building on Clark's work, have shown that the formation of such oppositional identities is a common psychological adaptation whenever a powerless minority group is systematically subordinated by a dominant majority. "Subordinate minorities like black Americans develop a sense of collective identity or sense of peoplehood in opposition to the social identity of white Americans because of the way white Americans treat them in economic, political, social, and psychological domains. . . . The oppositional identity of the minority evolves because they perceive and experience the treatment by whites as collective and enduring oppression. They realize and believe that, regardless of their individual ability and training or education, and regardless of their place of origin . . . , they cannot expect to be treated like white Americans."

As a protection against the persistent assaults to self-esteem that are inherent in ghetto life, black street culture has evolved to legitimate certain behaviors prevalent within the black community that would otherwise be held in contempt by white society. Black identity is thus constructed as a series of oppositions to conventional middle-class "white" attitudes and behavior. If whites speak Standard American English, succeed in school, work hard at routine jobs, marry, and support their children, then to be "black" requires one to speak Black English, do poorly in school, denigrate conventional employment, shun marriage, and raise children outside of marriage. To do otherwise would be to "act white."

By concentrating poor people prone to such oppositional identities in racially homogeneous settings, segregation creates the structural context for the maintenance and perpetuation of an ongoing oppositional culture "which includes devices for protecting [black] identity and for maintaining boundaries between [blacks] and white Americans. [Blacks] regard certain forms of behavior and certain activities or events, symbols, and meanings as *not appropriate* for them because . . . [they] are characteristic of white Americans. At the same time, they emphasize other forms of behavior and other events, symbols, and meanings as more appropriate for them because they are *not* a part of white Americans' way of life."

Ogbu and Fordham are educational specialists who have specifically documented the effect of oppositional black culture on educational achievement among black children. Their investigations show how bright, motivated, and intellectually curious ghetto children face tremendous pressure from their peers to avoid "acting white" in succeeding in school and achieving academic distinction. The pressure for educational failure is most intense during the teenage years, when peer acceptance is so important and black young people live in fear of being labeled "Oreos," "Uncle Toms," or "Aunt Jemimahs" for speaking Standard English or doing well in school. If they actually achieve academic distinction, they risk being called a "brainiac," or worse, a "pervert brainiac" (someone who is not only smart but of questionable sexuality as well).

Black children who do overcome the odds and achieve academic success in inner-city schools typically go to great lengths, and adopt ingenious strategies, to lessen the burden of "acting white." Some deliberately fail selected courses, others scale back their efforts and get B's or C's rather than the A's they are capable of, and still others become class clowns, seeking to deflect attention away from their scholarly achievements by acting so ridiculous that their peers no longer take them seriously. Better to be called "crazy" or a "clown" than a "pervert brainiac."

The powerful effect of oppositional ghetto culture on black educational performance is suggested by the recent work of James Rosenbaum and his colleagues at Northwestern University. Working in the Chicago area, they compared low-income black students from families assigned to scattered site housing in a white suburb (under the *Gautreaux* court decision) with comparable students from families assigned to public housing in Chicago's ghetto. Although the two groups were initially identical, once removed from ghetto high schools black students achieved higher grades, lower dropout rates, better academic preparation, and higher rates of college attendance compared with those who remained behind in ghetto institutions.

Another study by Robert Crain and Rita Mahard, who used a nationwide sample, found that northern blacks who attended racially mixed schools were more likely to enter and stay in college than those who went to all-black high schools. Susan Mayer followed students who attended the tenth grade in poor and affluent high schools in 1980 and determined the likelihood of their dropping out before 1982. Controlling for family background, she discovered that students who went to affluent schools were considerably less likely to drop out than those who attended poor schools, and that girls in affluent schools were much less likely to have a child. Moreover, white students who attended predominantly black high schools were considerably more likely to drop out and have a child than those who attended predominantly white schools.

All too often, whites observe the workings of black oppositional culture and conclude that African Americans suffer from some kind of "cultural defect," or that they are somehow "culturally disadvantaged." In doing so, they blame the victims of segregation rather than the social arrangements that created the oppositional culture in the first place. It is not a self-perpetuating "culture of poverty" that retards black educational progress but a structurally created and sustained "culture of segregation" that, however useful in adapting to the harsh realities of ghetto life, undermines socioeconomic progress in the wider society.

As Kenneth Clark pointed out in 1965, "the invisible walls of a segregated society are not only damaging but protective in a debilitating way. There is considerable psychological safety in the ghetto; there one lives among one's own and does not risk rejection among strangers. One first becomes aware of the psychological damage of such 'safety' when the walls of the ghetto are breached and the Negro ventures out into the repressive, frightening white world. . . . Most Negroes take the first steps into an integrated society tentatively and torn with conflict. To be the first Negro who is offered a job in a company brings a sense of triumph but also the dread of failure." More recently, Shelby Steele has written of the "integration shock" that envelops blacks who enter white society directly from the isolated world of the ghetto.

The origins of black oppositional culture can be traced to the period before 1920, when black migration fomented a hardening of white racial attitudes and a systematic limiting of opportunities for African Americans on a variety of fronts. Whereas urban blacks had zealously pursued education after the Civil War and were making great strides, the rise of Jim Crow in the south and de facto segregation in the north severed the links between hard work, education, sobriety, and their presumed rewards in society. Although black elites continued to promote these values, the rise of the ghetto made them look increasingly pathetic and ridiculous to the mass of recent in-migrants: in the face of pervasive barriers to social and residential mobility, the moral admonitions of the elites seemed hollow and pointless. If whites would not accept blacks on the basis of their individual accomplishments and if hard work and education went unrewarded, then why expend the effort? If one could never be accepted as white, it was just demeaning and humiliating to go through the motions of "acting white." Malcolm X summed up this attitude with his sardonic quip, "What do you call a Negro with a Ph.D.? A nigger."

Unlike other groups, the force of oppositional culture is particularly powerful among African Americans because it is so strongly reinforced by residential segregation. By isolating blacks within racially homogeneous neighborhoods and concentrating poverty within them, segregation creates an environment where failure to meet the ideal standards of American society loses its stigma; indeed, individual shortcomings become normative and supported by the values of oppositional culture. As transgressions lose their stigma through repetition and institutionalization, individual behavior at variance with broader societal ideals becomes progressively more likely.

The culture of segregation arises from the coincidence of racial isolation and high poverty, which inevitably occurs when a poor minority group is residentially segregated. By concentrating poverty, segregation simultaneously concentrates male joblessness, teenage motherhood, single parenthood, alcoholism, and drug abuse, thus creating an entirely black social world in which these oppositional states are normative. Given the racial isolation and concentrated poverty of the ghetto, it is hardly surprising that black street culture has drifted steadily away from middle-class American values.

The steady divergence of black street culture from the white mainstream is clearly visible in a series of participant observer studies of ghetto life conducted over the past thirty years. Studies carried out during the 1960s and 1970s—such as Elliot Liebow's *Tally's Corner*, Lee Rainwater's *Behind Ghetto Walls*, Ulf Hannerz's *Soulside*, and Elijah Anderson's *A Place on the Corner*—were remarkably consistent in reporting that ghetto dwellers, despite their poverty and oppression, essentially subscribed to the basic values of American society. What set ghetto blacks apart from other Americans was not their lack of fealty to American ideals but their inability to accomplish them. Specifically, the pervasiveness of poverty, unemployment, and dependency in the ghetto made it nearly impossible for them to live up to ideals they in fact held, which in turn undermined their self-esteem and thus created a psychological need for gratification through other means.

The **participant observer** studies indicated that feelings of personal inadequacy led black men to reject the unskilled and poorly paid jobs open to them, to denigrate the kind of work these jobs represented, and to seek gratification through more accessible channels, such as sexual liaisons or intoxication. Women and men tended to begin sexual relations at a young age, and woman generally found themselves pregnant as teenagers. Childbirth was typically followed by marriage or some informal living arrangement, at least for a time; but eventually the woman's demands for financial support undermined her partner's self-esteem, and family responsibilities blocked his access to the alternate status system of the streets. Given the cross-cutting pressures of poverty, joblessness, low self-esteem, family demands, and the allure of the streets, most male-female relationships were short-lived and devolved sooner or later into female-headed families.

Once they had been through this cycle of romance, pregnancy, family formation, and dissolution, black men and women came to see romantic relationships as a mutually exploitative contest whose pleasures were temporary and whose stability could not be relied upon. At the same time, the pervasive poverty of the ghetto meant that families were constantly bombarded with energy-sapping demands for assistance and debilitating requests for financial aid from extended family, friends, and neighbors. Given the association of poverty with crime and violence, moreover, they were constantly at risk of criminal victimization, injury, or even death.

In this social world, ghetto dwellers acquired a tough, cynical attitude toward life, a deep suspicion of the motives of others, and a marked lack of trust in the goodwill or benevolent intentions of people and institutions. Growing up in the ghetto, blacks came to expect the worst of others and to experience little sense of control over their lives. They adapted to these feelings by confining relationships of trust to close kin, especially maternal relatives.

Underlying this bleak portrait of ghetto life painted by studies carried out during the 1960s and 1970s was a common thread. Early participant observers saw ghetto culture as rooted in the structural conditions of poverty, dependency, and joblessness, over which ghetto residents had little control, and all characterized ghetto culture as essentially oppositional. That is, the attitudes and behaviors of ghetto blacks were fundamentally defined in opposition to the ideals of white society. Underneath the jaded rejection of conventional mores, ghetto dwellers, at least in the first or second generations, still clung to the basic values of American society. Indeed, it was because they judged themselves so harshly by broader standards that the psychological need for an oppositional identity arose in the first place.

Over time, however, as intense racial isolation and acutely concentrated poverty have continued, ghetto attitudes, values, and ideals have become progressively less connected to those prevailing elsewhere in the United States. More and more, the culture of the ghetto has become an entity unto itself, remote from the rest of American society and its institutions, and drifting ever further afield. As conditions within the ghetto worsen, as the social environment grows more hostile, and as racial isolation deepens, the original connection of ghetto culture to the broader values of American society—even if only in opposition—has faded.

The new culture of the ghetto increasingly rejects the values of American society as a farce and a sham, and traits that were once clearly oppositional and therefore somehow *linked* to the rest of American society have become ends in themselves, esteemed in their own right and disconnected from their relationship to the surrounding "white" society. Under the combined pressure of isolation and poverty, black street culture has increasingly become an autonomous cultural system. Participant observer studies of ghetto life done in the 1980s have an even darker and more pessimistic tone than those carried out in earlier decades. The contrast is clearly illustrated by two studies conducted by the sociologist Elijah Anderson: one carried out in the ghetto of Chicago during the early 1970s and the other conducted in a poor black neighborhood of Philadelphia during the late 1980s.

In Anderson's first study, *A Place on the Corner,* basic American values such as hard work, honesty, diligence, respect for authority, and staying out of trouble were still very much in evidence in the thoughts and words of the poor black men gathered around the corner bar he studied. Indeed, these values provided the basis for an alternative status system that arose to confer esteem when broader standards were not met, and to encourage young men to live up to ideals despite the long odds. As a result, Anderson's subjects—who would be considered of "no account" by conventional standards—acquire a certain nobility for their pursuit of dignity and honor in the face of adversity.

In contrast, the subjects of Anderson's latest study, *Streetwise,* scorn and ridicule conventional American ideals. Symbolic of the disappearance of traditional values from the ghetto is the breakdown of the long-standing relationship between "old heads" and young boys. According to Anderson, "an old head was a man of stable means who was strongly committed to family life, to church, and, most important, to passing on his philosophy, developed through his own rewarding experience with work, to young boys he found worthy. He personified the work ethic and equated it with value and high standards of morality; in his eyes a workingman was a good, decent individual."

In the ghetto environment of earlier decades, the old head "acted as a kind of guidance counselor and moral cheerleader who preached anticrime and antitrouble messages to his charges," and "the young boy readily deferred to the old head's chronological age and worldly experience." In contrast, today, "as the economic and social circumstances of the urban ghetto have changed, the traditional old head has been losing prestige and credibility as a role model. . . . When gainful employment and its rewards are not forthcoming, boys easily conclude that the moral lessons of the old head concerning the work ethnic, punctuality, and honesty do not fit their own circumstances."

In the past, black ghettos also used to contain numerous "female old heads," who served as "neighborhood mothers," correcting and admonishing children in the streets and instructing them in proper behavior. They "were seen as mature and wise figures in the community, not only by women and girls, but also by many young men" because of their motherly love and concern for children. According to Anderson, however, these role models also have increasingly disappeared, indicating "a breakdown in feelings of community. Residents . . . keep more to themselves now, [and] no longer involve themselves in their neighbors' lives as they did as recently as ten years ago."

In place of traditional mores that assign value to steady work, family life, the church, and respect for others, a drug culture and its economy have arisen, with profound effects on community well-being. Anderson and others have studied and written on the appeal of the underground drug economy to young men and women from the ghetto. According to Anderson, "the roles of drug pusher, pimp, and (illegal). hustler have become more and more attractive. Street-smart young people who operate this underground economy are apparently able to obtain big money more easily and glamorously than their elders, including traditional male and female old heads. Because they appear successful, they become role models for still younger people."

The proliferation of the drug culture within the ghetto has exacerbated the problems caused by segregation and its concentration of poverty, adding a powerful impetus to the cycle of neighborhood decline. Given the financial gain to be had from drugs, ghetto dealers establish aggressive marketing strategies to capture business from disillusioned young people who see little hope for improvement through work, education, or staying out of trouble. Because limited economic opportunities in the ghetto as well as drug use itself make it difficult for drug users to support themselves, the spread of drug use leads inevitably to the escalation of crime and violence. As a by-product of the new drug culture, the violent death rate has skyrocketed among black men, prostitution has spread among black women, and the number of drug-addicted babies has mushroomed. The old social order of the ghetto has increasingly broken down and veered off on an independent path dramatically different from that prevailing in the rest of American society.

At the same time, relations between the sexes, which were already antagonistic and mutually exploitative in the ghetto world of the 1960s, had by the 1980s lost all connection to conventional family values. According to Anderson, by the late 1980s sexual relations in the ghetto had degenerated into a vicious, competitive contest in which young men and women exploited each other with diametrically opposed goals. For young ghetto men, sex had become strictly a means of enhancing status among male peers and of experiencing pleasure at the expense of women. "To the young man the woman becomes, in the most profound sense, a sexual object. Her body and mind are the object of a sexual game, to be won for personal aggrandizement. Status goes to the winner, and sex is prized not as a testament of love but as testimony to control of another human being. Sex is the prize, and sexual conquests are a game whose goal is to make a fool of the young woman."

In the ghetto of the 1960s, a pregnancy growing out of such casual sexual encounters was relatively likely to be followed by a marriage or some other housekeeping arrangement, however unstable or short-lived it might have been. By the late 1980s, however, this bow to conventional culture had been eliminated in black street culture. "In the social context of persistent poverty, [black men] have come to devalue the conventional marital relationship, viewing women as a burden and children as even more of one." Even if a young man "admits paternity and 'does right' by the girl, his peer group likely will label him a chump, a square, or a fool."

Ghetto women, for their part, seek gratification less through sex than through pregnancy and childbirth. They understand that their suitors' sweet words and well-honed "rap" are fabrications being told in order to extract sex from them, and despite a few romantic self-deceptions along the way, they realize that if they become pregnant the father is unlikely to support their child. Nonetheless, they look forward to getting pregnant, for in the contemporary ghetto "it is becoming socially acceptable for a young woman to have children out of wedlock—supported by a regular welfare check."

These findings are corroborated by other ethnographic interviews gathered as part of William Julius Wilson's larger study of urban poverty in Chicago. When the sociologist Richard Taub examined the interview transcripts, he found that marriage had virtually disappeared as a meaningful category of thought and discourse among poor blacks. Informants consistently stated that husband-wife relationships were neither important nor reliable as a basis for family life and childrearing, and they were deeply suspicious of the intentions of the opposite sex.

The disappearance of marriage as a social institution was underscored by field observations that Taub and his associates undertook in black and Mexican neighborhoods. Whereas a four-block shopping strip in one of Chicago's poor Mexican neighborhoods yielded fifteen shops that provided goods or services explicitly connected to marriage, a trip to a comparable black shopping area uncovered only two shops that even mentioned marriage, and not very prominently at that.

Elijah Anderson argues that childbearing has become increasingly disconnected from marriage in the ghetto; black women now seek childbirth to signal their status as adults and to validate their worth and standing before their own peer group—namely, other young black women. A baby is a young girl's entry ticket into what Anderson calls "the baby club." This "club" consists of young black mothers who gather in public places with their children to "lobby for compliments, smiles, and nods of approval and feel very good when they are forthcoming, since they signal affirmation and pride. On Sundays, the new little dresses and suits come out and the cutest babies are passed around, and this attention serves as a social measure of the person. The young mothers who form such baby clubs develop an ideology counter to that of more conventional society, one that not only approves of but enhances their position. In effect, they work to create value and status by inverting that of the girls who do not become pregnant. The teenage mother derives status from her baby; hence, her preoccupation with the impression that the baby makes and her willingness to spend inordinately large sums toward that end."

According to Anderson, sex is thus a key component in the informal status system that has evolved in the street culture of America's urban ghettos. In the absence of gratification through the conventional avenues of work and family, young men and women have increasingly turned to one commodity that lies within their reach. Through sex, young men get pleasure and a feeling of self-esteem before their peers, whereas young women get a baby and a sense of belonging within the baby club. This relationship of mutual exploitation, however, has come at a price. It has further marginalized black men from black women and has escalated the war of the sexes to new heights, a fact that is clearly revealed in the music of black street culture—rap.

An unabashedly misogynist viewpoint is extolled by rap groups such as N.W.A. ("Niggers with Attitude"), whose song "A Bitch Iz a Bitch" depicts black women as scheming, vain, whining mercenaries whose goal is to deprive black men of their self-esteem, money, and possessions. In the view of N.W.A., women are good for little more than sex, and their incessant demands for attention, constant requests for money and support, and their ever-present threats to male pride can only be checked through violence, ". . . 'cause a bitch is a bitch."

The female side of the issue is aired by the female rap group H.W.A. ("Hoes [Whores] with Attitude") in songs such as "A Trick Is a Trick," "Little Dick," and "1-900-BITCHES," which attack men as vain, superficial creatures who are incompetent in their love-making, ill equipped to satisfy, and prone to meaningless violence when their inflated pride is punctured. Their metaphor for the state of male-female relations in the ghetto is that of a whorehouse, where all women are whores and men are either tricks or pimps. The liner notes leave little doubt as to the group's message: "Everybody is a pimp of some kind and pimpin' is easy when you got a Hoe Wit Attitude."

The war of words between black men and women has also been fought in the black press, exemplified in 1990 by the appearance of *The Blackman's Guide to*

Understanding the Blackwoman, by Shaharazad Ali, which presents a vituperative attack on black women for their supposedly historical emasculation of black men. The book advocates the violent subjugation of women by black men, advising male readers that "there is never an excuse for ever hitting a Blackwoman anywhere but in the mouth. Because it is from that hole, in the lower part of her face, that all her rebellion culminates into words. Her unbridled tongue is a main reason she cannot get along with the Blackman. . . . If she ignores the authority and superiority of the Blackman, there is a penalty. When she crosses this line and becomes viciously insulting it is time for the Blackman to soundly slap her in the mouth." Ten black scholars answered to the attack in a pamphlet entitled *Confusion by Any Other Name,* hoping "to respond to the range of insulting myths, half-truths and generalized personal experiences by the author."

From a sociological point of view, the specific content of these works is less important than what they illustrate about the state of relations between the sexes within the black community. After evolving for decades under conditions of intense social and economic isolation, black street culture has become increasingly divorced from basic American ideals of family, work, and respect for others. By confining large numbers of black people to an environment within which failure is endemic, negative role models abound, and adherence to conventional values is nearly impossible, segregation has helped to create a nihilistic and violent counterculture sharply at odds with the basic values and goals of a democratic society. As Kenneth Clark presciently noted in 1965, "the pathologies of the ghetto community perpetuate themselves through cumulative ugliness, deterioration, and isolation."

The social environment created by segregation places a heavy burden on black parents aspiring to promote conventional attitudes and behavior in their children and increase the odds for their socioeconomic success. Although the problem is most acute for the poor, segregation confines all blacks to segregated neighborhoods regardless of social class, so working- and middle-class blacks also have a very difficult time insulating their children from the competing values and attitudes of the street. Compared with children of middle-class whites, children of middle-class blacks are much more likely to be exposed to poverty, drugs, teenage pregnancy, family disruption, and violence in the neighborhoods where they live.

As a result, it requires a great deal of concerted effort by committed parents, and no small amount of luck, to raise children successfully within the ghetto. Given the burden of "acting white," the pressures to speak Black English, the social stigma attached to "brainiacs," the allure of drug taking, the quick money to be had from drug dealing, and the romantic sexuality of the streets, it is not surprising that black educational achievement has stagnated.

Although participant observer studies and rap lyrics illustrate the harsh realities of black street life, they do not "prove" the harmful effects of growing up in a ghetto. Hard evidence about segregation's ill effects requires statistical studies using nationally representative data. Linda Datcher estimates that moving a poor black male from his typical neighborhood (66% black with an average income of $8,500) to a typical white neighborhood (86% white with a mean income of $11,500) would raise his educational attainment by nearly a year. Mary Corcoran and her colleagues found similar results when they considered the effect of moving a man from a typical black to a typical white neighborhood; and Jonathan Crane shows that the dropout probability for black teenage males increases dramatically as the percentage of low-status workers in the neighborhood rises, going from about 8% in areas where three-quarters of the workers are in low-status occupations to nearly 35% when the percentage reaches 97%.

Growing up in a poor neighborhood also undermines the odds of success in the labor market. Linda Datcher's statistical estimates suggest that growing up in a poor black area lowers a man's earnings by at least 27%. Although Mary Corcoran and her colleagues put the percentage loss at about 18%, both teams of researchers agree that black men suffer a loss in earning ability simply for the misfortune of having grown up in a ghetto.

Exposure to conditions typical of the ghetto also dramatically increase the odds of pregnancy and childbirth among teenagers. According to estimates by Jonathan Crane, the probability of a teenage birth increases dramatically as the percentage of low-status workers in the child's neighborhoods increases from 70% to 95%, ultimately reaching a likelihood of about 20%. Similarly, Dennis Hogan and Evelyn Kitagawa found that living in a very poor neighborhood raised the monthly pregnancy rate among black adolescents by 20% and significantly lowered the age at which they became sexually active; and Frank Furstenburg and his colleagues have shown that attending school in integrated rather than segregated classrooms substantially lowers the odds that fifteen- to sixteen-year-old black girls will experience sexual intercourse.

The quantitative evidence thus suggests that any process that concentrates poverty within racially isolated neighborhoods will simultaneously increase the odds of socioeconomic failure within the segregated group. No matter what their personal traits or characteristics, people who grow up and live in environments of concentrated poverty and social isolation are more likely to become teenage mothers, drop out of school, achieve only low levels of education, and earn lower adult incomes.

One study has directly linked the socioeconomic disadvantages suffered by individual minority members to the degree of segregation they experience in society. Using individual, community, and metropolitan data from the fifty largest U.S. metropolitan areas in 1980, Douglas Massey, Andrew Gross, and Mitchell Eggers showed that group segregation and poverty rates interacted to concentrate poverty geographically within neighborhoods, and that exposure to neighborhood poverty subsequently increased the probability of male joblessness and single motherhood among group members. In this fashion, they linked the structural condition of segregation to individual behaviors widely associated with the underclass through the intervening factor of neighborhood poverty, holding individual background characteristics constant.

Their results are summarized in Table 6.2, which traces what happens to levels of black poverty concentration, male joblessness, and single motherhood when the black poverty rate is systematically increased from 10% to 40% under conditions of no segregation and high segregation (where the latter condition is defined to occur with a black-white dissimilarity index of 90). In the absence of segregation, changing the overall rate of black poverty has a relatively modest effect on the neighborhood environment that blacks experience. By increasing the number of poor blacks, the degree of poverty within neighborhoods where blacks live rises somewhat, but under integrated conditions the additional poor families are scattered evenly throughout the urban area, so the level of poverty concentration does not increase much in any single neighborhood. Overall, it rises modestly from about 8% to 17% as a result of shifting the rate of black poverty from 10% to 40%.

Table 6.2

Predicted neighborhood poverty concentrations, probabilities of male joblessness, and likelihoods of single parenthood, assuming different group poverty rates and levels of segregation

Group's poverty rate and level of segregation	Predicted poverty concentration in neighborhood	Predicted probability that a young black man is jobless	Predicted probability that a young black woman heads a family
No residential segregation			
Poverty rate 10%	7.8%	35.8%	22.8%
Poverty rate 20%	10.2	39.9	28.0
Poverty rate 30%	13.3	39.9	28.0
Poverty rate 40%	17.2	39.9	28.0
High residential segregation			
Poverty rate 10%	10.2	39.9	28.0
Poverty rate 20%	17.2	39.9	28.0
Poverty rate 30%	27.5	43.0	31.6
Poverty rate 40%	40.9	53.3	40.6

Source: Douglas S. Massey, Andrew B. Gross, and Mitchell L. Eggers, "Segregation, the Concentration of Poverty, and the Life Chances of Individuals," *Social Science Research* 20 (1991):415.

Note: No segregation means black-white dissimilarity index equals 0 and high segregation means this index equals 90; predicted probabilities control for age, nativity, education, marital status, and English-language ability.

Although the probabilities of male joblessness and single motherhood are sensitive to the rate of poverty that people experience in their neighborhoods, this modest change in the concentration of neighborhood poverty is not enough to affect these individual outcomes very much. The probability of male joblessness rises only from 36% to 40% as a result of the increased poverty concentration, and the likelihood of single motherhood goes from 23% to 28%. In the absence of racial segregation, therefore, even substantial increases in the overall rate of black poverty (from 10% to 40%) would not greatly affect the welfare of individual blacks, because the additional black poverty would not be concentrated but spread widely around the metropolitan area.

In a highly segregated urban area, in contrast, increasing the rate of black poverty causes a marked increase in the concentration of poverty within the neighborhoods where blacks live. As the overall rate of poverty increases from 10% to 40%, the poverty rate in black neighborhoods goes from 10% to 41%. The degree of poverty concentration increases so dramatically because all of the additional poverty must be absorbed by a small number of geographically isolated black neighborhoods. . . . Segregation and poverty interact to yield geographically concentrated poverty.

This sharp increase in neighborhood poverty has profound consequences for the well-being of individual blacks, even those who have not been pushed into poverty themselves, because segregation forces them to live in neighborhoods with many families who are poor. As a result of the increase in neighborhood poverty to which they are exposed, individual probabilities of joblessness and single motherhood rise substantially. As the overall black poverty rate rises from 10% to 40%

and the amount of poverty concentrated within black neighborhoods experiences a comparable increase, the probability of joblessness among young black males rises from 40% to 53% and the likelihood of single motherhood increases from 28% to 41%.

Increasing the rate of poverty of a segregated group thus causes its neighborhood environment to deteriorate, which in turn causes individual probabilities of socioeconomic failure to rise. The same rise in poverty without segregation would hardly affect group members at all, because it would have marginal effects on the neighborhoods where they live. Segregation, in other words, is directly responsible for the creation of a harsh and uniquely disadvantaged black residential environment, making it quite likely that individual blacks themselves will fail, no matter what their socioeconomic characteristics or family background. Racial segregation is the institutional nexus that enables the transmission of poverty from person to person and generation to generation, and is therefore a primary structural factor behind the perpetuation of the urban underclass.

How to Build an Underclass

The foregoing analysis of segregation and its consequences constitutes a primer on how to construct an urban underclass. To begin, choose a minority group whose members are somehow identifiably different from the majority.

Once the group has been selected, the next step in creating an underclass is to confine its members to a small number of contiguous residential areas, and then to impose on them stringent barriers to residential mobility. These barriers are effectively created through discrimination buttressed by prejudice. Those who attempt to leave the enclave are systematically steered away from majority neighborhoods and back to minority or racially mixed areas. If they inquire about homes in other areas, they are treated brusquely and told none are available, and if they insist on seeing an advertised unit, little information is provided about it and no other units are shown. If these deceptions are overcome and a minority homebuyer succeeds in making an offer on a home in a majority neighborhood, the sales agent provides as little information as possible about the options for financing the sale and makes no effort to assist the customer in obtaining a mortgage. At the same time, the seller is discouraged from coming down in price to meet the offer that has been made.

If, despite these efforts, a minority family succeeds in having its offer to buy a majority home accepted, financial institutions take over the task of enforcing the barriers to residential mobility by attempting to deny the family's application for a mortgage, either on the basis of "objective" criteria such as the applicant's income, employment, or family history or because of more subjective concerns about neighborhood "quality" or "stability." Through whatever means, minority loan applications are rejected at a rate several times that of majority applications.

If the foregoing barriers are still somehow overcome and a minority family actually succeeds in moving into a majority neighborhood, then the fallback mechanisms of prejudice come into play. The minority family is systematically harassed by threatening phone calls, rocks thrown through windows, property vandalism, burning crosses, and if these crass measures are unacceptable, through more genteel mechanisms of social ostracism. If acts of prejudice do not succeed in dislodging the family, the ultimate weapon is the avoidance by majority members of the neighborhood. Those in the immediate area seek to leave as soon as they are able and no potential majority homebuyers are shown properties in the area. As a result, the neighborhood rapidly turns from a majority to a minority population.

Through the systematic application of these principles, areas where members of the minority manage to gain entry can be restricted in number and confined largely to locations adjacent to existing minority neighborhoods, thereby maintaining the residential structure of the ghetto. Moreover, prejudice and discrimination applied in the manner just discussed have the additional effect of undermining minority self-esteem, because they make it very clear that no matter how much money or education a minority person may have, he or she will never be accepted or treated as an equal by majority neighbors.

Once a group's segregation in society has been ensured, the next step in building an underclass is to drive up its rate of poverty. Segregation, paradoxically facilitates this task, because policies that harm a highly segregated minority group and its neighborhoods will have few untoward side effects on other racial or ethnic groups. Geographic isolation translates into political isolation, making it difficult for segregated groups to form political coalitions with others to end policies inimical to their self-interests or to promote policies that might advance their welfare. Racial segregation thus makes it politically easy to limit the number of government jobs within the ghetto, to reduce its public services, to keep its schools understaffed and underfunded, to lower the transfer payments on which its poor depend, and to close its hospitals, clinics, employment offices, and other social support institutions.

With the political marginalization of minority members ensured by their segregation, the only thing required to set off a spiral of decay within the ghetto is a first-class economic disaster that removes the means of subsistence from a large share of the population. If the minority migrated to cities largely to take industrial jobs vacated by upwardly mobile majority immigrants, the inner-city manufacturing base provides a particularly opportune point at which to undercut the economic supports of the minority community, thereby bringing about the necessary increases in minority poverty.

Through a combination of corporate disinvestments in older plants and equipment, a decentralization of blue-collar employment from city to suburban areas, the relocation of manufacturing processes to nonmetropolitan areas, the transfer of production jobs to the sunbelt or overseas, and the setting of high real interest rates to produce an overvalued dollar and relatively expensive U.S. products, inner-city manufacturing industries can effectively be driven out of the urban economy. As manufacturing employment falls and employment suburbanizes, thousands of ghetto dwellers, primarily men with little formal education, will be displaced from jobs that pay them relatively high wages and sent into a two-tiered service economy that generates a larger number of menial, low-paying jobs but few high-paying positions for people without education or training.

These inner-city economic dislocations drive up the rate of minority poverty. The additional deprivation created by the economic flux is concentrated geographically within isolated ghetto neighborhoods. As neighborhood poverty concentrations rise, income is withdrawn from minority neighborhoods, and the resulting increase in dilapidation and abandonment sets off physical decay that soon spreads to surrounding stable neighborhoods. If, owing to the constraints of fiscal austerity and the political isolation of these neighborhoods, fire service to ghetto areas is simultaneously reduced, then the process of neighborhood decay will be substantially accelerated. The increase in poverty concentration also brings a sharp constriction of demand density within the ghetto, leading to the collapse of its retail sector and the elimination of most nonessential goods and services.

The interaction of poverty and segregation acts to concentrate a variety of deleterious social and economic characteristics, creating an environment where male joblessness, female welfare dependency, crime, drug abuse, teenage childbearing, and single parenthood are common or even normative. The ghetto comes to house an abundance of negative role models who exemplify attitudes and behaviors detrimental to success in the emerging post-industrial service economy.

Given the lack of opportunity, pervasive poverty, and increasing hopelessness of life in the ghetto, a social-psychological dynamic is set in motion to produce a culture of segregation. Under the structural conditions of segregation, it is difficult for ghetto dwellers to build self-esteem by satisfying the values and ideals of the larger society or to acquire prestige through socially accepted paths. Precisely because the ghetto residents deem themselves failures by the broader standards of society, they evolve a parallel status system defined in opposition to the prevailing majority culture. As new generations are born into conditions of increasing deprivation and deepening racial isolation, however, the oppositional origins of the status system gradually recede and the culture of segregation becomes autonomous and independent.

A sure sign that the culture of segregation is well advanced occurs when the language of the segregated group diverges sharply from the standard dialect spoken in the wider society. Not only will the breakdown in intergroup communications enhance feelings of racial separation between the underclass and the rest of society, but the lack of facility in the standard dialect will undermine the minority group's prospects for success in education and employment.

The emergence of a culture of segregation also limits the number of minority families who aspire to leave the ghetto. As "minority" culture becomes more firmly established and deeply rooted, members of the minority who seek integration within the larger social and economic institutions of the society will come under increasing pressure from others to stop acting like a majority member. Those who succumb to this pressure, or who themselves promote self-segregation in language, culture, and housing, will be unlikely to meet with socioeconomic success in the larger society and will be limited to a life of persistent poverty and deprivation. Through prolonged exposure to life in racially isolated and intensely poor neighborhoods, this poverty will quite likely be passed to children in the next generation. When this point is reached, a well-functioning and efficient social structure for the creation and maintenance of an urban underclass will have been created.

Integration Anxiety

Lise Funderburg is a freelance writer working on a book about race and class in integrated communities.

How many of you who are white think about being white all the time?" asks Michelle Fine, speaking to a racially integrated class of seventh graders last spring at Renaissance Middle School in Montclair, N.J. Fine, a white woman and Montclair resident, is a nationally regarded social psychologist who specializes in education issues. Today she's wrapping up an oral history course she has volunteered to teach along with the school's principal, Bernadette Anand.

For nine weeks, these students have considered nothing less than the meaning of race in Montclair as they have documented the town's 40-year history of school desegregation. They have interviewed residents, reviewed court cases, read mountains of newspaper clippings and watched segments of the civil rights documentary "Eyes on the Prize." Yet none of these students connect to feeling white, and Fine's question is met with silence. She tries a different tack.

"White kids, when you go into a store, do you feel like you are white?"

Dust particles drift into the rays of light spilling through the classroom's tall, arched windows. Students look down at their desks and stare into space. Finally, Kendra Urdang, a white girl with a South African mother and a Canadian father, answers yes, sometimes, when she's in a store filled with black people. No one else speaks. Fine tries again.

"Kids who are African-American," she says, "when you go into a store, are you reminded about being black?"

Suddenly, several students leap from their chairs, clamoring to give examples of local stores where they have been followed, searched, accused of stealing, asked to leave. Daryl Shelton, a serious-faced 12-year-old, names a toy shop in town, and three other black students nod their heads vigorously, "mm-hmming" in recognition.

"I was with him, right?" Daryl begins, pointing to his best friend in school, a tall white boy named Kyle O'Donnell. Kyle's mother was giving Daryl a ride home when she stopped for an errand. All the kids piled out of the car. "His younger sister went into this store," Daryl says. "Then when I try to go in, I can't. They always bring up, 'You have to be 18 or older.' "

In most cities and towns across the country, Daryl's tale of being singled out because he's black would be regarded as sad but not surprising. But this is Montclair, a suburban enclave 12 miles west of New York City that is renowned for being racially and socioeconomically integrated, for welcoming everyone who is willing to mow their lawns and pay their taxes. That reputation has attracted blacks and whites—including the presidential hopeful Bill Bradley—who have chosen not to default into more common patterns of racial segregation. In most of the country's metropolitan areas, 79 percent of whites and 33 percent of blacks live exclusively among members of their own racial groups: they borrow sugar from people who would check the same box on a census form or file in the same tax bracket.

All Americans are going to have to face integration sooner or later, whether they want to or not. Although in the 1990 United States census, whites made up 84 percent of the population, some demographers now project that this figure will drop to 50 percent in the next half-century. People can retreat to only so many gated communities, themed dorms and homogenous executive lounges.

For more than a century, Montclair residents have struggled to live the integrated life. When newcomers buy houses, they often assume that they have put a down payment on diversity. Yet once you get past the Kumbaya hype, self-congratulatory civic boosterism and media accolades, stories like Daryl's appear with disturbing frequency. Montclair's experience, then, holds lessons for the rest of the nation. Diversity is still a concept very much under construction here.

No one has defined what constitutes a truly integrated community. But Montclair (pop. 36,313) is a serious contender. In a landmark study published last year [1998], researchers for the Department of Housing and Urban Development (HUD) identified some of the characteristics that undergird a "successful, stable, racially and ethnically diverse" neighborhood. Montclair fits HUD's criteria; it has, among other things, a mixed racial balance since at least 1980 and the willingness of residents to identify their community as diverse.

During the last 30 years, while other communities became all black or all white as industrial decline, white flight and gentrification took their toll, Montclair has remained roughly 30 percent black and 65 percent white. A varied housing stock has helped preserve its socioeconomic mix. Home prices may average $334,000, but rambling Victorians with sprawling lawns often stand a stone's throw from apartment buildings and tiny clapboard homes where more than 2,200 people live below the poverty line. And while most of the town's poor are black, many of its middle- and upper-class residents are black as well.

Like many of the towns and neighborhoods in the HUD study, Montclair is older and physically attractive and has more than its share of amenities. It has a nationally recognized art museum, four movie houses, six theaters, four bookstores, 48 religious congregations, 154 acres of parkland, Montclair State University and a heavenly fried porgy sandwich made to order at the Fin and Feather. And while it's a point of civic pride—and of tax-revenue woe—that Montclair has no mall, it does have five shopping districts, a Gap and two Starbucks.

Culture, food and lattes may boost the community's appeal, particularly to integration-tolerant ex-urbanites (and a stunning number of celebrities, from the tap dancer Savion Glover to the makeup mogul Bobbi Brown, as well as Bill Bradley). But it's the enduring mix of race and class that sets Montclair apart from prototypical suburbia. "Racial and economic exclusion continue to be hallmarks of suburbanization," writes W. Dennis Keating in "The Suburban Racial Dilemma." Although most residents will argue that the town has yet to achieve the physical, social and spiritual integration Martin Luther King Jr. once described as "the be-loved community," hardly any of its streets are totally racially isolated.

The HUD study also notes that in diverse communities, schools typically offer a rallying point for people to come together—the place where "social seams" are stitched together. And indeed, Montclair's 11 public schools are perhaps the town's most integrated institutions. Thanks to zealous compliance with a 1976 state-levied desegregation order, the district's 5,930 students all have significant exposure to kids of different races and classes. Montclair operates a "controlled choice" program that relies on magnet schools, a lottery and town-subsidized busing. And unlike a similar, recently abandoned program in Boston, it has largely gone undisputed over the years. But the schools are also where the pressures on racial harmony are the greatest, threatening to fray those seams beyond repair.

"I need seats in the middle," Michelle Fine calls out, trying to make room for Marvyn Rice, today's guest and one of 25 black parents who successfully brought suit against the school district in the mid-1960's. Rice is among a parade of subjects, most of them still Montclair residents, whom Fine and Bernadette Anand have invited to the school and whose stories have helped personalize the abstractions of the town's history for students.

Volunteers bring chairs into the center of the room with an eagerness that probably won't last into high school. Rice responds generously to students' questions, carefully unfolding rich anecdotes. Between inquirers, she sits primly, hands folded in her lap. "I just want to mention that Mrs. Rice is a real, live hero," Fine says, when the students have exhausted the list of scripted questions. "So take the moment!"

Those involved in the early days of school desegregation in Montclair still shudder at the battles fought. "Those were **Armageddon** arguments," Montclair's mayor, William Farlie, remembers. But in those days, the principle at stake—that barriers to equal education should be removed—bore a noble, if naïve, simplicity. Nowadays things are messier. Fully sharing power and resources across race and class lines—often called relational diversity—is something no one has done before. The skirmishes over educational access that fill P.T.A. meetings and op-eds in The Montclair Times are inevitably complex: Is a budget cutback racist, for example, if it affects more blacks than whites? More whites than blacks? Should district resources be dedicated to keeping the school population "stable," which is often code for "middle class" and "not too black"?

Nationwide, Fine says, perceptions of an institution's worth shift depending on whether whites or blacks are in the majority. Consequently, the slight black majority (53 percent) at Montclair High sometimes sets off alarms for real estate agents who show prospective buyers around town and for some white and black parents deciding where to send their children. "There are a lost of whispers about tipping," Fine says, referring to concern over maintaining current racial percentages. "I get calls from friends who say, 'My kid's class is imbalanced.' I know right away that means there are too many black people in the room."

In 1993, for instance, some parents became panicked when Bernadette Anand, then the head of the Montclair High School English department, along with some of her colleagues, devised a world literature class that was open to everyone. By jettisoning prerequisites, world lit renounced the ability-based groupings that in Montclair and across the country too often default into racial equations—advanced placement equals white; remedial equals black, especially black and male. The town is striving to close the achievement gap between black and white students (which also exists nationally).

To that end, Anand had declared war on "tracked classes," but in so doing, assaulted the protected inner sanctum that allows middle- and upper-middle-class parents to comfortably keep their children in the public schools. After acrimonious debate, the school board voted to go forward with the class, but a swell of parents—mostly but not all white—plucked their children from advanced-placement classes and out of the system altogether.

Many liberals in town characterize those who left the system as cloaking their racism in a pro-meritocracy argument. But Brenda Farrow White, an African-American woman whose husband, Herman, was the school board president for two years, and whose children attend Montclair schools, is more generous toward parents who put their own needs in front of larger social justice issues. "Parents are, by nature, not objective when it comes to matters regarding their children," she says. "All that matters to them is what is good for Johnny or Susie. Or Laquesha or Tanesha."

The board of ed also noticed that an increasing number of students—again, mostly but not exclusively white—were leaving the district, particularly at the middle-school level. Many transcript requests indicated parochial- or private-school destinations. The white kids were clearly middle and upper middle class. (Montclair's white working-class stronghold virtually disappeared during the 60's and 70's.) But black kids also departed, and administrators surmised that they, too, were from well-heeled families. People in town have come to call this exodus "bright flight," unwittingly equating economic standing and intelligence.

With the explicit goal of "stabilizing" the district, the superintendent and school board opened a third middle school in 1997, which became Renaissance. This one would be smaller than the others—75 children per grade versus 200—and would offer educational innovations normally identified with private schools. The hope, says Michael Osnato, the superintendent, was that these components would "retain and return" the education-savvy middle class. The school was designed, in other words, by the district to stanch bright flight, but this goal created new tensions.

Anand, for one, was interested in creating a learning environment that valued achievement and equal access for all students. She remembers how white attrition dominated school board discussions. "That's what they cared about," she says. "They felt that if the whites left, the whole town would go down. Then we'd have a whole bunch of blacks here, and I'd be perfectly happy to teach them." Anand's first planning meeting was with Fine, whose older son is now a Renaissance seventh grader. The two women quickly became allies, promoting their vision of the school. "We're people you don't invite to parties," Anand jokes, referring to their fierce commitment to social justice.

Fine says that together they decided that the school would only succeed if its curriculum tapped the talents of every child—a familiar tenet of progressive education. The tendency to value certain kids over others is so endemic to school systems, Fine insists, "it's in the air-conditioning." Disproportionately, she explains, "kids who have had the cultural capital and the social reinforcements for getting it right tend to be elite kids, and in this town, that means white—or some middle-class black—kids. And then kids who learn that they don't quite get it right, who would be more hesitant in the class, who wouldn't feel as entitled to speak their minds, tend to be working-class African-American kids."

In its third year, Renaissance offers rigorous instruction, longer school days, innovative field trips and an extensive community-service program. This is an increasingly complicated endeavor in the jumbled classrooms of Montclair, as a new wave of poorer blacks move into town, and children who can't afford class outings sit next to the children of millionaires. Anand's strategy has proven popular, but at a potentially disturbing price. As of last year, Renaissance was the only middle school in the district with a majority of whites. If the school continues to attract whites disproportionately, Osnato's aim to "recapture the market share" may be met, but Fine counters that the school will have failed in a different way. "What does that say about poor and working-class kids?" she asks. "Are those kids not valued as much?"

Others voice different concerns. One white parent, who describes herself as "an old leftie," complains that Renaissance's good intentions have gone too far. She says her child has "gotten lost" despite Renaissance's small classes and links this neglect to race. "I'm happy that race is an issue in a positive sense, as a topic of discussion," says the woman, who asked not to be identified for the sake of her children. "But there does seem to be a feeling that if your child is white, he or she doesn't need any extra help. Now, it's a correct assumption that if you're white, you're likely to be privileged; but it's also assumed that you don't need any support in learning."

And middle-class whites aren't the only ones who are worried about their kids getting lost. Debra Jennings, 41, says that the African-American parents she knows have different reasons than whites for pulling out of the public schools. "I would say only one out of 10 feel like their supergifted child is not going to be sufficiently challenged," she estimates. "The other nine are worried about teachers' *low* expectations, particularly if the child is a boy. Those parents will tell you that their child was being painted with a certain brush, and they did not want that to happen."

Jennings has sat on the school board, run for mayor and co-founded a watchdog group called Concerned African American Parents (CAP). She's currently the associate executive director of an education support group, the Statewide Parent Advocacy Network. In Montclair, many blacks are reluctant to discuss the tensions of intraracial class divisions, and Jennings is known for specifically representing the town's working-class and poor blacks. "There's no such thing as 'bright flight,' " she says with a scowl. "It's 'I-can-afford-it flight.' "

On the theory that power lies in the hands of the informed, CAP focuses on information dissemination—mostly through a quarterly newsletter and biennial Parents' Expo. Jennings says even white parents rely on CAP's school-budget analyses to understand how money is being spent in the district. Yet communication gaps between the races persist.

Despite Renaissance's explicit mission to raise the bar for everyone, CAP had serious reservations about the district's starting a new middle school. "We had two questions," Jennings recalls. The first was about how, in a year of draconian budget cuts, the district could afford a new program. The second, she says, was why Renaissance didn't do a better job of including poor black parents when planning the school. "There were attempts made to reach out to African-American parents," she concedes, "but most of the parents they reached out to were middle to upper middle class. There was really no outreach to African-American parents who were more typical—more working and middle class."

Socioeconomic status matters, Jennings says, because wealthier families often have the luxuries of time and resources to lobby on behalf of their children's needs. "When I look at the parents who are at Renaissance," Jennings explains, "I don't criticize them, but almost all have been heavily involved in their children's education. I felt like that kind of energy should have gone into some of the other schools—because we need more African-American parents in the other schools. We don't need a concentration in one school."

Elliott Lee is part of that concentration. An Ivy League graduate and a senior program officer of a locally based foundation, he has a daughter, Andrea, who is an eighth grader at Renaissance, and has been an involved parent, joining Anand's curriculum development committee and participating in a loosely organized lobby against budget cuts. He has even considered seeking a seat on the school board.

Thirteen years ago, when Lee and his family moved onto a predominantly black street in Montclair, he wasn't prepared for the chilly reception from his new black neighbors. "I thought because we were black and they were black, they would welcome us," he says. "But we weren't just black people, we were the outsiders driving up property values and forcing the old folks out."

Class-consciousness is creeping into all of Montclair, he contends, and no one wants to admit it. "Most people are willing to talk about the folks with resources coming in and supplanting those who've been here a long time," Lee says. "What isn't talked about are the new black folks coming in who aren't well off, trying to get their kids into better schools. That would send the wrong message about Montclair. A lot of people—white and black, but maybe more white folks—want Montclair to be less diverse than it is. They want it to be middle class. It's one thing to have poor people who've been here for years, but it's another thing to be known as a place that attracts them."

A teacher's aide walks through the Renaissance hallway last spring, ringing a hand bell to signal the period's end. It's lunchtime, and students in the oral history class lunge for the door. Kids fill their plates—it's pizza day—and then make a beeline for their seats in the basement cafeteria. Day after day, the long tables fill up according to a carefully worked-out calculus of race and class.

"I sit at the semipopular/unpopular white girls' table," explains Susana Polo cheerfully.

"I think it has to do with the music people listen to," says Trevor Sage-El, the student council president at the time and a biracial boy who sits at the popular black boys' table.

"My friends are 75 percent black and 25 percent white," says Ashley Carter-Robinson, who is black and chooses to sit at a table that's all black and all girl, except when Daryl Shelton's friend Kyle O'Donnell invites himself over, seemingly oblivious to whether he's welcome.

"Four of my black friends sit with us," says Kendra Urdang, "and the rest of us are white at my table. I have mixed friends, but honestly, my best friends, more of them are white because in this school it is a bit more separated. When there's a clique of only black people, one time I went over to that crowd and they just ignored me."

In these social striations, the children are not much different than the adults. Despite all that Montclair has going for it, despite the widely expressed desire for relational integration, if you ask residents, black or white, whether people cross the color line socially, most will say no, not really, or not very often. Maybe at Watchung Booksellers or Sharron Miller's dance studio or the Luna Stage theater—but they're exceptions. Even supermarkets have the reputation of being patronized along racial lines. (King's is white, Pathmark is black, Fresh Fields is for anyone with a full wallet.)

Not even the HUD researchers could calculate whether living together leads to social integration. But as community life atrophies everywhere, true relational integration seems ever more difficult to imagine.

"There's an impoverishment in relatedness in America," says Mindy Thompson Fullilove, a public health research psychiatrist at Columbia-Presbyterian Medical Center. Where we once raised barns to build commonality, we now pay property taxes. Normal patterns of socializing have eroded because people no longer live, work and socialize in the same place. Overlay race, and the challenge of integration is heightened.

"I find communities like Montclair hopeful," says the sociologist Douglas Massey. "But the sorts of forces that produce segregation in American society don't happen at the community level. Basically, places like Montclair are forced to adapt to a racially segregated world and undertake heroic efforts, often, to keep themselves these islands of integration in the broader sea of segregation."

Renaissance's principal, Anand, says, "School is the one place where you can really break down the patterns of sameness that exist within our communities." But perhaps because it is one of the town's few arenas for change, progress continues to come slowly.

"It's not our fault if we don't like people," says Susana Polo, who is half Irish and half Puerto Rican. "We want to sit with our friends. I'm not saying this racistly, but black people are brought up different, because of persecutions and slavery and stuff—they're brought up to feel different things than white kids, which makes their personalities different. I don't get along with the black kids in my school. I get along with my friends, who are mostly white, and Michelle, who's black. And it's just like that."

A seating chart Anand implemented to break up the cafeteria's race- and class-based groupings stood little chance against the undertow of elaborate and steadfast allegiances—kids who live in Upper Montclair as opposed to those who live in Frog Hollow, who listen to rap as opposed to Hanson, who come home at night to play basketball as opposed to Battle Squad. After less than a month, Kendra Urdang observes, "everyone was just sitting back where they wanted to."

Still, Montclair offers reason for optimism. One of Daryl Shelton's classmates, a white boy named Ian Bandes, tells me the most important thing he learned in Fine and Anand's oral history class was about the relationship between time and social progress. "I learned that very recently, maybe 20 years ago, the town was very racist. And it's kind of scary, but it also taught us that we've come so far in that short time."

Renaissance, one suspects, deserves only partial credit for Ian's enlightened attitude. After all, many schools, even in the most segregated neighborhoods, teach racial tolerance. If Montclair's white students are more open to racial diversity than other kids, it's probably because their families are, too; that's why they chose this town in the first place.

Absolute integration may still be unrealized in Montclair, says Joan Pransky, the white mother of a 12th grader at the high school, but that's no reason to despair. "I don't think it happens in your lifetime," she says. "The long and short of it is the contribution you make along the way and the fervor you bring to it. The fact that a lot of things around here are wrong doesn't mean for a minute you change doing your best to do right."

The town is still very much a work in progress. True integration, Mayor Farlie observes, demands an acceptance that no town will ever be perfect and that people will always disagree. "One of the challenges of suburban and urban life these days in America," he says, "is you either believe in diversity and are prepared to sometimes be disappointed and other times be elated, or you move to suburban Connecticut."

A week after Daryl tells his story in class, I ask him to talk about the episode at the toy store. "I was distressed that they were singling me out because of my race," he says as we sit on the stairwell outside the cafeteria. "It's never happened before. I thought Montclair was perfect." Now, partly because of the class project, he says: "I'm starting to notice that other people are looking at me more often. I don't think it's very fair."

On his own, Daryl has come up with a plan for returning to the store, a combined appeal to human decency and market forces. "I was thinking I should just go over there and talk to them about it and tell them how it makes people feel," he explains. "And tell them how many kids actually don't want to come to their store." He is thinking about the profits, he says, because the store should want to attract as many customers as possible.

His resolve fulfills Fine's goals for the class. "Young people need to know that they can produce history," she says, "and hopefully, that's the legacy of this town. It's not just about raising kids to be good citizens or good boys and girls, it's actually a town committed to raising young people who know how to live in a multiracial, multiethnic community."

Daryl's tale of hometown discrimination makes a case for Montclair's failure—that even in such small moments of interaction, the community can't break free of segregationist, prejudiced patterns. But a stronger case can be made that, here, the stage for real progress is continually being set. With Daryl's plan, the town takes one more small but meaningful step toward the beloved community.

6.6   Michael Eric Dyson

In a Color-Blind Society, We Can Only See Black and White: Why Race Will Continue to Rule

Michael Eric Dyson is author of Making Malcolm: The Myth and Meaning of Malcolm X, Reflecting Black: African-American Cultural Criticism, *and* Between God and Gansta Rap: Bearing Witness to Black Culture. *He is the Ida B. Wells-Barnett University Professor of religious studies at DePaul University in Chicago.*

The rules may be color-blind, but people are not. The question remains, therefore, whether the law can truly exist apart from the color-conscious society in which it exists, as a skeleton devoid of flesh; or whether law is the embodiment of society, the reflection of a particular citizenry's arranged complexity of relations.

—Patricia J. Williams, *The Alchemy of Race and Rights,* 1991

Michael Eric Dyson . . . any sense of why these things are going on?" Charlie Gibson, the literate host of *Good Morning America,* asked me.

He was referring to the recent rash of burnings that have gutted nearly seventy black churches since January 1, 1995. In the brief time I had—shared with eloquent guests Deval Patrick, U.S. Assistant Attorney General for Civil Rights, and Morris Dees, Director of the Southern Poverty Law Center—I suggested two factors. First, black churches are vulnerable targets for white rage, especially since even rural churches symbolize black presence and progress. Second, the burnings are an outgrowth of our nation's s lethal racial climate.

To be honest, no one can say for certain why black churches are being targeted for fiery destruction, mostly in the South. In the '60s black churches were the headquarters for those enlisted in the army of nonviolent resistance to state-sponsored apartheid. The church kitchen provided nourishment to famished troops, offices became war rooms to develop strategies, and sanctuaries became rallying posts where the charge to battle was sounded. In the perverse reasoning of white supremacists, it made sense to bomb and burn churches as a way to terrorize blacks, to discourage them from fighting for racial justice.

While the church remains at the center of black life in the '90s, it is now more venerable than threatening. In part, that's a reflection of how our times have evoked less dramatic demonstrations of the church's role in social transformation. In that light, it is curious that black churches—not the large, urban, affluent ones, but mostly modest, rural houses of worship—are once again being consumed by more than the Holy Spirit.

The fact that we can't get a good grip on what's going on, that we can't draw from these church burnings the clear conclusions that old-style racism made possible, is an ironic sign of progress. In the '60s and before, acts of hatred had symbolic clarity because blacks and whites shared an ecology of race. I'm not suggesting that blacks and whites agreed about what each group saw as the source of racial conflict. In fact, like today, they often didn't even agree about what they saw: many whites saw roses where many blacks saw thorns. Blacks and whites also bitterly disagreed about what they should do about the problems that existed. Still, the racial environment they inherited and shaped made the discerning of racist symbols easier. A church burning was undisguised racial hatred. A cross burning was meant to intimidate "uppity" blacks. And a lynching was the ultimate expression of a white supremacist desire to control the black body.

But in our more racially murky era—an era in which the ecology of race is much more complex and choked with half-discarded symbols and muddied signs—our skills of interpretation have to be more keen, our readings more nuanced. There's little doubt that most of the vitriolic expressions of racism have been forced underground by the success of '60s black freedom struggles. But symptoms of racial antipathy persist, even if they're harder to prove and far more difficult to analyze.

Our current racial climate, which encourages the belief that we do, or should, live in a color-blind society, has made many commentators wary of claiming a connection between the church burnings. Some commentators claim that these burnings are more religious than racial, since so many white churches have also been burned. Some commentators believe that claiming a connection between the burnings might give heart to isolated racists by exaggerating the degree to which a concerted effort to rattle black folk even exists among the perpetrators. In other words, these commentators seek to avoid claiming that a conspiracy to destroy black churches exists. Well, if not all racial meanings have been driven underground, some of them are hidden in plain sight. We miss them because they're right in front of our faces.

There are various reasons for some of the black church burnings: teenage vandalism, mental derangement, and, in a couple of cases, insurance fraud. (Though we should ask why a black church is viewed as a viable target for a disgruntled teen or a confused young adult.) Among those twelve arsonists already convicted of burning black churches in the '90s, however, there is a definite pattern of racial hostility. A couple of them felt they were being cheated at a black-owned juke joint in Tennessee, while another was angered that his daughter had run off with a black man. Torching a black church was a way to get revenge.

All twelve of the arsonists are white, and all of them were convicted under a 1965 federal civil rights law. Two other arsonists, both white, are in jail awaiting trial, as federal prosecutors prepare to charge them under civil rights law.

The twelve share other similarities. Ten didn't finish high school. Half were unemployed, while others were stuck in low-paying jobs. Ten are young, ranging in age from seventeen to twenty-three. Half lived at home with their parents, most in rural areas near the churches they burned. And three had explicit ties to racist groups.

The perpetrators' profiles made it clear that black churches symbolize to them—and perhaps to other arsonists as well—not the civil rights threat of old, but a local sign of black survival, of black success. The rural black church in particular captures the utility—it is a major outlet for social recreation—and the invincibility of black Christian faith. Ironically, those very qualities have made it newly vulnerable to another generation of confused, disgruntled, racist whites. We need not hunt for a Grand Conspiracy to explain what's going on. It would then be easy to scapegoat poor whites. Rather, our very racial ecology—littered with code words, hidden racial meanings, thinly veiled racial assumptions, and confused racial rules, while witnessing the emergence of racist militias and the resurgence of white hate groups—conspires against racial justice. Church burnings are merely the most obvious sign of a more dangerous racial fire raging in our nation.

To make matters worse, many of the guardians of our legal and political culture are busy retarding real racial progress by invoking the same principles of justice and equality for which blacks heroically fought and often died. One of the bitter ironies of this situation is that many of the former opponents of racial equality are now charged with dispensing racial justice in local, state, and federal governments. The fox who once terrorized the chicken coop is now expected to be fair to the chickens—to know best what they need, and to determine what measures are just in their pursuit of equality with the foxes.

That bitter irony is compounded by the fact that laws aimed at equality and justice are often interpreted by those who have done little of the suffering that brought the laws into existence. As a result, the spirit of struggle that helped make the laws a vibrant fulfillment of democracy is nullified. And the history of racial conflict that shaped how those laws should be understood and applied is obscured, distorted, or simply erased.

I'm certainly not arguing that one has to have been victimized by slavery, a denial of rights after Reconstruction, or the rule of Jim Crow to interpret or apply laws meant to realize racial justice. That kind of petty identity politics is harmful to historically wronged blacks who are much larger and more complex than the labels of suffering they wear. Neither am I arguing that blacks should demonize those who disagree with us about how to bring about justice and equality. It's one thing to say let freedom ring. It's another matter to determine who gets to strike the liberty bell, when it should be rung, and what our responses should be to what we hear. Still, there's no denying that, in terms of racial politics, where you stand— and the history that makes that stance both possible and plausible—determines what you see and hear. If the Rodney King beating, and the riots that followed his molesters' acquittal, didn't make that clear, then the O. J. Simpson trial and its aftermath should leave little doubt that it's true.

The most recent example of our tragic confusion about how racial justice should be conceived and applied is the 1996 Supreme Court decisions that ruled four congressional districts—one in North Carolina and three in Texas—unconstitutional. The Court invalidated the districts because race played a predominant role in their creation. The four districts had been created after the 1990 census to give minorities more just electoral representation. The Supreme Court's 5–4 rulings buttress three previous decisions in which the Court said race should not be the main reason for drawing odd-shaped districts that pull together minority voters to maximize their electoral strength. So while districts may be legally redrawn to protect political incumbents, they cannot be drawn to support previously and presently excluded minority voters.

What's tragic about the Court's decision is that it is based in large part on an ahistorical interpretation of the Fourteenth Amendment. We should recall that the Fourteenth Amendment was passed after the Civil War to extend to former slaves equal protection under the law. In his majority decision against the district (in the North Carolina case, *Shaw v. Hunt*), Chief Justice William Rehnquist argued that racial "classifications are antithetical to the **Fourteenth Amendment**, whose central purpose was to eliminate racial discrimination emanating from official sources in the States."

But what Rehnquist fails to address is how congressional districts drawn with race in mind are a response to the 1965 Voting Rights Act, passed to guarantee the right to vote for blacks who should already have been protected by the Fourteenth Amendment. If that amendment was insufficient to help enforce legal enfranchisement for blacks, it is ironic that the supposed failure to abide by it is now evoked by the Supreme Court to further erode electoral representation for those same blacks.

Before the 1990 census led to the creation of majority-minority districts, there were 26 black members in Congress. In 1992 that number rose to 39, and in 1994 there were 41 black members in Congress. In North Carolina, two majority-minority districts helped send the first two black North Carolina legislators to Congress since George White was forced out of Congress in 1901 by the state's ratification of a disfranchisement amendment. In the words of white turn-of-the-century North Carolina Democratic leader Charles Aycock, the ratification of the disfranchisement amendment was "the final settlement of the negro problem." Unsurprisingly, Aycock was elected governor of North Carolina in the same election in 1901. When Congresswoman Eva Clayton, of North Carolina's first district, and Congressman Melvin Watt, of the twelfth district, took their seats in the House in 1993, the promise of the Fourteenth Amendment, reinforced by the Voting Rights Act of 1965, was at long last realized.

An even greater irony is that the Court ruled against the majority-minority districts because they failed to satisfy the Court's criteria, established in a 1993 ruling, that a "compelling state interest" be reflected in the drawing of the districts, and that the districts should be drawn in a way that was "narrowly tailored" to serve that interest. Certainly the proportional representation of black voters is a "compelling state interest." But Rehnquist wrote: "an effort to alleviate the effects of societal discrimination is not a compelling interest."

And according to Justice Sandra Day O'Connor's opinion for the majority in the Texas case, *Bush v. Vera,* more judicial weight is given to the geographical shape of a district than to its political utility in realizing the aims of the Fourteenth Amendment and the Voting Rights Act. "The bizarre shape and noncompactness demonstrated by the districts . . . cause constitutional harm insofar as they convey the message that political identity is, or should be, predominantly racial," O'Connor writes. With one stroke of her pen, O'Connor denies the role that race has historically played in shaping political identity. She also completely ignores how racial identity is politicized, since it doesn't exist in a protected zone outside our nations profound political conflicts. One can only conclude that, at least when it comes to racial politics and majority-minority districts, Freud was right. Anatomy *is* destiny.

Of course, alternatives to district-based representation, and hence, to racial redistricting, have been put forth. Alas, they have gone the way of all political flesh, or at least such ideas have been castigated as "profoundly antidemocratic." Lani Guinier, for instance, suggested that geographically based constituencies deny individual representation of the voter. She has written that "the use of geographic districts as the basis for establishing representational constituencies is at its very heart a system of group-based representation."

What to do? Guinier suggested an alternative to the winner-take-all manner of our current single-member congressional districts. Instead, we might have multiseat congressional districts where each voter has several votes that can be distributed among many candidates. Or we might have preference voting, where voters rank their votes in order of preference. But Guinier's notions of cumulative and preference voting got her dubbed a "quota queen" in the *Wall Street Journal.* She was widely dismissed as a fringe radical whose ideas made her unfit for the Assistant Attorney General for Civil Rights post, for which her nomination was withdrawn by President Clinton in 1993. A year later, without any controversy, Supreme Court Justice Clarence Thomas, in an opinion for a voting rights case, wrote that in "principle, cumulative voting and other non-district-based methods of effecting proportional representation are simply more efficient and straightforward mechanisms for achieving what has already become our tacit objective: roughly proportional allocation of political power according to race."   ·

It is clear from the Supreme Court's decisions about majority-minority districts and other recent decisions severely undermining the scope of affirmative action, and from the effect its decisions have had on black communities, that the Court is failing miserably as the guardian of racial justice. Justice O'Connor is worried that by creating majority-minority districts, we will forget that "voters are more than racial statistics." What she fails to understand is that without legal guarantees of equal protection and just representation, the interests of black voters will remain largely unrepresented. The Supreme Court's judgments underscore a dilemma the Court has failed to successfully address: how our nation can overcome racism without taking race into account.

The Supreme Court has consistently, at least recently, argued for the ideal of a color-blind society. Ironically, that ideal has led the Court, and other would-be advocates of black interests, to overlook the history of sacrifice, suffering, and struggle that made the Fourteenth Amendment and the Voting Rights Act necessary. (In fact, Robinson Everett, the Duke law professor who instigated the North Carolina suit, and who argued it before the Supreme Court, is a self-described "yellow dog Democrat" who believes in a color-blind politics inspired by 1960s social activism. Everett and other southern white Democrats are heartened by the Supreme Court ruling because it will spread blacks throughout districts where white politicians have a better chance of being elected, since blacks vote overwhelmingly Democratic. This is another instance where alleged black allies inflict the deepest wounds to black interests with the double-edged sword of political opportunism sharpened on either side by race.)

Over the last decade, the Supreme Court has consistently failed to appreciate the complexities of the history of race in America. As Justice John Paul Stevens writes in his dissenting opinion, it is unfortunate that the Court should intervene "into a process by which federal and state actors, both black and white, are jointly attempting to resolve difficult questions of politics and race that have long plagued North Carolina." Stevens recognizes that the Court's ruling means, in effect, that all sorts of political interests can be legally protected save those that are based on race. Stevens doesn't "see how our constitutional tradition can countenance the suggestion that a State may draw unsightly lines to favor farmers or city dwellers, but not to create districts that benefit the very group whose history inspired the Amendment that the Voting Rights Act was designed to implement."

The disagreement about race in America's highest court reflects the fatal disagreements that continue to bewitch our nation. Those courageous black souls who fought to make America all that it should be were not interested in what is presently meant by a color-blind society. True enough, they were interested in shaping an American society that wasn't obsessed with race, that didn't use race to unfairly dispense goods or allocate resources. But most were not naive enough to believe that we could ever, in the foreseeable future, arrive at a place where race didn't make a huge difference in how we live our lives, how we view one another, how we are granted or denied social privilege.

The tragedy of our condition is that we have a Supreme Court, and many other Americans, who have ignored the rules of race, how race continues to shape American life. Worse yet, they blame those who resist the color-blind myth for extending, rather than exposing, the hold race still has on American character. But we cannot overcome the history of racial oppression in our nation without understanding and addressing the subtle, subversive ways race continues to poison our lives. The ostrich approach of burying our collective head in the sands of historical amnesia or political denial will not work. We must face race head on.

The ideal of a color-blind society is a pale imitation of a greater, grander ideal: of living in a society where our color won't be denigrated, where our skin will be neither a badge for undue privilege nor a sign of social stigma. Because skin, race, and color have in the past been the basis for social inequality, they must play a role in righting the social wrongs on which our society has been built. We can't afford to be blind to color when extreme color consciousness continues to mold the fabric and form of our nation's history. Color consciousness is why black churches continue to burn. Color consciousness is why Supreme Court justices bend over backwards to repress the memory and present manifestation of racial inequality.

But we can strive for a society where each receives his or her just due, where the past in all its glory and grief is part of the equation of racial justice and social equality. Then we won't need to be blind to color, which in any case is a most morbid state of existence. Then we can embrace our history and our ideals with the sort of humane balance that makes democracy more than a distant dream.

6.7   Ron Nixon

Turning Back the Clock on Voting Rights

Ron Nixon is a Virginia-based investigative reporter.

Greene County, Alabama

The knock on the door in the summer of 1995 surprised the Rev. James Carter. He wasn't expecting company. It was a Sunday evening, and he'd planned to catch up on some well-deserved rest. He walked toward the door, peeking out the window before answering. The two men outside were dressed in dark suits. "The FBI" Carter thought to himself. "It's about time." As he opened the door and invited the two agents in, he assumed they were there about the church burnings. Four black churches, including the one where Carter worshiped, Little Zion Baptist, had been burned down days apart just a few weeks before. The burnings had taken an emotional toll on churchgoers like Carter, whose forebears, just out of slavery, had laid the foundation of the church in the late 1800s.

Inside, the agents informed Carter that they weren't there about the church burnings alone. They were there for something else as well—a multicounty voter-fraud investigation that alleged the misuse of absentee ballots by black voters. The agents began questioning Carter about his role in registering voters. Had he signed an absentee ballot for his elderly uncle? Did he know of anyone who had signed an absentee ballot for another person? "They were clearly more concerned about the voter-fraud investigation than the church burnings," Carter remembers.

Carter wasn't the only one targeted following the 1994 elections. In all, nearly 1,000 people in three counties were questioned and asked to submit handwriting samples to state and federal officials. The investigation was a joint state and federal undertaking spearheaded by Alabama Attorney General Jefferson Beauregard Sessions III, a politician with a history of making racist comments about blacks and launching voter-fraud investigations in predominantly black counties. He would go on to win a seat in the US Senate in 1996.

The investigation culminated earlier this year, when nine people, all black, pleaded guilty to several charges related to the fraudulent use of absentee ballots. Two others, who had been convicted earlier on similar charges, have appealed their convictions. The trial and verdicts have widened the already fragile racial divide in these mostly rural counties. And they have radically changed the perception of the Justice Department, which was once seen as the protector of black citizens from Southern white segregationists. Attorneys representing the black activists prosecuted for voter fraud call it a case of selective prosecution. They note several instances in which whites were accused of the same crimes but never investigated, even though there was ample evidence. And, they say, each of the counties where voter-fraud investigations are taking place or have taken place is majority African-American.

Government officials and many white residents of the counties dismiss such comments as unfounded. The investigations, they say, are not about race but about crimes. Indeed, the Justice Department has treated voter fraud as a serious crime— for example, a mayoral election in Miami was overturned and indictments were handed down because of voter fraud. But an investigation shows that African-American voters' complaints about the Justice Department's activities in Alabama have considerable merit. While there do appear to be some instances where African-Americans have engaged in voter fraud, numerous interviews and court records show that blacks have borne the brunt of voter-fraud investigations. The records show that even in cases where there was evidence that whites had engaged in similar activities, those individuals were not investigated or even questioned by state or federal agencies.

The investigations, in many cases, appear to be the result of a Reagan-era Justice Department policy to go after black voting-rights activists. The policy was inherited by current officials, many of whom were appointed by Alabama Republicans who have called for voter-fraud investigations in black counties. Author David Burnham describes Alabama Republican prosecutors as "local hit men for a larger plan."

Records also show a history of voter-fraud investigations initiated by white citizens and elected officials dating back to the late seventies. These investigations in many cases have turned up little: Charges have been dismissed in numerous cases, while in others those accused have been acquitted of any wrongdoing. "It's an abusive effort to crush a successful black voting bloc," said Margaret Carey-McCray, formerly director of the Center for Constitutional Rights in Greenville, Mississippi, who has worked on voter-fraud cases across the South. "They know the best way to crush the vote is to go after the advocates."

Nor are such tactics unique to Alabama. For years, voting-rights activists and black voters in the South have complained to federal officials that their rights have been denied through such tactics as harassment at the voting booth in the form of having their pictures taken or their license-plate numbers recorded by white poll workers. Officials at the Justice Department's Washington headquarters even warned the State of Mississippi and the Republican Party of Georgia—the former in 1996 and the latter in 1998—about allowing such practices. In a similar vein, Republican North Carolina Senator Jesse Helms, trailing a black opponent in 1990, mailed out postcards to 125,000 black voters implicitly threatening them with jail if they went to the polls. Helms's campaign settled a complaint with the Justice Department in 1992, but not before he had won another term.

But it is here in Alabama, the state that boasts the largest number of black elected officials, that voter intimidation has taken on its greatest significance. The voter-fraud investigations are concentrated in counties that make up the so-called Black Belt of the state: Greene, Wilcox, Hale, Sumter, Perry, Marengo, Pickers and Dallas. These counties served as the backdrop for some of the hardest-fought battles of the civil rights movement and the struggle for black voting rights. The brutal beating of civil rights marchers as they attempted in 1965 to cross the Edmund Pettus Bridge in Selma, the seat of Dallas County, was televised nationally and became the catalyst for the Voting Rights Act of 1965. Today, although the counties rank among the most impoverished in the state, blacks, largely because of the civil rights movement, have made enormous political gains. Most of the elected officials are African-American, even though economic power remains largely in the hands of whites.

The voter-fraud cases in Alabama may be a harbinger of things to come if they are allowed to continue, said Ron Daniels of the Center for Constitutional Rights in New York. "This could have political ramifications across the South," he said. "Blacks, who have worked hard to get the basic right to vote, could find themselves, once again, at the mercy of the very people who opposed them in the fifties and sixties."

The first voter-fraud investigation in the Black Belt counties came after African-Americans began to hold office in significant numbers for the first time as a result of the civil rights movement's success in insuring blacks the right to vote. The case, which started in 1979, involved Maggie Bozeman, a young teacher in Pickens County, Alabama, and Julia Wilder, a local voting-rights activist. After complaints of voter fraud by local whites, federal investigators charged both women with voter fraud after they assisted voters with absentee ballots.

Bozeman and Wilder were convicted, but the decision was eventually overturned in 1985 with the assistance of Lani Guinier, then a lawyer with the NAACP Legal Defense and Educational Fund and later, briefly, Clinton's nominee to be Deputy Attorney General for Civil Rights. "Absentee ballots have always been used in these countries, even when whites were in control," said J.L. Chestnut, an attorney in Selma and former chairman of the Alabama New South Coalition, an African-American-led group that advocates voting rights. "Only when blacks began to win did they become a problem." (The use of absentee ballots is common in areas where many voters are elderly or work elsewhere because of high local unemployment.)

In the same year as the Bozeman and Wilder case, a federal investigation of the Federation of Southern Cooperatives, a group established to help black farmers in the rural South, began after whites in the surrounding counties said blacks were using illegal means to elect officeholders. In May 1979 more than 100 influential white citizens of Sumter County gathered at the Cotton Patch Restaurant in Greene County. Among those at the meeting were several local and state elected officials, the local newspaper editor, both of Alabama's US senators and then–US Representative Richard Shelby, who is now a US senator. The purpose of the meeting, which was later called the Cotton Patch conspiracy, was to determine whether black staffers at the federation were using federal money to register voters. Representative Shelby was asked by attendees to initiate a General Accounting Office investigation of the federation—to stop the alleged "government-funded activism." But the state comptroller general at the time, Elmer Staats, said a full-scale investigation by the GAO was unwarranted, because the federal agencies giving money to the federation had their own inspectors general to monitor the use of federal dollars. Undeterred, the Cotton Patch attendees managed to get the local US Attorney's office in Birmingham to investigate. The office spent more than a year poring over federation records and questioning hundreds of people. In the end, nothing was found. In May 1981 the US Attorney issued a statement saying, "I have decided to decline prosecution."

But just four years later, in 1985, the federal government launched another investigation of voting-rights activists that would also end in acquittals. This time the investigation was two-pronged. In the Southern District of Alabama, the US Attorney in Mobile began a probe of three veteran civil rights activists: Albert Turner, a local activist and former aide to Martin Luther King Jr.; his wife, Evelyn Turner; and Spencer Houge Jr., all of Perry County, Alabama. As in other cases, the government alleged that the Turners and Houge had illegally obtained absentee ballots and had forged the signatures of voters. All three defendants denied the charges and called the investigation an attempt to undermine black voting power. The case got national attention, and the three activists became known as the Marion Three. The NAACP Legal Defense and Educational Fund and several other civil rights organizations provided legal counsel. After a long trial, a jury found the three activists not guilty on all counts.

The investigation proved an embarrassment for the US Attorney, Jeff Sessions. A year later, in 1986, when Sessions was being considered for a federal judgeship, witnesses recalled his treatment of the Marion Three and several alleged racist remarks he had made about blacks during his tenure as US Attorney. A black former attorney who worked under Sessions said he was once called "boy" by Sessions and that Sessions once spoke fondly of Ku Klux Klan members who lynched a black man. Another witness said Sessions once called a white civil rights attorney a "traitor to his race." Sessions said the remarks about the Klan and the white attorney were jokes. The Senate Judiciary Committee did not find the jokes funny; Sessions was denied a judgeship, becoming the only one of Ronald Reagan's 269 nominees to the federal bench to be rejected. He did go on to become the Attorney General of Alabama.

Sessions, a Republican, later won the Senate seat vacated by Senator Howell Heflin, an Alabama Democrat who had voted against his judgeship. In the Senate, Sessions was one of the biggest critics of President Clinton's temporary appointment of Bill Lann Lee to the Justice Department's top civil rights post in 1997. Lee was at the time of his appointment the western regional counsel for the NAACP Legal

Defense and Educational Fund, the same group that opposed Sessions in his voter-fraud campaigns.

While Sessions was leading the case against the Marion Three, Frank Donaldson, the US Attorney in Birmingham, was trying to make a voter-fraud case against Spiver Gordon, a local official in Greene County and an activist with the Southern Christian Leadership Conference, a group co-founded by Martin Luther King Jr. Gordon was found guilty of four counts of voter fraud: two counts of mail fraud and two counts of providing false information to an election manager. But the US Court of Appeals later overturned the charges, ruling that Gordon had been denied equal protection because the government had used all its peremptory challenges to strike every black potential juror from his trial. The court also held that Gordon's lawyers had proved that voter-fraud investigations had occurred only in those counties where blacks made up a significant part of the population and that those indicted were affiliated with majority-black groups. But perhaps the most damning piece of evidence in overturning Gordon's conviction was a statement by an unidentified Justice Department spokesman in Washington who said that the prosecution of black political activists in Alabama's Black Belt without prosecution of whites was "a new policy . . . brought on by the arrogance on the part of blacks in these counties."

The US Attorney did not seek to retry Gordon. Gordon, however, along with several other black voting-rights advocates, did plead guilty this past February [1999] to charges of voter fraud in connection with the case in which Reverend Carter was questioned. Attorneys would not say why they allowed their clients to plead guilty to lesser charges in the case. But in motions filed with the court, they wrote that their attempts to prove selective prosecution had been limited by the government's refusal to share information and thus by an inability to review all the material relating to the fraud investigation. As a result, "We did what we thought was in the best interest of our clients," said Laura Hankins, an attorney with the NAACP Legal Defense and Educational Fund, who refused to elaborate further on the case.

Most whites in Alabama, as elsewhere, maintain that investigations of voter fraud are about corruption in local government, not race. Pam Montgomery, co-founder of Citizens for a Better Greene County, a majority-white organization, points out that the county is the poorest in the state and that a recent audit showed a $3 million budget shortfall, which raises questions about the financial accountability of local officials, most of whom are black. "They keep saying that this is about whites wanting to take control," Montgomery said. "People in the North want to believe that, so the South gets stuck with a bum rap of being racist."

G. Douglas Jones, the US Attorney in Birmingham who prosecuted the latest voter-fraud case—the one involving the questioning of Reverend Carter—says that absentee ballots have become a way for some black leaders to build their power base by illegally signing and submitting ballots that have been filled out or changed without the voter's permission. Jones also says his office found that absentee ballots were being mailed to several people on trial for voter fraud. The ballots, he says, are supposed to be filled out and then sent to the local elections office. He added, "We also had witnesses who said that their names were written on ballots that they didn't sign. All this stuff about intimidation [of black voters by government officials] was brought up at the trial, and there was no merit to it." As far as the number of blacks investigated for voter fraud is concerned Jones said, it's because of the racial makeup of the voting population. "I think if you look at the voting population, it's over 80 percent black," he said. Jones's office denied that race was a motive in the investigations, adding in a statement that "the right to vote is an essential guarantee under the Constitution and it must be protected. That is our purpose in bringing these investigations—and it is our sole purpose."

Still, federal and state court records show that the investigations have been uneven. Despite years of investigation into voting abuses, only one white has been indicted and prosecuted for voter fraud—and she was helping a black voter. One of the most vivid examples came after the 1992 mayoral election in Selma, Alabama. Incumbent Mayor Joe Smitherman, who is white and has been Mayor of the majority-black town since the sixties, won a controversial re-election with the aid of absentee ballots. His challenger quickly sued, charging fraud. In several affidavits taken in preparation for the suit, numerous people said that workers for the Mayor's office either bribed them for their votes or forged their signatures on absentee ballots. For example, a man named Henry Kirk said in a sworn statement that a worker for Smitherman offered him "a half gallon of Thunderbird wine, a half case of Milwaukee's Best Beer and two packs of Newport cigarettes" in exchange for his vote. Conec Walker, Kirk's roommate, said he was offered the same thing. Another resident, Leo Mitchell, said he signed his name on an absentee ballot but didn't fill it out. "I was not sick or out of town that day," Mitchell said in his statement. Several black citizens filed complaints with the state Attorney General's office about these alleged violations.

But neither state nor federal officials ever investigated the complaints against Smitherman. Instead, as part of a settlement with his challenger, he agreed to establish a voting oversight panel to which he would appoint half the members and his challenger the other half. The Mayor's office did not return calls seeking comment about the fraud allegations. "We've said for years that [he] was operating like this, buying votes," said J.L. Chestnut, who lives in Selma. "This is the one time he got caught, and even then the government did nothing. Is this selective prosecution? You tell me."

While black citizens in Selma were calling for the state to investigate voting irregularities, in nearby Wilcox County, Sheriff Prince Arnold was also receiving complaints about voter fraud. A subsequent investigation found evidence that two people, both white males, had forged signatures on absentee ballots, stolen several ballots and voted in the names of several people without their permission. Arnold, who is African-American, thought he had an open-and-shut case. The results of the investigation were presented to the Alabama Attorney General's office with witnesses and documents. But to Arnold's surprise, the Attorney General refused to present the case to the grand jury that had already been convened to look into alleged voter fraud by two African-Americans. "The office informed me that no cases would be presented to the grand jury, and the jury would be dismissed," Arnold said. "However, I learned the next day that the grand jury was in fact called together, and cases were presented against the two African-American individuals."

Furious, Arnold confronted the Assistant Attorney General and insisted that his investigation be presented to the grand jury. As a precaution, he placed a deputy outside the grand jury door. Finally, the deputy was allowed to present the case to the grand jury. But no prosecutors from the Attorney General's office went along to present the case. After hearing the deputy, the jury requested guidance but was given none. Arnold angrily fired off a letter to the Attorney General's office and to the Justice Department calling the investigation "racially charged, political." Said Arnold: "If you're going to send a message to people that voter fraud is illegal and that they could go to jail, then you need to send that to all people, not just black people."

Reverend Carter said blacks in Greene County experienced frustrations similar to Arnold's when they tried to get government investigators to look at illegal voting activities by whites. For example, during the voter-fraud trials and in later court documents it was revealed that members of Citizens for a Better Greene County used video cameras at polling booths to tape black voters as they entered to vote in the 1994 elections. And Pam Montgomery, the group's co-founder, engaged in what critics regarded as an attempt to intimidate black voters by sending out a letter days before the November elections saying that the group was investigating voter fraud. In October 1994 two members of Citizens for a Better Greene County, Rosie Carpenter and Annie Thomas, were arrested by the Greene County Sheriff Department (which is presided over by an African-American) for attempting to influence voters by physical threats and offers of money and for marking ballots contrary to voters' choices, according to arrest warrants. One witness said Carpenter offered her $5 for her vote. Still, federal investigators, already involved in a massive voter-fraud investigation in the county, brought no charges after being presented with the evidence against the group.

Montgomery adamantly denies that anyone associated with her organization has engaged in any wrongdoing. "There may have been some people who thought that they should fight fire with fire," she said. "But we did not encourage anyone to do anything illegal." Nevertheless, court records show that a handwriting expert and state and federal judges believed that there was sufficient evidence of wrongdoing by at least five people associated with the group to warrant a closer look, even though the judges did not believe the government had engaged in the selective prosecution of blacks. So far, no additional investigations by the state or federal governments have taken place. US Attorney Jones said his office would look into further allegations, but he said he didn't think additional indictments would be forthcoming.

Blacks say the voter-fraud investigations have had a profound impact on voting in Alabama's Black Belt counties, causing a dramatic reduction in voter turnout even while the number of people registered to vote has climbed. Dozens of blacks say they are simply afraid of voting for fear of being investigated. The impact is felt most in Greene County. In a June 2, 1998, primary election, the overall voter turnout declined to 3,928—down from 4,691 in 1994. Most striking was the fall in absentee ballots. In a similar primary in 1994, 1,118 absentee ballots were filed. In the 1998 primary, just 147 were cast. In nearby Marengo County, many believe that fear on the part of black voters cost Barrown Lankster, the first black elected District Attorney in Alabama, his seat in 1998. Lankster lost by 256 votes to a white prosecutor whom he had ousted in the previous election.

Voting rights, civil rights and black Congressional leaders met with US Attorney General Janet Reno in June 1998 to complain about what they called gross misconduct and abuse by the local US Attorneys and the FBI. Winnett Hagens of the Southern Regional Council, a racial-justice organization in Atlanta, said Reno has yet to respond to their complaints. In a recent interview, Justice Department civil rights division press officer Christine DiBartolo said she didn't know about the voter-fraud investigations or what action, if any, the division would take.

Voting-rights activists say that if something isn't done soon to stop what they see as abusive prosecution, the rights that blacks have fought hard for may be in fundamental danger. The Voting Rights Act was a landmark piece of legislation. It ended arbitrary voting tests in seven Southern states, and black voting registration soared. Almost overnight, citizens who had been shut out of the political process took control of it in many areas. Activists like J.L. Chestnut see the voter-fraud investigations and other attempts to intimidate black voters as a stunning reversal of the goals of voting rights, aided by a willing Justice Department. "In this climate, not only are we going to lose cases," he said, "but we're going to lose all the things that we have gained over the past thirty years."

6.8   Joe R. Feagin

The Continuing Significance of Race: Antiblack Discrimination in Public Places

Joe Feagin, professor of sociology at the University of Florida, is author of Living with Racism: The Black Middle-Class Experience. *He was nominated for a Pulitzer Prize for* Ghetto Revolts *in 1975. He has served as scholar-in-residence for the U.S. Commission on Civil Rights.*

Title II of the 1964 Civil Rights Act stipulates that "all persons shall be entitled to the full and equal enjoyment of the goods, services, facilities, privileges, advantages, and accommodations of any place of public accommodation . . . without discrimination or segregation on the ground of race, color, religion, or national origin." The public places emphasized in the act are restaurants, hotels, and motels, although racial discrimination occurs in many other public places. Those black Americans who would make the greatest use of these public accommodations and certain other public places would be middle-class, i.e., those with the requisite resources. . . .

Discrimination can be defined in social-contextual terms as "actions or practices carried out by members of dominant racial or ethnic groups that have a differential and negative impact on members of subordinate racial and ethnic groups" (Feagin & Eckberg 1980, pp. 1–2). This differential treatment ranges from the blatant to the subtle (Feagin and Feagin 1986). Here I focus primarily on blatant discrimination by white Americans targeting middle-class blacks. Historically, discrimination against blacks has been one of the most serious forms of racial/ethnic discrimination in the United States and one of the most difficult to overcome, in part because of the institutionalized character of color coding. I focus on three important aspects of discrimination: (1) the variation in sites of discrimination; (2) the range of discriminatory actions; and (3) the range of responses by blacks to discrimination.

547

6.8 The Continuing Significance of Race: Antiblack Discrimination in Public Places

Sites of Discrimination

There is a spatial dimension to discrimination. The probability of experiencing racial hostility varies from the most private to the most public sites. If a black person is in a relatively protected site, such as with friends at home, the probability of experiencing hostility and discrimination is low. The probability increases as one moves from friendship settings to such outside sites as the workplace, where a black person typically has contacts with both acquaintances and strangers, providing an interactive context with greater potential for discrimination.

In most workplaces, middle-class status and its organizational resources provide some protection against certain categories of discrimination. This protection probably weakens as a black person moves from those work and school settings where he or she is well-known into public accommodations such as large stores and city restaurants where contacts are mainly with white strangers. On public streets blacks have the greatest public exposure to strangers and the least protection against overt discriminatory behavior, including violence. A key feature of these more public settings is that they often involve contacts with white strangers who react primarily on the basis of one ascribed characteristic. The study of the micro-life of interaction between strangers in public was pioneered by Goffman (1963, 1971) and his students, but few of their analyses have treated hostile discriminatory interaction in public places. A rare exception is the research by Gardner (1980; see also Gardner 1988), who documented the character and danger of passing remarks by men directed against women in unprotected public places. Gardner writes of women (and blacks) as "open persons," i.e. particularly vulnerable targets for harassment that violates the rules of public courtesy.

The Range of Discriminatory Actions

In his classic study, *The Nature of Prejudice,* Allport (1958, pp. 14–5) noted that prejudice can be expressed in a series of progressively more serious actions, ranging from antilocution to avoidance, exclusion, physical attack, and extermination. Allport's work suggests a continuum of actions from avoidance, to exclusion or rejection, to attack. In his travels in the South in the 1950s a white journalist who changed his skin color to black encountered discrimination in each of these categories (Griffin 1961). In my data, discrimination against middle-class blacks still ranges across this continuum: (1) avoidance actions, such as a white couple crossing the street when a black male approaches; (2) rejection actions, such as poor service in public accommodations; (3) verbal attacks, such as shouting racial epithets in the street; (4) physical threats and harassment by white police officers; and (5) physical threats and attacks by other whites, such as attacks by white supremacists in the street. Changing relations between blacks and whites in recent decades have expanded the repertoire of discrimination to include more subtle forms and to encompass discrimination in arenas from which blacks were formerly excluded such as formerly all-white public accommodations.

Prior to societal desegregation in the 1960s much traditional discrimination, especially in the South, took the form of an asymmetrical "deference ritual" in which blacks were typically expected to respond to discriminating whites with great deference.... Such rituals can be seen in the obsequious words and gestures—the etiquette of race relations—that many blacks, including middle-class blacks, were forced to utilize to survive the rigors of segregation (Doyle 1937). However, not all responses in this period were deferential. From the late 1800s to the 1950s, numerous lynchings and other violence targeted blacks whose behavior was defined as too aggressive (Raper 1933). Blauner's (1989) respondents reported acquaintances reacting aggressively to discrimination prior to the 1960s.

Deference rituals can still be found today between some lower-income blacks and their white employers. In her northeastern study Rollins (1985, p. 157) found black maids regularly deferring to white employers. Today, most discriminatory interaction no longer involves much asymmetrical deference, at least for middle-class blacks. Even where whites expect substantial deference, most middle-class blacks do not oblige. For middle-class blacks contemporary discrimination has evolved beyond the asymmetrical deference rituals and "No Negroes served" type of exclusion to patterns of black-contested discrimination....

Some white observers have suggested that many middle-class blacks are paranoid about white discrimination and rush too quickly to charges of racism (Wieseltier 1989, June 5; for male views of female "paranoia" see Gardner 1988). But the daily reality may be just the opposite, as middle-class black Americans often evaluate a situation carefully before judging it discriminatory and taking additional action. This careful evaluation, based on past experiences (real or vicarious), not only prevents jumping to conclusions, but also reflects the hope that white behavior is not based on race, because an act not based on race is easier to endure. After evaluation one strategy is to leave the site of discrimination rather than to create a disturbance. Another is to ignore the discrimination and continue with the interaction, a "blocking" strategy similar to that Gardner (1980, p. 345) reported for women dealing with street remarks. In many situations resigned acceptance is the only realistic response. More confrontational responses to white actions include verbal reprimands and sarcasm, physical counterattacks, and filing lawsuits. Several strategies may be tried in any given discriminatory situation. In crafting these strategies middle-class blacks, in comparison with less privileged blacks, may draw on middle-class resources to fight discrimination.

The Research Study

To examine discrimination, I draw primarily on 37 in-depth interviews from a larger study of 135 middle-class black Americans in Boston, Buffalo, Baltimore, Washington, D.C., Detroit, Houston, Dallas, Austin, San Antonio, Marshall, Las Vegas, and Los Angeles....

Although all types of mistreatment are reported, there is a strong relationship between type of discrimination and site, with rejection/poor-service discrimination being most common in public accommodations and verbal or physical threat discrimination by white citizens or police officers most likely in the street. [Table 1]....

Table 1

549

6.8 *The*
Continuing
Significance of
Race: Antiblack
Discrimination
in Public Places

Percentage Distribution of Discriminatory Actions by Type and Site: Middle-Class Blacks in Selected Cities, 1988–1990

| | Site of Discriminatory Action | |
Type of Discriminatory Action	*Public Accommodations*	*Street*
Avoidance	3	7
Rejection/poor service	79	4
Verbal epithets	12	25
Police threats/harassment	3	46
Other threats/harassment	3	18
Total	100	100
Number of actions	34	28

Table 2

Percentage Distribution of Primary Responses to Discriminatory Incidents by Type and Site: Middle-Class Blacks in Selected Cities, 1988–1990

| | Site of Discriminatory Action | |
Response to Discriminatory Incident	*Public Accommodations*	*Street*
Withdrawal/exit	4	22
Resigned acceptance	23	7
Verbal response	69	59
Physical counterattack	4	7
Response unclear	—	4
Total	100	99
Number of responses	26	27

The most common black responses to racial hostility in the street are withdrawal or a verbal reply [Table 2]. In many avoidance situations (e.g., a white couple crossing a street to avoid walking past a black college student) or attack situations (e.g., whites throwing beer cans from a passing car), a verbal response is difficult because of the danger or the fleeting character of the hostility. A black victim often withdraws, endures this treatment with resigned acceptance, or replies with a quick verbal retort. In the case of police harassment, the response is limited by the danger, and resigned acceptance or mild verbal protests are likely responses. Rejection (poor service) in public accommodations provides an opportunity to fight back verbally—the most common responses to public accommodations discrimination are verbal counterattacks or resigned acceptance. Some black victims correct whites quietly, while others respond aggressively and lecture the assailant about the discrimination or threaten court action. A few retaliate physically. Examining materials in these 37 interviews . . . we will see that the depth and complexity of contemporary black middle-class responses to white discrimination accents the changing character of white-black interaction and the necessity of continual negotiation of the terms of that interaction.

Responses to Discrimination:
Public Accommodations

Two Fundamental Strategies:
Verbal Confrontation and Withdrawal

In the following account, a black news director at a major television station shows the interwoven character of discriminatory action and black response. The discrimination took the form of poor restaurant service, and the responses included both suggested withdrawal and verbal counterattack.

He [her boyfriend] was waiting to be seated. . . . He said, "You go to the bathroom and I'll get the table. . . ." He was standing there when I came back; he continued to stand there. The restaurant was almost empty. There were waiters, waitresses, and no one seated. And when I got back to him, he was ready to leave, and said, "Let's go." I said, "What happened to our table?" He wasn't seated. So I said, "No, we're not leaving, please." And he said, "No, I'm leaving." So we went outside and we talked about it. And what I said to him was, you have to be aware of the possibilities that this is not the first time that this has happened at this restaurant or at other restaurants, but this is the first time it has happened to a black news director here or someone who could make an issue of it, or someone who is prepared to make an issue of it.

So we went back inside after I talked him into it and, to make a long story short, I had the manager come. I made most of the people who were there (while conducting myself professionally the whole time) aware that I was incensed at being treated this way. . . . I said, "Why do you think we weren't seated?" And the manager said, "Well, I don't really know." And I said, "Guess." He said, "Well I don't know, because you're black?" I said, "Bingo. Now isn't it funny that you didn't guess that I didn't have any money" (and I opened up my purse) and I said, "because I certainly have money. And isn't it odd that you didn't guess that it's because I couldn't pay for it because I've got two American Express cards and a Master Card right here. I think it's just funny that you would have assumed that it's because I'm black." . . . And then I took out my card and gave it to him and said, "If this happens again, or if I hear of this happening again, I will bring the full wrath of an entire news department down on this restaurant." And he just kind of looked at me. "Not [just] because I am personally offended. I am. But because you have no right to do what you did, and as a people we have lived a long time with having our rights abridged. . . ." There were probably three or four sets of diners in the restaurant and maybe five waiters/waitresses. They watched him standing there waiting to be seated. His reaction to it was that he wanted to leave. I understood why he would have reacted that way, because he felt that he was in no condition to be civil. He was ready to take the place apart and . . . sometimes it's appropriate to behave that way. We hadn't gone the first step before going on to the next step. He didn't feel that he could comfortably and calmly take the first step, and I did. So I just asked him to please get back in the restaurant with me, and then you don't have to say a word, and let me handle it from there. It took some convincing, but I had to appeal to his sense of, this is not just you, this is not just for you. We are finally in a position as black people where there are some of us who can genuinely get their attention. And if they don't want to do this because it's right for them to do it, then they'd better do it because they're afraid to do otherwise. If it's fear, then fine, instill the fear.

This example provides insight into the character of modern discrimination. The discrimination was not the "No Negroes" exclusion of the recent past, but rejection in the form of poor service by restaurant personnel. The black response indicates the change in black-white interaction since the 1950s and 1960s, for discrimination is handled with vigorous confrontation rather than deference. The aggressive black response and the white backtracking underscore Brittan and Maynard's (1984, p. 7) point that black-white interaction today is being renegotiated. It is possible that the white personnel defined the couple as "poor blacks" because of their jeans, although the jeans were fashionable and white patrons wear jeans. In comments not quoted here the news director rejects such an explanation. She forcefully articulates a theory of rights—a response that signals the critical impact of civil rights laws on the thinking of middle-class blacks. The news director articulates the American dream: she has worked hard, earned the money and credit cards, developed the appropriate middle-class behavior, and thus has under the law a *right* to be served. There is defensiveness in her actions too, for she feels a need to legitimate her status by showing her purse and credit cards. One important factor that enabled her to take such assertive action was her power to bring a TV news team to the restaurant. This power marks a change from a few decades ago when very few black Americans had the social or economic resources to fight back successfully. . . .

The confrontation response is generally so costly in terms of time and energy that acquiescence or withdrawal are common options. An example of the exit response was provided by a utility company executive in an east coast city:

> I can remember one time my husband had picked up our son . . . from camp; and he'd stopped at a little store in the neighborhood near the camp. It was hot, and he was going to buy him a snowball. And the proprietor of the store— this was a very old, white neighborhood, and it was just a little sundry store. But the proprietor said he had the little window where people could come up and order things. Well, my husband and son had gone into the store. And he told them, "Well, I can't give it to you here, but if you go outside to the window, I'll give it to you." And there were other [white] people in the store who'd been served [inside]. So, they just left and didn't buy anything.

. . . This site differed from the previous example in that the service was probably not of long-term importance to the black family passing through the area. In the previous site the possibility of returning to the restaurant for business or pleasure, may have contributed to the choice of a confrontational response. The importance of the service is a likely variable affecting black responses to discrimination in public accommodations. . . .

The complex process of evaluation and response is described by a college dean, who commented generally on hotel and restaurant discrimination encountered as he travels across the United States:

> When you're in a restaurant and . . . you notice that blacks get seated near the kitchen. You notice that if it's a hotel, your room is near the elevator, or your room is always way down in a corner somewhere. You find that you are getting

the undesirable rooms. And you come there early in the day and you don't see very many cars on the lot and they'll tell you that this is all we've got. Or you get the room that's got a bad television set. You know that you're being discriminated against. And of course you have to act accordingly. You have to tell them, "Okay, the room is fine, [but] this television set has got to go. Bring me another television set." So in my personal experience, I simply cannot sit and let them get away with it [discrimination] and not let them know that I know that that's what they are doing. . . .

When I face discrimination, first I take a long look at myself and try to determine whether or not I am seeing what I think I'm seeing in 1989, and if it's something that I have an option [about]. In other words, if I'm at a store making a purchase, I'll simply walk away from it. If it's at a restaurant where I'm not getting good service, I first of all let the people know that I'm not getting good service, then I [may] walk away from it. But the thing that I have to do is to let people know that I know that I'm being singled out for a separate treatment. And then I might react in any number of ways—depending on where I am and how badly I want whatever it is that I'm there for.

This commentary adds another dimension to our understanding of public discrimination, its cumulative aspect. Blacks confront not just isolated incidents—such as a bad room in a luxury hotel once every few years—but a lifelong series of such incidents. Here again the omnipresence of careful assessments is underscored. The dean's interview highlights a major difficulty in being black—one must be constantly prepared to assess accurately and then decide on the appropriate response. This long-look approach may indicate that some middle-class blacks are so sensitive to white charges of hypersensitivity and paranoia that they err in the opposite direction and fail to see discrimination when it occurs. In addition, as one black graduate student at a leading white university in the Southeast put it: "I think that sometimes timely and appropriate responses to racially motivated acts and comments are lost due to the processing of the input." The "long look" can result in missed opportunities to respond to discrimination.

Using Middle-Class Resources for Protection

One advantage that middle-class blacks have over poorer blacks is the use of the resources of middle-class occupations. A professor at a major white university commented on the varying protection her middle-class status gives her at certain sites:

If I'm in those areas that are fairly protected, within gatherings of my own group, other African Americans, or if I'm in the university where my status as a professor mediates against the way I might be perceived, mediates against the hostile perception, then it's fairly comfortable. . . . When I divide my life into encounters with the outside world, and of course that's ninety percent of my life, it's fairly consistently unpleasant at those sites where there's nothing that mediates between my race and what I have to do. For example, if I'm in a grocery store, if I'm in my car, which is a 1970 Chevrolet, a real old ugly car, all those things—being in a grocery store in casual clothes, or being in the car—sort of advertises something that doesn't have anything to do with my status as far as people I run into are concerned.

Because I'm a large black woman, and I don't wear whatever class status I have, or whatever professional status [I have] in my appearance when I'm in the grocery store, I'm part of the mass of large black women shopping. For most whites, and even for some blacks, that translates into negative status. That means that they are free to treat me the way they treat most poor black people, because they can't tell by looking at me that I differ from that.

This professor notes the variation in discrimination in the sites through which she travels, from the most private to the most public. At home with friends she faces no problems, and at the university her professional status gives her some protection from discrimination. The increase in unpleasant encounters as she moves into public accommodations sites such as grocery stores is attributed to the absence of mediating factors such as clear symbols of middle-class status—displaying the middle-class symbols may provide some protection against discrimination in public places. . . .

Responses to Discrimination: The Street

Reacting to White Strangers

As we move away from public accommodations settings to the usually less protected street sites, racial hostility can become more fleeting and severer, and thus black responses are often restricted. The most serious form of street discrimination is violence. Often the reasonable black response to street discrimination is withdrawal, resigned acceptance, or a quick verbal retort. The difficulty of responding to violence is seen in this report by a man working for a media surveying firm in a southern industrial city:

> I was parked in front of this guy's house. . . . This guy puts his hands on the window and says, "Get out of the car, nigger." . . . So, I got out, and I thought, "Oh, this is what's going to happen here." And I'm talking fast. And they're, "What are you doing here?" And I'm, "This is who I am. I work with these people. This is the man we want to put in the survey." And I pointed to the house. And the guy said, "Well you have an out-of-state license tag, right?" "Yea." And he said, "If something happened to you, your people at home wouldn't know for a long time, would they?" . . . I said, "Look, I deal with a company that deals with television. [If] something happens to me, it's going to be a national thing." . . . So, they grab me by the lapel of my coat, and put me in front of my car. They put the blade on my zipper. And now I'm thinking about this guy that's in the truck [behind me], because now I'm thinking that I'm going to have to run somewhere. Where am I going to run? Go to the police? [laughs] So, after a while they bash up my headlight. And I drove [away].

Stigmatized and physically attacked solely because of his color, this man faced verbal hostility and threats of death with courage. Cautiously drawing on his middle-class resources, he told the attackers his death would bring television crews to the town. This resource utilization is similar to that of the news director in the restaurant incident. Beyond this verbal threat his response had to be one of caution. For most whites threatened on the street, the police are a sought-after source of protection; this is often not the case. . . .

Most middle-class blacks do not have such governmental authority as their personal protection. In fact, white police officers are a major problem. Encounters with the police can be life-threatening and thus limit the range of responses. A television commentator recounted two cases of police harassment when he was working for a survey firm in the mid-1980s. In one of the incidents, which took place in a southern metropolis, he was stopped by several white officers:

> "What are you doing here?" I tell them what I'm doing here.... And so me spread on top of my car. [What had you done?] Because I was in the neighborhood, I left this note on these peoples' house: "Here's who I am. You weren't here, and I will come back in thirty minutes." [Why were they searching you?] They don't know. To me, they're searching, I remember at that particular moment when this all was going down, there was a lot of reports about police crime on civilians.... It took four cops to shake me down, two police cars, so they had me up there spread out. I had a friend of mine with me who was making the call with me, because we were going to have dinner together, and he was black, and they had me up, and they had him outside.... They said, "Well, let's check you out."... And I'm talking to myself, and I'm not thinking about being at attention, with my arms spread on my Ford [a company car], and I'm sitting there talking to myself, "Man, this is crazy, this is crazy."
>
> [How are you feeling inside?] Scared. I mean real scared. [What did you think was going to happen to you?] I was going to go to jail.... Just because they picked me. Why would they stop me? It's like, if they can stop me, why wouldn't I go to jail, and I could sit there for ten days before the judge sees me. I'm thinking all this crazy stuff.... Again, I'm talking to myself. And the guy takes his stick. And he doesn't whack me hard, but he does it with enough authority to let me know they mean business. "I told you stand still; now put your arms back out." And I've got this suit on, and the car's wet. And my friend's hysterical. He's outside the car. And they're checking him out. And he's like, "Man, just be cool, man." And he had tears in his eyes. And I'm like, oh, man, this is a nightmare. This is not supposed to happen to me. This is not my style! And so finally, this other cop comes up and says, "What have we got here Charlie?" "Oh, we've got a guy here. He's running through the neighborhood, and he doesn't want to do what we tell him. We might have to run him in." [You're "running through" the neighborhood?] Yeah, exactly, in a suit in the rain?! After they got through doing their thing and harassing me, I just said, "Man, this has been a hell of a week."
>
> And I had tears in my eyes, but it wasn't tears of upset. It was tears of anger; it was tears of wanting to lash back.... What I thought to myself was, man, blacks have it real hard down here. I don't care if they're a broadcaster; I don't care if they're a businessman or a banker.... They don't have it any easier than the persons on skid row who get harassed by the police on a Friday or Saturday night.

It seems likely that most black men—including middle-class black men—see white police officers as a major source of danger and death. (See "Mood of Ghetto America" 1980, June 2, pp. 32–34; Louis Harris & Associates 1989; Roddy 1990, August 26.) Scattered evidence suggests that by the time they are in their twenties, most black males, regardless of socioeconomic status, have been stopped by the police because "blackness" is considered a sign of possible criminality by police officers

(Moss 1990; Roddy 1990, August 26). This treatment probably marks a dramatic contrast with the experiences of young white middle-class males. In the incident above the respondent and a friend experienced severe police maltreatment—detention for a lengthy period, threat of arrest, and the reality of physical violence. The coping response of the respondent was resigned acceptance somewhat similar to the deference rituals highlighted by Goffman. The middle-class suits and obvious corporate credentials (for example, survey questionnaires and company car) did not protect the two black men. The final comment suggests a disappointment that middle-class status brought no reprieve from police stigmatization and harassment. . . .

Conclusion

I have examined the sites of discrimination, the types of discriminatory acts, and the responses of the victims and have found the color stigma still to be very important in the public lives of affluent black Americans. The sites of racial discrimination range from relatively protected home sites, to less protected workplace and educational sites, to the even less protected public places. The 1964 Civil Rights Act guarantees that black Americans are "entitled to the full and equal enjoyment of the goods, services, facilities, privileges, advantages, and accommodations" in public accommodations. Yet the interviews indicate that deprivation of full enjoyment of public facilities is not a relic of the past: deprivation and discrimination in public accommodations persist. Middle-class black Americans remain vulnerable targets in public places. Prejudice-generated aggression in public places is, of course, not limited to black men and women—gay men and white women are also targets of street harassment (Benokraitis & Feagin 1986). Nonetheless, black women and men face an unusually broad range of discrimination on the street and in public accommodations.

The interviews highlight two significant aspects of the additive discrimination faced by black Americans in public places and elsewhere: (1) the cumulative character of an *individual's* experiences with discrimination; and (2) the *group's* accumulated historical experiences as perceived by the individual. A retired psychology professor who has worked in the Midwest and Southwest commented on the pyramiding of incidents:

> I don't think white people, generally, understand the full meaning of racist discriminatory behaviors directed toward Americans of African descent. They seem to see each act of discrimination or any act of violence as an "isolated" event. As a result, most white Americans cannot understand the strong reaction manifested by blacks when such events occur. They feel that blacks tend to "overreact." They forget that in most cases, we live lives of quiet desperation generated by a litany of *daily* large and small events that whether or not by design, remind us of our "place" in American society.

Particular instances of discrimination may seem minor to outside white observers when considered in isolation. But when blatant acts of avoidance, verbal harassment, and physical attack combine with subtle and covert slights, and these accumulate over months, years, and lifetimes, the impact on a black person is far more than the sum of the individual instances.

The historical context of contemporary discrimination was described by the retired psychologist, who argued that average white Americans

> ... ignore the personal context of stimulus. That is, they deny the historical impact that a negative act may have on an individual. "Nigger" to a white may simply be an epithet that should be ignored. To most blacks, the term brings into sharp and current focus all kinds of acts of racism—murder, rape, torture, denial of constitutional rights, insults, limited opportunity structure, economic problems, unequal justice under the law and a myriad of ... other racist and discriminatory acts that occur daily in the lives of *most* Americans of African descent—including professional blacks.

Particular acts, even antilocution that might seem minor to white observers, are freighted not only with one's past experience of discrimination but also with centuries of racial discrimination directed at the entire group, vicarious oppression that still includes racially translated violence and denial of access to the American dream. Anti-black discrimination is a matter of racial-power inequality institutionalized in a variety of economic and social institutions over a long period of time. The microlevel events of public accommodations and public streets are not just rare and isolated encounters by individuals; they are recurring events reflecting an invasion of the microworld by the macroworld of historical racial subordination.

References

Allport, Gordon. 1958. *The Nature of Prejudice.* Abridged. New York: Doubleday Anchor Books.

Benokraitis, Nijole, and Joe R. Feagin. 1986. *Modern Sexism: Blatant, Subtle and Covert Discrimination.* Englewood Cliffs, NJ: Prentice-Hall.

Blauner, Bob. 1989. *Black Lives, White Lives.* Berkeley: University of California Press.

Brittan, Arthur, and Mary Maynard. 1984. *Sexism, Racism and Oppression.* Oxford: Basil Blackwell.

Doyle, Bertram W. 1937. *The Etiquette of Race Relations in the South.* Port Washington, NY: Kennikat Press.

Feagin, Joe R., and Douglas Eckberg. 1980. "Prejudice and Discrimination." *Annual Review of Sociology* 6:1–20.

Feagin, Joe R., and Clairece Booher Feagin. 1986. *Discrimination American Style,* rev. ed. Melbourne, FL: Krieger.

Gardner, Carol Brooks. 1980. "Passing By: Street Remarks, Address Rights, and the Urban Female." *Sociological Inquiry* 50:328–56.

_____. 1988. "Access Information: Public Lies and Private Peril." *Social Problems* 34:384–97.

Goffman, Erving. 1956. "The Nature of Deference and Demeanor." *American Anthropologist* 58:473–502.

Griffin, John Howard. 1961. *Black Like Me.* Boston: Houghton Mifflin.

"The Mood of Ghetto America." 1980. *Newsweek,* 2 June, pp. 32–4.

Moss, E. Yvonne. 1990. "African Americans and the Administration of Justice." Pp. 79–86 in *Assessment of the Status of African-Americans,* edited by Wornie L. Reed. Boston: University of Massachusetts, William Monroe Trotter Institute.

Raper, Arthur F. 1933. *The Tragedy of Lynching.* Chapel Hill: University of North Carolina Press.

Roddy, Dennis B. 1990. "Perceptions Still Segregate Police, Black Community." *The Pittsburgh Press,* 26 August, p. B1.

Rollins, Judith. 1985. *Between Women.* Philadelphia: Temple University Press.

Wieseltier, Leon. 1989. "Scar Tissue." *New Republic,* 5 June, pp. 19–20.

The Illusion of Racial Equality: The Black American Dilemma

Robert Staples, professor of sociology at the University of California, San Francisco, is author of Black Masculinity, The Urban Plantation, *and* Families at the Crossroads.

Never in the history of *Homo sapiens* has a society brought together so many cultural, religious, and racial groups in one country as the twentieth-century United States. Protestants, Catholics, Jews, Buddhists, Muslims, Italians, Africans, Chinese, Mexicans, Indians, all live together under the same government and operate in the same economy. This diversity is all the more striking when it is noted that none of these groups are at war with each other, that they coexist peacefully. This situation runs counter to the experiences of other countries in the world, where conflicts between ethnic and religious groups are epidemic. In 1986, more than five million people worldwide died as a result of ethnic and religious conflicts.

As a society dominated by people of European ancestry, the U.S.A. appears to have accommodated people of different national origins while European governments are besieged and in danger of being toppled by the small number of non-European immigrants allowed into their countries. Whereas most countries, in the latter part of the twentieth century, have permitted immigration on the basis of labor demand and personal wealth, American immigration policies have favored the family ties and refugee status of American citizens. Consequently, 85 percent of the legal immigration to the United States for the last twenty years has involved citizens of Latin America, Asia, the Caribbean, and Africa. The white, non-Hispanic population in 1990 was recorded as 75 percent of the American population and, if current immigration and birthrate trends prevail, fewer than half of this country's citizens will be non-Hispanic whites in the year 2080. Further testament to the efficacy of the melting-pot theory is the high rate of intermarriage between these different groups. Most telling is the statistic that shows that Jews, a group that has faced persecution for most of its existence on this planet, have a minority of their members married within the same faith.

It is within the Afro-American community that America's blend of free-wheeling capitalism and political democracy has produced the most startling success stories—or so it seems. Having come to the American continent, first as indentured servants, later as slaves, suffering from the most vicious form of segregation and discrimination in the postslavery era, they have risen to heights never envisioned for any group that occupied such low status. Jesse Jackson's slogan "From the outhouse to the White House" belies the struggle of this nation to keep its black population in a perpetually subjugated condition since their arrival. Having used their labor, destroyed their culture and family life, the American version of apartheid and the caste system was erected after the official end of slavery. The white South created dual public institutions to degrade them, and states outside Dixie used informal rules to establish a ceiling on their aspirations and status. The black condition was best summed up in the saying: "No black shall ever rise above the lowest status of a white man."

Perforce, 1990s America has witnessed a dramatic turnaround of this country's determination to see and treat all black Americans as subhumans. This reversal did not come without a great deal of turmoil for a country whose self-definition is "the world's greatest democracy." It fought a bloody civil war over the issue of black slavery, perverted many of its institutions to protect racial inequality, endured mass demonstrations and protest against Jim Crow over a twenty-year period before officially eliminating the practice, and witnessed its major cities in flames during the 1960s as rebellions by blacks occurred throughout the nation. Because the civil rights movement and urban rebellions transpired during the expansionist and neo-colonial phase of capitalism, the pragmatic captains of industry and government decided that the caste line had to be abolished. Civil rights laws, recruitment of blacks into heretofore excluded positions, affirmative action regulations, loans, scholarships, social programs, set asides, and so on were gradually used to reduce the absolute caste line extant in 1940.

Those measures bore fruit in the 1990s when the world's largest black middle class was created. Overall, black Americans had a total income of $300 billion a year, a figure that equals the income of the twelfth-largest nation in the world. The median household income of black married couples, in 1990, was $33,893, giving them almost the highest standard of living in the world. Blacks also have a median educational level of 12.2 years, higher than most Europeans. More than a million blacks were enrolled in institutions of higher learning in 1991. More than other people of color, blacks appear to be integrated into the institutional life of American society. On the political level, they serve in the president's cabinet as his advisers, on the Supreme Court, as governors of states, as presidential candidates, as the head of the military, and as mayors of the nation's largest cities. In the major sports, amateur and professional, blacks dominate and earn millions of dollars in salaries and commercial endorsements. Three of the five wealthiest entertainers in America are black, the biggest box-office stars and highest-rated TV shows have, in the past, been black, and the largest sales of a record album are by a black performer. Not all blacks in the entertainment industry are performers. In 1991, two dozen theatrical films were directed by blacks, starring black actors and actresses.

One might think that 1990s America is a racial utopia—or close to it. Certainly a black sociologist from Harvard, Orlando Patterson, believed it to be true when he wrote in *The New York Times* that "the sociological truths are that America, while still flawed in its race relations and its stubborn refusal to institute a national, universal welfare system, is now the least racist white majority society in the world; has a better record of legal protection of minorities than any other society, white or black; offers more opportunities to a greater number of black persons than any other society, including those of Africa; and has gone through a dramatic change in its attitude toward miscegenation over the past 25 years." Professor Patterson is regarded as a colorblind neo-conservative, which helps to explain his pollyannaish view of race relations. Another view is held by an Afro-American filmmaker, who has earned millions in the movie industry. Douglas McHenry is quoted as saying: "Today there is probably more segregation and less tolerance than there was. More than ever, there are two Americas."

Ironically, both men are essentially correct. The U.S., with a white majority, has made more accommodations to its racial diversity than any other country largely composed of Europeans. Even South American countries, with their pervasive pattern of miscegenation, have reserved the most powerful and prestigious positions for those most clearly identified as of European ancestry. The Patterson argument is most flawed when it depicts the U.S. as "the least racist white majority society in the world." However one defines racism in the 1990s, this country is more racially segregated and its institutions more race driven than any country outside South Africa. This fact, at least for the Euro-American population, has been disguised by the emerging racial ideology of the "color-blind theory." This theory has as its main premise that after 365 years of slavery and legal segregation, only 25 years of governmental laws and actions were necessary to reverse the historical systematic and legalized segregation and inequality in this country, and no further remedial effort is needed. The net effect of the color-blind theory is to institutionalize and stabilize the status quo of race relations for the twenty-first century: white privilege and black deprivation. Most notable among the proponents of the color-blind theory are the ideological descendants of the theories that slavery was necessary to make Christians out of African savages, that the South could operate separate but equal facilities and Jim Crow could not be abolished because it interfered with states' rights.

The color-blind theory ignores the reality of 1990s America: that race determines everyone's life chances in this country. In any area where there is significant racial diversity, race impacts on where people live and go to school, whom they vote for, date, and marry, with whom they do business, who they buy from or sell to, how much they pay, and so on. This does not sound like the racial utopia Martin Luther King dreamed of. Indeed, it may have been his worst nightmare. Yet there could be a worse nightmare for the prophet of racial equality. How would he have felt if he had watched his former lieutenants endorse the right-wing Ronald Reagan for president in 1980, or the organization he founded, the Southern Christian Leadership Conference, remain neutral on the appointment of Clarence Thomas to the U.S. Supreme Court—a neutrality tantamount to the support provided by Strom Thurmond, Jesse Helms, and David Duke (former Grand Dragon of the Ku Klux Klan). The complexities of race in 1990s America are enough to confuse any outsider who has read the history of race relations in the U.S.

In part, to sort out the contradictions in American race relations, it is necessary to look at the other side of the black success story. Despite the largest black middle class in the world, the average black household income is only 56 percent of white household income. More than 32 percent of black households have incomes below the poverty line. The high income of black married-couple households is a function of multiple workers in those households. Moreover, poverty in the U.S. is increasingly synonymous with people of color. Only 8 percent of whites are considered poor, and they are disproportionately found among the elderly, women with children, and rural and farm families. Of all Western nations, the United States has the greatest inequality of wealth. According to an international study, poverty in the U.S. is more widespread and more severe: poor families here stay poor longer; and government programs of assistance are the least able to lift families with children out of poverty.

Poverty also is more likely to be spread among the nonelderly households and to be widely distributed across all age and family groups. It is this class of poor people of color that make up a majority. In the more racially homogeneous countries of Europe, Australia, and New Zealand, government welfare programs and subsidies have eliminated the kind of massive poverty found among young households in this country. The tolerance of pervasive poverty, malnutrition, and homelessness can only be related to the perception that it is people of color who bear the brunt of American poverty and the reasons attributed to are their failure to get an education and work hard. When asked if the Federal Government should see to it that every person has a job and a good standard of living, 65 percent of blacks said it should, but only 24 percent of whites thought so. Euro-Americans were more inclined to give support to the idea of "individuals getting ahead on their own," versus government intervention. Surely the racial differences in attitude toward government assistance are linked to the fact that unemployment, for white male heads of households, is less than 6 percent, and as many as 46 percent of black males sixteen to sixty-two years of age are not in the labor force. Moreover, money is not the only measure of wealth in 1990s America. Noncash assets are easily convertible to cash. They include stocks, bonds, businesses, property, and so on, a total of $10 trillion. Given the concentration of wealth in the U.S., Euro-Americans will control 97 percent of those assets. Most blacks have only their homes and automobiles as assets. Because black homes tend to be located in black neighborhoods, their value is inherently less than those of similar homes in white neighborhoods.

Based on any variable that can be statistically measured, blacks have not achieved racial equality in any area of American life. And they are overrepresented on every negative variable except suicide, itself a mixed blessing since black suicide rates are highest among its young people in contrast to white suicide rates weighted toward its oldest members. And the direction of change in the U.S. has made come conditions worse than in the era before the civil rights movement. In 1950 the black unemployment rate was double that of whites: in 1990 it was triple. Housing and school segregation are worse outside the South in 1990 than in 1950. The inequality of wealth is greater in 1990 than in 1950, when most people earned money from wages. In the 1990s, people earn money, in larger numbers, from stocks, bonds, property, leveraged buyouts, etc. The percent of intact black families vis-à-vis white families was much higher in 1950 than in 1990, as was the lower number of black children born in wedlock. The times they are changing but things remain the same.

For some reason this society documents but does not change many of its discriminatory practices. There are numerous studies, most of them conducted by Euro-Americans showing the retention of racial discrimination in employment, housing, education, health care, and so on. One study found that 75 percent of black men seeking employment were discriminated against. In another investigation of housing discrimination, it was discovered that blacks face discrimination 56 percent of the time they seek to rent a house and 59 percent of the time they try to buy a home. Other studies reveal that black patients in a hospital were more likely to be sent to inexperienced medical doctors and that car dealers were likely to charge Afro-Americans and women higher prices than white males. The number of studies showing racial discrimination in every facet of American life makes a mockery of the color-blind theory and Patterson's claim that this is the least-racist white majority society in the world.

Adding to the scholarly studies of racial discrimination are the TV shows, like *60 Minutes,* which showed an employment agency using special codes to avoid sending black applicants to employers for jobs. On September 26, 1991, the show

Prime Time Live showed a nationwide audience what it's like to be black in 1990s America. They sent two twenty-eight-year-old men, Glen Brewer, black, and John Kuhnen, white, to shop in the same stores, attempt to rent the same apartment, and apply for the same job. Here are the results of their experiment in the city of St. Louis:

> At several stores, Mr. Kuhnen gets instant service; Mr. Brewer is ignored except at a record store, where a salesman keeps a close eye on him, without offering any assistance. When they go for a walk, separately on the same street, a police car passes Mr. Kuhnen but slows down to give Mr. Brewer a once-over. At a car dealership, Mr. Kuhnen is offered a lower price and better financing terms than Mr. Brewer. Inquiring about a job at a dry cleaner that has advertised for help, Mr. Kuhnen is told jobs are still available; Mr. Brewer is told, "The positions are taken." Following up a for-rent sign, Mr. Kuhnen is promptly offered an apartment, which he does not take; ten minutes later, Mr. Brewer is told it has been rented for hours.

That program gave Euro-Americans a visual lesson in the mundane indignities that many Afro-Americans experience day after day. Of course, only the most naive white viewer should have been surprised at the results. Despite the color-blind theory, white claims of reverse racism and preferential treatment for blacks, there is no queue of whites claiming black heritage to qualify for the "benefits" of black membership. The color-blind theory is a smokescreen to mask the persistence of a racial hierarchy in American life. Blacks who buy into the theory are easily manipulated, compare themselves to their poorer brothers on the African continent, and measure their progress by those standards, and a small but increasing number of black opportunists who seek to reap the rewards of catering to Euro-American prejudices. The illusion of racial equality seems real because tokenism begins at the top and slowly trickles down to the bottom. Only a small number of elite positions are available in 1990s America and they are often visible to everyone. Few Euro-Americans make claims on the elite positions albeit they are very desired. Selection or appointment is very subjective and the qualifications ambiguous. Thus, it is easier to integrate the elite positions, such as Miss America or head of the military, involving a few thousand people than provide equal employment opportunities for millions of black and white workers. The blacks see their members in elite positions and take pride in their achievements, although their own situations have not improved—reflected glory. Euro-Americans see those same blacks and can rationalize a dramatic change in the racial character of American society while thinking that the poor, homeless, and criminals could have made similar achievements if they had gotten an education and worked hard.

The illusions of racial equality are best exemplified in the two areas in which blacks appear to dominate: entertainment and sports. While three of the five wealthiest entertainers are black (Oprah Winfrey, Bill Cosby, and Michael Jackson), they are not the wealthiest people in the entertainment industry. Those people are white and own and/or manage record companies, talent-management agencies, movie studios, and so on. Because black entertainers often have unique skills and American society highlights all black entry into elite positions, they have a visibility difficult for Euro-American entertainers to attain. However, there are thousands of Euro-Americans we do not know about earning millions yearly from the entertainment industry. There are comparatively few black millionaires in show business and we tend to know them all. Moreover, even among the wealthy black entertainers, their income is divided up among agents, attorneys, accountants, producers, and so on. In most cases those people are white. There is virtually no white entertainer who shares any significant portion of his/her income with a black person.

It is possible that Euro-Americans take 97 percent of the dollars spent on entertainment produced in this country and distributed to the rest of the world. Thus, black success in the entertainment world is racial tokenism at its worst. And the constraints of race dictate the kind of entertainment product that blacks are allowed to exhibit. Although people of color buy 38 percent of the movie tickets, almost all the blacks starring in movies are men and comedians. Former basketball star Wilt Chamberlain has written, "The movie industry is still back in the 1930's and 1940's. The Eddie ("Rochester") Andersons and Stepin Fetchits of today are the Eddie Murphys and Richard Pryors. Producers give starring roles to comedians and let them make a lot of money, but they never cast people of color in the roles of real heroes." The same is true of prime-time television, where blacks are frequently relegated to scattered token roles or the clownish context of a situation comedy. With the exception of the now defunct Cosby show, most of the prime-time sitcoms featuring blacks portray them in particularly stereotyped roles. One NAACP study found that "no Black executive makes final decisions in the motion picture or television industry, that only a handful of Afro-Americans hold executive positions with film studios or television networks."

Anyone watching the popular American sports on television would have to be impressed with the number of black athletes. In the case of basketball, the starting players are often all Afro-Americans. The sports pages are replete with the million-dollar salaries of professional athletes and their commercial endorsement deals. While the most popular sports, football, baseball, and basketball, are the ones dominated by blacks, those athletes do not necessarily earn the highest incomes. Because of sponsor tie-ins, endorsement deals, and appearance fees, the top ten of the highest-paid athletes are mostly whites in the less popular sports of tennis, golf, and racing. Since those sports appeal to a better demographic group (i.e., higher-status whites), corporations pay more per audience than in the more popular sports. It might be noted that the white-dominated sports have fewer injuries and greater longevity for their participants. As true of show business, black athletes share their incomes with agents, accountants, investors, and so on, almost all of them Euro-Americans. And it is essential that a black player be superior to any white rivals for his position. He will rarely be allowed to be a part-time or reserve player in any sport. Those positions are reserved for Euro-Americans. Few blacks can remain in their sports, after finishing their careers, as managers, coaches, or front-office employees. In sports where the top ten players are all Afro-Americans it was rare to find an Afro-American clerk-typist in the front office of most professional teams.

On the amateur level, the exploitation of black athletes is most blatant. Afro-Americans constitute almost 75 percent of the players in the major revenue sports at the collegiate level. While they ostensibly do not get paid except for tuition and expenses, the alleged advantage of college athletes is a college education for four years' sports performance and a chance to enter the lucrative professional sports arena. Yet only a fraction will join a professional sports team, and 70 percent of black college athletes do not attain a college degree within four years. Adding insult to injury, the revenues received from the black-dominated sports programs are generally used to subsidize the less-popular, Euro-American-dominated sports such as lacrosse, volleyball, baseball, wrestling, and tennis.

Throughout American society the illusion of racial equality is promoted as a reality. Although black political participation increased dramatically, once blacks were permitted access to the voting booths as a result of the Voting Rights Act of 1965, Afro-Americans hold less than 2 percent of all political offices in the United States while comprising 13 percent of its population. As a result of at-large elections and political **gerrymandering**, black candidates cannot win elective office in political districts where blacks are not a majority. With few exceptions, Euro-Americans vote for Euro-Americans, regardless of the political party, gender, or other variable. Race transcends everything in politics. Until recently, no Afro-American had been elected mayor of a major city with a majority of the Euro-American vote. That explains why blacks rarely win state-wide offices, because no American state has a majority black population. Afro-American politicians are generally dependent on getting 90 percent of the black vote and 20–40 percent of the white vote in order to win elective office. Once they are in office, their appointments are often of Euro-Americans to the most important positions—a tactic designed to reassure the business community of their "colorblindness" and to pacify Euro-American voters worried about black "domination." With a black mayor in charge, blacks lose the right to charge racism in their governance. Seemingly they also lose the desire to change black mayors, as relatively few black incumbents are ever voted out of office by their black constituents.

The structural inequality, based on race, poses a vicious circle for Afro-Americans. A high rate of unemployment creates a class of impoverished blacks, particularly males, who resort to illegal activity in order to survive. While representing less than 6 percent of the American population, Afro-American men comprise 47 percent of the prison population. Almost one of four black men aged twenty to thirty are in jail or on probation or parole. The United States has the highest percentage of its population behind bars of any country in the world, and a majority of them are poor and people of color. Blacks make up 40 percent of prisoners awaiting death penalties. The majority of those death-row black prisoners have been convicted of murdering Euro-Americans. In the last forty-seven years, no white person has been executed for murdering an Afro-American. The inescapable conclusion is that the American legal system, and its participants, place a greater value, on white life than on black life.

Other examples abound on racial difference and the question of value. In a bizarre case of a sperm-bank mixup resulting in a white woman's giving birth to a black child, the white "victim" was awarded $400,000 because of the mistake. Imagine the anguish of millions of black mothers who have no choice but to give birth to black children. Had the situation been reversed, a black woman inseminated with a white man's sperm, the baby would still be considered black, and it is doubtful that a jury would award a black woman $400,000 for giving birth to a biracial child. It is these countless racial insults that make most Afro-Americans feel they live in the United States at the discretion of Euro-Americans, even those most recently arrived. The case of Rodney King, the black male beaten by Los Angeles police officers, certainly did little to reassure Afro-Americans that they have the same citizenship rights as Euro-Americans. His case was not an isolated incident. A commission assigned to investigate the Los Angeles Police Department found over seven hundred racist, homophobic, and sexist remarks typed by officers into the department's car-communication systems over the previous eighteen months. One of the most eloquent testimonies to the legacy of racism is the number of prominent blacks stopped and abused by police officers in this country, ranging from famous athletes to singers and movie stars. Comparable situations with Euro-American celebrities are almost unheard of.

Racial indignities affect the black middle class the most. They have played by the rules, achieved some degree of success, and find they are still below the lowest-ranking Euro-American. As one Afro-American woman was quoted, "Life in general requires a lot of psychic energy for Black people on racial things." A professor of philosophy wrote an article entitled "In My Next Life, I'll Be White." He speaks of the fact that black men rarely enjoy the public trust of Euro-Americans, that they are always regarded as possible thieves, criminals, violent and dangerous until proven innocent. The essence of his argument is that while white males have committed more evil cumulatively than any other class of people in the world, a suit and tie suffice to make one of them respectable. Black women, while regarded as less dangerous, encounter the same suspicion that they are shoplifters or morally loose. The important point is that being denied the public trust leaves a deep psychic scar of discrimination, which festers and becomes the fountainhead of low self-esteem and self-hate for those who have no emotional salve.

Those Afro-Americans who do not have their self-esteem destroyed often suffer from a quiet anger at their treatment. This anger is currently being manifested in a racial chauvinism almost as virulent as its white counterpart. It is expressed in a kind of dysfunctional racial solidarity that has left the race victim to a series of charlatans and racial demagogues. Any black who yells racism when accused of misconduct is assumed to be innocent without being required to prove that innocence. This anger and this racial solidarity reached their most extreme form in the nomination of black jurist Clarence Thomas to replace Thurgood Marshall on the U.S. Supreme Court. Nominated by the titular head of the Republican party, the party which had captured the presidency of the nation largely through its use of racial appeals to white voters, Thomas had a record considered so anti-black that one black political scientist called him a "racist by proxy." Another columnist wrote, "Stripped of his color, Clarence Thomas is just another Republican conservative apparatchik come to Washington to seek his fortune by protecting the already powerful from the weak and disenfranchised."

That Thomas had the support of former and current arch segregationists, such as Strom Thurmond, Jesse Helms, and David Duke, seems not to have mattered or was not known to his black supporters. When Professor Anita Hill, an Afro-American woman, accused him of sexually harassing her, the low-esteem, angry black population rallied to his defense, representing 60 percent of the blacks polled on the matter. White Southern Democrats claimed their vote to appoint him was from the fear of black anger if they did not. Observers of the situation speculate that Thomas's anti–civil rights record will be reinforced by his anger at black groups for attempting to derail his appointment. Meanwhile, the party of Strom Thurmond, Jesse Helms, and David Duke is talking about a massive defection of blacks from the Democratic party because of their support of Clarence Thomas. One black leader's explanation for this weird marriage between blacks and the leaders of American racialism, Roger Wilkins, says, "Blacks have been terribly deprived throughout our history and we've been deprived among other things of symbols of pride occupying high places. So that when a Black is presented for such a position, there is an instinctive reaction to support that person."

The controversy over Clarence Thomas revealed some widening splits in the Afro-American community and the Euro-American political strategies for the twenty-first century. Those splits are along gender and class lines. Gender lines are dividing because some black men feel that black women are given preference over them, that white men like to put black women in between themselves and black men. Many blacks accused Anita Hill of acting as a tool for white men to ruin the life of a black man at the peak of his career. That many black leaders did not share that view is reflected in the statement of Jesse Jackson that Anita Hill will rank in history along with civil rights pioneer Rosa Parks. Representative Craig Washington put it best when he said, "It is not Black women who have lynched Black men. It is white racism that has been tolerated for so long by many of Judge Thomas's supporters. It is a problem that will not be addressed by attacking and demeaning Black women." Thomas's claim that he was the victim of racism was the real irony. Most of the racists in America were his supporters, and the white supporters of civil rights were his opponents.

Class divisions are a more serious matter. Since the desegregation of public facilities and the rise of racial tokenism, blacks have been less united as a race on many matters that affect one class more than the other. Younger blacks have become ahistorical and simply want to enter mainstream America. The Republican party has been in power for eighteen of the last twenty-two years, by controlling the White House. They attained power by developing a political strategy to appeal to southern whites resentful of the civil rights gains in the 1960s. In the 1980s the Republican presidents Reagan and Bush both had past histories of publicly supporting racial segregation. As the party of white America, there was little room for blacks, except those who supported the racist and classist views of the Republican party. Clarence Thomas was an opportunist who decided to jump on the Republican bandwagon at exactly the time this bandwagon was crushing millions of Afro-Americans into deeper economic misery. One columnist noted: "Thomas has spent a lot of his life seeking to please people who hate him, currying favor with the man, being available as a token and symbol." Thousands of other blacks, hungry for some political power, will join the Republican party because the line for political participation is shorter. Race traitors are in short supply, even in 1990s America. If the Republicans believe that replacing white overseers with black ones will make blacks accept slavery, that may be the greatest illusion of them all.

The double-consciousness that Du Bois wrote about still exists, except that the racial identity of blackness threatens to overtake the national identity of Americans. White America is imposing this choice upon many of its black inhabitants. Being human—also American—seems beyond the pale of consideration for people of African descent. For all the progress that has been made on so many fronts, it is still true that Afro-Americans have their worth measured by the darkness of their skin, not the content of their characters. In a society where there is no scarcity of decent jobs, housing, and education, nonracial factors may become the criteria for the perception and treatment of black Americans. Du Bois also recognized that the class factor was intertwined with the racial factor. It is unlikely that the problems of race and class will be resolved in this generation's lifetime. Until the problem of class division is resolved, the problem of the twenty-first century will continue to be the problem of the color line.

Blues-Collar Clarity

Stanley Crouch is author of The All-American Skin Game, or, The Decoy of Race *and* Always
in Pursuit: Fresh American Perspectives, 1995–1997. *A former jazz critic for the* Village Voice,
he is a contributing editor to The New Republic *and a columnist for the* New York Daily News.

*This essay was delivered as a talk at a conference held in Washington, D.C., in the spring of
1990, which was entitled "Second Thoughts on Race in America." It allowed me to work out
my sense of how supposedly new directions in Afro-American consciousness were actually old-time
stuff that missed, or denied, or repudiated a sturdy set of principles that underlay Negro-American
morale and achievement.*

Following my mentors, Albert Murray and Ralph Ellison, I have long maintained
that the influence of Afro-Americans on our cultural and political life is indelible
and ongoing. Just as it is quite easy to see how Negro style has affected our music,
our language, our humor, our dance, and even our ways of walking and performing
sports, we cannot deny the impact Afro-Americans have had on this country's movement toward the realization of the ideals that cluster in the heart of our democratic
conception. In a long and tragic series of confrontations, black Americans have had
to scale, bore through, or detonate the prejudicial walls that blocked access to the
banquet of relatively unlimited social advancement that we acknowledge as the
grand inspirational myth of American life.

This epic confrontation with bigoted policies reached its high heroic moment
during the Civil Rights Movement, bringing together troops that crossed all
racial lines, classes, religions, and political parties. At that point, our struggle
for greater democratic purity entered an arena of political engagement that demanded dousing redneck dragon fire, transforming segregationists like Lyndon
Johnson, battling the paranoid illnesses of men like J. Edgar Hoover, and holding at bay all of the hysterically cynical tendencies toward self-pity and defeatist
sulking or name calling within our ranks. The result was both a monumental
shift in the national perception of racial matters and an unprecedented entree
into the processes of democratic life. What we learned during those years is
that the role of American democracy has come to be one of constant expansion,
of inclusive motion beyond one group or one sex to all groups in both sexes.
And at this point in our history, the democratic idea has grown even to include
the idea that both the animate and inanimate environment should have the rights
that preclude callous exploitation.

But for all the expansions of our conception of democracy and for all the
victories against discriminatory attitudes and policies over the last twenty-five years,
we still find ourselves facing the job of improvising the best way of going about
making the democratic imperatives at the center of our society function with the sort
of vitality that inspires comprehensive engagement. From my position on the battlefield,
I have come to believe that a large part of what must he addressed is the nature of
the enemy within, the influential dimensions of what must finally be recognized as a

vision of American society that leads not toward democratic vibrance but the limitations of **Balkanization**. In fact, I now believe the discussion of race is far too influenced by a body of ideas reflecting the amount of decay that has taken place in the Afro-American intellectual, political, and lower-class communities.

The battle with so-called "white middle-class standards" that we still hear discussed when the subjects ranging from school performance to rap records are addressed is itself a distortion of the goals of the Civil Rights Movement. This battle would lead us to believe that there are differences so great in this society that we should actually accept a separatist vision in which the elemental necessity of human identification across racial, sexual, and class lines would be replaced by the idea that people from various backgrounds can identify only with those from their own groups. Such a conception avoids King's idea that people should be judged by the content of their character and not by the color of their skin or, if we extend that to include sex, by gender.

The nature of ethnic nationalism and of gender antagonism that has polluted so much contemporary discussion misses the point of the March on Washington in symbolic terms—that this culture is usually bettered when we have as many people as possible intelligently interacting, when quality takes precedence over point of social origin, class, race, sex, nationality, and religion. Those who came forward in the late sixties and began to trumpet the idea that there were two Americas—one black, one white—not only ignored all of the regional complexities of North, South, Midwest, Southwest, and West, but of Catholic and Protestant, Christian and Jew, as well as all of the variations that break down inside such large categories as white, black, Hispanic, Jew, and American Indian. Now those benumbing simplifications have pulled feminism into the task of making the white male the same thing that he is inside the cosmology of the Nation of Islam: the source of all evil.

This simplification is at odds with the realities of human interaction within our society, and it suggests that those removed from the proverbial seats of power are invariably limited in their freedom to be inspired. We can see that quite easily if we look at something like the controversy at Harvard, where the demand has been raised that a tenured black female be hired by the Law School. No one can be disturbed by a first-class black female professor's being hired by the department, but the argument that has begun to vibrate with hysteria about such matters implies a fundamental inferiority on the part of black female students. If we were to listen to the activists, we would conclude that black females are so incapable of identifying across racial lines that they cannot look at Sandra Day O'Connor on the Supreme Court and feel that there is a place for them in the American legal profession, perhaps one of extraordinary import someday.

Nothing in my own experience or in the experience of Afro-Americans I have met or read about corroborates the idea that, to any significant extent, people of color are capable of being inspired only by their own race or sex. To suggest that is to distort the heroic engagement that defines Negro history, a good measure of which has always been about struggling with any exclusive conception of human possibility or human identification. Yet we are now supposed to wolf down the idea that if a black child is looking at Kenneth Branagh's remarkable film of Shakespeare's *Henry V,* he or she will not be intrigued by the insights into the problems of power and struggle, of class and cultural clash, but will only be bored or feel left out because the work is something written by "a dead white man about dead white people." In its very provincialism and its racist conception of culture, such an idea opposes the richness of the best of Afro-American culture, regardless of class.

It is due to the distortions of people such as James Baldwin that we have come to believe in far too many instances that black people are such victims of racism that they are as limited as they are purported to be in the most provincial superstitions, those irrational undergirdings of discrimination. Having been born December 14, 1945, in Los Angeles, California, I can say that the people in my community, which was not so much blue-collar as *blues-collar,* were forever encouraging all of us to aspire to the very best that we could achieve and were always at war with any idea that would result in our accepting the ethnic limits encouraged by the traditions of segregated thought. Though my mother was a domestic worker who earned sometimes no more than $11 a day and often worked six days a week, she was always cutting out editorials for me to read, bringing home books that her employers either gave her or loaned, and wasn't above forcing me against my will to watch Laurence Olivier's *Richard III* when it came on, or doing the same thing when Orson Welles's *Macbeth* was shown nightly on *The Million Dollar Movie,* which I had to keep looking at until I came to understand what they were saying.

My blues-collar mother wasn't being pretentious or exhibiting the effects of having been brainwashed by a Eurocentric conception of cultural values. I was never given the impression that I was looking at some great white people strutting some great white stuff. That wasn't the idea at all. My mother knew that Olivier was a great actor and that Shakespeare was a great dramatist. She wanted me to know and experience those facts. She also told me about Marian Anderson, Duke Ellington, Jackie Robinson, and anybody else who represented exemplary achievement. The same was true in public school, where we read *Julius Caesar* aloud in class, saw films about Marian Anderson and Jackie Robinson, read Dickens, and so on. We were constantly taught that great significance was not the franchise of any single group and that we were supposed to identify with the best from whomever and wherever in the world it happened to come. We were not allowed to give any excuses for poor performance either. If we had come up with some so-called cultural difference excuse, we would have been laughed at, if not whacked on the boody, for disrespecting the intelligence of the teacher. Our teachers were tough and supportive. They knew well that the best way to respect so-called minority students was to demand the most of them.

It is not that the adults of my childhood were naive about racial matters. They knew that excellence and bulldog tenacity were the best weapons against the dragons of this society. That was the point of telling us about the struggles of the Andersons and the Robinsons. But the worst thing that you could be within that community at that time was a racist, no matter how obvious the social limitations were. Adults would say to you, "Boy, the lowest thing you can be is a man who spends all his time hating somebody he doesn't even know. You know, if you want to hold a man down in a hole full of mud, you got to get down there in that mud with him, which will make you just as dirty as the man you say you don't like because he's so damn filthy." Those Negroes I grew up under were always quick to tell you that there were just two kinds of people in the world: those who tried their best to be good and those who didn't care about being bad. They were true democrats, perhaps because they had learned the hard way what it meant when you submitted to the superstitions of discrimination. Those adults were just as proud of Branch Rickey as they were of Jackie Robinson, for each symbolized the will and the discipline necessary to expand the idea of democracy into the arena of practice.

The Afro-American tradition of which I speak is a continuation of what we learn from the life of Frederick Douglass, whose career makes it possible to see that all Americans, regardless of point of social origin, are capable of producing those who will do remarkable things. As Albert Murray points out in *The Omni-Americans*, a book all should read who really wish to know something about this country, the embodiment of the nineteenth-century self-made man is Douglass. Lincoln, the self-made Midwesterner, easily saw that. After Lincoln met with Douglass, the Great Emancipator told his secretary that, given Douglass's beginnings as a slave and his present achievements, he was probably "the most meritorious man in the United States." Murray also observes that Harriet Tubman is surely the best example of the pioneer woman, what my grandmother meant when she complimented someone on having "shit, grit, and mother wit." Yet neither of them can be reduced to mere racial heroes. They are symbols of great American achievement against extraordinary odds.

When we address the richness of our heritage, we will understand our national heritage in the context of Western civilization to the degree that we will acknowledge it for what it is—an astonishing gathering of information from the entire world, a gathering that had its impact at least partially because of the fight against provincialism that fresh information from other cultures demanded. The experiment that is American democracy is an extension of the ideas of the Magna Carta and the Enlightenment and is also a social development of the New Testament's motion away from the idea of a chosen people. That is why a reduction of the meaning of Western civilization to "the story of dead white men" and racist exploitation distorts the realities of the ongoing debate that has lifted our social vision beyond the provincial, whether that lifting meant the debate over slavery or women's suffrage or anything else that has hobbled this country's freedom to benefit from its human resources.

The kind of defeatism, paranoia, and alienation that is fomented by the "dead white men" version of Western and national history is dangerous because it is so far from the facts of what those who made so many of the achievements thought of themselves. I have a feeling that Isaac Newton and Galileo didn't spend too much time thinking about their skin color. It is hard for me to believe that Newton got up in the morning saying, "Well, here I am, white Isaac Newton in England and, as white Isaac Newton, I think I'll go over here and try and figure out something white about gravity." I also doubt that Galileo said to himself, "Well, as white Galileo, let me look out here as a white man and see how far I can see with my white eyes. I can't see far enough, so I guess I'll have to work on a white tool so I can have a white view of the cosmos." Or can one imagine Beethoven battling to get those string quartets right and thinking, "My job as a white man who will some day be dead is to write some white notes and provide the future with the work of a great white dead man." The work of those men was too hard to be limited by such concerns. The exploits of Negro and women aviators in the history of flying between the invention of the airplane and World War II prove that there were always those who could see past color and gender to the quality of the contribution and what that contribution might offer them in their own lives. And it is that sort of history that we must perpetually reiterate if we have any serious intention of combating Balkanization.

It is also easy to see that those who have promoted a reductive vision of Afro-American identity by posturing an antagonistic attitude toward "white middle-class standards" would do well to think about the differences between those students who come out of the business school at Florida A & M University and those students whom anthropologists Signithia Fordham of Rutgers University and John U. Ogbu of Berkeley studied at Capital High School in Washington, D.C. At the predominantly black Florida A & M, Sybil C. Mobley, dean and creator of the business school, has developed a program over the last sixteen years that is recognized by Hewlett-Packard recruiters as one of the top five in the country, one that can be counted on to produce first-level students of finance.

In the April 8, 1990, *New York Times* article about the program, it is observed that Mobley forged a curriculum that places as much emphasis on deportment, verbal skills, dress, grooming, and writing abilities as on the details of business. According to the article, Mobley's two-tiered curriculum is "one that some major American companies say the top business schools would do well to emulate." Given the high degree of interest in its business students, Florida A & M has shown that the best thing for so-called minority students is to demand that they engage the specifics of the world in which they live, not allow them to retreat into visions of victimization that diminish the will and thwart the discipline necessary to make one's own way in our society. As one of the female students says of what Mobley has built, "I know who I am. If you know who you are, you don't have to run around in a dashiki. There's a time to do that and a time to wear a suit." Eurocentric? Hardly. That is actually a reiteration of the Afro-American tradition of seeking to be the best within the terms of one's chosen arena.

Just one week later in the *Times,* the disturbing observations of the study of those high school students in Washington, D.C., were reported. The fundamental findings of Fordham and Ogbu give us important insights into some of the elements that explain what has become a noticeable performance gap between white and black students on Scholastic Aptitude Tests and in college work. Though neither the SAT scores nor college performances are discussed in the article, the idea that black students have about what constitutes ethnic authenticity says much about substandard academic achievement by Negroes. Such a circumscribed conception of "blackness" now so influences young black people that, according to the study of those high school students, "They chose to avoid adopting attitudes and putting in enough time and effort in their schoolwork because their peers (and they themselves) would interpret their 'white.' " It went on to say that there were more than a "dozen other types of behavior that the students considered 'acting white' "—including "speaking standard English, listening to so-called white music, going to the opera or ballet, studying in the library, going to the Smithsonian Institution, doing volunteer work, camping or hiking, putting on airs and being on time." In other words, anything short of the most provincial way of addressing and assessing the varieties of expression and the possibilities that education exists to illuminate meant rejecting one's ethnic identity. Such self-assured provincialism is, at best, self-destructive, and is a tendency that must be fought relentlessly.

It is more than odd that we should find ourselves as Americans faced with these bizarre ideas and their effects not only on the black lower class but, as Jeff Howard and Ray Hammond pointed out in the 1985 *New Republic* article "Rumors of Inferiority," on the Negro middle class as well. What we are seeing is a retreat from community expectations and personal demands of high quality in intellectual areas. As Howard and Hammond point out, "Black leaders too often have tried to explain away these problems by blaming racism or cultural bias in the tests themselves. These factors haven't disappeared. But for many middle-class black Americans who have had access to educational and economic opportunities for nearly 20 years, the traditional protestations of cultural deprivation and educational disadvantage ring hollow." That hollowness and those clichés are surely the result of the Balkanized sense of reality that remains at odds with the best of the Afro-American tradition.

We have some very good examples, however, of what can happen when a so-called minority doesn't find itself burdened with a separatist ideology, when its people choose—as black people once knew they should—to work at more than complaining and trying to subvert the standards that promote excellence. Asian students have shown that they are capable of confounding their fellow students by rising to the challenges of higher education so consistently and so well that they seem not to understand what too many others consider the most important aspects of the college experience. They don't know that when you go to college you're supposed to pledge a fraternity or sorority, go to as many beer busts as possible, sleep through your classes, fail to do your papers, and devote large amounts of time to the incredibly significant problem of becoming popular. They obviously have a misunderstanding. They think they're supposed to study. That's why they call the campus library at Berkeley "Chinatown." When the library opens, Asian students flood in; when the library closes, Asian students are told to leave. Yet there are those who continue to wonder at the high percentage of Asian students who do so well academically! Deduction is obviously not one of their stronger suits.

The defeatist undertow that so misshapes the thinking of black youth regarding intellectual and career engagement is about more than the lack of role models, which is usually the explanation. In a letter to Ann Landers published February 25, 1990, in *The Washington Post,* a black middle-class reader complained, "Black children need role models. We read and hear too much about black pimps and drug dealers and not enough about blacks who have made it. Maybe this is what happens when the press, radio, and TV are predominantly white." Landers responded, quite rightly, that "the problems facing black youths are the same ones white youth have—no core family unit, no parental guidance, inadequate education, and joblessness." She went on to write, again, quite correctly, "You lose me when you complain of bias in the field of communications and an absence of black role models. A few who come to mind are Oprah Winfrey, Bill Cosby, Lena Horne, Sidney Poitier, Michael Jordan, Magic Johnson, Walter Payton, Mike Singletary, publishing tycoon John Johnson, Supreme Court Justice Thurgood Marshall, General Colin Powell, attorney Marian Wright Edelman, and Dr. Louis Sullivan of Health and Human Services. I could go on, but I'm sure you get the idea."

What we must question is the nature of the voices that black youth choose to listen to when the difficulties facing our society are under discussion. We must look at the problems that exist as much in the black media as in the general media. It is incredible that neither of the two largest black papers in New York—*The Amsterdam News* and *The City Sun*—has ever done its job in assessing the scandal of the Tawana Brawley farce and the disreputable roles played by Al Sharpton, Vernon Mason, and Alton Maddox. Nor can we ignore the national trend in black radio to promote paranoid conspiracy theories and to submit to the kind of rabble-rousing that avoids the complexity of the various levels of opposition and the necessity of equally complex forms of combat. Nor can we fail to recognize the way in which too many irresponsible intellectuals—black and white—have submitted to the youth culture and the adolescent rebellion of pop music, bootlegging liberal arts rhetoric to defend Afro-fascist rap groups like Public Enemy on the one hand, while paternalistically defining the "gangster rap" of doggerel chanters such as Ice Cube as expressive of the "real" black community. The problem with these tendencies is the same problem that existed when racist iconography dominated media and folklore: semiliterates and illiterates quite often fail to see those things as distortions; they believe they are real. Therefore, it should come as no shock to us when black young people, the products of an oral culture that is ever vulnerable to the dominant voice, sink down into reductive ideas about what they can achieve in this culture.

What must be done is rather obvious. The values of civilized behavior must be reestablished and defined as fundamentals beyond race. No one in this society should be encouraged to believe that excellence, mastery of our national language, tasteful dress, reliability, or any of the virtues that bring vitality to a society are the sole province of the white population. Welfare laws should be changed so that irresponsible sexual behavior is discouraged by laying the burden of support on the teenage parents, making it in their interest to use birth control—if, in fact, they have sex at all. That is not as wild as it immediately sounds. If, for instance, there was a cut-off point—say, January 1, 1994—when it would become law that each teenage parent would be responsible for 45 percent of the support of his or her child and receive only 10 percent of that from welfare agencies, and, that if either parent refused, he or she would be incarcerated in a work-study program from which the monies paid would go to the child's support, the problem would diminish quite rapidly. Those who think that absurd have no understanding of human nature.

As an example, let us look at racial attacks in the South from the end of Reconstruction in 1877 until the middle of the 1960s. They were so frequent one would have been led to believe that Southern white men were genetically predisposed to assaulting black males. Yet those attacks, what journalist Jack Germond recalls as a tradition known as "nigger knocking," fell with true deliberate speed when those who committed such crimes were punished. If something that had gone on for ninety years could be largely reined in when the society refused to allow it, even think of it as normal behavior, are we to believe the problem of teenage pregnancy would sustain itself once black kids saw it as truly opposed to their self-interest?

At the same time, it is important to note that in a black youth film like *House Party,* Warrington and Reginal Hudlin did something very important: they made it quite clear that the hoodlum element that is so often celebrated in rap recordings is a bane on the black community, something the vast majority of young black people knows already. That vision must be reinforced constantly, as it was on *Hill Street Blues,* which never failed to show the suffocating social weight extensive crime imposed on so-called minority communities. Those kinds of decisions in mass media are very important because they counter the irresponsibility of those aforementioned intellectuals who champion or attempt to be sympathetic to anything that shocks or shows contempt for the supposed "white middle-class standards" Sybil C. Mobley is so successfully passing on to the students in the Florida A & M business school.

The Mobleys of this nation should be celebrated and nationally recognized, for they are doing the real work. The public schools of this nation should follow her example and they should get whatever monies are necessary to make them the extraordinarily important aspects of democratic success that they once were. We cannot allow our public schools to remain in such bad shape and then wonder why we are having so many social problems. First-class teachers, dressing codes, and the reiteration of the importance of the inner life that comes from intellectual development are fundamental to what we must have if this society is to move in the direction of its greatest potential.

We should also think about fresh ways of recognizing Afro-American authenticity. When those who have triumphed and who represent some of the best the country has to offer are discussed, their ethnic identity is often called into question. But when they are jerks, vulgarians, opportunists, and criminals, race is somehow always important. It is time to have the term "black criminal" reversed so that the defining aspect is the criminality, not the race. After all, during the Wall Street scandal the media didn't say "crooked Jewish stockholder Ivan Boesky" or "another group of Jewish stockbrokers was accused of insider trading." Even John Gotti isn't described as "purported Italian Mafia boss." Of course, part of the problem is that manipulators of racial paranoia such as Al Sharpton, Vernon Mason, Alton Maddox, and Marion Barry will inevitably introduce color as an escape hatch. But they must not be allowed to get away with it. The recent elections in Washington, D.C., prove that those who were so willing to support Barry before the cameras didn't at all express the real feelings of the city. The people didn't go for the color con. Lincoln was right: you can't fool all of the people all of the time.

Examples such as Mobley, such as Washington, DC's, Kimi Gray, such as the list of achievers that Ann Landers presented, and the country's willingness to embrace virtue and heroic engagement from every quarter of this nation on a scale that has no precedent make me quite optimistic. We must get back to the grandest vision of this society, which is that all exemplary human endeavor is the heritage of every person. It is the combination of one's ethnic and human heritage that is the issue. Every ethnic group has a heritage of its own and is also heir to symbols of inspiration as different as Michael Jordan and William Shakespeare. All people are heir to everything of wonder that anyone has produced, regardless of race, gender, and place. Anyone who would deny any person identification with the vastness of that marvelously rich offering of human achievement is not truly speaking as an American.

6.11   Randall Kennedy

My Race Problem—and Ours

Randall Kennedy was a law clerk for former Supreme Court justice Thurgood Marshall. He is the author of Race, Crime, and the Law. *Currently he is professor of law at Harvard University Law School.*

W hat is the proper role of race in determining how I, an American black, should feel toward others? One response is that although I should not dislike people because of their race, there is nothing wrong with having a special—a *racial*—affection for other black people. Indeed, many would go further and maintain that something would be wrong with me if I did not sense and express racial pride, racial kinship, racial patriotism, racial loyalty, racial solidarity—synonyms for that amalgam of belief, intuition, and commitment that manifests itself when blacks treat blacks with more solicitude than they do those who are not black.

Some conduct animated by these sentiments has blended into the background of daily routine, as when blacks who are strangers nonetheless speak to each other—"Hello," "Hey," "Yo"—or hug or give each other a soul handshake or refer to each other as "brother" or "sister." Other manifestations are more dramatic. For example, the Million Man March, which brought at least 500,000 black men to Washington, D.C., in 1995, was a demonstration predicated on the notion that blackness gives rise to racial obligation and that black people should have a special, closer, more affectionate relationship with their fellow blacks than with others in America's diverse society.

I reject this response to the question. Neither racial pride nor racial kinship offers guidance that is intellectually, morally, or politically satisfactory.

Racial Pride

I eschew racial pride because of my conception of what should properly be the object of pride for an individual: something that he or she has accomplished. I can feel pride in a good deed I have done or a good effort I have made. I cannot feel pride in some state of affairs that is independent of my contribution to it. The color of my skin, the width of my nose, the texture of my hair, and the various other signs that prompt people to label me black constitute such a state of affairs. I did not achieve my racial designation. It was something I inherited—like my nationality and socio-economic starting place and sex—and therefore something I should not feel proud of or be credited with. In taking this position I follow Frederick Douglass, the great nineteenth-century reformer, who declared that "the only excuse for pride in individuals . . . is in the fact of their own achievements." If the sun has created curled hair and tanned skin, Douglass observed, "let the sun be proud of its achievement."

It is understandable why people have often made inherited group status an honorific credential. Personal achievement is difficult to attain, and the lack of it often leaves a vacuum that racial pride can easily fill. Thus even if a person has little to show for himself, racial pride gives him status.

But maybe I am misconstruing what people mean by racial pride; perhaps it means simply that one is unashamed of one's race. To that I have no objection. No one should be ashamed of the labeling by which she or he is racially categorized, because no one chooses her or his parents or the signs by which society describes and sorts people. For this very same reason, however, no one should congratulate herself on her race insofar as it is merely an accident of birth.

I suspect, however, that when most black people embrace the term "racial pride," they mean more than that they are unembarrassed by their race. They mean, echoing Marcus Garvey, that "to be [black] is no disgrace, but an honor." Thus when James Brown sings "Say It Loud—I'm Black and I'm Proud," he is heard by many blacks as expressing not just the absence of shame but delight and assertiveness in valuing a racial designation that has long been stigmatized in America.

There is an important virtue in this assertion of the value of black life. It combats something still eminently in need of challenge: the assumption that because of their race black people are stupid, ugly, and low, and that because of their race white people are smart, beautiful, and righteous. But within some of the forms that this assertiveness has taken are important vices—including the belief that because of racial kinship blacks ought to value blacks more highly than others.

Racial Kinship

I reject the notion of racial kinship. I do so in order to avoid its burdens and to be free to claim what the distinguished political theorist Michael Sandel labels "the unencumbered self." The unencumbered self is free and independent, "unencumbered by aims and attachments it does not choose for itself," Sandel writes. "Freed from the sanctions of custom and tradition and inherited status, unbound by moral ties antecedent to choice, the self is installed as sovereign, cast as the author of the only obligations that constrain." Sandel believes that the unencumbered self is an illusion and that the yearning for it is a manifestation of a shallow liberalism that "cannot account for certain moral and political obligations that we commonly recognize, even prize"—"obligations of solidarity, religious duties, and other moral ties that may claim us for reasons unrelated to a choice," which are "indispensable aspects of our moral and political experience." Sandel's objection to those who, like me, seek the unencumbered self is that they fail to appreciate loyalties and responsibilities that should be accorded moral force partly because they influence our identity, such that living by these attachments "is inseparable from understanding ourselves as the particular persons we are—as members of this family or city or nation or people, as bearers of that history, as citizens of this republic."

I admire Sandel's work and have learned much from it. But a major weakness in it is a conflation of "is" and "ought." Sandel privileges what exists and has enlisted so much that his deference to tradition lapses into historical determinism. He faults the model of the unencumbered self because, he says, it cannot account for feelings of solidarity and loyalty that most people have not chosen to impose upon themselves but that they cherish nonetheless. This represents a fault, however, only if we believe that the unchosen attachments Sandel celebrates should be accorded moral weight. I am not prepared to do that simply on the basis that such attachments exist, have long existed, and are passionately felt. Feelings of primordial attachment often represent mere prejudice or superstition, a hangover of the childhood socialization from which many people never recover.

One defense of racial kinship takes the shape of an analogy between race and family. This position was strikingly advanced by the nineteenth-century blacknationalist intellectual Alexander Crummell, who asserted that "a race *is* a family," that "race feeling, like the family feeling, is of divine origin," and that the extinction of race feeling is thus—fortunately, in his view—just as impossible as the extinction of family feeling.

Analogizing race to family is a potent rhetorical move used to challenge those who, like me, are animated by a liberal, individualistic, and universalistic ethos that is skeptical of, if not hostile to, the particularisms—national, ethnic, religious, and racial—that seem to have grown so strong recently, even in arenas, such as major cosmopolitan universities, where one might have expected their demise. The central point of the challenge is to suggest that the norms I embrace will, or at least should, wobble and collapse in the face of claims on familial loyalty. Blood, as they say, is thicker than water.

One way to deal with the race-family analogy is to question its aptness on the grounds that a race is so much more populous than what is commonly thought of as a family that race cannot give rise to the same, or even similar, feelings of loyalty. When we think of a family, we think of a small, close-knit association of people who grow to know one another intimately over time. A race, in contrast, is a conglomeration of strangers. Black men at the Million Man March assuredly called one another brothers. But if certain questions were posed ("Would you be willing to lend a hundred dollars to this brother, or donate a kidney to that one?"), it would have quickly become clear that many, if not most, of those "brothers" perceived one another as strangers—not so distant as whites, perhaps, but strangers nonetheless.

However, I do not want to rest my argument here. Rather, I want to accept the race-family analogy in order to strengthen my attack on assumptions that privilege status-driven loyalties (the loyalties of blood) over chosen loyalties (the loyalties of will). In my view, many people, including legislators and judges, make far too much of blood ties in derogation of ties created by loving effort.

A vivid illustration is provided by the following kind of child-custody decision. It involves a child who has been separated from her parents and placed with adults who assume the role of foster parents. These adults nurture her, come to love her, and ultimately seek legally to become her new parents. If the "blood" parents of the child do not interfere, the foster parents will have a good chance of doing this. If, however, the blood parents say they want "their" child back, authorities in many jurisdictions will privilege the blood connection and return the child—even if the initial separation is mainly attributable to the fault of the blood parents, even if the child has been with the foster parents for a long time and is prospering under their care, even if the child views the foster parents as her parents and wants to stay with them, and even if there is good reason to believe that the foster parents will provide a more secure home setting than the child's blood parents. Judges make such rulings in large part because they reflect the idolatry of "blood," which is an ideological cousin to the racial beliefs I oppose.

Am I saying that, morally blood ties are an insufficient, indeed bad basis for preferring one's genetic relatives to others? Yes. I will rightly give the only life jacket on the sinking ship to my mother as opposed to your mother, because I love my mother (or at least I love her more than yours). I love my mother, however, not because of a genetic tie but because over time she has done countless things that make me want to love her. She took care of me when I could not take care of myself. She encouraged me. She provided for my future by taking me to the doctor when appropriate, disciplining me, giving me advice, paying for my education. I love her, too, because of qualities I have seen her exhibit in interactions with others—my father, my brother, my sister, neighbors, colleagues, adversaries. The biological connection helped to create the framework in which I have been able to see and experience her lovable qualities. But it is deeds, not blood—doing, not being—that is the morally appropriate basis for my preference for my mother over all other mothers in the world.

Solidarity with Viola Liuzzo

Some contend, though, that "doing" is what lies at the foundation of black racial kinship—that the reason one should feel morally compelled by virtue of one's blackness to have and show racial solidarity toward other blacks is that preceding generations of black people did things animated by racial loyalty which now benefit all black people. These advocates would contend that the benefits bestowed—for instance, *Brown v. Board of Education,* the Civil Rights Act of 1964, the Voting Rights Act of 1965, and affirmative-action programs—impose upon blacks correlative racial obligations. This is what many are getting at when they say that all blacks, but particularly affluent ones, have a racial obligation to "give back" to the black community.

I agree that one should be grateful to those who have waged struggles for racial justice, sometimes at tremendous sacrifice. But why should my gratitude be racially bounded? Elijah Lovejoy, a white man murdered in Alton, Illinois, in 1837 for advocating the abolition of slavery, participated just as fervently in that great crusade as any person of my hue. The same could be said of scores of other white abolitionists. Coming closer to our time, not only courageous black people, such as Medgar Evers, Vernon Dahmer, and James Chaney, fought white supremacy in the shadow of death during the struggle for civil rights in the Deep South. White people like James Reeb and Viola Liuzzo were there too, as were Andrew Goodman and Michael Schwerner. Against this history I see no reason why paying homage to the struggle for racial justice and endeavoring to continue that struggle must entail any sort of racially stratified loyalty. Indeed, this history suggests the opposite.

"One's People"

Thus far I have mainly argued that a black person should not feel morally bound to experience and show racial kinship with other blacks. But what do I say to a person who is considering whether to *choose* to embrace racial kinship?

One person who has made this choice is Stephen L. Carter, a professor at Yale Law School and a well-known author. In a contribution to an anthology titled *Lure and Loathing: Essays on Race, Identity, and the Ambivalence of Assimilation,* Carter writes about his racial love for black people, declaring at one point that "to love one's people is to crave a kind of familyhood with them." Carter observes that this feeling of racial kinship influences his life concretely, affecting the way in which he values people's opinions of him. "The good opinions of black people . . . matter to me more," he writes, than the good opinions of white people. "That is my choice, and I cannot imagine ever making another." In *Reflections of an Affirmative Action Baby,* Carter gives another example of how racial kinship affects his life.

> Each December, my wife and I host a holiday dessert for the black students at the Yale Law School. . . . Our hope is to provide for the students an opportunity to unwind, to escape, to renew themselves, to chat, to argue, to complain—in short, to relax. For my wife and myself, the party is a chance to get to know some of the people who will lead black America (and white America, too) into the twenty-first century. But more than that, we feel a deep emotional connection to them, through our blackness: we look at their youthful, enthusiastic faces and see ourselves. There is something affirming about the occasion—for them, we hope, but certainly for us. It is a reminder of the bright and supportive side of solidarity.

I contend that in the mind, heart, and soul of a teacher there should be no stratification of students such that a teacher feels closer to certain pupils than to others on grounds of racial kinship. No teacher should view certain students as his racial "brothers and sisters" while viewing others as, well, mere students. Every student should be free of the worry that because of race, he or she will have less opportunity to benefit from what a teacher has to offer.

Friends with whom I have debated these matters object to my position, charging that I pay insufficient attention to the complexity of the identities and roles that individuals assume in society, and that I thus ignore or minimize the ability of a black professor to be both a good teacher who serves all his students well *and* a good racial patriot who feels a special, racial affection for fellow blacks. These friends assert that I have no valid basis for complaint so long as the professor in his official duties is evenhanded in his treatment of students. By "official duties" they mean his conduct in the classroom, his accessibility during office hours, and his grading of students' academic performance. If these duties are met, they see no problem if the black professor, paying homage to his feelings of racial kinship, goes beyond what is officially required in his dealings with black students.

I see a variety of problems. For one thing, I find it inconceivable that there would be no seepage from the personal sphere into the professional sphere. The students invited to the professor's home are surely being afforded an opportunity denied to those who are not invited—an opportunity likely to be reflected in, for instance, letters of recommendation to judge So-and-So and Law Firm Partner Such-and-Such.

Another problem is that even in the absence of any tangible, dollars-and-cents difference, the teacher's racial distinctions are likely to make a difference psychologically to the students involved. I have had the great benefit of being taught by wonderful teachers of various races, including white teachers. I never perceived a racial difference in the way that the best of these teachers treated me in comparison with my white classmates. Neither John McCune nor Sanford Levinson nor Eric Foner nor Owen Fiss ever gave me reason to believe that because of my color I took a back seat to any of my classmates when it came to having a claim on their attention. My respect for their conduct is accompanied by disappointment in others who seemed for reasons of racial kinship to invest more in white than in black students—who acted, in other words, in a way that remains unfortunately "normal" in this society.

Am I demanding that teachers make no distinctions between pupils? No. Distinctions should be made. I am simply insisting that sentiments of racial kinship should play no role in making them.

Am I demanding that teachers be blind to race? No. It seems to me bad policy to blind oneself to any potentially useful knowledge. Teachers should be aware of racial differences and differentiations in our society. They should be keenly aware, for instance, that historically and currently the dominant form of racial kinship in American life, the racial kinship that has been best organized and most destructive, is racial kinship mobilized in behalf of whites. This racial kinship has been animated by the desire to make and keep the United States "a white man's country." It is the racial kinship that politicians like Patrick Buchanan and Jesse Helms openly nurture and exploit. This is also the racial kinship that politicians take care to avoid challenging explicitly. A teacher should be aware of these and other racial facts of life in order to satisfactorily equip students with knowledge about their society.

The fact that race matters, however, does not mean that the salience and consequences of racial distinctions are good or that race must continue to matter in the future. Nor does the brute sociological fact that race matters dictate what one's response to that fact should be.

Assuming that a teacher is aware of the different ways in which the race problem bears down upon his students, how should he react? That depends on the circumstances.

Consider a case, for instance, in which white students were receiving considerable attention from teachers while black students were being widely ignored. In this case it would be morally correct for a professor, with his eyes focused on race, to reach out with special vigor to the black students. In this circumstance the black students would be more in need than the white students, whose needs for mentorship were already being abundantly met. This outreach, however, would be based not on racial kinship but on distributive justice.

Our Problems

The distinction is significant. For one thing, under the rationale of giving priority of attention to those most in need, no racial boundary insulates professors from the obligation to attend to whatever maldistribution of mentorship they are in a position to correct. White professors are at least as morally obligated to address the problem as are black or other professors.

This is a point with ramifications that reach far beyond the university. For it is said with increasing urgency by increasing numbers of people that the various social difficulties confronting black Americans are, for reasons of racial kinship, the moral responsibility of blacks, particularly those who have obtained some degree of affluence. This view should be rejected. The difficulties that disproportionately afflict black Americans are not "black problems" whose solutions are the special responsibility of black people. They are *our* problems, and their solution or amelioration is the responsibility of us all, irrespective of race. That is why it is proper to object when white politicians use the term "you people" to refer to blacks. This happened when Ross Perot addressed the NAACP annual convention during the 1992 presidential election campaign. Many of those who objected to Perot's reference to "you people," however, turned right around and referred to blacks as "our people," thereby replicating the racial boundary-setting they had denounced.

A second reason why the justification for outreach matters is that unlike an appeal to racial kinship, an appeal to an ideal untrammeled by race enables any person or group to be the object of solicitude. No person or group is racially excluded from the possibility of assistance, and no person or group is expected to help only "our own." If a professor reaches out in response to student need, for instance, that means that whereas black students may deserve special solicitude today, Latino students, or Asian-American students or white students may deserve it tomorrow. If Asian-American students have a greater need for faculty mentorship than black students, black professors as well as other professors should give them priority.

Some will argue that I ignore or minimize the fact that different groups are differently situated and that it is thus justifiable to impose upon blacks and whites different standards for purposes of evaluating conduct, beliefs, and sentiments. They will maintain that it is one thing for a white teacher to prefer his white students on grounds of racial kinship and a very different thing for a black teacher to prefer his black students on grounds of racial kinship. The former, they will say, is an expression of ethnocentrism that perpetuates racist inequality, whereas the latter is a laudable expression of racial solidarity that is needed to counter white domination.

Several responses are in order.

First, it is a sociological fact that blacks and whites are differently situated in the American polity. But, again, a brute fact does not dictate the proper human response to it. That is a matter of choice—constrained, to be sure, but a choice nonetheless. In choosing how to proceed in the face of all that they encounter, blacks should insist, as did Martin Luther King Jr., that acting with moral propriety is itself a glorious goal. In seeking to attain that goal, blacks should be attuned not only to the all too human cruelties and weaknesses of others but also to the all too human cruelties and weaknesses in themselves. A good place to start is with the recognition that unless inhibited, every person and group will tend toward beliefs and practices that are self-aggrandizing. This is certainly true of those who inherit a dominant status. But it is also true of those who inherit a subordinate status. Surely one of the most striking features of human dynamics is the alacrity with which those who have been oppressed will oppress whomever they can once the opportunity presents itself. Because this is so, it is not premature to worry about the possibility that blacks or other historically subordinated groups will abuse power to the detriment of others.

Moreover, at long last blacks have sufficient power to raise urgent concerns reegarding the abuse of it. Now, in enough circumstances to make the matter worth discussing, blacks are positioned to exploit their potential racial power effectively. Hence black attorneys wonder whether they should seek to elicit the racial loyalties of black jurors or judges in behalf of clients. Black jurors and judges face the question of whether they should respond to such appeals. Black professors face the question of whether racial loyalty should shape the extent to which they make themselves available to their students. Black employers or personnel directors face the question of whether racial loyalties should shape their hiring decisions. Were blacks wholly bereft of power, as some commentators erroneously assert, these and similar questions would not arise. Thus I evaluate arguments in favor of exempting blacks from the same standards imposed upon whites and conclude that typically, though perhaps not always, such arguments amount to little more than an elaborate camouflage for self-promotion or group promotion.

A second reason I resist arguments in favor of asymmetrical standards of judgment has to do with my sense of the requirements of reciprocity. I find it difficult to accept that it is wrong for whites to mobilize themselves on a racial basis solely for purposes of white advancement but morally permissible for blacks to mobilize themselves on a racial basis solely for purposes of black advancement. I would propose a shoe-on-the-other-foot test for the propriety of racial sentiment. If a sentiment or practice would be judged offensive when voiced or implemented by anyone, it should be viewed as prima facie offensive generally. If we would look askance at a white professor who wrote that on grounds of racial kinship he values the opinions of whites more than those of blacks, then unless given persuasive reasons to the contrary, we should look askance at a black professor who writes that on grounds of racial kinship he values the opinions of blacks more than those of whites.

In some circumstances it is more difficult for blacks to give up the consolations of racial kinship than for whites to do so, insofar as whites typically have more resources to fall back on. But that should not matter, or at least should not matter decisively, if my underlying argument—that the sentiments and conduct of racial kinship are morally dubious—is correct. After all, it is surely more difficult for a poor person than for a rich one to give up the opportunity to steal untended merchandise. But we nevertheless rightly expect the poor person to give up that opportunity.

A third consideration is prudential. It is bad for the country if whites, blacks, or any other group engages in the politics of racial kinship, because racial mobilization prompts racial countermobilization, further entrenching a pattern of sterile racial competition.

Beyond Racial Loyalty

I anticipate that some will counter that this is what is happening, has happened, and will always happen, and that the best that blacks can expect is what they are able to exact from the white power structure through hard bargaining. In this view, racial unity, racial loyalty, racial solidarity, racial kinship—whatever one wants to call it—is absolutely essential for obtaining the best deal available. Therefore, in this view, my thesis is anathema, the most foolhardy idealism, a plan for ruination, a plea for unilateral disarmament by blacks in the face of a well-armed foe with a long history of bad intentions.

This challenge raises large issues that cannot be exhaustively dealt with here. But I should like to conclude by suggesting the beginning of a response, based on two observations.

First, it is noteworthy that those who have most ostentatiously asserted the imperatives of black racial solidarity—I think here particularly of Marcus Garvey, Elijah Muhammad, and Louis Farrakhan—are also those who have engaged in the most divisive, destructive, and merciless attacks on "brothers" and "sisters" who wished to follow a different path. My objection to the claims of racial pride and kinship stems in part from my fears of the effect on interracial relations. But it stems also in large part from my fears of the stultifying effect on intraracial relations. Racial pride and kinship seem often to stunt intellectual independence. If racial loyalty is deemed essential and morally virtuous, then a black person's adoption of positions that are deemed racially disloyal will be seen by racial loyalists as a supremely threatening sin, one warranting the harsh punishments that have historically been visited upon alleged traitors.

Second, if one looks at the most admirable efforts by activists to overcome racial oppression in the United States, one finds people who yearn for justice, not merely for the advancement of a particular racial group. One finds people who do not replicate the racial alienations of the larger society but instead welcome interracial intimacy of the most profound sorts. One finds people who are not content to accept the categories of communal affiliation they have inherited but instead insist upon bringing into being new and better forms of communal affiliation, ones in which love and loyalty are unbounded by race. I think here of Wendell Phillips and certain sectors of the abolitionist movement. I also think of James Farmer and the early years of the Congress of Racial Equality, and John Lewis and the early years of the Student Nonviolent Coordinating Committee. My favorite champion of this ethos, however, is a person I quoted at the beginning of this article, a person whom the sociologist Orlando Patterson aptly describes as "undoubtedly the most articulate former slave who ever lived," a person with whose words I would like to end. Frederick Douglass literally bore on his back the stigmata of racial oppression. Speaking in June of 1863, only five months after the Emancipation Proclamation and before the complete abolition of slavery, Douglass gave a talk titled "The Present and Future of the Colored Race in America," in which he asked whether "the white and colored people of this country [can] be blended into a common nationality, and enjoy together . . . under the same flag, the inestimable blessings of life, liberty, and the pursuit of happiness, as neighborly citizens of a common country." He answered: "I believe they can."

I, too, believe we can, if we are willing to reconsider and reconstruct the basis of our feelings of pride and kinship.

Additional Resources

Suggested Readings

Gates, Henry Louis, Jr., and Cornel West. *The Future of the Race.* New York: Alfred A. Knopf, 1996. A collaboration that addresses the hopes, fears and responsibilities of the black community. The future of blacks in the twenty-first century is addressed from two very different points of view.

Hacker, Andrew. *Two Nations: Black and White, Separate, Hostile, Unequal.* New York: Ballantine Books, 1992. A candid book on present-day racism. Hacker argues that despite all efforts to increase understanding and expand opportunities, black and white Americans still lead separate lives, continually marked by tension and hostility.

Lipsitz, George. *The Possessive Investment in Whiteness: How White People Profit from Identity Politics.* Philadelphia: Temple University Press, 1998. A study of the ways that race determines life chances and structures experience in contemporary America. Insightful in the ways that the color line works in the realm of public policy, politics, and culture.

Massey, Douglas, and Nancy A. Denton. *American Apartheid: Segregation and the Making of the Underclass.* Cambridge: Harvard University Press, 1993. Links the persistence of poverty among blacks in the United States to the degree of deliberate segregation they experience in American cities.

Patterson, Orlando. *The Ordeal of Integration: Progress and Resentment in America's "Racial" Crisis.* Washington, D. C.: Civitas/Counterpoint, 1998. Challenges the views of conservatives and liberals looking at the contemporary paradoxes of integration.

Shipler, David. *A Country of Strangers: Blacks and Whites in America.* New York: Vintage Books, 1998. A revealing look at the sometimes imaginary line that divides black and white in America. The book shows how ordinary people struggle with bias in everyday life.

Tatum, Beverly Daniel. *"Why Are All the Black Kids Sitting Together in the Cafeteria?"* New York: Basic Books, 1997. A sensitive treatment of subtleties of racial interaction and racial barriers that exist in American society.

West, Cornel. *Race Matters.* New York: Vintage Books, 1993. Blending philosophy, theology, sociology, and political commentary, this is a collection of essays on post–civil rights issues.

Williams, Patricia. *The Rooster's Egg: On the Persistence of Prejudice.* Cambridge: Harvard University Press, 1995. A critical and insightful collection of essays on popular events citing segregation and prejudice in contemporary America. The author suggests that the problem of race is a constant yet to be addressed by the powers that be.

Wilson, William Julius. *When Work Disappears.* New York: Alfred A. Knopf, 1997. Looks at the consequences of public policy concerning work and its impact on poor areas of cities. Wilson argues that the victories of the civil rights movement created opportunities for middle-class blacks but did little for employment in the urban ghetto.

Web Sites

www.auaa.org/library/

This is the Web site of Americans United for Affirmative Action. It contains a great deal of information including an affirmative action timeline and the full texts of major legal decisions on affirmative action. There are special sections for *University of California v. Bakke* (reverse discrimination) and *Steelworkers v. Weber* (employment).

http://aad.english.ucsb.edu/

This is the Web site for the Affirmative Action and Diversity Project. It contains different opinions and perspectives on affirmative action. The site includes on-site articles, theoretical analyses, policy documents, and an annotated bibliography.

www.law.harvard.edu/groups/civilrights/publications/lawsurvey.html

The Civil Rights Project at Harvard University created this first-rate Web site. It explores the central propositions set out by the Supreme Court in the *Bakke* decision. Using data from a Gallup poll survey, Gary Orfield and Dean Whitle wrote "The Impact of Diversity on the Experiences of Law Students." This lengthy study looks at student experiences in leading law schools.

www.usdoj.gov/crt/

This is the site of the Civil Rights Division of the U.S. Department of Justice, which is responsible for enforcing federal statutes that prohibit exclusion and discrimination. It offers access to publications, public statements and briefs dealing with civil rights.

www.mcgill.pvt.k12.al.us/jerryd/cm/black.htm

This site is made up of a collection of resources related to discrimination against African Americans. The Theological Library provides the Web site. There are over 60 links to related sites. A good site to use when beginning a research project.

www.prrac.org

The Poverty and Race Research Action Committee is a nonpartisan, national nonprofit organization. Its Web site "Race and Poverty" links social science to advocacy work in order to address problems at the intersection of race and poverty. The committee supports progressive solutions to the problems of racism and poverty. The site offers academic resources on poverty, race, welfare, employment, housing, and immigration.

www.gsd.harvard.edu/archseg

This is the Web site for "Architecture of Segregation," a traveling multidisciplinary project that looks at race and the built environment. The project, which will include a traveling exhibition and book, explores the structures that maintain divisions between whites and blacks in American society. The site offers teachers and students the opportunity to explore their own neighborhoods and contribute to an online map that documents the separation of races in urban, suburban, and rural landscapes.

Glossary

≈≈

Aid to Families with Dependent Children a federal program to support unmarried, unemployed women and their dependent children. **388**

American Friends Service Committee (AFSC) a Quaker organization committed to pacifism and racial integration. The AFSC was a strong supporter of the Southern civil rights movement. **291**

Armageddon prophesied in the Bible to occur at the end of the world, it is the scene of a final battle between the forces of good and evil. **528**

assimilationism Du Bois and others argued against this viewpoint, which, they felt, overlooked the uniqueness of black cultural identity and advocated black integration with mainstream white culture. **252**

bailiwick the jurisdiction of a bailiff. **87**

Balkanization division into small, sometimes hostile, units; from the political division of the Balkans in the early twentieth century. **146**

Bell Curve, The the highly controversial study of race and intelligence published in 1994 by Richard Herrnstein and Charles Murray. **353**

blue bomb blue pamphlets distributed the Sunday before the Nixon-Kennedy election in 1960 describing what Kennedy had done to get Martin Luther King released from prison the previous week. Two million copies were distributed among black churches across the country, presenting a positive picture of Kennedy. **281**

bourgeois liberalism political philosophy of the liberal middle classes emphasizing individual freedom, improvement, and progress. **458**

cathartic the act of cleansing or release of emotions. **372**

cold war the political, and threatened military, conflict between communism (the Soviet Union) and capitalism (the United States and Western Europe) for world domination and influence between the 1950s and 1991. **57**

credentials committee the committee that determines official eligibility for seats at the national conventions for the national political parties. **373**

Daughters of the American Revolution a politically conservative group of descendants of colonial patriotic society in the United States. Open to women having one or more ancestors who aided the cause of the American Revolution. **331**

debt peonage a system where laborers were bound in servitude until they discharged their debt. **160**

dialectical the process of change in which a concept passes over into its opposite. **126**

division of labor the way in which work-roles are divided among people in a social system or an organization. **150**

Dixiecrats Southern Democrats who formed the State's Rights Democratic Party, which supported each state's right to decide on issues of race, during the 1948 presidential election; the party was a right-wing split from Truman. During the 1950s and 1960s the movement was directed toward massive resistance to civil rights and violent attacks on blacks and white integrationists. **66**

Don Quixote written in 1605 by Cervantes, a superb burlesque of the popular romances of chivalry, contrasting man's idealism and realism. **427**

ecclesia pertaining to a church as an organization, including its congregation. **329**

ecumenical worldwide representation, or general in extent. **87**

Fellowship of Reconciliation (FOR) a pacifist organization founded in England in 1914 and established in the United States in 1915, FOR was responsible for introducing the method of nonviolent protest to Southern black communities. **291**

Fifteenth Amendment passed in 1970, gives blacks the right to vote (removing race as a qualification for voting). **158**

Fourteenth Amendment passed in 1868, defines citizenship to include blacks and provides equal protection for all under the law. **158**

gerrymandering the rearrangement of voting districts so as to give unfair advantage to one party in elections. **563**

Great Society the social and economic domestic program of Lyndon Johnson during the 1960s constituting part of the war on poverty. **175**

Harlem Renaissance the period between World War I and the Great Depression; an era of great cultural change for African Americans, characterized by the expression "New Negro," intended to define blacks in new terms, outside convenient stereotypes. Tremendous outpouring of literature, art, and music. **162**

Harrington, Michael author of *The Other America: Poverty in the United States,* an influential book of the early 1960s, which argued that America's prosperity had missed the poor. **343**

Highlander Folk School originally established by Esau Jenkins, Septima Clark, and Myles Horton in the 1950s in South Carolina as a citizenship training center. Acting as an adult education movement, the Highlander center in Monteagle, Tennessee, ran workshops in nonviolent direct action. Martin Luther King and Rosa Parks attended meetings and workshops at Highlander. **294**

infrapolitics the daily confrontations, evasive actions, and stifled thoughts, such as individual acts of protest by blacks during the Reconstruction and after, which influence organized political movements **122**

jail-no-bail the Southern civil rights movement protest strategy of declining bail when arrested, electing to spend the full sentence in jail, thereby crowding the jails and drawing attention to segregation. **281**

jeremiad from Jeremiah, Hebrew prophet of the seventh and sixth centuries B.C.; an elaborate and prolonged tale of woe. **382**

jurisprudence the philosophy of law. **233**

legal realism the only reality is what the law stipulates. **233**

leumpenproletariat Marxist terminology for the underclass. **382**

Levison, Stanley close friend of Martin Luther King and supporter of the civil rights movement; lawyer and Communist Party member. **317**

manumission formal release from slavery. **333**

Pan Africanism W. E. B. Du Bois's ideology of black integration with mainstream America; a controversial concept, it was opposed by black leaders such as Marcus Garvey and A. Phillip Randolph. **163**

panegyric elaborate praise (formal eulogistic composition intended as public compliment). **332**

participant observer sociologist who spends time interacting, and often living with those in the community being studied. A participant-observation study is based upon the observations of the researcher. **515**

peonage a condition in which laborers are bound in servitude because of debt. **32**

Popular Front Spain's fledgling democratic government overthrown by the fascist government of Generalissimo Franco during the Spanish civil war. The communists (Soviet Union) supported the people's government, while Hitler (Germany) and Mussolini (Italy) supported the fascists. **167**

Populist Party a new party created in the 1890s by labor, feminist, farm, and other reformists, which would be free from corporate influence, sectionalism, and racial tension.

Their 1892 party platform promised to return government "to the hands of the people." 43

Progressive Era   the period between the mid-1890s and early 1900s, when reformers reacting to the excesses of industrialization and urbanization used the techniques of the new industrial order—organization, management, and science—to redeem traditional American values such as opportunity for the individual and the spirit of public service.   43

Progressive Movement   the early-twentieth-century political movement promoting political and social reform. The NAACP was marginal to the Progressive Movement.   158

Progressive Party   a split in the Republican Party, formed by Theodore Roosevelt in the 1912 presidential election.   83

Project C   the code name for the planned movement that the SCLC prepared for Birmingham, Alabama, in 1963. The "C" stood for planned confrontation with Birmingham's white power structure.   282

racial tipping   concerning race and housing, when an integrated residential block or neighborhood turns from a majority of white families to predominantly black or all-black families.   469

red-baiting   attacking or persecuting a person as a communist.   61

restrictive covenant   a binding agreement that is part of a contract; used in housing to discriminate against blacks, when, for example, owners restrict future sales to whites.   164

Road to Damascus   a reference to the conversion of Saul of Tarsus (St. Paul) who was converted to Christianity when a bolt of light struck him off his horse as he rode to Damascus to persecute Christians, and a voice spoke to him urging him to repent.   257

Rule Twenty-Two   a rule to restrict unlimited debate in the Senate. It is a way to invoke cloture to end a filibuster with two-thirds of those present voting to end a debate.   347

sharecropping   postslavery social and economic arrangement common among poor, rural blacks and plantation owners. The tenant farmer gives a share of his crop to the landowner.   160

social engineer   one whose policy will affect the behavior of many.   165, 176

stool pigeon   a person acting as a decoy; for example, a spy for the police.   124

stretch-out system   a system of industrial operation in which workers are required to do extra work with slight or no additional wages.   45

symbiosis   a cooperative relationship between two dissimilar factions.   238

teleological   the use of design or purpose as an explanation of natural phenomena.   145

trope   the use of a word or expression in a figurative sense.   125

Truman Doctrine   President Truman's 1947 proclamation that the United States needed to protect the free world against the threat of expanding communist and totalitarian regimes; it marked a departure in U.S. foreign policy from the Monroe Doctrine's nonintervention.   62

untouchable   the group that is below the lowest caste in the Hindu Indian caste system. Members of this caste perform the most menial tasks.   455

Zeitgeist   the spirit, taste, and outlook characteristic of a particular period in a culture.   326

zoot suit   a suit in fashion during World War II, which had a thigh-length jacket with wide, padded shoulders and pants with narrow cuffs.   99

References

Bloom, Jack. 1987. *Class, Race and the Civil Rights Movement*. Bloomington: Indiana University Press.

Branch, Taylor. 1988. *Parting the Waters: America in the King Years 1954–63*. New York: Simon & Schuster.

_____. 1998. *Pillar of Fire: America in the King Years 1963–65*. New York: Simon & Schuster.

Burns, Stuart. 1997. *Daybreak of Freedom: The Montgomery Bus Boycott*. Chapel Hill: University of North Carolina Press.

Carmichael, Stokely, and Charles V. Hamilton. 1967. *Black Power: The Politics of Liberation in America*. New York: Vintage.

Carson, Clayborne. 1981. *In Struggle: SNCC and the Black Awakening of the 1960s*. Cambridge: Harvard University Press.

Cleaver, Eldridge. 1968. *Soul on Ice*. New York: Dell.

Cose, Ellis. 1993. *The Rage of a Privileged Class*. New York: HarperCollins.

Davis, Allison, Burleigh Gardner, and Mary Gardner. 1941. *Deep South*. Chicago: University of Chicago Press.

Dittmer, John. 1995. *Local People: The Struggle for Civil Rights in Mississippi*. Urbana and Chicago: University of Illinois Press.

Dollard, John. 1957. *Caste and Class in a Southern Town*. Garden City, NY: Doubleday.

Du Bois, W. E. B. 1903. *The Souls of Black Folk* Chicago: A. C. McClurg..

Dyson, Michael Eric. 1995. *Making Malcolm: The Myth and Meaning of Malcolm X*. New York: Oxford University Press.

Eskew, Glenn T. 1997. *But for Birmingham: The Local and National Movements in the Civil Rights Struggle*. Chapel Hill: University of North Carolina Press.

Fairclough, Adam. 1990. *Martin Luther King, Jr*. Athens: University of Georgia Press.

Foner, Eric. October/November 1983. "The New View of Reconstruction." *American Heritage*. Vol. 34, No. 6.

_____. 1998. *The Story of American Freedom*. New York: W. W. Norton.

Grant, Joanne. 1998. *Ella Baker, Freedom Bound*. New York: John Wiley.

Hampton, Henry, and Steve Fayer. 1990. *Voices of Freedom: An Oral History of the Civil Rights Movement from the 1950s through the 1980s*. New York: Bantam Books.

Higginbotham, Evelyn. 1993. *Righteous Discontent: The Women's Movement in the Black Baptist Church, 1880–1920*. Cambridge: Harvard University Press.

Howard, John R. 1999. *The Shifting Wind, the Supreme Court and Civil Rights from Reconstruction to* Brown. Albany: State University of New York Press.

Kasher, Steven. 1996. *The Civil Rights Movement: A Photographic History, 1954–68*. New York: Abbeville Press.

Kelley, Robin. June 1993. "We Are Not What We Seem: Rethinking Black Working Class Opposition in the Jim Crow South." *Journal of American History*. Vol. 80.

King, Martin Luther, Jr. 1958. *Stride toward Freedom: The Montgomery Story*. New York: Harper.

King, Mary. 1987. *Freedom Song: A Personal Story of the 1960s Civil Rights Movement*. New York: Quill Books, a division of William Morrow.

Kluger, Richard. 1975. *Simple Justice*. New York: Knopf.

Korstad, Robert, and Nelson Lichtenstein. December 1988. "Opportunities Lost and Found: Labor, Radicals, and the Early Civil Rights Movement." *Journal of American History.* Vol. 751.

Lipsitz, George. 1998. *The Possessive Investment in Whiteness: How White People Profit from Identity Politics.* Philadelphia: Temple University Press.

Litwack, Leon. 1998. *Trouble in Mind: Black Southerners in the Age of Jim Crow.* New York: Knopf.

Martin, Waldo. 1998. *The* Brown *Decision: A Brief History with Documents.* Boston: Bedford Books.

Massey, Douglas and Nancy Denton. 1993. *American Apartheid: Segregation and the Making of the Underclass.* Cambridge: Harvard University Press.

McAdam, Doug. 1999. *Political Process and the Development of Black Insurgency, 1930–1970,* 2nd ed. Chicago: University of Chicago Press.

_____. 1988. *Freedom Summer.* New York: Oxford University Press.

Meier, August, and Elliot Rudwick. 1973. *CORE: A Study in the Civil Rights Movement, 1942–1968.* New York: Oxford University Press.

Mills, Nicholas. 1994. *Debating Affirmative Action: Race, Gender, Ethnicity, and the Politics of Inclusion.* New York: Delta.

Morris, Aldon. 1984. *The Origins of the Civil Rights Movement: Black Communities Organizing for Change.* New York: Free Press.

Myrdal, Gunnar. 1944. *An American Dilemma: The Negro Problem and Modern Democracy.* New York: Harper & Row.

Patterson, Orlando. 1997. *The Ordeal of Integration: Progress and Resentment in America's "Racial" Crisis.* Washington: Civitas.

Report of the National Advisory Commission on Civil Disorders. 1968. New York: E. P. Dutton.

Savage, Barbara. 1999. *Broadcasting Freedom: Radio, War and the Politics of Race, 1938–1948.* Chapel Hill: University of North Carolina Press.

Seale, Bobby. 1968. *Seize the Time: The Story of the Black Panther Party and Huey P. Newton.* New York: Random House.

Schaefer, Richard. 1995. *Race and Ethnicity in the United States.* New York: HarperCollins.

Sitkoff, Harvard. 1993. *The Struggle for Black Equality, 1954–1992.* New York: Hill & Wang.

Steinberg, Stephen. 1981. *The Ethnic Myth, Race, Ethnicity and Class in America.* New York: Atheneum.

Sullivan, Patricia. 1996. *Days of Hope, Race and Democracy in the New Deal Era.* Chapel Hill: University of North Carolina Press.

Watters, Pat. 1993. *Down to Now: Reflections on the Southern Civil Rights Movement.* Athens: University of Georgia Press.

Weber, Max. 1947. *The Theory of Social and Economic Organizations.* Ed. Talcott Parsons. New York: Free Press.

Wexler, Sanford. 1993. *The Civil Rights Movement: An Eyewitness History.* New York: Facts on File.

Wilson, William J. 1987. *The Truly Disadvantaged: The Inner City, the Underclass, and Public Policy.* Chicago: University of Chicago Press.

_____. 1997. *When Work Disappears.* New York: Knopf.

Woodward, C. Vann. 1974. *The Strange Career of Jim Crow,* 3rd ed. New York: Oxford University Press.

Young, Andrew. 1996. *An Easy Burden: The Civil Rights Movement and the Transformation of America.* New York: Harper Collins.

Zinn, Howard. 1965. *SNCC: The New Abolitionists.* Boston: Beacon Press.

Acknowledgments

Chapter 1

Introduction
Table 1: From *The Statistical History of the United States* by Ben J. Wattenberg, Introduction and User's Guide. Copyright © 1976 by Ben J. Wattenberg. Reprinted by permission of Basic Books, a member of Perseus Books, L.L.C.

Reading 1.1
Booker T. Washington, "The Atlanta Exposition Address," September 18, 1895.

Reading 1.2
W. E. Burghardt Du Bois, "Of Mr. Booker T. Washington and Others," *The Souls of Black Folk,* (New York: Fawcett, 1968) pp. 42–54.

Reading 1.3
Charles Flint Kellogg, "Lynching and Mob Violence," *NAACP, A History of the National Association for the Advancement of Colored People, Vol. 1 (1909–1920)* (Baltimore, MD: Johns Hopkins Press, 1967). Copyright © 1967 by the Johns Hopkins Press. Reprinted by permission.

Reading 1.4
Patricia Sullivan, "On the Eve of the New Deal," *Days of Hope: Race and Democracy in the New Deal Era* (Chapel Hill: University of North Carolina Press, 1996). Copyright © 1996 by the University of North Carolina Press. Reprinted by permission.

Reading 1.5
Asa Philip Randolph, "Call to Negro America to March on Washington for Jobs and Equal Participation on July 1, 1941," *The Black Worker* (May 1941). Reprinted by permission of A. Philip Randolph Institute.

Reading 1.6
Jack M. Bloom, "Nineteen Forty-Eight: The Opening of the Breach," *Class, Race, and the Civil Rights Movement* (Bloomington: Indiana University Press, 1987), pp. 74–86. Copyright © 1987 by Jack M. Bloom. Reprinted by permission of Indiana University Press.

Reading 1.7
John Dittmer, "We Return Fighting;" *Local People: The Struggle for Civil Rights in Mississippi* (Champaign: University of Illinois Press, 1994), pp. 1–18. Copyright © 1994 by the Board of Trustees of the University of Illinois. Reprinted by permission of the University of Illinois Press.

Reading 1.8
John Dittmer, "Rising Expectations, 1946–54," *Local People: The Struggle for Civil Rights in Mississippi* (Champaign: University of Illinois Press, 1994), pp. 19–40. Copyright © 1994 by the Board of Trustees of the University of Illinois. Reprinted by permission of the University of Illinois Press.

Reading 1.9
Barbara Dianne Savage, "Radio and the Political Discourse of Racial Equality," *Broadcast Freedom: Radio, War, and the Politics of Race, 1938–1948* (Chapel Hill: University of North Carolina Press, 1999) pp. 194–222. Copyright © 1999 by the University of North Carolina Press. Reprinted by permission.

Chapter 2

Reading 2.1
Robin D. G. Kelley, " 'We Are Not What We Seem': Rethinking Black Working-Class Opposition in the Jim Crow South," *Journal of American History* (June, 1993), pp. 75–112. Copyroght © 1993 by the Organization of American Historians. Reprinted by permission.

Reading 2.2
Aldon D. Morris, "Domination, Church, and the NAACP," *The Origins of the Civil Rights Movement: Black Communities Organizing for Change* (New York: Free Press, 1984) pp. 1–16. Copyright © 1984 by the Free Press. Reprinted by permission of The Free Press, a division of Simon & Schuster, Inc.

Reading 2.3
August Meier and John H. Bracey Jr., "The NAACP as a Reform Movement, 1909–1965: 'To Reach the Conscience of America' " *Journal of Southern History,* LIX, no. 1 (February 1993), pp. 3–30. Copyright © 1993 by the Southern Historical Association. Reprinted by permission of the Managing Editor.

Reading 2.4
Genna Rae McNeil, "Charles Hamilton Houston: Social Engineer for Civil Rights," John Hope Franklin and August Meier, eds. *Black Leaders of the Twentieth Century* (Champaign: University of Illinois Press, 1982), pp. 221–240. Copyright © 1982 by the Board of Trustees of the University of Illinois. Reprinted by permission of the University of Illinois Press.

Reading 2.5
Thurgoood Marshall, "The Legal Attack to Secure Civil Rights." Speech delivered July 13, 1944, at the NAACP Wartime Conference.

Reading 2.6
August Meier, "On the Role of Martin Luther King," August Meier and Elliot Rudwick, eds. *Along the Color Line: Explorations in the Black Experience* (Champaign: University of Illinois Press, 1976). Copyright © 1965 by New Politics Associates, Inc.

Reading 2.7
Clayborne Carson, "Martin Luther King Jr.: Charismatic Leadership in a Mass Struggle," *Journal of American History,* vol. 74 (September 1987), pp. 448–454. Reprinted by permission of the Organization of American Historians.

Reading 2.8

Charles Payne, "Ella Baker and Models of Social Change," *Signs: Journal of Women and Society,* vol. 14, no. 4 (1989), pp. 885–899. Copyright © 1987 by the University of Chicago Press. Reprinted by permission.

Reading 2.9

Ella Baker, "Organization without Dictatorship," Emily Stoper, ed. *The Student Nonviolent Coordinating Committee: The Growth of Radicalism in a Civil Rights Organization* (Brooklyn, NY: Carlson Publishing, 1989). Copyright © 1989 by Emily Stoper. Reprinted by permission of Carlson Publishing Inc.

Ella Baker, in Ellen Cantarow, Susan Gushee O'Malley, and Sharon Hartman Strom, eds., *Moving the Mountain: Women Working for Social Change* (New York: Feminist Press at the City University of New York, 1980). Copyright © 1980 by Ellen Cantarow, Susan Gushee O'Malley, and Sharon Hartman Strom. Reprinted by permission of Ellen Cantarow and the Feminist Press at the City University of New York.

Chapter 3

Reading 3.1

Waldo E. Martin, "Shades of *Brown*: Black Freedom, White Supremacy and the Law," *Brown vs. Board of Education* (New York: Bedford/St. Martin's Press, 1998) Copyright © 1998 by Bedford/St. Martin's, Inc. Reprinted by permission.

Reading 3.2

"The Southern Manifesto: Declaration of Constitutional Principles," *Congressional Record,* 84th Congress, 2nd session (March 12, 1956).

Reading 3.3

John White, "Nixon *Was* the One: Edgar Daniel Nixon, the MIA and the Montgomery Bus Boycott," Brian Ward and Tony Badger, eds., *The Making of Martin Luther King and the Civil Rights Movement* (New York: New York University Press, 1996), pp. 45–63. Copyright © 1996 by New York University Press. Reprinted by permission.

Reading 3.4

Rosa Parks, " . . . I Tried Not to Think about What Might Happen," Rosa Parks with Jim Haskins, *Rosa Parks: My Story* (New York: Dial Books, 1992) pp. 113–116. Copyright © 1992 by Rosa Parks. Reprinted by permission of Dial Books for Young Readers, a division of Penguin Putnam, Inc.

Reading 3.5

Elizabeth Eckford, "The First Day: Little Rock, 1957," Chris Mayfield, ed., *Growing Up Southern: Southern Exposure Looks at Childhood Then and Now* (New York: Pantheon Books, 1981). Copyright © 1976, 1978, 1980, 1981 by the Institute for Southern Studies. Reprinted by permission of Pantheon Books, a division of Random House, Inc.

Reading 3.6

David L. Kirp, "Retreat to Legalism: The Little Rock School Desegregation Case in Historic Perspective," *PS: Political Science and Politics* 29 (September, 1997), pp. 443–447. Copyright © 1997 by David Kirp and the American Political Science Association. Reprinted by permission of the American Political Science Association.

Chapter 4

Reading 4.1

Joanne Grant, "Political Mama," *Ella Baker: Freedom Bound* (New York: John Wiley, 1998). Copyright © 1998 by Joanne Grant. Reprinted by permission of John Wiley & Sons, Inc.

Reading 4.2

John Lewis, Hank Thomas, and James Farmer, "Freedom Riders," Howell Raines, ed., *My Soul Is Rested: Movement Days in the Deep South Remembered* (New York: G. P. Putnam's Sons, 1977). Copyright © 1977 by Howell Raines. Reprinted by permission of Putnam Berkley, a division of Penguin Putnam, Inc.

Reading 4.3

Adam Fairclough, "Confrontation: Albany and Birmingham," *Martin Luther King, Jr.* (Athens: University of Georgia Press, 1990). Copyright © 1990, 1995 by Adam Fairclough. Reprinted by permission of Little, Brown & Company (U.K.).

Reading 4.4

Martin Luther King Jr., "Letter from Birmingham City Jail," (New York: Harper & Row, 1964). Copyright © 1963 by Martin Luther King Jr., © renewed 1991 by Coretta Scott King. Reprinted by arrangement with The Heirs to the Estate of Martin Luther King Jr., c/o Writers House, Inc. as agent for the proprietor.

Reading 4.5

Keith Miller and Emily Lewis, "Touchstones, Authorities and Marion Anderson: The Making of 'I Have a Dream,' " Brian Ward and Tony Badger, eds., *The Making of Martin Luther King and the Civil Rights Movement* (New York: New York University Press, 1996). Copyright © 1996 by Keith Miller and Emily Lewis. Reprinted by permission of New York University Press.

Reading 4.6

Bayard Rustin, "From Protest to Politics: The Future of the Civil Rights Movement," *Commentary* (February 1965). Copyright © 1965 by *Commentary*. Reprinted by permission; all rights reserved.

Reading 4.7

Lyndon B. Johnson, "The Voting Rights Act Should Be Passed," *Congressional Record,* 89th Congress, 1st sess. vol. 3, no. 47 (March 15, 1965).

Reading 4.8

Douglas A. Blackmon, "Silent Partner: How the South's Fight to Uphold Segregation Was Funded Up North," *Wall Street Journal* (June 11, 1999). Copyright © 1999 by Douglas A. Blackmon. Reprinted by permission; permission conveyed through Copyright Clearance Center.

Chapter 5

Reading 5.1

Allen J. Matusow, "From Civil Rights to Black Power: The Case of SNCC, 1960–1966," Barton J. Bernstein and Allen J. Matusow, eds., *Twentieth Century America: Recent Interpretations* (New York: Harcourt Brace Jovanovich, 1969). Copyright © 1969 by Allen J. Matusow. Reprinted by permission of Allen J. Matusow, Rice University.

Reading 5.2
Jack M. Bloom, "Ghetto Revolts, Black Power, and the Limits of the Civil Rights Coalition," *Class, Race, and the Civil Rights Movement* (Bloomington: Indiana University Press, 1987), pp. 186–213. Copyright © 1987 by Jack M. Bloom. Reprinted by permission of Indiana University Press.

Reading 5.3
Michael Eric Dyson, "Meeting Malcolm," *Making Malcolm: The Myth and Meaning of Malcolm X* (New York: Oxford University Press, 1996). Copyright © 1996 by Michael Eric Dyson. Reprinted by permission of Oxford University Press, Inc.

Reading 5.4
Malcolm X, "The Ballot or the Bullet," George Breitman, ed., *Malcolm X Speaks: Selected Speeches and Statements* (New York, Pathfinder Press, 1965). Copyright © 1965, 1989 by Betty Shabazz and Pathfinder Press. Reprinted by permission.

Reading 5.5
Henry Hampton and Steve Fayer, "The Meredith March, 1966: 'Hit Them Now,' " *Voices of Freedom: An Oral History of the Civil Rights Movement from the 1950s through the 1980s* (New York: Bantam, 1990). Copyright © 1990 by Blackside, Inc. Reprinted by permission of Bantam Books, a division of Random House, Inc.

Reading 5.6
Stokely Carmichael (Kwame Ture), "Toward Black Liberation," *Massachusetts Review,* (Autumn, 1966). Copyright © 1966 by The Massachusetts Review. Reprinted by permission.

Reading 5.7
Howard Zinn, "The Limits of Nonviolence," *Freedomways* (Winter 1964). Copyright © 1964 by Howard Zinn. Reprinted by permission of the author.

Reading 5.8
Charles Payne, "Mrs. Hamer Is No Longer Relevant: The Loss of the Organizing Tradition," *I've Got the Light of Freedom: The Organizing Tradition and the Mississippi Freedom Struggle* (Berkeley: University of California Press, 1996) pp. 363–390. Copyright © 1995 by the Regents of the University of California. Reprinted by permission of the University of California Press.

Chapter 6

Reading 6.1
Raymond S. Franklin, "From Civil Rights to Civic Disgrace," *Shadows of Race and Class* (Minneapolis: University of Minnesota Press, 1991), pp. 1–21. Copyright © 1991 by the Regents of the University of Minnesota. Reprinted by permission of the University of Minnesota Press.

Reading 6.2
Randall Kennedy, "Persuasion and Distrust: The Affirmative Action Debate," *Harvard Law Review* (April 1986), pp. 48–67. Copyright © 1986 by the Harvard Law Review Association. Reprinted by permission of the author and the Harvard Law Review Association.

Reading 6.3
Stephen L. Carter, "Racial Preference? So What?" *Wall Street Journal,* September 13, 1989. Copyright © 1989 by Stephen L. Carter.

Reading 6.4
Douglas S. Massey and Nancy A. Denton, "The Perpetuation of the Underclass," *American Apartheid: Segregation and the Making of the Underclass* (Cambridge, MA: Harvard University Press, 1993). Copyright © 1993 by the President and Fellows of Harvard College. Reprinted by permission of Harvard University Press.

Reading 6.5
Lise Funderburg, "Integration Anxiety," *New York Times Magazine* (November 7, 1999), pp. 83–87. Copyright © 1999 by Lise Funderburg. Reprinted by permission of the author.

Reading 6.6
Michael Eric Dyson, "In a Color-Blind Society, We Can Only See Black and White: Why Race Will Continue to Rule," *Race Rules: Navigating the Color Line* (Reading, MA: Addison-Wesley Longman, 1996), pp. 213–224. Copyright © 1996 by Michael Eric Dyson. Reprinted by permission of Perseus Book Publishers, a member of Perseus Books, L.L.C.

Reading 6.7
Ron Nixon, "Turning Back the Clock on Voting Rights," *The Nation* (November 15, 1999), pp. 11–12, 14–17. Copyright © by Ron Nixon. Reprinted by permission of *The Nation.*

Reading 6.8
Joe R. Feagin, "The Continuing Significance of Race: Antiblack Discrimination in Public Places," *American Sociological Review* (February 1991) pp. 101–116. Copyright © 1991 by the American Sociological Association. Reprinted by permission of the author.

Reading 6.9
Robert E. Staples, "The Illusion of Racial Equality: The Black American Dilemma," Gerald Early, ed., *Lure and Loathing: Essays on Race, Identity and the Ambivalence of Assimilation* (New York: Penguin Putnam, 1993), pp. 227–244. Copyright © 1993 by Robert E. Staples. Reprinted by permission of the author.

Reading 6.10
Stanley Crouch, "Blues Collar Clarity," *The All-American Skin Game, or, The Decoy of Race* (New York: Vintage Books, 1997). Copyright © 1995 by Stanley Crouch. Reprinted by permission of Pantheon Books, a division of Random House, Inc.

Reading 6.11
Randall Kennedy, "My Race Problem—And Ours," *Atlantic Monthly* (May 1997), pp. 55–66. Copyright © 1997 by Randall Kennedy. Reprinted by permission of the author and the Atlantic Monthly.